Language Acquisition and Development

Language Acquisition and Development
Proceedings of GALA2005

Edited by

Adriana Belletti, Elisa Bennati, Cristiano Chesi, Elisa Di Domenico, and Ida Ferrari

CAMBRIDGE SCHOLARS PRESS

Language Acquisition and Development: Proceedings of GALA2005, edited by Adriana Belletti, Elisa Bennati, Cristiano Chesi, Elisa Di Domenico, and Ida Ferrari

This book first published 2006 by

Cambridge Scholars Press

15 Angerton Gardens, Newcastle, NE5 2JA, UK

TABLE OF CONTENTS

ACKNOWLEDGEMENTS

The GALA2005 Conference took place at the University of Siena from September 5 to September 10. We all, participants and organizers, share a very good memory of this event for both its intellectual quality and the friendly atmosphere which has characterized it during all three (rainy!...) days. The University of Siena is proud to have hosted this significant event.

I want to take the opportunity of these few lines to thank all the speakers and the participants who presented a poster, for their decisive role in enhancing the overall quality of the conference. Most of the presenters have then submitted their paper for publication in these Proceedings. The outcome is an extremely rich piece of work, which promises to become a crucial up to date tool for all researchers working on language acquisition and pathology from a theoretically sophisticated formal perspective. I sincerely thank all the authors for their contributions to this volume.

Finally, I want to thank the colleagues and the doctoral students who effectively participated in the various organizational steps during the preparation of the conference and during its development. In particular, my warmest thanks go to Giulia Bianchi and Giuliano Bocci for their excellent work as the main editors of the booklet of the conference. And, last but not least, I thank my co-editors of these Proceedings for the generosity and care which has characterized each and every aspect of their editing work. Without their enthusiastic and careful involvement this publication would have hardly seen the light.

Adriana Belletti
April 2006

LIST OF CONTRIBUTORS

Flavia Adani	*University of Milano-Bicocca*
Sharon Armon-Lotem	*Bar Ilan University*
Fabrizio Arosio	*University of Milano-Bicocca*
Larisa Avram	*University of Bucharest*
Sergey Avrutin	*Universiteit Utrecht*
Elisa Bennati	*University of Siena*
Sigal Birka	*Bar Ilan University*
Elma Blom	*University of Amsterdam*
Ute Bohnacker	*Lund University*
Laura Bontempi	*University of Urbino*
Irena Botwinik-Rotem	*Tel Aviv University, Ben Gurion University of the Negev*
Gerald Bullock	*University of Hawai'i; Kobe Women's University*
Claudia Caprin	*University of Milano Bicocca*
Anna Cardinaletti	*Ca' Foscari University of Venice*
Pritha Chandra	*University of Maryland at College Park*
Paolo Chinellato	*University of Padua; University of Venice*
Myong-Hee Choi	*Georgetown University*
Vicky Chondrogianni	*University of Cambridge*
Martine Coene	*Leiden University; Antwerp University (CNTS)*
Cécile De Cat	*University of Leeds*
Kamil Ud Deen	*University of Hawai'i*
Maria Dimitrakopoulou	*University of Thessaloniki*

Caterina Donati	*University of Urbino*
Arnold Evers	*Universiteit Utrecht*
Olga Fedorova	*Moscow State University*
Ida Ferrari	*University of Siena; University of Florence*
Francesca Foppolo	*University of Milano-Bicocca*
Georgia Fotiadou	*University of Thessaloniki*
Naama Friedmann	*Tel Aviv University*
Alison Gabriele	*University of Kansas*
Letizia Gasperoni	*University of Urbino*
Giuliana Giusti	*Ca' Foscari University of Venice*
Roberta Gozzi	*Ca' Foscari University of Venice*
Maria Teresa Guasti	*University of Milano-Bicocca*
Gvion Aviah	*Tel Aviv University*
Jeremy Hartman	*Harvard University*
Belma Haznedar	*Bogazici University*
Julia Herschensohn	*University of Washington*
Christopher Hirsch	*Massachusetts Institute of Technology - MIT*
Barbara Höhle	*University of Potsdam*
Bart Hollebrandse	*University of Groningen*
Holger Hopp	*University of Groningen*
Nina Hyams	*University of California, Los Angeles - UCLA*
Chiara Ioghà	*University of Milano-Bicocca*
Jacqueline van Kampen	*UiL OTS, Utrecht University*
Leontine Kremers	*University of Groningen*
Edva Lavi	*Tel Aviv University*
Joke de Lange	*Universiteit Utrecht*
Donna Lardiere	*Georgetown University*

Chiara Leonini	*University of Siena; University of Florence*
Paolo Lorusso	*Universitat Autònoma de Barcelona*
Simona Matteini	*University of Siena; University of Florence*
Utako Minai	*University of Maryland*
Vincenzo Moscati	*University of Siena*
Anja Müller	*Humboldt-University Berlin*
Rama Novogrodsky	*Tel Aviv University*
Michèle Oliviéri	*Université de Nice - CNRS UMR 6039*
Akira Omaki	*University of Maryland*
Katérina Palasis-Jourdan	*Université de Nice - CNRS UMR 6039*
Maren Pannemann	*University of Amsterdam*
Despina Papadopoulou	*University of Thessaloniki*
Lydia Pelzer	*University of Potsdam*
Alexandra Perovic	*Massachusetts Institute of Technology - MIT*
Cristina Pierantozzi	*University of Urbino*
Mihaela Pirvulescu	*University of Toronto at Mississauga*
Anna Roussou	*University of Patras*
Dominik Rus	*Georgetown University*
Tetsuya Sano	*Meiji Gakuin University*
Ana Lúcia Santos	*Universidade de Lisboa / Onset – CEL*
Michaela Schmitz	*University of Potsdam*
Barbara Schulz	*University of Hawai'i; University of Maryland*
Bonnie D. Schwartz	*University of Hawai'i*
Neal Snape	*University of Essex*
Antonella Sorace	*University of Edinburgh*
Nelleke Strik	*Université de Paris 5-CNRS-FRE2929; Paris,8-CNRS-UMR7023*

Annie Tremblay	*University of Hawai'i*
Ianthi-Maria Tsimpli	*University of Thessaloniki*
George Tsoulas	*University of York*
Marina Tzakosta	*University of Crete*
Akira Watanabe	*University of Tokyo*
Fred Weerman	*University of Amsterdam*
Jürgen Weissenborn	*Humboldt-University Berlin*
Marit R. Westergaard	*University of Tromsø*
Kyoko Yamakoshi	*Senshu University*
Maki Yamane	*Kanagawa University*
Igor Yanovich	*Moscow State University*
Boping Yuan	*University of Cambridge*

THE ACQUISITION OF RELATIVE CLAUSES IN HEBREW: PREPOSITIONS AND RESUMPTIVE PRONOUNS

SHARON ARMON-LOTEM, IRENA BOTWINIK-ROTEM, AND SIGAL BIRKA

1. Introduction

A number of recent studies have shown that children, crosslinguistically, tend to rely on resumption (resumptive pronouns (RPr), and resumptive DPs (RDPs)) in their early relative clauses (RC). This is particularly conspicuous in so-called "intrusive pronoun" languages (Sells (1984)), like English or French, where resumption is permitted only in positions disallowing (pied-piped) movement (i.e. islands). The extensive use of resumption alongside complete lack of pied-piping gave rise to various analyses bearing on the availability of A'-movement, the existence of linking operators, and the specification of the empty category in early RCs (Labelle (1990, 1996), Guasti & Shlonsky (1995), Pérez-Leroux (1995), Friedmann, Novogrodsky, Szterman & Preminger (to appear), among others).

Focusing on Hebrew, "a true resumptive language" (Shlonsky (1992)), the aim of the present study is to explore and explain where and why children acquiring Hebrew (or Arabic, Bshara (2004)) tend to omit obligatory RPrs or replace them by RDPs. Examples of children's production, including such errors are shown in (1).

(1) a. *ha-ec   she-ha-gamad   tipes   alav /*ø / *al ha-ec*   Hebrew
       the-tree that-the-dwarf climbed on-it / ø / **on the-tree**
     b. *iz-zalami illi l-walad khaf   mino /*ø / *min (iz)-zalami* Arabic
       the-man   that the-boy feared from-him / ø / **from the-man**

Nonetheless, our findings and analysis will shed light on the more general questions bearing on the production of RCs as well. But before that, a few words regarding the distribution of RPrs in Hebrew are in place.

As mentioned, unlike in languages such as English, where RPrs are used only as a salvation mechanism when movement is impossible, in Hebrew, they are obligatory for indirect object (IO) and PP extraction sites, ungrammatical in the highest subject position, and optional for direct objects (DO) and embedded subjects (Table 1).[1]

Table 1. Distribution of RPr in Hebrew RC

Extraction site	RPr
Highest S	Ungrammatical
Embedded S	Optional
DO	Optional
IO (Dative)	**Obligatory**
PP (Oblique and Locative)	**Obligatory**

2. Method and Results

2.1 Methodology

Participants. 20 Hebrew speaking children aged 3;4-6;00 participated in the experiment. The children, all from middle SES, attended different preschools in the central region of Israel, and were tested individually in their respective preschools. All subjects showed normal language development and had no hearing impairment.

Procedure. An elicited production task, involving at least three identical toy-figures participating in different actions was used in order to elicit the relative clauses (Hamburger & Crain (1982), Crain & Thornton (1998)). The experimenter maneuvers the toy props, while a blindfolded puppet tries to understand what goes on. Being blindfolded, the puppet needs the child's help. Deictics cannot be used to identify one of the three objects, so the child has to use a relative clause to identify it. The present study included 12 stories targeting relativization sites where RPrs are obligatory:

4 stories targeting dative PPs (*natan le-*, 'gave to', *azar le-*, 'helped to')
4 stories targeting oblique PPs (*paxad me-* '[was] afraid from [of]', *nigen be-* 'played music in [on]', *ka'as al* 'angered on [at]', *ba'at be-* 'kicked in [at]')
4 stories targeting locative PPs (*leyad* 'near', *al* 'on')
The stories were presented in a randomized order. Examples for the different PP extraction sites with an obligatory RPr are given in (2):

(2) a. *ha-xazir she-pinokio natan lo   perax*   Dative
        the-pig that-Pinokio gave to-him flower
     b. *ha-gamad she-shilgiya ka'asa   alav*   Oblique
        the-dwarf that-Snowhite angered on-him
     c. *ha-xazir she-saba   omed leyado*   Locative
        the-pig that-granddad ṣtands near-him

The children's responses were analyzed for grammaticality, focusing on the use of RPrs, gaps and RDPs in their responses, for each item and within each category. Findings are given in percentage and raw numbers were applicable.

2.2 Results

The experiment yielded 180 RCs with PP relativization sites, distributed as follows: 65 with dative, 61 with oblique and 54 with locative PP relativization sites. Despite our wide age range, responses were qualitatively similar across the age-span and therefore are treated as a single group. Errors were found for 17 out of the 20 children.

The main finding of our study is that children treat the three relativization sites differently. There were no errors in RCs with a Dative PP (as has also been reported by Varlokosta and Armon-Lotem (1998)). While omission errors occurred in both RCs with oblique PPs and RCs with locative PPs, RDPs were found only in the latter. An accusative RPr was never used to replace a prepositional RPr. This is shown in Figure 1 giving the distribution of the responses by preposition type (in percentage):

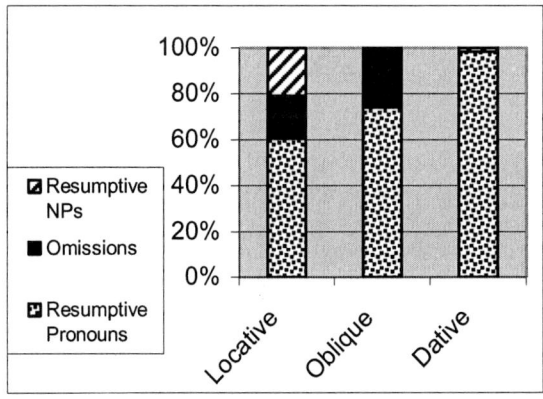

Figure 1. Distribution of responses by preposition type

As shown in Figure 1, most of the responses involved RPrs; they were used at ceiling with dative PPs, and less with the other PPs. The mean omission rate in RCs with oblique PPs was 26%, and in RCs with locative PPs the mean was 20%. RDPs are found only in RCs with locative PPs and their mean rate was also 20%.

Figures 2 and 3 show that the error rate varies across the different prepositions. Figure 2 presents the distribution of responses for the 4 different prepositions of oblique PPs, while Figure 3 gives the error rate for the two locative prepositions used in the experiment. Findings are presented in percentage:

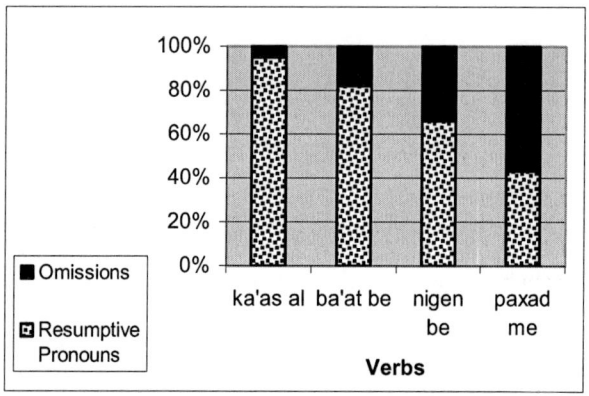

Figure 2. Distribution of responses for Oblique PPs

Figure 2 shows that while the mean omission rate in RCs with oblique PPs was 26%, omission rate varied from 5% for *ka'as al* 'was angry at' to 57% for *paxad me* 'was afraid of'. It also shows that no RDPs were used with oblique PPs.

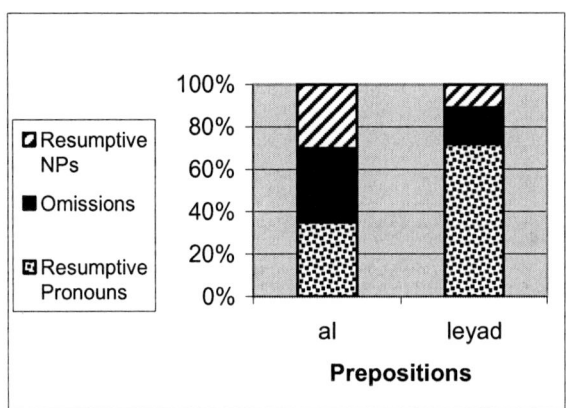

Figure 3. Distribution of responses for Locative PPs

Figure 3 shows once more that the omission rate and RDP rate depend on the preposition (and the verb). Though both prepositions allow omissions and RDPs, *al* 'on' shows a higher error rate than *leyad* 'near, next to'. That is, children used RDPs in 30% of their responses with *al* 'on', but only in 11% of their responses with *leyad* 'near, next to'. Similarly, they omitted the RPr in 35% of their responses with *al* 'on', but only in 17% of their responses with *leyad* 'near'.

3. Discussion

3.1 The main questions

As mentioned earlier, our goal is to explain what underlies the omission of RPrs and the occurrence of RDPs in the acquisition of Hebrew relatives. Based on the above findings, achieving this goal amounts to answering the following questions: (i) Why are RDPs attested only in relatives with locative PPs? (ii) What is the source for the different omission rates in relatives with (oblique) PPs? (iii) Why is there no omission in relatives with Dative PPs?

3.2 Background assumptions and main claim

Adopting the conventional analysis of RC formation (cf. Sells (1984)), Hebrew relative clauses are derived either:
(i) by movement of the null operator (Op) (3a) (or relative pronoun (3b, c)) (Hebrew does not allow P-stranding).[2]

(ii) without movement, with the null operator (Op) base-generated in spec-CP binding an overt RPr in situ (3d, e) (Hebrew does not allow null resumptive PPs).

(3) **RC formation in Hebrew**

    a. *ze   ha-sefer* Op$_i$ *she-dan kara t$_i$*
       this the-book   that-Dan read

    b. *ze   ha-sefer* $_i$ *(she)-oto$_i$ dan kara t$_i$*
       this the-book (that)-it Dan read

    c. *ze   ha-sefer (she)- alav$_i$/*Op$_i$ dan diber*   t$_i$/*[*al* t$_i$]
       this the-book (that)-about-it   Dan talked   /about

    d. *ze   ha-sefer* Op$_i$ *she-dan kara oto$_i$*
       this the-book   that-Dan read it

    e. *ze   ha-sefer* Op$_i$ *she-dan diber   alav$_i$/*$[_{PP} e]_i$*
       this the-book   that-Dan talked about-it/ ø

Given the above, combined with the (null) hypothesis that children derive RCs like adults (Guasti (2002)), we take omission of an obligatory RPr in children's data (4a) to be on a par with (3a), namely involving (Op)-movement to spec-CP (4b).

    (4) a. *ze ha-gamad she-shilgiya ka'asa   alav$_i$/ø*
          this the-dwarf that-Snowhite was-angry on-it/ø

        b. *ze ha-gamad* Op$_i$ *she-shilgiya ka'asa* t$_i$

We hold that, as in adult grammar, Op moving to spec-CP is nominal (a bare DP, rather than a PP or a Case-marked DP) (Cinque (1990)) (also classified as PRO in Bennis & Hoekstra (1989), Den Dikken (1995), among others). In what follows it will be symbolized as Op/PRO. In contrast to adults, we assume that children's base generated operator is generalized, binding either a DP or a PP argument-variable, to the exclusion of a referential DP, which cannot serve as a variable (Fiengo and May (1994)) (this will be made explicit below). Finally, we assume some version of (lexical) V-P reanalysis to be employed by children. Specifically, a non-predicative preposition (i.e. a preposition not specifying a two-place relation) does not necessarily project. Rather, it is analyzed as part of the verb, with its content being deleted under recoverability. Consequently, our main claim is that omission of RPr in children's relatives in Hebrew has the representation in (5), involving lexical V-P reanalysis and syntactic Op/PRO-movement:

    (5) $[_{CP}$ Op/PRO$_i$ ... $[V_{+P\emptyset}]$ $[_{DP}$ t$_i]]$

With this in mind, let us turn now to the three aforementioned questions.

3.3 Locative vs. oblique PPs: the case of RDP

A locative PP can be an argument, receiving a Θ-role from the verb (6a), or a modifer (an adjunct) (6b).[3] It is commonly assumed that a locative P is a predicate, and the following DP is its (Θ-) argument.

(6)   a. [$_{VP}$ V$_{Θi}$ [$_{PP}$ P$_{Θj}$ DP$_j$]$_i$]   locative PP-argument
      b. [$_{V'}$ [$_{V'}$ [V] [$_{PP}$ P$_{Θj}$ DP$_j$]]]]   locative PP-modifier

An oblique PP, though a complement of the verb, is not its argument, i.e. the Θ-role of the verb is assigned to the nominal complement of P, not to the PP (7) (cf. Neeleman (1997), Botwinik-Rotem (2004)). (The semantic relation of an oblique P to its nominal complement is not easily identifiable (e.g. *Dan relies on Dina*), which is suggestive of the formal nature of this instance of P, arguably Case-related, Botwinik-Rotem (2004)).

(7)   [$_{VP}$ V$_{Θi}$ [$_{PP}$ P   DP$_i$]]   oblique PP

RC formation of (6a) gives rise to two binding patterns (8). In (8a) the Op binds the PP-argument, whereas in (8b) it binds the DP-argument of P. Since the DP argument of P in (8a) is not bound by the Op, it is free and can be realized as a referential DP, namely an RDP.

(8)   a. Op$_i$ ... [$_{VP}$ V$_{Θi}$ [$_{PP}$ P$_{Θj}$ DP$_j$]$_i$]   locative PP-argument → RDP
      b. Op$_j$ ... [$_{VP}$ V$_{Θi}$ [$_{PP}$ P$_{Θj}$ DP$_j$]$_i$]   locative PP-argument → RPr

Relativization of the locative PP-modifier and of the oblique PP results in a single binding pattern (9), (10), respectively. As neither in (9) nor in (10) the PP is an argument, only the DP within the PP can be bound by the Op. Being Op-bound, namely a variable, it cannot be realized as a referential DP (i.e. an RDP).

(9)   Op$_j$ ... [$_{V'}$ [$_{V'}$ [V] [$_{PP}$ P$_{Θj}$ DP$_j$]]]   locative PP-modifier (→ RPr)
(10) Op$_i$ ... [$_{VP}$ V$_{Θi}$ [$_{PP}$ P DP$_i$]]   oblique PP (→ RPr)

To sum up, an RDP occurs only in relatives with locative PPs, as only when the locative PP (which functions as the argument of the verb) is relativized binding of the DP is obviated. In this respect, it this worth noting that the clearly limited distribution of RDPs in Hebrew cannot be accounted for either by Pérez-Leroux's (1995) proposal that views the empty category in children's RCs as resulting from movement but having the status of a Null Constant, equally realizable by RPrs and RDPs, or by the head-raising analysis in Guasti and Shlonsky (1995), where RDPs are assumed to move at LF (for the sake of argument, we can assume that movement out of a PP is possible at LF). Both proposals predict a much wider distribution of RDPs than is actually attested. Regarding Pérez-Leroux's (1995) proposal, our findings suggest that children acquiring a "true resumptive" language like Hebrew know from the start that pronouns, but not referential DPs, can function as semantic variables. Therefore, the use of RDPs in child Hebrew is restricted to syntactic contexts where binding of the RDP is obviated.

3.4 Omission of RPr

3.4.1 Locative PPs

In our proposal, Op/PRO-movement that gives rise to relatives without an RPr can take place if the P is analyzed as part of the verb and not projected. As this kind of V-P reanalysis is reasonably limited to non-predicative prepositions (i.e. Ps that are not Θ-assigning), it is unlikely to target the P of a locative PP-modifier. The DP complement of this P is necessarily Θ-marked by the P. Omission of the locative RPr, thus, is most likely to result from perceiving the locative P of the PP-argument (6a) on a par with an oblique P, namely not as a Θ-assigner (7), resulting in the derivation given in (11):

(11) Op/PRO$_i$ ... [$_{VP}$ [V$_{\Theta i}$ + P$_{loc}$ø] [$_{DP}$ t$_i$]]

Viewed this way, a locative PP has, in principle, three possible analyses. It can be analyzed as the argument of the verb (12a), as its modifier (12b), or as its (obligatory) PP-complement (12c) (borrowing the term from Neeleman (1997)). In (12a, b) P is a Θ-assigning predicate, not undergoing reanalysis. (12a) can give rise to an RDP, (12b) is the RPr representation, and (12c) underlies omission of the RPr:

(12) a. Op$_i$ ... [$_{VP}$ V$_{\Theta i}$ [$_{PP}$ P$_{\Theta j}$ [$_{DP}$ **RDP**$_j$]$_i$]]   locative   PP-argument
     b. Op$_j$ ... [$_{VP}$ V$_{(\Theta i)}$ [$_{PP}$ P$_{\Theta j}$ [$_{DP}$ **RPr**$_j$]]]   locative PP-modifier
     c. Op$_i$ ... [$_{VP}$ [V$_{\Theta i}$ + Pø] [$_{DP}$ t$_i$]]   locative PP-complement

To what extent a locative P is susceptible to be analyzed as a non-Θ-assigning P depends on the P itself, and on its combination with the verb.

Table 2. Distribution of responses with locative PPs

	RPr	RDP	ø
*tipes **al*** ('climbed on/'up')	35%	30%	35%
kofec/omed/yoshev **leyad** ('jumps/stands/sits near')	72%	11%	17%

As shown in Table 2, children's performance regarding *tipes al* ('climbed on/up') is distributed almost evenly between the options in (12). The preposition *al* in this context is clearly locative, projecting a locative PP that can be analyzed either as the argument of *tipes* ('climbed') or as its modifier. Moreover, its combination with the particular verb is unique (13a) vs. (13b)):

(13) a. *ha-yeled tipes   al/*leyad/*meal*/mitaxat ha-bait*
        the-boy climbed on/near/above/under   the-house
     b. *ha-yeled yashav al/leyad/meal/mitaxat ha-bait*
        the-boy   sat   on/near/above/under the-house

Since, when combined with *tipes*, the content of *al* ('on') is fully recoverable, the plausibility of the analysis in (12c) is on a par with (12a,b), resulting in the evenly distributed performance. In contrast, *leyad* ('near') is much less likely to be reanalyzed giving rise to (12c), as its content not being fully determined by the verb, is not easily recoverable. Consequently, the omission rate of the RPr is much lower (17%). From the fact that the rate of the RDP is rather low as well (11%), we can deduce that the PP headed by *leyad* ('near') is analyzed correctly by most children as a modifier (12b).

3.4.2 Oblique PPs

The content of an oblique P is fully recoverable from the verb (e.g. *ka'as al/*be/*me*, 'angered on/*in/*from'), and arguably, it is not involved in Θ-assignment. Therefore it can undergo the V-P reanalysis assumed here (which in turn underlies RPr-omission). The distribution of responses with oblique PPs (Table 3) suggests, however, that this may not be the only factor that plays a role in the omission of RPrs.[4]

Table 3. Distribution of responses with oblique PPs

	RPr	ø
ka'as al ('angered on [at]')	95%	5%
ba'at be- ('kicked in')	82%	18%
nigen be- ('played music in [on]')	66%	33%
paxad me- ('[was] afraid of/from')	43%	57%

Following Botwinik-Rotem (2004), the internal arguments of verbs occurring with oblique PPs in Hebrew are Goal or Subject Matter (SM), rather than Theme or Experiencer (14). The latter are the only internal arguments realized in adult Hebrew as bare (accusative) DPs (i.e. DO), undergoing Op-movement in RC formation. The former (IO) relativize without movement, by means of RPr.

(14) a. *dan ba'at be-/azar   le-yosi* [Goal]
        Dan kicked in-/helped to-Yosi

'Dan kicked/helped Yosi.'
b. *dan ka'as al/paxad   me-yosi* [SM]
   Dan angered on/feared of/from-Yosi
   'Dan was angry at/afraid of Yosi.'
c. *dan raxac   et   yosi* [Theme]
   Dan washed Acc Yosi
   'Dan washed Yosi.'
d. *dan hifxid   et   yosi* [Experiencer]
   Dan scared Acc Yosi
   'Dan scared Yosi.'

Judging by their adult-like performance regarding *ka'as al* ('angered at'), we assume that children are aware of the distinction between the Theme/Experiencer (realizable as bare DPs) on the one hand, and Goal/SM on the other hand. That is, since the internal argument of *ka'as* is SM, rather than Theme, it is not relativized via Op/PRO-movement (and V-P reanalysis).

Given this and the claim that omission of RPr involves Op/PRO-movement, we suggest that omission of RPrs realizing Goal and SM results from perceiving them on a par with Theme/Experiencer. In what follows we elaborate briefly on what can possibly bring this about.

3.4.2.1 Interpretation of certain Θ-roles
Following Reinhart (2002), Θ-roles are not atomic notions, but rather clusters of two binary specified (±) Θ-features:

(15) /c = cause change
      /m = mental state relevant

Some Θ-roles are fully specified, whereas others are not (i.e. only one of the features has a specific value, the value of the other feature is not determined). Theme, Experiencer, Instrument, as well as the object of a locative P (Marelj 2004), belong to the former (16a), Goal and SM exemplify the latter (16b):

(16) a. Theme/object of P_{loc} [-c-m]
         Experiencer   [-c+m]
         Instrument   [+c-m]
      b. Goal   [-c]
         SM   [-m]

The interpretation of the fully specified Θ-roles is fixed, as both their features are specified. In contrast, the underspecified clusters have some freedom of interpretation, as their non-specified feature is assumed to be consistent with either value. Thus, a Θ-cluster like [-c] corresponding to the traditional label Goal, is, in fact, consistent with either [-c-m] or [-c+m] interpretations, and the SM cluster [-m] is consistent with either [-c-m] or [+c-m] interpretations. If children have not yet mastered this distinction (i.e. assignment of a fully specified Θ-cluster vs. consistency with a fully specified Θ-cluster), they are expected to apply relativization via Op/PRO-movement not only to fully specified arguments, but also to underspecified ones (e.g. to the Goal of *ba'at be-*, or to the SM of *paxad me-*). [5]

We take the attested omission of locative PPs (e.g. *tipes al*, 'climbed up') and of the PP realizing the Instrument Θ-role ([+c-m]), (e.g. *nigen be-*, 'played music on') to indicate that at some stage children may apply relativization via Op/PRO-movement to any fully specified argument (rather than only to Theme and Experiencer), provided that the P can be reanalyzed with the verb.

It should be noted that the arguable relevance of the thematic role to the omission of an RPr is assumed here to be secondary. Once the option not to project a non-predicative (oblique) P (i.e. the $[V_{+P\emptyset}]$ representation) ceases to exist, relativization via Op-movement will be applicable only to bare DPs, regardless of their thematic role (assuming that the accusative marker *et* is not P).

3.5 The dative RPr (which is never omitted)

The dative morpheme *le-* ('to') in Hebrew is not a syntactic head P, but rather a Case-marking affix of the DP (Landau (1994), Botwinik-Rotem (2004)). The status of the dative *le-* as a nominal affix prevents it from being analyzed as part of the verb. Therefore, a dative argument in Hebrew is never a bare DP. Since the omission of an RPr crucially involves Op/PRO-movement, and since Op/PRO cannot be conceived with a non-bare DP, omission of the dative RPr is not attested.

Summary

Assuming that children acquiring Hebrew derive RCs essentially like adults, we analyzed the omission of obligatory (oblique and locative) RPr in the acquisition of Hebrew RCs as Op/PRO-movement enabled by a particular and clearly limited version of V-P reanalysis. Both the availability of V-P reanalysis and children's conception of the kind of argument that can be relativized via Op/PRO-movement (a fully specified bare DP) give rise to the deviations attested in the acquisition of Hebrew RCs, namely the omission of obligatory RPrs, to the exclusion of the dative RPr. The attested distribution of RDPs supports our assumption that children acquiring Hebrew know that a referential DP, unlike an RPr, cannot be a variable, allowing it only in contexts where its binding by the base-generated generalized Op can be obviated.

Notes

[1]For further discussion bearing on the optionality of RPr, see Sharvit (1999), Shlonsky (1992) and references cited therein.

[2] The derivation involving movement of the RPr (3b, c), not being attested in children's data, is not addressed here. Note that in Hebrew the relative operator is homophonous with a pronoun rather than with a *wh*-phrase. Whether the fronted RPr is a moved operator or rather a sub-case of topicalization is debatable (Borer (1984) vs. Doron (1982), Shlonsky (1985)).

[3] The status of the locative PP depends on the verb (e.g. *put* vs. *sleep*), or on the verb-PP combination (e.g. *sleep in bed* vs. *sleep in the forest*) (for further discussion see Hornstein & Weinberg (1981), Baker (1988) and references cited therein).

[4] It seems unreasonable to attribute the attested variability to the P-morphemes, as quite distinct omission rates are attested with the same P-morpheme (e.g. *ba'at be-* (17%) vs. *nigen be-* (33%); *tipes al* (35%) vs. *ka'as al* (5%)).

[5]The exceptionally high omission rate with *paxad me-* ('was afraid of') is probably due to an additional and independent factor. The combination of *me-* ('from'/'of') with a pronoun is morphologically irregular and quite complex (e.g. *me + hu* ('he') → *mimeno* ('from him') vs. *be + hu* → *bo, leayd + hu* → *leyado*) (Dromi (1979)). Thus, it is reasonable to assume that the omission of this RPr results, to some extent, from avoidance of it. (It is therefore highly desirable to check the omission rate of this RPr in clearly directional contexts (e.g. *ha-gamad she-dan barax mimeno,* 'the dwarf that Dan escaped from him').)

References

Baker, M. (1988) *Incorporation,* University of Chicago Press, Chicago.

Bennis, H. and T. Hoekstra (1989) "PRO and the Binding Theory," in H. Bennis and A. van Kemanade, eds., *Linguisitics in the Netherland,* Foris, Dordrecht, 11-20.

Borer, H. (1984) *Parametric Syntax,* Foris, Dordrecht.

Botwinik-Rotem, I. (2004) *The Category P: Features, projections, interpretation,* Doctoral dissertation, Tel Aviv University.

Bshara, R. (2004) "The Acquisition of Relative Clauses in Palestinian Arabic," Seminar paper, Bar-Ilan University.

Cinque, G. (1990) *Types of A'-Dependencies,* MIT Press, Cambridge, Massachusetts.

Crain, S. and R. Thornton (1998) *Investigations in Universal Grammar: A Guide to research on the acquisition of syntax and semantics,* MIT Press, Cambridge, Massachusetts.

Den Dikken, M. (1995) *Particles,* Oxford University Press.

Doron, E. (1982) "The Syntax and Semantics of Resumptive Pronouns," in *Texas Linguistics Forum 19*, Department of Linguistics, University of Texas, Austin.

Dromi, E. (1979) "More on the Acquisition of Locative Prepositions: An analysis of Hebrew data," *Journal of Child Language* 6, 547-562.

Fiengo, R. and R. May (1994) *Indices and Identity,* MIT Press, Cambridge, Massachusetts.

Friedmann, N., R. Novogrodsky, R. Szterman and O. Preminger (to appear). "Resumptive Pronouns as a Last Resort When Movement is Impaired: Relative clauses in hearing impairment," in S. Armon-Lotem, G. Danon and S. Rothstein, eds., *Generative Approaches to Hebrew Linguistics,* John Benjamins.

Guasti, T. (2002) *Language Acquisition: The Growth of Grammar,* MIT Press, Cambridge, Massachusetts.

Guasti, M.T. and U. Shlonsky (1995) "The Acquisition of French Relative Clauses Reconsidered," *Language Acquisition* 4, 257-276.

Hamburger, H. and S. Crain (1982) "Relative acquisition," in S. Kuczaj, ed., *Language Development: Syntax and Semantics,* Lawrence Erlbaum Associates, Hillsdale, N.J.

Hornstein, N. and A. Weinberg (1981) "Case Theory and Preposition Stranding," *Linguistic Inquiry* 12, 54-91.

Landau, I. (1994) *Dative Shift and Extended VP-Shell,* M.A. thesis, Tel Aviv University.

Labelle, M. (1990) "Predication, Wh-movement and the Development of Relative Clauses," *Language Acquisition* 1, 95-119.

—. (1996) "Wh-movement and the Development of Relative Clauses," *Language Acquisition* 5, 65-82.

Marelj, M. (2004) *Middles and Argument Structure across Languages,* LOT series.

McKee, C. and D. McDaniel (2001) "Resumptive Pronouns in English Relative Clauses," *Language Acquisition* 9, 113-156.

Neeleman, A. (1997) "PP-Complements," *Natural Language and Linguistic Theory* 15, 89-137.

Pérez-Leroux, A. T. (1995) "Resumptives in the Acquisition of Relative Clauses," *Language Acquisition* 4, 105-138.

Reinhart, T. (2002) "The Theta-System – An Overview," *Theoretical Linguistics* 28, 229-290.

Sells, P. (1984) *Syntax and Semantics of Resumptive Pronouns,* Doctoral Dissertation, University of Massachusetts, Amherst.

Sharvit, Y. (1999) "Resumptive Pronouns in Relative Clauses," *Natural Language and Linguistic Theory* 17, 613-671.

Shlonsky, U. (1985) "The Syntax of COMP in Hebrew and the ECP," ms., MIT, Cambridge, Massachusetts.

—. (1992) "Resumptive Pronouns as a Last Resort," *Linguistic Inquiry* 23, 443-468.

Varlokosta, S. and S. Armon-Lotem (1998) "Resumptives and Wh-movement in the Acquisition of Relative Clauses in Modern Greek and Hebrew,"

Proceedings of the 22nd Boston University Conference on Language Development, Cascadilla Press, Boston, MA.

CHILDREN'S PROCESSING OF SUBJECT AND OBJECT RELATIVES IN ITALIAN

FABRIZIO AROSIO, FLAVIA ADANI, AND MARIA TERESA GUASTI

1. Introduction

Children's comprehension and production of Relative Clauses (RCs, henceforth) has been extensively studied. In her pioneering work, Sheldon (1974) found that these structures are difficult to comprehend even at 6 years. Further research has shown that, once disturbing factors are removed from the experimental setting, children's performance improves significantly (Hamburger & Crain, 1982). Studies on adult processing have established that subject RCs are easier to process than object RCs (Frauenfelder, *et al.* 1980; King & Just 1991; Traxler *et al.* 2002; Schrifers, *et al.* 1995 among others). In this article, we aim to bring these two traditions together by examining how children process subject and object RCs disambiguated through different devices. We will do so, by looking at Italian RCs since in this language there are two kinds of object RCs, one with the embedded subject in the preverbal embedded position and another with the embedded subject in the postverbal position.

2. Italian facts

An Italian RC such as in (1) is ambiguous between a subject and an object reading, that is, it can correspond to the English sentences in (1a) and (1b).

(1) La volpe$_1$ [che insegue il gatto$_2$] zoppica
    The fox$_1$ [that chase-3sg the cat$_2$] limp-3sg

    (1a) The fox that is chasing the cat is limping   SUBJECT READING
    (1b) The fox that the cat is chasing is limping   OBJECT READING

For the sake of argument, we assume the standard analysis of RCs (Cinque, 1982), according to which the subject reading in (1) is obtained by coindexing the head-NP with a null operator in Spec-CP that has moved there from the embedded subject position as shown in (2). The object reading of (1) is also obtained by coindexing the head-NP_1 with the null operator in Spec-CP moved there from the embedded object position, as shown in (3); in addition, in this structure, we also have a chain between the embedded-NP_2 and an empty expletive pronoun in the embedded subject position (Rizzi, 1986).

(2) La volpe$_1$ [Op$_1$ che t$_1$ insegue il gatto$_2$] zoppica

(3) La volpe$_1$ [Op$_1$ che pro$_2$ insegue t$_1$ il gatto$_2$] zoppica

Thus, the ambiguity in (1) comes about because Italian allows postverbal subjects and both the embedded-NP_2 "il gatto" and the head of the RC NP_1 "la volpe" (or the trace of the Op) potentially agree with the embedded verb "insegue", thus both could be its subject.

Interestingly, sentence (1) is not the only way Italian speakers can convey (1b). Actually, as in English, it is also possible to have the embedded subject in the preverbal position as in (4)

(4) La volpe$_1$ [che il gatto$_2$ insegue] zoppica
    The fox$_1$ [that the cat$_2$ follow-3sg] limp-3sg

Sentence (4) is unambiguously an object RC. Clearly, since Italian post verbal subjects agree in number features with the verb, RCs with post verbal subjects are not ambiguous in cases in which the head-NP_1 and the embedded-NP_2 do not share the same number features, as in (5) and (6). In (5) only the embedded-NP_2 in postverbal position agree with the embedded verb and thus this is unambiguously an object RC. In (6) only the head-NP_1 or more accurately its trace agrees with the embedded verb and thus only a subject RC is possible.

(5) La volpe$_1$ [che insegu**ono i gatti**$_2$] zoppica
    The fox$_1$ [that follow**^{3Pl} the ^{Pl} cats**$_2$] limp^{3Sing}
    Lit: The fox that the cats are following is limping   OBJECT READING ONLY

(6) **La volpe**$_1$ [che insegue i gatti$_2$] zoppica
    The ^{Sing} fox$_1$ [that follow^{3Sing} the cats$_2$] limp^{3Sing}
    Lit: The fox that is following the cats is limping   SUBJECT READING ONLY

Summing up, Italian subjects can engage in an object RC analysis if they see an NP after the complementizer "che" ("that") (see 4) or if the morphological information on the embedded verb is incompatible with the feature of the head-NP, as in (5). If the feature of the head-NP and that of the embedded verb are the same, a subject RC analysis is possible.

The fact that Italian speakers make use of two different grammatical devices while interpreting RCs is particularly interesting since it offers an intriguing set of data to test some of the processing theories. Looking at the problem in children might provide some data not available in a fully developed system.

3. Italian RCs and processing theories

In this paragraph we will consider some of the processing theories which make distinct predictions for Italian subject RCs and object RCs.

According to the *Dependency Locality Theory* (Gibson 1998, 2000) storage resources are required to keep track of the syntactic dependencies that are needed to complete a grammatical sentence and the number of temporary incomplete syntactic dependencies determines the memory load of a computation. Let us see the prediction of this theory for Italian. After processing the complementizer "che" ("that") a RC is postulated and the parser attempts to posit as few elements as possible. Thus, to complete a subject or an object RC the minimal set of constituents required includes three elements (the parser does not distinguish at this point between subject and object RC, but attempts the simpler analysis, which includes the least number of elements): the trace in the embedded subject position bound by the empty operator, the embedded verb (an intransitive one would be enough) and the matrix verb (also an intransitive one would be enough). When the next, the verb, element is processed the set of expected elements in a subject RC in (6) repeated in (6a), will include an NP object, as the verb turns out to be transitive, and the matrix verb.

Subject relative

(6a) La volpe₁ [Op₁ che   t₁ insegue   i gatti₂] zoppica
     The^{Sing} fox₁ [Op₁ that   t₁ follow^{3Sing} the cats₂] limp^{3Sing}

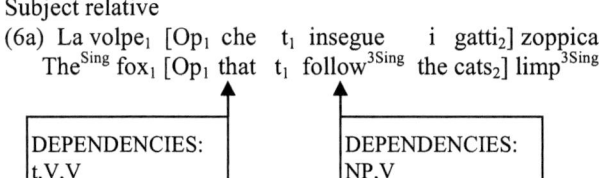

DEPENDENCIES:	DEPENDENCIES:
t,V,V	NP,V

For the object relative in (4), repeated in (4a), at the "che" the minimal set necessary to complete the sentence is as before, while the next element processed is the definite article "il". At this point, the minimal set includes a NP, a verb, a trace and the matrix verb (a subject RC is not possible):

Object relative preverbal-Subj
(4a) La   volpe₁ [Op₁ che il gatto₂ insegue   t₁] zoppica
     The-sg fox₁ [Op₁ that the cat₂ follow-3sg t₁] limp-3sg

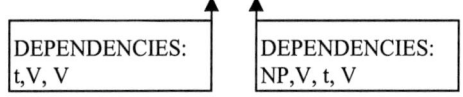

DEPENDENCIES:	DEPENDENCIES:
t,V, V	NP,V, t, V

Consider now sentence (5), repeated in (5a), which also contains an object RC. No difference with respect to the previous cases exists at the complementizer. When processing the first word after the complementizer, namely the embedded verb "inseguono" ("follow-3PL"), the minimal set includes just two elements: the trace of the object and a matrix verb. Italian is a Pro-drop language and a null subject should already have been postulated before the verb. This is shown in the picture below:

Object relative postverbal-Subj
(5a) La   volpe₁ [Op₁ che pro₂ insegu**ono** t₁ **i**   **gatti**₂] zoppica
     The-sg fox₁ [Op₁ that pro₂ follow-3pl   t₁ **the-pl cats**₂] limp-3g

DEPENDENCIES:	DEPENDENCIES:
t,V,V	NP,V

Thus, according to the *Dependency Locality Theory*, we expect that subject RC and object RCs with a postverbal subject are equally difficult to analyze at the embedded verb: they require the same number of incomplete dependencies. Object RCs with a preverbal subject are more difficult than both subject RCs and object RCs with a postverbal subject.

According to the *Competition Model* (Bates & MacWhinney, 1987), different languages use different sources of information to determine the outcome of sentence processing. The different outcome depends on the relative strength of the cues which varies from one language to another. Adults base their interpretation of sentences on the most valid and reliable cues in their language. For instance, English is a language in which word order is high in cue validity while Italian speakers prefer subject-verb agreement. Since agreement is a stronger cue than position in Italian, this model predicts that (6) is unproblematic and that (5) is easier than (4).

According to the *Minimal Chain Principle* (De Vincenzi 1991), the human processor decides for an interpretation as soon as possible, without waiting for a disambiguation which can arrive soon, later or never. De Vincenzi's principle states that we do not postulate unnecessary traces, but if necessary, we do not delay their postulation. This means that, in the course of the processing, mono-argumental chains are preferred than longer chains, but, if the parser has to posit a trace, it does so as soon as possible. This principle predicts that subject RC are easier than object relatives, because at the complementizer the parser inserts a null operator and builds the shortest chain by inserting a trace in the preverbal subject position immediately after the complementizer.

(6ii) La volpe$_1$ [Op$_1$ che t$_1$ insegue i gatti$_2$] zoppica
The^{Sing} fox$_1$ [Op$_1$ that t$_1$ follow^{3Sing} the cats$_2$] limp^{3Sing}
        |_____|

Consider now an object RC with preverbal a subject as the one in sentence (4). After the parser has built the minimal chain as before, it sees the NP "il gatto" that disconfirms this analysis. It deletes the trace of the moved operator and after it has seen the verb it inserts the trace of the operator in object position and builds a chain, as shown below:

(4ii) La volpe$_1$ [Op$_1$ che ⱦ il gatto$_2$ insegue t$_1$] zoppica
The^{Sing} fox$_1$ [Op$_1$ thatⱦt$_1$ the cat$_2$ follow^{3Sing} t$_1$] limp^{3Sing}
        |_____|

Now, consider sentence (5). After having built the minimal chain as before, the parser sees the verb disconfirming this choice. It deletes the inserted trace, it inserts a pronominal entity in the embedded subject position and a trace of the moved operator in the position of direct object of the embedded verb. At this point the parser sees the NP "i gatti" that, as postverbal subject, needs to be coindexed with the pronominal element in the preverbal subject position.

(5ii) La volpe$_1$ [Op$_1$ che ⱦ pro$_2$ insegu**ono** t$_1$ i   **gatti**$_2$] zoppica
The^{Sing} fox$_1$ [Op$_1$ that ⱦ$_1$ pro$_2$ follow$^{\underline{3Pl}}$ t$_1$ **the** $^{\underline{Pl}}$ **cats**$_2$] limp^{3Sing}
        |_____|_____|

As we can easily see, in (4ii) we find a longer chain then in (6ii). This predicts that (6ii) is easier then (4ii). Moreover, we find two chains in (5ii). This predicts that (5ii) is more difficult than (6ii) and (4ii). In general, the prediction of MCP is the following: subject RCs are easier then object RCs; object RCs with a preverbal subject are easier than object RCs with a postverbal subject.

PREDICTIONS OF THE PROCESSING THEORIES ("<" means easier)					
DEPENDENCY LOCALITY THEORY	SUBJECT RCs	=	OBJECT RC POSTVERBAL SUB	<	OBJECT RC PREVERBAL SUB
COMPETITION MODEL	SUBJECT RCs	<	OBJECT RCs POSTVERBAL SUB	<	OBJECT RC PREVERBAL SUB
MINIMAL CHAIN PRINCIPLE	SUBJECT RCs	<	OBJECT RCs PREVERBAL SUB	<	OBJECT RC POSTVERBAL SUB

In the following paragraph we will present an experiment testing how Italian children process subject and object RCs and how data from children processing can help us to parse apart different theories of processing and, furthermore, to explain how different cues to disambiguation are used by Italian children during development.

4. Our Study

Our study was composed of: (1) a picture selection task aimed at testing the comprehension of subject and object RCs, (2) a grammaticality judgement task whose aim was to establish whether participants are sensitive to number agreement violations between the inflected lexical verb and its subject, (3) two memory tests to control for possible effects of working memory.

4.1. Participants

A group of 79 Italian monolingual children took part in the study. The experimental group was divided into 3 age groups as reported in the table below:

Age group	N	Age range (m)	Mean age (m)	SD
5	31	61-77	70,35	3,92
7	35	88-99	94,64	3,45
9	13	97-110	105,77	3,94

The children were recruited from kindergartens and primary schools in the Areas of Milano, Modena and Como (Italy). A control group of 24 undergraduate students was also tested. They were all students at the Università di Milano-Bicocca. Before starting the experiment children were familiarized with a puppet that was learning Italian; the puppet asked for their help in the enterprise. Experiments were all carried out in a quiet room in which children were tested individually. Adults were tested with the same procedure used for children, except for the puppet mediation.

4.2. The Grammaticality Judgment Task (GJT)

In the GJT (McDaniel & Cairns, 1996) participants were asked to listen to a series of sentences pre-recorded on a computer and delivered through loudspeakers. Children were told that the sentences had been recorded by the puppet and they had to say whether what the puppet said was correct or not. In the case children answered that what the puppet said was not correct they were asked to correct it. We presented 18 sentences, 9 with singular subjects, 9 with plural subjects. Eight of the 18 sentences were grammatical and 10 were ungrammatical because of number agreement violations. Sentences were presented in a pseudo-random order. An example of a sentence is given below:

(7) * I cuochi cuoce la pasta   NOT CORRECT: AGREEMENT MISMATCH
        The cooks make-3sg the pasta
        Lit: The cooks is making pasta

(8)   I bambini mangiano la mela   CORRECT: AGREEMENT IS MET
        The children eat-3pl the apple
        Lit: The children are eating the apple

4.3. The picture selection task (PST)

In this experiment we wanted to test childrens' comprehension of subject and object RC of the kind in (4), (5) and (6) above. Our material included

- 18 unambiguous **subject** RCs (SR) as below

    (9) Fammi vedere il cane che rincorre i cavalli
        Let-me   see   the dog that chease-3sg the horses
        Lit: Show me the dog that is chasing the horses

- 18 unambiguous **number marked object** RCs (ORN) as below

    (10) Fammi vedere il cane che rincorrono i cavalli
        Let-me   see   the dog that chease-3pl the horses
        Lit: Show me the dog that the horses are chasing

- 18 unambiguous **position marked object** RCs (ORP) as below

    (11) Fammi vedere il cane che il cavallo rincorre
        Let-me   see   the dog that the horse chease-3sg
        Lit: Show me the dog that the horse is chasing

The above structures were obtained in the following way. We singled out 18 lexical verbs controlled for length and familiarity. Out of these 18 verbs we created 18 item sentences containing an SR, 18 item sentences containing an ORN, 18 item sentences containing an ORP. From these three sets we created three different lists, each containing 6 sentences from each condition for a total of 18 experimental sentences. The items were randomized and interspersed with 18 fillers. Each sentence in the lists was then associated to two pictures, as in the figure 1. Subject were randomly assigned to each list and were tested individually. The experiment was run on a portable computer connected to external loudspeakers in a quiet room in the subjects' schools. During the experimental trials the children heard a sentence trough the loudspeakers and immediately afterwards two pictures were presented on the computer screen. They were asked to point out which picture matched the sentence.

Picture 1: The above picture appeared after the participant heard one of the three following sentences: *Show me the dwarf that is painting the children* or *Show me the dwarf that the children are painting* or *Show me the dwarf that are painting the children*

Before starting the experiment a familiarization session was run until the children had understood the task.

4.4. Memory tests

In order to see if development in the memory resources plays a role in childrens' processing of RCs, we administrated the following memory tests: (i) Ciccarelli's *Backward Repetition Span* (1998), which requires to maintain in memory an ordered sequence of words and to repeat them back in the reverse order, (ii) a *Dual Span Test* aimed at evaluating not only storage resources but also the capability of performing a dual task and thus of allocating resources to different tasks.

4.5. Results

4.5.1 The Grammaticality Judgement Test

The main purpose of the grammaticality judgement task was to identify children who failed to demonstrate any sensitivity to number agreement, as number agreement on the verb is crucial for understanding object RCs with a postverbal subjects. We found that the mean overall accuracy rate for GJT in the children groups was .92 (SD=.13). In more details, the 5-year-olds' accuracy rate was .81 (SD=.16), the 7-year-olds's was .98 (SD= .04) and the 9-year-olds's was 1. The results of a Tukey post-hoc comparison show that 5-year-olds are significantly different from both 7 and 9. Given the main purpose of GJT, we excluded 17 of 31 5-year-old children (those with less than .85 of correct answers in the grammaticality judgement task). The new mean overall accuracy rate is .97 (SD=.04), while 5-year-old group rate is .94 (SD=.05).

4.5.2 The Picture Selection Task

A two way repeated-measures ANOVA was conducted with age as the between-subjects factor, type of sentence as the repeated measure and accuracy as the dependent variable. The analysis revealed a main effect of age (F[3,99]= 41,58, p<.001), as well as type of sentence (F[2, 198]= 129,58, p<,001) and also an interaction between the two (F[6,198]= 16,353, p <0,001. Since we could not safely assume that this is a normal distribution, another repeated-measures ANOVA with standardised values was conducted. It yielded similar results. The overall results are summarised in Table 1 below where SUBJ stands for *subject RC*, Onum stands for *Number marked object RC* and Opos stands for *Position marked object RC*

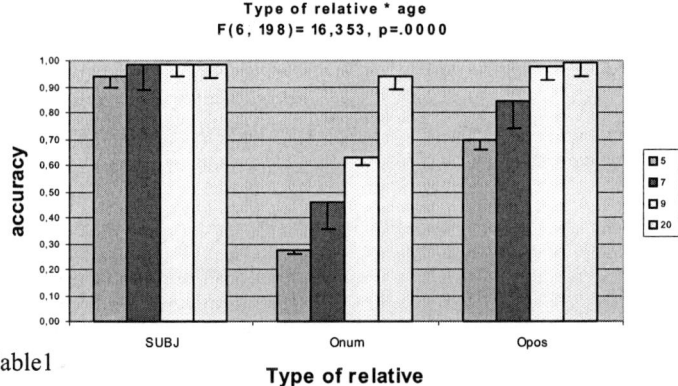

Type of relative * age
F(6, 198)= 16,353, p=.0000

Table1

Type of relative

We used the Tukey test for all comparisons within each group. Subject relatives are the easiest with no difference observed among age groups. Position marked object RCs at 5 are different from position marked object RCs at 9 years and in adulthood and at 7 they are different from position marked object RCs at 9 and in adults. Number marked object RCs are different at 5 from all the other groups, at 7 and 9 they are different from number marked object RCs in adulthood.

We used the Mann-Whitney test for single-sample comparisons to chance (0.5). The results reveal that, with number marked object RCs, the 5-year-olds perform significantly below chance (z =-4,2); the 7 and 9 year-olds perform at chance (respectively, $z = -1,15$ and $z = 0.37$), while the adult group performs above chance ($z = 6,5$). With the position marked object RCs, all children groups and adults perform above chance (respectively, $z = 5,08$ at 5; $z = 5,90$ at 7; $z = 4,88$ at 9 and $z = 6,7$ at 20). It can be argued that the very poor performance on number marked object RCs could depend on the insensitivity to number agreement by a small group of children. In order to safely assume that this is not the case, we excluded the 17 children who did not reach 85% in the GJT. A new ANOVA was conducted, with age as the independent variable and correct answer in number marked object RCs as dependent variable. The difference between 5 and 7 is still highly significant ($F[2,59]=6,5457$, $p<.00271$).

4.5.3 The memory tests

Two one-way ANOVAs were conducted with age groups as the independent variable and, respectively, backward repetition span and dual span as the dependent variables. Both ANOVAs show a significant effect of age: first ANOVA (age*backward span) ($F[1,64]=9,5307$, $p<.005$) and second ANOVA (age*dual span) ($F[2,76]=26,393$, $p<.0001$). Although there is an expected improvement in memory abilities as a function of age, no significant correlation was found between the score on memory tests and the performance in the Picture Selection Task.

5. Discussion

As expected, Italian children have less difficulty in interpreting subject RCs than object RCs, and this is consistent with the findings of a number of studies on adults on a variety of languages. This first result is compatible with the predictions of all the processing theories we discussed above. We also found that object RCs with postverbal subjects are more difficult than and object RCs with preverbal subjects. Crucially, this result is only predicted by the *Minimal Chain Principle* and not by the other processing theories. Moreover, this finding is consistent with De Vincenzi et al.'s (1999) results about comprehension of Italian wh-questions which show that semantically reversible object questions are more problematic than subject questions for children up to 9. This is not surprising as wh-questions in Italian present similar properties to RCs. Consider (12). The sentence (12a) is ambiguous between a subject and an object question. (12b) is an object question, in which the verb "inseguono" agrees with the post-verbal subject "i gatti" and (12c) is a subject question with the verb agreeing with the trace of the wh-operator

(12) a. Chi insegue il gatto?
      Who chases the cat?
      (=Who does the cat chase? or Who chases the cat?)
   b. Chi inseguono i gatti?
      Who chase-3PL the cats?
      Who do the cats chase?
   c. Chi insegue i gatti?
      Who chases the cats?

Our data support the hypothesis that children adhere to the MCP, that is, when they parse a RC (or a question) they attempt a subject analysis by positing a gap in the subject position. For position marked object relative clauses, this analysis is abandoned immediately, when children encounter the NP subject. Although there is improvement across ages, we have seen that from age 5, childrens performance on position marked object relative is above chance. In the case of number marked object RCs, instead, children perform at chance even at 9 years. Assume that they have started with a subject analysis and posited a gap in the embedded subject position. When they see the verb, it seems as though they understand that there is a clash between their hypothesis and number agreement on the verb, but are unable to perform a reanalysis. It is clear that number marked object RCs are more complex than position marked object RCs, as they involve two chains, something that may be memory demanding. Although memory may be implicated, we did not find any correlation between scores on the working memory tests and performance on the picture selection task. Other studies, such as Felser et al. (2003), (see also Booth, MacWhinney & Harasaky, 2000), have found a relation in 7-year-olds between score in memory tests and performance in comprehension of sentences. Unlike ours, in this study an on-line measure was used. This may be the source of the discrepancy and in future work we are planning to examine this possibility.

   The increased difficulty with number marked object RCs with respect to position marked object RCs may be related to the different operations required to check the agreement on the embedded verb (see Guasti & Rizzi, 2002; Franck, Lassi, Frauenfelder, & Rizzi, in press). From these works, it emerges that subject-verb agreement is more fragile in VS structures (as number marked object relatives) than in SV structures (as position marked object RCs), that is, in VS structures the subject may fail to agree with the verb (as in "lo ha fatto i bambini" lit. "it has done the children"). In addition, attraction errors (in which a noun close to the verb interfere with the subject-verb agreement relation, e.g., the friend of the neighbours always come late) increase in OVS structures with respect to OSV. This asymmetry stems from the fact that agreement is checked twice in SV structures and thus is less prone to interferences while once in VS

(Franck et al, in press). Our results seem to suggest that when agreement is checked twice it is more reliable and led to reanalysis. When it is checked once, it is less reliable and children err.

References

Bates, E., A. Devescovi and S. D'Amico (1999) "Processing complex sentences: a cross-linguistic study", *Language and Cognitive Processes*, 14, 69-123.

Booth, J.R., B. MacWhinney and Y. Harasaky (2000) "Developmental differences in visual and auditory processing of complex sentences" *Child Development* 4, 981-1003.

Ciccarelli, L. (1998) *Comprensione del linguaggio, dei processi di elaborazione e memoria di lavoro: uno studio in età prescolare*, PhD dissertation, University of Padua.

Cornoldi C., R. De Beni and B. Carretti (2003) "Studio sul ruolo della memoria di lavoro nella comprensione del testo", *Psicologia dello sviluppo cognitivo linguistico : tra teoria e intervento*. Firenze : Firenze University Press, 39-46.

Daneman, M., and P. Carpenter (1980) "Individual differences in working memory and reading". *Journal of verbal learning and verbal behaviour* 19, 450-466.

De Vincenzi, M., L. Arduino, L. Ciccarelli and R. Job (1999) "Parsing strategies in children comprehension of interrogative sentences", *Proceeding of ECCS '99, Siena*.

Felser, C., T. Marinis and H. Clahsen (2003) "Children's processing of ambiguous sentences: a study of relative clause attachment", *Language Acquisition*.

Frauenfelder, U.H., J.Segui and J. Mehler (1980) „Monitoring around the relative clause" *Journal of Verbal Learning and Verbal Behavior*, 19, 2.

Franck, J., G. Lassi, U. Frauenfelder and L. Rizzi (in press) Agreement and movement: A syntactic analysis of attraction.

Guasti, M.T. and A. Cardinaletti (2003) "Relative clause formation in Romance child production" *Probus* 15, 47-88.

—. and L. Rizzi (2002) "Agreement and tense as distinct syntactic positions. Evidence from acquisition" in G. Cinque, ed., *The structure of DP and IP. The cartography of syntactic structures*. Vol. 1. New York:Oxford University Press.

Hamburger, H., and S.Crain (1982) "Relative acquisition", in S. Kuczaj, ed., *Language development: Syntax and semantics*. Hillsdale, N.J.: Lawrence Erlbaum.

King, J., and M.A., Just (1991) "Individual differences in syntactic parsing: the role of working memory", *Journal of memory and language*, 30, 580-602.

Labelle, M. (1996) "The acquisition of relative clauses: movement or no movement?" *Language Acquisition* 5, 65-82.

Love, T. E. and D. A. Swinney (1997) "Real-time processing of object relative constructions by pre-school children" *Proceeding of the 10th annual CUNY conference on human sentence processing.*

MacWhinney, B., and E. Bates (1989) *The crosslinguistic study of sentence processing*, NY: CUP.

Palladino, P. (2004) "Uno strumento per esaminare la memoria di lavoro verbale in bambini di scuola elementare: taratura e validità", MS University of Pavia.

Schriefers, H., A.D. Friederici and K. Kühn (1995) "The processing of local ambiguous relative clauses in German", *Journal of Memory and Language*, 34, 499-520.

Sheldon, A. (1974) "The role of parallel functions in the acquisition of relative clauses in English", *Journal of verbal learning and verbal behaviour* 13, 272-281.

Tavakolian, S. (1981) "The conjoined clause analysis of relative clauses and other structures" in S. Tavakolian, ed., *Language acquisition and linguistic theory*. Cambridge, Mass.: MIT Press.

Traxler, M.J., R.K.Morris and R.E. Seely, (2002) "Processing Subject and Object Relative Clauses: Evidence from Eye-Movements", *Journal of Memory and Language*, 47, 69-90.

THE CP IN CHILD ROMANIAN: AN EARLY DISCOURSE-ANCHOR

LARISA AVRAM AND MARTINE COENE

1. On the C-domain: predictions for acquisition

In this paper we focus on the developmental pattern which characterizes the acquisition of the CP in Romanian. Following Rizzi (1997) we assume that the C-domain consists of two systems: the Force-Finiteness system, and the Topic-Focus system. The articulated structure of this split CP is given in (1):

(1) ForceP....(TopicP)....(FocusP)...FinP...IP

The acquisition of the CP domain could then be seen as (i) the valuation process of two different sets of features (as a natural reflex of the dual semantics incorporated in this domain) and (ii) the identification of their realization in the target language.

2. The Romanian C-domain in a nutshell

In order to understand what exactly can count as evidence in favour of an active CP in early grammar one has to identify first the properties of the CP domain in the target grammar, in our case in Romanian. The standard generative analysis of the CP in Romanian has associated this layer with complementizers and moved *wh*-phrases. Hill (2003) argues that the complementizers *că* (indicative "that") and *dacă* ("if") occupy ForceP, while *ca* (subjunctive "that") and *de* (the equivalent of the Italian *di*) are in FinP. The mood markers *să* (marker of the subjunctive) and *a* (marker of the infinitive) are in Mood if the Fin position is occupied by a lexical complementizer but, in the absence of a lexical complementizer, they raise to Fin:

(2) **ForceP**... TopicP .... **FinP**...IP
     ⬇   ⬇
     că, dacă   *ca, de* (*să, a*)

Romanian allows multiple *wh*-checking and all the *wh*-phrases cluster together. This has been taken to indicate a unique host for all the displaced *wh*-phrases, which is, in most studies, [Spec CP] (Dobrovie-Sorin 1994). Given word order facts (a *wh*-phrase may intervene between a topic and the finite verb) we will assume that fronted *wh*-phrases possibly land in FinP. The Romanian CP is also the landing site of topics (topicalized subjects, direct objects, pronominal clitics, etc.) which have been analysed as occupying [Spec TopicP] (Cornilescu 2002). Relative clauses project as high as ForceP (Hill 2003).

3. Data

Our analysis relies on data coming from two longitudinal corpora of monolingual Romanian (B. 1;3-3;2 and A.1;9-3;6), consisting of 60 minute audio recordings of natural unstructured conversations. Some of the B. files have been transcribed according to the CHILDES system (MacWhinney 2000). For the present study we analysed 13 files (age 1;05 – 2;05) from the B. corpus and 12 files (age 1;09- 2;07) from the A. corpus. All the CP-related constructions mentioned in the previous section were identified and analysed. The age of onset was considered the first productive use of a CP-related construction with more than one verb.

4. Results and analysis

The following stages were identified: (i) the "no active C-domain" stage; (ii) the "uncertain C-domain" stage; (iii) the activation of the C-domain (see Table 1 and Table 2 in the Appendix).

Stage 1: the "no active C-domain" stage [up to approx. 1;09] (MLU<1.5) is the stage when no complementizers or displaced *wh*-phrases are attested. Actually, *wh*-phrases may be omitted even in repetitions and the first (rarely) attested *wh*-questions are formulaic. No *wh*-phrases *in situ* exist in the early files. No topic-like elements or relative clauses are attested. All these data prove that the C-domain is not active yet.

Stage 2: the "uncertain C-domain" stage [the B. corpus 1;09-2;0.11// the A. corpus 1;09-2;01.22] (MLU >1.5//2) is the stage when various constituents associated with the C-domain begin to emerge. But the qualitative analysis of the data reveals that some of these elements are neither used in a target-like manner nor do they always occur in a context which can allow us to infer that the C-domain is already active. This is the stage when the first complementizer is found in one corpus (B. 1;10), but the context is unclear and non-target like (the complementizer takes a DP as its complement). In the A. corpus, on the other hand, there is no complementizer associated with either ForceP or with FinP until 2;03. As can be seen in (3), complementizers are omitted even in imitations or repetitions:

(3)   Adult : de ce, ca să-l strici tu ?
       Why, so that *să*-subj. marker it-ACC break-2nd sg you
       "Why, so that you can break it?"
       Child: strici tu.
       break-2nd sg you   [A. 1; 11]

Wh-phrases are no longer omitted in imitation and the first moved *wh*-phrase (*unde* "where") is attested in the B. corpus. Since there is no question in which the overt subject is placed in between the *wh*-phrase and the verb, in violation of the *wh*-criterion, we believe that *wh*-movement may be already present in the early grammar from the onset of the EMWS. However, the first four *wh*-questions in the B. files (1;10-2;0.11) are all *unde* "where" questions with omitted *be*. No overt verb is attested in these *wh*-questions. Moreover, three of them are used in a sort of hide and seek playing situation. In the A. corpus, the first displaced *wh*-phrase is attested at 2; 01. This is why we believe that one cannot take these early questions as evidence that *wh*-questions are already target-like. The data available for this short stage (corresponding to 1;10-2;0.11 in the B. corpus) cannot clearly show whether the *wh*-element moves to the C-domain or simply adjoins to IP/VP. Further evidence suggesting that the C-domain may be turning active comes from the first preverbal subjects (1;10.01 in the B. corpus // 1;09 in the A. corpus). However, preverbal subjects can be taken as evidence that the C-domain is active only if one adopts an analysis according to which preverbal subjects in Romanian are always topics, and hence in the C-domain. Also, the acquisition data seem to indicate that the *pro*-drop parameter has not been set at this stage (Avram and Coene 2004). The rare early preverbal subjects cannot be taken to indicate with certainty that a TopicP is active. They could well be in [Spec IP] or simply adjoined to VP/IP.

Fronted direct objects are also attested after the first *wh*-questions and they are compatible with a topic (or informative focus) interpretation. The existence of such fronted DPs (in both corpora) together with the existence of preverbal subjects suggests an early mastery of pragmatic rules associated with the encoding of topics. Children have, from the onset of the EMWS, the ability to distinguish between new and old information (see also, for similar conclusions for French de Cat 2002 or for Japanese Okada & Grinstead 2003). There might be a time lapse between the acquisition of the Force-Finiteness-related elements and the acquisition of the Topic-Focus-related ones. The existence of topicalized constituents, however, does not automatically indicate that they move to the left periphery of the clause. For solid evidence that this is indeed the case we would need to find structures containing a fronted DO (TopP) followed by a *wh*-phrase (presumably in FinP) or by a complementizer defined as occupying FinP. But such structures are not attested. This is why we have labelled this stage the "uncertain C-domain stage".

Stage 3: The activation of the left periphery [after age 2, MLU approx. 2.00]
During this stage, the first relative clauses (ForceP) are attested, at 2;02 in both corpora:

(4) Altu(l) care scrie
    other-the which writes.   [A. 2;02.19]

Also the first complementizer (*că* "that") used to introduce a clausal constituent is attested (in the B. corpus at 2;0.11, in the A. corpus only three months later, at 2;03):

(5) Aicea, că pus.
    Here, that put-past part.   [B. 2;0.11]

One can notice that there is individual variation in the acquisition of complementizers, on the one hand, and that the activation of the C-domain does not automatically entail the target-like use of CP-related elements. In the B. corpus a *complementizer spread* takes place: *că* "that" is used in a variety of contexts, in front of DPs and PPs included. The complementizer is used as a sort of clause delimiter in contexts in which its presence is not required in the adult grammar, even in relative clauses (8) (though adult-like relative clauses are already attested):

(6) aicea , **că** tu aicea **că** n-ai pove(s)tit.
    here, that you here that not have-2nd sg narrated   [B. 2;05.18]
(7) nu, **că** jucăm cu balonu (l).
    No, that we play with the balloon.   [B. 2;02.13]
(8) Adult: şi Robert unde doarme?
    "And where does Robert sleep?"
    Child: la pătuţ **că** e galben.
    at little bed that is yellow   [B. 2;02.13]

Că "that" seems to represent the default CP-related element in noninterrogative contexts in the beginning in the B. files. Other complementizers emerge later. In the A. corpus the first complementizers (*că* "that" and *dacă* "if/whether"), as already mentioned, *are* attested relatively late, but they are used in a target-like fashion from the beginning.

There is individual variation with respect to the order of emergence of displaced *wh*-phrases. But in both corpora different verbs are attested in *wh*-questions.

We also find evidence that topicalized subjects may be moved to [Spec TopP]; when they are topicalized in a *wh*-question they are correctly placed in front of the *wh*-phrase:

(9)   leu (l) unde e?
      lion-the where is   [B. 2;01.18]

The first preverbal object clitics (analysed as moved to a Topic position in the left periphery) also emerge during this stage (Avram & Coene 2004).

The data show that complementizers, displaced *wh*-phrases and displaced topicalized constituents emerge at approximately the same time, indicating that ForceP, TopicP, and FinP are activated during the same stage, with no time lapse between matrix CPs and embedded CPs.

5. Summing up

The developmental pattern which characterizes the acquisition of the Romanian CP provides evidence in favour of a split-CP (Rizzi 1997) from a very early stage: ForceP, TopicP, and FinP. All these projections are activated at approximately the same time, with no root/embedded asymmetry. Children seem, however, to deal differently with the two types of features associated with the left-periphery: topic/focus features on the one hand and force-finiteness features on the other, showing early sensitivity to pragmatic rules associated with the encoding of topics. Children seem to have, from the onset of the EMWS, the ability to distinguish between new and old information.

Appendix

Table 1. Complementizers, displaced *wh*-phrases, relative clauses in the B. files

File	MLU	Relative clauses	Displaced *wh*-phrases	Complementizers	
1;5.12 - 1;8.01		0	0	0	Stage 1
1;9.03	1.350	0	2	0	Stage 2
1;10.01	1.091	0	0	0	
1;10.29		0	2	1	
1;11.26	1.410	0	1	2	
2;0.11	1.384	0	1	3	Stage 3
2;1.18	2.069	0	4	8	
2;2.13	1.819	3	4	6	
2;3.23	1.869	3	7	1	
2;5.18	2.811	4	28	44	

Table 2. Complementizers, displaced *wh*-phrases, relative clauses in the A. files

File	Relative clauses	Displaced wh-phrases	Complementizers	
1; 9	0	1	0	Stage 2
1;10- 2;01.08	0	0	0	
2;01.22	0	1	0	Stage 3
2;02.19	3	1	0	
2;03.14	3	3	2	
2;04.11	1	4	2	
2;05.07	1	7	3	
2;06.10	3	16	8	
2;07.	0	31	18	

References

Avram, L. and M. Coene (2004) "What Early Clitics Can Tell Us about Early Subjects," in J. van Kampen and S. Baauw, (eds.) *Proceedings of GALA 2003*, 93-102, Utrecht: LOT.

Cornilescu, A. (2002) "At the Romanian Left Periphery," *Bucharest Working Papers in Linguistics* IV, 1, 89-107.

De Cat, C. (2002) *French Dislocation*, PhD thesis, University of York, UK.

Dobrovie-Sorin,C. (1994) *The Syntax of Romanian*, Mouton de Gruyter, Berlin.

Hill, V. (2003) "Reduced VP Fields and Phases," *Bucharest Working Papers in Linguistics* V, 1, 44-53.

MacWhinney, B. (2000) *The CHILDES Project: Tools for Analyzing Talk*. Third edition, Lawrence Erlbaum Associates, Mahwah, NJ.

Okada, K. and J. Grinstead (2003) "The Emergence of the CP in Child Japanese," Juana M. Liceras et al.,eds., *Proceedings of the 6th Generative Approaches to Second Language Acquisition Conference (GASLA 2002)*, 213-218, Cascadilla, Somerville, Massachusetts.

Rizzi, L. (1997) "The Fine Structure of the Left Periphery," in L. Haegeman, ed., *Elements of Grammar: Handbook of Generative Syntax*, Kluwer Academic Publishers, Dordrecht, 281-339.

OBJECT CLITIC CLIMBING IN L2 LEARNERS OF ITALIAN

ELISA BENNATI AND SIMONA MATTEINI

1. Introduction

This study explores the acquisition of Object Clitic Climbing (OCC henceforth) in adult L2 learners of Italian, focusing in particular on third person singular accusative clitics. One of the main purposes of this research was to re-visit the traditional theoretical approaches on causative constructions and restructuring predicates through L2 evidence, following the analyses proposed by Rizzi (1982), Burzio (1986), Guasti (1997) and Cinque (2004) among others. We analysed OCC both in i. obligatory and in ii. optional contexts. As for i. we tested auxiliary + past participle contexts and "da" causative constructions (see Kayne 1975, Burzio 1986 and Guasti 1996, 1997), as shown in (1) and (2):

(1) a. **L'ho mangiato/a**
        "I it(cl) have eaten"
        "I have eaten it"
     b. *Ho mangiato **lo/la**
        "I have eaten it(cl)"
(2) a. **Lo** fa correggere dal maestro (il tema)
        "He/She it(cl) make-s correct(inf) by the teacher (the composition)"
     b. **??** Fa corregger**lo** dal maestro (il tema)
        "He/She make-s correct(inf)-it(cl) by the teacher (the composition)"
        "He/she makes the teacher correct it"

As for ii. we concentrated on the contexts displaying either motion or modal verbs, on the basis of Rizzi's (1982) classification of restructuring verbs, as exemplified in (3) and (4)[1]:

(3) a. **Lo/la** vado a prendere da mia sorella
   "I it(cl) go to get from my sister"
   b. Vado a prender**lo/la** da mia sorella
   "I go to get-it(cl) from my sister"
   "I'll go and get it from my sister"

(4) a. **Lo/la** devo pulire
   "I it(cl) must clean"
   b. Devo pulir**lo/la**
   "I must clean-it(cl)
   "I must clean it"

Our experiment aimed at testing the level of mastery of OCC in Italian L2 both in English and German-speaking learners, whose L1s lack clitics[2], and in Spanish-speaking learners, where the L1 and L2 are alike both with respect to the clitic system and clitic placement[3].

2. Experimental subjects

Two groups of speakers participated in the experiment: a control group consisting of 8 native speakers of Italian and an experimental group consisting of 5 Spanish, 6 English and 7 German L2 learners of Italian, who had been resident in Italy for periods of varying length. The age range was from 18 to 48. All L2 learners had attended upper-intermediate/advanced Italian classes in their own countries before coming to Italy. At the time we administered the experiment the L2 learners were all attending Italian classes in Siena at an advanced level of proficiency, as determined by a standardized proficiency test which was run at the beginning of their courses. On the basis of a screening procedure adapted from Belletti&Leonini (2004)[4] we included in our study only the L2 learners who resorted to clitics. The screenining material consisted of two short movies at the end of which the subjects were asked a couple of questions some of which were designed to elicit object clitics, as illustrated below in scene (a) and (b) and in the examples from (5) to (7):

Scene (a)   Scene (b)

(5) Describe the scene
(6) What did the boy do with the lamp?
(7) What does the boy look like?

3. Procedure

The experiment consisted of a written elicitation task where OCC was tested in the four structural conditions which are mentioned in the introduction. Five items per condition were administered (20 experimental items in total). 20 fillers were also inserted. Subjects were tested individually and items were randomized at each run. Each item consisted of a picture and a question about it, as exemplified in (A), (B), (C) and (D):

(A) auxiliary+past participle

Che cosa ha fatto il bambino con la porta?
"What has the boy done with the door ?"

Nella risposta:
Sostituisci "porta" con un pronome
(In the answer replace "door" with a pronoun)

(B) "da" causatives

Da chi fa correggere il tema la bambina?
"Whom does the girl make correct the composition?"
Nella risposta: ripeti la costruzione "fare + verbo" e sostituisci "tema" con un pronome
(In the answer: repeat "*fare* + verb" construction and replace "composition" with a pronoun)

(C) motion verbs

Dove va la nonna a comprare il prosciutto?
"Where does Grandma go to buy some ham?"

Nella risposta: ripeti la costruzione "andare + verbo" e sostituisci "prosciutto" con un pronome
(In the answer: repeat "*andare* + verb" construction and replace "ham" with a pronoun)

(D) modal verbs

Che cosa deve fare Gianni con il vaso?
"What does John have to do with the vase?"

Nella risposta: deve essere presente il verbo "dovere"; sostituisci "vaso" con un pronome
(In the answer: repeat "*dovere* and replace "vase" with a pronoun)

The choice of a written elicitation procedure was due to the difficulty in eliciting the constructions under investigation orally. For this reason the subjects were provided with written instructions.

4. Data analysis

Before discussing the results in detail, we would like to point out that the English and German L2 learners of Italian have been included in the same group since they showed a similar performance in all elicited contexts. In order to give a clear overview we present the results of each structural condition separately.

Obligatory OCC in auxiliary + past participle contexts

Table 1

L2 learners	aux+ past participle		other
	climb	no climb	
Spanish L1 (5)	100% (25/25)	0% (0/25)	0% (0/25)
English/ German L1 (13)	97% (63/65)	1,5% (1/65)	1,5% (1/65)
Control group (8)	100% (40/40)	0% (0/40)	0% (0/40)

Figure 1

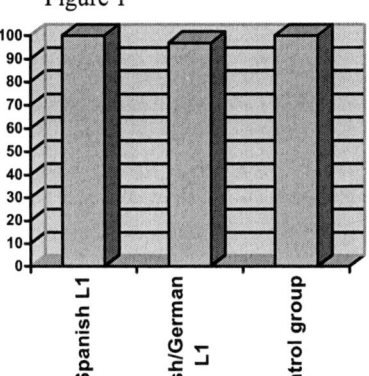

Example of experimental items:
(8) a. *Che cosa ha fatto il bambino con la porta?*
   "What has done the child with the door ?"
   Expected answer:
   b. *L'ha chiusa*
   "(He) it(cl) has closed"

Table 1 and Figure 1 indicate a target-like performance of both Spanish L1 and English/German L1 speakers of Italian with respect to OCC. Furthermore we observed a lack of object clitic misplacement. Indeed the clitic appeared to the left of the highest finite verb, i.e. the auxiliary. Only one case of ungrammatical order (*aux–past participle–cl) was attested in a German-speaking L2 learner, as shown in (9):

(9) Ha chiusa-la.
   "(He) has closed it(cl)"

Obligatory OCC in "da"causative constructions

Table 2

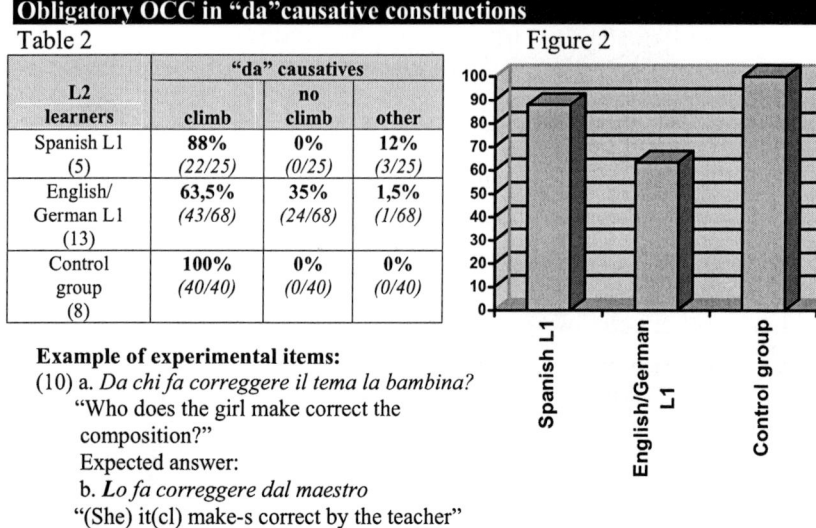

Figure 2

L2 learners	"da" causatives		
	climb	no climb	other
Spanish L1 (5)	88% *(22/25)*	0% *(0/25)*	12% *(3/25)*
English/ German L1 (13)	63,5% *(43/68)*	35% *(24/68)*	1,5% *(1/68)*
Control group (8)	100% *(40/40)*	0% *(0/40)*	0% *(0/40)*

Example of experimental items:
(10) a. *Da chi fa correggere il tema la bambina?*
   "Who does the girl make correct the
   composition?"
   Expected answer:
   b. *Lo fa correggere dal maestro*
   "(She) it(cl) make-s correct by the teacher"

Table 2 and Figure 2 illustrate the L2 results with respect to obligatory OCC in causative constructions. While Spanish-speaking subjects showed a native like performance (88% vs. 100%; the difference between the two groups is not statistically significant[5]; $\chi^2=1,2387$; p=0,2657), English/German-speaking subjects' performance was not target-like, as statistically attested ($\chi^2= 17,1245$; p<0,00001). However, if we analyse the Germanic subjects' answers individually, it emerges that only two speakers constantly avoid OCC, as clearly indicated in diagram 3:

Figure 3. "Da" causatives. English/German-speaking subjects' data

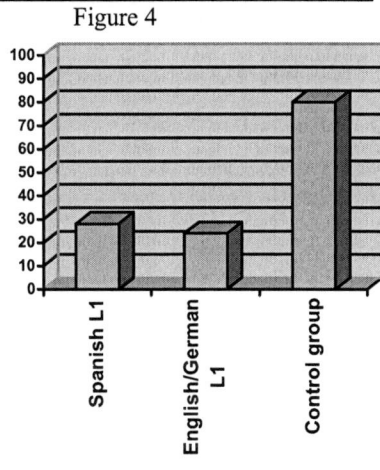

	other
	no climbing
	climbing

Optional OCC with motion verbs
Table 3

L2 learners	Motion verbs		
	climb	no climb	other
Spanish L1(5)	28%	68%	4%
	(7/25)	(17/25)	(1/25)
English/ GermanL1(13)	24%	76%	0%
	(16/68)	(52/68)	(0/68)
Control group(8)	80%	20%	0%
	(32/40)	(8/40)	(0/40)

Figure 4

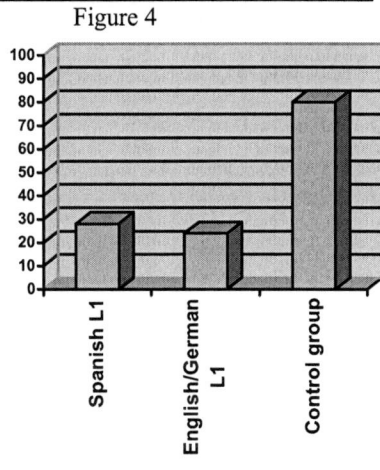

Example of experimental items:
(11) a. *Dove va a comprare il prosciutto?*
"Where does she go to buy some ham?"
Expected answers:
b. *Lo va a comprare dal salumiere*
"(She) it(cl) go-es to buy to the grocery"
c. *Va a comprarlo dal salumiere*
"(She) go-es to buy-it(cl) to the grocery"

Contrary to the results obtained in obligatory contexts, both Spanish and English/German-speaking subjects, despite their different L1s, tended to avoid OCC with motion verb constructions. The object clitic appeared on the infinitival verb at considerable rate (28%/24% vs. 80%; χ^2=14,2178/30,2802; p=0,0002/p<0,0001).

Optional OCC with modal verbs

Table 4   Figure 5

L2 learners	Modal verbs		
	climb	no climb	other
Spanish L1(5)	24% (6/25)	64% (16/25)	4% (3/25)
English/ German L1(13)	40% (27/67)	60% (40/67)	0% (0/67)
Control group(8)	93% (38/40)	3,5% (1/40)	3,5% (1/40)

Example of experimental items:
(12) a. *Che cosa deve fare Gianni con il vaso?*
"What does John have to do with the vase?"
Expected answers:
b. *Lo deve incollare*
"(He) it(cl) has to glue"
c. *Deve incollarlo*

As for modal verbs, English/German speaking subjects adopted OCC at higher rate than Spanish-speaking subjects (40% vs 24%). The difference between both L2 groups and the controls is statistically significant. (χ^2=31,0437; p<0,0001 Spanish-speaking subjects and the controls; χ^2=31,5642; p<0,0001 English/German-speaking subjects and the controls).

5. Discussion

In this section we will discuss the data we collected adopting the traditional theoretical approach to restructuring which is based on the dichotomy monoclausality vs. biclausality (following Rizzi 1982, Burzio 1986, Guasti 1996, 1997 among others). We assume that OCC is the result of a monoclausal analysis.

As a starting point we will focus on the split between obligatory vs. optional contexts with respect to OCC in L2 speakers, as indicated in table 5:

Table 5. OCC in obligatory and optional contexts

	obligatory OCC contexts		optional OCC contexts	
	aux+past part	causatives	motion verbs	modals
Spanish-speaking subjects	100% (25/25)	88% (22/25)	28% (7/25)	24% (6/25)
English/German-speaking subjects	97% (63/65)	63.5% (43/68)	24% (16/68)	40% (27/67)
Control Group	100% (40/40)	100% (40/40)	80% (32/40)	93% (38/40)

Overall, the performance of both L2 groups in obligatory contexts, i.e. aux.+past participle and causatives, shows evidence that OCC is active, regardless of L1, and that the object clitic is mostly located onto the highest inflected verb (Aux, caus). Whereas Spanish-speaking subjects and English/German-speaking subjects do not differ in auxiliary + past participle contexts, they seem to diverge in causatives:

- Hispanophones' native-like performance in causatives (88% vs. 100%) is not unexpected, since Spanish requires clitic climbing with "hacer" (to make) like the Italian "fare". It is reasonable to hypothesize that Spanish L2 learners, like native Italian speakers, process causatives as single verbal units, where OCC applies obligatorily (following Guasti 1996,1997). On the basis of these facts L1 properties seem to favour L2 respresentations.

- English/German-speaking subjects' lower percentage of OCC in causatives (63.5%) provides no absolute evidence of non native-like performance since an analysis of the individual tendencies highlights that most L2 learners produced 100% OCC. Only **2** of them adopted the no climbing option to a large extent (see Diagram 3). In light of these facts it seems to be quite uncontroversial to claim that **OCC** is **not optional/random** in interlanguage grammars and it gives us reason to speculate that once a monoclausal structure is available, OCC is mostly applied. In this respect the proposal we put forth is that the two L2 learners who do not resort to OCC process Italian causatives as two distinct verbal complexes, thus spelling out the clitic on the lower infinitival verb. Compare the example in (13):

(13) ?? Fa corregger**lo** dal maestro (il tema)
        "(She) make-s correct(inf) it(cl) by the teacher (the composition)"

The English/German group's data concerning OCC in obligatory contexts support the **No Impairment Hypothesis,** according to which UG is **operational** in interlanguage grammars and functional categories which are absent in L1 can be instantiated in L2. These results go in the same direction as previous work on this topic (see Duffield, White, Bruhn-Garavito, Montrul and Prévost 2002, Belletti&Leonini 2004 among others).

As far as optional contexts (i.e. motion/modal verb contexts) are concerned, both L2 groups diverge from the control group in adopting clitic climbing to a lower extent. It is reasonable to assume that the controls' tendency to resort to OCC in optional contexts depends on their dialects/idiolecs (as noticed in Cinque 2004 and Cardinaletti & Shlonsky 2004). Actually, all of them come from Central and Southern Italian regions where OCC is almost obligatory. On the contrary, the L2 learners' preference for no clitic climbing cannot be related to their geographical/dialectal varieties. Rather, we claim that the difference between Italian native speakers and L2 learners may be attributed to different structures at work. Whereas the former process motion and modal contexts as mono-clausal structures, the latter seem to parse them mainly as bi-clausal configurations where the object clitic is located in the internal argument position of the lexical infinitival predicate.

Going into detail, we found a slightly higher production of OCC in modal contexts vs. motion verb structures both in controls (80% vs. 93%; χ^2=4,3452; p=0,0371; the difference is statistically significant) and in English/German-speaking subjects (24% vs. 40%; χ^2=4,3720; p=0,0365; the difference is statistically significant). We would like to speculate on different theoretical reasons involved. As for the controls, this fact may find a suitable explanation in Cinque's (2004) remark on the usage of the two predicates. Indeed, while motion verbs can be used either as "restructuring" or lexical verbs in Italian, modals only have a functional usage. According to that, we assume that a monoclausal configuration, hence OCC, is expected to be more readily accessible with modals than with motion verbs. An analysis along these lines could be tentatively proposed for the German-speaking subjects as well. Following Wurmbrand's (2004) analysis on restructuring, we assume that modals in German are functional restructuring verbs which undergo a monoclausal processing[6], whereas motion verbs belong to the class of lexical restructuring predicates in which restructuring, hence a monoclausal structure, is optional. In this light the slightly higher rate of OCC with modals (40%) than with motion verbs (24%) is not surprising. As a final remark on English-speaking subjects' performance, a possible reason for their preference of OCC with modals than with motion verbs may lie in the fact that English modals form a special class and their usage is similar to auxiliary verbs which require a mono-clausal structure. As far as Spanish-speaking subjects are concerned, the tendency to avoid OCC with motion verbs is not unexpected giving the fact that in Spanish the climbing of clitics in this context seems to be favoured by the presence of a cluster of clitics as opposed to a single clitic (see the contrast between IVb and IVc in footnote n.3). A possible explanation for such result could be related to some sort of "selective" L1 transfer which affects this class of verbs. Contrary to motion verbs, the tendency found with modals is quite puzzling because Spanish and Italian share the same OCC optionality (cfr. footnote n.3, i.e. IIa and b), hence an hypothesis based on L1 transfer has to be probably discarded here. We argue that this result could be related to other facts such as different processing strategies at work or the experimental design[7].

A further consideration is prompted by the comparison between the results found in obligatory OCC contexts and the ones observed in optional OCC contexts. The more frequent occurrence of OCC with causatives than with motion or modal verbs could be related to the less complex structure involved. Indeed, causative verbs, like simple predicates (i.e. auxiliary + past participle constructions), select a VP (following Manzini 1983, Guasti 1997) rather than a CP as motion/modal predicates in non restructuring configurations. Compare the examples in (14) and (15):

(14) [IP La bambina **lo** fa [VP correggere] dal maestro]
     "The girl   it(cl) make-s correct(inf) by the teacher"
(15) [IP Maria deve [CP pulir**la**]]
     "Mary has to   clean(inf)-it(cl)"

This asymmetry could be taken to suggest that L2 learners are sensitive to clause boundaries (namely VP complements vs. CP complements) and OCC is the visible result of a mono-clausal structure.

6. Conclusions

Our study provides a twofold contribution:
i. On the one hand it shows how different theoretical analyses on restructuring proposed over the years contribute to the interpretation and disambiguation of experimental data concerning SLA.
ii. On the other hand it provides cues on the role of UG and L1 in SLA supporting the no impairment hypothesis.

Notes

[1] Aspectual verbs are not discussed in this work.

[2] In English and German tonic and atonic pronouns are used instead of clitic pronouns.
Compare the following examples.
I. Aux.+ Past participle
a. **L'ho mangiato/a**
b. I have eaten **it**
c. Ich habe **ihn/es/sie** gegessen
II. "da" Causatives
a. La mamma **lo** (il bambino) fa accompagnare a scuola dal nonno
b. Mum makes Grandfather take **him** (the boy) to school
c. Die Mutter läßt **es** (das Kind) vom Großvater zur Schule begleiten
III. Motion verbs
a. **Lo** (il prosciutto) va a comprare dal salumiere/Va a comprar**lo** dal salumiere
b. She goes to the grocery to buy **it** (some ham)
c. Sie geht in die Metzgerei, um **ihn** (den Schinken) zu kaufen
IV. Modal verbs
a. **Lo** vuole mangiare (il panino)/Vuole mangiar**lo**
b. He/she wants to eat **it** (the sandwich)
c. Er/Sie will **es** (das Brötchen) essen
[3] Even though OCC is a widespread phenomenon in Romance languages, it is worth
pointing out that there are some differences in the two languages under investigation.
Whereas Italian and Spanish have the same pattern with auxiliary + past participle
(where OCC is obligatory) and modals (where OCC is optional), they show some
language specific properties in causatives and with motion verbs, as illustrated in the
following examples:
I. Aux.+ Past participle
a. **L'ho** mangiato (il panino)
b. **Lo** he comido (el bocadillo)
II. Modal verbs
a. **Lo** vuole mangiare (il panino)/Vuole mangiar**lo**
b. **Lo** (el bocadillo) quiere comer/Quiere comer**lo**
III. "da" Causatives
a. **Lo** fa correggere dal maestro (il tema)
b. **Se lo** hace corregir al maestro/(??) por el maestro
Spanish causative constructions are "a" causatives and require the clitic cluster **se lo/la**.
Causative constructions with "por", which is the Spanish counterpart of the Italian "da",
are marginally accepted.
IV. Motion verbs
a. **Lo** (il prosciutto) va a comprare dal salumiere/Va a comprar**lo** dal salumiere
b. ?? **Lo** (el jamón) va a comprar a la charcutería
c. Va a comprar**lo** a la charcutería
In Spanish OCC constructions with motion verbs the clitic cluster "**se lo**" as opposed to
"**lo**" alone sounds more natural, as shown in IV.b:
d. **Se lo** va a comprar a la charcutería.
[4] Previous studies on object clitics in L2 Italian (see Leonini&Belletti 2004b and Leonini
2005) pointed out that non near-native L2 learners mainly produce full lexical noun

phrases in complement position instead of object clitics, which are extensively used by Italian native speakers. On the basis of these results we decided to focus only on upper-intermediate/advanced L2ers who displayed a productive use of object clitics at least in simple contexts such as aux+past participle.

[5] The data we collected were statistically analysed through the "Chi-squared test", which is one of the most widely used statistical procedures. It can be applied to test whether an experimental group and a control group behave similarly with respect to an observable phenomenon.

[6] For a detailed discussion of the difference among deontic, epistemic and dynamic modals, see Wurmbrand (2001).

[7] Gábor (2002) pointed out how different variables may play a crucial role in forcing the climbing of the clitic in Spanish infinitival constructions. Among the numerous aspects under investigation (verb classes, clitic classes, clitic clusters, animacy/inanimacy of clitics and so on and so forth), he found a significant difference in the frequency of clitic climbing with modal verbs in spontaneous production corpora as opposed to written tests, where the percentage of long clitic movement is considerably lower. Turning to our results, it could be even the case that this group of Spanish L2 learners of Italian may adopt some transfer strategies for Italian modal infinitival constructions as well. However, in order to verify this hipothesis, some extra work needs to be done. It should to be tested whether Spanish speakers show a significant discrepancy in resorting to clitic climbing in oral tasks.

References

Belletti,A. (1999) "Italian/Romance clitics: Structure and derivation", in Henk van Riemsdijk, eds., *Clitics in the Languages of Europe*, Mouton de Gruyter, 543-579.

—. (2004a) "Extended Doubling and the VP Periphery", in *Probus* 17.1, 1-36.

Burzio,L. (1986) *Italian Syntax*, Dortrecht: Reidel.

Cardinaletti,A. & U. Shlonsky, (2004) "Clitic positions and Restructuring in Italian", in *Linguistic Inquiry* 35.4, 519-557.

Cinque,G. (1999) *Adverbs and Functional Heads*, Oxford University Press, New York.

—. (2004) "Restructuring and Functional Structure", in A.Belletti, ed., *Structures and Beyond. The Cartography of Syntactic Structure*, Vol 3. New York: Oxford University Press, 132-191.

Duffield,N., White,L., Bruhn De Garavito,J., Montrul,S. & P. Prévost, (2002) "Clitic Placement in L2 French: evidence from Sentence Matching", in *Journal of Linguistics*, 38, 487-525.

Ferrari,I. (2005) "Acquisition of object clitics in Italian by two German/Italian bilingual children", talk given at GALA2005, Siena, to appear in the Proceedings.

Gábor, K. (2002) "Subida de clíticos en corpus electrónicos ", ms. University of Szeged.

Guasti,M.T. (1996) "Semantic restrictions on Romance causatives and the incorporation approach", in *Linguistic Inquiry* 27.2:294-313.

—. (1997) "Romance causative", in L.Haegeman (ed) *The new comparative syntax*, London: Longmans Linguistics Library, 124-144.

Kayne, R.S. (1989). "Null Subjects and Clitic Climbing", in Jaeggli,O. & Safir,K., eds., *The Null Subject Parameter*, Reidel, Dordrecht, 239-261.

—. (1991) "Romance Clitics, Verb Movement, and PRO" in Linguistic Inquiry 22, 647-686.

Leonini,C. & A. Belletti, (2004b) "Subject inversion in L2 Italian", in S.Foster-Cohen, M.Sharwood Smith,A.Sorace, M.Ota, eds., Eurosla Yearbook. 95-228 Benjamins.

—. (2005) "Object clitics and Determiners in the acquisition of Italian as L2 and L1", poster presented at GALA2005, Siena, to appear in the Proceedings.

Manzini,R. (1983) "Restructuring and reanalysis", Doctoral Dissertation, MIT, Cambridge, Mass.

Rizzi, L. (1982) "A Restructuring Rule" in Rizzi,L. *Issues in Italian Syntax*, Foris, Dordrecht, 1-48.

Roberts, I. (1997) "Restructuring, head movement, and locality", in *Linguistic Inquiry* 28:423-460.

Sportiche,D. (1996) "Clitic Constructions", in Rooryck, Johann &Zaring, Laurie, eds., *Phrase structure and the lexicon*, Dordrecht: Kluver, 213-276.

Torrego, E. (1998). "The Dependencies of Objects", *Linguistic Inquiry*, Monograph 34, The MIT Press.

Wurmbrand, S. (2001) *Infinitives. Restructuring and Clause Structure*, Studies in Generative Grammar 55, Berlin – New York: Mouton de Gruyter.

—. (2004) "Two types of restructuring – Lexical vs. functional", *Lingua* 114, 991-1014.

AGREEMENT INFLECTION IN CHILD L2 DUTCH

ELMA BLOM

1. Introduction

Grammaticality judgement tasks show that second language learners of English who started to learn English during childhood are significantly more accurate on judging English inflection than learners who started after puberty (Johnson and Newport, 1989, 1991; McDonald, 2000). Focussing on the acquisition of (inflectional) morphology, Goldowsky and Newport (1993: 236) observe that: "Native speakers make very few errors; they are characterized by extremely consistent use of the rules of the language. [...] Adult learners, in contrast, are characterized by variable and inconsistent use of rules; much of their behavior appears to be probabilistic." In her case study of a Chinese L2 learner of English, Lardiere (1998) found that the production of English 3rd person singular –s remains problematic even though knowledge of English syntax is advanced and stable. A comparison of the types of errors in English L2 learners of German indicates that adults substitute the inflectional suffix –en, which is not used as a finite substitute by child (L1 and L2) learners of German (Prévost, 2003).

The above observations suggest that acquisition of inflection is influenced by age. There is, however, no study that focuses on this particular issue. In this contribution, we compare child L2 learners of Dutch to child L1 and adult L2 learners of Dutch in order to investigate effects of age on the acquisition of verbal and adjectival inflection.[1] We compare the amount of errors, types of errors and between as well as within subject variability in the three learner groups. Our empirical basis consists of results obtained in a series of production experiments.

2. Participants

We crucially focus on child L2 learners, and compare a sample of this population to child L1 and adult L2 learners (Schwartz, 2004; Unsworth, 2005). Assuming that the critical period ends around the age of 6/7 (DeKeyser, 2000;

Johnson and Newport, 1989, 1991), child L2 learners are like the child L1 learners exposed to the target language within the critical period, but they do not learn Dutch from birth and Dutch is their second language. For the adult learners, Dutch is their second language as well. Thus, child L2 and adult L2 learners may show similar effects of L1 transfer. The child L2 and adult L2 learners differ in that the children started to learn Dutch within the critical period, whereas the adults started after the critical period (after puberty).

The (cross-sectional) L1 data are taken from Polišenská (2005), who tested monolinguals with an experimental design that is highly similar to the design described in sections 3.1 and 4.1. L2 participants are selected from the two largest immigrant populations in the Netherlands: Turks and Moroccans (mainly Berbers that speak Tarifit). The adults received no Dutch input before puberty. The children were born in the Netherlands, but had hardly any Dutch input before the age of four i.e. when they start to attend primary school.[2] All participants have Dutch lessons, either at school or at specific courses. To test the level of Dutch proficiency, each subject participated in a sentence-repetition task (Verhoeven et al, 1986, 2002). As there are still too little data per proficiency level for valid comparisons, we have collapsed results from different levels.[3] All samples contain Turks and Moroccans, except for adults with a high level of proficiency (only Turkish participants).

Table 1: Participants

Sample	Proficiency Level	Age of Arrival	Starting Age	Testing Age	Instructed learning	N
Child L1 (n = 31)	not tested	0	0	3-6	not relevant	31
Child L2 (n = 31)	Low	0	4	5	12 mos	2
	Moderate	0	4	5-7	24-36 mos	15
	High	0	4	5-8	24-36 mos	14
Adult (n = 18)	Low	21-39	>15	22-58	12-36 mos	9
	Moderate	23-31	>15	24-35	12-24 mos	7
	High	16-24	>15	25-32	12-36 mos	2

3. Finite verbal inflection (IP)

In standard Dutch declarative main clauses, the finite verb moves to second position where it precedes the object, negation, particles, etc. The Dutch infinitive remains in final base position. The infinitival verb is morphologically similar to finite plural verbs and is marked with the suffix –en.[4] Table 2 gives the Dutch finite verbal paradigm:

Table 2: Dutch finite verbal paradigm

Context	Suffix	Example
1SG	-ø	Ik loop (I walk)
2/3SG	-t	Jij/hij loopt (you walk/he walks)
1/2/3PL	-en	Wij/jullie/zij lopen (we/you/they walk)

3.1. Method

All participants have been tested with a sentence-completion task. We collected data on 1SG, 2SG, 3SG, 1PL and 3PL contexts in declarative main clauses. Embedded clause and inversion conditions tested knowledge of Dutch verb placement, which is relevant for distinguishing between finite and non-finite verbs. We targeted on verbs denoting the actions of calling, cleaning, drinking, painting, playing, pulling, reading and stirring. To control for lexical storage of unanalyzed finite verbs (Peters, 1983; Pinker, 1984) – which is relevant in case participants make very few errors - we included the nonsense verbs *pieren*, *zippen* and *kluken*. Verbal inflection items and verb placement items were presented in random order. Items of the adjectival inflection test (see section 4.1) have been included as filler items.

3.2. Data analysis

The counts are limited to responses in the main clause conditions containing simple, i.e. non-periphrastic, lexical verbs. Various participants, especially children of the youngest age groups, used periphrastic verbs that consisted of auxiliary + infinitive to denote ongoing actions (Jordens, 1990; Van Kampen, 1997; Zuckerman, 2001). We excluded such responses: the finite auxiliaries, being highly frequent verbs, may be stored as unanalyzed vocabulary items.

We performed two accuracy analyses and a substitution analysis. The question of the first accuracy analysis is: how many errors do learners make? In the second accuracy analysis, we compare conditions. The question that underlies the substitution analysis is: if learners make errors, what types of errors do they make? Via the substitution analysis, the preferred substitute ("default") can be determined.

With regard to errors, the common strategy in child L1 research is to distinguish between incorrect finiteness marking or absence of finiteness marking as in so called root infinitives. In a language like Dutch (which is OV +V2), the finite verb stands in second position whereas the non-finite verb is placed sentence-finally. For L1 Dutch it has repeatedly been shown that verb placement is acquired early (De Haan, 1987; Jordens, 1990; Zuckerman; 2001). The child L2 learners show also good performance on the verb placement task

(Blom and Polišenská, 2006). Thus, in child Dutch, verb placement is a reliable criterion for singling our finite verbs. We nevertheless analysed verbal inflection regardless of verb placement: nearly all adults performed poorly on the verb placement task, and therefore we cannot distinguish between finite and non-finite verbs in this sample.[5]

3.3. Results

The child L1 learners show an accuracy of 96% correct usage (n=334), the Turkish child L2 learners (child L2T) show an accuracy of 83% (n=260) and verbal inflection is in 85% of the cases correctly used (n=485) by Moroccan child L2 learners (child L2M). The difference between the child L1 and child L2 samples is not statistically significant (χ^2 = 0.45). High accuracy in the child groups reflects productivity of rules: nonsense verbs are correctly inflected in respectively 93% (n=256), 78% (n=67) and 82% (n=127) of the cases. The adult learners show an accuracy of 57% correct (n=166) and 56% correct (n=392) for respectively the Turks and Moroccans. The difference between the child L2 and adult L2 sample is statistically significant (χ^2 = 69.005, p ≤ 0.001).

Table 3: Accuracy and substitutions per condition, child L2 (existing verbs)

Child L2 T				Child L2 M			
	−ø	-t	-en		−ø	-t	-en
1SG	**73 %**	9 %	18 %	1SG	**72 %**	11 %	17 %
2SG	4 %	**77 %**	19 %	2SG	11 %	**75 %**	14 %
3SG	10 %	**75 %**	15 %	3SG	7 %	**85 %**	8 %
1PL	5 %	0 %	**95 %**	1PL	2 %	2 %	**97 %**
3PL	2 %	7 %	**91 %**	3PL	2 %	11 %	**87 %**

Table 4: Accuracy and substitutions per condition, adult L2 (existing verbs)

Adult L2 T				Adult L2 M			
	−ø	-t	-en		−ø	-t	-en
1SG	**67 %**	20 %	13 %	1SG	**73 %**	6 %	20 %
2SG	50 %	**35 %**	15 %	2SG	20 %	**55 %**	25 %
3SG	42 %	**35 %**	23 %	3SG	34 %	**33 %**	33 %
1PL	8 %	0 %	**92 %**	1PL	5 %	5 %	**89 %**
3PL	19 %	4 %	**78 %**	3PL	23 %	13 %	**64 %**

Tables 3-4 give the accuracy per condition. We did not perform this analysis on the child L1 learners, because their errors are too marginal. The bold-faced percentages represent target-like responses. At first glance, 2SG and 3SG (that both require $-t$) are more difficult than the other conditions (that either require – $\emptyset$ or $-en$). The two adult groups, although they differ in L1, show a similar patterning. In the adult sample, the difference between singular and plural (χ^2 = 13.45, p $\leq$ 0.001), and the difference between 1SG, on the one hand, and 2/3SG, on the other hand, is significant (χ^2 = 20.57, p $\leq$ 0.001). For the child groups, there are no significant differences between conditions.

Given the Dutch paradigm, a learner can substitute the suffix $-en$ in 1SG, 2SG and 3SG contexts, substitute the suffix $-t$ in 1SG, 1PL and 3PL contexts and/or substitute the suffix $-\emptyset$ in 2SG, 3SG, 1PL and 3PL contexts. In the experiment, the conditions in which $-en$, $-t$ or $-\emptyset$ can be substituted are not equally distributed. To compare the three suffixes, we calculated therefore the number of conditions in which this suffix is substituted as a proportion of the number of conditions in which this suffix can be substituted. A comparison of the obtained proportions tells us which suffix is most frequently used as a substitute ("default").

Table 5: Probabilities of substitution of suffixes $-en$, $-t$ and $-\emptyset$

Substitute	−en		-t		-ø	
Context	SG		1SG, PL		2/3 SG, PL	
Child L1	3 %	n=437	2 %	n=267	1 %	n=337
Child L2 T	17 %	n=211	3 %	n=172	6 %	n=271
Child L2 M	11 %	n=396	8%	n=286	5%	n=548
Adult L2 T	57 %	n=305	4 %	n=161	18 %	n=360
Adult L2 M	40 %	n=405	6 %	n=232	22 %	n=479

Adults substitute $-en$ significantly more often than the children. The child L2 learners substitute $-en$ more often than the child L1 learners. If we delimit the counts in the child samples to $-en$ substitutions in second (i.e. finite) position,$-en$ substitutions drop to nearly 0%.[6] Thus, child overuse of $-en$ reflects use of root infinitives. In the adult data, $-en$ substitutions may or may not be root infinitives.

Figure 1: Variability in probabilities of substitutions of suffixes *–en*, *-t* **and –** *ø* (T=Turkish, M=Moroccan, lower numbers within a group correspond to lower proficiency, higher numbers within a group to higher proficiency).

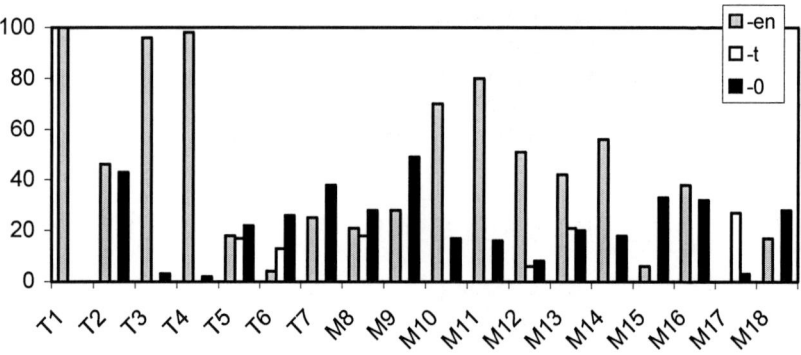

Table 5 masks the amount of variation, as shown in Figure 1: some adults prefer *–en* as a substitute (T1, T3, T4, M11, M14), others prefer *–ø* (M9, M15) or *–t* (M17). There are also participants that use two (T2, T7, M16, M18) or three (T5, M8, M13) different substitutes. Individual variation seems unrelated to level of proficiency. For instance, M10 has a low level of proficiency, whereas T7 has a high level of proficiency. Figure 1 indicates that particularly the Turks with a low level of proficiency substitute *-en*. Substitution of *–en* seems to decrease with increasing proficiency. Few adult learners substitute *–t*.

3.4. Interpretation of results

Differences in variability and accuracy suggest effects of age in the acquisition of verbal inflection. This is partially supported by a comparison of error types: the adults substitute *–t* infrequently. If children "substitute" *–en*, this is a root infinitive. The child L2 learners use more root infinitives than the child L1 learners, which is expected given their relatively short period of exposure to Dutch in combination with the observation that root infinitives in child L1 Dutch characterize early developmental stages (Wijnen and Bol, 1993; Blom, 2003). It is unclear if the adult *–en* substitutions are root infinitives. A first impression does suggest that *–en* substitutions negatively correlate with level of proficiency.

If the adult *–en* substitutions are root infinitives, adult development resembles child development (Jordens and Dimroth, to appear). Such a similarity does not necessarily contradict the occurrence of age effects. Wijnen et al. (2001) argue that the early across the board use of –en by Dutch children is the effect of input frequency, semantic transparency, information load and insertion of –en in a perceptually salient (i.e. final) position. Frequency is important in adult as well as in child language acquisition (Ellis, 2002). All other factors mentioned by Wijnen et al. represent general learning strategies that are applied by children and adults. By implication, –en is picked up early by children as well as adults. In the light of this, the early frequent overuse of –en in especially the Turkish adult L2 learners can be understood as an effect of focus on the final position in Dutch due to L1 transfer. In Dutch main clauses, this final position is filled by the infinitive (Lalleman, 1986; Klein and Perdue, 1997).[7]

4. Attributive adjectival inflection (DP)

The rule is: always add a schwa (-e) except in [indefinite, neuter, singular] contexts. In this special case, the bare adjective (-ø) must be used:

Table 6: Attributive adjectival inflection in Dutch

Context	Suffix	Example	
DEF, NEUT, SG	-e	Het mooie huis	'the nice house'
INDEF, NEUT, SG	-ø	Een mooi huis	'a nice house'
DEF, COM, SG	-e	De mooie auto	'the nice car'
INDEF, COM, SG	-e	Een mooie auto	'a nice car'
DEF, NEUT, PL	-e	De mooie huizen	'the nice houses'
INDEF, NEUT, PL	-e	Mooie huizen	'nice houses'
DEF, COM, PL	-e	De mooie autos	'the nice cars'
INDEF, COM, PL	-e	Mooie autos	'nice cars'

4.1. Method

The sentence completion task contained 16 singular nouns: 8 neuter and 8 common gender nouns. Each noun is tested in definite and indefinite conditions. Previous work on L1 and L2 Dutch indicates that gender is problematic (Van der Velde, 2005; Snow and Hoefnagel-Höhle, 1978; Sabourin, 2003). Therefore, we included a control test for gender attribution to the nouns in the adjectival inflection test. In this control test, we elicited for each noun a gender-marked definite determiner: *de* for common nouns, and *het* for neuter nouns. Gender attribution was tested at the beginning of each session. The same test, with differently ordered items, was repeated at the end of the session.

4.2. Data analysis

Results that are not corrected for gender attribution (Table 7) are followed by results that are corrected (Table 8). The corrected results are restricted to nouns with stable gender. To determine if a noun's gender is stable, we excluded nouns for which we collected less than two overt gender markings. Since we collected maximally three "gender responses" (twice in the gender attribution test and once in the adjectival inflection test), stable gender marking comprises four possibilities: *de/de* or *de/de/de* (=common gender) and *het/het* or *het/het/het* (=neuter gender). Instable gender marking comprises *de/het*, *de/de/het* and *het/het/de*.

4.3. Results

A learner can substitute –*e* in [indefinite, neuter] condition and/or substitute –*ø* in [definite, common], [indefinite, common] and [definite, neuter] conditions.

Table 7: Accuracy (% correct) in adjectival inflection test

	Target –ø		Target –e	
Child L1	33	50/152	96	353/368
Child L2T	16	21/132	93	267/287
Child L2M	11	30/263	97	568/585
Adult L2T	46	38/82	70	133/191
Adult L2M	68	80/117	33	94/283

Table 8: Accuracy (% correct) in adjectival inflection test, corrected results

	Target –ø		Target –e	
Child L1	73	27/37	93	341/367
Child L2T	*		94	211/224
Child L2M	11	1/9	97	360/371
Adult L2T	*		61	49/80
Adult L2M	83	5/6	28	28/101

With regard to the correct realization of –*e*, the children are highly accurate, before as well as after corrections for gender attribution. Hence, they hardly substitute –*ø*. The adults are less accurate and do substitute –*ø*, particularly the Moroccans. Correct realization of –*ø* shows a different picture. A * indicates the absence of responses, due to absence of stable neuter nouns, which is, in turn, an effect of the overuse of the common gender definite determiner *de*. This overuse characterizes all groups. Only the (older) child L1 learners use a fair number of stable neuter nouns. If the child L1 learners use stable neuter nouns, they also use most often the correct adjectival suffix in the special case ($-\emptyset$).[8] The low percentage of 33% correct in Table 7 comes from neuter nouns that are common according to the child: after corrections accuracy goes up to 73% correct. For the adults, corrections do not lead to any improvement. Adult responses in all conditions show substitutions in both directions. The Turks tend to substitute $-e$ whereas the Moroccans substitute $-\emptyset$ most frequently.

Figure 2: Variability in probabilities of substitutions of suffixes $-e$ and $-\emptyset$

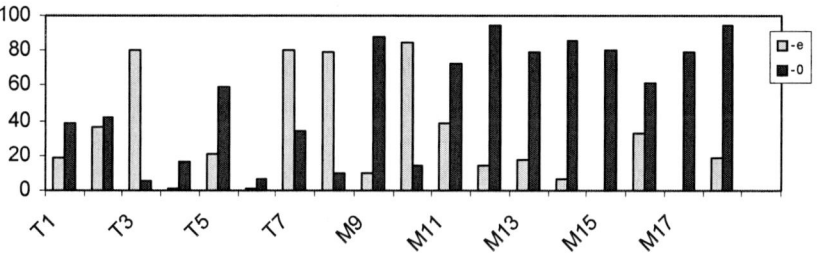

4.4. Interpretation of results

The children are more accurate than the adults, they make different errors and show hardly any variability between and within participants. Children's errors with adjectival inflection are in fact errors in gender attribution that are caused by the "overattribution" of common gender. For adjectival inflection this results in application of the default rule, and, hence, $-e$ substitutions. Thus, in the child sample adjectival inflection is consistent with gender attribution. The adults also overattribute common gender. However, unlike the children, they substitute both $-e$ and $-\emptyset$. In the adult sample adjectival inflection and gender attribution are inconsistent. The Moroccans' preference to substitute $-\emptyset$ may be an effect of the impossibility to have a final unstressed vowel in their L1. Although the L1 of the Moroccans marks gender, and Turkish does not, the Moroccans do not profit from their L1; this may be because their masculine-feminine system does not map unto the Dutch common-neuter gender system.

5. Conclusion

If there are age effects in the acquisition of inflection, it is expected that that child L2 learners behave like child L1 learners and unlike adult L2 learners. This prediction is borne out by our data. Child and adult learners differ in the amount of errors, types or errors, consistency of gender in determiner and inflection and variability between and within participants. Differences between children and adults can only partially be related to L1 transfer. The other differences indicate that the two groups acquire inflectional morphology in a different way.

6. Discussion: child L2 learners and ultimate attainment

We have seen that child L1 and child L2 learners follow a similar developmental path. Results of a pilot study suggest that the two groups differ in ultimate attainment of adjectival inflection, though.

Laloi et al. (2005) tested 15-16 year-old adolescents: 8 Moroccan child L2 learners of Dutch and 7 Dutch monolingual controls. Verbal inflection, adjectival inflection and gender attribution have been tested with the methods described here. With respect to finite verbal inflection the two groups performed at ceiling. Results of the adjectival inflection/gender attribution tasks show that the child L2 learners still overuse of –e in the special case: only 9% is correctly marked with a zero-suffix (10/111). Of the neuter nouns, however, 64% (36/56) is assigned correct gender. Thus, ten years of extra exposure to Dutch did not suffice for catching up with the child L1 learners. For adjectival inflection 'late start effects' seem more severe than for gender attribution.

Three types of factors may play a role: (i) external factors i.e. a learner's input situation, (ii) internal factors i.e. does a learner start within or after the critical period? and (iii) linguistic factors i.e. properties of a particular linguistic variable. The assumption that there is no difference between the child L1 and child L2 learners with regard to the internal factor is supported by the observation that both groups make the same types of errors. The child L1 and child L2 learners differ with regard to the external factor: the child L2 learners receive later -from four onwards- and less -only outside their homes- Dutch input. We may now hypothesize that the difference in input situation causes early age effects. However, only in combination with linguistic factors, since early age effects are limited to adjectival inflection. Adjectival inflection, in contrast to verbal inflection, requires knowledge of gender: acquisition of the special case involves mapping of -ø to [indefinite, *neuter*, singular].

What makes gender so problematic? In the special case, indefiniteness and singular are overtly marked on resp. indefinite determiner and noun. Gender is *not* overtly spelled out. Dutch indefinite determines are not marked for gender, and a noun's gender is neither phonologically nor semantically transparent. Hence, to deduce the special case a learner must know lexical gender. In Dutch, gender of simple nouns is to a large extent unpredictable. Therefore, the acquisition of this piece of indirect evidence may take long. We may now speculate that in the case of adjectival inflection external factors magnify the effect of linguistic factors (or vice versa). As a consequence, child L2 learners do not reach a certain critical mass of input or threshold within the critical period and fossilize in the default stage (Locke, 1997; Hulk and Cornips, 2006).

Notes

[1] We use the notion 'acquisition' here in a broad way. It may include possible effects of storage or selection; our production tests do not enable us to make a distinction.

[2] Inquiries have been made with the teacher(s), who, in turn, consulted the parents of the children in case of uncertainty. For the inquiries we used a questionnaire. The criterion for inclusion is that the parents did/do not speak Dutch to the child, so that the home-situation is clearly pre-dominant monolingual Turkish or Moroccan Arabic/Tarifit. If the children heard Dutch at home, this was via siblings and/or television. In our task, we did not find any significant differences between oldest children and children with older siblings (and who may have heard Dutch at home from their siblings). Moroccan Arabic and Tarifit have been collapsed because often the parents speak both languages, and with respect to the linguistic variables in our study, the two languages do not differ.

[3] Overall, the children represent a higher proficiency level than the adults. Consequently, qualitative analyses of errors may be more telling than comparisons of the amounts of errors. Also, effects of L1 transfer may be more present in the adult sample than in the child sample.

[4] The two syntactically dissociated morphemes –*en* may, morphologically, be one and the same underspecified vocabulary item.

[5] The adults showed effects of L1 transfer in combination with a general tendency to overuse the SVO order (Clahsen and Muysken, 1986; Meisel, Clahsen and Pienemann, 1981).

[6] 0% (n=424) for child L1, 0% (n=176) for child L2T and 2% (n=358) for child L2M.

[7] The Turkish base order is head-final (resulting in OV), and contrasts in this respect with the Moroccan-Arabic/Tarifit base order (VO).

[8] The 27% incorrect responses come from the younger L1 learners.

References

Blom, E. (2003) *From root infinitive to finite sentence*, Doctoral dissertation, Utrecht University.

—. and D. Polišenská, (2006) "Verbal inflection and verb placement in first and second language acquisition", in M. Vliegen, ed., *Variation in Sprachtheorie und Spracherwerb*, Peter Lang Publishing Group.

Clahsen, H. and P. Muysken, (1986) "The availability of Universal Grammar to adult and child learners: a study of the acquisition of German word order", in *Second Language Research* 2, 93-119.

DeKeyser, R (2000) "The robustness of critical period effects in second language acquisition", in *Studies in Second Language Acquisition* 22, 499-533.

Ellis, N. C. (2002) "Frequency effects in language acquisition: A review with implications for theories of implicit and explicit language acquisition", in *Studies in Second Language Acquisition*, 24, 143-188.

Goldowsky, B.N. and E. Newport, (1993) "Modeling the effects of processing limitations on the acquisition of morphology: The less is more hypothesis", in J. Mead, ed., *The Proceedings of the 11th WCCFL*, Stanford, CA: CSLI.

Haan, G. de (1987) "A theory-bound approach to the acquisition of verb placement in Dutch", in G. de Haan and W. Zonneveld (Eds.) *Formal parameters of generative grammar: OTS Yearbook 1987*, Dordrecht: ICG.

Hulk, A. and L. Cornips, (2006) "Neuter gender determiners and interface vulnerability in child L1/2L1 Dutch", in S. Unsworth, T. Parodi, A. Sorace and M. Young-Scholten, eds., *Paths of Development in L1 and L2 acquisition*, Amsterdam: John Benjamins.

Johnson, J. and E. Newport, (1989) "Critical period effects in second language learning: the influence of maturational state on the acquisition of English as a second language", in *Cognitive Psychology* 21, 60-99.

—. and E. Newport, (1991) "Critical period effects on universal properties of language: the status of subjacency in the acquisition of a second language", in *Cognition* 39, 215-258.

Jordens, P. (1990) "The acquisition of verb placement", in *Linguistics* 28, 1407-1448.

—. and C. Dimroth (to appear) "Finiteness in Children and Adults learning Dutch", in D. Bittner and N. Gagarina, eds., *Acquisition of Verb Grammar and Verb Arguments*, Kluwer.

Kampen, J. van (1997) *First steps in WH movement*, Doctoral Dissertation, Utrecht University.

Klein, W. and C. Perdue, (1997) "The Basic Variety (or: Couldn't natural languages be much simpler?)", in *Second Language Research* 13 (4), 302 – 347.

Lalleman, J. (1986) *Dutch language proficiency of Turkish children born in the Netherlands*, Doctoral dissertation, University of Amsterdam.

Laloi, A., R. Spanjaard and J. Styczynska, (2005) "Verbal and adjectival flexion by child L2 learners of Dutch", Ms. University of Amsterdam.

Lardiere, D. (1998) "Dissociating syntax from morphology in a divergent end-state grammar", in *Second Language Research* 14, 359-375.

Locke, J. (1997) "A Theory of Neurolinguistic Development", in *Brain and Language* 58: 265-326.

McDonald, J. (2000) "Grammaticality judgements in a second language: influences of age of acquisition and native language", in *Applied Psycholinguistics* 21, 395-423.

Meisel, J., H. Clahsen and M. Pienemann, (1981) "On determining developmental stages in natural second language acquisition", in *Studies in Second language Acquisition*, 3 (2), 109-135.

Peters, A.M. (1983). *The Units of Language Acquisition*, Monographs in Applied Psycholinguistics, Cambridge University Press.

Pinker, S. (1984) *Language Learnability and Language Development*, Harvard University Press, Cambridge MA.

Prévost, P. (2003) "Truncation and missing surface inflection in initial L2 German", in *Studies in Second Language Acquisition* 25, 65-97.

Polišenská, D. (2005) "Dutch children's acquisition of inflection", paper presented at IASCL 2005, Berlin.

Sabourin, L. (2003) *Grammatical Gender and Second Language Processing*, Doctoral dissertation, Groningen University.

Snow, C. and M. Hoefnagel-Höhle (1978) "The critical period for language acquisition: evidence from second-language learning", in *Child Development* 49, 1114-1128.

Schwartz, B. (2004) "Why child L2 acquisition?", in J. van Kampen and S. Baauw, eds., *Proceedings of GALA 2003*, Utrecht University.

Unsworth, S. (2005) *Child L2, adult L2, child L1: differences and similarities*, Doctoral dissertation, Utrecht University.

Velde, M. van der (2005) "Gender acquisition across languages: Dutch and French compared", paper presented at IASCL 2005, Berlin.

Verhoeven, L., Vermeer, A. and C. van de Guchte, (1986, 2002) *Taaltoets allochtone kinderen: diagnostische toets voor de mondelinge vaardigheid Nederlands bij allochtone kinderen van 5-9 jaar (TAK onderbouw)*. Tilburg: Zwijsen.

Wijnen, F. and G. Bol, (1993) "The escape from the optional infinitive stage", in A. de Boer, J. de Jong and R. Landeweerd (eds.) *Language and cognition 3: Yearbook of the research group for theoretical and experimental linguistics of the University of Groningen*.

—., M. Kempen and S. Gillis, (2001) "Bare infinitives in Dutch early child language: an effect of input?", in *Journal of Child Language* 28(3), 629-660

Zuckerman, S. (2001) *The acquisition of "optional" movement*, Doctoral dissertation, Groningen University.

DEVELOPMENTAL SEQUENCES AND (IN)VULNERABLE DOMAINS IN GERMAN INTERLANGUAGE SYNTAX

UTE BOHNACKER

1. Introduction

German and Swedish are both V2 languages, with the finite verb in main clauses in second position, and with the subject or an argument or a nonargument in first position. Concerning the order of nonfinite verbs (infinitives, participles, particles) vis-à-vis objects/complements (VP headedness), German is OV and Swedish VO, at the relevant level of abstraction. The nonnative acquisition of verb placement in German(ic) has often been characterised in the following terms (e.g. Clahsen & Muysken 1986; Platzack 2001; Pienemann 1998):

(1) a. It is hard or impossible to fully acquire V2, irrespective of L1.
   b. Targetlike finite verb placement (V2) is dependent on targetlike nonfinite verb placement (VO/OV) having been acquired first.
   c. Learners start out with (and stick to) so-called "canonical" SVO word order.
   d. Learners of German follow a universal developmental sequence (2).

(2) Stage 1: S (AUX/Modal) V O
   Stage 2: (ADV/PP) S (AUX/Modal) V O
   Stage 3: (ADV/PP) S V_{finite} O $V_{nonfinite}$
   Stage 4: XP V_{finite} S O ($V_{nonfinite}$)
   (Stage 5: S V_{finite} (ADV) O ($V_{nonfinite}$))
   Stage 6: main clauses as above, embedded clauses: *daß* SOV_{finite}

The notions in (1) rest on more general, but not uncontroversial, assumptions about (nonnative) acquisition of syntax, namely that

(3) i. syntactic structure at the initial state is rudimentary, only comprising lexical projections (VP) (e.g. Vainikka & Young-Scholten 1994).

   ii. functional categories and their projections, particularly CP, are "vulnerable", i.e. absent from interlanguage grammars at the initial state, and morphemes and grammatical operations associated with CP are mastered late (e.g. Platzack 2001; Bhatt-Hancin & Bhatt 2002).

   iii. acquisition of syntax always takes place from the bottom up, i.e. first VP, then IP, then CP (e.g. Vainikka & Young-Scholten 1994, 1996).

Here I will argue against the notions in (1)-(3), making use of quantified production data from native Swedish speakers learning German after puberty. Their behaviour concerning finite verb placement (V2) and nonfinite verb placement (VO/OV) is interpreted as evidence in favour of transfer-based theories (e.g. Schwartz & Sprouse 1994, 1996). I will argue that there are no universal developmental sequences, no universally vulnerable and no universally invulnerable syntactic domains in L2 acquisition. Instead I will argue that nonnative developmental paths vary, and that much of this variation can be predicted on the basis of the typological differences between and isomorphisms of the languages involved.

2. L1 Swedish, nonnative German: Finite verb placement (V2)

Most studies of Swedish-native learners of German only look at Swedes learning German as a *third* language, after substantial exposure to English (4-7 years). These learners appear to follow the developmental sequence in (2) and sometimes violate V2 (e.g. Håkansson, Pienemann & Sayehli 2002). Bohnacker (2005, in press), however, arrives at a very different conclusion, on the basis of a larger-scale investigation of Swedish-speaking learners of German as a *second* and as a *third* language. The results of her study are summarised here.

Bohnacker recorded 6 ab initio learners of German (old age pensioners) after 4 months and after 9 months of classroom German (3 hours/week), three learners with *no* English (Märta, Algot, Signe) and three *with* L2 English (Rune, Gun, Ulf). At 4 months, monologues on a given topic were recorded in the language lab, with 100-150 utterances each. Also at 4 months, 120-min dialogues of 2 informants were recorded in interaction with a monolingual German native speaker (ca. 1000 utterances each). At 9 months, language lab monologues were recorded again (100-350 utterances each). This elicitation technique led to a high ratio of complete sentences and non-subject-initial declaratives, i.e. a high ratio of utterances relevant to the investigation of V2 (for details, see Bohnacker, in press). Not surprisingly for data collected at such an early stage of nonnative acquisition, all learners show heavy lexical interference from Swedish, and the 3 learners who had learnt English prior to German also show heavy lexical interference from English, see e.g. (4).

(4) **and then I** # *denn ich geh ein studiecirkel*   *und wi* *mache sidenmåleri.*
[and then I]$_{ENG}$ then I   go   a study-circle$_{SWE}$ and we make silkpainting$_{SWE}$
'And then I, and then I do a course where we do silk painting.'

(Gun, 4 months)

Bohnacker (2005, in press) also collected cross-sectional data from 23 native speakers of Swedish. For these 16-year-old 9th grade pupils at Swedish secondary school, German was their third language, they had had 4 years of English before starting German and 7 years of English at the time of testing (3 years of classroom German). 23 language lab monologues were recorded in the same fashion as for the ab initio learners, and written productions were collected too (not reported on here).

2.1. V2 results for the adult ab initio learners

The ab initio learners produce both SVX and non-subject-initial main clauses (Bohnacker 2005, in press). At 4 and 9 months, the learners who do not know English adhere 100% to the V2 constraint in their L2 German (white rows in Table 1), whilst those learners who do know English sometimes violate V2 in their L3 German, producing non-subject-initial declaratives with V2 word order *and* with V3 word order (cf. grey shaded rows in Table 1). Examples are given in (5)-(6).

Table 1. Ab initio L2 and L3 German: Word order in main clauses.

4 months German	SVX	V1	V2	V3
Märta	**62%**	9%	**29%**	**0%**
	157/253	22/253	74/253	0
Algot	**69%**	0	**31%**	**0%**
	43/62	0	19/62	0
Rune	**61%**	4%	**19%**	**17%**
	136/224	8/224	43/224	37/224
Gun	**74%**	0%	**14%**	**12%**
	58/78	0	11/78	9/78

9 months German	SVX	V1	V2	V3
Märta	**68%**	**0%**	**32%**	**0%**
	125/184	0	59/184	0
Algot	**81%**	**0%**	**18%**	**1%**
	104/128	0	23/128	1/128
Signe	**62%**	**1%**	**37%**	**0%**
	128/206	2/206	76/206	0
Rune	**74%**	**0%**	**15%**	**11%**
	126/171	0	26/171	19/171
Gun	**65%**	**0%**	**20%**	**15%**
	120/185	0	37/185	28/185
Ulf	**70%**	**0%**	**16%**	**14%**
	58/83	0	13/83	12/83

(5) ***denn ich gehen** ein promenad # en   promenad, ja.*
then I go a walk$_{SWE}$ a$_{SWE}$ walk$_{SWE}$ yes
'Then I go for a walk, a walk, yeah.'
(Gun, 4 mts, *denn*: novel form = *dann*)

(6) *ich habe viel hören um   Bodensee,   **so ich will** gerne sehen das.*
I   have much hear about Lake-Constance, so I want gladly see it
'I've heard a lot about Lake Constance, so I'd like to see it.'
(Gun, 9 mts)

The difference between the two groups is even more striking when only non-subject-initial main clauses are considered (i.e. when SVX utterances are detracted). As shown in Table 2, the learners with no English do not violate V2 (0%, white rows), whereas those with prior knowledge of English do so 42%-41% of the time (grey rows). Only aggregated results are presented here; for the individual figures see Bohnacker (in press). The difference between the two groups indicates that prior knowledge of English (non-V2) is a confounding factor.

Table 2. *Non*-subject-initial main clauses: Ab initio L2 and L3 German.

4 months German	V1	V2	nontarget V3
Märta, Algot	19%	81%	0%
	22/115	93/115	0/115
Rune, Gun	7%	51%	42%
	8/107	55/107	45/107

9 months German	V1	V2	nontarget V3
Märta, Algot, Signe	1%	99%	0%
	2/160	158/160	0/160
Rune, Gun, Ulf	0%	59%	41%
	0/128	76/128	52/128

2.2. V2 results for the intermediate learners

The intermediate learners produce 32% non-subject-initial V2 clauses (Table 3). V2 is targetlike, possible earlier interference from English has virtually disappeared. V3 is rare (4.7%) and attested for only 12 of the 23 informants. Most of these V3 cases are not violations of V2, but declaratives with subject-verb-inversion (XXVS word order), for details see Bohnacker (2005).

Table 3. Word order in main clauses: Oral intermediate, 23 16-year-olds.

3 years German	SVX	V1	V2	V3
23 informants	62%	1.5%	32%	4.7%
	(754/1220)	(18/1220)	(386/1220)	(57/1220)

(plus 0.4% (5/1220) wh-questions)

2.3. Conclusions so far

Swedish ab initio learners of German adhere to the V2 constraint. This is strikingly different from what we know about learners with a non-V2 L1. The CP domain does not appear to be absent or vulnerable. Swedish learners of German do not only have rudimentary syntactic structure (VP). For them, the implicational hierarchy/developmental sequence of L2 German verb placement (2) does not hold, and therefore, the sequence cannot be universal. Rather, it is likely that the L1 syntax of Swedish has transferred. Lexical *and* functional projections (VP, IP, CP) and their L1 features can be assumed to exist at the initial state. For those learners of German who know English, the non-V2 English L2 syntax may interfere with the acquisition of V2 in the L3. Prior knowledge of languages should therefore be taken into account when investigating the initial state of nonnative acquisition.

3. L1 Swedish, nonnative German: nonfinite verb placement

3.1. VP headedness in the interlanguage of the ab initio learners

Despite the high frequencies of targetlike non-subject-initial V2, the ab initio learners are not advanced. Other aspects of their syntax are nontargetlike, e.g. VP headedness. Bohnacker (2005, in press) determined the position of nonfinite verbs (infinitives, participles) in the learner data in relation to other constituents ($V_{nonfin}X$ versus XV_{nonfin}). Many utterances with a nonfinite verb had to be excluded because of too few telltale constituents. Still, the remaining utterances show a striking pattern (Table 4). At 4 months, the learners exhibit 85%-90% $V_{nonfin}X$, whilst at 9 months, $V_{nonfin}X$ is down to ca. 30%, irrespective of whether the informants are learning German as a L2 (white rows) or as a L3 (grey rows). Having started out with a head-initial VP (VO, as in their L1 Swedish), they seem to be well underway towards head-final OV. For reasons of space, only group results are reported here; for the individual results, see Bohnacker (in press). Examples are given in (7).

Table 4. Ab initio L2 and L3 German: Nonfinite verb placement in infinitival clauses, sentence fragments, and main clauses with complex verb.

4 months German	nontarget $V_{nonfin}X$	XV_{nonfin}
Märta, Algot	85%	15%
	(105/124)	(19/124)
Rune, Gun	90%	10%
	(94/104)	(10/104)
9 months German	nontarget $V_{nonfin}X$	XV_{nonfin}
Märta, Algot, Signe	29%	71%
	(30/103)	(73/103)
Rune, Gun, Ulf	30%	70%
	(26/88)	(62/88)

(7) a. *nun haben ich **spielt Boule** vier Jahr.*
     now have I   played boules four year
     'I've now been playing boules for four years.' (VO, Märta, 4 months)

   b. *und dann solln ich **Boule spielen.***
     and then shall I   boules play
     'And then I'll play boules.'   (OV, Märta, 9 months)

All informants are doing worse on nonfinite verb placement than on V2; e.g. Märta and Algot produce 85% $V_{nonfinite}X$ at 4 months, at a time when their non-subject-initial main clauses show perfect V2 (100%). Thus, the acquisition of V2 is not developmentally dependent on target VP headedness having been acquired first.

3.2. VP headedness in the interlanguage of the intermediate learners

The findings from the ab initio learners concerning nonfinite verb placement suggest that they are resetting the VP parameter from head-initial to the target German head-final setting. Recall however that by 9 months, they have not yet achieved 100% OV, but only ca. 70% (Table 4). A similar picture emerges when we consider the intermediate teenage learners, who have had 3 years of classroom German. As shown in Table 5, the intermediate learners' nonfinite verb placement is still 26% nontargetlike at 3 years, at a time when V2 is near perfect.

Table 5. Nonfinite verb placement: Oral intermediate L2 German.

3 years German	nontarget $V_{nonfin}X$	XV_{nonfin}
23 informants	26%	74%
	(100/389)	(289/389)
which break down into		
3 years German	$V_{nonfin}X$	XV_{nonfin}
5 informants	-	100%
		(0/46)
11 informants	16%	84%
	(31/198)	(167/198)
7 informants	48%	52%
	(69/145)	(76/145)

As the breakdown in Table 5 shows, the aggregated figure of 26% nontarget $V_{nonfin}X$ masks individual differences: The 23 learners are heterogeneous with regard to VP headedness; for a subgroup of 7 learners, VP is head-final only 52% of the time (Bohnacker 2005). Such VO productions are illustrated in (8)-(11).

(8) ... *und mein Traum ist zu* **dans** **mit ihm.**
    and my   dream is to dance$_{SWE}$ with him
    '... and my dream is to dance with him'   (Dagny, 3 years)
    (cf. target: ... *mit ihm zu tanzen*)

(9) *aber meine Freund Mona kann nicht deutsch sprechen, so ich glaubt,*
    but my   friend Mona can not German speak   so I   think
    dass meine Deutsch kann **helfen uns.**
    that my   German can help   us
    'But my friend Mona doesn't speak German, so my German will come in
    handy.'   (cf. target: ... *mein Deutsch uns helfen kann*) (Greta, 3 years)

(10) *ich sollte   nach Indien fahren und da   sollten*
     I   should to   India go   and there should
     M.M. **lernen mich Meditation.**
     M.M. teach me   meditation
     'I'll go to India and there MM will teach me how to meditate.'
     (cf. target: ... *MM mich Meditation lehren*)   (Kåge, 3 years)

(11) *ich will auch nach Las Vegas fahren und* **gehen auf alle Klube da.**
     I   want also to   Las Vegas go   and go   on all clubs there
     'I also want to go to Las Vegas and go to all the clubs there.'
     (cf. target: ... *und in alle Klubs dort gehen*)   (Kåge, 3 years)

When the learners are looked at individually, there is no correlation between nontarget VP and V2 violations, nor between targetlike VP and perfect V2. Just as for the ab-initio learners, V2 in the intermediate learners is not developmentally dependent on a targetlike VP having been acquired first. This result contradicts the predictions of the implicational hierarchy (2) and theories of language acquisition that assume that syntax is always acquired from the bottom up.

3.3. A closer look at VP headedness

As we have seen, VPs with different head directions coexist for extensive periods in at least some of the intermediate learners' interlanguages. How this is to be captured formally in parameter (re)setting models is not entirely straightforward – from what the ab initio findings tell us, it can be surmised that the learners early on in their development adopt an "additional" head-final parameter setting for VP, but without getting rid of the old, head-initial VP setting.

Bohnacker (2005) does not really discuss why nontarget VO lingers on for so long in her informants. Considering that L2 knowledge of English was shown to have a "detrimental effect" on the acquisition of V2 in her ab initio learners, one might speculate whether L2 English, being a VO language, also has an effect on the learners' acquisition of OV. If so, the transfer of the Swedish L1 setting of the VP headedness parameter (VO) to the L3 German would receive a boost from the learners' L2 English, which is also VO, resulting in delayed acquisition of OV. Unfortunately we cannot test this hypothesis, since all the intermediate learners had English as their L2 and German as their L3. As for the ab initio learners, all of them are producing both VO and OV at 9 months, irrespectively of prior knowledge of English. What we would need to find out is whether those who do *not* speak English will be faster and/or more successful in "shedding" the remaining head-initial VPs than the learners who do speak English, *after* the 9-month testing point. I must leave this issue for future research.

Of course, there might also be quite different reasons for why nontarget $V_{nonfin}X$ productions linger on in some of the intermediate learners: A qualitative analysis of the learner data reveals that VP headedness does not correlate with lexical verb choice, verb type or morphological type of complement. Thus, it is not the case for a certain learner that a particular lexical verb always occurs as VX, and another verb always as XV. Also, the choice of VX vs. XV does not seem to correlate with whether the verb is transitive or ditransitive, or whether it takes a case-marked or a prepositional complement. Rather, the learners who produce $V_{nonfin}X$ use one and the same verb sometimes in a head-initial VP and sometimes in a head-final VP. Neither does it appear to matter whether the complement of the verb is a pronominal or a lexical DP, or whether this complement is particularly light or heavy. However, these observations are based on oral production data and on only 389 nonfinite constructions from 23 informants. A larger data base, and in particular production data from learners like those 7 informants who produce VX about half of the time, or an acceptability judgment task, may reveal patterns that I have failed to observe in the corpus at hand. I did however observe a tendency for VP headedness to interact with syntactic context in construction-specific ways. In the learner data, nonfinite VPs occur in four different syntactic contexts:

(12) i.   as a stand-alone VP, e.g. a subjectless root infinitive or elliptic
           utterance,

     ii.   as a VP in an infinitival subordinate clause (e.g. (8)),

     iii. as a VP embedded under an auxiliary or modal (e.g. (9)-(10)),

iv. as the second conjunct of a coordination construction, i.e. a VP coordinated with a preceding VP, which in turn may be embedded under an auxiliary or modal (e.g. (11)).

Only 2% of the VPs produced by the intermediate learners are stand-alone VPs (8/389), 8% are infinitival subordinate clauses (30/389), 10% are coordinated second-conjunct VPs (40/389), but by far the most, 80%, are VPs embedded under an auxiliary or modal (311/389).

The frequency of head-final vs. head-initial VPs varies greatly across the four different syntactic contexts in (12). In Figure 1, solid black bars indicate targetlike head-final XV_{nonfin}, and grey bars nontargetlike head-initial $V_{nonfin}X$. There are also a few cases of nontarget VXV (white bars, which will not be discussed here). 75% of the few stand-alone VPs are target XV_{nonfin}, though this figure is not particularly telling because of the low raw figures (6/8). 72% (21/30) of the infinitival subordinate clauses are target XV_{nonfin}. However, coordinated VPs show a radically different pattern: Only 14% (32/40) of the second-conjunct VPs show targetlike XV_{nonfin} order, by far the majority are nontarget $V_{nonfin}X$. By contrast, most of the numerous VPs embedded under an auxiliary or a modal (81%, 311/389) are targetlike XV_{nonfin}.

Figure 1. VP headedness and type of VP, percentages Swedish L1, L2 English, L3 German learners, 3 years German

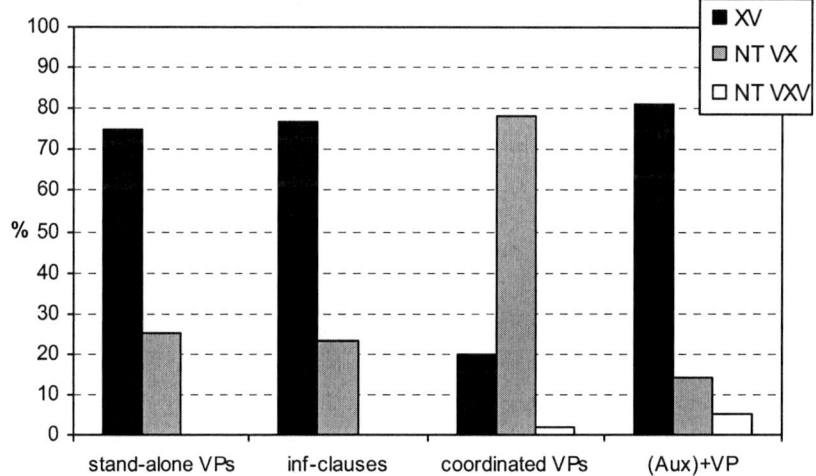

No matter how coordination is to be modelled formally (e.g. Johannessen 1998), it should be noted that the nontarget coordination cases are indeed instances of a nonfinite phrase (VP, V', or equivalent) and another nonfinite phrase (VP, V', or equivalent) being conjoined with each other, as sketched in (13'a). That is, we are *not* dealing with coordination of finite clauses at IP or CP level (13'b) (with an omitted subject and nontargetlike morphology on the verb in the second conjunct).

(13)   Coordinated VP (second conjunct)
  *ich will mehr de Beauvoir lesen und **schreiben** Poesie und Dichte.*
  I   want more de Beauvoir read and write   poetry and poems
  'I'd like to read more de Beauvoir and write poetry and poems.'
                    (target: ... *und Poesie und Gedichte schreiben*)
(13')   a. *ich will*
        [[$_{nonfin}$ *mehr de Beauvoir lesen*] & [$_{nonfin}$ *schreiben Poesie und Dichte*]]
     b. [$_{fin}$ *ich will mehr de Beauvoir lesen*] & [$_{fin}$ _ *schreiben Poesie und
        Dichte*]

That the analysis in (13'a) is to be preferred has to do with the interpretation of (13). The discourse context of (13) is a 16-year-old describing her plans for a future bohemian life in Paris. Thus, she intends both events (reading more de Beauvoir and writing poetry) to take place in the future. However, such an interpretation can only be assigned if the modal *will* takes scope over both events. Therefore the second conjunct [*schreiben Poesie und Dichte*] is not an IP or CP, but it is coordinated with [*mehr de Beauvoir lesen*] at a low projection level, such as VP.

Most of the nontargetlike head-initial coordinated VPs (81%, 26/32) are produced by 5 informants in the group of the 7 learners with an overall fifty-fifty distribution of head-final and head-initial VPs (recall Table 5). These learners also produce head-initial VPs in other syntactic contexts. The remaining head-initial VPs are distributed more evenly across the intermediate learners. However, caution is advised when drawing conclusions as to which learners allow nontarget head-initial coordinated VPs and which learners do not: Compared to the 311 instances of Aux + VP, the raw totals for coordinated second-conjunct VPs are low (40). 10 of the 23 informants happen not to produce any relevant coordinations in the corpus, so we do not know what might or might not be acceptable in their interlanguage grammar. (These informants, like the others, frequently do produce nonfinite VPs followed by a conjunction and a (nonfinite) verbs without a complement, but as such cases do not tell us anything about VP headedness, they have not been included in any of the counts here.) A much larger corpus, an elicitation task focusing on coordination, or an acceptability judgment task would be needed to clarify these matters. The corpus at hand was collected mainly for exploratory purposes concerning main clause word order (V2).

Why would head-initial VPs mainly be produced in coordination constructions? Perhaps, this has to do with the *on-line oral production* of coordinated nonfinite phrases. Note that it is predominantly the *second* conjunct that exhibits nontargetlike word order. Thus we find, often embedded under an auxiliary or modal, a targetlike head-final first VP conjoined with a nontargetlike head-initial second VP, we also find a few cases of a head-initial first VP conjoined with a head-initial second VP, but we very rarely find a head-initial first VP conjoined with a head-final second VP. We might conjecture then that in on-line production, the auxiliary or modal "reminds" the speaker to immediately continue with a head-final VP, but when s/he later gets to the conjunction and the second VP, the "reminder" is too far away.

Moreover, it is not clear where exactly, i.e. at which syntactic node, L2 speakers coordinate the two conjuncts. For instance, it might be possible that the speaker, having uttered the (head-final) verb of the first conjunct, directly conjoins this verb simply with the next *verb* (...V *und* V ...), instead of closing the first VP and conjoining it with the verb *phrase* (or equivalent) of the second event ([VP] *und* [VP]). If in online planning and production a speaker has come as far as producing ...V *und* V, like ... *fahren und gehen* in (11), repeated here, the only way of completing the utterance is to produce the complement of the second conjunct after the verb, resulting in "head-initial" nontarget word order.

(11)   *ich will auch nach Las Vegas **fahren und gehen** auf alle Klube da.*
        I   want also to   Las Vegas go   and go   on all clubs there
        'I also want to go to Las Vegas and go to all the clubs there.'

(Kåge, 3 years)

Little is known about online production of coordination, and at present, my suggestions concerning the L2 production data are mere speculation. I hope to investigate this issue further in future work.

4. Conclusions

Whatever the explanation for the prolonged existence of nontarget $V_{nonfin}X$ word order in German interlanguage grammar may turn out to be, it is clear that the learners in this study have greater problems mastering OV than mastering V2. The acquisition of targetlike nonfinite verb placement (a syntactic phenomenon involving the VP domain) thus lags behind the acquisition of V2 (involving the C-domain) in native speakers of Swedish learning German as their second or third language. We could call VP their "vulnerable domain" and

CP their "invulnerable domain", but this is quite the opposite of what has been proposed in the literature, namely that VP is universally invulnerable and that CP is universally vulnerable (e.g. Platzack 2001). We might perhaps be better advised to scrap the terms "(in)vulnerable domains", and return to those transfer-based L2 theories that predict divergent developmental routes with respect to the same target language for groups of learners with typologically distinct L1s. For instance, according to Schwartz & Sprouse's (1994, 1996) Full Transfer/Full Access model, learners initially produce and process L2 utterances entirely through the L1 grammar, and only later change their interlanguage syntax by acquiring new constraints or parameter settings. Native speakers of a V2-L1 should thus transfer the V2 property from their L1 and master V2 in a V2-L2 early on, and this is exactly what I have found for the Swedes learning German as a *second* language. As for the nontarget V3 main clauses, which occur in the informants learning German as a *third* language, existing models of syntactic transfer (such as Schwartz & Sprouse 1994) would need to be enriched to also allow for *L2* transfer. Concerning the VP domain, L1 transfer of a head-initial VP is predicted to result in the production of nontargetlike head-initial VP utterances, and this is documented for the Swedish learners of German irrespective of whether they know English or not.

References

Bhatt, R. M. and B. Hancin-Bhatt (2002) "Structural minimality, CP and the initial state in second language acquisition," in *Second Language Research*, 18, 348-392.

Bohnacker, U. (2005) "Nonnative acquisition of Verb Second: On the empirical underpinnings of universal L2 claims," in: M. den Dikken & C. Tortora, eds., *The function of function words and functional categories*, Amsterdam, John Benjamins, 41-77.

—. (in press) "When Swedes begin to learn German: From V2 to V2," in *Second Language Research*.

Clahsen, H. and P. Muysken (1986) "The availability of universal grammar to adult and child learners: A study of the acquisition of German word order," in *Second Language Research* 2, 93-119.

Håkansson, G., M. Pienemann and S. Sayehli (2002) "Transfer and typological proximity in the context of second language processing," in *Second Language Research* 18, 250-273.

Johannessen, J. B. (1998) *Coordination,* New York, Oxford University Press.

Pienemann, M. (1998) *Language processing and second language development: Processability Theory.* Amsterdam, John Benjamins.

Platzack, C. (2001) "The vulnerable C-domain" in *Brain and Language* 77, 364-377.

Schwartz, B. D. and R. Sprouse, (1994) "Word order and nominative case in nonnative language acquisition: A longitudinal study of (L1 Turkish) German interlanguage," in T. Hoekstra and B. D. Schwartz, eds., *Language acquisition studies in generative grammar*. Amsterdam, John Benjamins, 317-368.

—. and R. Sprouse (1996) "L2 cognitive states and the Full Transfer/Full Access model" in *Second Language Research* 12, 40-72.

Vainikka, A. and M. Young-Scholten (1994) "Direct access to X' theory: Evidence from Korean and Turkish adults learning German," in T. Hoekstra and B. D. Schwartz, eds., *Language acquisition studies in generative grammar*, Amsterdam, John Benjamins, 265-316.

—. and M. Young-Scholten (1996) "Gradual development of L2 phrase structure," in *Second Language Research* 12, 7-39.

NULL PREPOSITIONS IN L2 ENGLISH AND L2 HEBREW

IRENA BOTWINIK-ROTEM

1. Null prepositions in L2 English

1.1 Wild grammar

The phenomenon of null prepositions in the acquisition of L2 English was discovered and analyzed in Klein (1993). While showing knowledge of a particular verb for its prepositional complement (1), L2 learners of English freely accept omission of the very same preposition in related questions (Qs) and relative clauses (RCs) (2) (Table 1). Omission of this kind is what Klein calls *null-prep*:

(1) The student is worrying *(about) the exam.
(2) a. Which exam is the student worrying?
     b. Here's the exam that the student is worrying.

Table 1. Acceptance of null prep in Qs and RCs (Klein (1993, 1995))

	Qs (9)	RCs (9)
Beginners	69%	78%
Intermediate	52%	57%
Advanced	30%	35%
Native speakers (Native)	1%	2%

Assuming that Qs are derived obligatorily by movement (unlike RCs, for which a non-movement analysis is conceivable, (3)), Klein (1993, 1995) was lead to conclude that null prep Qs indicate a wild intergrammar, since their representation involves a null P which is unable to govern, leading to an ECP violation (4).

(3) **Null prep in *non-movement* RCs**: [PP [P e [DP pro]]]

(4)   **Null prep in Qs:** *$[_{PP} [_P e [_{DP} t]]]$

1.2 Well-behaved null prep grammars

1.2.1 Non-movement analysis of Qs

Challenging Klein's (1993) assumption that null prep Qs are absent across languages, Dekydspotter, Sprouse and Anderson ((1998), DSA henceforth) argue that such Qs are bound construals, including an A'- bound *pro*, rather than a trace of a moved element, licensed by V upon P-incorporation (5).

(5)   **Null prep in construal Qs:** wh_i ... $[V+Pø]$ P_{copy} pro_i

Positing that null prep grammars is a generalized procedure in L2 development, **DSA (1998) predict that null prep grammar should be attested in the acquisition of any L2.**

1.2.2 Op-movement analysis of null prep Qs

In response to DSA (1998), Klein (2001) claims that the proposed P-incorporation is untenable, because it should only be possible in cases of complementation, but null prep is also attested in adjunct Qs ((6) and Table 2):

(6)   a. Which library did he read the book?
      b. Which cafeteria did she eat her lunch?

Table 2. Null prep in adjunct vs. argument Qs (Klein and Casco (1999))

	Beginners	Intermediate	Advanced	Native
Adjuncts	64%	59%	**33%**	0%
Arguments	50%	44%	**14%**	0%

In Klein's (2001) proposal null prep Qs involve pied-piped movement of an empty operator (Op) to spec-FocP, with the actual *wh*-phrase base generated in spec-CP:

(7) **Null prep after spell-out:** $[_{CP} wh_i$ $[_{FocP} [_{PP} Pø Op]_i [_{Foc}$ ..... $[_{PP} t_i]]]]$

Klein (2001) suggests that null prep in L2 English (L2E) results from the learners' need to resolve a conflict: a constraint against P-stranding in the majority of languages vs. its frequency in the input. She, thus, **predicts that null prep grammars should not be evidenced in non-stranding L2s.**

1.2.2.1 Interim remarks on Klein (2001): (i) Klein's argument against the validity of P-incorporation in DSA's (1998) analysis is not well-founded. The possibility/impossibility to incorporate should correlate with the availability of pseudopassive, and stranding under *wh*-movement (Baker (1988)). However, locative PPs headed by small Ps (like those used in Klein and Casco (1999)) allow both pseudopassive and P-stranding under *wh*-movement (8), perhaps making an incorporation-based account tenable. (ii) Acceptance rate in adjunct Qs is systematically higher than in argument Qs, in all proficiency levels; the difference is significant in the advanced group ($\chi^2 = 5.41$, $p = .02$). This is not accounted for by Klein (2001).

(8)   a. New York was slept in by many politicians.
       b. Which cafeteria did she eat her lunch in?

Focusing on DSA (1998) and Klein (2001), I set up to check the aforementioned predictions and underlying claims bearing on the derivation of Qs and RCs in L2 Hebrew (L2H), a non-stranding language, with overt *wh*-movement.

2. L2 Hebrew experimental data: methods and results

2.1 Experiment 1: Null Prep in L2 Hebrew

Subjects: 40 adults (aged 19-25) from two proficiency levels (intermediate and advanced), and 9 native speakers serving as controls.
Languages: various L1 (predominance of L1 Russian in the advanced group); L2H.
Task: Grammaticality judgment of RCs and Qs including obligatory PPs (*mexake le-,* 'waits for', *diber al,* 'talked about', *somex al,* 'relies on', and *poxed me-,* 'afraid of'), and locative PP-modifiers (*be-,* 'in', *leyad,* 'near') (knowledge of subcategorization frame was controlled).
Scale: 1 – ungrammatical; 2 - don't know; 3 – grammatical
Sample stimuli (ungrammatical):
RC: *ze   ha-otobus she-dani mexake*   Q: *mi   dani mexake?*
    this the-bus   that-Dani waits   Who Dani waits?

Results: As shown in Table 3, there is virtually no acceptance of null prep in Qs. Acceptance of null prep in RCs is rather low, but significantly different from Qs ($\chi^2 = 16.39$, $p < .0001$). The difference between the two proficiency levels is insignificant.

Table 3. Acceptance of null prep in Qs and RCs

	Responses	Qs (6)	RCs (6)
Intermediate	82	1%	12%
Advanced	125	3%	15%
Native	54	2%	2%

Further, as shown in Table 4, null prep in RCs was accepted only with three verbs. However, its rate with the verbs *mexake le-* ('waits for') and *poxed me-* ('afraid of') is probably influenced by LI. The high rate with the former is clearly due to predominance of L1ers of Russian, where this verb assigns accusative, and as for the latter, in a variety of languages it is not necessarily realized as V (e.g. English or French), or occurs with a DP complement (e.g. in Russian it assigns Genitive with no P). Thus, in fact, null prep in L2H is clearly accepted only in RCs including the locative PP adjunct headed by *be-* ('in').

Table 4. Influence of L1 Russian on acceptance of null prep in RCs, intermediate and advanced level

	Total	Russian	Other	χ^2	p
poxed me-	21% (7/33)	4/17	3/16	0.11	0.7
mexake le-	27% (8/30)	**7/17**	**1/13**	**4.22**	**0.04**
nosea be-	24% (9/38)	3/20	6/18	1.76	0.18
other	3% (3/106)				

2.2 Experiment 2: Subjacency effects in L2 Hebrew

Subjects, Scale and Languages as in experiment 1.
Task: Grammaticality judgment of grammatical (up to two embeddings)
and ungrammatical Qs (including islands and resumptive pronouns).
Sample stimuli (ungrammatical):
et mi ha-isha   nishka ota?   et mi dan pagash et ha-isha she-nishka (oto)?
who the-woman kissed her?   who Dan met Acc the-woman that-kissed (him)?
Results: There was no acceptance of ungrammatical Qs (336/336 correct judgments).

3. Discussion

The attested sensitivity to islandhood shows that Qs in L2H are derived by movement (Klein (2001) contra DSA (1998)), and support Klein's (2001) prediction that in the absence of P-stranding in the target language, null prep grammar is not attested (no null prep in Qs). What is, then, the source of null prep in L2H RC with the locative PP (adjunct PP), and why is it not attested in

Qs? Recall also that the rate of null prep in adjunct Qs in L2E is higher than in argument Qs (see 1.2.2.1). This fact is not accounted for in Klein (2001), and I take it to fall together with the acceptance of null prep with adjunct PPs in L2H RCs. Assuming that (i) **the locative relation** is instantiated via an abstract noun *Place* with an empty D(eterminer) (cf. Kayne (2004)) (9), and that (ii) null prep grammar results from the need to resolve the stranding/pied-piping conflict (Klein (2001)), I propose that null prep in L2 acquisition may have two sources: **(a)** (Mis)analyzing a small **locative P** like *in* as an (empty) D of the NP-*Place* (10); **(b)** V-P reanalysis of a recoverable P, triggered by P-stranding in the input.

(9) $[_{PPLoc} P_{in} [_{DP} D_{\varnothing} [_{NP} [_{DP} wh/Op] [_N Place]]]]$
(10) $[_{DP} D_{\varnothing}\text{-}P_{in\text{->} \varnothing} [_{NP} [_{DP} wh/Op] [_N Place]]]$

L2 Hebrew: In the absence of the trigger (P-stranding) null prep can result only from option **(a)**. N-to-D movement is required for Case-licensing of the DP merged in the specifier of NP (cf. Siloni (1997)). N-raising is blocked when D is merged with an empty P, resulting in lack of Case-licensing. Hence, the operator can be realized as *Op,* but not as an invariably overt Q-operator. Consequently, null (locative) prep in L2H is attested only in RCs.

(10') $[_{DP} D_{\varnothing}\text{-}P_{in\text{->} \varnothing} [_{NP} [_{DP} *wh/Op] [_N Place]]]$

L2 English: N-raising is not required (Longobardi (1994)); hence **(a)** does not affect the realization of the operator, giving rise to null (locative) prep in L2E in RCs and Qs. **(b)** is another source for null prep in L2E, argument and adjunct Qs alike - whatever licenses P-stranding in (8) (repeated in (11)), can license reanalysis of these locative Ps in L2E. Obligatory P's content is fully recoverable from the verb (*rely on/*in*), and the content of locative P is determined either by the verb or by the nominal head of its complement (*in/*at bed*, cf. van Riemsdijk (1998)).

(11) a. New York was slept in by many politicians.
     b. Which cafeteria did she eat her lunch in?

Notes

[1]DSA (1998) cite two natural languages (French and Yoruba) that apparently exhibit null prep Qs. However, the constructions illustrating null prep questions involve elements whose status as prepositions is highly controversial (*de* in French, *ni* in Yoruba). For a detailed argumentation against this claim see Klein (2001) and references cited therein.

References

Baker, M. (1988) *Incorporation,* University of Chicago Press, Chicago.

Dekydspotter, L., R. Sprouse and B. Anderson (1998) "Interlanguage A-bar Dependencies: Binding Construals, Null Prepositions and Universal Grammar," in *Second Language Research* 14, 341-358.

Kayne, R. S. (2004) "Here and There," in C. Leclère, E. Laporte, M. Piot and M. Silberztein, eds., *Syntax, Lexis and Lexicon-Grammar. Papers in Honour of Maurice Gross,* Amsterdam, John Benjamins, 253-273.

Klein, E. (1993) *Toward Second Language Acquisition: A Study of Null-prep,* Dordrecht, Kluwer.

—. (1995) "Evidence for a 'Wild' Grammar: When PPs Rear their Empty Heads," in *Applied Linguistics* 16, 88-117.

—. (2001) "(Mis)construing Null Prepositions in L2 Intergrammars: A Commentary and Proposal," in *Second Language Research* 17, 37-70.

—. and M. Casco (1999) "Optionality in English Non-native Grammars: Differences between L1 and L2 Acquisition," in *Proceedings of the 23rd BUCLD,* Somerville, MA, Cascadilla Press.

Longobardi, G. (1994) "Reference and Proper Names," in *Linguistic Inquiry* 25, 609-665.

Riemsdijk van, H. C. (1998) "Categorial Feature Magnetism," in *Journal of Comparative Germanic Linguistics,* 2, 1-48.

Siloni, T. (1997) *Noun Phrases and Nominalizations: The Syntax of DPs,* Dordrecht, Kluwer.

WHERE DO L2ERS ATTACH INTERCLAUSAL ADVERBIALS?[*]

GERALD BULLOCK, AKIRA OMAKI, BARBARA SCHULZ, BONNIE D. SCHWARTZ, AND ANNIE TREMBLAY

1. Introduction

Dekydtspotter, Schwartz, Sprouse & Liljestrand (2005) presented a reanalysis of Garcia (1998), a study which examined the L2 English construal of interclausal temporal and locational PP adverbials, as exemplified in (1):

(1) a. Charles told Anne   in the winter that he played tennis.   [PP-Comp]
     b. Charles told Anne that in the winter   he played tennis.   [Comp-PP]
     c. Charles told Anne   in the winter   he played tennis.   [No overt Comp]

To explain the asymmetrically nontargetlike L2 behavior, they offer a processing account whereby universal processing mechanisms lead to the favoring of the embedded-clause construal of the interclausal adverbial. This paper reconsiders the Dekydtspotter et al. proposal by way of two experiments, both focusing on the previously unexplored class of deictic temporal adverbials such as *yesterday*, with high-beginning Japanese L2ers of English as well as native English speakers.

The paper is organized as follows: Section 2 reviews previous research on L2ers' construal of interclausal adverbials; Section 3 presents the method and results of our acceptability judgment task; and Section 4 presents the method and results of our self-paced reading task. Section 5 discusses (a) implications of our findings vis à vis related studies, and (b) other factors that might have influenced our results. We close by highlighting our main conclusion: In the area under investigation, native processing and nonnative processing are fairly closely aligned.

2. Previous Research

Garcia (1998) tested low-level Arabic- and Chinese-speaking L2ers of English and English native speakers (NSs). Participants heard, one by one, audio-recorded English sentences of the types in (1), with distinct pauses around the adverbial PP and the complementizer, and chose from three pictures (one a distracter) the one that best represented each sentence. The two relevant pictures depicted the adverbial construed with either the matrix clause or the embedded clause. The Dekydtspotter et al. reanalysis of the results showed that L2ers were more accurate on Comp-PP sentences (1b) than on PP-Comp sentences (1a), and had a preference for embedded-clause construal in sentences with no overt complementizer (1c).

Dekydtspotter et al. reasoned that although these asymmetries argue for the existence of CP in the L2ers' Interlanguage (cf. Bhatt & Hancin-Bhatt 2002), the poorer performance on PP-Comp sentences requires explanation. To this end, they appealed to a general processing principle (2a) and three parsing strategies (2b-d):

(2) a. *Principle of Incremental Comprehension* (Crocker 1996:106): The Sentence Processor operates in such a way as to maximize comprehension of the sentence at each stage of processing.

   b. *Attach Quickly* (Fodor & Inoue 2000:23): On receiving a word of the input sentence, connect it to the current partial phrase marker as quickly as possible.

   c. *Minimal Attachment* (Frazier 1979:76): Attach incoming material into the phrase marker being constructed with the fewest nodes consistent with the well-formedness rules of the language.

   d. *Attach (Anyway)* (Fodor & Inoue 2000:26): On receiving a word of the input sentence, connect it to the current partial phrase marker for the sentence wherever it least severely violates the grammar, subject to preference principles.

Relying on (2), Dekydtspotter et al. suggest that the sentences in (1) are parsed as follows. As participants encounter the verb *tell*, the parser immediately posits an unspecified theme complement—XP, which can be either DP or CP—due to the selectional properties of the verb. Upon encountering the PP, the parser selects CP, since PP cannot intervene between a verb and its DP complement in English. At this point, because of *Attach Quickly* and *Minimal Attachment*, PP is inserted into the CP (the current phrase marker), and not the matrix VP, creating the misconstrual in PP-Comp sentences and the preference for embedded-clause construal in sentences with no complementizer. Given *Attach (Anyway)*, L2ers tend to stick with this analysis, because it is less costly than reanalyzing the sentence; by contrast, NSs usually reanalyze the sentence, because it violates their grammar.

Recognizing the need for online data to back up the processing account, Dekydtspotter & Liljestrand (in press) designed a self-paced reading task, using similar sentences with interclausal locational PP adverbials, but this time in French. After reading a paragraph providing a context that forced either a matrix- or embedded-clause construal of the PP, 80 L1 English-speaking L2ers of French read sentences such as those in (3) online, where slashes indicate region boundaries.[1]

(3) a. Marie / a dit /   dans la maison / que / Thomas / mangeait / de la glace.
    b. Marie / a dit / que / dans la maison /   Thomas / mangeait / de la glace.
       'Marie said (that) in the house (that) Thomas was eating ice cream.'

Their results showed that on PP-Comp sentences (3a), the L2ers' reading times for the PP region were significantly slower with matrix-clause contexts than with embedded-clause contexts. By contrast, on Comp-PP sentences (3b), no significant difference was found between matrix-clause and embedded-clause contexts. This asymmetry thus added support to the Dekydtspotter et al. processing account.

Our study builds on these findings. It aims to determine if similar asymmetrical performances can be demonstrated with a different constellation of L1 and target language and with different experimental designs: an offline acceptability judgment task (Experiment 1) and an online non-cumulative self-paced reading task (Experiment 2).[2] Contrary to the previous studies, the experimental sentences used in the two tasks contain deictic temporal (DT) adverbials (e.g. *yesterday, tomorrow*, etc.), whose construal is established on the basis of tense-meaning (mis)matches between, on the one hand, the tense of the matrix or embedded verb and, on the other, the temporal meaning of the adverbial. The acceptability judgment task serves to assess L2ers' knowledge of the structural constraints governing the construal of interclausal DT adverbials in sentences with an overt complementizer and an embedded clause. The self-paced reading task is used to establish whether L2ers' asymmetrical performances (if also attested here) reflect their online processing of (DT) adverbials, as claimed by Dekydtspotter et al.

3. Experiment 1: Acceptability Judgment Task

3.1. Participants

Thirty adult NSs of American English living in Hawai'i and 30 adult high-beginning Japanese L2ers of English living in Japan participated in the acceptability judgment task. Prior to the experiment, the L2ers had received between 6 and 11 years of English instruction but had never lived in an English-speaking country. The L2ers' proficiency level was determined with a cloze test (Brown 1980). The NS scores previously reported for that test (Omaki 2005) range from 39 to 49 out of 50. The L2ers in this study scored between 5 and 15 out of 50. Participants were paid $10 or ¥1000 in compensation for their time.

3.2. Materials

The acceptability judgment task comprised a total of 80 items. Twenty (4x5) consisted of simple sentences with a tense-meaning (mis)match between the verb and the DT adverbial, as in (4). These sentences were included to ensure that L2ers know that the meaning of DT adverbials must match the tense of the verb. Another 20 (4x5) items consisted of complex sentences with a matrix verb, an interclausal DT adverbial, and an embedded clause. Since these items all had an overt complementizer, the meaning of the adverbial therefore (mis)matched with the tense of either the matrix verb or the embedded verb, as illustrated in (5).[3]

(4) a. Nancy studied with Brian yesterday.   [Past, Match]
    b. *Nancy studied with Brian tomorrow.   [Past, Mismatch]
    c. Nancy is going to play tennis tomorrow.   [Future, Match]
    d. *Nancy is going to play tennis yesterday.   [Future, Mismatch]

(5) a. Joe told Ann last year that he is going to move to China.   [Adv-Comp, Match]
    b. *Joe told Ann next year that he is going to move to China. [Adv-Comp, Mismatch]
    c. Joe told Ann that next year he is going to move to China.   [Comp-Adv, Match]
    d. *Joe told Ann that last year he is going to move to China. [Comp-Adv, Mismatch]

The DT adverbials in both item sets were *yesterday, tomorrow, last week, next week, last month, next month, last year* and *next year*. These 40 experimental items were pseudo-randomized with 40 filler sentences.

3.3. Predictions

Recall that according to Dekydtspotter et al., upon encountering the adverbial after the verb *tell*, L2ers anticipate an embedded clause, which leads them later to construe the interclausal adverbial as modifying the embedded clause. If this proposal is correct, the L2ers in this task should perform worse on Adv-Comp items (5a, 5b) than on Comp-Adv items (5c, 5d), because they will position the adverbial in the embedded clause in Adv-Comp sentences, despite the fact that the complementizer *that* should block that analysis. This should lead them to reject grammatical Adv-Comp sentences (5a) and accept ungrammatical ones (5b).

3.4. Procedure

The sentences were presented visually. The participants were instructed to rate the sentences on a scale of 1 to 4 (1=horrible, 2=awkward, 3=okay, 4=perfect). They were told to select X (=I don't know) if they had no judgment.[4] They had a maximum of 20 seconds to rate each sentence, but were encouraged to make a decision as quickly as possible. Since the sentences were presented one at a time, the participants could not go back and change their answers.

3.5. Analysis

We first collapsed the sentences rated 3 and 4 as grammatical and those rated 1 and 2 as ungrammatical (those with no judgment were excluded). We compiled the accuracy rates by calculating the percentages of grammatical sentences rated as grammatical and of ungrammatical sentences rated as ungrammatical.

3.6. Results

Table 1 presents the percentage and standard deviation of *correct* judgments for NSs and L2ers on grammatical and ungrammatical simple sentences (4).

Table 1. Percentage (Standard Deviation) of Correct Judgments: Simple Sentences

Sentence Type	NSs	L2ers
Past, Match (4a)	98.0 (6.1)	98.0 (6.1)
Past, Mismatch (4b)	99.3 (3.7)	96.0 (9.7)
Future, Match (4c)	97.3 (10.1)	92.7 (12.3)
Future, Mismatch (4d)	97.3 (8.7)	93.3 (10.9)

The results show that L2ers perform almost as well as NSs on simple sentences containing a tense-meaning (mis)match between DT adverbial and verb tense. A 2x2 repeated-measures ANOVA with match and tense as within-subject variables reveals a main effect of tense for only the L2ers ($F(1,29)=6.566$, $p=.016$), who do not perform quite as well on future sentences. No significant effect of match or tense-match interaction was found for either group ($Fs<1$). The reasonably low standard deviations indicate that there is little individual variation in each group.

Table 2 summarizes the percentage and standard deviation of *correct* judgments for NSs and L2ers on grammatical and ungrammatical complex sentences (5).

Table 2. Percentage (Standard Deviation) of Correct Judgments: Complex Sentences

Sentence Type	NSs	L2ers
Adv-Comp, Match (5a)	88.0 (19.4)	54.0 (34.1)
Adv-Comp, Mismatch (5b)	74.7 (23.4)	68.0 (31.3)
Comp-Adv, Match (5c)	93.3 (13.2)	75.3 (30.5)
Comp-Adv, Mismatch (5d)	86.0 (20.4)	80.7 (20.0)

These results show a different pattern. In the case of NSs, a 2x2 repeated-measures ANOVA with word order and match as within-subject variables reveals main effects of word order ($F(1,29)=7.932$, $p=.009$) and match ($F(1,29)=6.590$, $p=.016$), with a numerical advantage for Comp-Adv sentences, on the one hand, and for Match sentences, on the other. Similarly, a 2x2 repeated-measures ANOVA run on the L2ers' accuracy rates reveals main effects of word order ($F(1,29)=7.260$, $p=.012$) and match ($F(1,29)=4.928$, $p=.034$), also with a numerical advantage for Comp-Adv sentences, but with a numerical disadvantage for Match sentences. No significant tense-match interaction was found for either group ($Fs<1$). The moderately high standard deviations suggest that there is considerable individual variation in the data, especially in the L2 group.

3.7. Discussion

As these results indicate, both NSs and L2ers performed very well on simple sentences containing a tense-meaning (mis)match between DT adverbial and verb tense. While not surprising for NSs, for L2ers it at least confirms they know that the meaning of DT adverbials must match the tense of the verb. On complex sentences, NSs failed to reject some Mismatch sentences when they should have (which is perhaps unexpected on the part of NSs), whereas L2ers rejected some Match sentences when they should not have. Importantly, the accuracy rates of both groups are significantly higher for the two types of Comp-Adv sentences than for their respective Adv-Comp counterparts. These latter results are precisely what the Dekydtspotter et al. analysis would predict. We return to implications of these findings in Section 5.

4. Experiment 2: Self-Paced Reading Task

4.1. Participants

The participants in the self-paced reading task were exactly the same as those in the acceptability judgment task, with the exception of one NS who was excluded for failing to meet the inclusion criterion (see Section 4.5).

4.2. Materials

The self-paced reading task comprised a total of 75 items. Of these, 30 (6x5) were experimental sentences containing an interclausal DT adverbial and an embedded clause, but no overt complementizer. The first two sentence types, exemplified in (6a)-(6b), did not evince any mismatch between the meaning of the adverbial and the tense of either the matrix verb or the embedded auxiliary (Match). These are the control sentences against which the mismatch counterparts are compared. The next two sentence types, illustrated in (6c)-(6d), had a mismatch between the tense of the matrix verb and the meaning of the adverbial (M(atrix)-Mismatch). The last two sentence types, illustrated in (6e)-(6f), had a mismatch between the meaning of the adverbial and the tense of the embedded auxiliary (E(mbedded)-Mismatch). To ensure that the participants were reacting to the tense-meaning mismatch and not to the specific verb tense, we fully crossed the verb tenses to create the (mis)matches. The slashes indicate the region boundaries.

(6) a. Joe / told   / Ann / yesterday / he / did not / play / tennis.   [Past, Match]
    b. Joe / will tell / Ann / tomorrow/ he / will not/ play / tennis.   [Future, Match]
    c. Joe / told   / Ann / tomorrow/ he / will not/ play / tennis.   [Past, M-Mismatch]
    d. Joe / will tell / Ann / yesterday / he / did not / play / tennis. [Future, M-Mismatch]
    e. Joe / told   / Ann / yesterday / he / will not/ play / tennis.   [Past, E-Mismatch]
    f. Joe / will tell / Ann / tomorrow/ he / did not / play / tennis. [Future, E-Mismatch]

The DT adverbials in the experimental sentences were *yesterday*, *tomorrow*, *last week*, *next week*, *last month* and *next month*. The 30 experimental items were counterbalanced across 6 lists and pseudo-randomized with 45 distracter sentences.

4.3. Predictions

Dekydtspotter et al. predict that upon reading the adverbial after *told/will tell*, L2ers (and NSs) should immediately anticipate an embedded clause, which should then lead to their construing the interclausal adverbial with the embedded clause. If this analysis is correct, the reading times (RTs) in this task should be longer at the auxiliary + *not* region for E-Mismatch sentences (6e)-(6f) than for Match sentences (6a)-(6b), because the meaning of the adverbial conflicts with the tense of the embedded auxiliary. Crucially, no significant difference should be found in the RTs at the adverbial region between M-Mismatch sentences (6c)-(6d) and Match sentences (6a)-(6b), even though the meaning of the adverbial in M-Mismatch sentences conflicts with the tense of the matrix verb. In this case, significantly longer RTs at the M-Mismatch adverbial region would indicate that the adverbial had been construed as modifying the matrix predicate, *contra* Dekydtspotter et al.

4.4. Procedure

The self-paced reading task was run on individual computers. At the start of each trial, the symbol "+" appeared on the left side of the screen. Participants were instructed to press a button to make the first region of the sentence appear, and, as soon as they had read that region, to press the button again to make the next region appear. Each region disappeared from the screen as the next region appeared. Participants were told to repeat this procedure until they finished reading the entire sentence. Each trial was followed by a true-or-false comprehension question to ensure the participants were paying attention to the sentences.[5] Participants occasionally received feedback on their answers, but never on experimental items. The main experimental session was preceded by a practice session of 5 sentences.

4.5. Analysis

Our inclusion criterion was set at 24 correct answers out of the 30 true-or-false comprehension questions on the experimental sentences. This criterion was met by all but one NS whose data were therefore excluded. Individual RTs of experimental items for which the comprehension question was incorrectly answered were also excluded from the analyses. Between-subject outliers were trimmed at 3 standard deviations from the mean. Since the error rates were approximately the same for all sentence types, they are not reported here.

4.6. Results

Given the possibility of spill-over effects, we report RTs and statistical analyses on the combined adverbial and subject regions, on the one hand, and on the combined auxiliary + *not* and verb regions, on the other. Table 3 summarizes the mean RTs and standard deviations of NSs and L2ers. Recall that to test the effect of matrix mismatch, the adverbial and subject regions of M-Mismatch sentences (6c-6d) are compared to the adverbial and subject regions of the corresponding Match sentences (6a-6b), and that to test the effect of embedded mismatch, the auxiliary + *not* and verb regions of E-Mismatch sentences (6e-6f) are compared to the auxiliary + *not* and verb regions of the corresponding Match sentences (6a-6b).

Table 3. NSs' and L2ers' Mean Reading Times (Standard Deviations) by Region

Sentence Type		NSs		L2ers	
		Adverbial + Subject	Aux. + *not* + Verb	Adverbial + Subject	Aux. + *not* + Verb
Past	Match (6a)	1031 (248)	1041 (285)	2659 (1046)	2027 (562)
	M-Mismatch (6c)	1092 (308)	1048 (430)	2899 (1099)	2434 (1000)
	E-Mismatch (6e)	1039 (272)	1150 (358)	2619 (1041)	2453 (842)
Future	Match (6b)	1120 (310)	1140 (301)	3030 (1415)	2238 (755)
	M-Mismatch (6d)	1241 (430)	1155 (404)	3175 (1444)	2010 (636)
	E-Mismatch (6f)	1106 (253)	1128 (352)	2570 (932)	2107 (723)

Note: M-Mismatch=Matrix Mismatch; E-Mismatch=Embedded Mismatch

As can be seen in Table 3, NSs' RTs are slower at the combined adverbial and subject region of M-Mismatch sentences (6c, 6d) than of Match sentences (6a, 6b) for both past and future conditions. A 2x2 repeated-measures ANOVA conducted on the combined adverbial and subject region of Match and M-Mismatch sentences with tense and match as within-subject variables reveals significant effects of tense ($F_1(1,28)=14.779$, $p<.001$; $F_2(1,27)=10.764$, $p=.003$) and match ($F_1(1,28)=5.181$, $p=.031$; $F_2(1,27)=4.089$, $p=.053$), but no tense-match interaction (Fs<1).

Conversely, the NSs' RTs at the combined auxiliary + *not* and verb region are slower only for E-Mismatch sentences in the past (viz. (6e) vs. (6a)). A 2x2 repeated-measures ANOVA conducted on the combined auxiliary + *not* and verb region of Match and E-Mismatch sentences fails to reveal a significant effect of tense ($F_1(1,28)=1.509$, $p=.229$; $F_2(1,27)<1$) or match ($F_1(1,28)=3.365$, $p=.077$; $F_2(1,27)<1$), but it does reveal, only in the subject analysis, a marginally significant tense-match interaction ($F_1(1,28)=4.134$, $p=.054$; $F_2(1,27)=1.832$, $p=.187$). Subsequent paired-sample t-tests adjusted with the Bonferroni correction show a significant effect of match for only the past condition ($t(28)=-2.740$, $p=.011$).

In comparison to NSs, L2ers' RTs and standard deviations are much larger, as expected given their low proficiency. Their RTs for M-Mismatch sentences (6c, 6d) in comparison to Match sentences (6a, 6b) are numerically longer at the combined adverbial and subject region in both the past and future conditions. However, a 2x2 repeated-measures ANOVA conducted on the combined adverbial and subject region reveals only a marginally significant effect of tense ($F_1(1,29)=3.845$, $p=.06$; $F_2(1,27)=3.354$, $p=.078$) but not of match, and no tense-match interaction (Fs<1).

Similar to NSs, L2ers also show slower RTs at the combined auxiliary + *not* and verb region of E-Mismatch sentences than of Match sentences in the past condition (viz. (6e) vs. (6a)) but not the future condition (viz. (6f) vs. (6b)). A

2x2 repeated-measures ANOVA conducted on the combined auxiliary + *not* and verb region reveals no significant effect of tense ($Fs<1$), a marginally significant effect of match only in the subject analysis ($F_1(1,29)=3.639$, $p=.066$; $F_2(1,27)=2.598$, $p=.119$), and a significant tense-match interaction only in the subject analysis ($F_1(1,29)=8.847$, $p=.006$; $F_2(1,27)=2.339$, $p=.138$). Subsequent paired-sample t-tests adjusted with the Bonferroni correction show a significant effect of match in only the past condition ($t(29)=-3.293$, $p=.003$).

4.7. Discussion

NSs' results show significantly slower RTs at the combined adverbial and subject region of M-Mismatch sentences than of Match sentences in both the past and future conditions, which strongly suggests they had construed the adverbial as modifying—hence had attached it to—the matrix predicate. These findings, which are consistent with the idea that words are attached as closely as possible to the most recently parsed predicate (e.g. Gibson, Pearlmutter, Canseco-Gonzales & Hickok 1996), therefore run counter to the Dekydtspotter et al. proposal. Despite the lack of significance in the L2ers' results, they, too, showed a tendency to slow down at the combined adverbial and subject region of M-Mismatch sentences.

NSs' results also show significantly slower RTs at the combined auxiliary + *not* and verb region of E-Mismatch sentences than of Match sentences, but only in the past condition. Possibly, this slow down was caused by a tense-chain violation, where the tense of the embedded auxiliary (i.e. *will* in (6e)) conflicts with the tense of the matrix verb (e.g. *told*). While the embedded auxiliary in past M-Mismatch sentences (i.e. *will* in (6c)) also creates a tense-chain violation, the future meaning of the adverbial (e.g. *tomorrow*) might reduce that effect. Since no slow down was found in the future condition of E-Mismatch sentences, it cannot be argued that the slow down in the past condition was caused solely by a tense-meaning mismatch.

Like NSs, L2ers exhibit slower RTs at the combined auxiliary + *not* and verb region of E-Mismatch sentences than of Match sentences in only the past condition. This time, however, the future tense seems to be the cause, as L2ers' RTs are faster in all items in which the embedded clause contains the past auxiliary *did* compared to the future auxiliary *will* (viz. (6a) vs. (6b), (6d) vs. (6c), and (6f) vs. (6e)). A subsequent paired-sample t-test confirms that this is the case ($t(145)=4.243$, $p<.001$). Since this effect is blurring the picture, it is unclear whether the L2ers' E-Mismatch results support the Dekydtspotter et al. hypothesis.

5. General Discussion

Experiment 1 investigated the acceptability of Adv-Comp and Comp-Adv sentences, in which DT adverbials were controlled to (mis)match the tense of, respectively, the matrix verb and the embedded verb. As Dekydtspotter et al. predicted, both the NSs and the L2ers were more accurate in judging Comp-Adv sentences than Adv-Comp sentences: The accuracy of NSs was far above chance in both conditions, while that of L2ers was around chance-level in the Adv-Comp condition and above chance-level in the Comp-Adv condition. Experiment 2 employed a self-paced reading task to investigate the time course of DT adverbial attachment, when the adverbial can modify only the matrix predicate or only the embedded clause. The RT data showed that NSs slowed down when the DT adverbial mismatched the tense of the matrix verb, but not across tense conditions when it mismatched the tense of the embedded verb; for L2ers, there was a tendency to construe the adverbial as modifying the matrix predicate, but no clear evidence for embedded-clause construal. We now turn to implications of these findings in relation to the Dekydtspotter et al. proposal.

With respect to NSs, the self-paced reading data clearly show that they initially interpret the adverbial as modifying the matrix predicate, *contra* the Dekydtspotter et al. prediction. This leaves us with the question of why their accuracy rates were lower on Adv-Comp sentences than Comp-Adv sentences in the acceptability judgment task. It is important to note that NSs were much more accurate on Adv-Comp Match items (88.0%) than on Adv-Comp Mismatch items (74.7%). Given this asymmetry, we suggest that it is not the Adv-Comp structure *per se* which causes processing difficulties, but rather the particular structure of Adv-Comp Mismatch sentences, repeated in (7).

(7) *Joe told Ann next year that he is going to move to China.   [Adv-Comp, Mismatch]

Let us assume that NSs initially attach *next year* to the matrix predicate. At this point, the tense-meaning mismatch between matrix verb and DT adverbial prompts reanalysis of this first parse, such that *next year* is repositioned in the embedded clause. However, this revision encounters a further snag, as it is incompatible with the presence of the complementizer *that*, which should trigger another instance of reanalysis, i.e. reattaching *next year* to the matrix predicate (which should lead to a judgment of "unacceptable"). Given that reanalyses are generally costly, NSs may sometimes fail in the second reanalysis, leaving the adverbial in the embedded clause, which in turn leads to the incorrect judgment that this sentence is acceptable (given the tense-meaning match between adverbial and embedded auxiliary).

With respect to L2ers, the results of the self-paced reading task, while not conclusive, numerically suggest that sometimes L2ers initially construe the adverbial as modifying the matrix predicate. This conclusion, if correct, also leaves unexplained the L2ers' asymmetrical performances on Adv-Comp sentences vs. Comp-Adv sentences in the acceptability judgment task. Unlike NSs, however, L2ers performed worse on Adv-Comp Match sentences than on Adv-Comp Mismatch sentences. Therefore, in regard to the L2ers' results, the processes about which we speculated above for NSs are insufficient. One possibility is that the L2ers, for some reason, had a "no"-bias on the acceptability judgment task, rejecting grammatical sentences more often than accepting ungrammatical ones. Combining the speculation given above for the NSs—i.e. initially attach the adverbial to the matrix predicate and subsequently attach it within the embedded clause—with this "no"-bias can accommodate both the online and offline L2 results, including chance performance on Adv-Comp Match sentences.

Of importance are the differences in empirical findings between this study and previous ones (Garcia 1998; Dekydtspotter & Liljestrand in press). Several factors may figure into the divergent results. First, locational and DT adverbials might be processed differently. It is possible, for instance, that upon processing the DT adverbial, the parser, guided by the grammar, sets the reference time for the adverbial as soon as possible by checking its temporal information against the tense of the matrix verb, whereas no such grammatical relation characterizes verbs and locational adverbials (e.g. *in the house*). Another possible influence on the results is differential frequencies with which locational and DT adverbials modify matrix vs. embedded predicates. For example, it might well be the case that matrix predicates (or rather, verbs of reporting in general) are not often modified by a post-VP locational adverbial.[6] A third point is the issue of presentation modes used across studies (in addition to other methodological differences). For instance, the prosody of Garcia's (1998) experimental sentences, with pauses before and after both the adverbial and the complementizer, might have biased the participants to interpret the adverbial as modifying the embedded clause. Finally, it is quite possible that sentences with vs. without a complementizer differ in the way they are processed.[7]

6. Conclusion

In this paper, we investigated the construal of interclausal deictic temporal adverbials on the part of native and nonnative speakers of English. The theoretical backdrop of our study was the processing account of Dekydtspotter et al. (2005), the first specific attempt to explain L2ers' asymmetrical treatment of interclausal adverbials, i.e. with the embedded-clause construal favored. Our 30 low-level Japanese L2ers of English and 30 native speakers participated in two tasks. The L2 results of our acceptability judgment task replicated earlier findings that L2ers prefer to construe interclausal adverbials as modifying the embedded clause. Interestingly, very similar results were found for NSs (albeit at higher levels of accuracy). The results of our self-paced reading task, however, revealed that the embedded-clause construal is not the initial analysis that NSs and L2ers give to interclausal (DT) adverbials. Instead, despite the much more robust NS data, both groups evince reading time patterns that show initial attachment of the adverbial to the matrix predicate, i.e. to the most recently parsed predicate (e.g. Gibson et al. 1996). These findings indicate that the processing sequence proposed by Dekydtspotter et al. cannot explain our NS and L2 data, since this sequence fails to capture the first parse of interclausal adverbials (at least interclausal DT adverbials). These findings furthermore suggest that for the phenomena at issue, NSs and even low-level L2ers are using very similar processing strategies.

Notes

* Our thanks to Cécile De Cat and Laurent Dekydtspotter for very useful discussions as well as to all those who took part in the study for their good-natured cooperation. For comments on earlier versions of the paper, we also thank: the audience at the 5th annual conference of the Japan Second Language Association; participants at GALA 2005, especially Luigi Rizzi; members of the University of Hawaii's Psycholinguistic Sanji-no Oyatsu discussion group, particularly William O'Grady and Amy Schafer. We are grateful to the University of Hawai'i for support from the Endowment for the Humanities Summer Research Program (awarded to Bonnie D. Schwartz) and from the Elizabeth Holmes-Carr Research Scholarship Fund (awarded to Annie Tremblay). The authors are listed in alphabetical order.
[1] The French variant of (1c) is ungrammatical and so was not used.
[2] Experiment 2 was administered before Experiment 1 so as to guard against participants' acceptability judgments influencing their reading times on the self-paced reading task.
[3] In these sentences, *is going to* was used instead of *will*, because it was judged that a tense-chain violation involving *is going to* (e.g. sentences (5a) and (5c), where *was going to* satisfies the tense-chain) is less noticeable than a tense-chain violation involving *will* (where *would* satisfies the tense-chain). Since all experimental sentences contained *is going to*, the tense-chain violation (if noticed) should affect all the results equally.
[4] The instructions defined the rating categories and illustrated them with several examples.
[5] No true-or-false question drew attention to the interclausal adverbial.
[6] Many thanks to Ted Gibson (p.c., 15 July 2005) for mentioning this to us.
[7] It should also be noted that our online study is the first to compare native and nonnative processing of interclausal adverbials. Dekydtspotter & Liljestrand, for example, might also have found online evidence for matrix construal with French NSs, contrary to what they found with their English-French L2ers. Such a result would suggest that, somehow, NSs and low-level L2ers differ in their treatment of interclausal adverbials, and it would challenge the Dekydtspotter et al. hypothesis that in these interclausal configurations, universal processing principles initially favor embedded-clause attachment, where the difference between NSs and L2ers lies in how successful they are in their reanalyses to matrix-predicate attachment.

References

Bhatt, R. M. and B. Hancin-Bhatt (2002) "Structural Minimality, CP and the Initial State in Second Language Acquisition," in *Second Language Research* 18, 348–392.

Brown, J. D. (1980) "Relative Merits of Four Methods for Scoring Cloze Tests," in *Modern Language Journal*, 64, 311–317.

Crocker, M. (1996) *Computational Psycholinguistics: An Interdisciplinary Approach to the Study of Language*, Kluwer, Dordrecht.

Dekydtspotter, L. and A. Liljestrand, (in press) "(Mis)interpretations of Adverbials at the Left-Edge in Early English-French as a Reflex of the Sentence Processor," in K. U. Deen, J. Nomura, B. Schulz and B. D. Schwartz, eds., *Proceedings of the Inaugural Conference on Generative Approaches to Language Acquisition—North America*, UConnWPiL, Storrs, CT.

—., B. D. Schwartz, R. Sprouse and A. Liljestrand, (2005) "Evidence for the C-domain in Interlanguage," in S. H. Foster-Cohen, M. García-Mayo and J. Cenoz, eds., *EUROSLA Yearbook, Volume 5*, Benjamins, Amsterdam.

Fodor, J. D. and A. Inoue, (2000) "Garden Path Re-analysis: Attach (Anyway) and Revision as Last Resort," in M. de Vincenzi and V. Lombardo, eds., *Cross-linguistic Perspective on Language Processing*, Kluwer, Dordrecht.

Frazier, L. (1979) *On Comprehending Sentences: Syntactic Parsing Strategies*, Indiana University Linguistics Club, Bloomington.

Garcia, B. (1998) *The L2 Initial State: Minimal Trees or Full Transfer/Full Access?*, MA thesis, University of Durham.

Gibson, E., N. J. Pearlmutter, E. Canseco-Gonzales and G. Hickok (1996) "Recency Preference in the Human Sentence Processing Mechanism," in *Cognition* 59, 23–59.

Omaki, A. (2005) *Working Memory and Relative Clause Attachment in First and Second Language Processing*, MA thesis, University of Hawai'i.

ARTICLE OMISSION AND THE ROLE OF THE ROOT

CLAUDIA CAPRIN AND CHIARA IOGHÀ

1. Introduction

In the earliest stages of language acquisition young children typically omit function morphemes, such as articles, pronouns, auxiliaries. Such omissions have received great attention and have been object of various analysis by psycho-linguistic research. Nevertheless, our understanding of why function morphemes are missing is still a matter of discussion. Two general classes of explanations have been offered. One assumes that children's speech reflects their linguistic competence; as a consequence the omission of function morpheme depends on an immature grammar. The alternative view is that children have limits on the complexity of the utterances that they can produce (Gerken, 1991).

In this work, we will focus on the acquisition of articles in Italian children (Chierchia et al. 1998; Crisma & Tomasutti 2000; Bottari et al. 2001; Guasti & Gavarrò 2003). Although articles appear early in Italian children speech, since the emergence of first words combinations (D'Odorico & Carubbi, 1997), for a long time they are optionally omitted, though when used they are used appropriately (Antelmi, 1997; Pizzuto & Caselli 1993). Generally the mastery of Italian articles system is acquired over the third year of life (Cipriani et al. 1993/1994).

It is important to say that some researches found that children omission of the articles adheres to a systematic pattern: article omission is neither an across-the-board nor an haphazard phenomenon. In fact Gerken (1996) showed that children acquiring English tend to not omit the article when it is in object position (see A), while they do it when it is in subject position and in nominal expressions uttered in isolation (see B) (see also Lleò and Demuth, 1999).

(A) I want THE toy → lower omission rate
(B) Who is outside? THE dog (is outside) → higher omission rate

She explains this subject/object asymmetry of article omission in early English in terms of prosodic constrains on the output of the speech production system (the Trochaic Template Hypothesis). The child applies a trochaic prosodic template (a metrical unit formed by a strong syllable (S) followed by a weak syllable (W)) on her intended utterance that results in the omission of all weak syllables that do not fit the template. Therefore, in an utterance like (C) below, the article accompanying the noun in subject position is omitted since it is a weak syllable that does not fit the trochaic template. By contrast, the article in object position is produced given that it forms a trochaic foot with the monosyllabic verb preceding it:

(C) THE zebra kicks THE cat   clause
     w   S w   S   w   S   metrical structure
     *   [S w] [S   w] [S]   trochaic template

Considering this hypothesis in relation to Italian language, it is possible to predict that articles will be omitted more frequently in subject position and in nominal expressions uttered in isolation than in object position provided that the verb would be a monosyllabic word in the last case. Let's consider the following clauses:

(D) *Maria fa la torta* ('Maria makes the cokie')   clause
     w S   S w S w   metrical structure
     w [S] [S w] [S w]   trochaic template

(E) *Maria mangia   la torta* ("Maria eats the cokie")   clause
     w S   S w   w S w   metrical structure
     w [S] [S w] * [S w]   trochaic template

In (D) the article LA (feminine singular) in object position is a weak syllable and it forms a trochaic foot with the preceding monosyllabic verb, a strong syllable. On the contrary in an utterance like (E) the article LA may not form a prosodic unit with the preceding disyllabic verb; as a consequence the article might tend to be omitted more frequently.

Extending the prosodic approach to Italian, Crisma & Tomasutti (2000) experimentally investigated the omission of the article LA from object position of verbal utterances and from nouns uttered in isolation. They found that in verbal utterances omission was contingent on the prosodic properties of the preceding verb: it was higher when the verb was disyllabic than when it was monosyllabic.

Based on the spontaneous production of 59 Italian learners Caprin et al. (2003) found a tendency to omit more articles from subject position (and from nouns uttered in isolation) than from object position. However, in object position no difference emerged depending on the prosodic structure of preceding verbs, contrary to Crisma & Tomasutti (2000). A subject/object asymmetry is found in agrammatic speech and in some special registers of Italian, as for example headlines, according to Guasti et al. (2004), and this fact does not seem to depend on prosodic constraints. For these reasons and because Caprin et al.'s data and Crisma & Tomasutti's data are not directly comparable (the former come from spontaneous production, while the latter from elicited production), we designed two experiments with the aim to further investigate whether articles omission in early Italian adheres to a specific pattern and to find out whether and to what extent prosodic constrains rule article omission.

2. Study 1

2.1. Method

2.1.1. Participants
The participants were 42 children, 22 males and 17 females, living in Milan (Italy). They were equally distribuited in three age groups: G1 from 2;0 to 2,6 years (mean=2.283 ds=.158), G2 from 2;6 to 3;0 years (mean=2.814 ds=.241) and G3 from 3;0 to 3,6 years (mean=3.17 ds=.133).

Approximately each group included the same number of males and females. All children came from middle-class families. Children were recruited from local day-care centers and from preschools and were reported by their teachears to be developing language normally.

2.1.2. Procedure
The experimenter visited the children in their classrooms several times before the experimental session in order to familiarize with them. At the beginning of the session the experimenter introduced a puppet to the children named Max, who was said to be acquiring Italian. The experimenter and the child played with the puppet for about 10 minutes before beginning the experimental task. After this period the experimenter asked the child if he wants to teach Italian to the puppet, explaining that in order to do it, he should repeat some utterances to the puppet. Before the test a training session was performed, during which the experimenter uttered some items and asked the child to imitate them.

2.1.3. Experimental design and material

Experiment 1 analysed the repetition of determiners with nouns uttered in isolation, e.g., *il cane* (the dog). The material was comprised of 52 utterances. 28 items were conceived in order to investigate differences among the production of determiners. The determiners were: LA, IL, UN, I, GLI, LE, UNA, DUE. There were 4 items for each of the determiners.

The other 24 items were conceived in order to investigate differences between LA and UNA. The former is a monosyllabic article, that is prosodically a weak syllable (W) and the second is disyllabic and its prosodic structure is a trochaic foot, that is a strong-weak syllables unit (SW). Following the Trochaic Template Hypothesis it might be expected a higher omission of LA than UNA, since LA is a weak syllable and UNA a trochaic foot. The articles LA and UNA might appear before a disyllabic or a trisyllabic common noun. The prosodic structure of the disyllabic nouns was SW, while the structure of the trisyllabic nouns might be WSW (for istance: *caròta*, carrot) or SWW (for istance: *pàpera*, duck). There were 4 items for each prosodic noun structure.

The presentation order was the same for all the children. To facilitate the task, the child was presented with the object named by the utterance (e.g., she was shown a dog while the experimenter uttered "the dog").

2.1.4. Scoring and Analysis

Children were generally successful at imitating the experimental items, refusing to respond to only 0.36 %, but the number of scorable items sometimes differed from child to child; for this reason the percentage of correct imitations rather than the number of correct imitations was used as dependent measure. Utterances that children attempted to imitate were coded as being in one of these categories: correct imitations, article omission and substitutions.

2.2 Results

In order to investigate differences among determiners, a mixed model ANOVA was performed with age as a between-subjects variable and determiner type as a within-subjects variable. A significant main effect for age was observed (F(2,12)=29.130 p=.001), but the differences among the determiners and the interaction of age by determiner type were not significant.

Moreover some specific analyses were conducted to investigate the differences in the determiner omission rate in relation to its prosodic structure, comparing LA (W) and UNA (SW) omission. A mixed model ANOVA was performed with age as a between-subjects variable and prosodic structure of determiner as a within-subjects variable. The analyses were conducted distinguishing the items with disyllabic and trisyllabic nouns. A significant main effect for age was observed (disyllabic F(2,39) = 4.886 p=.013 ; trisyllabic F(2,39) = 6.290 p=.004), but contrary to the expectations we did not find a different rate omission between LA and UNA neither before disyllabic (F(1,39) =1.429 p=.239) nor before trisyllabic nouns (F=6.260 p=.004). No interaction effects between age and number of determiner syllables were found (disyllabic F (2,39) =.580 p=.565; trisyllabic F(2,39) =.580 p=.565).

The analyses conducted in order to investigate the effect of the prosodic stress of the following noun on the omission rate of LA revealed only the main effect of age (F(2,39)= 4.267 p=.021). No effects concerning nouns stress (F (1,39) =1.731 p=.196) or interaction between age and nouns stress were found (F (2,39) =1.120 p=.337). Similar results were found concerning UNA (Age F(2,39)= 6.851 p=.003; nouns stress F(1,39)=.102 p=.752 ; age*nouns stress F(2,39)=.483 p=.621).

3. Study 2

3.1. Method

3.1.1. Participants

The participants were 37 children, 16 males and 21 females, living in Milan (Italy). They were distribuited in the same three age groups of the first experiment: 10 children in G1 (mean=2.33 ds=.132), 11 children in G2 (mean=2.76 ds=.22) and 16 children in G3 (mean=3.27 ds=.26). Approximately the same number of males and females comprised each age group.

All children came from middle-class families. Children were recruited from the same local day-care centers and preschools of Study 1 and were reported by their teachears to be developing language normally.

3.1.2. Procedure

The adopted procedure was the same of Study 1.

3.1.3. Experimental design and material

Experiment 2 analysed the repetition of the article LA (feminine singular) in 48 verbal utterances. The article might appear in front of nouns in subject and object position. We wanted to investigate whether omission rate varies in relation to syntactic position. Moreover the utterances included a monosyllabic or a disyllabic verb. Following the Trochaic Template Hypothesis it might be predicted that article omission in postverbal position should depend on the prosodic status of the verb: mono- or disyllabic.

To facilitate the task (and to not tax working memory resources), the experimenter acted out the action described by the verbal utterance in front of the child (e.g. using props and toys, the experimenter acted out the action of a child washing a cat while uttering the sentence *la bimba lava la gatta*, the child washes the cat, or the action of a child eating an apple for the sentence *la bimba mangia la mela*, the child eats the apple).

3.1.4. Scoring and Analysis

Children were generally successful at imitating the experimental items, refusing to respond to only 0.9%.

Utterances that children attempted to imitate were coded as being in one of two categories: correct and incorrect imitations. The last category includes three types of imitation errors: NP omissions, article omission, and substitutions. Omissions of articles include cases of failure to provide an article in front of a common NP.

Due to occasional unscorable responses, the number of scorable items sometimes differed from child to child, and thus the percentage rather the number of correct imitations was used as dependent measure.

3.2. Results

In order to investigate the effect of pre-post verbal position of the article, a mixed model ANOVA was performed with age as a between-subjects variable and syntactic position as a within-subjects variable. A significant main effect for position ($F(1,34) = 4.9$ p=.034) was found, but neither for age ($F(2,34)=2.392$ p=.154) nor for the interaction ($F(2,34)= 2.183$ p=.149). Post-hoc testing indicated that omission rate of LA was higher in subject than in object position.

Moreover an analysis was performed to test whether the omission of LA in object position might depend on the prosodic status of the verb, using a mixed model ANOVA with age as a between-subjects variable and verb syllabic structure (mono or disyllabic) as a within-subjects variable. Contrary to what was expected in relation to the Trochaic Template Hypothesis, it was found a significant main effect for age ($F(2,34)=3.270$), but neither for the verb syllabic structure ($F(1,34)=.302$ p=.586). nor for the variables interaction ($F(2,34)=1.1$ p=.344).

Finally a comparison between the two experiments data was conducted, in order to analyze whether LA omission rate in isolated NPs and in clauses differs. It was found that LA omission rate does not differ between isolated NPs and subject position (utterance type $F(1,78)=1.022$ p=.315; age $F(2,78)=4.647$ p=.013; age*utterance type $F(2,78)=1.450$ p=.241) but does it between isolated NPs and object position (utterance type $F(1,78)=7.452$ p=.008; age $F(2,78)=7.072$ p=.002; age*utterance type $F(2,78)=1.809$ p=.171).

4. General discussion

We did not find significant differences among the articles used in our experiment; omission was not more frequent with some articles than with others. An effect of age was observed with older children omitting less than younger ones.

Interestingly the hypothesis that article omission might depend on phonological constrains (Gerken 1996, Crisma & Tomasutti 2000) is not confirmed by our data. In fact following the Trochaic Template Hypothesis the determiner LA - a weak sillable - should be omitted more than the determiner UNA – a trochaic foot. But contrary to the expectations in Study 1 we did not find different omission patterns between LA and UNA. Moreover, in Study 1, no differences were found in LA and UNA omission as a function of the prosodic structure of the following nouns. Finally it is interesting to notice that in Study 2 contrary to what we expected based on the Trochaic Template Hypothesis the omission of LA in object position did not depend on the prosodic status of the verb that precedes it, and so on the possibility for La to form a trochaic foot with it; in fact we did not find significant differences between clauses with monosyllabic or disyllabic verbs.

Although not dependent on prosody, we found a higher omission of LA in subject than in object position. Moreover children omitted the entire NP more frequently from subject position (29.8%) than from object position (1.8%).

A comparison between the two experiments reveals that omission of LA is higher in subject position and from nouns uttered in isolation than in object position. Finally, these patterns of omission are observed in the three age groups, although omission tend to decrease with age (and with linguistic development).

A generalization that could be made is that article omission is higher from the *First Position* (and this would include also Nouns uttered in isolation) than inside clauses. It is interesting to observe that this phenomenon is not limited to articles but it has already been observed for early subject omission in languages that require overt subjects, such as English, French, German, Dutch, and so on (e.g., Rizzi, 1993/4; 2000; Haegeman, 2000). In these early languages, subject omission is generally an option limited to main declarative clauses, where the subject should occupy, if overt, the first syntactic position. Taken together, our results suggest that omission of functional material is possible from the highest clausal position, either because this position does not have any clausal internal antecedent or because this is the most accessible position for discourse identification. Exploiting the option of omitting functional material is adopted under a condition of limited processing resources and provided this option does not violate the grammar of the child (Rizzi, 2000). In conclusion, omission of articles is not the expression of an incomplete grammatical system, but of a system that under reduced capacity adopts options that are regulated by syntactic constraints.

References

Antelmi, D. (1997) *La prima grammatica del bambino*, Bologna, Il Mulino.
Bottari, P., P. Cipriani, A.M. Chilosi, L. Pfanner, (2001) "The Italian determiner System in Normal Acquisition, Specific Language Impairment, and Childhood Aphasia," in *Brain and Language*, *77*, 283-293.
Caprin, C., M.T. Guasti, D. Varin, (2003) "Is article omission a casual or ruled phenomenon", Paper presented at the XI of European Conference on Developmental Psychology, University of Milano Cattolica, Milan.
Chierchia, G., M.T. Guasti, A. Gualmini (1998) "The nominal mapping parameter article omission across languages", Paper presented at the Gala Congress 1998, University of Postdam, Potsdam.
Cipriani, P., A.M. Chilosi, P. Bottari, L. Pfanner, (1993/1994) *L'acquisizione della morfosintassi: Fasi e processi*, Unipress, Padova.
Crisma, P., E. Tomasutti, (2000). "Phonological Effects on Article Omission in the Acquisition of Italian," in *BUCLD 24 Proceedings,* S. Catherine Howell et al., ed., Cascadilla Press, 220-231.
D'Odorico, L. and S. Carrubbi, (1997) "Dalle espressioni di una sola parola alle prime combinazioni di parole. Forme di transizione linguistica nel processo di acquisizione della lingua italiana," in *Età evolutiva*, 26-39.
Guasti, M. T., A. Gavarrò, J., de Lange, C. Caprin, (2004) "Articles omission: across child language and across special registers," in Van Kampen, J. and S. Baauw, eds, in *Proceedings of GALA Congress 2003, vol 1.*
—., F. Foppolo, C. Luzzatti, C. Caprin, (2004) "The priviledge of the first position in agrammatism, child speech and headlines," poster presented at the Science of Aphasia V Conference, University of Postdam, Potsdam.
Gerken, L.A. (1991). "The Metrical Basis for Children's Subjectless Sentences" in *Journal of Memory and Language,* 30, 431-451.
—. (1996). "Prosodic structure in young children's language production," in *Language,* 72, 683-712.
Haegeman, L. (2000). "Adult null subjects in non pro-drop languages" in Friedemann, E. and L. Rizzi, eds., *The Acquisition of Syntax,* Harlow Longman Editors.
Lleó, C. and K. Demuth, (1999) "Prosodic constraints on the emergence of grammatical morphemes: crosslinguistic evidence from Germanic and Romance languages," in *Proceedings of the 23rd BUCLD*, Somerville, Cascadilla Press, 407–418.

Pizzuto, E. and M.C. Caselli, (1992) "The acquisition of Italian morphology. Implications for models of language development, " *Journal of Child Language*, *19*, 491-557.

Rizzi, L., (1993/1994) "Some Notes on linguistic theory and Language Development: The Case of Root Infinitives," in *Language Acquisition,* 384, 371-393.

—. (2000) "Remarks on early null subjects," in Friedemann, E. and L. Rizzi, eds., *The Acquisition of Syntax,* Harlow Longman Editors.

VERBAL AGREEMENT IN TWO DEAF ADULTS

ANNA CARDINALETTI AND PAOLO CHINELLATO

1. Introduction

Hearing impairments affect the normal development of language acquisition. They drastically reduce both the quantity and quality of linguistic input available and accessible to deaf children.

Studies on the production by Italian deaf children and adults have pointed out that inflection errors, especially on verbs, are among the most frequent types of errors (Caselli *et al*. 1994: Ch. 6).

In this paper, we analyse subject-verb agreement discussing data from an experimental investigation on some aspects of the syntactic competence of two Italian deaf adults. The experiments have been conducted by Francesca Volpato, from October 2001 to September 2002 and reported in Volpato (2002). The two deaf adults (FR, GR) are University students, age 24, 22. They have been recovered with an oralist method, and do not know Italian Sign Language.

The tests used are elicited production in a sentence completion task and a grammaticality judgement task.

The results are very interesting. The two deaf adults are extremely competent in Italian and provide a very high percentage of correct responses.[1] With subject-verb agreement, they only show some deficiency with dative subjects in the grammaticality judgment task.

2. The experiment

2.1. The subjects

The two deaf subjects are brothers and both profoundly deaf since birth. FR (age 24) was diagnosed as deaf when he was one year old. He spent one year at the John Tracy Clinic (Los Angeles). GR (age 22) was diagnosed as deaf at birth and began recovery after six months. In Italy, they attended the audiological centre in Mogliano Veneto (Treviso). The speech therapy was very intensive and lasted from the time of individuation of the hearing impairment until they were 19.

Two control subjects, matched for age and education, were also tested. They were University students, aged 22 and 24.

2.2. Preliminary test

The subjects underwent a preliminary neuropsychological assessment test, based on Miceli *et al.* (1994) (B.A.D.A. test). It consisted in a Short Term Memory test (Repetition of (series of) words, RSW, and Sentence Repetition, SR) and in a Visual Comprehension test (Picture Matching Task, PMT). The deaf subjects showed no significant difference ($p > 0.05$) with the control subjects in the RSW task. In the SR task subject GR performed at ceiling like the control subjects, whereas FR made only two errors (31/33; 93.9%). In the PMT tasks all four subjects performed at ceiling.

2.3. The tasks

A grammaticality judgement task and a sentence completion task were administered to the four subjects of the experiment. All the items of every task were proposed with a visual stimuli to avoid potential comprehension problems deriving from incorrect lip-reading.

The sentences to be judged consisted in 84 sentences with Left Dislocation of both the subject and the object (55 grammatical, and 29 ungrammatical), as in examples (1), and 43 sentences with unaccusative verbs with preposed dative subject (22 grammatical; 21 ungrammatical), as in examples (2) (the star in (1b) and (2b) is present for expository reasons):[2]

(1) a.   Il ladro, i poliziotti l'hanno arrestato ieri sera.
          (the thief, the policemen him$_{CL}$ have arrested last night)
   b.   *Mio fratello, le mele le hanno mangiate.
          (my brother, the apples [he] them$_{CL}$ have eaten)
          (cf. *Mio fratello, le mele le ha mangiate*)
(2) a.   A loro piace il documentario.
          (to them like-*sg.* the documentary film=they like the documentary film)
   b.   *A loro piacciono il film.
          (to them like-*pl.* the film = they like the film)
          (cf. *A loro piace il film*)

The sentences to be completed consisted in a total of 97 sentences with Left Dislocation of both the subject and the object, as in (3), and 5 sentences with unaccusative verbs with preposed dative subjects, as in (4):[3]

(3) a.   I carabinieri, il ladro, lo ___ (arrestare).
         (the policemen, the thief, [they] him ___ (arrest-*inf.*))
    b.   Io e tuo zio, la casa, ___ (dipingere) di rosso.
         (I and your uncle, the house, [we] ___ (paint-*inf.*) of red)
(4)   A me le ciliegie ___ (piacere) mature
         (to me the cherries ___' (like-*inf.*) mature)

2.4. The results

In the sentence completion task, FR produced only two errors with subject-verb agreement. In the task in (5), FR has inserted the 1st person plural auxiliary *abbiamo* instead of the 2nd plural *avete*:

(5)   *Tu e tuo fratello, la luce, *l'abbiamo accesa* perché la stanza era completamente al buio.
         (you and your brother, the light, [we] it have turned-on because the room was completely dark)

In (6), FR has inserted the 1st person plural auxiliary *abbiamo* instead of the 3rd person plural *hanno*:

(6)   *Il telefonino, i miei amici, *l'abbiamo comprato* ieri in un grande negozio di Padova.
         (the mobile phone, the my friends, [we] it have bought yesterday in a big store in P.)

In both cases, the error concerns agreement with an auxiliary verb, while no error was found with lexical verbs in simple tenses (in both present and simple past).

As FR himself interpreted (5), he placed himself in the pragmatic situation as if the action (to turn on the light) had been really performed by him and his brother. In this case, the role of the coordinated DP subject has been misinterpreted; this incorrect sentence is thus probably not significant for the present investigation. Similarly in (6), it could be that FR felt involved in the situation and interpreted my friends as "I and my friends", so that the 1st person plural agreement could somehow be motivated.

Apart from these two cases, which represent the 2% of the sentences, FR did not produce any other instance of incorrect subject-verb agreement.

In GR's elicited productions, subject-verb agreement was correct 100% of the times with all verbal tenses and in both types of sentences, with both nominative and dative subjects.[4]

Both FR and GR however made a few errors in the grammaticality judgment task. These errors are restricted to the cases in which the grammatical subject occurs in postverbal position, and the preverbal position is occupied by a preposed dative argument.

FR made the following two errors out of 43 sentences (4,65%). On the one hand, he considered (7a) grammatical while the sentence with plural agreement is ungrammatical; the grammatical sentence contains the singular verb *serve*, as in (7b), which he however judged ungrammatical (the judgments here are by FR):

(7) a. A me e a mia mamma servono il biglietto per l'autobus.
        (to me and to my mother need-*pl.* the ticket for the bus)
    b. *A me e a mia mamma serve il biglietto per l'autobus.
        (to me and to my mother need-*sg.* the ticket for the bus)

GR made the following three errors out of 43 sentences (7%): he considered (8a) ungrammatical with singular agreement on the verb, while he considered (8b-c) grammatical, which they are not (GR's judgments are reported):

(8) a. *A lei e suo zio interessa molto la casa in riva al mare.
        (to her and her uncle interest-*sg.* a lot the house at the seaside)
    b. A loro piacciono il film d'azione.
        (to them like-*pl.* the action movie)
    c. Ai due poliziotti spettano una grossa ricompensa per aver catturato i ladri.
        (to-the two policemen are-due-*pl.* a great reward for have caught the thieves)

Both subjects thus seem to accept plural agreement with a plural preposed dative subject, and to consider ungrammatical a sentence in which the verb does not agree with a plural preposed dative.[5]

3. Towards an explanation

Since the total amount of errors is extremely small and all errors are very selective, chance or lack of linguistic competence cannot be the explanation of the errors. Both the fact that the two deaf subjects underwent rehabilitation since they were very young and the fact that the speech therapy was long and intensive allowed them gain a very good knowledge of Italian.[6]

Since the errors by the deaf subjects are not due to interference with the dialect (contrary to what happens with one control subject, see note 5), partial knowledge of Italian cannot be the explanation either. Although we do not have an explanation for the task-sensitive behaviour of one of the two deaf subjects (GR),[7] we suggest that the analysis of the errors in the grammaticality judgment task must be searched within linguistic theory.

Following Belletti and Rizzi (1988) and Cardinaletti (1997), (2004), we take the preposed dative experiencer to occupy the preverbal subject position. Although nominative and dative subjects can occupy the same structural position, they check different features. With preverbal nominative subjects, all subject properties are displayed by the DP itself, which checks the subject-of-predication feature, nominative case, and phi-features, thus agreeing with the verb. With preverbal dative subjects, the subject properties are dissociated: the preverbal dative subject only checks the subject-of-predication feature, while the postverbal nominative subject checks nominative case and phi-features and agrees with the verb.

We assume that dissociate checking is cognitively more costly than checking by a single DP. The two deaf subjects thus sometimes avoid dissociate checking by reanalysing dative subjects as nominative subjects.[8]

Notice that this reanalysis is within the possibilities made available by UG. In this respect, consider the language change with English psych verbs like *to like*, which underwent the same kind of reanalysis: the preposed dative experiencer has been reanalysed as a nominative subject (Allen 1995, Roberts 2006).

Notes

[1] The language of very competent deaf adults has been studied a number of times. See e.g. Volterra and Bates (1989) for Italian and Tuller (2000) for French.

[2] All the sentences contained 3rd person agreement (singular and plural).

[3] Most of the items were 3rd person, but there were also 12 items with 1st person pl., 10 items with 2nd person pl., 4 items with 2nd person sing., and 2 items with 1st person sing.

[4] It is noteworthy that no tense error is ever found in FR's and GR's responses.

[5] The errors made by one control subject are of different nature. As shown in (ia-c), Control Subject #2 accepts singular agreement with a plural postverbal subject (only (id) is similar to FR and GR's judgments in that plural agreement with a plural preposed dative and a singular postverbal DP is considered grammatical):

(i) a.   A me manca pochi pezzi per completare la raccolta.
          (to me lack-*sg.* few items to complete the collection)
     b.   A te interessa quei libri sugli animali per la ricerca di scienze.
          (to you interest-*sg.* those books on animals for the paper in Sciences)
     c.   A te interessa i libri di storia dell'arte.
          (to you interest-*sg.* the books of history of arts)

d. A loro mancano un esame per finire l'università.
   (to them lack-*pl.* an exam to finish the university)
Apart from (id), which we consider to be a careless mistake, the three errors in (ia-c) have probably to be ascribed to the influence of the Venetian dialect spoken by Control Subject #2 (the dialect of Preganziol, Treviso), where the verb is never marked for plural in the 3rd person. In other words, in (ia-c) the verb does not agree with the preposed dative.

[6] Early identification and intervention of hearing loss, as well as systematic and careful speech therapy have been recognised as crucial in developing good syntactic abilities. For Italian see Caselli *et al.* (1994: 351); for other languages, see Friedmann and Szterman (to appear) and the references cited therein.

[7] On the discussion of dissociations between grammaticality judgment tasks and other tasks in pathological and non-native competence, see Altenberg and Vago (2004: 114).

[8] A similar reanalysis was found with a bilingual aphasic patient in both languages (Italian and German) and in both tasks (grammaticality judgment and sentence completion). Cf. Cardinaletti and Chinellato (2006).

References

Allen, C.L. (1995), *Case marking and reanalysis: Grammatical Relations from Old to Early Modern English*, New York, Oxford University Press.

Altenberg E.P., R.M. Vago (2004), "The role of grammaticality judgments in investigating first language attrition. A cross-disciplinary perspective", in M.S. Schmid, B. Köpke, M. Keijzer, L. Weilemar, eds., *First Language Attrition*, Benjamins, Amsterdam, 105-129.

Belletti A., L. Rizzi (1988), "Psych verbs and θ-theory", *Natural Language and Linguistic Theory* 6, 291-352.

Cardinaletti A. (1997), "Subjects and Clause Structure", in L. Haegeman, ed., *The New Comparative Syntax*, Longman, London, 33-63.

—. (2004), "Toward a cartography of subject positions", in L. Rizzi, ed., *The Structure of CP and IP. The Cartography of Syntactic Structures, Volume 2*, Oxford University Press, Oxford – New York, 115-165.

—., P. Chinellato (2006), "L'accordo verbale nell'afasia bilingue non fluente (tedesco – italiano). Lo studio di un caso", Paper presented at the *Zweite Tagung „Deutsche Sprachwissenschaft in Italien"*, February 9, 2006, Rome.

Caselli M.C., S. Maragna, L. Pagliari Rampelli, V. Volterra (1994), *Linguaggio e sordità*, La Nuova Italia, Firenze.

Friedmann N., R. Szterman (to appear), "Syntactic movement in orally-trained children with hearing impairment", *Journal of Deaf Studies and Deaf Education*.

Miceli G., A. Laudanna, C. Burani, R. Capasso (1994), *Batteria per l'Analisi dei Deficit Afasici - B.A.D.A.*, CEPSAG, Università Cattolica del S. Cuore.

Roberts I. (2006), *Diachronic Syntax*, Oxford, Oxford University Press.

Tuller L. (2000), "Aspects de la morphosyntaxe du français des sourds", *Recherches linguistiques de Vincennes* 29, 143-156.

Volpato F. (2002), *Clitic Pronouns and Verbal Agreement in Two Deaf Adults: an Experimental Investigation*, Graduation Thesis, University of Venice.

FUNCTIONAL CATEGORIES IN ITALIAN AGRAMMATISM

PAOLO CHINELLATO

1. Introduction

Recent neurolinguistic research proposed that the syntactic tree is impaired in agrammatic aphasia. More precisely, dissociations between the Tense Phrase and the AgrS Phrase lead Friedmann & Grodzinsky (1997) to the formulation of a structural explanation for agrammatism. They proposed the Tree-Pruning Hypothesis, which is reported in (1):

(1) The tree-pruning hypothesis:
(a) T is underspecified in agrammatic production.
(b) An underspecified node cannot project any higher.

Other approaches to agrammatism based on generative grammar have been made. Hagiwara (1995) claimed that cognitive limitations in the syntactic derivation (i.e. in the operation of Merge) are responsible for several syntactic disorders. According to other scholars, the syntactic deficits does not rely on the operation of Merge, but involves the operation Move. Gavarrò (1993:9) motivates the inflectional deficit in agrammatism as an "incapacity of keeping track of the application of move-α […] to explain case assignment and agreement". This approach has been recast in minimalist terms by Gavarrò (2002): following Chomsky (2000), she claimed that "agrammatism results from an inability of the application of Agree." Finally, other studies on agrammatism have proposed a characterization of the deficit in terms of a failure in the feature checking operation (Chinellato 2003, Wenzlaff & Clahsen 2004).

The aim of this paper is to sketch a linguistic description of some agrammatic disorders in Italian. I will consider data from sentence production and I will compare them with early reports in other languages. When comparative data will be relevant for the discussion, I will use data from

bilingual aphasia (Italian- Northern Italian Dialects, henceforth NIDs, see Chinellato 2003, 2004).
The paper is organised as follows: in section 2 I will present the theoretical framework; section 3 presents experimental data on tense and agreement production in italian agrammatism; section 4 deals with clitics whereas section 5 presents data on negation. Section 6 concludes the work.

2. Theoretical Background

I assume a theory of movement as a computational operation which takes place in narrow syntax and which operates to check features in the lexical entries before the morphophonological spell-out (Chomsky 1995). Following a recent treatment of verbal inflection proposed by Manzini & Savoia (2002, 2005) for Standard Italian and NIDs, I assume that person features (or categories, in Manzini & Savoia's terms) are interpretable (contra Chomsky 2000) and lexicalized in functional categories above the inflectional domain (IP for Manzini & Savoia 2002, 2005; TP for Chomsky 2000). Therefore, the functional projection of AgrS is eliminated since its sole contribution in the previous model was a mediating relation between the subject and the verb. The AgrS field becomes a set of multiple functional projections where syntactic properties are checked (e.g person and quantification; see Manzini & Savoia 2002, 2005)

3. Verb movement in agrammatism (V° to I°)

It is well established that functional categories in agrammatic aphasia are not absent. Lonzi & Luzzatti (1993) convincingly showed that Italian and French agrammatics can handle the correct order "finite verb – adverb". Subsequent works on agrammatism clearly showed that a dissociation between tense morphology (severly impaired) and agreement mophology (less impaired or spared) really exists. In particular, it has been observed that an agrammatic patient can show an impairment on both tense and agreement or only on tense. A dissociation between a spared tense and an impaired agreement has never been reported in the literature.
Tense impairments have been reported cross-linguistically: Gavarrò & Martinez-Ferreiro (2005) for Ibero-Romance (Spanish, Catalan and Galician), Benedet et. alii (1998) for Spanish and English, Wenzlaff & Clahsen (2004) for German; Stavrakaki & Kouvava (2003) for Greek; Friedmann (2000) for Hebrew and Palestian Arabic; Bastiaanse & Van Zonnneveld (1998) for Dutch.
As for Italian, Miceli & Caramazza (1988) reported a case study of a dissociation between derivational and inflection in an aphasic patient (FS). The

spontaneous speech of the agrammatic control subject (CDA) was more impaired in tense than agreement. Chinellato (2002, 2003, 2004) studied the agrammatic production in a group of Broca's bilingual aphasics (Italian and NIDs) with sentence completion and delayed repetition tasks.

I studied the production of the present tense (2) in its habitual use. Each sentence has been presented with the infinitive form, as you can see in (3):

(2) verb *amare*, 'love'

Root +		1	2	3	4	5	6
am- +		-o	-i	-a	-[j]amo	-ate	-ano

(3) Ogni mattina io _____ un cappuccino (bere)
     (Every morning I _____ a cappuccino) (drink-inf.)

The same procedure has been used for imperfect (4), future[1] (5) and present perfect (see 6; simple past 'passato remoto' cannot be used because it does not belong to the competence of nothern Italian speakers):

(4) verb *amare*, 'love'

Root + T+	1	2	3	4	5	6
am- + av	-o	-i	-a	-amo	-ate	-ano

(5) verb *amare*, 'love'

Root + T+	1	2	3	4	5	6
am- + er	-ò	-'ai	-à	-'emo	-'ete	-'anno

(6) verb *amare*, 'love'
     io ho amato
     (I have loved)

3.1 Agreement

As far as agreement is concerned, our result are consistent with Grodzinsky's (1990, 2000) approach to agrammatic errors in the verbal domain, namely that agrammatic patients produce substitution errors instead of omissions. Moreover, it has been found that plural is more impaired than singular in all tenses (see table 1), even when agreement does not involve person and quantification, but also gender and quantification (i.e. in the case of past participle agreement with unaccusatives; see table 3). Furthermore, auxiliaries, since they are not bound morphemes, are omitted (see table 2).

Table 1 Completion (% correct)

N=7	Singular	Plural
Present	92.5	50.86
Imperfect	83.43	9.03
Future	55.73	19.63

When agreement is related to present and imperfect (compare (2) and (4)), it shows the same morphological endings and it is above chance (in the singular). When it is related to the future, it is at chance level. This is probably due to the fact that the present and imperfect are actually 'non-tenses', but rather 'aspects' (which are lower than tense in the clausal struture; see Cinque 1999). This is also consistent with a structural approach of agrammatism (see 1)

Table 2 Completion (% correct)

N=7	Singular	Plural
Aux	34.8	2.93

Table 3 Completion (% correct)

N=7	Gender	Number
Past Participle agreement	100	11.11

(7) α^2 Noi (siamo) andato
     target   Noi siamo andati
            (We are gone-pl-masc.)
(8) α Loro (sono) andata
     target   Loro sono andate
            (They are gone-pl-fem.)

The first question that arises is: why is plural more impaired than singular in italian agrammatism? A phonological problem cannot be an explanation, since in Italian we find the same phonological structure both with plural (in the case of present tense) and with singular (in the case of the imperfect) as it is shown in (9). We have seen in table 1 that singular in imperfect tense is above chance.

(9)

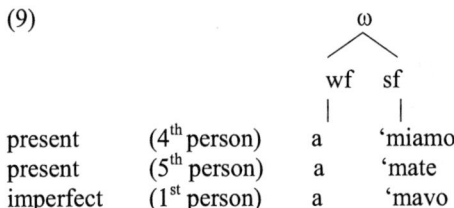

present	(4th person)	a	'miamo
present	(5th person)	a	'mate
imperfect	(1st person)	a	'mavo

Furthermore, a morphological problem cannot be responsible for the impairment with verbal morphology. If it were a problem of lexical retrieval of the verbal forms in the plural, we would expect a dissociation between the first, sencond, third and sixth person, at least in the case in which there is a morphological distinction as it is shown in (10), but this dissociation is never attested in this group-study:

(10) 1	2	3	4	5	6
vado	vai	va	*andiamo*	*andate*	vanno

Following (and extending) Kayne's (2000) idea, I propose that the morphemes
-*mo* and -*te* (4th and 5th person) are enclitics which are spelt out in a functional projection (PersP; see also Manzini & Savoia, 2005), higher than TP, because they have to check interpretable *deictic features* (and not number features):

(11) PersP

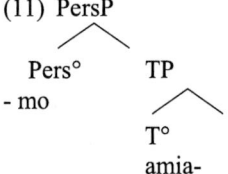

The 6th person (3rd + no) checks the uninterpretable number feature on T° (which is lexicalized as –*no*) post-syntactically (e.g. in a morphological structure MS, according to Halle & Marantz 1993)

3.2. Tense

In table (4) data on tense errors are presented. Given a target, the substitution pattern involves only the present and the imperfect. The most impaired tense is the present perfect, which is the only real 'past tense' in the linguistic competence of the Italian speakers who live in the north-east of the country (in this case, in the Veneto region)

Table 4 Completion (% errors)

N=7	
Target	Substitution
Present	3.03
Imperfect	11.36
Present Perfect	*86.36*
Future	23.49

To sum up, as it is shown in table 5, if we compare the agreement production (in the singular, since plural morphologically realizes not only number features but also deictic features) with tense production, we see that our results are consistent with early reports: tense is more impaired than agreement in Italian agrammatism.

Table 5 Completion (% correct)

N=7	Agreement (singular)	Tense
	87.96^3	13.64

4. Clitics

Early reports on clitics (object and subject) convincingly showed that they are severly impaired. All data come from spontaneous speech. Stavrakaki & Kouvava (2003) reported a 29.16% of correct production for object clitics in Greek agrammatism; as for French, Nespoulous et al. 1990 showed same results for Mr.Clermont's production of object clitics (33% correct). The same holds for Mr.Rossi's production in Italian (17% correct; see Miceli & Mazzucchi 1990). Fabbro & Frau (2001) found an impaired production of subject clitics (38% correct) in Friulian, another northern italian dialect.

4.1 Object Clitics in Italian

Table 6 shows the results of a sentence completion task in which the patients had to substitute a full DP with an object clitic before a modal verb (proclitic form, see (12)) or after the infinitive (enclitic form (see 13)). As it is shown, the production of object clitics is at chance level (although it is better in the enclitic form)

Table 6 Completion (% correct)

N=7	Proclitic	Enclitic
Clitic+ modal + infinitive + clitic	22.5	43.75

(12) Lo voglio vedere
     (him want-1ps see-inf)
     I want to see him
(13) Voglio veder-lo
     (Want-1ps see-inf him)
     I want to see him

4.2 Pronominal subject Clitics in NID

If we compare the production of object clitics in Standard Italian and the production of subject clitic in the NIDs (see table 7) we can see that subject clitics (14) are below chance both in the declarative and in the interrogative form (15):

(14)   1   2   3   4   5   6
        pro   **t(e)** (e)l   *pro*   *pro*   **i**

(15) a.   te   bevi.
           (you-cl   drink)
     b.   bevi-to?
           (drink you-cl?)

Table 7 Completion (% correct)

N=7	Proclitic (declarative)	Enclitic (interrogative)
(Clitic)+ finite verb + (clitic)	1.57	2,4

Our data support previous findings on bilingual aphasia in Italian and NIDs (Fabbro & Frau, 2001 for Italian and Friulian). Nevertheless vocalic clitics are not all equally impaired. Northern italian dialects show another type of 'clitic' (see 16) which is higher than person clitic (but it does not belong to the Comp domain, see (17); see also Cardinaletti & Repetti 2004 for Piacentine, Chinellato 2002 for Vicentino) and it is spared in agrammatic production (see Chinellato 2002, spontaneous speech data)

(16) 1   2   3   4   5   6
     a   ep^4 ep   a   a   i
                                         (Cardinaletti & Repetti 2004)
     a   a   ep   a   a   i
                                         (Chinellato 2002)

(17) Ti a te bevi
     (You 'a' you-2cl drink)

Fabbro & Frau (2001) showed that in Friulian the third person singular pronoun '*al*' is omitted:

(18) El frut *al* bev   (Fabbro & Frau (2001))
     (The boy 3-cl drinks)

This result is compatible with the one found in table (7) if data are supported by a linguistic theory claiming that in Friulian the '*a*' in '*al*' is not the morphological realization of an *a* clitic plus the person clitic *l*, but rather it is part of the personal pronoun (an epenthetic vowel, as it is claimed in Cardinaletti & Repetti 2004 or a monomorphemic unit, as it is claimed in Vanelli 1984).

We can try to propose an answer to the following question: why are object and subject clitics impaired in agrammatism? A pure phonological problem cannot be an explanation. This was already been claimed by Nespoulous et al. (1990) who noted a dissociation between subjects and objects in French. Although they are clitics from a phonological point of view, the former are spared whereas the latter are impaired. A problem with the phonological tree as in (19) cannot explain the asymmetries found in French, Italian and NIDs:

(19)   CG
       ◻╱‾‾‾╲

      wω   sω
      | |
      il   mange   French   (spared)   'he eats'
      el   magna   NID   (impaired)   'he eats'
      a   magno   NID   (spared)   'I eat'
Je   le   vois   French (obj)   (impaired)   'Isee him'
Io   lo   vedo   Italian (obj)   (impaired)   'I see him'

French and NID subject clitics are phonological clitics but they have different syntactic status: the former are DPs (weak pronouns, see Kayne 1975,

Rizzi 1986; Cardinaletti & Starke 1999), the latter are X° (syntactic clitics, see Rizzi 1986, Brandi & Cordin 1989). If we recast Nespoulous'(1990) observations about subjects and objects into linguistic terms, we could say that weak pronouns (XPs) are spared whereas clitics (X°) are impaired. Data are consistent with another dialectal weak pronoun (*elo*, contrast 20a with 20b) which is spared in agrammatic aphasia (see Chinellato 2004)

(20) a.   NID: *Elo*   magna   weak   spared
     b.   NID: *El*   magna   clitic   impaired
                   (He   eats)

5. Negation

Early reports on agrammatism showed that the negative marker is impaired only if it is a syntactic head. When negation is lexicalized by an XP, it is less impaired (or spared). Stavrakaki & Kouvava 2003 reported only the 17.6% of correct production of *den* and *min*. Bastiaanse et al. (2000) found with a sentence anagram task that English agrammatics had more problems with *not* than Dutch agrammatics with *niet*. Ramshoj-Christensen (2005) found that Danish agrammatics did not show any problem in a grammaticality judgement task with NegP such as *ingen* and *ikke....nogen*.

5.1. Negation in Italian

Table 12 shows the agrammatic production of several types of negative markers in Italian. In a sentence completion task, the preverbal negative marker which negates the whole sentence (see 21a) is below chance, whereas the negation in a negative imperative (see 21b) is absent. When the negation is an NegP, namely in a postverbal context (morhologically realized by the negative adverb *mica*, see 21c) or when the negative marker is a constituent negation (see the context of a small clause, 21d) it reaches the ceiling effect.

Table 12 Completion

N= 7	% correct
a. sentential negation	13.6
b. negative imperative	0
c. postverbal negation (mica)	100
d. constituent negation	100

(21) a. Gianni *non* mangia   (lit. John not eats)
     b. *Non* mangiare!   (lit. Not eat!)
     c. Gianni non mangia *mica*   (lit. John not eats not)

d. Considero[Gianni *non* degno di fiducia]
(lit.I consider John not trust-worthy)

6. Conclusions

In this paper I gave a linguistic sketch of certain impairments in Italian agrammatic production, namely tense and agreement disorders, omission of clitics, omission of the negative marker. They are well-known phenomena in the literature of agrammatism.

I took a comparative perspective and I showed that the same impairments found in other languages are present in Italian. Italian agrammatism can be identified by the following morpho-syntactic disorders: tense is more impaired than agreement. When agreement is tense-dependent (e.g. in the future tense), it is at chance level; when it is at the end of an aspectual head (e.g. present, imperfect), it is above chance. Maximal projections, namely XPs, are spared, whereas moved syntactic heads, namely X°s, are severly impaired.

Notes

[1] Future tense and agreement morphology derive from medieval latin forms: cantare habeo (sing-inf 'I have to sing) > cantar h(abe)o > canterò (I will sing); see Väänänen 1963
[2] α indicates aphasic production
[3] Average between present and impefect.
[4] ep= epenthetic vowel

References

Bastiaanse, R. and R. Van Zonneveld, (1998) "Verb retrieval in action naming and spontaneous speech in agrammatic and anomic aphasia," in *Aphasiology* 12(11), 951-969.
Bastiaanse, R. et al., (2000) "Verb retrieval, verb inflection and negation in agrammatic aphasia" in Bastiaanse and Grodzinsky, eds., in *Grammatical Disorders in Aphasia. A neurolinguistic perspective,* London, Whurr.
Benedet, M.J. et al., (1998) "A cross-linguistic study of grammatical morphology of Spanish- and English-speaking agrammatic patients," in *Cortex* 34, 309-336.

Brandi, L. and P.Cordin, (1989) "Two Italian Dialects and the Null Subject Parameter," in O.Jaeggly and K.Safir, eds., in *The Null Subject Parameter,* Dordrecht, Kluwer, 111-142.

Cardinaletti, A. and L. Repetti, (2004) "Clitics in Northern Italian Dialects: Phonology, Syntax and Microvariation," in *Venice Woorking Papers in Linguistics*, XIV, University of Venice, 7-111.

Cardinaletti, A. and M. Starke, (1999) "The typology of structural deficiency. A case-study of the three classes of pronouns" in Henk van Riemsdijk, ed., *Clitics in the Languages of Europe*, Berlin, Mouton de Gruyter, 145-233

Chinellato P., (2002) "Agreement Disorders, Subject Clitics and the Structure of IP in dialectal agrammatism: the Field Damage Hypothesis. Short Paper,2 in *Cortex,* 38, 5, 837-840.

Chinellato P., (2003) "Agreement Disorders in Broca's Aphasia sentence production: a bilingual Case study" in Fava, E. and A. Mioni, eds., *Issues in Clinical Linguististics*, Unipress, Padova, 71-89.

Chinellato P., (2004) "Disturbi di sintassi nell'afasia non fluente: un'analisi linguistica dell'agrammatismo italiano e dialettale" *Ph.D. Dissertation*, University of Padua.

Chomsky, N. (1995) *The Minimalist Program*, MIT Press, Cambridge, Mass.

Chomsky, N. (2000) "Minimalist Inquires: the framework" in R. Martin, D. Michaels and J. Uriagereka, eds., *Step by Step. Essays on Minimalist Syntax in Honor of Howard Lasnik*, Cambridge, MA, MIT Press.

Cinque, G. (1999) *Adverb and Functional Heads. A Cross-Linguistic perspective*. New York, Oxford, Oxford University Press.

Fabbro F. and G. Frau, (2001) "Manifestations of aphasia in Friulian," in *Journal of Neurolinguistics,* 14, 2-4, 255-279.

Friedmann, N, (2000) "Moving Verbs in Agrammatic Production" in R. Bastiaanse and Y. Grodzinsky, eds., *Grammatical disorders in aphasia: A neurolinguistic perspective*, 152-170, London, Whurr.

Friedmann, N. and Y. Grodzinsky, (1997) "Tense and Agreement in Agrammatic Production Pruning the Syntactic Tree," in *Brain and Language*, 56, 397-425.

Friedmann , N. and Y. Grodzinsky, (2000) "Split Inflection in Neurolinguistics," in M.-A. Friedemann and L. Rizzi, eds., *The Acquisition of Syntax*, 84-104, Geneva, Switzerland, Longman Linguistics Library Series.

Gavarró, A. (1993) A note on Agrammatism and the Minimalist Program. Ms., University of Barcelona.

Gavarrò, A. (2002) "Failure to Agree in Agrammatism," in Fava, E., ed., *Clinical Linguistics – Theory and Applications in Speech Pathology and Therapy*.

Gavarrò, A. and S.Martinez-Ferreiro (2005) Tense and agreement impairment in Ibero-Romance, Ms, submitted.

Grodzinsky, Y., (1990) *Theoretical perspectives on language deficits*, Cambridge, Mass., MIT press.

Grodzinsky, Y. (2000) "The Neurology of Syntax: Language Use without Broca's Area," in *Behavioral and Brain Sciences*, 23, 1-71.

Hagiwara, H. (1995) "The Breakdown of Functional Categories and the Economy of Derivations," in *Brain & Language*, 50, 92-116.

Halle, M. and A.Marantz, (1993) "Distributed Morphology and Pieces of Inflection" in K. Hale and S. J. Kayser, eds., *The View form Building 20,*. Moyer Bell, Wakefield, London, 111-176.

Kayne, R. (1975) *French Syntax*, Cambridge, Mass, MIT Press.

Kayne, R. (2000) "Person Morpheme and Reflexives in Italian, French and Related Languages" in *Parameters and Universals*, Oxford University Press, New York / Oxford.

Lonzi, L. and C. Luzzatti, (1993) "Relevance of adverbs distribution for the analysis of sentence representation in agrammatic patients," in *Brain & Language*, 45, 306-317.

Manzini, M.R. and L. Savoia, (2002) "Parameters of subject inflection in Italian dialects" in P. Svenonius, ed., *Subjects, Expletives, and the EPP*, Oxford University Press, New York, Oxford.

Manzini, M.R. and L. Savoia, (2005) *I dialetti italiani e romanci. Morfosintassi generativa*. Edizioni Dell'Orso, Alessandria.

Miceli, G. and A. Caramazza, (1988) "Dissociation of inflectional and derivational morphology: Evidence from aphasia," *Brain and Language,*35, 24-65.

Miceli, G and A. Mazzucchi, (1990) "The speech production deficit of so-called agrammatic aphasics: evidence from two Italian patients," in Menn L., Obler L.K., eds., *Agrammatic aphasia: Cross-language narrative source book*, Philadelphia, John Benjamin's Publishing Company.

Nespoulous, J.L et al. (1990) "Agrammatism in French: two case studies," in Menn L. and L. Obler, *Agrammatic Aphasia: A Cross-language Narrative Sourcebook*, Philadelphia, John Benjamin's Publishing Company.

Ramshøj Christensen, K. (2005) "Interfaces and syntactic movement," talk given at the 2nd LPIA meeting, Vienna, 2005.

Rizzi, L., (1986) "On the status of subject clitics in Romance," in *Studies in Romance Linguistics*, ed., Osvaldo Jaeggli and C. Silva-Corválan, Dordrecht, Foris, 391-419.

Stravrakaki, S. and S. Kouvava, (2003) "Functional categories in agrammatism: evidence from Greek," in *Brain and Language*, 90, 423-433.

Väänänen, V. (1963) *Introduction au latin vulgaire*, Paris, Klincksieck.

Vanelli, L. (1984) "Il sistema dei pronomi soggetto nelle parlate ladine" in Messner, D., ed., *Das Romanische in den Ostalpen*, Verlag der Oesterreichischen Akademie der Wissenschaften, Wien, 147-160.

Wenzlaff, M. and M. Clashen, (2004) 2Tense and Agreement in German Agrammatism" in *Brain and Language*, 89, 57-68.

THE INTERPRETATION OF WH-IN-SITU IN KOREAN SECOND LANGUAGE ACQUISITION

MYONG-HEE CHOI AND DONNA LARDIERE

1. Introduction

A large number of studies (e.g., Hawkins and Chan, 1997; Martohardjono, 1993; Schachter, 1990) in generative second language research have investigated the acquisition of overt wh-movement by native speakers of wh-in-situ languages, primarily to test for UG-derived knowledge of constraints on such movement (e.g., 'subjacency' effects). The acquisition of wh-in-situ by native speakers of overt wh-movement languages, on the other hand, has been largely ignored in second language studies, presumably on the grounds that such learners have little problem acquiring wh-in-situ expressions, compared with overt movement which is considered more costly, or 'difficult' (Platzack, 1996; Kim, 2003), and knowledge of movement constraints is considered irrelevant. However, second language research has so far barely acknowledged the complexity of the conditions governing the interpretation of wh-expressions in wh-in-situ languages. For instance, in Korean, wh-(in-situ) expressions can be interpreted as indefinite pronouns (*someone, something, somewhere*) or wh-question words (*who/whom/whose, what, where*) depending on the context in which they occur.

This study addresses that research gap, by investigating whether speakers of an overt wh-movement language are able to correctly interpret L2 Korean wh-in-situ expressions according to the contextual co-occurrence of sentential licensing particles. In this paper, we report on the acquisition of the interpretations of Korean wh-expressions in L2 grammars of adult native English speakers.

An analysis and comparison of the distribution of wh-expressions in Korean and English are discussed in the next section. In Section 3, we review other current second language approaches with respect to their predictions for wh-acquisition. In Section 4, we describe an experiment which tested English-speaking learners' interpretation of Korean in-situ wh-expressions, and report the findings in Section 5. Finally, in the last section, we present a general discussion of the experimental results and our conclusions.

2. Korean WH-(in-situ) expressions

It is widely assumed that Korean[1], like Chinese and Japanese, is a wh-in-situ language, and therefore Korean wh-phrases do not move to the Spec of CP because they lack a strong (uninterpretable) wh-feature. As can be seen from comparing the English sentence in (1) and its Korean counterpart in (2), Korean wh-phrases do not have to raise overtly to the Spec of CP, while English wh-phrases must be displaced overtly.

(1)   I know [$_{CP}$ who$_i$ [$_{IP}$ John liked t_i]]

(2)   Na-nun [$_{CP}$ [$_{IP}$ John-i   nuku-lul   cohahaessnun]-ci] an-ta.
       I-Top   John-Nom WHO[2]-Acc liked-Q   know-Decl[3]
       'I know who John liked'

However, it is not enough to explain the distribution of Korean wh-words in terms of overt versus covert movement. As shown in (3), the same wh-expression may have two readings.

(3)   a. John-un   Mary-ka   mues-ul   sass-ta-(ko)   an-ta
          John-Top   Mary-Nom WHAT-Acc bought-Decl-C know-Decl
          'John knows (that) Mary bought something'

       b. John-un   Mary-ka   mues-ul   sassnun-ci   an-ta
          John-Top   Mary-Nom WHAT-Acc bought-Q   know-Decl
          'John knows what Mary bought'

That is, *mues* 'WHAT' in (3a) has an obligatory noninterrogative indefinite reading, when the declarative particle *-ta* occurs. In contrast, the same form in (3b) has the wh-question reading, when the Q-morpheme *-ci* occurs. These examples show that wh-movement is not the only crucial issue in Korean wh-structures. This requires us to examine the nature of wh-interpretation in Korean.

As shown in (3), the particle *-ta* which bears [-Q] plays a role in determining the interpretation of the wh-element. Because the presence of the *-ci* particle in (3b) requires that we interpret the embedded clause as a question, following Aoun & Li (1993, 2003), we assume that this particle bears a [+Q] feature. We adopt the proposal of Nishigauchi (1990), Kim (1989) and Aoun & Li (1993,

2003), that Korean wh-words are variables which do not have an inherent wh-operator, and thus they require appropriate licensing environments which are morphologically realized as sentential particles in Korean.

English also has [Q] and wh-operator features. Consider the English counterparts, as in (4):

(4) a. John knows [CP that Mary bought something].
     b. John knows [CP what_i [∅ [Mary bought t_i]].

The feature [-Q] is spelled out by the functional lexical item *that*, in (4a). In contrast, the [+Q] morpheme of a wh-question is null, as in (4b).

Table 1 shows a comparison of the properties of wh-constructions in Korean and English. With respect to uninterpretable features, according to Chomsky (1995) and Adger (2003), an uninterpretable [wh] feature in C is strong in English and weak in Korean.

Table 1. Differences and Similarities in Wh-construction between Korean and English

Properties	Korean	English
C [uwh]	Weak (no movement)	Strong (movement)
C [+Q]	Q-particle (e.g. -ci)	Null
[Wh-operator]	Null (Spec of C)	Part of Wh-phrase (e.g. what = [wh, non-human])
D [Variable]	Wh-expression	A copy of the wh-phrase

As far as relevant interpretable features are concerned, the [Q] feature is morphologically realized in Korean but not in English. The [wh-OP] feature is generated with the wh-phrase in English but in Spec of C in Korean. Additionally, a wh-expression is itself a variable in Korean, whereas the copy of a moved wh-phrase is the variable in English.

3. Relevant Second Language Hypotheses?

In studies focusing on UG constraints such as subjacency and superiority effects on wh-movement, the difference between wh-movement and wh-in-situ languages has been characterized as a parametric difference involving the selection of a strong vs. weak uninterpretable wh-feature in C. Current approaches in second language acquisition (e.g., Schwartz & Sprouse 1996, 2000; White & Juffs, 1998; Hawkins, 2005; Hawkins & Liszka, 2003) differ as to whether selection of a new feature—parameter setting—is possible after a hypothesized critical period.

The Full Transfer/Full Access (FT/FA) model of Schwartz & Sprouse (1996), for example, assumes that, although L1 features initially transfer into the L2 in their entirety, the selection of new features is possible on the basis of available positive evidence. Accordingly, though one would expect native English speakers to initially transfer their L1 feature values into Korean, positive evidence will indicate that different sentential interpretations obtain according to the overt presence of different morphological particles (e.g., *-ta*, *-ci*). Under the "Full Access" part of the model, there appears to be nothing standing in the way of acquiring the different interpretations of wh-expressions in Korean associated with the sentential particles.

Under another approach—the Representational Deficit Hypothesis of Tsimpli (2003) and Hawkins (2005)—parameter-resetting is impossible if it involves the selection of an uninterpretable feature or feature value that is absent from the L1. Because interpreting wh-expressions involves knowledge of *interpretable* features, the Representational Deficit approach has little to say about whether or not these can be acquired easily—because only *un*interpretable features are considered to be unacquirable in this model. As observed in the previous section, it requires more than a single parameter to define the interpretive differences between English and Korean wh-constructions.   Presumably there is nothing standing in the way of acquiring interpretable features, especially those that are in fact selected by both languages in question.

In this paper, we would like to consider a somewhat different approach, which focuses on the assembly of features within lexical items rather than simply their possible selection from a feature inventory. We will refer to it as a Feature-Reassembly Approach—which is not necessarily incompatible with either of the above two models, especially in assuming L1 transfer. However, we think that it is the required re-distribution or re-clustering of features within and across different lexical items that is likely to cause the learner considerable difficulty in acquisition. This perspective is supported by recent work of Lardiere (2005, to appear), in which an end-state learner of English was shown to exhibit variability in the production of overt plural marking in English obligatory contexts. Although the speaker's L1 Chinese and L2 English select quantificational features such as [+number], these are conditioned and configured very differently in each language. Lardiere argues that accounts of parameter resetting as simple feature-selection are not sufficient to describe the actual cross-linguistic differences that must be acquired. Rather, the acquisition problems confronting the language learner involve figuring out how the relevant features are specifically conditioned and realized in the target language.

The interpretation of Korean wh-expressions by native English speakers provides another case in point. Both English and Korean select the relevant features for interpreting wh-expressions, but these are assembled differently in each language. In English, both the wh-operator and [Q] feature are merged into a single lexical item (the wh-word), whereas wh-expressions in Korean are variables and the wh-operator and [Q] features are realized on different lexical items, -ci and -ta—the morphological particles that license the appropriate interpretation. To test our hypothesis that these differences would cause considerable learning difficulties for adult native English speakers acquiring Korean, we designed the experiment described in the following section.

4. Experiment

4.1. Subjects

The participants in the experimental group consisted of 80 adult native English speakers, at an intermediate level of L2 Korean (as determined by prior proficiency testing). As shown in Table 2, the adult L2ers were late learners of Korean; on average, their length of studying Korean was about 11 months. Additionally, none of the learners had Korean-speaking parents. In other words, they were all non-heritage Korean learners.

Table 2. Summary of (Mean) Background Information of Subjects

Subjects	Gender (F/M)	Age	Length of study	Age of first exposure to L2
N = 80	20/60	23.2 (18-40)	11.2 mos.	22.6 (17-39)

Additionally, ten monolingual native speakers of Korean served as controls for the truth value judgment task, while six (native Korean-speaking) Korean-English bilinguals served as a control comparison group for the translation task. We now turn to a description of the tasks.

4.2. Materials and Procedures

In this study, two tasks were administered to investigate L2 grammars of native English speakers learning Korean: a written translation task and a truth value judgment task. The written translation task preceded the judgment one in order to minimize the subjects' awareness of the focus of the experiment. It was made clear to the participants that the goal of the test was not to assess their level of grammar and that they should rely on their intuition. They were instructed not to go back to previous sentences or judgments.

In the translation task, subjects were asked to translate Korean complex sentences containing wh-expressions into English. Because intonation plays a role in how wh-expressions are interpreted in simple interrogative clauses, we were required to test them in embedded clauses, where intonation plays no role. The test items comprised two types of constructions: wh-forms along with either the declarative particle *–ta* or the question particle *–ci* in an embedded clause. In these contexts, the closest sentential particle plays a role in disambiguating the two readings of Korean embedded wh-words, as in examples (5–6).

(5) WH-Decl(arative) Construction:
John-nun   [Mary-ka   nuku-lul   cohahaess-ta-(ko)]   an-ta.
John-Top   Mary-Nom   WHO-Acc   liked-Decl-C   know-Decl
'John knows that Mary liked *somebody*'

(6) WH-Q(uestion) Construction:
John-nun   [Mary-ka   nuku-lul   cohahaessnun-ci]   an-ta.
John-Top   Mary-Nom   WHO-Acc   liked-Q   know-Decl
'John knows *who* Mary liked'

In the truth value judgment task, the subjects were presented with short story contexts supporting either an indefinite or wh-Q reading of wh-expressions (see Figure 1 for an example of an indefinite context),[4] each followed by a set of four related statements (two of which were distracters). Participants were asked to judge whether each statement was 'true', 'false' or 'don't know'. These contexts were presented to the experimental group in their L1 English, with the test sentences in Korean; for the Korean monolingual controls, the contexts were also given in Korean.

Figure 1: Indefinite Context

John and Mary are close co-workers working in the financial division. One day John saw a large and beautiful flower basket delivered to Mary. Mary was not there at the time. John was very curious about it, and then opened a card attached to the flower basket. A love message was written on the card. But there was no name of the sender on the card.

a. John-nun   nu(ku)-ka   Mary-lul   coahan-ta-ko   an-ta.
['John knows that *somebody* likes Mary.']

True [X]   False [   ]   Don't Know [   ]

b. John-nun nu(ku)-ka Mary-lul coahanun-ci an-ta.
   ['John knows *who* likes Mary']

True [   ]   False [X]   Don't Know [   ]

Distracters:

c. John-un cikcangtonglyo chung han salam-i Mary-lul cohahan-ta-ko an-ta.
   ['John knows that one of his co-workers likes Mary']

d. John-un Mary-ka ku-lul coahhanun-ci an-ta.
   ['John knows whether Mary likes him']

If the L2ers have acquired the role of sentential particles in the interpretation of Korean wh-words, they should answer 'true' for the sentences containing the indefinite meaning of Korean wh-expressions in the indefinite context in Figure 1, and 'false' for the sentences with a wh-question reading.

5. Results

5.1. Results of the Written Translation Task

Results from the translation task are reported in Table 3, which shows the mean accuracy of sentences containing Korean wh-(in-situ) forms in relation to the interpretation of wh-expressions.

Table 3. % Mean Accuracy on Interpretations of Wh-forms

Sentence Type (Reading)	WH-Decl (Indefinite)	WH-Q (Wh-phrase)
	Mean	Mean
Learners (N = 80)	31 (134/428)	76 (325/428)
Controls (N = 6)	100 (36/36)	100 (36/36)

Results from the control group confirm that Korean speakers construe wh-elements differently depending on the types of sentential particles associated with them. As Table 3 shows, they had perfectly accurate results in the written translation task, 100% correct interpretations for both Question and Declarative constructions.

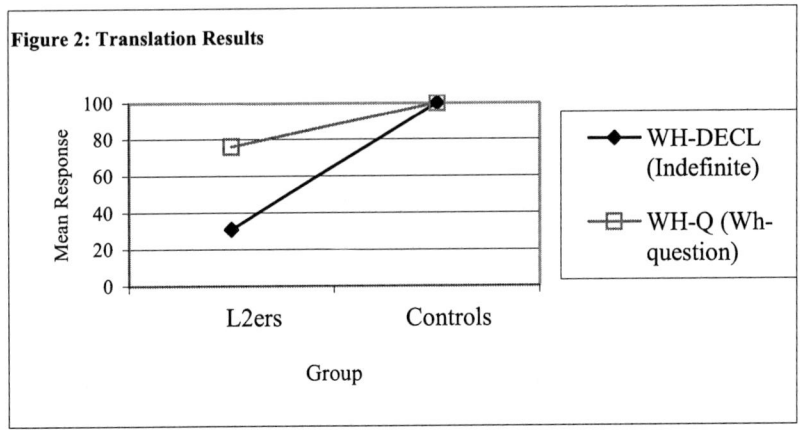

Figure 2: Translation Results

However, as shown in Table 3 and Figure 2, the learners performed significantly better in the case where the Korean wh-expressions receive the question interpretation than in the case where they should receive the indefinite interpretation, $t(79) = -6.83, p < .0001$.

5.2. Results of the Truth-Value Judgment Task

Turning now to the results of the truth-value judgment task, recall that if a learner has acquired Korean wh-expressions, s/he is expected to answer 'true' for the WH-Decl construction with an indefinite reading, while rejecting a WH-question reading, when the indefinite context is provided. The following scores were given for the judgment task. When a participant judged a test item as 'true', s/he received +1 points; when s/he answered 'false', s/he received −1 points. Accordingly, learners' negative mean responses indicate that they were likely to reject a test construction, and positive mean responses show that they were likely to accept a test structure (Wh-Decl or Wh-Q).

Table 4 shows the mean of judgments in the Declarative and Question sentence types in the indefinite contexts.

Table 4. Mean of Judgments in the Interpretation of Korean WH-forms

Indefinite Context		
Sentence Type	WH-Decl*(True: +1)	WH-Q** (False: −1)
	Mean	Mean
L2 Learners (N=80)	− 0.34	− 0.11
NS Controls (N=10)	+ 0.67	− 0.97

Note: * indefinite reading; ** wh-question reading

As expected, the control group strongly preferred the Declarative statement in the indefinite contexts, $t(9) = 15.58, p < .0001$.

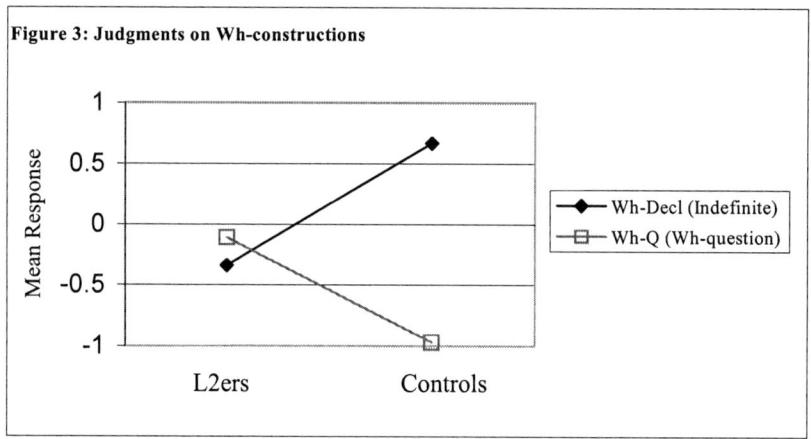

Figure 3: Judgments on Wh-constructions

On the other hand, the learners' group behaved in almost the opposite manner. As Figure 3 illustrates, unlike the controls, the learners more strongly incorrectly rejected the Declarative than the Question statement. They significantly preferred the question reading, as in Table 4: $t(79) = - 0.23, p < .05$. This shows that the learners were incorrectly likely to construe the wh-elements in the Declarative construction as wh-questions.

6. Summary and Discussion

These results suggest that English native speakers through at least an intermediate proficiency level were not yet sensitive to the contingency between sentential particle types and the appropriate interpretation of wh-in-situ expressions in Korean. We suggest that this result cannot be easily accounted for under current approaches to parameter-resetting-failure in second language acquisition. Instead, the data are better accounted for under a feature-reassembly approach, in which the learning problem confronting English-speaking acquirers of Korean can be defined in terms of the differences in how these features are assembled in lexical items in each language.

Our study, because it does not include data from end-state or highly proficient learners, cannot be used to draw conclusions about whether the correct interpretations of Korean wh-expressions are *ultimately* acquirable or not by native English speakers (and in fact, we would assume that they are ultimately acquirable). However, we wonder why their acquisition appears to be so difficult and late. It is this point we think our approach can address more effectively than other approaches. One of the next steps will be to locate end-state or highly advanced native English speakers of Korean to see if, in fact, the correct interpretations of wh-expressions are acquired.

Notes

[1] Note that basic Korean word order is subject-object-verb (SOV).

[2] The capitalized WHs indicate wh-elements that are not specified for meaning. Thus, for example, WHAT indicates that the element can be the wh-question pronoun 'what' or the indefinite counterpart 'someone'.

[3] In Korean glosses, the Yale romanization is followed, which reflects the Korean spelling system without reflecting pronunciation. The following abbreviations are used: Nom-nominative case marker; Acc-accusative case marker; C-complementizer; Decl-Declarative marker; Q-question marker; Top-topic marker.

[4] We report only on the indefinite context responses in this paper because these are the only kind for which the wh-Q reading can reliably be ruled out as 'False'. In the wh-Q contexts, both the wh-Q and indefinite readings could conceivably be 'True', since, for example, knowing 'who likes Mary' entails knowing that 'someone likes Mary'.

References

Adger, D. (2003) *Core syntax: a minimalist approach,* Oxford, Oxford University Press.

Aoun, J. and Li, Y.-H. A. (1993) "Wh-elements in Situ: Syntax or LF?" in *Linguistic Inquiry* 24, 199-238.

—. and Li, Y.-H. A. (2003) *Essays on the representational and deriva-tional nature of grammar: the diversity of wh-constructions*, Cambridge, MA, MIT Press.

Chomsky, N (1995) *The Minimalist Program*, MIT Press, Cambridge.

Hawkins, R. and C. Chan. (1997) "The partial availability of Universal Grammar in second language acquisition: the 'Failed Functional Features Hypothesis'" in *Second Language Research* 13, 187-226.

—. (2003) "Representational deficit' theories of adult SLA: evidence, counterevidence and implications," invited plenary address presented at EuroSLA, Edinburgh, September 2003.

—. (2005) "Revisiting wh-movement: the availability of an uninterpretable [wh] feature in interlanguage grammars," in L. Dekydtspotter et al., eds., *Proceedings of the 7th Generative Approaches to Second Language Acquisition Conference*, Somerville, MA, Cascadilla Press, 124-137.

—. and S. Liszka. (2003) "Locating the source of defective past tense marking in advanced L2 English speakers", in R. van Hout et al., eds., *The lexicon-syntax interface in second language acquisition*, Amsterdam, John Benjamins.

Kim, J. (2003) "L2 initial syntax: Wh-movement and the most economical syntactic derivation," in B. Beachley et al., eds., *BUCLD 27 Proceedings*, Somerville, MA, Cascadilla.

Kim, S. (1989) "Wh-phrase in Korean and Japanese are QPs," *MIT Working papers in Linguistics* 11, 119-138.

Lardiere, D. (2005) "On morphological competence," in L. Dekydtspotter et al.,eds., *Proceedings of the 7th Generative Approaches to Second Language Acquisition Conference,* Somerville, MA, Cascadilla Press, 178-192.

—. (to appear) "Feature-assembly in second language acquisition," in J. Liceras, H. Zobl and H, Goodluck, eds., *The role of formal features in second language acquisition*, Mahwah, NJ, Erlbaum.

Martohardjono, G. (1993) *Wh-movement in the Acquisition of a Second Language: A Crosslinguistic Study of Three Languages with and without Movement*, Doctoral dissertation, Cornell University.

Nishigauchi, T. (1990) *Quantification in the theory of grammar*, Dordrecht, Kluwer.

Platzack, C. (1996) "The initial hypothesis of syntax: a minimalist perspective on language acquisition and attrition," in H. Clahsen, ed., *Generative perspectives on language acquisition*, Amsterdam, John Benjamins.

Schachter, J. (1990) "On the issue of completeness in second language acquisition," in *Second Language Research* 6, 93-124.

Schwartz, B. D., and R. Sprouse. (1996) "L2 cognitive states and the Full Transfer/Full Access model" in *Second Language Research* 12, 40-72.

Tsai, W.-T. D. (1994) On economizing the theory of A-bar dependency, Doctoral dissertation, MIT, Cambridge, MA.

Tsimpli, I.-M. (2003) "Features in language development," invited plenary address presented at EuroSLA, Edinburgh.

THE ACQUISITION OF CLITICS AND DETERMINERS BY CHILD L2 LEARNERS OF MODERN GREEK

VICKY CHONDROGIANNI

1. Introduction

Recent second language acquisition (L2A) theories within the Minimalist Program (Chomsky 1995 onwards) place the burden of acquisition on feature interpretability as this is the locus of crosslinguistic variation. The present paper explores this issue by looking into the acquisition of two categorically similar D-elements, that is, third person direct object (DO) clitics and the definite determiner by child Turkish-speaking L2 learners of Modern Greek. Data show that, although the acquisition of their φ-features is parallel, the two D-elements have a differential status in the learners' interlanguage.

2 Determiners and pronominal elements in Modern Greek and Turkish

2.1 Clitics and determiners in Modern Greek

Modern Greek has a definite determiner which inflects for case, number and gender and agrees in φ-feature specification with the following adjective and noun. The obligatory presence of the definite determiner before count nouns as well as proper names in argument positions points to the fact that it is not inherently definite, but it rather has an expletive use and serves as a mere spell-out of uninterpretable φ-features within the noun phrase. As such it is merged at a position lower than D, at the FP head (locus of Agr) and moves to the D head in order to get the definiteness specification (Alexiadou 2005).

Turning to pronominal elements, Modern Greek has strong and clitic pronouns. The morphophonological similarity between third person direct object (DO) clitics and the definite determiner in Modern Greek has also argued for their structural similarity. It is thus put forward that clitics are also a spell-out of φ-features, i.e. person, number and gender (Tsimpli 2003). Clitics being deficient elements need to move from their canonical object position and merge in a preverbal position in order to check their case features and become visible. This is possible due to their XP/X status, thus moving both as maximal and minimal categories (cf. Mavrogiorgos (2005) on clitics as ΦP/φs and cliticization in Modern Greek).

2.2 DP layers in Turkish

Turkish has no definite article and formal features (case, number but no gender) are marked on the noun. Accusative case marking is linked to definiteness/specificity of (in)definite objects (Enç 1991). This interaction between case, definiteness and plural marking on the noun has been considered as evidence for the presence of a DP layer in the Turkish noun phrase, since number under certain readings and case can block syntactic operations possible with NPs but not DPs (e.g. incorporation of the noun into the verb) (see Ketrez 2003 for DP, although see Öztürk 2005 for lack of DP in Turkish).

In the pronominal system, Turkish has strong pronouns and allows a null element *pro* to appear in D-linked contexts, in order to recover a referent already introduced in discourse (Kornfilt 1997).

3 Child L1, child L2 and second language acquisition theories

Child L1 acquisition research of clitics and determiners in Modern Greek has showed that both elements are partially present in the child grammar from the age of 1;09 onwards and that their rate of acquisition is rather fast, with both elements being fully acquired by the age of 3;00 (Tsakali and Wexler 2003, Marinis 2003).

Turning to child L2 acquisition it has been argued that the interlanguage of child L2 learners can exhibit properties different from their L1 counterparts due to L1 transfer and the domain to be acquired (morphology vs. syntax) (Schwartz 2004). At the same time most L2A theories place the burden of acquisition on feature interpretability as this is the locus of crosslinguistic variation (Chomsky 1995), whereas syntactic operations (Merge, Move) remain intact both in L2A. Thus, according to the Failed Feature Hypothesis (FFH) (Hawkins and Chan 1997; Tsimpli 2003) uninterpretable features in the L2 not present in the L1 will remain unlearnable. Furthermore, the categorical similarity between two elements (i.e. clitics and determiners in the present study) will also lead to a parallel (impaired) acquisition pattern both with respect to their formal features (φ-features) and their acquisition rate. Conversely, the Full Transfer/Full Access (FT/FA) Hypothesis (Schwartz and Sprouse 1994/6) predicts that feature interpretability can affect initial stages of language acquisition, as the L1 feature inventory is transferred at the initial stage, but later UG constrained restructuring is possible

Similarly, the acquisition of cliticization per se has been agued to be susceptible to principles of economy in computation (Jakubowicz et al. 1998), sensitive to age of exposure as a child or an adult (Granfeldt & Schlyter 2004).

Given that child L2 learners in the present study are exposed to the L2 after the age of 5-6 years, i.e. when most relevant L1 structures are in place, we expect to find properties of the L1 grammar in the child L2 learners' interlanguage. It is also investigated whether the acquisition of the two D-elements and their morphological properties will be similar.

4 Present study

4.1 Subjects

The participants in the present study were 106 Turkish-speaking children attending primary minority schools in Thrace, that is, Greek-Turkish bilingual schools in North-eastern Greece. L2 children attended grades 2 to 6 of the minority school and were aged from 7 to 12 years old at the time of testing. Subjects had been exposed to Greek primarily at a school setting and their age of first exposure was at the age of 5 or 6 years.

A control group of 50 Greek native children of the same age and corresponding school grades was selected. The control group was given all experimental tasks and exhibited a ceiling effect across tasks.

4.2 Method

4.2.1 Placement Test

Subjects were divided into proficiency levels based on tests developed for measuring young learners' language proficiency in Greek (Tzevelekou et al. 2004). The tests follow the specifications of the Common European Framework of Reference and categorize young learners into five proficiency levels, from -A1, which is considered the lowest one, to B2, when all grammatical properties are supposed to be in place. Table 1 illustrates the distribution of subjects across ages, grades and proficiency levels.

Proficiency level	Grade	Age range	N of subjects
-A1	2	7 - 8	9
A1	2-4	8-10	21
A2	2-6	7-12	44
B1	3-6	9-12	24
B2	6	11-12	8
Total			106

Table 1 Distribution of subjects across proficiency levels

4.2.2 Experimental materials

The production of the definite determiner was tested through a story telling task based on Mayers (1969) 'Oh Frog, where are you?' picture story. The production of third person DO clitics was examined in the story-telling task (results are not presented here) and through an Elicited Production task. The elicited production task was a partial replication of Schaeffer's (2000) Truth-Value Judgment Task and Elicited Production task based on the elicitation question of the form *"What is X doing to Y?"*, where the response prompts the production of the clitic in a D-linked environment. A picture-based and an act-out version of the elicited production task were administered.

5 Results

Table 2 shows the production of 3rd person DO clitics and the definite determiners across tasks. The production of the definite determiner is initially quite low but increases at the post-initial level (A1) and is fully acquired at advanced proficiency levels. A one-way ANOVA also showed that there is an overall significant interaction between proficiency level and structure ($F(4, 102)=7.868$, $p<.001$) especially between –A1 and subsequent levels (-A1 to A1, A2, B1 and B2, $p<.001$).

	Picture-based task			Act-out task			Story telling	
	Lex. NP	Øobj	Clitic	Lex. NP	Øobj	Clitic	DP	ØDP
-A1	57%	43%	0%	52%	48%	0%	31%	69%
A1	46,3%	45%	8,7%	50%	39%	11%	65.5%	34.5%
A2	32%	33%	35%	30%	31%	39%	75.5%	24.5%
B1	30%	30%	40%	30%	21%	47%	86.5%	13.5%
B2	7,5%	5,5%	87%	16,7%	8,3%	75%	100%	0%

Table 2 Production of clitics and determiner in %

Contrary to the acquisition pattern and rate of the definite determiner, clitics are initially completely absent and require longer time for the child L2 learners to acquire. A one-way ANOVA showed that although an overall interaction between clitics and proficiency level is attested for each task $(F(4,102)=7.312$, $p<.001$ and $F(4,102)=4.775$, $p<.01$ for picture-based and act-out task respectively), significant difference between proficiency levels is attested after the A2 level (A2 to –A1, $p<.03$, to A1, $p<.00$, to B1 and B2 n.s.).

	Gender DP	Number DP	Case DP	Gender Cl.	Number Cl.
A1-	10.4%	2.1%	3%	-	-
A1	29.2%	1%	0%	28.6%	9%
A2	13.9%	0%	0%	26.2%	2%
B1	6%	0%	0%	5%	0%
B2	0%	0%	0%	12%	0%

Table 3 erroneous production of φ-features

Turning to phi-features (Table 3), the acquisition of number and case seem to be almost error-free, whereas gender is more problematic, although ultimate convergence is possible.

6 Discussion and conclusions

The results of the present study partially argue for the presence of L1 features in the initial stages of child L2 learners' interlanguage, since both clitics and the definite determiner are initially absent to a different degree. The asymmetrical pattern though observed in the acquisition of the two categorically similar D-elements poses problems for both the FFH and the FT/FA Hypothesis. The FFH cannot explain how two elements with similar uninterpretable features are distinct in the learner's grammar. Similarly, mere transfer fails to capture delayed clitic production, as well as the presence of other non felicitous structures such as full lexical noun phrases, apart from null objects.

The question that arises then is why child L2 learners differentiate between these two morphophonologically similar elements and exhibit this asymmetrical acquisition pattern. The present study shows that L2 learners do not drop the object, as full lexical noun phrases are also produced, but it is the pronominal element, whose omission is persistent. This finding, in relation to the fact that the feature specification of the D-category is already in place, as the acquisition of the definite determiner shows, could point to the fact that it is the properties of cliticization per se that pose problems to child L2 learners. It could be argued that the complexity imposed by the deficient nature of the element being merged as an object and the factors regulating its occurrence (discourse properties) impose learnability limitations on its acquisition, leading to its initial treatment as a full lexical XP element before merging it as an X^0. Additionally, persistent erroneous feature specification after the two D-elements are correctly produced points to a direction of a mapping problem than of lack of a syntactic category.

References

Alexiadou, A. (2005) "Possessors and (in)definiteness", in *Lingua*, 115, 6, 787-819.

Chomsky, N. (1995) *The Minimalist Program*, MIT Press, Cambridge, Mass.

Enç, M. (1991) "Semantics of Specificity," in *Linguistic Inquiry* 22, 1, 1-25.

Granfeldt, J. and S. Schlyter (2004) "Cliticization in the acquisition of French as L1 and L2," in P. Prévost and J. Paradis, eds., *The Acquisition of French in Different Contexts*, John Benjamins, Amsterdam, 333-370.

Hawkins, R. and C.Y. Chan (1997) "The partial availability of Universal Grammar in Second Language Acquisition: The 'failed functional features hypothesis'," in *Second Language Research* 13, 3, 187-226.

Jakubowicz, C., L. Nash and C. Gerard (1998) "Determiners and Clitic Pronouns in French-Speaking Children with SLI.," in *Language Acquisition* 7, 113-160.

Ketrez, N. (2003) "-*lAr*-marked nominals and three types of plurality in Turkish" in Proceedings of CLS 39, Chicago.

Kornfilt (1997) *Turkish*, Longman, London.

Marinis, T. (2003) *The Acquisition of the DP in Modern Greek*, John Benjamins, Amsterdam.

Mavrogiorgos, M (2005) "Clitics as morphosyntactic independent phrases," paper presented at the MIT-Harvard Workshop on Greek Morphosyntax, 22-23 July 2005, Cambridge, Massachusetts.

Öztürk, B. (2005) *Case, Referentiality and Phrase Structure*, John Benjamins, Amsterdam.

Schaeffer, J. C. (2000) *The Acquisition of Direct Object Scrambling and Clitic Placement*, John Benjamins, Amsterdam.

Schwartz, B. and R. Sprouse (19994/96) "L2 cognitive states and the Full Transfer/Full Access Model," in *Second Language Research* 12, 1, 40-72.

—. (2004) "Child L2 acquisition: Paving the way," in J. van Kampen and S.Baauw, eds., *Proceedings of GALA 2003*, LOT Publications.

Tsakali, V. and K. Wexler (2003) "Why do children omit clitics in some languages but not in others?," in J. van Kampen and S.Baauw, eds., *Proceedings of GALA 2003*, LOT Publications.

Tsimpli, I.M. (2003) "Clitics and Determiners in L2 Greek," in J. M. Liceras et al., eds., *Proceedings of the 6th GASLA*, Cascadilla Press, Somerville, Massachusetts, 331-339.

Tzevelekou M. et al. (2004) *Greek as a Second Language: Assessing Greek Language Proficiency in the Minority Schools in Thrace*, Ms. University of Athens.

THE STRUCTURE OF FRAGMENTS IN (CHILD) FRENCH

CÉCILE DE CAT AND GEORGE TSOULAS

Elliptical utterances are beginning to attract an important amount of attention in the generative literature. As a result, several categories of elliptical utterances with specific properties have been recognised. We will focus here on so-called *fragments*. On the surface, fragments are *non-sentential* utterances consisting typically of a DP or a PP:

(1)   A pint of Guiness.   (meaning: I would like a pint of Guiness.)

As has been observed, such fragments are interpreted as if they were full propositions with the unpronounced, yet understood surrounding linguistic environment somehow retrieved from the context. This state of affairs has led a number of researchers to propose that fragmentary utterances derive from fully specified syntactic structures, so as to preserve the standard view of the syntax-semantics mapping (e.g. Merchant 2005). On the other hand it has also been proposed that fragmentary utterances consist syntactically of no more than what is pronounced (e.g. Stainton 2004). Theories of the latter type must and do rely heavily on pragmatic enrichment in order to account for the observed interpretations. In this paper, we will focus on a sub-class of fragments: those that are more complex than a simple DP/PP as they present an information structural partition. The analysis that we are going to outline will rely on the presence of a functional category mediating between the two parts of the fragment. We will argue that the child has an adult-like representation of these structures from the beginning.

The data set used in this study comes from two French corpora of spontaneous interaction between children and adults: the York corpus (available on CHILDES) and the Cat corpus. They contain speech from 4 children (between the ages of 1;10 and 3;6) and adults from Belgium, Canada and France. Recordings took place fortnightly (York corpus) or monthly (Cat corpus) and lasted 30 minutes. For details regarding the transcription and coding procedures, see Plunkett & De Cat (2002) and De Cat (2002).

Complex fragments consist in a verbless phrase (the *nucleus* – in bold in all our examples) and a peripheral phrase (the *satellite*). The nucleus conveys the main information (and is therefore in focus).

(2)   [$_{Focus}$ XP] satellite   (XP = *nucleus*)
        satellite [$_{Focus}$ XP]

The satellite expresses what the utterance (or fragment) is about (3), or it restricts the (temporal or spatial) domain within which the predication holds (4).

(3)   **Les   voilà,**   les   petits copains.   (Adult)
        them PRESENTATIVE the   little   friends
        'Here (are) the little friends.'

(4)   **De   la   tomate,** maintenant.   (Adult)
        PART   the   tomato   now
        'Now (let's add) some tomato.' .

The fact that fragments can contain elements that typically modify full sentences is symptomatic of the general puzzle they represent for the theory: in spite of consisting of essentially a DP or a PP, fragments are interpreted as if they were full propositions with assertoric force (Stainton 2004, Merchant 2005), e.g. questions, requests, statements etc. Thus, although they are highly reduced, fragments are interpreted like sentences and behave like sentences. The fragments below are representative of those found in the speech of the children from the York and Cat corpora.

(5)   Moi,   **pas   l'hippopotame.**   (Anne 2;2.20)
        me   not   the-hippopotamus
        'I (don't want to draw) the hippopotamus.'

(6)   **Quoi,** ma   gauche?   (Lea 2;9.21)
        what   my   left
        'What('s the matter with) my left? '

(7)   **Méchant,** la feuille.   (Tom 2;4.9)
        nasty   the leaf
        'The leaf (is) nasty.'

On the assumption that syntactically non-propositional XPs cannot be mapped onto semantic propositions, Merchant (2005) proposes that fragments are in fact fully propositional in syntax, but that most of the structure remains unpronounced. He argues that the fragment occupies the specifier of a left-peripheral phrase (which he suggests may be FocusP) whose head is endowed with an E feature. This feature has two functions: (i) it instructs PF not to parse its complement (and hence not to pronounce it) and (ii) it consists of a "partial identity function over propositions", which is supposed to ensure that the complement of an E-endowed head has an appropriate antecedent in the discourse (which essentially ensures that the content of the unpronounced structure is identifiable/recoverable). In principle, this account could be extended to fragments with satellites, if one assumes that satellites are dislocated elements situated at the periphery of the clause.   Despite its many merits, this analysis runs into a number of problems which we do not have space to elaborate on. The interested reader is referred to De Cat & Tsoulas (2006) for details. From an acquisition point of view, Merchant's ellipsis analysis of fragments is rather implausible for two reasons. The first arises from learnability considerations. When presented with fragments in the input, all the child hears is a verbless XP, or, in the case of our complex fragments a sequence of two XPs which do not contain a verbal predicate. Nothing indicates that it is part of a larger syntactic structure: the nucleus (which for Merchant constitutes the whole fragment) is not endowed with a distinctive prosody, nor with any kind of morphology that would force the child to assume that this XP has been fronted. Even instances of fragments displaying connectivity (e.g. case) do not *per se* require a fronting analysis and could in principle be accounted for by truncation - an option which has been independently argued to be heavily exploited in child grammars (see e.g. Rizzi 1994). (Note incidentally that no case connectivity effect is observable in spoken French.) The second fact which renders Merchant's ellipsis analysis implausible is that fragments are heavily used by children from the onset of expressive syntax, well before there is any evidence that CP can be implemented. Children in the York corpus (i.e. the only ones for whom data collection started early enough) produce fragments at least 4 months before they start fronting *wh*-phrases.

(8)

	First moved WH	First fragments
Anne	2;4.2	2;0.13
Max	2;5.1	1;11.0

Table 1: Age of first use of WH-fronting vs. fragments (with satellites)

If Merchant's analysis was to account for the (early) child data, the only evidence of complex syntax involving the left-periphery at that point in development would in fact be invisible (as most of the postulated structure is unpronounced).

Is it then possible for the child to reconstruct the interpretation given the limited resources at his/her disposal, and, crucially, to do so without recourse to any extraneous pragmatic enrichment that would violate presumably innate principles governing the syntax-semantics mapping?

A central property of complex fragments is that the relation between the nucleus and the satellite has to remain vague (i.e. potentially ambiguous), given that several interpretations are possible depending on the context. A fragment like (5), for instance, could be interpreted as *I don't want to have/be/draw/make/take/... the hippopotamus* depending on what is salient in the context. This is true of all fragments, both in adult and in child speech.

Universal grammar makes available devices for the expression of vague relations, relations that need contextual supplementation in order to be fully specified and interpreted. In other words, it is possible to encode an *aboutness* relation without further specifying from the lexicon the terms in which this *aboutness* is to be cashed out. One such example is to be found in the semantics of the possessive. Williams (1982) proposed the Det-Rule in order to capture the inherent vagueness of the possessive relation:

(9)   **The Det-Rule**   (Williams 1982:283)
        The relation between a possessive NP and the following N' can
        be any relation at all

Williams cites examples like *John's* cat which can be interpreted as the cat John owns, the cat sitting on John's lap, etc... Without wanting to make any specific proposals about the nature and the semantics of the possessive, one could think of the vagueness that the Det-rule encodes as being part of the possessive determiner.

In the same spirit as the above, we would like to propose that for fragments with satellites, the relationship between the satellite and the nucleus is mediated by a functional head whose interpretation is vague and context-dependent in the same way as for the possessive D. Postulating an extra functional head has the merit of facilitating syntactic composition on the one hand, and on the other it allows a straightforward syntax-semantics mapping without having to postulate excessive amounts of structure for which we find little or no empirical support. The functional head (which we label *Act*, loosely following Ross (1972)) is interpreted as some relation R that holds between the nucleus and the satellite. *Act* does not in itself inherently and unambiguously encode any particular relation. Rather, it allows the retrieval of the relational semantic content from the context. *Act* then must contain an anaphoric feature: it is a deep predicate anaphor in the sense of Hankamer (1979). *Act* must also be specified for a *force* feature to account for the assertoric properties of fragments. Thus, *Act* corresponds not only to the syntactic and semantic glue between nucleus and satellite, but also, as the head of the construction which carries the features allowing the fragment's syntactic independence. *Act's* selectional requirements are underspecified, because its argument can be of many types (usually DP or PP, but also AdvP – see De Cat & Tsoulas (2006)).

In spite of the disagreement regarding their exact nature, the presence of constraints on the structures children are initially able to express is uncontroversial. It is therefore not surprising that children should exploit early the availability in the target grammar of a highly efficient device that maximises the interpretive potential of a syntactically simple structure (relying heavily on the ability of the hearer to identify the unexpressed information). Indeed, children have been shown to make informationally judicious choices regarding what they (do not) express, even at the one-word stage (Greenfield et al 1985).

References

De Cat, C. (2002) *French Dislocation,* Unpublished Doctoral Dissertation, University of York.

—. and G. Tsoulas, (2006) *Complex fragments,* Ms. Universities of Leeds/York.

Greenfield, P., Reilly, J., Leaper, C. and Baker, N. (1985) "The structural and functional status of single-word utterances and their relationship to early multi-word speech", in M. Barrett, ed., *Children's single-word speech,* New York, Wiley, 233-67.

Hankamer, J. (1979) *Deletion in coordinate structures*, New York, Garland.

Merchant, J. (2005) "Fragments and ellipsis," in *Linguistics and Philosophy, 6,* 661-738.

Plunkett, B., and C. De Cat, (2001) « Root specifiers and null subjects revisited" in A. H.-J. Do et al, eds., *Proceedings of BUCLD 25,* Somerville, MA, Cascadilla, 611-622).

Rizzi, L. (1994) "Early null subjects and root null subjects," in B. Lust, G. Harmon, J. Kornfilt, Eds., *Syntactic theory and first language acquisition - Crosslinguistic perspectives,* Hillsdale, NJ, Lawrence Erlbaum Associates, vol. 2, 249-272.

Ross, J. R. (1972). "ACT," in D. Davidson and G. Harman, eds., *Semantics of Natural Language,* Dordrech, *D. Reidel.*

Stainton, R. (2004) In defence on non-sentential assertion," in Z. Szabo, Ed., *Semantics vs. Pragmatics*. Oxford,Oxford University Press, 383-457.

Williams, E. (1982) "The NP Cycle," in *Linguistic Inquiry, 13,* 277 – 295.

A NOVEL POVERTY OF THE STIMULUS ARGUMENT FROM SWAHILI

KAMIL UD DEEN

1. Introduction

A central argument for the existence of innate, domain-specific knowledge that aids in the acquisition of language is the so-called Poverty of the Stimulus argument (PoS argument). The logic of this argument goes something like this.

(1) a. The process of language acquisition can either be purely data-driven, or it can be aided by some pre-existing knowledge.
   b. Certain principles of language that are not evidenced in the input, are nevertheless acquired by children.
   c. Therefore pure data-driven models of acquisition are inadequate, and pre-existing knowledge must be available to the child.

The vast majority of linguists (if not all) these days agree that language acquisition is not a purely data-driven process and that there is some pre-existing knowledge that aids in language acquisition. However, deep divisions remain as to the scope and the precise nature of that pre-existing knowledge. One approach to this problem is that these PoS facts may be accounted for by appealing to abilities and principles that are domain-general, not specific to language. Such approaches encounter significant problems, as PoS facts often reflect highly specialized principles that appear to be specific to language. A second position holds that the pre-existing knowledge is in fact specific to language, but that all relevant principles are derivable from very basic, fundamental principles of language such as dominance relations, constituency, etc. A third position holds that even this is insufficient to account for all of the PoS facts, and thus not only is the pre-existing knowledge domain-specific, but it is also highly articulated, and probably (at some abstract level) of the precise form postulated by modern linguists.

In this paper I present evidence of a novel PoS argument from Swahili, and argue for an approach to nativism that involves domain-specific, highly articulated knowledge of language. I begin by reviewing an influential example of the Poverty of the Stimulus argument from the literature and some recent criticisms. I then provide an overview of the relevant facts about adult Swahili, including my theoretical assumptions, and finally I present the child Swahili facts. The essence of my argument is this: Swahili children produce a clause type that is utterly unmodeled (and ungrammatical) in adult Swahili – an error of sorts. And yet within this unmodeled, ungrammatical clause type, children exhibit knowledge of the abstract relationship between tense and grammatical subjects – a principle that is clearly specific to language.

2. The Debate on the Poverty of the Stimulus Arguments

The most widely cited PoS argument in the literature is that of Structure Dependent yes-no question formation, discussed by Chomsky (1971) and then later tested by Crain & Nakayama (1987). Another well-known PoS argument that has received much recent attention is the case of anaphoric *one*, exemplified in (1). This was first discussed by Baker (1978), and more recently up by Lidz, Waxman and Freedman (2003). The crux of this argument is that anaphoric *one* must refer back to a constituent bigger than just N, say an N', as shown in example (2).

(1)   This box is bigger than the other one.
(2)   Context: John has a blue glass
          Alice has a yellow glass

Sentence: 'John has a blue glass but Alice doesn't have one.'

Given the context indicated, the sentence in (2) is felicitous. If *one* referred to just an N, in this case *glass,* then this sentence should be ungrammatical because both John and Alice *do* have glasses. However, because *one* refers to a larger N' constituent (*blue glass*), the sentence is acceptable. Sentence (3) shows that not only is it possible for anaphoric one to refer to an N', but it in fact *must* refer to an N'. Baker states that the only evidence that would inform the child of this fact are sentences such as (4). He claims that such sentences are very rare in child directed speech, and thus this is a good case of the poverty of the stimulus.

(3)   *The student of chemistry is better prepared than the one of physics.

(4)   (Context: Chris had a red ball and Max had a yellow ball.)
          → Chris had a red ball but Max doesn't have one

Lidz et al. (2003) investigate this issue, showing two important things. First, they show that the relevant kinds of evidence for the acquisition of anaphoric *one* (as in 4) in the speech of two children are in fact very rare: of the 792 tokens of anaphoric uses of *one,* only 2 unambiguously indicate that *one* must refer to an N'. This constitutes a rate of evidence of 0.253%. Second, using a preferential looking paradigm, they demonstrate that children as young as 1;6 show knowledge of the anaphoric properties of anaphoric *one*.[1]

In response to this, Akhtar, Callanan, Pullum & Scholz (2004) question what they refer to as the *inaccessibility evidence*. They argue that while an evidence rate of 0.253% sounds exceedingly low, in their view this is actually sufficient for a child to acquire language. They calculate that an average child should hear approximately 33 tokens of utterances such as those in (4) by about age 1;6. They argue that while this is not a huge amount, it is sufficient.

It is true that 33 tokens give the impression of significance more so than a paltry 0.253%, but this is deceptive. One must keep in mind that these 33 tokens are counterbalanced by 12,967 tokens of the *wrong* kind of evidence, indicating that anaphoric *one* can refer back to just an N (not an N'). But nonetheless, it raises the question: How much evidence is enough to drive language acquisition?

Traditional acquisitionists assume that anything below roughly 5% is *noise* on the reasonable assumption that normal human language is fraught with slips-of-the-tongue, false-starts, mid-sentence shifts, and other speech errors. Thus if small percentages of input were sufficient to trigger any sort of acquisition, we expect at least some children to be fooled by the noisy input, contrary to fact. However, apparently for Akhtar et. al. 0.253% is sufficient enough to motivate a purely data-driven model of language acquisition. While their position is clearly logically flawed and empirically unsupported, a debate about what precise percentage of evidence in the input is sufficient is always going to be a subjective one.

Rather than entering into such a debate, I propose avoiding this problem entirely by focusing on contexts in which the relevant input is *zero*, and thus beyond subjectivity. I will provide an example of a PoS argument in which evidence in the input is entirely absent, both empirically and logically. Thus the question of *how much is enough* simply does not apply because the crucial evidence cannot and does not occur in the input. First I sketch out the relevant facts of adult Swahili, the theoretical assumptions I make, and some background acquisition facts.

3. Swahili

Swahili is a Bantu language spoken in Eastern Africa. It is an SVO language, with agglutinative morphology on the verbal complex. The indicative verbal complex consists of Subject Agreement–Tense–Verb Root–Indicative, as schematized in (6).

Verbal Complex

(5) Juma ⎧ a - na - m – pend - a ⎫   Mariam   S-V-O
    Juma   SA₃ₛ-PRES- OA₃ₛ- like - IND   Mariam
    'Juma likes Mariam'

(6) SA – T – (OA) – Verb – MOOD   Indicative
    a – na – m – pend – a   Verbal Complex

Subject agreement marks person, number, and animacy (table 1), and there
are various tense markers (table 2). Swahili is a null subject language (7), like
Italian. Additionally, speakers of this dialect of Swahili produce clauses that I
call [-SA] because they are missing Subject Agreement (8). The syntax of these
clauses is not important for our purposes here (although see Deen 2003; 2006),
but it is important to know what the input to children consists of: that is, it
consists of full clauses and [-SA] clauses, and no other kind of indicative clause.

Table 1. Subject Agreement paradigm

SA prefix	
ni-	1st person singular
u-	2nd person singular
a-	3rd person singular
tu-	1st person plural
mu-	2nd person plural
wa-	3rd person plural

Table 2. Some tense/aspect prefixes

T/A marker	Meaning
li	past
na	present on-going
ta	future
ka	Narrative, resultative
me	pres perf.
sha	pres perf. completive
Ku	infinitival

(7) A – na – m – pend–a   Mariam   Null Subject
    SA₃ₛ–PRES–OA₃ₛ– like–IND   Mariam
    'He likes Mariam'

(8) a. Ø – na – tak – a   ch–ai?   [-SA] Clause
       pres–want–IND 7–tea
    '(Do you) want tea?'

    b. Ø – ta–ku – chun – a   [-SA] Clause
       fut–OA₂ₛ–pinch–IND
    '(I) will pinch you'

3.1 Theoretical Assumptions

I assume a strong version of Baker's (1988) Mirror Principle in which the overt order of morphemes is a direct indicator of the hierarchical order of phrase structure, as in 9.

(9) Order of Morphemes   Hierarchical phrase structure
     A-B-C   →   [A [B [C]]]   (or the exact reverse)

From (5-6) and (9), I assume a structure of the Swahili clause as shown in (10a), in which AgrSP dominates a syncretic, or unitary, category of TP and MoodP in the sense of Giorgi & Pianesi, 1997; Bobaljik & Thrainsson, 1998; Deen & Hyams, 2006). This syncretic nature of TP/MoodP will not have any direct bearing on this paper, which deals only with indicative clauses in Swahili in which MoodP is not activated, and thus we may simply assume that in all the examples in this paper, the syncretic category is equivalent to TP, as shown in (10b).

(10)   a.   b.

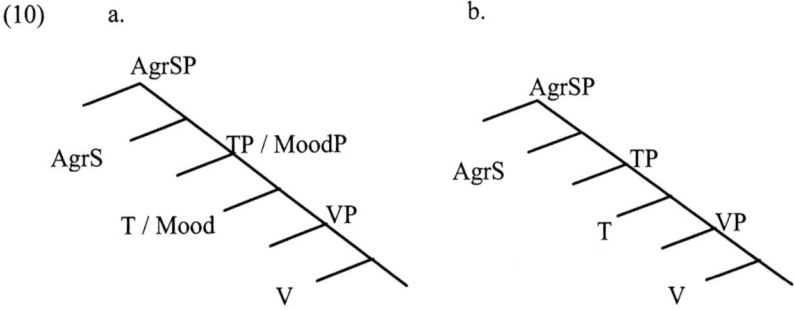

Finally, because Swahili is a null subject language of the familiar sort, I assume that null subjects are identified by the presence of rich agreement, and licensed by the presence of tense (as in Rizzi, 1986 and elsewhere).

(11)   Identification Requirement: rich agreement *identifies* null subjects
            Licensing Requirement: Tense *licenses* all subjects   (Rizzi, 1986)

The Licensing Requirement may be recast in alternative terms such as case checking or case licensing, but the underlying principle that motivates the Licensing Requirement is that there exists an abstract relationship between the specification of tense and the presence of a subject. So irrespective of which approach to the Licensing Requirement one wishes to take, this relationship is acknowledged and accepted by all approaches to generative syntax.

4. Data and Results

The data come from biweekly recordings of naturalistic speech in the homes of four children in Nairobi, Kenya (see table 3). The data were audio recorded and transcribed using CHAT format. The data were organized into four developmental stages based upon MLU, Verb-Ratio and the rate of monosyllabic place holders that occurred in the speech of each child.

Table 3. Subject information

Child	Haw	Mus	Fau	Has
Age range	2;2 – 2;6	2;0 – 2;11	1;8 – 2;2	2;10 – 3;1
#of recordings	7	23	10	5
MLU	1.54–2.46	1.52–3.57	2.97–3.93	3.15–4.23
V Ratio	.07-.14	.05-.17	.20-.36	.30-.40

An analysis of the child speech in these recordings reveals that Swahili children, just like adults, do indeed produce full clauses and [-SA] clauses. However, in addition to these two clause types, Swahili children also produce two clause types not attested in adult Swahili, all four of which are shown in (12). The rates of each clause type are given in table 4, organized by developmental stage. Note the second-to-last column which shows that Root Infinitives are NOT attested in child Swahili. For more details on these results and their implications for modern generative theories of the acquisition of inflection, see Deen (2006).

(12)　　Attested Indicative Clause types in child Swahili

　　　　a.　　Full Clause　　　　　　　　SA – T – V
　　　　b.　　[-SA] Clause　　　　　　　Ø – T – V
　　　　c.　　[-T] Clause　　　　　　　　SA – Ø – V
　　　　d.　　Bare Stem　　　　　　　　　Ø – Ø – V

Table 4. Proportion of different clause types in stages 1 though 4

Stage	Full clause	[-SA] clause	[-T] clause	Bare stem	RI	Total
	SA-T-V	Ø-T-V	SA-Ø-V	Ø-Ø-V	INF-V	
1	18% (39)	29% (60)	**20% (42)**	32% (67)	0.9% (2)	210
2	20% (58)	52% (154)	**8% (25)**	19% (55)	1% (3)	295
3	51% (235)	36% (166)	**5% (21)**	7% (34)	0.9% (4)	460
4	60% (225)	28% (104)	**7% (26)**	4% (15)	1.8% (7)	377

The focus of our attention for this paper are the [-T] clauses (12c), which are verbs that contain Subject Agreement, but are missing the tense morpheme. These clause types are utterly unattested in adult speech, except a few tokens that occur purely and very clearly as speech errors. Additionally, adult Swahili

speakers categorically reject [-T] clauses as utterly ungrammatical. I therefore conclude that [-T] clauses do not exist in the input because:
(i)   they are ungrammatical in adult Swahili, and
(ii)   the few *apparent* tokens that occur are clearly speech errors.

So if [-T] clauses are not modeled in the input, what exactly are they? An examination of child [-T] clauses reveals the following properties. First, in terms of their morphological structure, they contain SA, no Tense marker, and the mood final vowel is always indicative. Furthermore, the interpretation of these clauses (which is determined from context), is always temporal and not modal, and it is not restricted to either past or present. Finally, there does not appear to be any discourse restriction on their occurrence, although I do not rule out such a possibility. These properties are summarized in (13). In (14) I provide a few examples of [-T] clauses taken from various corpora.[2] However, the most interesting property of [-T] clauses is their occurrence with grammatical subjects, to which we now turn.

(13)   Properties of [-T] clauses (in child Swahili):
a. Contain SA, but not T: SA – Ø – V – IND
b. The final vowel, which marks mood, is always INDICATIVE
c. The interpretation of these clauses is always temporal.
d. The intended temporal interpretation is both past as well as present.
e. No apparent discourse condition associated with their occurrence.

(14)   a.   ni – Ø – kw – ambi – a   Fau, 1;10.02
target: ni – na – kw – ambi – a
                SA_{1s}–pres–OA_{2s}–tell–IND
                'I am telling you.'

         b.   ni – Ø – pit – a   Mus, 2;3.05
target: ni – me – pit – a
                SA_{1s}– p.perf. – pass – IND
                'I have passed (through).'

         c.   alafu a – Ø – rud – i   Haw, 2;6.05
target: alafu a – li – rud – i
                then SA_{3s}–past–return–IND
                'Then he returned.'

We can start with the *rate* of overt subjects in adult full clauses. As shown in table 5, adults use overt subjects in full clauses at a rate of about 16.7%. The rate of overt subjects in child full clauses is a little higher, but roughly the same, as shown in the first column of data in table 6. But as shown in the right-most column of table 6, overt subjects almost never occur in [-T] context – of the 114 tokens of [-T] clauses, only four occur with an overt subject. These four tokens are listed in (15).

Table 5. Subjects in adult full clauses

	Adults
Overt Subjects	230 (16.7%)
Null Subjects	1150
Total	1380

Table 6.Subjects in child [-T] clauses

Subject	Full Clauses	[-T] Clauses
Overt	132 (23.6%)	4 (3.5%)
Null	425	110
Total	557	114

Of these four, three may potentially be eliminated from consideration, for various reasons. (15b) is more likely a case of a misanalyzed verb root (the child misanalysing the verb root *namaza* as consisting of present tense *na* and verb root maza); (15b) is likely an incorrect final vowel (given the target subjunctive meaning) and (15c) is likely a case of phonological coalescence. Space prevents a full explication of the reasoning for each example, but it is sufficient to state that 4 out of 114 is a conservative count.

(15)   a.   mimi ni – fungu – a
               I SA_{1s}– open –IND
      Target =   mimi ni – na – fung– a
               I SA_{1s}–pres–open–IND
               'I am closing (it)'

      b.   mimi ni – namaz – a
               I SA_{1s}–be quiet–IND
      Target =   mimi ni – na – namaz – a
               I SA_{1s} – pres – be quiet – IND
               'I am being quiet'

      c.   dadi   ni – um – a
               Daddy SA_{1s}–hurt–IND
      Target =   Daddy, ni – ku – um – e
               Daddy SA_{1s}–OA_{2s}–hurt–SUBJ
               'Daddy, I will/want to hurt you'

      d.   taa   iy – ek – a   ndani
               light-9 SA_9–be on–IND in
      Target =   Taa   i – na –wak– a   ndani
               light-9 SA_9–prs–be on–IND in
               'The light is on inside'

How do we account for the absence of overt subjects in [-T] clauses? There are several possibilities. First, this could be mere chance or a fluke of the data. In order to assess this possibility, two chi-square tests were performed. First, the difference between the rate of overt subjects in full clauses and the rate of overt subjects in

[-T] clauses was found to be statistically significant (chi-square = 21.833, p<0.001). The difference, moreover, was massively significant.

Furthermore, a hypothetical distribution was generated in which zero overt subjects out of 114 tokens occur and the difference between this hypothetical zero distribution and that of [-T] clauses was found NOT to be significant (chi-square = 2.290, p=0.10, 2.706). Given these statistical indications, as well as the fact that at least three of the four overt subject tokens are questionable, I conclude that this low rate of subjects in [-T] clauses is in fact an *absence* of subjects, and that this absence is not due to chance.

A second possibility is that this absence of subjects in [-T] clauses is modeled from the input, and thus this is a simple case of data-driven acquisition. However, as has been stated several times already, [-T] clauses are utterly ungrammatical in the adult language. Furthermore, of the total 1614 indicative clauses coded from the adult tiers of the corpora, only 8 potential [-T] clauses occur, all 8 of which are clear cases of speech error. Additionally, all 8 of these speech errors are essentially mispronounced subjunctives (as indicated by their modal meanings). The fact that none of the *[-T] clauses* are modal indicates that these 8 adult errors are not the model for [-T] clauses. Unless one assumes that children are oblivious to the intentional properties of child-directed speech, these 8 tokens of errors cannot possibly constitute a reasonable model for [-T] clauses.

An advocate of data-driven acquisition may argue that additional sources of generalization may still be available. Specifically, perhaps this relationship between tense and subjects is manifested elsewhere in the input, and the child is simply generalizing from that alternative construction. The only possible candidate constructions of this sort are those in which tense is absent. These are listed in (16). Thus the contention is that perhaps the absence of subjects in tenseless environments is modeled in subjunctives (or imperatives or infinitives), and children generalize this principle from subjunctives to [-T] clauses.

(16)   Tenseless clauses in Swahili: a.   Subjunctives
                                            b.   Imperatives
                                            c.   Infinitives

The first, initially plausible, source from which the child might draw knowledge of the Licensing Requirement is subjunctives, exemplified in (17), and whose morphological structure is schematized in (18a). Subjunctives occur with subject agreement, no tense marking, and a subjunctive final vowel. When compared to the structure of a [-T] clause, schematized in (18b), these two clause types are strikingly similar, with the only difference being the final vowel. Thus the subjunctive is an excellent candidate for a model for the child.

(17)   tafadhali ni - pat - i - **e**   ch – ai
         please OA_{1s}–give–APPL–SUBJ 7-tea
         'Please give me (some) tea'

(18)   a. Morphological structure of a subjunctive: SA – Ø – V – SUBJ
         b. Morphological structure of a [-T] clause: SA – Ø – V – IND

However, there are two good reasons to discount this possibility. First, subjunctives are always associated with a modal or irrealis meaning in Swahili, while [-T] clauses are never associated with irrealis. As we saw earlier, almost all [-T] clauses are associated with a temporal meaning, either past or here and now. So interpretive differences suggest that subjunctives are not the model for [-T] clauses. Secondly, subjunctives in adult Swahili occur with subjects. Thus if children were modeling [-T] clauses after subjunctives, we would expect children to produce some overt subjects, just as in subjunctives.

The second potential source for generalization is imperatives (see 19, schematized in 20a). However, just as in the case of subjunctives, imperatives are always associated with deontic modality, and none of the [-T] clauses are used in this way. Furthermore, imperatives in Swahili (as in English) allow overt emphatic subjects, which again serves as exactly the wrong model for the child. So it is remarkable that children in fact ignore this conflicting data and exhibit a much less obvious, a much less modeled pattern in their subject use.[3]

(19)   nunu – a   m – kate
         buy – IND   3 – bread
         'Buy bread!'

(20)   a. Morphological structure of an imperative: Ø – Ø – V – IND
         b. Morphological structure of a [-T] clause: SA – Ø – V – IND

A third possible source of modeling in the input is infinitives (exemplified in 21, schematized in 22a). There are several reasons to be skeptical that infinitives are the source of the Licensing Requirement in [-T] clauses. First, infinitives in the child-directed speech occur almost exclusively in embedded clauses, unlike [-T] clauses. And perhaps because of this, infinitives are almost always associated with some kind of modal meaning, depending on the matrix verb under which it is embedded. Third, infinitives differ from [-T] clauses in that the absence of tense is overtly marked in the case of infinitives. It is unclear why children would assume that an infinitive is the equivalent of a [-T] clause in terms of the absence of tense (one is overtly marked for the absence of T in the form of an infinitive morpheme, the other is not), but not in terms of meaning or syntactic distribution. Related to this, infinitives also sometimes allow overt subjects (e.g., "I want *John* to leave now"). If the child were using the infinitive as the source for generalization, one might reasonably suppose that children would produce at least some Root Infinitives, contrary to fact. Thus there are significant syntactic, semantic and morphological differences between infinitives and [-T] clauses that make a straight-forward generalization unlikely.

(21)   Ni - na - tak - a **ku** - ondok - a sasa
         SA$_{1s}$–pres–want–IND   INF-leave-IND now
         'I want to leave now.'

(22)   a. Morphological structure of an infinitive: INF – V – IND
         b. Morphological structure of a [-T] clause: SA – Ø – V – IND

5. Concluding Remarks

In this paper I have shown that children acquiring Swahili produce utterances that are unmodeled in the input. Moreover, within this unmodeled utterance type, children adhere to an abstract principle of syntax for which there is no direct evidence. We investigated the possibility that this knowledge was derived through some sort of generalization from other utterances in the input, and we conclude that not only is there no feasible alternative model in the input from which the child could derive the Licensing Requirement, but that there are several tenseless clause types in the input which would lead the child in exactly the wrong direction.[4]

So what does this leave? The final possible explanation of this absence of subjects in [-T] clauses is a natural one for generative linguists because this absence of subjects in [-T] clauses follows immediately and directly from a principle of language that we have known of for many years now: the Licensing Requirement of Rizzi (1986). Thus Swahili children produce tenseless clauses that are:

(i)   Utterly unmodeled in the input
(ii)   Express knowledge of the Licensing Requirement on subjects.

I believe that this constitutes evidence for innate knowledge that appears to be highly specific to language, and indeed of a very detailed, articulated nature. It is highly unlikely that the evidence for this knowledge is the result of chance or statistical fluke, and this knowledge could not reasonably have been derived from any model in the input. This constitutes a novel perspective on the Poverty of the Stimulus in that knowledge of abstract principles of language are attested in the errors of children, thereby bypassing any subjective debate regarding how much evidence is sufficient in the input.

Notes

[1] For a critical re-assessment of this result, see Gualmini (2006). I don't wish to focus on the veracity of Lidz et. al's result, but rather the contention that a low rate of evidence in the input is sufficient to acquire language (see ensuing discussion in the text).

[2] Please note that [-T] clauses are *not* the equivalent of root infinitives in Swahili. There are several reasons for this, including structural and interpretive differences, although this depends on one's definition of RI/OI. [-T] clauses may be counted as OIs if one adopts Wexler's (1998) definition as including all those non-adultlike tenseless clauses.

[3] The fact that adult Swahili allows subjects in imperatives and subjunctives appears (on the surface at least) to violate the Licensing Requirement since these are tenseless clauses that allow overt subjects. However, I contend that the Licensing Requirement is subject to parametric variation in terms of which features participate in this licensing relationship. In some languages, tense is the only functional head that participates in this relationship, while in other languages, it may be other categories that license subjects, e.g., agreement, aspect, or mood. Imperatives and subjunctives in Swahili are fully specified for mood, and thus mood in Swahili licenses overt subjects. For more on this point see Deen & Hyams (2006).

[4] Thanks to Takuya Goro for discussion on this point.

References

Akhtar, N., Callanan,M., Pullum, G. & B. Scholz (2004) Learning antecedents for anaphoric one. *Cognition*, 93, 2, Sept, 141-145.

Baker, C. L (1978) *Introduction to Generative-Transformational Syntax*. Englewood Cliffs, NJ: Prentice-Hall.

Baker, M. (1988) *Incorporation: A Theory of Grammatical Function Changing*. Chicago: University of Chicago Press.

Bobaljik, J., & H. Thrainsson, (1998) Two heads aren't always better than one. *Syntax* 1:37-71.

Chomsky, N. (1971) *Problems of Knowledge and Freedom*. London: Fontana.

Crain, S. & M. Nakayama, (1987) Structure dependence in grammar formation. *Language* 63: 522.543.

Deen, K. U (2003) Underspecified verb forms and subject omission in Nairobi Swahili. in Beachley, B., A. Brown and F. Conlin, eds., *The Proceedings of the 27th Annual Boston University Conference on Language Development*, Somerville, MA: Cascadilla Press, 220-231.

—. (2006) *The Acquisition of Swahili*. Amsterdam, Netherlands: John Benjamins Publishing.

—. & N. Hyams, (2006) The morphosyntax of mood in early grammar with special reference to Swahili. To appear in a special issue of *First Language*, 2006.

Giorgi, A. & F. Pianesi, (1997) *Tense and Aspect: from Semantics to Morphosyntax*. Oxford: Oxford University Press

Gualmini, A. (2006) On that *One* Debate. Unpublished ms. McGill University.

Lidz, J., Waxman, S. and J. Freedman, (2003) What infants know about syntax but couldn't have learned: experimental evidence for syntactic structure at 18 months. *Cognition* 89, B65–B73.

Rizzi, L. (1986) Null objects in Italian and the theory of pro. *Linguistic Inquiry* 17, 501-557.

Wexler, K. (1998) Very early parameter setting and the unique checking constraint: A new explanation of the optional infinitive stage. *Lingua* 106:23-79.

FEATURES AND *AGREE* RELATIONS IN L2 GREEK

MARIA DIMITRAKOPOULOU, GEORGIA FOTIADOU, ANNA ROUSSOU, AND IANTHI MARIA TSIMPLI

1. Introduction

Variation in the linguistic performance of L2 speakers of various L1s in terms of morphological production is attested even at advanced stages of acquisition and has been accounted for by alternative views in the generative framework. According to representational deficit accounts (Hawkins & Chan 1997, Tsimpli 2003), inconsistent use of target forms is viewed as evidence of an underlying deficit in syntactic representations since inaccuracy, although less frequent at more advanced stages of acquisition, qualitatively differentiates the L2 learner from the native speaker. With respect to the relation between narrow syntax and the morpho(pho)nological component, Smith & Tsimpli (1995) argue that the two develop independently in L2A and the mapping between them is not a straightforward process.

The alternative view, the Missing Surface Inflection Hypothesis (Haznedar & Schwartz 1997, Lardiere 1998, Prévost & White 2000), maintains that syntax and morphology in L2A do not develop in a parallel fashion (see also Smith & Tsimpli ibid). This dissociation is reflected by the inaccurate production of functional free or bound morphemes, which, as proponents of this theory argue, is caused by the inability to access the target morphological form and not of a problem with underlying syntactic representations. Finally, it has been suggested that variation at the syntax/morphology interface is the result of a conflict between the grammar and the parser, which is responsible for mapping syntactic objects into phonetic realizations and on which processing constraints and memory limitations apply (Juffs 1998, Felser et al 2003, a.o.).

This paper seeks to evaluate the two hypotheses by examining the production of morphological agreement in different domains (TP and DP) by L1 Slavic/L2Greek speakers and by analysing cases of agreement mismatch in terms of locality and the type of features involved. Furthermore, by looking at the developmental pattern, it aims to establish a correlation between length of stay and L2 development.

2. Agreement morphology in Greek and Slavic

Agree is an operation of the computational system and, as such, universally available, while there are cross linguistic differences in terms of spell-out properties of agreement features. In Greek, morphological agreement is found in the following domains: verbal (TP), realized as subject agreement suffix on the verb, nominal (DP), realized on all the elements found in the DP, and long-distance, namely, between a (null) subject and a predicate or between a clitic and its DP-antecedent. In each agreement relation, different features may be involved. Case, which is an uninterpretable feature both on the head noun and on the elements that agree with it, is morphologically realized in the DP domain and also on clitics. Person and number are found in all instances of verbal agreement as well as on clitics. Gender is relevant to the nominal domain and is also realized on 3rd person accusative and possessive clitics but not in the verbal domain.

In the Slavic L1s of our subjects, all of the above features also take part in agreement relations albeit differently in some cases. For instance, Russian possessive modifiers agree with the possessor and with the head noun in whose domain they are merged (Rappaport 1998). Specifically, 1st and 2nd person possessive forms agree with the head NP in number/case and in gender - when in singular. In contrast, all Greek possessive clitics only agree with the possessor.

3. Predictions

Since *Agree* is a UG operation of the computational component, it is expected to be available in L2A (cf. Smith & Tsimpli 1995, who argue for the availability of UG operations in second language development). Thus, learners should show evidence of agreement in various types of dependencies where agreement is required. Variation in the L2 output may be due to either feature-specification at the syntactic level or a mapping problem (MSI). In the former case, we expect differential use of agreement morphology depending on the interpretability of the feature (Tsimpli & Dimitrakopoulou in press) while in the latter case there should be effects of locality between the head and the agreeing elements.

4. The study

The data were collected in the period between 2002 and 2004 and came from oral interviews with 39 adult Slavic (Russian and Serbian) speakers of Greek, all immigrants and learning Greek in a naturalistic setting (see Table 1). The interviews consisted of four parts: i) conversation on biographical details relevant to the subject's exposure to the L2 etc, ii) story-telling through the description of eight sets of pictures, iii) two instruction-giving tasks and iv) general discussion on every-day life topics.

Table 1. Information on the participants (Mean / Standard Deviation)

	Length of stay	Age at time of test	MLU
Group 1	2.7 (SD: .70)	37 (SD: 10.1)	4.25 (SD: 1.18)
Group 2	6.9 (SD: .96)	39.5 (SD: 9.36)	5.43 (SD: 1.71)
Group 3	13.6 (SD: 5.20)	46 (SD: 9.35)	5.97 (SD: 1.71)

5. Results

5.1. Between-group results

Table 2 shows the percentages of agreement mismatches in the types of dependencies investigated.

Table 2. % of agreement mismatches for each type of dependency

Agreement domains	Group 1	Group 2	Group 3
Subject-Verb	4.5	3	2.1
inside DP	19.3	14.5	11.1
Subject-Predicative adjective	19	25.6	23.1
Acc. clitic-DP antecedent	26	25.3	19.3
Poss. clitic- DP antecedent	58.3	35.9	33.3

The almost target performance in the case of subject agreement indicates that this is the least problematic agreement relation. Furthermore, there is a developmental pattern since there are significant differences across groups (Groups 1/2: χ^2= 8.50, p< .01; Groups 2/3: χ^2= 4.61, p<.05).

The nominal domain seems to be more vulnerable than the verbal one as the percentages of mismatches are generally higher. However, groups differ significantly in the case of agreement within DP, indicating effect of length of exposure to language on performance (Groups 1/2: χ^2= 10.52, p< .01, Groups 2/3: χ^2= 37.56, p<.01). Agreement between the possessive clitic and the possessor seems to be the most problematic, as is shown by the comparatively high percentage of agreement mismatches. This could be due to the fact that possessive clitics are embedded within a DP and are morphophonologically influenced by the features of the head noun. In fact, in 60% of errors in Group 2 and over 90% in Group 3, the possessive clitic agrees in gender or/and number with the host DP instead of the antecedent. However, groups show a developmental pattern as group 1 differs significantly from group 2 ($\chi^2 = 6.24$, $p < .01$) and group 3 ($\chi^2 = 6.44$, $p < .01$).

5.2. Within-group results

Effect of features on performance: Table 3 is informative with respect to the features responsible for most agreement mismatches.

Table 3. Distribution of agreement errors according to features (% and cases)

	Gender	Number	Person	Case
Group 1	57.4% (191)	30.6% (102)	8.7% (9)	3.3% (11)
Group 2	70.8% (252)	23.6% (84)	2.8% (10)	2.8% (10)
Group 3	73.9% (215)	21.3% (62)	1% (3)	3.8% (11)

Gender causes the most learnability problems even for group 3 (with the longest exposure to Greek). On the other hand, person and the uninterpetable feature of case are the least problematic in production.

Effect of locality/complexity on performance: Agreement mismatches in the DP-domain are mostly related to determiners (48-56%) and are not affected by the complexity of the DP (i.e. the number of elements in the DP).

For the rest of the dependencies, we examined the distribution of agreement errors on the basis of the distance of the antecedent, i.e. whether it was in the same clause as the agreeing element or not (see Table 4).

Table 4. Agreement mismatches with a non-local antecedent (% and cases)

	Group 1	Group 2	Group 3
Subj.-Verb	63.5% (68/107)*	60% (52/87)	71.5% (45/63)*
Subj-Pred.	28.6% (8/28)*	25% (11/44)*	31.8% (7/24)*
Clitic-DP	82.2% (32/45)*	85% (34/40)*	83% (39/47)*

*= significant effect of locality on performance.

Generally, effect of locality on performance was found in the TP domain and in the object clitic-DP dependency but not in the subject-predicate dependency.

It might be the case that a *pro* subject improves predicate agreement (presumably a spell-out economy constraint). Note that in the case of subject-verb agreement, most of the mismatches occur in null-subject contexts. There, however, agreement is spelled out on the verb only.

6. General conclusions

Generally, analysis of the data showed that verbal agreement is acquired, in line with other studies that show low percentages of verbal agreement errors (cf. Bruhn de Garavito 2003). A developmental pattern was also attested in the nominal domain and in possessive clitic dependencies.

Effects of locality were found to affect performance. More specifically, mismatches occurred mostly when the antecedent was outside the clause that included the agreeing element. Moreover, the morphological features of head nouns in DPs including possessive clitics were found to influence the feature marking of the clitic. Effects of morphophonological influence on grammatical processing were attested in a study that investigated the production of subject-verb number agreement by native speakers of Dutch and German (Hartsuiker et al 2003). The data thus point to a processing difficulty in L2A that might cause failure to access the correct morphophonological form.

With respect to the role of features in the production of inaccurate morphology, it was found that gender is largely responsible for the problems in the nominal domain. Although gender is also a feature of the participants' L1s, gender agreement seems to follow two strategies in L2 learners: (a) phonological agreement (phonological harmony, amounting to 31% of cases, or by analogy with frequent phonological combinations of Det+N, amounting to 51.4%) or (b) default use of (neuter) determiner (13%). Hence, inaccuracy in gender agreement may be due to the phonological information of the head noun, which affects the retrieval of the target morphophonological form.

In view of the above, we would like to suggest that the Missing Surface Inflection hypothesis is a plausible explanation for the agreement errors reported in the study.

References

Bruhn de Garavito, J. and L., White (2000) "L2 Acquisition of Spanish DPs: the status of grammatical features," in C. Howell, S. Fish and T. Keith-Lucas, eds., *Proceedings of the 24ᵗʰ Annual BUCLD*, Cascadilla P., Somerville, MA, 164-175.

Felser, C., L. Roberts, R. Gross and T. Marinis (2003) "The processing of ambiguous sentences by first and second language learners of English," in *Applied Psycholinguistics* 24, 453-489.

Hartsuiker, R, J., H. J. Schriefers, K. Bock and G. M. Kikstra (2003) "Morphological influences on the construction of subject verb agreement," in *Memory and Cognition* 31, 1316-1326.

Hawkins, R. and Y. Chan (1997) "The partial availability of Universal Grammar in second language acquisition: the 'failed functional features hypothesis'," in *Second Language Research* 13, 187-226.

Haznedar, B. and B. D. Schwartz (1997) "Are there optional infinitives in child L2 acquisition?" in E. Hughes, M. Hughes and A. Greenhill, eds., *Proceedings of the 21st Annual BUCLD*. Cascadilla P., Somerville, MA, 257-268.

Juffs, A. (1998) "Some effects of first language argument structure and morphosyntax on second language sentence processing," in *Second Language Research* 14, 406-424.

Lardiere, D. (1998) "Dissociating syntax from morphology in a divergent L2 end-state grammar," in *Second Language Research* 14, 359-375.

Prévost, P. and L. White (2000) "Missing Surface Inflection or Impairment in second language acquisition? Evidence from tense and agreement," in *Second Language Research* 16, 103-133.

Rappaport, G. (1998) "The Slavic Noun Phrase," Position paper in the *Comparative Slavic Morphosyntax* Workshop, Spencer, Indiana. Available at http://www.indiana.edu/~slavconf/linguistics/rapp.pdf

Smith, N. and I. M. Tsimpli (1995) *The Mind of a Savant: Language Learning and Modularity*, Blackwell, Oxford.

Tsimpli, I .M. (2003) "Clitics and determiners in L2 Greek," in J. M. Liceras, H. Zobl and H. Goodluck, eds., *Proceedings of the 6th Generative Approaches to Second Language Acquisition Conference,* Cascadilla P., Somerville, MA, 331-339.

—. & M. Dimitrakopoulou (in press) "The Interpretability Hypothesis: Evidence from *wh*-interrogatives", in *Second Language Research.*

EMERGENCE OF PRINCIPLE B: A VARIABLE-FREE APPROACH

OLGA FEDOROVA AND IGOR YANOVICH

1. Acquisition of Principle B: The standard approach.

Since the first experiments on the acquisition of pronominal reference it is well known that children respond to Principle A sentences nearly as good as adults, with the error rate around 10%, while children's performance in Principle B sentences is much worse. The main focus in Principle B acquisition studies since Chien & Wexler (1990) has been the difference between children's performance in contexts with referential or quantified DPs as illicit antecedents. Chien & Wexler (1990) found that children aged 5-6 in the mismatch condition of the Truth-Value Judgment task correctly rejected sentences with quantified antecedents in 80% of cases and only in 50% of cases with referential antecedents.

This effect has been explained with the help of the Binding Theory of Reinhart (1983). Under this version of the Binding Theory (and its descendants), there is a crucial difference between bound-variable and coreference construals of pronouns: while the former are directly banned by the syntactic part of the binding theory, Chomsky (1981), the latter cannot be ruled out in the syntax, because the syntax just cannot "see" the fact that the pronouns are actually coreferential with their antecedents: it can be seen in the semantics only. What rules out the coreference construal for sentences like $Bill_i$ hit him_i under these theories is some version of Principle I (Grodzinsky & Reinhart (1993): the coreference construal is always banned if there is a banned bound-variable construal with the indistinguishable meaning. Note that this principle is crucially trans-derivational: to check if a coreference construal is possible, we must check the corresponding (possibly ungrammatical!) bound-variable construal. It is obvious that such a computation is extremely costly. However, this very fact allows for the standard, by now, explanation of Chien & Wexler's (1990) data: since checking the well-formedness of a coreference construal is much harder than checking that of a bound-variable construal, we expect children to make more errors with coreference construals. Coreference construals are possible when the antecedent is a referential DP and not possible when it is a quantified DP. Thus we expect more errors with referential DPs: in this case children are forced to compute the grammaticality of a coreference construal, but can hardly accomplish this difficult computation.

However, this important pattern of results is not the only interesting thing about the acquisition of Principle B. Here, we examine a different set of data, namely, the children's performance in one-clause and two-clause Principle B sentences that, despite the fact that the results were obtained long ago, has not, to our knowledge, received attention in the literature.

Solan (1987) presented Act-Out data from 5 and 6 year-olds: they performed correct acting-out only in 50% cases for 2-clause sentences like *The dog said that the horse hit him.* Similar chance-level results were reported in Jacubowicz (1984) for younger children. However, Chien & Wexler (1990) who tested Principle B in children aged 2;6-7;10 using 1-clause stimuli like *This is Mama Bear. This is Goldilocks. Is Mama Bear touching her?* in the Truth-Value Judgment task, received 90% right answers in the 'match'-condition, i.e. when the right answer to the question was "yes". (The well-known difference between quantified and referential DPs obtained in that study affects the mismatch condition only.) Similar results were presented in Kaufmann (1987) and Grimshaw & Rosen (1990).

The Act-Out task corresponds to the match condition of the Truth-Value task, since in both cases children do not need to decline anything, and it is exactly the need to reject something that makes the mismatch condition harder for children. But still we have a huge difference between the 1-clause Act-Out data and the 2-clause Truth-Value Judgment match condition data, namely, **50% of errors** in the former case vs. **10% of errors** in the latter.

Can this difference be caused by the methodology? No, it cannot: First, in Thornton & Wexler's (1999) Truth-Value Judgment Task with 2-clause sentences like *Every Cabbage Patch boy said that Superman likes him*, the children's performance was around 50%, as in the early Act-Out 2-clause stimuli experiments.

Secondly, we conducted a pilot study on 20 Russian children aged 2;11 to 6;3 with the 1-clause stimuli analogous to those of Chien & Wexler (1990): *Eto slon, eto kot. Pokazhi, kak slon potrogaet ego* 'This is an elephant, this is a cat. Show how the elephant touches him'. Each child was asked to act out 6 reflexive sentences and 6 pronominal sentences. There were no errors at all in reflexive sentences, and there were only 3 errors (out of 120 trials) with pronominals, that is, 97.5% of answers were adult-like. It is comparable to Truth-Value Judgment results for 1-clause stimuli.

We conclude that the 10%-50% difference is caused not by the choice of methodology, but by the structure of stimuli: children make around 50% of errors with 2-clause stimuli and only around 10% of errors with 1-clause stimuli.

The problem with these data is that none of the existing theories can explain them. Reinhart (1983) can explain the differences between quantified and referential contexts, and that is why every current theory used in the field of Principle B acquisition is its descendant. However, while it explains the referential vs. quantificational differences, it fails to explain the 1- vs. 2-clause differences.

Under (any variant of) Reinhart (1983), anaphora in the 1-clause sentences is predicted to be more complex for the child than in the 2-clause sentences. In the 1-clause stimuli, the proper antecedent is in the preceding sentence and thus cannot c-command the pronoun; if the antecedent does not c-command the pronoun, than only the coreference construal is possible, not the bound-variable one; coreference construals involve more resource-consuming computation, and thus the child makes more errors when forced to compute the possibility of such a construal. On the other hand, in the 2-clause stimuli case the antecedent does c-command the pronoun, and the bound-variable construal is possible. Cf. Reinhart (2004): "binding is a more efficient way to obtain anaphora than coreference. So whenever possible (in configurational terms), it is the only anaphora option ..." Thus the 2-clause stimuli in which the pronoun is in a configuration when a bound-variable construal is possible are predicted to be much easier than the 1-clause stimuli in which no bound-variable construal is available (and according to the latest Reinhart's work, we must find a chance-level error rate with such stimuli). However, the actual pattern is precisely the reverse: children make around 50% of errors in the 2-clause type predicted to be easier, and only 10% of errors in the 1-clause type that is predicted to be more complex.

2. Variable-free binding theory

Instead of trying to accommodate the problematic data above into the standard theory, we develop an extension to an alternative binding theory of Jacobson (1999). Jacobson's variable-free binding theory was shown to be superior to the Chomsky-Reinhart binding theory in explaining such phenomena as across-the-board binding, paycheck pronouns, implicit variable binding, parasitic gaps, etc. Under Jacobson's original theory, pronoun meanings are identity functions, and there are several type-shift rules that allow to perform the binding. However, Jacobson does not account for Principles A and B effects.

We propose an extension to her theory, analyzing binding conditions as *parts of the meanings of the pronouns* rather than filter restrictions introduced in

Principles A and B of Chomsky (1981). We define PRON and REFL predicates and use them in our pronoun meanings, narrowing the domain of the identity function in the same way as it is narrowed by the animacy and gender conditions. For instance, [[he]] = λx.[human(x) & male(x) & **PRON(x)**]. The predicates REFL and PRON are dynamically updated, so that at any point of the derivation REFL is true of discourse referents denoted by all DPs c-commanding the current node in the binding domain, and PRON is true of discourse referents correspondent to DPs outside of the binding domain. So in a sense, we move the job of defining binding domains from syntax to semantics. Moreover, a new architecture for semantics is needed, including a fine-grained context allowing dynamic predicates to be updated in the course of the derivation, see Fedorova & Yanovich (2005) for discussion.

We argue that these two predicates and the mechanism for their update are an innate part of the human computational system, and that binding conditions work not on abstract structural domains, as in the standard theory, but on the speaker's representation of these domains—these constantly updated predicates.

Note that the crucial stage in the process of PRON and REFL update is the crossing of clause boundaries. Namely, when an adult speaker starts the processing of a new clause, she performs the following: she 1) erases the old contents of REFL (so that it would be true of no referent) and 2) updates PRON for the erased referents (so that PRON would be true of those referents that have just been erased from REFL).

A child that performs well on the 1-clause stimuli but performs poor on the 2-clause ones is definitely able to cope with the first part of the procedure, that is, she can successfully clear REFL (if she could not, then REFL would be true both of new referents and those introduced earlier, and the child would make errors with reflexives, which she does not do.) We argue that while she can successfully add new elements to PRON during the big pause associated with the whole sentence boundary, she fails to update PRON when she encounters a clause boundary within the sentence, because she is busy with the processing: the structure is more complex; the computational load is high; the resources, such as working memory, are very limited, as compared to those of adults; and moreover, there is no time.

Consider (1) and (2). In the *sentence boundary* case in (1) the child encounters *her* being in state$_2$, when PRON is true of Goldilocks only. So she rightly chooses Goldilocks as the referent, with the accuracy above 90%. The crucial difference between (1) and (2), the *clause boundary* case, is that in (2) the child often fails to update PRON, so it is true of no individual. Thus when the child encounters *her*, she looks if there are referents of which PRON is true, but there are not any. To save the derivation, the child tries to pick up just any discourse referent for *her*, and resorts to guessing. Since there are two referents present the performance is at the chance level, around 50%.

(1)   This is Mama Bear. This is Goldilocks.
        state₁ Mama Bear is washing **state₂** her.
        state₁   REFL: {}   PRON: {MB, G}   All referents: {MB, G}
        state₂   REFL: {MB}   PRON: {G}   All referents: {MB, G}

(2)   Goldilocks **state₃** said that **state₄** Mama Bear is washing **state₅** her.
        state₃   REFL: {G}   PRON: {}   All referents: {MB, G}
        state₄   REFL: {}   PRON: {}   All referents: {MB, G}
        state₅   REFL: {MB}   PRON: {}   All referents: {MB, G}

Thus the variable-free binding theory of Jacobson (1999) combined with our extension to it, stating that binding conditions make reference not to structural domains, but to dynamic predicates corresponding to these domains, allows us to explain the 10%-50% error rate difference between the 1-clause and the 2-clause stimuli. Of course, many open questions remain, the most important of which on the psycholinguistic side is whether such a theory can explain the differences between quantified and referential contexts for which the standard theory provides a viable explanation. We leave this and other questions for future research.

References

Chien, Y.-Ch. and K. Wexler (1990) "Children's Knowledge of Locality Conditions on Binding as Evidence for the Modularity of Syntax and Pragmatics", in *Language Acquisition* 1, 225-295.

Chomsky, N. (1981) *Lectures on Government and Binding*, Foris, Dordrecht.

Fedorova, O. and I. Yanovich (2005) "Lexically modifying binding restrictions: Case for a variable-free binding theory", talk given at CSSP 2005.

Grimshaw, J. and S.T. Rosen (1990) "Knowledge and Obedience: The Developmental Status of the Binding Theory", in *Linguistic Inquiry* 21, 187-222.

Grodzinsky, Y. and T. Reinhart (1993) "The Innateness of Binding and the Development of Coreference", in *Linguistic Inquiry* 24, 69-102.

Jacobson, P. (1999) "Towards a Variable-free Semantics", in *Linguistics and Philosophy* 22, 117-184.

Jacubowicz, C. (1984) "On Markedness and Binding Principles", in *Proceedings of the North Eastern Linguistics Society* 14, 154-182.

Kaufman, D.K. (1987) "Who's him? Evidence for Principle B in child's grammar", in *BUCLD Proceedings* 12, Cascadilla Press, Somerville, Mass.

Reinhart, T. (1983) *Anaphora and Semantic interpretation*, Chicago University Press, Croom-Helm.

—. (2004) "The Processing Cost of Reference-Set Computation: Acquisition of Stress Shift and Focus", in *Language Acquisition* 12, 109-155.

Solan, L. (1987) "Parameter Setting and the Development of Pronouns and Reflexives", in T. Roeper and E. Williams, eds., *Parameter Setting*, Reidel, Dordrecht.

Thornton, R. and K. Wexler (1999) *Principle B, VP Ellipsis and Interpretation in Child Grammar*, MIT Press, Cambridge, MA.

ACQUISITION OF OBJECT CLITICS BY TWO ITALIAN/GERMAN BILINGUAL CHILDREN

IDA FERRARI

1. Introduction

The present study is concerned with the acquisition of object clitics in Italian by two Italian/German bilingual children.

If we assume that German doesn't dispose of this class of pronouns, following Cardinaletti & Starke (1999), in the case under examination, the analysis of the acquisition of clitics becomes particularly interesting in order to verify the early access to two different grammars and possible cross-linguistic influences between them.

2. Data

The corpus of spontaneous production I collected and analysed consists of ten recordings, about 60 minutes each, for the child V. (2.05.28-3.00.18) and nine recordings, about 50 minutes each, for the child E. (2.10.08-3.05.21)[1].

As for the linguistic status of the two children, V. is a nearly balanced bilingual or, adopting the definition of Meisel (1989), a Bilingual First Language Acquirer, since the child has regularly been exposed to both languages from birth. On the other hand, E. can be considered an early German L2 learner or, adopting the definition of De Houwer (1996), a Bilingual Second Language Acquirer as the child has regularly been exposed to German from the second year of life.

However, the linguistic production of the two children is very similar, as it emerges from the data analysis.

3. Quantitative analysis

As object clitics in Romance languages need a verbal host, I first checked if there was a considerable production of verbal utterances in the overall production of the two children. I then considered the verbal utterances that, in target Italian, obligatorily take a direct object complement (accusative case) or an indirect one (dative case) or both.

The charts in 1 report the distribution of object clitics over the period under examination, and we can observe a considerable production of them by both children. The charts in 2, illustrate that during this period both children are acquiring object clitics, as indicated by the decrease of the omissions/occurrences ratio for both of them. At the end of the recordings, we still find some omissions, thus indicating that the acquisition process is still going on. Moreover, these data seem to confirm the average age of object clitics productive use individuated in other studies: two and a half years of age, maybe with some delay for E., (Hamann et al., 1996; Granfeldt & Schlyter, 2004).

(1)

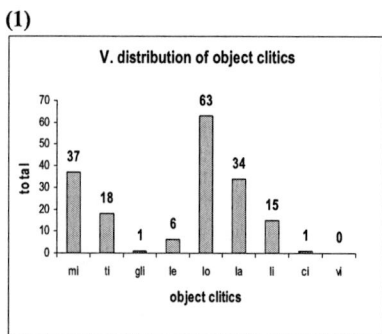

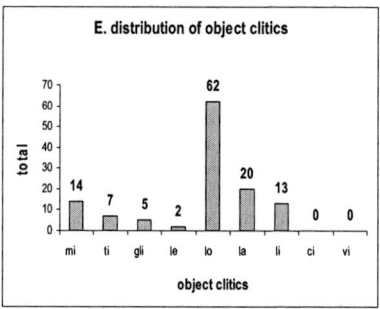

(2)

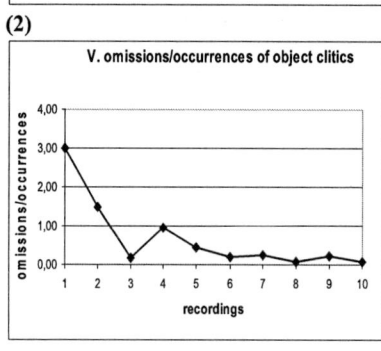

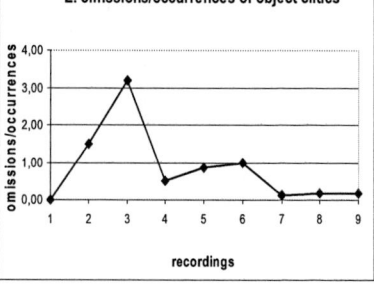

4. Qualitative analysis

From the analysis it emerges that:

➤ Clitics are correctly placed in proclisis with finite verbs.

(1) *V.: ...così li perdi.*
   ...in this way Obj. Cl.$_{3rd\ p.\ pl.}$ lose$_{2nd\ p.\ s.\ ind.\ pres.}$
   '...in this way you lose them.'

➤ They are correctly placed in enclisis with non-finite verbs and in the few cases of affirmative imperatives found in the corpus[2].

(2) *V.: come si fa a aprirlo?*
   How Imp. Subj. make$_{3rd\ p.\ s.\ ind.\ pres.}$ to open$_{inf.}$ Obj. Cl.$_{3rd\ p.\ s.}$?
   'How can you open it?'

(3) *V.: guardalo!*
   Look$_{imper.}$ Obj. Cl.$_{3rd\ p.\ s.}$!
   'Look at it!'

➤ Clitics are not correctly placed in some of the Modal + Infinitive constructions.

(4) *V.: anche tu vuoi lo mangiare?*
   Also you want$_{2nd\ p.\ s.\ ind.\ pres.}$ Obj. Cl.$_{3rd\ p.\ s.}$ eat$_{inf.}$?
   'Do you also want to eat it?'

5. Clitics in Modal + Infinitive constructions

Concerning the non-target occurrences both children produce:
modal + clitic + infinitive (the clitic is in the non-target intermediate position). That happens with accusative clitics and in one occurrence in the E. corpus with a reflexive clitic, as reported in (5).

(5) *E.: voglio mi mettere.*
   Want$_{1st\ p.\ s.\ ind.\ pres.}$ Ref. Cl.$_{1st\ p.\ s.}$ put on$_{inf.}$
   'I want to put on.'

As one of the non-target utterances occurs with a reflexive clitic, we will consider both object and reflexive clitics in the more detailed analysis of the Mod + Inf constructions.

(3a)

	V. clitic placement in mod+inf constructions
Enclisis	2
Proclisis	2
Intemediate position*	7 (63%)
Total	11
Omissions	15
Lexical Complements occurrences	30 + 2^ + 2* + 3#

^ omission of *ne* partitive   * in intermediate position
# topicalized in 1st position

(3b)

	E. clitic placement in mod+inf constructions
Enclisis	/
Proclisis	8
Intemediate position*	3 (27%)
Total	11
Omissions	24
Lexical Complements occurrences	55 + 1* + 1^ + 1#

^ omission of *ne* partitive   * in intermediate position
# topicalized in 1st position

Table (3a) indicates that V. correctly places the clitic in enclisis on the non-finite verb in 2 occurrences. The clitic is correctly located in proclisis on the main verb in 2 cases and it is located in the intermediate position in 7 occurrences, that constitute 63% of the production. Also two lexical complements occur in intermediate position.

In the E. corpus (see table 3b), we do not find any clitics occurring in enclisis, 8 clitics are located in proclisis and 3 in intermediate position constituting 27% of the production. Also in E's data, one lexical complement occurs in intermediate position.

Moreover, some lexical complements occur topicalized in first position in both corpus. This is found throughout the corpora. Indeed it seems that in these cases both children often use German topicalization, that is a complement or an adverb occurring in first position followed by the verb as reported in (6).

(6) *V.: questo voglio attaccare.*
     This I want paste$_{inf.}$
     'I want to paste this one.'

In order to better understand this peculiar production, I compared the occurrences of lexical complements, object clitics and cases of omissions in this specific context, with those in the overall production. As reported in the charts in 4, it emerges that clitic omissions are twice as frequent in the modal + infinitive constructions if compared with those of the overall production, though the occurrences of lexical objects are nearly the same in the two cases. In details if we observe the charts in 4 in the V. corpus the omissions are 9% in the overall production and 24% in modal + infinitive. In the E. corpus omissions constitute 12% in the overall production and 26% in modal + infinitive constructions[3].

(4)

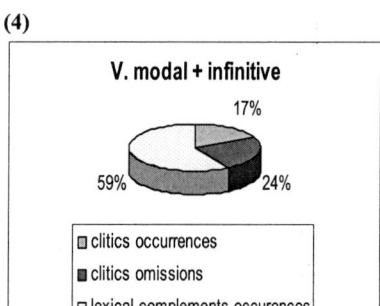

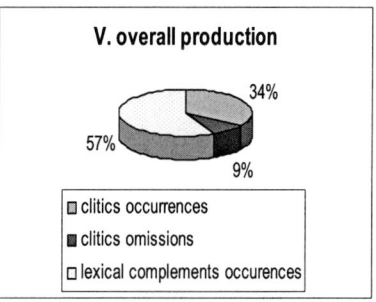

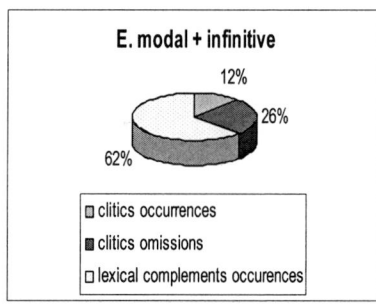

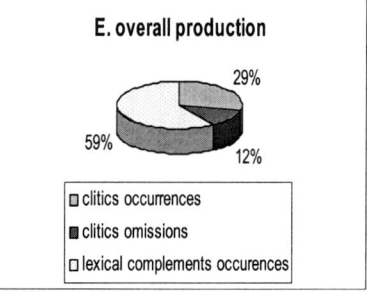

The values above and the non-target placement suggest that:

➢ The modal+infinitive construction is rather problematic for the two children as for the placement of the clitic is concerned.

➢ The two children seem to adopt an avoiding strategy.

6. Clitic placement in other OCC contexts

As modal + inf constructions optionally admit clitic-climbing in Italian, the performance of the two children in other OCC contexts has been checked. The results are that in obligatory contexts clitics are correctly located. Indeed, I found 28 occurrences of the clitic in proclisis on the auxiliary in aux + past participle structures in the V. corpus and 24 in the E. one. In *fare* + infinitive contexts the clitic is correctly located in proclisis on the main verb by both children in the few occurrences I found (3 in E. and 1 in V. corpus). Concerning other optional contexts, I didn't find any occurrences in V. corpus. In the E. one, the clitic correctly occurs in proclisis on the main verb in 3 occurrences of *venire* + infinitive and it is correctly located in enclisis on the main verb in affirmative imperative form in 1 occurrence of *andare* + infinitive.

(7) *E.: ti ho mangiato tutta, tutta, tutta.*
    Obj. Cl.$_{2nd p. s.}$ have$_{1st p. s. ind. pres.}$ eaten all, all, all.
    'I have eaten you all'

(8) *E.: ti faccio vedere dove sta.*
    Obj. Cl.$_{2nd p. s.}$ make see where is.
    'I show you where it is.'

(9) *E.: mi viene a prendere Susanne.*
    Obj. Cl.$_{1st p. s.}$ come$_{3rd p. s. ind. pres.}$ to get Susanne
    'Susanne comes and get me.'

(10) *E.: tu, vatti a prendere un po' di sole.*
    You, go$_{imper.}$ Refl. Cl.$_{2nd p. s.}$ to get some sun.
    'Go and get some sun.'

7. Interpretative hypothesis for the non-target placement

As for the interpretation of these data, I excluded a direct transfer from German where the pronoun is located in the intermediate position. This would lead us to conclude that the two children hadn't recognised the syntactic status of Italian clitics. (Following the tripartition of pronouns proposed by Cardinaletti & Starke, 1999)
This hypothesis has been excluded, as

➢ clitics are correctly placed in all other contexts in which German admits this position;

(11) *E.: ...l'ho comprato ieri...*
> ...Obj Cl._{3rd p. s.} have_{1st p. s. ind. pres.} bought yesterday.
> '...I bought it yesterday.'

➤ none of these pronominal forms is separated from the verb as illustrated in (12), where the child has problem concerning the placement of *tutti* and in order not to separate the Cl from the V, she repeats the Auxiliary;

(12) *E.: io ho tutti li ho mangiati.*
> I have all Obj. Cl._{3rd p. pl.} have eaten.
> 'I have eaten them all.'

➤ their final vowel is mostly elided in front of a following vowel;

(13) *E.: io l'ho tagliato.*
> I Obj. Cl._{3rd p. s.} have cut.
> 'I cut it'

➤ they are not stressed or contrastively used, as indicated by the use of the strong pronoun in the case of topicalization reported in (14). It's interesting to note that in the same sentence the child omits the resumptive clitic;

(14) *E.: no, lei non portiamo.*
> No, her not bring_{1st p. pl. ind. pres.}
> 'No, we don't bring her.'

➤ there are some cases of clitic-doubling.

(15) *E.: io la posso aiutare a mamma.*
> I Obj. Cl._{3rd p. s.} can help to mummy.
> 'I can help mummy'

I then hypothesise that both children place the clitic close to the verb to which it is thematically related, i.e. the infinitive, and that the infinitive does not raise to Agr, as expected in Italian, but remains in Inf, the head where the non-finite morphology is verified, (see the tree below). Since this head is lower than AgrO, the clitic landing-site (assuming Belletti, 1999), this yields the Mod+Cl+Inf construction produced by the two children.

This construction is grammatical in, e. g., French, a language whose object clitics have the same status as Italian ones, but where the raising of the non-finite verb is optional and targets a lower head (T).

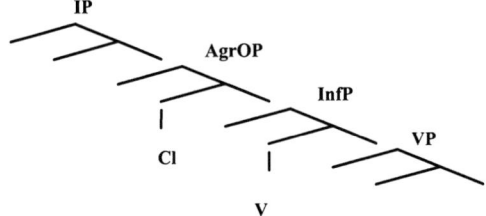

8. Adverbs placement

In order to verify the hypothesis above, I analysed the placement of adverbs in the data (assuming Belletti, 1990, if the non-finite verb does not raise to Agr, we should find adverbs preceding non-finite verbs). Though not many adverbs are produced by the two children, it emerges that they are located both before and after the non-finite verb as illustrated in (16) and (17).

(16) *E.: sì ancora sentire.*
      Yes, Adv. listen$_{inf.}$

V.: ...e insieme mangiare.   *V.: così, così fare.*
   ...and Adv. eat$_{inf.}$ Adv., Adv., make$_{inf.}$

(17) *V.: (x) stare così.*   *E.: vieni a vedere veloce.*
     (x) stay$_{inf.}$ Adv.   Come$_{2nd\ p.\ s.\ imper.}$ to see$_{inf.}$ Adv.

Thus it seems that, for the two children, raising of the non-finite verb is optional and not obligatory as in target Italian.

This conclusion seems also to be supported by one of V. non-target utterances where both the adverb and the clitic appear.

The child produces:

(18) V.: *voglio anche la macinare.*
        I want$_{1st\ p.\ s.\ ind.\ pres.}$ also Obj. Cl.$_{3rd\ p.\ s.}$ grind$_{inf.}$
        'I also want to grind it.'

that is **Mod   Adv   Cl Inf**
If he had not recognised the syntactic status of Italian clitics, he would have probably separated the pronoun from the verb producing:
Mod   Pron   Adv   Inf
as it happens in German. (*Ich will die auch hacken.*)
Note that the construction he produces is non-target consistent in Italian but grammatical in French. (*Je veux aussi la moudre.*)

9. Conclusions

This analysis indicates that both children correctly realized the syntactic status of Italian clitic pronouns.

In fact the non-target constructions seem to be due to the optional raising in Italian of the non-finite verb for the two children.

We can suppose that this behavior can be influenced by the German verbal syntax under the assumption that German non-finite verbs do not raise at all or they raise to a low head.

More generally this analysis suggests that given that bilingual children have two partial inputs of two different grammars, they may adopt a UG options selection strategy that proceeds by parallel attempts. Therefore, by exploring UG, they may produce both alternatives in one of the two languages at the same time.

This phenomenon can be explained assuming that bilingual children have prompter access to UG options as they can have more evidence available through the simultaneous exposure to two different grammars[4].

Notes

[1] The following tables report the details of the recordings:

Vincenzo		
rec.	age (y. m. d.)	rec. time
1	[2.05.28-2.06.01]	50 min. ca
2	[2.06.27]	65 min. ca
3	[2.08.08]	60 min. ca
4	[2.08.26]	70 min. ca
5	[2.09.16]	70 min. ca
6	[2.10.07]	60 min. ca
7	[2.10.26]	60 min. ca
8	[2.11.14]	70 min. ca
9	[2.11.29]	70 min. ca
10	[3.00.18]	70 min. ca

Elisa		
rec.	age (y. m. d.)	rec. time
1	[2.10.08]	25 min. ca
2	[2.11.13]	55 min. ca
3	[3.00.17]	70 min. ca
4	[3.01.06]	50 min. ca
5	[3.02.01]	60 min. ca
6	[3.02.21]	40 min. ca
7	[3.04.12]	60 min. ca
8	[3.05.01]	50 min. ca
9	[3.05.21]	45 min. ca

[2] In this case it is worth noting that both children mostly use the non-finite form of the verb also in affirmative imperative contexts.

[3] The following tables report the absolute values.

V.	Occurrences of Clitics	Omissions of Clitics	Occurrences of Lexical Complements
Overall production	238	60	393
Modal + infinitive	11	15	37

E.	Occurrences of Clitics	Omissions of Clitics	Occurrences of Lexical Complements
Overall production	160	68	327
Modal + infinitive	11	24	58

[4] See also Hamann C. & A. Belletti, (2005).

References

Belletti, A. (1990) *Generalized Verb Movement: Aspects of Verb Syntax*, Rosenberg e Sellier, Torino.

—. (1999) "Italian/Romance Clitics: Structure and Derivation," in H. Van Riemsdijk, ed., *Clitics in the Languages of Europe,* Mouton De Gruyter, Berlin, 543-579.

—. (forthcoming) "Kinds of Evidence for Linguistic Theory," in E. Agathopoulou, M. Dimitrakopoulou, D. Papadopoulou, eds., *Proceedings of the 17th International Symposium on Theoretical & Applied Linguistics*, University of Thessaloniki.

—. and C. Hamann, (2004) "On the L2/Bilingual Acquisition of French by Two Young Children with Different Sources Languages," in P. Prévost, J. Paradis, eds., *The Acquisition of French in Different Context: Focus on Fuctional Categories*, John Benjamins Publishing Co., Amsterdam, 147-173.

Cardinaletti, A. and M. Starke, (1999) "The typology of Structural Deficiency: A case Study of Three Classes of Pronouns," in H. Van Riemsdijk, ed., *Clitics in the Languages of Europe,* Mouton De Gruyter, Berlin, 145-233.

Cinque, G. (2004) ""Restructuring" and Functional Structure," in A. Belletti, ed., *Structures and Beyond. The Cartography of Syntactic Structures,* vol. 3, Oxford University Press, New York, 132-191.

De Houwer, A. (1996) "Bilingual Language Acquisition," in P. Fletcher, B. Mac Whinney, *The Handbook of Child Language*, Blackwell Publisher Ltd, Oxford UK, 219-250.

Granfeldt, J. and S. Schlyter, (2004) "Cliticization in the Acquisition of French as L1 and L2," in P. Prevost, and J. Paradis, eds., *The Acquisition of French in*

Different Contexts: Focus on Fuctional Categories, John Benjamins Publishing Co., Amsterdam, 333-369.

Hamann, C. and A. Belletti, (2005) "Developmental patterns in the acquisition of French clitics: comparing monolinguals, early and adult L2ers, bilingual children and French children with SLI," ms. University of Oldenburg, University of Siena.

—., L. Rizzi, U. Frauenfelder, (1996) "On the Acquisition of Subject and Object Clitics in French," in H. Clahsen, ed., *Generative Perspectives on Language Acquisition*, John Benjamins Publishing Co., Amsterdam, 309-334.

Hulk, A. (2000) "L'acquisition des pronoms clitiques français par un énfant bilingue français-néerlandais," in *Canadian Journal of Linguistics/Revue canadienne de linguistique,* 45, 97-117.

—. and N. Mueller, (2000) "Bilingual First Language Acquisition at the Interface between Syntax and Pragmatics," in *Language and Cognition,* 3, 227-244.

Kayne, R. S. (1975) *French Syntax,* MIT Press, Cambridge, Mass.

—. (1991) "Romance Clitics, Verb Movement and PRO," in *Linguistic Inquiry*, 22, 647-689.

Meisel, J. M., (1989) "Early Differentation of Language in Early Bilingual Children," in K. Hiltenstam, L. Obler, *Bilingualism across the Lifespan*, Cambridge University Press, 13-40.

—., ed., (1990) *Two First Languages-Early Grammatical Development in Bilingual Children*, Foris, Dordrecht.

Mueller, N. (1998) "Transfer in Bilingual First Language Acquisition," in *Language and Cognition*, 1, 151-171.

—. and A. Hulk, (2001) "Crosslinguistic Influence in Bilingual Language Acquisition: Italian and French as Recipients Languages," in *Language and Cognition*, 4 (1), 1-21.

Pollock, J. Y. (1989) "Verb Movement, Universal Grammar and the Structure of IP," in *Linguistic Inquiry*, 20, 365-424.

Rizzi, L. (1982) *Issues in Italian Syntax*, Foris, Dordrecht.

Sportiche, D. (1998) *Partitions and Atoms of Clause Structure. Subjects, Agreement, Case and Clitics*, Routledge, New York.

HOW THE ACTIVATION OF THE SCALE IMPROVES PRAGMATIC PERFORMANCE

FRANCESCA FOPPOLO

1. Theoretical perspectives on Scalar Implicatures

In this paper, I will present an experimental study on the emergence of a special kind of pragmatic inference, i.e. scalar implicature (SI henceforth), such as those evoked by the speaker's use of certain quantifiers, connectives or aspectual verbs. This topic has been the source of much debate in the last years and such interest is interacting in intriguing ways with developments in the semantic/pragmatic theorizing. It seems to be a well documented fact in the literature that young children are not competent in deriving pragmatic inferences associated to scalar items such as *some*. According to some authors, this ability seems to develop later than others because of its connection with extra-linguistic knowledge factors, such as the ability to meet relevance expectations, and/or memory limitation. My aim in this paper is to present some experimental data showing that children as young as five are in fact quite competent with pragmatic inferencing despite the limitations of their cognitive system, contrary to the results presented in the literature. These new results support the idea proposed in Chierchia (2004) that settles pragmatics as part of the general process of the computation of the meaning of sentences, operating in tandem with the semantic module. According to this view, SIs are to be considered a UG driven process, thus the mechanism to draw implicatures should be available to the child from the beginning. Along these lines, the delay in the ability to deal with pragmatic inferencing must be accounted for in terms of factors that can undergo a developmental process, such as lexicon formation.

To illustrate the issues I will be dealing with in this paper, consider the examples in (1) through (3). Following Grice (1975) and much literature inspired by him, it is argued that when a speaker utters sentences like the ones labelled (a) in contexts (1)-(2)-(3), then the hearer is entitled to assume that the speaker intended to convey the (b) version of the sentences in those contexts respectively:

(1) At the kindergarten
      (a)   *Some* children had spaghetti for lunch
      (b)   *Not all* children had spaghetti for lunch
(2) After dinner
      (a)   Nick paid *two coins* for the pizza
      (b)   He did *not* pay *three coins* (only two coins)
(3) Housework
      (a)   The painter painted *a piece of* the barn
      (b)   He did *not* paint *the whole* barn (only a piece)

The basic idea here is the following. Uttering sentences involves choosing from a range of reasonable alternatives. In particular, the (a)-sentences in (1)-(3), typically may evoke the following alternative possibilities:

      (1c)   *All* children had spaghetti for lunch
      (2c)   Nick paid *three* coins for the pizza
      (3c)   The painter painted *the whole* barn

The (a)-sentences are semantically compatible with the (c)-sentences; in fact, it can be argued that the (c)-sentences entail the (a)-sentences. In a situation where, for example, (1c) is true, (1a) would have to be too. As a consequence, choosing to utter (1a) over the stronger (1b) is taken to convey that the alternative (1c) does not hold in that context. Simplifying somewhat, I will refer to the (b)-sentences as to the (canonical) SI associated with the (a)-sentences. The existence of a contrast between the (a)-sentences and the (b)-sentences seems crucial. In fact, items like the quantifiers or the numbers can be seen as forming scales of the following sort: some < many < most < all; one < two < three < …n < n+1; a piece < (half) < whole. Using a generalized notion of entailment, we can view the elements in a scale as in a subset/superset relationship (*all* $\subseteq$ *some*; *n+1* $\subseteq$ *n*; *whole* $\subseteq$ *a piece*) because a statement including the upper elements in the scale asymmetrically entail (i.e. are true in a smaller set of circumstances) than a sentence containing the lower elements (*some, n, a piece* in the scales considered). This makes stronger elements in a scale more informative than weaker ones and this is crucial to understand the reason why implicatures are derived: to exploit something like Gricean maxim of quantity, according to which speakers should make their contribution as informative as it is required. It is important to realize that the existence of lexical entailments such as those from the (c)-sentences above to the (a)-sentences is necessary but not sufficient for SIs to come about (cf. Horn, 1972). Consider for example the following pair:

(4)

    (a)   John ate

    (b)   John ate in the kitchen

The (b)-sentence in (4) entails the (a)-sentence, as in examples (1)-(3) the (c)-sentences entail the (a)-sentences. Yet, uttering (4a) typically does not convey any particular intention about (4b). Stating that John ate does not tell us anything as to how, where or when he did it and therefore we have no reason to infer, from (4a), that John ate, but not in the kitchen, i.e., to deny (4b). Thus, scalar interpretation seems to be somehow lexically driven, a consideration that reveals crucial to the approach I intend to adopt here.

Going back to examples (1)-(3) above, the distinction between a first level of propositional (or basic) meaning (in which the (a)-sentences are compatible with the (c)-sentences) and a second level of pragmatically enriched meaning (in which the (a)-sentences are understood as excluding the (c)-sentences, as stated in the (b)-sentences) is widely agreed upon. On the contrary, the actual steps of the inference that leads from the (a)-sentences to the (b)-sentences remain controversial.

For the purpose of considering developmental work on SI, it may be useful to briefly review some of the ongoing theoretical debates. Of the various theoretical perspectives on SIs that have been inspired by Grice, it may be worth keeping in mind three families of approaches. The first, which I will jointly refer to as Canonical Neo-Gricean and include, a.o., Horn (1972), Levinson (2000), Chierchia and Mc. Connell Ginet (2000), might be characterized by a set of assumptions of the following tenor:

(5)

    (a)   SIs are added to a fully specified basic meaning by default in a cost free way

    (b)   SIs may be cancelled or suspended

    (c)   Although SIs are computed "globally" at the level of whole utterances, they may also intrude (i.e. occur in embedded position)

These are often contrasted with Relevance Theoretic approaches which are designed to derive the following assumptions (Sperber & Wilson, 1986):

(6)

    (a)   SIs are really explicatures, i.e., part of a pragmatically driven process of enrichment of an underspecified semantic representation.

(b)   SIs are not derived by default, but they are effortfully drawn to meet an expectation of optimal relevance.

(c)   SIs are computed globally, and the phenomenon of intrusion must be accounted for as part of the explicature process.

More recently, there have been proposals that revive the idea that SIs are computed compositionally as part of a grammatically driven process, an idea that hadn't been pursued after Gazdar (1979). A characteristic common to such approaches is that the alternatives relevant to SIs computation (e.g., (1-2-3c) are the alternatives computed upon hearing (1-2-3a), which are processed and possibly factored in as part of the compositional semantics by analogy with what has been proposed for focus by Rooth (1985). An example of an approach of this sort is Chierchia (2004) (see also Sauerland (in print), Spector (2003), Fox (2004) who share this general take). The term Semantic Core Models has been adopted to refer to such compositional approaches (see Chierchia et al. 2001), which share the following assumptions:

(7)

(a)   simultaneous computation of alternatives (by default)

(b)   factoring in of alternatives into meaning at various stages of the computation

Along these lines, building upon the consideration I made above that scalar interpretation seems to be somehow lexically driven, one way of thinking about this is that the scalar interpretation is part of the grammaticized information associated with certain lexical entries that are members of a scale, so that the relevant alternatives tend to be automatically activated whenever such entries are used. In other words, we can think of the lexical entry of each scalar item as consisting of two components: the representation of the basic meaning, which in the case of *some* is the representation of the existential quantifier, and the scale. Consider (8) as an example, illustrating the lexical entry associated to *some*:

(8)   Representation of the basic meaning:
        $\|some\| = \lambda P \lambda Q \exists x[P(x) \wedge Q(x)]$
        Scale:
        $\|some\|^{S\text{-}ALT} = \{$ some < many < most < all $\}$

Crucially, in order to derive a SI, one should have in the lexicon the complete lexical entry associated to that particular scalar item, consisting of the representation of its basic meaning plus the scale, whose elements have to be placed and ordered for each different scalar item. This makes SIs different from other kind of pragmatic inferences that do not require a lexicalization of a special component added to the basic meaning.

It is useful to consider the developmental work on SIs against this background of different approaches, as they lead to different expectations about children's behaviors and they are bound to explain differences between children and adults in distinct ways. For example, Canonical Neo-gricean or Relevance Theoretic positions are consistent with the view that the emergence of pragmatic inferences is not tied to that of other principles of the grammar, in particular to compositional processes that derive the meaning of sentences. Thus, it is possible that at a given time children can compute the basic meaning of a sentence but not the enriched one. For Relevance Theoretic approaches, it is also possible that children have different relevance expectations than adults and therefore derive SIs less than adults. In addition, since SIs are part of a pragmatically driven process governed by principles of effort and benefit, it is not in principle expected that children compute the enriched meaning of some scalar items but not of others. By contrast, on the Semantic Core Models, the derivation of SIs is part of the compositional processes that derive the meaning of sentences, and thus is part of the grammar. On this view, it's yielded by a compositional process similar to the one involved in deriving the meaning of a simple sentence like *John is eating an apple*. The two compositional processes only differ in their complexity, as the derivation of SIs requires the computation of alternatives, a process that is similar to what happens if an element in the sentence gets focused. On the Semantic Core Models it is not expected that there is a temporal difference in computing the meaning of simple sentences and the one of sentences involving SIs. Differences between children and adults in the derivation of SIs can be attributed to limitations of extra-linguistic cognitive systems, such as the working memory system, which is likely to be involved in the computation of the alternatives, or to differences in the lexicon.

At this point, it's interesting to move to the acquisition data and see how and when children are able to deal with this special kind of pragmatic inferences.

2. Acquisition works on SIs

In recent years, different experimental works on the acquisition of SIs have been carried out with children of different ages (from 5 to 11 years) and languages using different experimental methods, but all authors seem to agree on the observation that overall children do not derive pragmatic inferences as much as adults. Back in the eighties, investigating the logical competence of children from 4 to 7 year of age, Carol Smith (1980) found that children consistently interpreted *some* as meaning *some and possibly all*. In the same period, Braine and Rumain (1981) concluded that 7- to 9-year-olds tend to assign *or* an inclusive reading, taking sentences of the kind *A or B* to mean *A or B and possibly both*. More recently, Noveck (2001) presented a first systematic investigation of the emergence of SIs in children, modeled on the previous work by Smith (1980). In one of the experiments presented in that paper, he showed that otherwise logically competent children do not derive the SI associated to *some* up to age 11 by means of a Statement Evaluation Task (SET) in which the subject had to evaluate a series of sentences containing *some* and *all*. For example, 7 year old children rejected the underinformative statements *Some elephants have trunks* only 11% of the time. These same children did not have any problem in rejecting false statement including *all* and in accepting true statements including *some* or *all*. Using a different task, the Truth Value Judgment Task (TVJT, Crain & Thorton, 1998) Guasti et al. (2005) tested the youngest age group investigated by Noveck on *some*, i.e., 7 year olds, and showed that these children were as competent as adults in deriving the SI related to that scalar item. However, it seems that SIs remain problematic for 5 year olds, as emerged from the study by Papafragou and Musolino (2003). Always using the TVJT, these authors investigated the interpretation of three different scalar items (*some, two, start*) in 5 year old Greek speaking children and found a low percentage in the derivation of the SIs associated to *some* and *start* (12,5% and 10%, respectively) and a better performance on the numeral scale (65% of derivation of the SI). They conjectured that children's poor performance was due to a failure to understand that they were not being asked about the truth or falsity of statements (which were in fact true, given that *some* is in a subset relation with *all*), but about the pragmatic appropriateness of the statements. To test this conjecture, they designed a second experiment in which the experimental goals were made as explicit as possible, by adding a training session before the test started. After the training, children performance improved, and the computation of SIs rose to 52,5% in the case of *some*, 47,5 % in the case of *start* and 90% in the case of numerals. However, these results have to be taken with some caution, as children's performance with *some* and *start* remains well below adults' performance (which is around 90% of derivation of SIs) and is likely to be not different from chance. Poor performance with another scalar item, *or*, is reported in Chierchia et al. (2001 and 2004). Always using a TVJT, Chierchia and colleagues found that *or* tends to be interpreted inclusively by children (about 50% of the time without any training) even in a context in which the exclusive interpretation is more appropriate and thus favoured by adults. Finally, Doitchinov (2003) reported that 8 year olds fail in the derivation of the pragmatic inferences associated to the use of epistemic modals (see also Noveck, 2001), although they behaved like adults with respect to the SI associated to *some*. Finally, I carried out a developmental study on *some* testing four different age groups (4 to 7 year old children) and adults trying to establish which can be considered the critical age for the emergence of an adult-like behavior with respect to SIs (cf. Foppolo et al. (submitted)). The main finding of that experiment is that there is a developmental effect: while the group of older children (6 and 7 years olds) behaved like the adults and accepted the critical statements less than 20% of the time, the group of younger children (4 and 5 years olds) accepted these same statements around 50% of the time. Examining individual responses to the five critical trials presented per each session, subjects were divided in two groups: one group was comprised of the subjects who accepted the critical statements 3 or more times, and the other group was comprised of subjects who accepted the critical statements less than 3 times. It turned out that 58% of the 4- and 58% of the 5-year-olds, respectively, accepted the critical statements three or more times, while only 17%, 13% and 8% of the 6- and 7-year-olds and adults, respectively, accepted them. An analysis of proportions applied to these data revealed a reliable difference between the group of the 4- and 5-year-olds on the one hand and the group of the 6- and 7-year-olds and adults on the other (p<.05). Thus, a developmental effect was found: 6 and 7 year old children behave as adults in mostly rejecting the critical statement with s*ome* when a parallel description with *all* would be more appropriate; by contrast, the responses of the 4- and 5-year-olds give rise to a bimodal distribution; roughly half of the children of this age behave like older children and adults, mostly rejecting the critical statements, while the other half behave differently from them, mostly accepting the critical statements. This bimodal distribution of the younger children shows that they were not answering randomly (note that the same bimodal distribution displays also in experiments conducted by other authors (see e.g. Papafragou and Musolino, (2003), fn. 9), but went unnoticed or uncommented in those works). Moreover, those results show that by the age of 6 children can derive the SI associated to *some* as much as adults when the appropriate evidence for the evaluation of the statements is available, confirming and extending what was previously found in Guasti et al. (2005) with 7-year-old children. Then, by means of a series of different experiments, Foppolo and colleagues also investigated some possible factors that might be responsible for the non-adult like performance displayed by children with respect to SIs, finding that: it is not the case that children have insufficient or incorrect general knowledge of the items involved in the scale and their uses in felicitous contexts (see also Foppolo and Guasti, 2005); moreover, it is not the case that they lack awareness that items differ with respect of informational strength, that they fail to meet relevance expectations and/or they are prevented from deriving implicatures by working memory limitations (see Foppolo et al. (submitted) for a detailed discussion on this).

Summarizing the previous findings on SIs, these general conclusions seem to emerge from the acquisition literature so far: children at 4 and 5 have some difficulties in deriving pragmatic inferences, even when the task is designed to favour the derivation of SIs; subjects split: either always or never derive implicatures; children at 6 seem to be as competent as adults in the derivation of SIs if the task is appropriate (at least for *some*); children seem to respond differently to different scalar items. Yet, we still don't know precisely how to account for the differences observed between young children's and adults' performance. Another factor which is worth investigating, and that I will investigate in the experiment I'm going to present in the next session, is that the actual recovery of the scale by children is affected and/or masked by the particular experimental design that has been adopted in all the experiments conducted so far.

3. A new experimental design

Let us return to one intriguing observation on the distribution of subjects' responses. As reported, younger children are not uniformly less prone than adults in deriving SIs, but are split into two groups: one group that, like adults, always derives SIs, and one that never does. In fact, children persevere in the answers they offer the first time, given that the response we get to the first target statements (and the explanation provided) is reiterated for all the other target statements of the same form (remember that, in all those experiments, each subject was shown 4 or 5 critical items of the same kind interspersed with fillers). This outcome is rather puzzling and is a hint that children may have adopted some sort of strategy to which they stick during the whole experimental session. As a consequence of this observation, it becomes difficult to interpret previous results. Children may have simply guessed the answer to the first scalar statement and then maintained the same response through the whole session. Notice that the distribution of subjects reported above is just what one would expect from a guessing situation (see Reinhart, in press). If this is correct, it means that all the experiments carried out so far are either underestimating or overestimating children's competence and readiness in deriving SIs. Those children who accepted underinformative statements may indeed be able to generate SIs, but because of their tendency to persevere they did not display it after they chose the "wrong" answer the first time; similarly, children who computed SIs may find it hard to do so, but this difficulty did not come out during the experimental session, as children could simply reiterate the same "right" answer they gave to the first item across similar items. In connection to this, it is worth pointing out that in reasoning tasks involving SIs, such as the one carried out by Noveck et al. (2002), the repetition of the same problem is avoided as "repeated problems can make participants readily aware of the experimenter's intent and can easily affect participants' interpretations. In order to encourage spontaneous reactions, no problem is presented twice." It's plausible that this concern holds not only for reasoning tasks, but also for the task in question. If the particular design adopted in previous works is responsible for children's answers distribution, one expects that an appropriate change in the design will eliminate the tendency to persevere, thus eliminating the bimodal distribution of subjects. The change introduced in the design of this new experiment is based on Noveck et al.'s insight reported above and consists in the fact that each subject was presented with only one critical sentence per item type, instead of testing four or five target statements containing the same item in the same session as it was done before. In addition, three different scales were tested within the same subject: numerals, *some* < *all* and *a piece of* < *whole*. In this way, a mixed design was used, with different scales operating as a within subject factor (not as a between-subject factor, as it was in the Papafragou and Musolino's (2003) study) and different sentences of the same type as a between subject factor. Each subject was also presented with control items for all the different scalar items to check for comprehension and attention. Adopting this design was a way to block the tendency to persevere that children displayed in previous experiments. Moreover, it was a way to test if a lexical component is involved in the generation of SIs. In fact, if children have the general ability to draw Sis, i.e., they know the maxim of quantity, have no memory limitations in representing alternatives, can meet relevance expectations but do not have a complete representation of the lexical entry of a given scalar item (or the memory traces are not well established), we expect to find different behaviours on the part of the same subject depending on the scalar item tested, and thus differences in performance between children and adults on some, but not necessarily all, scales.

3.1 Methods

A group of forty-seven 5-year-olds and forty adult native speakers of Italian participated in the experiment. Children were recruited from different nursery schools in the Milan Area: nursery schools Cesalpino and Soffredini (Milan municipality) and nursery school in Cornate D'Adda. Adults were undergraduate and graduate students at the University of Milano-Bicocca. Subjects that, for any reason, didn't complete the task, were excluded from the analysis. This was the case for seven children, so that data analysis is based on a total of forty 5-year-olds (Age range: 4,11-5,11; Mean Age: 5,4; SD: 0,15).

The material consisted of 48 statements based on three scales: *<alcuni dei, tutti>* (some of, all), *<due, tre>* (two, three), and *<un pezzo, tutto>* (a piece of, whole). It included 16 critical statements, 8 containing *some of* (4 in subject and 4 in object position), 4 containing *two* and 4 containing *a piece of*. In addition, there were 32 control statements; of these, 20 were true statements, 4 for each of the items involved in the scales: *all, some of, two, a piece of, whole* and 12 were false statements, 4 for each of the following scalar items: *all, two* and *whole*. The 48 statements were divided in 4 lists of 12 statements each, so that each list included one statement per each type. Subjects were randomly assigned to one of the four lists, so that each subject was presented with only one sentence per type, but saw sentences from all the three scales. Items were presented semi-randomly, to avoid that two consecutive trials contained the same type of scalar item. A digital version of the TVJT was used: the stories were previously recorded with a digital video camera and then played on a laptop. Children answers were directly reported on a score sheet by the experimenter and the whole test session was also tape–recorded for further control. Adults were shown the video in small groups and were given a score sheet to write their comments on the puppet's statement.

3.2 Results

With respect to individual scales, we can observe that children rejected critical statements 97,5% of the time for numerals, 62,5% of the time for *a piece of*, 70% for *some* in subject position and 75% for *some* in object position. Adults, instead, rejected critical statements between 97% and 100% for all scales. Statistical analysis, by means of test Q of Cochran, revealed a significant difference across scalar items in children (Q= 17.67, df=3, p<.001); pairwise comparisons across items in children data by means of Pearson Chi-Square Test revealed that numbers differ from all the other the scalar items tested, in particular: they differ from *a piece of* (χ^2=15,313, df=1, p<.0001), from *some* in subject position (χ^2=11,114, df=1, p<.001) and from *some* in object position (χ^2=8,538, df=1, p<.003). The proportion of children who generated the SI for *some* (both in object and subject position) and for numerals is significantly different from one predicted by chance based on the binomial distribution (p<.05), while it is not so for *a piece of*. Interestingly, no difference is found between children and adults with respect to the number scale. By contrast, differences still exist between children and adults with respect to the other items, in particular with respect to *a piece of* (χ^2=15,598, df=1, p<.0001), to *some* in subject position (χ^2=11,114, df=1, p<.001) and to *some* in object position (χ^2=9,722, df=1, p<.002).

On control items, adults gave correct responses 100% of the time for all items, except for true statements containing *a piece of*, for which the percentage of correct answers was 97,5%. Children gave correct responses 100% of the time to numerals (true) and *all* (false); 97,5% of the time to *all* (true), to numerals (false) and to *whole* (true and false); 92,5% to *some* (true); 80% to *a piece of* (true). Statistical analysis, by means of test Q of Cochran revealed a significant difference across items in children (Q= 27. 64, df=7, p<.001). Pairwise comparisons showed a reliable difference between *a piece of* (true) and all the other control items. In fact, some children rejected true statements including *a piece of* because they interpreted this item in a numerical sense. For example, in a situation in which a character had built a piece of the puzzle (and not the whole puzzle), some children said that the puppet was wrong because the character had used *three* pieces of the puzzle and not just one. In Italian, in fact, there's no phonological distinction between *un pezzo* (lit. *a* piece of) in which *un* is used as an indefinite, and *un pezzo* (lit. *one* piece of) in which *un* is used as the numeral "one". Given that in some of the stories the pieces of the objects used could effectively be counted (like in the stories where the character managed a puzzle or a paddock), this fact could have led some children to take the expression *un pezzo* in its numerical sense, thus rejecting the otherwise true proposition. If we leave the data on *a piece of* aside, we can say that children performed in an adult-like way on all control items, showing that they have no problems in evaluating sentences containing scalar items in contexts where these are felicitous.

The distribution of children as a function of the number of times they rejected critical statements (i.e., derived the SI associated to each scalar item) is different from one predicted by chance (χ^2=10,80, df = 3, p<.01). Overall, most of the children, i.e., 75%, computed SIs 3 or 4 times; 87,5% did so at least 2 times. However, a difference with adults is still attested, given that 95% adults generate SIs 3 or 4 times. These proportions are significantly different (χ^2=6,27, df=1, p<.05). This suggests that there still is a percentage of children who do not derive the implicatures and that do not benefit from this new experimental design.

3.3 Conclusion

Three major results of this experiment are worth taking into consideration: the distribution of children is not bimodal anymore; children's rejection of critical statements is much higher than in previous experiments; differences exist across the three scales in children, but not in adults. More specifically, changing the experimental design was very effective in eliminating the tendency to persevere and thus the ensuing bimodal distribution. Moreover, the findings reported above clearly show that mixing scalar items is very effective overall in eliciting more rejections of critical statements. For example, if we analyse children's performance on *some* we can see that this was much better than in previous works: if SIs with *some* were inferred only 12,5% of the time in the first study in Papafragou and Musolino (2003) and 42% in the developmental study by Foppolo et al. (submitted), in this new experiment they were derived 72,5% of the time overall. This suggests that the retrieval of the scale can be primed by the use of different scalars, at least for those children that have the scale already available in their lexicon but fail to automatically retrieve it. Although an improvement is observed, we still find that children are less prone than adults to generate SIs, with the exception of numerals, as it was already found in Papafragou and Musolino (2003).

If we want to interpret these data along the lines of a UG driven approach, the difficulty to derive SIs observed in some children cannot be accounted for in terms of a delay of the pragmatic module over the semantic module. Rather, differences between children and adults in the derivation of SIs, and differences among scalar items, are to be attributed to differences in the lexicon. Recall that, in the model proposed, a scalar item is encoded in the lexicon with two pieces of information: the representation of its basic meaning plus the scale. In order to derive SIs, children must have the scale in the first place and then retrieve it. But, to have the scale, children need to establish which items of their language instantiate the various elements of each scale, a process that can be assimilated to the process of acquiring an inflectional paradigm. It's plausible to assume that the acquisition of this lexical component may take time and may vary depending on the scalar item itself. In the end, children that fail in deriving SI for a given scalar item may have not lexicalised the scale component yet-and those are the children that will fail in any task-or they simply have not automatic access to the scale component and have difficulty in retrieving it in general-and these are the ones that can improve in a cross-scalar setting, as the one used in the experiment reported here.

References

Chierchia, G. (2004) "Scalar Implicatures, Polarity Phenomena, and the Syntax/Pragmatics Interface", in A. Belletti, ed., *Structures and Beyond: The Cartography of Syntactic Structures*, Vol. 3. Preprint, Oxford University Press.

—., M. T. Guasti, A. Gualmini, L. Meroni, S. Crain and F. Foppolo (2004) "Semantic and pragmatic competence in children and adults' comprehension of "or"", in I. Noveck and D. Sperber, eds., *Experimental Pragmatics*, Palgrave Macmillan, New York.

Foppolo, F., M.T. Guasti and G. Chierchia. (Submitted) "Scalar Implicatures in Child Language: failure, strategies and lexical factors".

—. and M.T. Guasti (2005) "Children comprehension of sentences involving scalar items", in: *Proceedings of the 30ᵗʰ "Incontro di Grammatica Generativa"*. Cafoscarina, Venezia.

Guasti, M.T., G. Chierchia, S. Crain, F. Foppolo, A. Gualmini and L. Meroni (2005) "Why children and adults sometimes (but not always) compute implicatures" *Language and Cognitive Processes,* 20 (5), 667-696.

Noveck, I. (2001) "When children are more logical than adults: Experimental investigations of scalar implicatures" *Cognition,* 78, 165-188.

Papafragou A. and J. Musolino (2003) "Scalar Implicatures at the Semantic-Pragmatics Interface", *Cognition,* 80, 253-282.

SYNTACTIC MOVEMENT IN AGRAMMATISM AND S-SLI: TWO DIFFERENT IMPAIRMENTS

NAAMA FRIEDMANN, AVIAH GVION, AND RAMA NOVOGRODSKY

Individuals with agrammatic aphasia and children with syntactic SLI (Specific Language Impairment) have difficulties understanding object relative clauses, difficulties that have been ascribed to a deficit in phrasal movement. The aim of the current study was to explore the nature of this deficit in movement in the two populations, and to examine whether the underlying deficit in the two populations is the same.

Individuals with Broca's agrammatic aphasia show significant difficulties in the comprehension of object relative clauses, object Wh-questions, and topicalized structures (Friedmann & Shapiro, 2003; Grodzinsky, 1989, 2000; Schwartz, Linebarger, Saffran, & Pate, 1987; Zurif & Caramazza, 1976; see Grodzinsky, Piñango, Zurif, & Drai, 1999 for a review). Difficulties in these structures have also been reported for children with SLI (Adams, 1990; Ebbels & van der Lely, 2001; Friedmann & Novogrodsky, 2003, 2004; Stavrakaki, 2001; van der Lely & Harris, 1990). These impaired structures share a syntactic property: they are all derived by movement of a phrase that results in a non-canonical order of the arguments. This led researchers of agrammatism to suggest that individuals with agrammatism have an impairment in phrasal movement (Grodzinsky, 1990, 2000). Similarly, some researchers of SLI suggest that the deficit in these structures in SLI is related to a deficit in movement (Friedmann & Novogrodsky, 2004; Novogrodsky & Friedmann, in press; van der Lely, 2005; van der Lely & Harris, 1990; see also Bishop, 1979 for an earlier suggestion that the difficulty is in sentences in which the surface structure is different from the deep structure).

Yet, the exact nature of the deficit in movement is still an open question. What exactly is impaired when movement is impaired in these two populations? Is the deficit related to the construction of syntactic structure and traces, or is the structure constructed correctly and the deficit relates to a failure to transfer thematic roles via chains?

According to syntactic theory (e.g. Chomsky, 1981, 1995), the comprehension of movement-derived sentences requires the assignment of thematic roles to the moved element. The assignment of thematic roles to a moved element is taken to include two related components - a trace (or a copy) at the position from which the element has moved, and a process of thematic role assignment via a chain that is constructed between the trace and moved element (the antecedent) (see example (1)). Namely, in order to correctly understand a sentence that includes syntactic movement, the syntactic structure of the sentence has to be constructed, the position of the trace has to be created, and a trace should be placed. For example, in (1), a structural node for the object of the verb *drew* has to be created, and an empty element should be placed there. This is not enough, though. In order for the sentence to be interpreted, and for the relation between the verb and its moved argument to be established, the thematic role should be assigned to the moved element via a chain (illustrated by the large arrow in (1)), and in relative clauses a further step of co-indexing the moved operator with the relative head has to take place. An impaired comprehension of movement-derived sentences can result from a deficit in either of these abilities.

(1)   The man$_1$ [Op$_1$ that Dudu drew t$_1$] is a clerk

The current study will try to examine, in the two populations, whether the syntactic structure of the relative clause including the trace is constructed and whether thematic roles can be assigned via chain to the moved element. For this aim, a special task was created. This task used the fact that in reading noun-verb heterophonic homographs, i.e., words that are written the same but sound differently (like *lives, tears, wind,* and *dove*), the correct reading requires the analysis of the syntactic position of the homograph. For example, in sentence (2), the word *lives* appears as the object, and is therefore read as a noun, whereas in sentence (3), it appears as the verb, and read as a verb.

(2)   Lifeguards save *lives*.
(3)   The woman *lives* in Italy.
(4)   The woman$_1$ [that the lifeguard saved t$_1$] *lives* in Italy.

We used this phenomenon and tested reading of object relative sentences that included noun-verb heterophonic homographs positioned immediately after the trace position. In object relatives, like in simple sentences, the correct reading of the homograph depends on the syntactic structure that the reader assigns to the sentence. Crucially, in order to understand this structure and to read the homograph correctly, the construction of an empty category as the object of the embedded verb and the identification of the homograph as the main verb are required. In order to read correctly the homograph *lives* in sentence (4), for example, the reader has to understand that the object of *saved* is *the woman*, or actually its trace, and therefore *lives* is the main verb. However, if the trace is not identified, the embedded verb *saved* might be missing an object, so the homograph might be read as a noun, the object of *saved*.

The Hebrew orthography usually does not represent vowels, and some consonant letters are ambiguous. This creates numerous heterophonic homographs, many of them representing different grammatical categories like nouns and verbs, and for many of them the two meanings are very different from one another and familiar even to young children, so they can be used also in a study of children's comprehension.

For example, because of the underrepresentation of vowels, the written word GZR (גזר) can be read either as the verb /gazar/, cut-past-3rd-masc., or as the noun /gezer/, carrot. Incorporated after the trace position in a relative clause as in (5), it can be used to test the construction of the trace. Again, if the reader assigns the correct structure to the sentence, she should know that the trace is the argument of the embedded verb and thus read the homograph as the main verb *cut*. However, if the reader cannot construct the trace at the required position, the embedded verb *liked* would appear to be lacking an argument, and this might lead to an incorrect reading of the homograph as the object of *liked*, *carrot*.

(5)   ha-more$_1$ she-ha-yeled ahav t$_1$ GZR itonim yeshanim.
       The-teacher$_1$ that-the-boy liked t$_1$ *cut/carrot* newspapers old.
       "The teacher that the boy liked cut old newspapers."

The crucial point here is that even the assumption of an empty category at the correct structural position (manifested by the correct reading of the homograph) does not guarantee the correct interpretation of the sentence. If there are difficulties in the assignment of thematic roles to the displaced NP, the interpretation of the sentence might still be flawed (for example, understanding sentence (5) as if the teacher liked the boy). Or, in processing terms (see for example Nicol & Swinney, 1989; Zurif, Swinney, Prather, Solomon, & Bushell, 1993), the correct antecedent (in the above example, *the teacher*) may not be accessed at the trace. These difficulties in assignment of thematic roles can be identified by asking the reader to paraphrase the sentence.

Thus, reading of the homograph immediately after the trace position might serve as a sensitive indicator for the construction of the syntactic position of the object and the assumption of an empty category in this position, whereas paraphrasing of the sentence can serve as a litmus for whether or not the thematic roles were correctly assigned to the moved element.

If the difficulties in the comprehension of object relatives are due to inability to construct the trace, poor performance in the reading task is expected, with a tendency to read the homographic verb as the object noun. But if the difficulties are due to thematic role assignment deficit, with unimpaired trace identification, correct reading of the homograph is expected, accompanied by difficulties in the paraphrasing task with respect to the thematic roles in the sentence. Thus, the comparison between reading and paraphrasing performance can shed light on the component of syntactic movement that is impaired in agrammatism and syntactic SLI (S-SLI).

Participants

The participants were 9 individuals with agrammatism, 15 school-age children with syntactic SLI, and 68 control participants.

Agrammatic group: The participants with agrammatic aphasia were 4 women and 5 men. They were all native speakers of Hebrew, diagnosed as Broca's aphasics with agrammatism. Five of them had left hemisphere CVA, 3 had left hemisphere infarct following head trauma, and one had a right hemisphere CVA. Age range was 19-67 (mean=38). All had characteristic agrammatic speech production. In sentence-picture matching comprehension tasks of right-branching subject and object relative clauses, topicalization structures, and Wh questions, they performed well on the subject relatives and subject questions, and at chance on object relatives, object questions and topicalized sentences. Their performance was compared to 9 individuals with conduction or anomic aphasia without agrammatism, and 9 matched individuals without language impairment.

S-SLI group: The 15 participants in the S-SLI group were 11 boys and 4 girls, in 4th to 8th grade, aged 9;3 to 14;6 years (mean age 11;7). All of them were attending regular classes in regular schools. All of them had a syntactic deficit, and were therefore diagnosed with syntactic SLI (S-SLI). Their comprehension of noncanonical sentences with Wh-movement, as measured by 3 tasks of auditory comprehension was severely compromised. They performed poorly on object relative sentences and object Wh questions, significantly poorer than younger controls. In the sentence-picture matching task they had an average comprehension of 73% of object relatives and 73.5% on referential object questions. They performed 73.7% in comprehension questions task on object relatives. The participants in the control group for the S-SLI study were 50 typically developing children, 25 in fourth grade (mean age = 9;8, SD = 0;5), and 25 in sixth grade (mean age = 11;8, SD = 0;5).

Procedure

The sentences were presented one by one on a paper in large print. The participants were asked to read each sentence aloud as accurately as possible, and then paraphrase it. Each sentence remained in front of them until they finished reading and paraphrasing it. If the paraphrase was unclear to the experimenter, a direct question was asked (for example, if the participant said "He cuts newspapers", we asked "Who cuts?").

The adults with agrammatism read 116 sentences: 87 sentences with a homograph, and 29 filler sentences. The 87 sentences with a homograph included 3 sentences per each homograph: a target center-embedded relative clauses with a homograph after the trace, and two length-matched control simple sentences without movement, one included the homograph as a verb and one as a noun (see examples (6)-(8)).

(6) *Relative*:   Ha-more   she-ha-yeled ohev **gazar**   itonim   yeshanim
                       *the-teacher that-the-boy loves **cut**-past newspapers old*
(7) *Control-verb:* Ha-more   im   ha-se'ar ha-kacar **gazar**   dapim civ'oniim
                       *the-teacher with the-hair the-short **cut**-past papers colorful*
(8) *Control-noun:* Ha-talmid me-ha-kibuz   axal **gezer** be-yom rishon
                       *the-pupil from-the-Kibbutz ate **carrot** on-Sunday*

The children with S-SLI read 24 sentences, 12 relatives with a homograph, and 12 control sentences with the same homographs but without movement. The sentences were randomized and presented in two sessions so that each homograph appeared only once in each session.

Constructing the sentences with the relative clauses was a delicate task. The relative clauses were constructed so that their main verbs were heterophonic-homographs of nouns, and appeared immediately after the trace of the relative clause. The embedded verbs were chosen so that the incorrect (noun) reading of the homograph could serve as their object. We chose only homographs for which the verb and the noun meanings were different enough to permit reliable judgment of which meaning was selected in the speakers' paraphrases (like *tear* and *presents* in English). The homographs were simple and frequent words that are known to school age children both for their verb and for their noun meaning. In order to prevent reliance on semantic and world knowledge cues in the interpretation of the sentences, all relative clauses that were presented to the S-SLI group were semantically reversible, i.e., the subject and the object of the embedded verb could semantically serve both as the agent and as the theme. For further details on the procedure, material and analyses see Friedmann and Novogrodsky (2003).

Results

Agrammatic group

The individuals with agrammatism were severely impaired in reading the homographs when they appeared after the trace in object relative clauses, and consequently failed to paraphrase the object relatives.

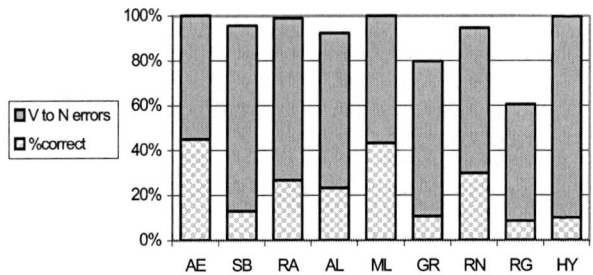

Figure 1. Agrammatic aphasics: Reading homographs in object relatives.

Agrammatism-reading aloud. The individuals with agrammatism read only 21% of the homographs in the relative clauses correctly, and the vast majority (87%) of their errors was reading the verb as a noun (see Figure 1). As shown in Table 1, the reading of the same homographs incorporated in simple sentences as either nouns or verbs was significantly better than when they were incorporated in object relatives. Repeated measure one way ANOVA showed a significant main effect of sentence type, $F(2, 23) = 118.400$, $p < .0001$. The analysis of correct reading showed significantly better reading of the homograph in the verb control than in the relative clause, $t(7) = 16.91$, $p < .0001$, and significantly better reading of the homograph in the noun control than in the relative clause, $t(7) = 12.87$, $p < .0001$. This difference was significant also for each individual agrammatic participant, using Fisher's Exact Test, $p < .0001$.

Table 1. Average % correct reading of homographs (standard deviation), and average number of grammatical category errors in the homographs.

	Relative Clause		Verb Control		Noun Control	
	%correct	V to N	%correct	V to N	%correct	N to V
Agrammatic	21% (14)	20	86% (12)	3	97% (4)	1
Conduction	93% (5)	2	100% (1)	0	100% (0)	0
Control	99% (0)	0	100% (0)	0	100% (0)	0

Similarly, the analysis of the number of noun-verb substitutions in the homograph reading yielded a significant main effect of sentence type,

$F(2, 23) = 210.53$, $p < .0001$. Paired comparisons showed significantly more noun-verb errors in the relative clause than in the verb control, $t(7) = 15.71$, $p < .0001$, and significantly more noun-verb errors in the relative clause than in the noun control, $t(7) = 18.76$, $p < .0001$. No preference was found in the simple sentences to read the homographs as nouns or as verbs. The comparison of the reading of homographs in the relative clauses to the control sentences is crucial, because it shows that they did not have a specific deficit in reading homographs, but that it rather relates to the syntactic structure in which the homograph is incorporated.

A comparison between the reading of the agrammatic group and the two control groups can be seen in Table 1. The participants with conduction or anomic aphasia performed well on these tests (mean 93% correct in the relative clauses). The participants without language impairment who were matched to the agrammatic participants in age, gender and education also performed well on all sentence types. One way between-group ANOVA for the relative clause reading yielded main effect of group, $F(2,26) = 159$, $p < .0001$. The percentage of correct reading of the homograph in the relative clauses in the agrammatic group was significantly lower than in the conduction aphasia group, $t(16) = 13.67$, $p < .0001$, and significantly lower than the healthy group, $t(16) = 15.80$, $p < .0001$. The agrammatic participants made significantly more errors of reading the homograph in the relative clause as a noun than the participants in the conduction and the healthy group, $t(16) = 13.57$, $p < .0001$ and $t(16) = 16.19$, $p < .0001$, respectively.

Agrammatism-paraphrasing. Analysis of the agrammatic participants' comprehension of the relative clauses as measured by their paraphrases yielded two main findings: Firstly, they did not understand most of the sentences with relative clauses, and performed on the average only 11.9% correct (SD = 18%) in paraphrasing. Even in the rare cases in which they read the homograph aloud correctly, they did not always understand the sentence. For the sentences in which they read the homograph as the object, they either tried to make sense of the sentence somehow, and reached an interpretation in which all NPs in the sentence receive a role, trying to combine the head of the relative clause and the subject in the clause to one entity, or combining the homograph (as an object) and the main object to one noun phrase. Otherwise, when they read the homograph incorrectly as object and could not reach an interpretation in which all NPs in the sentence receive some role, they insisted that the sentences were "incorrect", "illogical", or just "bad sentences", but usually could not correct their reading, although they were given unlimited time (see (9) and (10) for examples of reading and paraphrasing of two of the agrammatic participants).

(9)   *Target*: ha-tinok she-ha-yeled ohev **GZR** (gazar=cut,gezer=carrot) et ha-iton
          the-baby that-the-boy loves **cut** ACC the-newspaper

GR reads: tinok....she...ha-yeled...ohev...ohev...eh... **gezer** shel... lo.. et ha-iton.
ha-mishpat lo beseder! (lama?) eh... tinok, yeled. ohev gezer. ve-ex iton?
baby...that... the-kid loves.. loves... eh... **carrot** of... no... ACC the-newspaper.
The-sentence not right! (why?) eh... baby, boy. loves carrot. and-how newspaper?

(10) *Target*: Ha-shokolad she-ha-yalda axla **PITH** (pità=tempted, pìta=pita bread) et
ha-yeled
the-chocolate that-the-girl ate **tempted** ACC the boy
RA: Ha-shokolad she-hayalda axla **pìta**... no no. lama ze –shin? lama ze??? efshar
lada'at ma ze omer? ma ma shin po? (ma ha-yalda axla?) ulai shokolad, ulai pita.
the-chocolate that-the-girl ate **pita-bread**... no no. why this- "that" (points to the
complementizer) why this??? possible to-know what this means? what "that" here?
(experimenter: What did the girl eat?) maybe chocolate, maybe pita-bread.

To summarize, the individuals with agrammatism could not construct the
syntactic structure of the object relatives, and therefore failed to identify the
trace position, failed to read the homograph, and consequently failed to interpret
the sentences.

S-SLI group

Unlike the individuals with agrammatism, the children with SLI read the
homographs after the trace correctly, and not significantly different from their
age-matched controls, but failed to interpret the object relative sentences.

SLI - Reading aloud. The children with S-SLI read the homographs
similarly to the age-matched control participants, and all the groups read the
homographs correctly more than 90% of the time. The rate of reading errors in
the younger control group was significantly higher than that of the older control
group, $t(48) = 2.41$, $p = .02$. We therefore divided the SLI group accordingly
into two groups, a younger group with 7 children in 4th-5th grade, and an older
group of 8 children in 6th grade and on. In the SLI groups too, the younger
participants made more errors of reading the homograph verb as a noun than the
older group, $t(13) = 2.47$, $p = .03$. Importantly, when each group of children with
SLI was compared to its age-matching control group, the SLI and the control
groups did *not* differ in the rate of reading errors, both for the younger age
groups, who made 9% and 7% errors respectively, $t(30) = 0.94$, $p = .36$, and for
the older groups, who made 5% and 3% errors respectively, $t(31) = 1.40$,
$p = .17$. The homographs in the control sentences were read correctly by both
the control and SLI group.

SLI - Paraphrasing. Crucially, unlike the reading errors, the paraphrasing
task yielded significant differences between the S-SLI and the control group, as
can be seen in Figure 2. The control group showed good performance in the
paraphrasing task, and the two age groups did not differ in the rate of

paraphrasing errors, which was 7% for the 4th graders and 9% for the 6th graders, t(48) = 0.89, p = .38. Their data were therefore lumped together and compared to the SLI group.

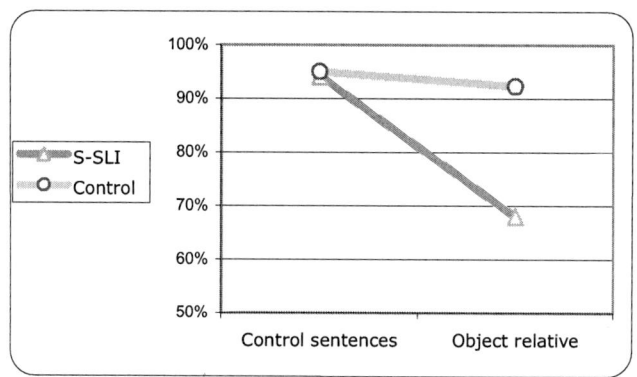

Figure 2. **The difference in performance between relative clauses and control sentences in the paraphrase task, % of correct paraphrasing.**

The difference in performance between the relative clauses and the control sentences was significantly larger in the S-SLI group than in the control group, as can be seen in the significant interaction between sentence type (object relative versus simple sentence) and group (S-SLI versus control), F(1, 129) = 26, p < .0001. Namely, the object relative sentences were more difficult than simple sentences for both groups, but the difficulty in this structure was significantly larger for the SLI group.

The paraphrasing errors constituted the most substantial difference between the SLI and the control group. The participants in the SLI group made an average of 34% paraphrasing errors in the sentences that they read correctly, whereas the control group made such errors in only 8% of the sentences they read correctly, yielding a significant difference, t(63) = 7.76, p < .0001.

The S-SLI participants produced various paraphrases, all sharing the misassignment of thematic roles to the arguments. The error types demonstrated all the possible combinations of the two arguments and the roles assigned by the two verbs (the main verb and the embedded verb), see examples under (11), and the distribution of the paraphrasing errors in the SLI group in Table 2.

In addition to the wrong paraphrases, the SLI and the control children provided some incomplete paraphrases that did not include a paraphrasing error, which appeared in a similar rate in the SLI and in the control group, t(63) = 0.11, p = .91.

(11) Target sentence: ha-baxur she-ha-yeled ahav gazar itonim yeshanim

the-guy that-the-boy loved cut old newspapers
a. Interpretation: ha-baxur she-ohev et ha-yeled gazar itonim
the guy that-loves acc the-boy cut newspapers
The guy that loves the boy cut newspapers.
b. Interpretation: ha-yeled gazar itonim yeshanim, biglal ze ha-baxur ahav oto
the-boy cut newspapers old, for this the-guy loved him
The boy cut old newspapers, that's why the guy liked him.
c. Interpretation: ha-yeled ha-tinok ahav ligzor itonim yeshanim
the-boy the-baby liked to-cut newspapers old
The baby boy liked to cut old news papers.

Table 2. SLI: Types of thematic role assignment errors in the paraphrases

Error type	% of paraphrasing errors
Theta role reversal in the relative clause	22%
Ascribing the predicate of the main clause to an argument in the relative clause	24%
Theta role reversal and ascribing the main predicate to an argument in the relative clause	35%
Ascribing the predicate of the main clause to an argument in the relative clause and not assigning a role to the main subject	6%
Deletion of the relativizer	14%

After the task was completed, we asked each child to describe which test sentences were most difficult to paraphrase. Here, too, the replies of the children in the SLI group differed from that of the children in the control group. The children with SLI pointed to the relative clauses as the most difficult sentences and noted that they were harder to understand, whereas the children in the control group usually pointed to the control sentences and said they were harder to paraphrase because they were not complex and therefore they could not paraphrase them by breaking them into clauses, but rather had to look for synonyms.

To summarize, the children with SLI read the homographs well and similarly to the control group, but their paraphrases showed poor comprehension of object relative clauses, and mainly errors of thematic roles. This pattern suggests that it is the incorrect assignment of thematic roles, rather than inability to construct the structure, that leads to the poor comprehension of relative clauses in S-SLI.

Discussion

The current study suggests that although both individuals with agrammatism and children with S-SLI have difficulties understanding sentences derived by phrasal movement, the underlying deficit in the two populations is different. In agrammatism the syntactic structure is impaired and the trace is not constructed in the first place, and therefore both reading aloud of the homograph and the interpretation of the relative clause are impaired. Unlike them, in S-SLI the syntactic structure is created correctly, and an empty category is assumed at the trace position, as the correct reading of the homographs indicated. The deficit in SLI lies elsewhere: in the assignment of thematic roles to the moved element.

With respect to agrammatic aphasia, apart from suggesting a new method for assessing comprehension of relative clauses, only through reading aloud and without explicitly requiring the participant to perform a comprehension task, this study also sheds light on the nature of the deficit in agrammatism. Grodzinsky (1990, 2000) argued that traces of phrasal movement are deleted from the agrammatic representation, and this proves to be exactly the case – the individuals with agrammatic aphasia do not assume a trace at the original position of the moved element when they build the syntactic structure of the relative clause they hear.

Why can't they build the trace? One possibility is that their deficit is related to the CP node. A reason for why traces are not created in agrammatism might be related to a failure to construct the syntactic tree correctly. If individuals with agrammatism fail to assign the relative head above CP and the relative operator in CP their position on the syntactic tree, they will not know that they should assume a trace, or where to locate it. For agrammatic production, it has been claimed that the construction of the syntactic tree, and specifically CP (and for some individuals also IP) is impaired (Tree Pruning Hypothesis, Friedmann, 2001, 2005a, 2006a; Friedmann & Grodzinsky, 1997). This can be extended to comprehension as well, to account for the deficit in traces of Wh-movement. If CP is inaccessible for comprehension, then when individuals with agrammatism hear a sentence that should include an operator in CP as an antecedent, they cannot construct the operator in spec-CP, because CP is not projected. Later, when they get to the sentential position in which a trace should be assumed, they do not assume a trace there, because there is no antecedent that hints that a trace should be constructed. Furthermore, the head of the relative clause should be situated above CP and be connected to the operator in CP which, in turn, is connected to the trace. If CP is not accessible in comprehension, they would also not know where to put the relative head above CP, neither will they be able to connect it to elements in the CP or to the trace. This possibility, of a deficit in CP in comprehension, accounts not only for the results reported in the current study, but also for reports that resumptive pronouns at the embedded object position do not assist in comprehension (Friedmann, 2005b). It also has the additional advantage of giving a unified account for comprehension and production (see Friedmann, 2006b).

The study also bears on the underlying deficit in syntactic SLI. It suggests that the deficit in SLI relates to inability to assign thematic roles to the moved element rather than to syntactic structure building. The correct reading of the homographs indicates that an empty category is assumed at the embedded object position, but the thematic role errors in paraphrasing suggest that this is not enough, and that the deficit lies in inability to assign thematic roles via a chain to the moved Theme. Namely, an empty category was created as the object of the embedded verb, but then the children with SLI did not know to which NP they should transfer the thematic role. This generalization is consistent with the general picture we now have on the production and comprehension of movement-derived sentences in SLI. Studies of production show that they can produce the syntactic structure of embedding and that they produce well-formed relative clauses, including the embedding markers in CP, and do not produce ungrammatical sentences, but they make errors of thematic roles (Novogrodsky & Friedmann, in press). The deficit in thematic roles that was reflected in the current task is also consistent with the difficulty evinced in other comprehension tasks such as sentence-picture matching, where the children with SLI make errors of pointing to the picture that describes reversed thematic roles (Friedmann & Novogrodsky, 2004; Stavrakaki, 2001; van der Lely & Harris, 1990).

Thus, a deficit in the comprehension of relative clauses can derive from (at least) two different deficits, in agrammatism it is related to a structural deficit that hinders the construction of the trace, whereas in S-SLI the structure, including the empty category, is built correctly, and the failure relates to a deficit in the transmission of thematic roles to a displaced element.

References

Adams, C. (1990) "Syntactic comprehension in children with expressive language impairment," *British Journal of Disorders of Communication* 25, 149-171.

Bishop, M. V. D. (1979) "Comprehension in developmental language disorders," *Developmental Medicine and Child Neurology* 21, 225-238.

Chomsky, N. (1981) *Lectures on Government and Binding*, Foris, Dordrecht.

—. (1995) *The Minimalist Program*, MIT Press, Cambridge, Massachusetts.

Ebbels, S. and H. K. J. van der Lely (2001) "Metasyntactic therapy using visual coding for children with severe persistent SLI," *International Journal of Language and Communication Disorders* 36, Supplement, 345-350.

Friedmann, N. (2001) "Agrammatism and the psychological reality of the syntactic tree," *Journal of Psycholinguistic Research* 30, 71-90.

—. (2005a) "Degrees of severity and recovery in agrammatism: Climbing up the syntactic tree," *Aphasiology* 19, 1037-1051.

—. (2005b) "Traceless relatives: Agrammatic comprehension of relative clauses

with resumptive pronouns," Manuscript submitted for publication
—. (2006a) "Speech production in Broca's agrammatic aphasia: Syntactic tree pruning," in Y. Grodzinsky and K. Amunts, eds., *Broca's region* (pp. 63-82), Oxford University Press, New York.
—. (2006b) "Generalizations on variations in comprehension and production: A further source of variation and a possible account," *Brain and Language 96*, 151-153.
—. and Y. Grodzinsky (1997) "Tense and agreement in agrammatic production: Pruning the syntactic tree," *Brain and Language 56*, 397-425.
—. and R. Novogrodsky (2003, May) *Syntactic movement in Hebrew-speaking children with G-SLI*. Presented at EUCLIDES conference, Wales, UK.
—. and R. Novogrodsky (2004) "The acquisition of relative clause comprehension in Hebrew: A study of SLI and normal development," *Journal of Child Language 31*, 661-681.
—. and L. P. Shapiro (2003) "Agrammatic comprehension of simple active sentences with moved constituents: Hebrew OSV and OVS structures," *Journal of Speech Language and Hearing Research 46*, 288-297.
Grodzinsky, Y. (1989) "Agrammatic comprehension of relative clauses," *Brain and Language 37*, 480-499.
—. (1990) *Theoretical perspectives on language deficits*, MIT Press, Cambridge, Massachusetts.
—. (2000) "The neurology of syntax: Language use without Broca's area," *Behavioral and Brain Sciences 23*, 1-71.
—., M. Piñango, E. Zurif, and D. Drai (1999) "The critical role of group studies in neuropsychology: Comprehension regularities in Broca's aphasia," *Brain and Language 67*, 134-147.
Nicol, J. and D. Swinney (1989) "The role of structure in coreference assignment during sentence comprehension," *Journal of Psycholinguistics Research 18*, 5-24.
Novogrodsky, R. and N. Friedmann (2003) "The movement deficit in SLI: Trace deletion or thematic role transfer impairment?" in Y. Falk, ed., *IATL 19th Proceedings*.
—. and N. Friedmann (in press) "The production of relative clauses in SLI: A window to the nature of the impairment," *Advances in Speech-Language pathology*.
Schwartz, M. F., M. C. Linebarger, E. M. Saffran, and D. Pate (1987) "Syntactic transparency and sentence interpretation in aphasia," *Language and Cognitive Processes, 2*, 85-113.
Stavrakaki, S. (2001) "Comprehension of reversible relative clauses in SLI and normally developing Greek children," *Brain and Language 77*, 419-431.

van der Lely, H. K. J. (2005) "Domain-specific cognitive systems: Insight from grammatical specific language impairment," *Trends in Cognitive Sciences* 9, 53-59.

—. and M. Harris (1990) "Comprehension of reversible sentences in specifically language impaired children," *Journal of Speech and Hearing Disorders* 55, 101-117.

Zurif, E. and A. Caramazza (1976) "Psycholinguistic structures in aphasia: Studies in syntax and semantics," in H. Whitaker and H. A. Whitaker, eds., *Studies in neurolinguistics* (Vol. I), Academic Press, New York.

Zurif, E. B., D. Swinney, P. Prather, J. Solomon, and C. Bushell (1993) "An on-line analysis of syntactic processing in Broca's and Wernicke's aphasia," *Brain and Language* 45, 448-464.

Acknowledgement

The research was supported by the Joint German-Israeli Research Program grant GR01791 (Friedmann) and by the Adams Super Center for Brain Studies research grant (Friedmann). We thank Michal Biran for fruitful discussions and comments.

ON THE ORDER OF ACQUISITION OF
A-MOVEMENT, WH-MOVEMENT AND
V-C MOVEMENT

NAAMA FRIEDMANN AND HEDVA LAVI

Syntactic movement is a central notion in syntactic theory, and an important factor in accounting for the acquisition of syntax. There are several distinct types of syntactic movement. The first classification relates to the type of element that moves, phrases undergo phrasal movement, and heads, such as verbs, undergo head movement. These movement types further divide by the position to which the constituent moves: phrases can move to an argument position (an argument movement, or A-movement), to spec-VP or spec-IP, or they can move higher up to a non-argument position, to spec-CP (A-bar movement, or Wh movement). Verbs move to I in order to collect (or check) inflection, but they can also move further to C, a movement that is obligatory in Germanic V2 languages, and is optional and stylistic in other languages, like Hebrew.

A substantial body of research has looked at the ability of children who are in the process of acquiring language to produce and understand sentences that are derived by various types of movement. With respect to A-movement, following the findings about children's difficulty in understanding passives (Maratsos et al., 1985), Borer and Wexler (1987, 1992) suggested that the ability to assign thematic roles to constituents that moved to another position in the sentence matures only at around the age of 4 or even 5 years. This hypothesis was termed "The maturation of A-chains". Other studies, of passives and unaccusatives, indicate that A-chains are actually acquired much earlier (Fox & Grodzinsky (1998), Friedmann (2004); Guasti (2002), Snyder, Hyams, & Crisma (1995)).

The numerous studies that focused on the acquisition of Wh movement found that structures that involve Wh movement do not occur from the onset of sentences production, and that relative clauses, for example, appear around age 2;6 in production (Berman, 1997; Crain, McKee, & Emiliani, 1990; de Villiers, de Villiers, & Hoban, 1994; Labelle, 1990, 1996; McKee, McDaniel, &

Snedeker, 1998; Varlokosta & Armon-Lotem, 1998). In comprehension relative clauses are mastered even later, at around the age of five or six (de Villiers et al., 1994; Friedmann & Novogrodsky, 2004; McKee et al., 1998; Roth, 1984; Sheldon, 1974; Tavakolian, 1981). These findings have been accounted for by reference to children's inability to handle the movement that occurs in this structure. Wexler (1992; and also Guasti & Shlonsky, 1995) suggested that linking operators, operators that must be co-indexed with an antecedent and transfer referential features, mature late. Namely, what matures later is the ability to co-index an operator that moves to a non-argument position with an element in the matrix clause. This is the case in object relatives: an empty operator moves from object position within the embedded clause to spec-CP of the embedded clause, and is co-indexed with an NP in the matrix clause, and therefore it can account also for the late acquisition of object relatives. Finally, studies that explored the acquisition of verb movement (thorough I) to C (V-C for short) showed that structures that involve this movement also do not occur early on. V-C movement was found to be acquired later than V-I (Déprez & Pierce, 1993; Soares, 2003), and in Hebrew after age 4 (Friedmann & Novogrodsky, 2003; Zuckerman, 2001).

However, not much is known about the order of acquisition of the three types of movement within a child, and whether the order is uniform across children, or whether each movement type kicks in at a different stage for different children. The current study tried to establish the order of acquisition of Wh movement, A-movement and V-C movement within the same child, using an imitation task that included 60 Hebrew-speaking children, each repeating 80 sentences derived by different types of movement.

Method

Participants. The participants were 60 Israeli children aged 2;2-3;10: 21 children aged 2;2-2;9, 19 children aged 2;10-3;2, and 20 children aged 3;3-3;10. All the children were monolingual native speakers of Hebrew, with normal language development and no hearing impairment.

Procedure. The children were asked to repeat sentences. In order to encourage them to repeat the sentences they received building blocks after each sentence they repeated, in order to build a block tower up "all the way up to the sky".

Material. Each child repeated 80 sentences, 10 sentences of each type. A-movement was tested using SV sentences with unaccusatives in which the subjects undergo A-movement, as they move from their base-generated object position to a position before the verb. This structure is frequent in Hebrew, and much more common than passive. The assessment of Wh movement used subject- and object relative clauses and topicalization, all involving movement to spec-CP. V-C movement was tested in sentences in which the verb appears right after a temporal adverb, with transitive and unergative verbs. We compared the movement-derived sentences to SV sentences with unergative and transitive verbs. All sentences included 4 words (counting prepositions, complementizers and case markers with the words they attach to), and were randomly ordered. The structures and their constituents were (given only in transliteration due to space limitation):

Basic SV	A-S-Vunergative-PP	*yesterday the-boy jumped in-the-garden*
	A-S-Vtransitive-O	*yesterday the-boy built tower*
A movement:	A-S-Vunaccusative-PP	*yesterday the-girl fell in-the-garden*
Wh	Topicalization O-S-V-	*ACC-the-tower the-boy built yesterday*
	Subject relatives	*(I)-saw ACC-the-girl that-kissed ACC-grandma*
	Object relatives	*(I)-saw ACC-the-girl that-grandma kissed*
V-C	A-Vunergative-S-PP	*yesterday jumped the-boy in-the-garden*
	A-Vtransitive-S-O	*yesterday built the-boy tower*

Results

The type of movement (A, Wh, V-C) had a significant effect on repetition performance, as can be seen in Figure 1. An analysis on the group level indicated that there were strong correlations between different structures with the same movement, that sentences with Wh and V-C movement were repeated significantly worse than their counterparts that did not include movement, and that there were significant differences in performance between movement types. The repetition of A-movement was better than Wh-movement, which in turn was better than V-C movement.

The correct repetition on the three structures that are derived by Wh movement – subject relative, object relative and topicalization – was strongly correlated, Cronbach's Alpha = 0.88; the two structures that involved V-C movement, with transitive and unergative verbs, also yielded a strong correlation, Cronbach's Alpha = 0.82.

The children showed mastery of A-movement of subjects of unaccusative verbs, and their repetition of SV sentences with unaccusatives did not differ from their repetition of SV sentences with unergative and transitive verbs (with a mean of 93% correct repetition for each of the 3 sentence types). The repetition of the 3 Wh-movement structures was poorer, with a mean of 71% correct, significantly poorer than the repetition of A-movement, $t(59) = 5.98$, $p < .0001$. The repetition of sentences with V-C movement was the poorest, with a mean of 32% correct. V-C movement was significantly poorer than both A-movement, $t(59)=14.34$, $p < .0001$ and Wh movement, $t(59)= 9.15$, $p < .0001$.

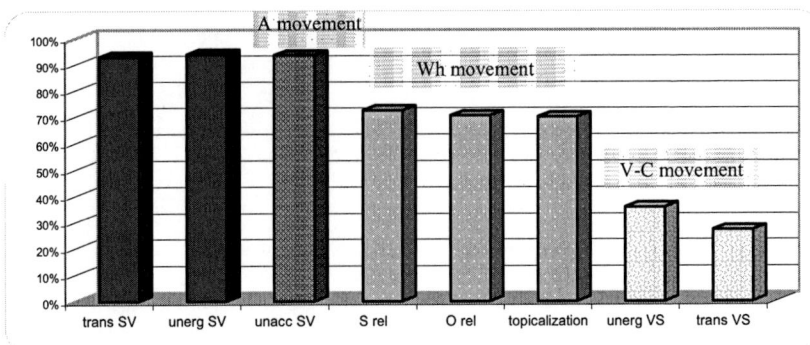

Figure 1. **Average percentage of correct repetition on the 8 sentence types.**

The errors in repetition of sentences with V-C movement were mainly SV order reversal: 67% of the target VSO with transitives and 60% of target VS sentences with unergatives were repeated in SV order.

No correlation was found between repetition of any of the movement types and age (Rpb < 0.22 for all the sentences with movement), and no significant difference in repetition was detected between the three age groups: For example, a 2;3 year old girl succeeded in repeating all the V-C sentences, whereas a 3;10 boy failed in them. Two girls aged 2;5 succeeded in repeating Wh sentences, whereas 4 children aged 3;7 failed in them.

Individual level analysis

Possibly the most important result of this study was that the repetition pattern of each of the 60 children revealed a hierarchical order of acquisition of the three movement types, which created a perfect Guttman scale: with a criterion of 80% correct repetition for "acquired structure", 56 children acquired movement of the subject of unaccusatives (A-movement); 34 children acquired Wh movement, and 8 acquired V-C movement. Importantly, **all children who already acquired V-C also acquired both Wh- and A-movement, and all children who already acquired Wh movement also acquired A-movement**. Namely, children who could repeat VS sentences with transitives and unergatives were also able to repeat relatives and topicalization sentences, as well as SV sentences with unaccusative verbs. All children who were able to repeat relative clauses and topicalization sentences were also able to produce the unaccusative subject in preverbal position. Thus, a very clear order of acquisition of the 3 types of movement within each child emerges from this study, presented in Figure 2:

1) A-movement in unaccusatives
2) Wh movement: subject relative, object relative and topicalization
3) Verb movement to C

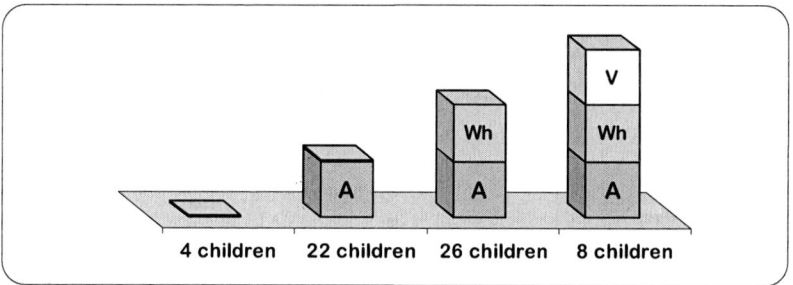

Figure 2. The gradual acquisition of movement types at the individual level:
Four stages of movement acquisition.

Some additional interesting results concern the omission of complements and temporal adverbs and the stage of movement acquisition of each participant. Omissions occurred almost exclusively in sentences with movement. Sentence-initial temporal adverbs were only omitted by children who have not yet acquired V-C movement. Children who already acquired V-C did not omit temporal adverbs. The non-omission of temporal adverbs was also correlated with the acquisition of Wh movement, r = 0.49, p < .0001. Children who acquired Wh movement omitted significantly less temporal adverbs than children who have not acquired Wh movement yet, χ^2 = 157.1, p < .0001, possibly because of the shared maximal projection, CP, that is required both for sentence-initial adverbs and for Wh movement. In addition, no complements were omitted from SVO sentences, but 11% of the complements were omitted from VSO target sentences. Importantly, complements were only omitted by children who have not yet acquired V-C movement, when they could not raise the verb to C and repeated VS as SV.

Summary

The study indicates that movement is an important tool in accounting for syntactic acquisition. The acquisition of movement is reflected not only in the ability to produce certain word orders but also in the ability to use complements in movement-derived sentences. Sentences that share the same movement types are acquired together, and although different children acquire movement at different ages, the order of acquisition of A, Wh and V-C movement is fixed across children. First they acquire A-movement, then Wh-movement, and only then V-C movement.

References

Berman, R. (1997) "Early Acquisition of Syntax and Discourse in Hebrew," in Y. Shimron, ed., *Psycholinguistic Studies in Israel: Language Acquisition, Reading and Writing*, Magnes Press, Jerusalem. (in Hebrew)

Borer, H. and K. Wexler (1987) "The Maturation of Syntax," in T. Roeper & E. Williams, eds., *Parameter-Setting and Language Acquisition*, Reidel, Dordrecht.

—. and K. Wexler (1992) "Bi-Unique Relations and the Maturation of Grammatical Principles," *Natural Language and Linguistic Theory* 10, 147-189.

Crain, S., C. McKee, and M. Emiliani (1990) "Visiting Relatives in Italy," in L. Frazier & J. de Villiers, eds, *Language Processing and Language Acquisition*, Kluwer, NY

de Villiers, J. G., P. A. de Villiers, and E. Hoban (1994) "The Central Problem of Functional Categories in the English Syntax of Oral Deaf Children," in H. Tager-Flusberg, ed., *Constraints on Language Acquisition: Studies of Atypical Children*, Erlbaum, Hillsdale, NJ.

Déprez, V. and A. Pierce (1993) "Negation and Functional Projections in Early Grammar". *Linguistic Inquiry* 24, 25-68.

Fox, D. and Y. Grodzinsky (1998) "Children's Passive: A View from the by-Phrase," *Linguistic Inquiry* 29, 311-332.

Friedmann, N. (2004) "The Acquisition of Hebrew Unaccusatives: Young Children and A-Chains," in Y. N. Falk, ed., *Proceedings of the Israel Association for Theoretical Linguistics 20,* Bar Ilan University.

—. and R. Novogrodsky, (2004) "The Acquisition of Relative Clause Comprehension in Hebrew: A Study of SLI and Normal Development," *Journal of Child Language* 31, 661-681.

Guasti, M. T. (2002) *Language Acquisition: The Growth of Grammar,* MIT Press Cambridge, MA.

Maratsos, M., D. E. C. Fox, J. A. Becker, and M. A. Chalkley (1985) "Semantic Restrictions on Children's Passives," *Cognition* 19, 167-191.

McKee, C., D. McDaniel, and J. Snedeker, (1998) "Relatives Children Say," *Journal of Psycholinguistic Research* 27, 573-596.

Snyder, W., N. Hyams and P. Crisma (1995) "Romance Auxiliary Selection with Reflexive Clitics: Evidence for Early Knowledge Of Unaccusativity," in E. Clark, ed., *Proceedings of the 26th Annual Child Language Research Forum,* Stanford, CA, CSLI.

Soares, C. (2003) "XP and X Movement to the Left Periphery in Child European Portuguese," *Probus* 15, 147-176.

Varlokosta, S. and S. Armon-Lotem (1998) "Resumptives and Wh-movement in the Acquisition of Relative Clauses in Modern Greek and Hebrew," *BUCLD*, 22, 737-746. Somerville, MA: Cascadilla Press.

Wexler, K. (1992) "Some Issues in the Growth of Control," in R. K. Larson et al., eds., *Control and grammar*, Kluwer, Dordrecht.

Zuckerman, S. (2001) *The Acquisition of "Optional" Movement*. Groningen Dissertations in Linguistics 34, Rijksuniversiteit Groningen.

Acknowledgements

The research was supported by the Joint German-Israeli Research Program grant GR01791 (Friedmann) and by the Adams Super Center for Brain Studies research grant (Friedmann).

WHY *IS ARRIVING* CAN ALSO MEAN *HAS ARRIVED* FOR JAPANESE LEARNERS OF ENGLISH[i]

ALISON GABRIELE

1. Introduction

Though aspectual distinctions are notoriously difficult for second language (L2) learners, there is little consensus as to exactly what factors are at the root of the difficulty. Surprisingly there have been very few controlled experimental studies systematically investigating, for example, the influence of native language aspectual properties or the influence of tense on the interpretation of aspectual forms such as the progressive. The present study addresses both of these factors in a controlled experimental study examining the interpretation of the English present and past progressive by native speakers of Japanese[ii].

We examine the learnability problem that crosslinguistic differences in the semantics of the progressive operator present to the L2 learner. The study addresses not only the role of native language transfer but also the issue of how transfer interacts with the input available to the learner in the course of L2 development. The overall picture presented here is that in interpreting the present progressive, it is easier for learners to *add* an interpretation to their grammar than it is to *preempt* an option that is available in the L1 and not in the L2. Preemption contexts appear to remain difficult even at very advanced levels of proficiency. However, I will also argue that there are aspectual forms, such as the past progressive, which present a challenge even when the goal is to add an interpretation due to the complexity of the semantic representation and the insufficiency of robust evidence.

2. The progressive in Japanese and English

While both Japanese and English have a grammatical form denoting the progressive, the two forms (*be+ing* in English and *te-iru* in Japanese) interact differently with the lexical aspect of the verb phrase to which they attach[iii]. In

English the relevant facts are simple: the progressive *be+ing* denotes an ongoing interpretation regardless of the lexical aspect of the verb phrase, as can be seen in (1-3).

(1) Sophia is running. (activity)
(2) Carlos is building a sandcastle. (accomplishment)
(3) My plane is arriving at the airport. (achievement)

Japanese *te-iru*, on the other hand, is more complex. With activity and accomplishments, as in (4-5), the preferred reading is strongly progressive, just as it is in English. With achievements, however, *te-iru* always denotes a perfective interpretation and a progressive reading is ruled out. The sentence in (6) literally means *the plane has arrived* or *the plane is at the airport* and crucially cannot mean *the plane is arriving at the airport*.

(4) Tarō-ga hasit-<u>te-iru</u>   (activity)
    Tarō-NOM run te-iru PRES
    Tarō is running.

(5) Tarō-ga hon-o yon<u>de-iru</u>   (accomplishment)
    Tarō-NOM book-ACC read te-iru PRES
    Tarō is reading a book.

(6) Hikōki-ga kūko-ni tui<u>te-iru</u>   (achievement)
    plane-NOM airport at arrive te-iru PRES
    The plane (arrived and) is at the airport.

In summary, achievements under *te-iru* in Japanese focus on the resulting state of the event (the arrival) while achievements under English *be+ing* focus on the process leading up to the change of state (the point just before arriving).

This crosslinguistic difference has been analyzed in the framework of truth conditional semantics. Traditional analyses of the English progressive such as Landman (1992) have analyzed the progressive as a semantic operator PROG that interacts with the verb stem to which it attaches as in (7).

(7) PROG[VP]

McClure (1995) extended this type of analysis and argued that the difference in the interpretation of the progressive in English and Japanese lies in the semantic representation of the aspectual operator PROG in the two languages[iv]. McClure's semantics makes reference to an interval of evaluation, which is the point at which the truth value of the sentence is computed. The semantics for English *be+ing* requires that any event that is a final event be manifested *after* the point of evaluation. In this way, English *be+ing* will never allow a resultative interpretation; the final event will always be manifested after evaluation. The semantics for *te-iru* on the other hand, requires that at least one complete event entailed by the predicate be manifested *before* the point of evaluation. On this approach, similar to Dowty (1979), achievements are defined by a single event, a change of state. Therefore, *te-iru* is only true when the final event has already occurred. The crucial difference between achievements under PROG in English and Japanese boils down to a difference in the manifestation of the final event.

Finally, we will consider the interaction of the past tense with the PROG aspectual operator as is represented in (8).

(8) PAST[PROG[VP]]

Most discussions of the past progressive sentence in English focus on the Imperfective Paradox (Dowty, 1979; Landman, 1992; Parsons, 1990). It is well known that a sentence such as (9) does not entail that the building of the house was in fact ever completed.

(9) Mary was building a house.

These facts fall out of the semantics we have presented for PROG. The sentence in (9) is true if and only if at some past time, PROG[build a house] is true. As we mentioned earlier, PROG[build a house] is true in English if the final event of house building is not realized before the point of evaluation. Therefore, PAST[PROG[build a house]] simply requires that at some past point, the event of building a house continued into the future. There is no formal entailment that the house building was in fact ever completed, only that at some point in the past, the house building was underway. However, the semantics is *also* compatible with the interpretation that the house building was completed at some point.

In Japanese, the past form of *te-iru* is *te-ita*. With activities and accomplishments the same patterns hold for *te-ita* that hold for the English past progressive. The truth conditions for the sentence in (10) are also compatible with the two outcomes outlined for its translational equivalent in English.

(10) Mari-wa uchi-o *tukut-te i-ta.*
Mari-TOP house-ACC build-ASP-PAST
Mari was building a house.

Achievements under *te-ita*, on the other hand, necessarily have different entailment patterns due to their distinctive interaction with *te-iru*. Achievements under *te-iru* denote resultative interpretations, therefore achievements under *te-ita* as in (11) necessarily do as well.

(11) Hikōki-ga kūkō –ni tuit-<u>te-i-ta</u>.
     plane-NOM airport at arrive ASP-PAST
     The plane had arrived at the airport.

The sentence in (11) is compatible only with an event in which the event of arriving was completely realized prior to the point of evaluation. The English sentence in (12), on the other hand, is compatible with dual outcomes.

(12) The plane was arriving at the airport.

Due to the semantics of *be+ing* in English, it is possible that the plane's arrival was never actually realized.

In summary, we have outlined an analysis for aspectual forms in English and Japanese using the general structure in (13) (cf. De Swart, 1998).

(13) [Tense [*Aspect [VP]]]

We have identified differences at the level of the aspectual operator, with specific reference to PROG in English and Japanese. This is the locus of crosslinguistic differences and thus the level at which we will make predictions with respect to L1 influence in second language acquisition.

2.1 Consequences for L2 Acquisition

By adopting the analysis above, we have identified the goal of the L2 learner in terms of the acquisition of the semantics for PROG. In this section we outline predictions for L2 acquisition if we assume a transfer model (cf. White, 1985; Schwartz and Sprouse, 1994, 1996). If we assume that L2 learners make use of L1 grammatical properties in their initial analysis of the L2, then we do not predict difficulty with accomplishments because English and Japanese denote similar interpretations with these verb phrases.

However we do predict difficulty with achievements. In order to successfully acquire the progressive in English, the Japanese learners will need to achieve two different goals. First the Japanese learners need to acquire the target representation. They need to learn that achievements under *be+ing* denote a progressive interpretation. We'll refer to this as the *adding* context because this interpretation does not exist in the L1 Japanese. Second, the learners need to preempt the interpretation that is available in the L1; they need to rule out a perfective interpretation for the English progressive. This is the *preemption* context.

Based on previous work in the domain of learnability (White, 1990/1; Juffs, 1996; Inagaki, 2001), we do not predict equal success with these two goals. With respect to adding, we predict that positive evidence will facilitate acquisition of the target. With respect to preemption on the other hand we predict that the learners will have more difficulty because there is usually very little evidence in the input as to what interpretations are not available. The experimental study we will outline in the next section is specifically designed to test both contexts.

3. Methodology

3.1 Participants

We tested 101 Japanese learners of English: they were divided into three groups, low (n = 46), intermediate (n = 39), and high (n = 16), based on the results of the Michigan listening comprehension test. We also tested a small group (n = 9) of Japanese near-native speakers of English who were living in New York. Participants were classified as near-native based on Michigan test scores (40/45 correct) and performance on an oral proficiency exam. We also tested a control group of native English speakers (n = 23).

3.2 Interpretation task

This task targeted accomplishments and achievements in the past, present progressive and past progressive[v]. Eight accomplishments (*paint a portrait, write a book, build a sandcastle, read a pile of books, eat a bowl of ramen, make a cake, drink a glass of coke, wash a pile of dishes*) and eight achievements (*arrive, go, die, stop, return, come, leave, close*) were tested. Learners listened to recorded stories and looked at two pictures. They were then presented with a sentence and asked to judge on a scale of 1-5 whether or not the sentence was compatible with the story (5 being highly compatible). For each verb, a complete context and an incomplete context were developed. Examples are given in (14) and (15). In (14) and (15) we also summarize the predicted responses for native speakers and L2 learners.

(14) *paint a portrait*: Complete Story Context
Picture 1: Ken is an artist. At 12:00 he begins to paint a portrait of his family.
Picture 2: At 8:00 he gives the portrait to his mother for her birthday.

	English Native	L1 Japanese
Ken is painting a portrait of his family.	1	1
Ken was painting a portrait of his family.	5	5

paint a portrait: Incomplete/Ongoing Story Context
Picture 1: Ken is an artist. At 12:00 he begins to paint a portrait of his family.
Picture 2: At 12:30 he paints his mother and father.

	English Native	L1 Japanese
Ken is painting a portrait of his family.	5	5
Ken was painting a portrait of his family.	5	5

(15) *arrive*: Complete Story Context
Picture 1: This is the plane to Tokyo. At 4:00 the plane is near the airport.
Picture 2: At 5:00 the passengers are at the airport.

	English Native	L1 Japanese
The plane is arriving at the airport.	1	5
The plane was arriving at the airport.	5	5

arrive: Incomplete/Ongoing Story Context
Picture 1: This is the plane to Tokyo. At 4:00 the plane is near the airport.
Picture 2: There is a lot of wind. At 4:30 the plane is still in the air.

	English Native	L1 Japanese
The plane is arriving at the airport.	5	1
The plane was arriving at the airport.	5	1

No differences between learners and native speakers are predicted with the accomplishments. Differences are predicted with the achievements. On the Complete context, we predict that native speakers will reject the present progressive. The L2 learners on the other hand, if they transfer the semantics of *te-iru*, will interpret this sentence as *The plane arrived at the airport* and will thus accept it. This is the *preemption* context.

On the Incomplete context, differences are predicted with both the present and past progressive. Native English speakers should accept these sentences but if the learners transfer the semantics of *te-iru*, they will reject them because they will interpret the form to mean that the plane is already at the airport. These are *adding* contexts.

We predict that the preemption context will remain difficult even for advanced learners due to the lack of evidence that would guide the learner in ruling out the L1 interpretation. The adding contexts, on the other hand, should in principle be acquired on the basis of positive evidence.

4. Results

In this section we present a general discussion of the main findings (refer to Gabriele (2005) for details of the statistical analyses). We first present results for the present progressive. For the accomplishments, as we predicted, all participants correctly give generally high scores to present progressive sentences in incomplete contexts and generally low scores in complete contexts. The L2 learners are not significantly different from native speakers. These results confirm the hypothesis that positive transfer facilitates acquisition.

Results for the achievements in the present progressive are summarized in Figure 1. We predicted on the basis of transfer that learners would reject the present progressive with the incomplete context and accept it with the complete context. This is the general pattern that is evident in the Low and Intermediate group. Results of individual samples t-tests revealed that both the Low and Intermediate group gave significantly higher scores to the present progressive with *complete* contexts (Low: t (44) = 2.723, p. < .01; Int: t (37) = 2.212, p. < .05). These results suggest that the lower level learners have difficulty assigning an ongoing interpretation to the present progressive with achievement verbs. More advanced learners do not have this difficulty. This is the result we expected given that this is the adding context. Learners can overcome transfer effects on the basis of positive evidence.

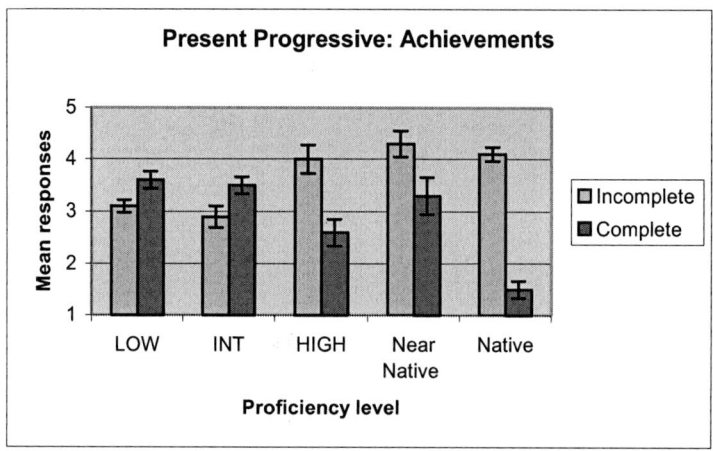

Figure 1. Mean responses to achievements in the present progressive

Results are different for the complete context. Results of a one-way ANOVA and post-hoc procedures indicate that all learner groups, including the Near-natives, accept the present progressive to refer to complete contexts to a greater degree than native speakers $(F(4, 64) = 20.479, p. < .001)$.

In summary, results indicate that accepting the present progressive with incomplete/ongoing contexts is difficult only for the lower level learners. As we predicted, we do not see the same pattern of emerging development on the complete context or the preemption context. All learner groups accepted the present progressive to refer to a complete event to a greater extent than the native speakers. As we predicted, preemption remains a problem. The advanced learners are very interesting in this respect because they seem to have acquired the target interpretation of the progressive but nevertheless also allow this additional perfective interpretation that is available in the L1. These results are compatible with the characterization of optionality proposed by Sorace (1999, 2003) in her recent work.

Next we present results for the past progressive. Results for the accomplishments are summarized in Figure 2. No differences between the L2 learners and native speakers were predicted for the accomplishments. However, results of a factorial ANOVA with context (incomplete, complete) and proficiency level as between-subjects factors indicated a significant interaction between context and proficiency level $(F(4, 123) = 3.568, p. < .01)$. This indicates that the distinction in responses to past progressive sentences with complete and incomplete contexts is not the same across proficiency levels.

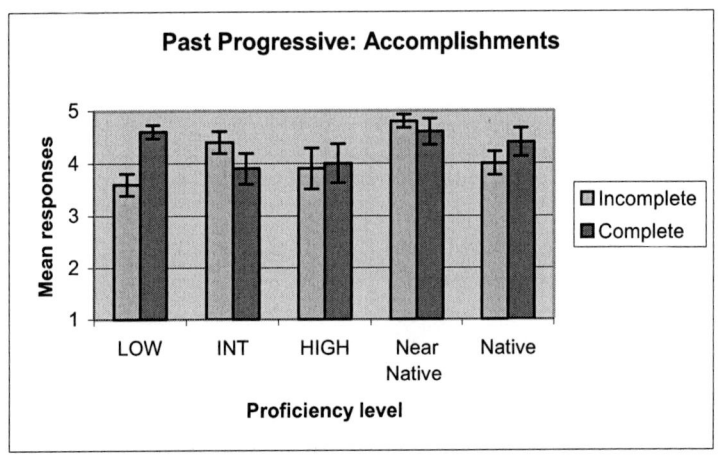

Figure 2. Mean responses to accomplishments in the past progressive

The graph in Figure 2 shows that the Low group has a tendency to give higher scores on the complete context. Results of an independent samples t-test revealed that the Low group gave significantly higher scores on the complete context, t (44) = 4.216, p. < .001. Results of t-tests with all other proficiency levels were not significant. This result was not predicted on the basis of positive transfer.

Results for the achievements in the past progressive are presented in Figure 3. We predicted difficulty in the lower level learners on the incomplete context but expected that learners in the more advanced groups would perform well due to the fact that this is an adding context. Surprisingly, a one-way ANOVA on the incomplete context and the follow-up post hoc procedures indicated that even learners in the High group had difficulty.

Further tests were conducted to examine the distinction between the incomplete and complete contexts. Results of independent samples t-tests showed that participants in the Low, Intermediate and Near-native group gave significantly higher scores to past progressive sentences with achievements in complete contexts (Low: t (44) = -4.903, p. < .001; Intermediate: t (37) = -5.552, p. < .001; Near-native: t (7) = -2.844, p. < .05). This is similar to the pattern found with the Low group on the accomplishments in the past progressive. Participants in the High group did not distinguish between the two contexts; this is also true of the native speakers, although there is variability in their responses.

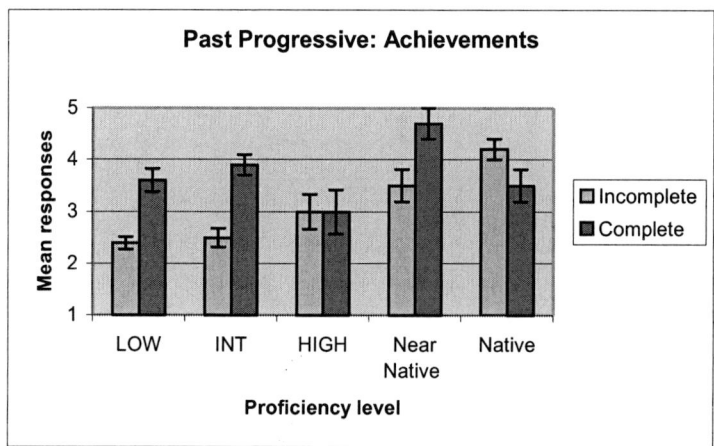

Figure 3. Mean responses to achievements in the past progressive

In summary, the results for achievements showed that most learners incorrectly rejected the past progressive on the incomplete context. This challenges the hypothesis that the *adding* contexts are easily acquirable. The results for the High group are important here. Though they performed like native speakers on the incomplete context with the present progressive, they had difficulty with the past progressive. There is a clear interaction with tense. In addition, with the accomplishments, the Low group rejected the past progressive with the incomplete context to some extent. This result challenges the hypothesis that positive transfer facilitates acquisition. This result again highlights the importance of the tense interaction because with accomplishments in the present progressive, all groups performed at the level of native speakers. There is a tendency for learners to prefer the past progressive to refer to completed events.

5. Discussion

If our study was restricted to crosslinguistic differences in the present progressive we would be able to propose a relatively simple model where consideration of the properties of the L1 and L2 grammar and learnability allow us to account for the data. Results for the present progressive suggested that the acquisition of some semantic properties in the L2 is facilitated by consistent input and positive evidence. It is easier to add an interpretation to the L2 grammar. On the other hand the ability to preempt possible interpretations in the

L2 that are available in the L1 remains difficult even for very advanced learners. It remains an empirical question whether negative evidence would be beneficial in these contexts (White, 1992; Schwartz, 1993). But when we consider the results for the past progressive, the model we just presented is challenged. There are contexts where positive evidence does not seem to drive acquisition: even advanced learners seem to reject achievements in the past progressive on the incomplete context. There are also contexts where the L1 and L2 grammar are equivalent and acquisition is still difficult: we did not predict the learners in the Low group would have difficulty with accomplishments in the past progressive on the incomplete context.

We suggested that there is a general tendency for learners to prefer for the past progressive to refer to a complete event; the tendency is stronger with the achievements. Wagner (2001) found a similar tendency with accomplishments in young children acquiring English as a first language. In her study two-year olds were more likely to allow a question such as *Where was Kitty building a sandcastle* to refer to a past event that had already been completed than a past event that was incomplete. To account for this finding, Wagner proposes that the children conflate tense and aspect so that they interpret any occurrence of the past tense as referring to perfective aspect. However in her study there is no independent test of the past, so the conflation proposal may be too strong. We have evidence from other tasks that the learners in this study do have knowledge of the past tense but we will nevertheless consider a proposal related to Wagner's where the learner's challenge lies in deciphering what semantic notions are encoded by what particular pieces of morphology.

In order to understand why a form such as the past progressive is so difficult we need to consider a rather complex semantic computation at three different levels: the VP, the progressive aspect marker and then the past tense. It is possible that the difficulty could arise at the lower level of the structure in (13) where the learner is trying to understand how to progressivize a telic VP[vi]. If this were the problem, then we should see difficulty with the progressive in general as long as the VP is telic; the difficulty should then be apparent in both the present and past progressive. However, results showed more pronounced difficulty in the past progressive so this can't be the whole story.

We could also consider that the difficulty could arise in the interpretation of the past. If the learner incorrectly maps perfective aspect onto the past tense, then the perfective aspect would take scope over the progressive aspect and the resulting interpretation would be perfective. This proposal predicts difficulty with past progressive forms in general and is thus compatible with my results for the Low group. However if the difficulty is all in the past tense, we still cannot explain why there is an effect for the VP: the difficulty is more pronounced with achievements.

It is more likely that a combination of the two proposals is needed. Learners may have a tendency to map perfective aspect onto past morphology but they may be more likely to do so when the VP is strongly telic. Achievements are arguably more telic than accomplishments in that they do not denote events that can be measured out along a direct object, process or path.

We propose for the past progressive that the learners are having difficulty mapping specific semantic distinctions onto specific pieces of morphology. This mapping difficulty may arise because the computation is so complex. It is also possible that the input to the learner is not robust. The past progressive is often used to provide background information and thus may not allow the learner to evaluate a given sentence against an observable real world context. In addition, there was variability even in the native speaker judgments.

In summary, we proposed for the past progressive that L2 learners follow the same developmental path as children. We've argued that the past progressive is so difficult due to a number of factors: the complexity of the semantic computation; the potential difficulty mapping particular semantic distinctions onto specific pieces of morphology; a lack of robust positive evidence.

We have shown that a comprehensive model of the acquisition of L2 aspect requires us to go beyond the question of whether or not aspect is acquirable given the properties of the L1 and L2 grammar. We also need to consider the input and general patterns of language development. Only by evaluating the interaction of these factors can we address the question of why the acquisition of aspect presents such a complex puzzle in L2 acquisition.

Notes

[i] The study reported here is part of the author's dissertation work completed at the CUNY Graduate Center. This research was supported by NSF grant #0345697 to Alison Gabriele and Gita Martohardjono and the Mario Capelloni dissertation fellowship at the CUNY Graduate Center. I would like to thank Gita Martohardjono, Bill McClure, Virginia Valian and Marcel den Dikken for their guidance and support on this project. Noriaki Yusa deserves special thanks for hosting me in Sendai and for making data collection possible. Thanks to Erika Troseth and Harold Torrence for comments on this paper.
[ii] This study is part of a bidirectional experiment where both Japanese learners of English and English-speaking learners of Japanese were tested. See Gabriele (2005) for details.
[iii] The interaction of the progressive with stative verb phrases is not relevant in this paper.
[iv] Due to space limitations details of the formal analysis will not be presented. See Gabriele (2005, in progress) for further discussion.

ᵛ The simple past was included primarily as a control and due to space limitations cannot be discussed here. Filler sentences and distractors were also included but will not be discussed.
ᵛⁱ Thanks to Roumyana Slabakova for discussion of this point.

References

De Swart, H. (1998) Aspect shift and coercion. *Natural Language and Linguistic Theory* 16(2), 347-385.

Dowty, D. (1979) *Word meaning and Montague grammar*, Dordrecht and Boston: D. Reidel Publishing Co.

Gabriele, A. (2005) *The acquisition of aspect in a second language: a bidirectional study of learners of English and Japanese*, Doctoral dissertation, CUNY Graduate Center.

—. (in progress) Learnability and transfer in the L2 acquisition of aspect: a bidirectional study of learners of English and Japanese. Ms. Univ. of Kansas.

Inagaki, S. (2001) Motion verbs with goal PPs in the L2 acquisition of English and Japanese. *Studies in Second Language Acquisition* 23, 153-170.

Juffs, A. (1996) *Learnability and the lexicon: theories and second language acquisition research,* Amsterdam: John Benjamins

Landman, F. (1992) The Progressive. *Natural Language Semantics* 1: 1-32.

McClure, W. (1995) *Syntactic projections of the semantics of aspect*, Tokyo: Hituzi Syobo.

Ogihara, T. (1998) The ambiguity of the *–te iru* form in Japanese. *Journal of East Asian Linguistics* 7, 87-120.

Parsons, T. (1990) *Events in the semantics of English: A study in subatomic semantics*. Cambridge, MA: MIT Press.

Schwartz, B. (1993) On explicit and negative data effecting and affecting competence and linguistic behavior. *Studies in second language acquisition* 15, 147-163.

—. and Sprouse, R. (1994) Word order and nominative case in non-native language acquisition: a longitudinal study of (L1 Turkish) German interlanguage. In T. Hoekstra and B. Schwartz (Eds.), *Language Acquisition Studies in Generative Grammar*. Amsterdam: John Benjamins.

—. and Sprouse, R. (1996) L2 cognitive states and the Full Transfer/Full Access model. *Second Language Research* 12: 40-72.

Sorace, A. (1999) Initial states, end states, and residual optionality in L2 acquisition. Proceedings of the *Boston University Conference on Language Development*. Somerville, MA: Cascadilla Press.

—. (2003) Near-nativeness. In C. Doughty and M. Long (Eds.), *The Handbook of Second Language Acquisition*. Oxford: Blackwell.

Wagner, L. (2001) Aspectual influences on early tense comprehension. *Journal of Child Language* 28: 661-681.

White, L. (1985) The pro-drop parameter in second language acquisition. *Language Learning* 35, 47-62.

—. (1990/91) The verb-movement parameter in second language acquisition. *Language Acquisition* 1: 337-60.

—. (1992) On triggering data in L2 acquisition: a reply to Schwartz and Gubala-Ryzak. *Second Language Research* 8, 120-137.

THE ACQUISITION OF DETERMINERS: EVIDENCE FOR THE FULL COMPETENCE HYPOTHESIS[*]

GIULIANA GIUSTI AND ROBERTA GOZZI

1. Introduction

This paper addresses the following question: Are functional projections subject to maturation or are they already present at the very earliest stages of acquisition?

Assuming that phonology is acquired in stages (cf. Demuth 1996, 2001, Selkirk 1996, Lleó 2000, and Gozzi 2004 a. o.), if PF "filters out" the production, functional words may be present in the syntactic structure even if missing at the interface level. We take this as the "null hypothesis".

In the minimalist program, syntax should at best be derivable from properties "imposed by the sensorimotor (S-M) system and the conceptual-intentional (C-I) system" (Chomsky 2005:10). The two interfaces (PF/LF) should therefore provide a "filtering effect" in language acquisition and language processing, as well as on the output in language production. In this paper, we focus on the "filtering" effect of PF in early productions and claim that even at the earliest stage there is no strong reason to doubt that syntactic structure is fully present.

Our claims are grounded on original data collected by Roberta Gozzi in 2003-4 in the *Gaia corpus*, which consists in 15 video-recordings of spontaneous speech of an Italian child from 19 to 30 months of age, complemented by diary notes.

We also claim that counting the occurrences of bare nouns and articles with no reference to the length of the lexical noun obscures one important fact, namely that articles and word-initial weak syllables appear at the same time and are at first in complementary distribution. If the phonological context is not taken into consideration, the Gaia corpus presents the same tendency that has grounded the hypothesis that early occurrences of articles are "fillers", that there is a stage in which article omission co-exists with article insertion, as shown in chart (1).

(1) Occurrences of articles (with no regard to syllable structure):

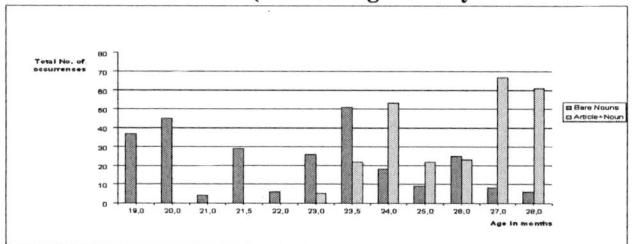

However, if utterance length is taken into consideration with regard to syllable structure, the results are more straightforward, as is shown in table (2):

(2) Occurrences of articles with regard to syllable structure

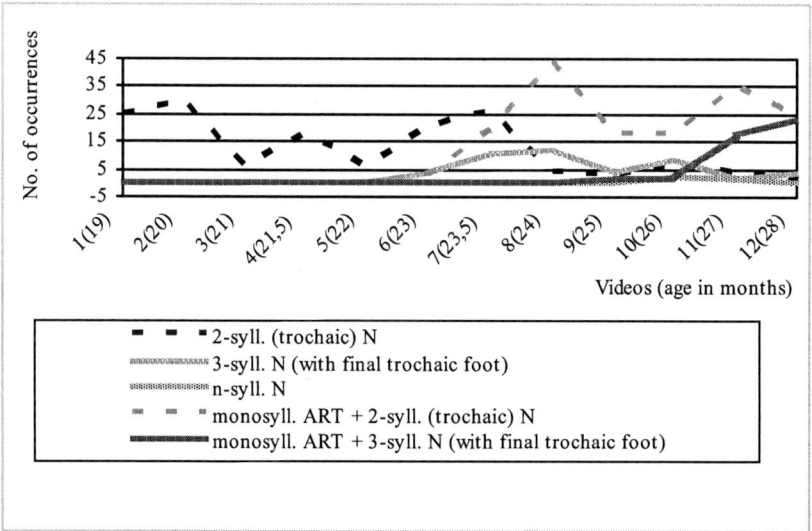

In graphic (2), recording #5, trisyllabic nouns (with a trochaic final foot) with no article and trochaic nouns with a monosyllabic article appear at the same time as the first occurrences of the article, which at this time only precedes trochaic nouns. The correlation is straightforward: in both cases the PF output is a structure with a weak syllable preceding a trochey. Only three months later, in #

9, we have the first occurrence of a monosyllabic article appearing with a trisyllabic noun. The second occurrence of which is in the next recording (#10), where polisyllabic nouns also appear for the first time, and where we also find the earliest occurrences of disyllabic articles, namely the indefinite *una and uno*. The option of the resulting polisyllabic structure with a weak trochaic foot preceding a strong trochaic foot is exploited in #11 and #12 respectively in many occurrences.

If we can show from the analysis of the context that after the stages in which the article is phonologically possible in a give syllabic structure its lack is due to independent semantic factors (e.g. maturation of semantic competence), we can claim that the functional structure to merge the article is there from the very beginning (Full competence) and what is to be acquired in order to obtain an adult-like distribution is its morphology, and its semantics but not its syntax. Unfortunately this cannot be done in this short paper, but at a first recognition it appears to be probably the case.

2. The acquisition of prosodic structure and the production of articles.

The Gaia corpus (Gozzi 2004) evidences a development in the acquisition of prosodic structure that reflects some stages already observed in the acquisition of Spanish (cf. Demuth 2001, Lleò 2000). Gaia's early production are clearly shaped on a prosodic basis: adult targets are accommodated through omission of weak syllables into distinct constrained prosodic units, that expand over time. Gozzi (2004) identifies four stages. These provide a unified account for a number of phenomena: a) the reduced shape of lexical items; b) the omission of definite articles; c) the omission of prepositions; d) the particular behaviour of the indefinite article (the much later appearance of the feminine form *una* with respect to the masculine form *un*). Our main contribution here is to observe the four stages of prosodic development in the perspective of the appearance of articles.

At Stage 1 (age 1;7-1;10), utterances do not extend beyond the Prosodic Word (PW) and consist in no more than one trochaic foot, as in table (3). Articles are never produced at this stage. Our claim is that this is because articles are weak proclitic syllables (σ_w) and cannot initiate the PW. For this reason they "get lost" at the PF interface in (3b,c,e) due to the same restructuring process which affects the word initial weak syllable/foot of lexical words such as those in (3a,f,g):[1†]

(3) *Child*	*Adult target*	*Gloss*	*Prosodic structure*
a. tàto	tabàcco	tobacco	
b. pùpo	[il] prosciùtto	[the] ham	
c. òa	[un']olìva	[an] olive	F/PW
d. tàta	àcqua	water	
e. ài/àli	[i] cereàli	[the] cereals	
f. nìni	fiorellìni	little flowers	σ_s σ_w
g. tènta	attènta	careful (fem.)	

Note that gender and number are always correctly represented, as in (3g) and (3e,f). This suggests that these features are already projected at this early stage.

At Stage 2 (age 1;10-1;11), the PW is still the maximal level available. At this stage the appearance of the earliest articles coincides with the first production of trisyllabic bare nouns as in (4). Definite articles and indefinite *un* appear at the same time. This is in favour of Full Competence interacting with a PF filter which blocks a prosodic structure such as (4b). We see no other reason for the avoidance of *una*, given that gender agreement is target-like already at the previous stage and the indefinite article (*un*) is attested and semantically appropriate to the context.

Articles only appear with trochaic nouns. Trisyllabic nouns with the prosodic structure in (4a) are produced freely; but none of them is preceded by any article. This would create (4b) which is not available yet, as shown by the restructuring of quadrisyllabic nouns such as *cucchiaino*. Bisyllabic *caffè*, with no article in (4g) is no counterexample. The syllabic structure enhanced by the insertion of an article would be a version of (4b), with a trochaic weak foot preceding a strong monosyllabic foot. Such a structure is predicted not to be present at this stage.

(4) *Child*	*Adult target*	*Gloss*	*Prosodic structure*
a. e nòci	le nòci	the nuts	
b. a tàta	la tàta	the little girl	a) PW b) • PW
c. un patto	un piatto	a dish	
d. soddìno	[un] soldìno	[a] coin	F
e. cuchìno	[il/un] cucchiaìno	[the/a] little spoon	(σ_w) σ_s σ_w σ_s σ_w σ_s σ_w
f. ontìna	[la] lontrìna	[the] little otter	
g. tattè	[il] caffè	[the] coffee	

Stage 3 (age 1;11-2;2) involves the possibility to prosodify an article at the level of Prosodic Phrase (PP), resulting in an unfooted syllable at the left of a PW, as in (5a). This procedure does not apply freely, but is a last resort to express functional features such as gender and number. In fact, the first articles to appear with trisyllabic nouns are inserted with nouns that do not bear overt gender (*pampam, baubàu*) or whose gender is ambiguous (*signoe* is either femm. pl. or masc. sing.). The ban on (4b) above persists, as in *Popìmo* (targ.: *Topolìno*). From this, we conclude that the PW is still constrained to no more than one unfooted syllable preceding either one trochaic foot or a single strong syllabe (5c):

(5) *Child*   *Adult target* *Gloss*   *Prosodic structures*

Popìmo   Topolino   Mickey Mouse
a nànna   a nanna   to bed
da sòla   da sola   by [my]self
i pampàm   i *onomat.*   the *on. for balls*
i baubàu   il *onomat.*   the *on. for dogs*
e signòe   le signore   the ladies
            cf. il signore vs. the gentelman

At this stage, simple Ps also appear for the first time. We conjecture that they do not appear at Stage 2 because they are only at the PP level. This level appears to be bootstrapped only at Stage 3 by the functional requirement of syntax to make gender and number features visible. When these uninterpretable features are visible on the noun, the occurrence of the article with trisyllabic words is still avoided. The semantic choice for definite or indefinite articles is arbitrary since both appear in turn in repetitions. This suggests that, at least in early syntax, articles are inserted only to realize uninterpretable features (cf. Giusti 2002) and are not directly related to interpretive properties of the C-I system, also subject to maturation (cf. Chierchia, Guasti and Gualmini 1999).

At stage 4 (from age 2;2 on), we finally find the appearance of words with four or more syllables, and of the indefinite articles *una* and *uno*. Now all articles are inserted independently from the phonological shape of the nouns. At this level, we also find articulated prepositions, adjectival modification, Quantifiers and Demonstratives merged in the DP, as in the examples given in (6) all target-like. This stage still misses the dactilic foot which is restructured into a trochey (7a). For this, verbal 3rd pers. pl. is non-target (7b):

(6)   a. *un tato con la sua mamma. [#] che ciuccia le poppe della sua mamma*
         a child with his mum. [#] that sucks the tits of his mum. (2;2.10)
      b. *un ciuccio grande del tato* (2;2.28)
         a pacifier big of the child (target-like)

c. *la gallina* + *... non c'è il suo amico,* # *il gallino* (syntax taget-like, *il gallino* non-target but morphologically well formed)

(7) a. àbo [target: albero, *tree*] pùnco/puzza [target: puzzola, *polecat*]
     b. bévo [target: bévono, *they drink*]   prènde [target: prèndere, *to take*]

We conclude that Stage 4 is not the final one in a multiple-phase spell-out system. Further research is needed to establish the stages of the maturation of multiple spell-outs.

3. Conclusions

With respect to the two functional layers of nominal structure (AgrP and DP), we conclude that they are both present in core syntax at the very earliest stage, according to the Full Competence Hypothesis. Articles can be missing for the following reasons: a) they are merged but not pronounced, due to incomplete maturation of the S-M system; b) their semantics is not yet acquired due to incomplete maturation of the C-I system; c) the lexical forms of articles are not yet acquired due to maturation of the lexicon. None of the reasons above have to do with maturation of core syntax, but are dependent on maturation at the interfaces.

Notes

* Thanks to Alessandra Giorgi and Maria Teresa Guasti for discussion and comments.

[1] Under the heading *Adult target*, the tables provide an article in brackets when needed by the context. Elements glossed without an article are target like as such.

References

Chomsky, N. (2005) "Three factors in language design" *Linguistic Inquiry* 36(1): 1-22.

Chierchia, G., M.T. Guasti and A. Gualmini (1999) "Noun and articles in child grammar and the syntax/semantcs map", Paper presented at GALA, Potsdam.

Demuth, K. (1996) "The prosodic structure of early words", in J.L. Morgan and K. Demuth (eds.) *Signal to syntax: Bootstrapping from speech to grammar in early acquisition*, Mahwah, New Jersey: Lawrence Erlbaum Associates, Publishers, 171-184.

—. (2001) "Prosodic constraints on morphological development", in Weissenborn and B Höhle (eds.) *Approaches to bootstrapping*, vol . 2 Amsterdam/Philadelphia, John Benjamins, 3-22.

Giusti, G. (2002) "The functional structure of noun phrases: A bare phrase structure approach". In Guglielmo Cinque (ed.) *Functional Structure in DP and IP. The Cartography of Syntactic Structures,* vol.1, Oxford University Press, 54-90.

Gozzi, R. (2004) *The Acquisition of Determiners. A longitudinal study on an Italian child.* Tesi di laurea. Università Ca' Foscari Venezia.

Lleó, C. (2000) "The interface of phonology and syntax. The emergence of the article in the early acquisition of Spanish and German" in *Approaches to bootstrapping,* Amsterdam/Philadelphia, John Benjamins.

Selkirk, E. (1996) "The prosodic structure of function words", in J.L. Morgan and K. Demuth (eds.) *Signal to syntax: Bootstrapping from speech to grammar in early acquisition,* Mahwah, New Jersey: Lawrence Erlbaum Associates, Publishers, 187-213.

DOES ASPECT MATTER IN CHILD L2 ACQUISITION? REVISITING THE RELATIONSHIP BETWEEN INHERENT ASPECT OF PREDICATES AND THEIR FINITENESS IN CHILD L2 ACQUISITION OF ENGLISH

BELMA HAZNEDAR

1. Introduction

It has long been noted that grammatical morphemes cause problems for learners both in first (L1) and second language (L2) acquisition (e.g. Brown, 1973; Dulay, Burt & Krashen, 1982). In most cases, learners exhibit optionality or variability in the use of morphology relating to tense, agreement, case and/or gender as well as functional elements such as determiners, complementizers and auxiliaries. While much work in recent child L2 acquisition literature has focused on the acquisition of tense and agreement morphology (e.g. Grondin & White, 1996; Haznedar, 2001; Ionin & Wexler, 2002), the development of tense-aspect morphology has also been studied extensively both in monolingual and bilingual language acquisition (e.g. Antinucci & Miller, 1976; Shirai and Andersen, 1995; ; Shirai, 1998), as well as in adult L2 acquisition (e.g. Robison, 1995; Bardovi-Harlig & Bergström, 1996).

With the exception of some studies (e.g. Rohde, 1996; Gavruseva, 2002, 2003, 2004), there has been little discussion of how tense/aspect morphology develops in child L2 acquisition. Based on longitudinal data from a Turkish-speaking child L2 learner of English, the primary aim of this paper is to investigate the acquisition of tense/aspect in child L2 acquisition of English with special reference to Gavruseva's underspecification of AspP hypothesis (Gavruseva, 2002, 2003, 2004).

The organization of the paper is as follows. Section 2 introduces Gavruseva's account of root infinitives in child L2 acquisition, with an emphasis on verb semantics and the notion of the underspecification of the

AspP. Section 3 presents the child L2 data and its analysis. Finally, Section 4 discusses the findings in terms of the Underspecification of the AspP hypothesis.

2. An aspectual account of root infinitives in child L2 acquisition

In recent work, Gavruseva (2002, 2003, 2004) proposes an analysis of the infinitive-like verb forms in finite contexts, a phenomenon known as the Optional infinitive (OI) stage or Root infinitive (RI) stage, during which children acquiring Dutch, German, Swedish, French, English use infinitives in root contexts (e.g. Wexler, 1994; Rizzi, 1994). Based on Hoekstra & Hyams' (1998) earlier work on child L1 acquisition which shows that optional/root infinitives in languages such as Dutch, German and French occur with eventive predicates, Gavruseva (2002, 2003, 2004) relates the OI/RI phenomenon to the aspectual properties of the verb. Following the aktionsart typology of verbs proposed by Vendler (1967), she proposes that stative verbs such as *like and love* are inherently atelic, as they are assumed to have no end point and that punctual verbs such as *break and fall* are inherently telic, as they have an intrinsic end point. The telicity of non-punctual verbs such as *eat*, on the other hand, is dependent on the other elements in the VP. Following Borer (1994), Gavruseva (2002) also assumes that telicity is a syntactic feature that is checked by the verb in an AspP. Under Gavruseva's account, only the non-punctual verbs, which are unspecified for telicity, moves in an AspP projection. Their telicity feature is determined by the argument in the specifier of AspP. In line with Guerón & Hoekstra (1995), Gavruseva also assumes that the temporal interpretation of the clause is given by a tense chain where AspP is included.

Under Gavruseva's approach, '*A Tense Operator cannot bind Tense unless a VP predicate is specified for syntactic aspectual features*' (Gavruseva, 2003: 64)

Root infinitives appear when AspP is underspecified, as a tense chain cannot be formed in the absence of Asp. Gavruseva's theory predicts that statives and punctual eventives which are inherently specified for telicity licence a tense chain. Non-finite clauses, root infinitives and bare verbs, on the other hand, will be restricted to non-punctual eventive verbs, as they require a grammatical specification of Asp to license a tense chain. These predictions are given in (1).

(1)   a.   Statives (e.g. love) occur in finite contexts.

       b.   Punctual eventives (e.g. fall) occur in finite contexts.

       c.   Non-punctual eventive verbs (e.g. run) occur in non-finite contexts.

In the next section, we discuss the child L2 data that will be used as an empirical source for testing the acquisition of tense-aspect morphology with special reference to the distribution of temporal and aspectual interpretation of verb forms in child L2 acquisition of English.

3. The present study

The data analyzed in this paper come from a Turkish-speaking child, Erdem, who started acquiring English at age 4 in the UK. The longitudinal data consist of 46 recordings, covering a period of approximately 18 months. Following the coding procedure used in Shirai and Andersen (1995) and Gavruseva (2002), verbs were classified according to aspectual types, stative or eventive, with eventive verbs being further broken down into punctual and non-punctual. As in Gavruseva (2002), accomplishments and activities are combined as non-punctual eventives and achievements are taken as punctual eventives. The lexical aspect of the verbs was determined through standard tests for aspect (e.g. Vendler, 1967; Shirai & Andersen, 1995). Only root declarative utterances with a VP predicate are coded as bare or past forms.

4. Results

4.1. Tense marking

In regard to the acquisition patterns found in the study, first it should be noted that past tense forms do not appear at the earliest point in Erdem's L2 English. Rather, the development of past forms is gradual (see, Haznedar, 2001). As in L1 acquisition of English (e.g. Brown, 1973), irregular past tense forms such as *did* and *bought* are produced prior to regular past tense forms such as *played* and *painted*. Regular past inflection -*ed* is supplied in fewer obligatory contexts, compared to irregular past forms. Past morphology is first and predominantly used with achievement verbs. Accomplishment verbs are marked with past tense in a lesser extent. Past tense morphology is then used with atelic verbs.

4.2. Testing Gavruseva's 'Underspecification of the Aspect Hypothesis'

As noted in Section 2, Gavruseva's Underspecification of the Aspect hypothesis makes specific predictions in regard to the distribution of root infinitives.

With regard to Prediction 1, that statives will be finite, Table 1 shows that only 58% of statives are finite.

Table 1. Finite and uninflected (bare) stative verbs

	Finite	Bare statives
Child	35/60 (58%)	25/60 (**42%**)

Prediction (2), that punctual verbs should occur in finite contexts, is not confirmed in the data. The proportion of bare punctuals in the corpus is %63 (478/759), which is rather high.

Table 2. Inflected (+Finite) vs. uninflected (bare, -Finite) punctual verbs

	Finite	Bare punctuals
Child	281/759 (37%)	478/759 (**63%**)

These results demonstrate that only 37% of punctual verbs are finite. This is in marked contrast to what is predicted in Gavruseva's model. Clearly, punctual verbs occur in non-finite form.

With regard to Prediction 3, we find that while non-punctuals occur in non-finite contexts, the proportion of bare non-punctuals is lower than that of bare punctuals. As can be seen in Table 3, the proportion of bare non-punctuals is 56% (264/468), as opposed to 63% bare punctuals.

Table 3. Finite and uninflected (bare) non-punctual verbs

	Finite	Bare non-punctuals
Child	204/468 (44%)	264/468 (**56%**)

Overall, the proportion of bare punctual verbs is unexpectedly high, and this contrasts with the lower proportion of bare non-punctuals. Gavrueseva's 'underspecification of the AspP' hypothesis does not predict a higher proportion of bare punctuals. On the contrary, bare verbs during the Optional/Root infinitive stage should have been virtually non-punctual eventives. These results are fully compatible with Torrence & Hyams' (2004) study on L1 English. While Gavruseva's approach to root infinitives is of interesting in itself, it fails to account for why more punctual verbs remain uninflected in comparison to uninflected non-punctual verbs. Overall, we conclude that Gavruseva's underspecification of aspectual features account is not supported by the child L2 data analyzed in this paper.

References

Antinucci, F. and R. Miller (1976) "How children talk about what happened", *Journal of Child Language,* 3, 169-189.

Bardovi-Harlig, K. and A. Bergström (1996) "The acquisition of tense and aspect in second language and foreign language learning: Learner narratives in English (SL) and French (FL)", *Canadian Modern Language Review,* 52: 308-330.

Borer, H. (1994) "The projection of arguments", in E. Benedicto and J. Runner (eds), *UMass Occasional Papers in Linguistics,* 17: 19–47, Amherst, MA: GLSA.

Brown, R. (1973) *A first language,* Cambridge, MA: Harvard University Press.

Dulay, H.C., M.K. Burt and S. Krashen (1982) *Language Two,* New York: OUP.

Gavruseva, E. (2002) "Is there primacy of aspect in child L2 English?", *Bilingualism: Language and Cognition,* 5 (2), 109-130.

—. (2003) "Aktionsart, aspect and the acquisition of finiteness in early child grammar" *Linguistics,* 41 (4), 723-755.

—. (2004)"Root infinitives in child second language English: an aspectual features account", *Second Language Research,* 20 (4), 335-371.

Grondin, N and L. White (1996) "Functional categories in child L2 acquisition of French" *Language Acquisition,* 1, 1-34.

Guerón, J. and T. Hoekstra (1995) "The temporal interpretation of predication", in A. Cardinaletti and M.T. Guasti (eds.) *Small clauses, syntax and semantics,* 77-107.

Haznedar, B. (2001) "The acquisition of the IP system in child L2 acquisition" *Studies in Second Language Acquisition,* 23, 1-39.

Hoekstra, T. and N. Hyams (1998) "Aspects of root infinitives", *Lingua,* 106, 81-112.

Ionin, T. and K. Wexler (2002) "Why is 'is' easier than '-s'?: Acquisition of tense/agreement morphology by child second language learners of English", *Second Language Research,* 18 (2), 95-136.

Lardiere, D. (1998) "Case and Tense in the 'fossilized' steady state" *Second Language Research, 14* (1), 1-26.

Prévost, P. and L. White (2000) "Missing surface inflection or impairment in second language? Evidence from Tense and Agreement", *Second Language Research,* 16 (2), 103-133.

Rizzi, L. (1994) "Early null subjects and root null subjects", in T. Hoekstra and B. D. Schwartz (eds.) *Language Acquisition Studies in Generative Grammar,* Amsterdam: John Benjamins, 151-76

Robison, R.E. (1990) "The primacy of aspect: Aspectual marking in English interlanguage" *Studies in Second Language Acquisition*, 12, 315-330.

Rohde, A. (1996) "The aspect hypothesis and the emergence of tense distinctions in naturalistic L2 acquisition" *Linguistics*, 34, 1115-1137.

Shirai, Y. (1998) "The emergence of tense/aspect morphology in Japanese: Universal disposition", *First Language*, 18, 281-310.

—. and R.W. Andersen (1995) "The acquisition of tense-aspect morphology: A prototype account", *Language*, 71 (4), 743-762.

Torrence, H. and N. Hyams (2004) "On the role of aspect in determining Finiteness and Temporal interpretation of early grammar" *Proceedings of GALA 10*, LOT. University of Utrecht, The Netherlands.

Vendler, Z. (1967) "Verbs and times", *Philosophical Review 56,* 143-160.

Wexler, K. (1994) "Optional Infinitives, head movement and the economy of derivations", in D. Lightfoot and N. Hornstein (eds.) *Verb movement*, Cambridge, Cambridge University Press, 305-50.

DEVELOPING INTERLANGUAGE MORPHOSYNTAX: A CASE STUDY OF L2 FRENCH

JULIA HERSCHENSOHN

1. Introduction

Two UG accessible approaches to L2A propose opposing possibilities for parameter resetting, dependent on the capacity of interlanguage grammars to gain new values for uninterpretable functional features. The Representational Deficit hypothesis (RDH, Hawkins & Chan 1997, Franceschina 2001, Hawkins & Franceschina 2004) maintains that parameter settings are limited to L1 values, the cause of L2 morphological errors, while Missing Surface Inflection (MSI, Lardiere 2000, Prévost & White 2000) allows acquisition of new values, attributing morphological errors to PF mapping difficulties. I examine accuracy of verb morphology and syntax in production and grammaticality judgement (GJ) of Chloe, an advanced anglophone learner of L2 French, in terms of these two theories, first describing the theoretical issues, then presenting the data and discussing it. I conclude that the results favor MSI over RDH.

2. Syntactic theory

In the bare phrase structure framework (Chomsky 2001, 2002, 2004), syntactic combinations result mainly from the operations Merge and Agree, building syntactic structure from an array of lexical items that combine from the bottom up (Epstein and Hornstein 1999, Ndayiragije 1999). Lexical items have interpretable features necessary for semantic interpretation that persist at LF, and uninterpretable features of functional categories that must be valued and deleted before Spell-out. Merge, an operation licensed by such a match, combines two elements that mutually select one another, while Agree matches features and deletes uninterpretable ones. As Chomsky (2001, 3) says "we therefore have a relation Agree holding between α and β, where α has interpretable inflectional features and β has uninterpretable ones, which delete under Agree."

Two factors related to verb agreement are the morphological form and feature configuration of verbs upon entry into a derivation. Lasnik (1999) suggests that the lexical entry for main verbs in English is their bare form, with the bare form and T joined at PF by "affix hopping." In opposition to the bare English forms (1b), French verbs enter the numeration fully inflected, with Tense specified as a feature (1a).

(1)   a. <u>Nous</u> (n')embrass<u>ons</u> *souvent / jamais* Marie.
       b. <u>We</u> *often / never* kiss Mary.

This distinction between the two languages reflects the well-accepted difference in richness of morphology that has been long cited as a criterion determining the verb raising parameter (Emonds 1978, Pollock 1989, Koeneman & Neeleman 2001). French, with its relatively rich morphology requires raising of all finite verbs to T to check agreement, whereas English main verbs remain in situ in VP and only auxiliaries and modals raise. A diagnostic for locating the position of the verb is the placement of negation, adverbs and quantifiers which are assumed to be in a left adjoined position to VP in both English and French. In English they remain left of the verb (1b), but in French they follow the inflected verb, indicating that the verb has moved above them to T. In infinitival clauses French thematic verbs without tense cannot raise, so negation and adverbs precede (2).

(2)   French unraised infinitives
       a. Ne pas embrasser Marie serait un supplice
       'Not to kiss Mary would be a torture.'
       b. Souvent embrasser Marie serait un plaisir.
       'Often to kiss Mary would be a pleasure.'

In a discussion of the parametric variation in verb raising, Thráinsson (2003, 166) provides a definition of morphological richness—"clearly separable tense and agreement morphemes in the verbal inflection"—and relates it to his Split IP Parameter:

(3)   Split IP Parameter (p. 164)
       Languages that have a positive value for the SIP have AgrSP and TP as separate functional projections whereas languages with a negative value of the SIP are characterized by an unsplit IP.

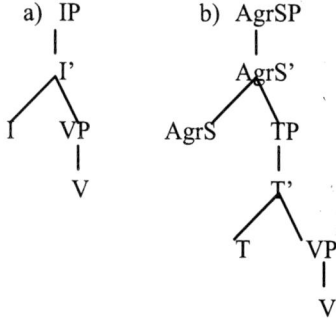

The trees illustrate that languages with the split (3b) require verb raising since VP is not in the checking domain of AgrSP (because TP intervenes), whereas with a simple IP (unsplit, (3a)) the verb can be checked in situ (the case for English). In the minimalist spirit of reducing the number of functional categories to *v*, T and C, the SIP can be interpreted as a description of features of T which allow additional projections. Recall that Chomsky's (2002) characterization of the EPP is as a feature that creates a landing place for a moved phrase. Similarly, in a [+SIP] language, T would carry features for both finite tense and person (AgrS), engendering the "split IP"; in [-SIP] languages T would only carry finite tense, and the impoverished agreement that does show up is a PF phenomenon. This analysis complements Lasnik's suggestions concerning French-English differences in verb morphology.

Using the probe-goal terminology, the verb raises in [+SIP] languages to check the uninterpretable [Agr] feature on T, which is subsequently deleted by the interpretable [+/- past] of the inflected verb; the inflected verb then raises to the second specifier of TP required by AgrS to check off that uninterpretable [Agr] feature with interpretable person features of the inflected verb. The raising of the subject entails that the uninterpretable nominative Case feature of the subject is also deleted in the match (Pesetsky & Torrego 2001).[1] Summarizing, main verbs in French are fully inflected, raised and checked for tense / person inflection in TP and AgrSP, while English main verbs do not raise and check only auxiliaries in TP (Lasnik 1999). The uninterpretable feature, [+Agr] is crucial to both tense and person agreement in French, with the interpretable features overtly marked on the verb valuing uninterpretable [+Agr] in the functional categories T and AgrS, the split IP.

3. L2A theory

For verb raising, anglophone learners need to gain a split IP for L2 French, with uninterpretable [Agr] on T and AgrS deleted by the raised inflected main verb (or auxiliary). How might learners go about this task, and how could their development be theoretically framed? I examine two approaches to L2A that I label RDH and MSI.

RDH encompasses a number of studies which generally attribute morphological errors in the L2 to a syntactic flaw, not a morphological one (Hawkins & Chan 1997, Hawkins 2001, Franceschina, 2001, Hawkins & Franceschina 2004). Following a proposal by Tsimpli & Roussou (1991) and Smith & Tsimpli (1995) that parameter setting can only take place during the Critical Period, the RDH (Hawkins & Chan, 1997, Franceschina, 2001) holds that parameterized L2 functional features may fail in post Critical Period L2 acquisition, leading to surface morphology errors. The authors maintain that the native values of uninterpretable functional features are available throughout life to the adult L2 learner, but that after the Critical Period parametric values that differ from L1 cannot be acquired. Hawkins & Franceschina (2004) suggest that the threshold of the Critical Period is nine years of age. For them inflectional errors are due in large part to a syntactic deficit in underlying competence in adults. Tsimpli & Roussou attribute superficially correct forms to misanalysis, the transfer of an L1 grammatical strategy which gives an interlanguage result resembling the target L2 superficial form, but which is not target–like in the interlanguage grammatical competence.

In contrast, MSI holds that the L2 grammar may access both native and L2 functional features (Schwartz & Sprouse 1996), but that syntax is not directly linked to the mastery of morphological inflection. Lardiere (1998), who studies an L2 learner of English (with Chinese as L1), shows that her subject Patty has very stable and accurate syntax, but that Patty's morphology is consistently flawed: she produces tense errors at a rate greater than 50%, yet makes no mistakes in her use of nominative pronouns. Lardiere subscribes to the idea of Missing Inflection (Haznedar & Schwartz 1997, Prévost & White 2000), attributing mistakes to a number of mapping difficulties in PF realization. Errors are then seen as superficial performance mistakes, not deep syntactic deficits. Since L2A is similar for children and adults on this theory, there is no Critical Period functional feature deficit to examine.

The two approaches to L2 morphosyntax predict opposite developments for the French VR parameter with respect to anglophone learners. For anglophones learning French, RDH expects no parameter resetting and misanalyzed syntax with concomitant morphological errors; whereas MSI allows eventual mastery of split IP (uninterpretable [Agr] on T and AgrS) and correct syntax with possible performance errors of morphology.

4. Data

In order to consider the relationship of explicit morphology and functional categories in the emerging L2, this study looks at the development of morphological competence—specifically verb inflection—in an advanced anglophone subject who spends nine months in France as a English language teaching assistant in a French lycée. The corpus consists of three interviews conducted before, during and after the period abroad.

Before becoming an an *assistante d'anglais* in the French department of Réunion after college graduation, Chloe, had studied French for nine years: two years in middle school, two years in high school, and six months residence in France at age 16 (Herschensohn 2001, 2003); subsequently she studied French in college and spent six months in France her junior year (age 20). During her nine months in France as an *assistante* she lived with a French housemate and worked daily with French speakers in the lycée.[2]

I document Chloe's development of French verb inflection and her syntactic control of verb raising in three interviews conducted over nine months. Table 1 tallies tokens of non-finite and finite verbs, and errors in use of finite verbs; Table 2 shows tokens of VP negation, adverbs, and quantifiers. The small number of adverb and quantifier diagnostics are supplemented by grammaticality judgements discussed below.

Table1. Chloe's TP data and errors

Interview	V-fin	V+fin	Total	Err's+fin	% Error
I	29	150	179	3	2%
II	33	231	264	3	1%
III	85	372	457	3	0%
Total	147	384	900	9	1

Table2. Chloe's VR diagnostics

Interview	Negation	Adverb	Quantifier	Err's VR	% Error
I	18	1	2	0	0%
II	28	5	0	0	0%
III	50	6	1	0	0%
Total	96	12	3	0	0%

These errors include only conjugational mistakes, not lexical errors (use of a pronominal verb as a non-pronominal, two; an incorrect non-finite, two;

incorrect auxiliary, one), or mistakes in choice of aspect; her non-finite verbs are all correct. Despite lexical and other grammatical errors, Chloe uses all verbal persons in a range of tenses (present, *passé composé*, imperfect, pluperfect, future, and conditional), increases her use of correct verbal morphology, and reduces errors from the first to the third interview. The principal finite verb error (7/9) is third singular for third plural (4), an apparent default since the mistake only goes in one direction. The Roman numeral indicates the interview.

(4)   Examples of singular-plural mistakes
  a. *les   trois ne   va pas marcher* (I)
       the-PL   three neg goes not to walk
       'the three are not going to walk' = v*ont*
       ils   prend   le travail (II)
       they-M-PL take-3-SG   the work
       'they take the work' = *prennent*
  b. *des   sujets   qui   doit   être enseignés* (III)
       some-PL subjects-PL   that must-3-SG to be taught
       'subjects that must be taught' = *doivent*

(5)   *ils prendent* (II)
       they   take-3-PL
       'they take' = *ils prennent*

The morphological error in (5) can be seen as an example of overregularization of an irregular verb *prendre* to the regular *rendre* ('render') paradigm (6); in the singular persons the regular and irregular verb are identical for the present tense.

(6)   *rendre / prendre*
       a. *ils rendent*
          they render-3-PL
          'they render'
       b. *il rend*
          he renders-3-SG
          'he renders'
       c. *il prend*
          he takes-3-SG
          'he takes'

The one instance of a null subject (*comment se fait [le vin]* 'how [wine] is made') is in the context of a middle voice construction which would prohibit an expletive subject in null subject languages; in spoken French null subjects are licit in certain impersonal constructions (7).

(7) *Faut   faire   attention!*
     be necessary-3-SG   to make   attention
     'It is necessary to pay attention.'

Chloe's essentially target-like morphological inflection indicates mastery of person / number / tense inflection in L2 French, as her inflectional mistakes diminish to less than 1% by the third interview (the only mistake is number at that point). The mistakes she makes often seem related to added processing load, as for example (4b) which is a long distance agreement, or (5) which she repeats twice, obviously searching for the correct irregular form.

As for other aspects of syntax, Chloe always uses nominative subjects and consistently raises the thematic verb / auxilary to Tense, as indicated by the 111 tokens of negation, adverb placement and quantifiers. The placement of these adverbials, which start out in a left adjoined VP position, serves as a clear diagnostic for VR. Often omitting *ne*, as is common in spoken French, Chloe uses not simply *pas* 'not,' but a number of other negations, including *jamais* 'never,' *aucun* 'not one,' *rien* 'nothing'and *plus* 'no more' (8).

(8) Negations
     a. *je ne suis jamais allée* (I)
         I neg am   never gone
         'I have never gone'
     b. *il n' y   a rien   que je veux* (II)
         it neg there has nothing that I want
         'there is nothing that I want'
     c. *je vois aucune façon* (III)
         I see   not-one way
         'I see no way [to get out]'
     d. *on avait   plus   d'eau* (III)
         one had-IMP-3-SG   no-more   of water
         'we had no more water'

Adverbs and quantifiers indicate correct placement of both thematic verbs and auxiliaries in French, even when it differs from English (9).

(9) Adverbs and quantifiers
    a. ils   sont   tous   allés à   l'   hôpital (I)
       they-M-PL are all-M-PL gone to the-SG hospital-M-SG
       'they all went to the hospital'
    b. j' aimerais   bien parler (II)
       I would like well to speak
       'I'd really like to speak'
    c. j'ai   récemment vu (III)
       I have-1-SG recently seen
       'I recently saw'

On a 37 sentence grammaticality judgement (GJ) task (modeled after Hawkins et al. 1993) using negation, adverb and quantifier placement (10), she correctly identifies and corrects 35 sentences as grammatical and ungrammatical, only making two mistakes with quantifier placement, one grammatical as ungrammatical and vice versa (11).

(10) GJ examples
    a. Marie n'écoute jamais   ses   disques.
       Mary neg listens never   her-PL disks
       'Mary never listens to her disks.'
    b. *Marc et Jeanne probablement viendront.
       Mark and Jean probably will come-FUT-3-PL
       'Mark and Jean will probably come.'
    c. Ils   relisent   tous   leurs notes.
       they reread-3-PL   all-M-PL their-PL notes-F-PL
       'They all reread their notes.'

(11) Chloe's GJ errors
    a. Les photographes   quittent   tous leurs voitures pour suivre P.
       the-PL photographers-M-PL leave all-M-PL their-PL cars for to follow
       P
       'The photographers all leave their cars to follow P.'
    b. *Les spectateurs tous regardaient   la famille royale.
       The-PL spectators all watched-IMP-3-PL the-F-SG family-F-SG royal-F-SG
       'The spectators all were watching the royal family.'

Her GJs are essentially correct, with very a small amount of indeterminacy for quantifier placement.

5. Discussion

What does the data on verb inflection and syntax indicate for the two hypotheses, RDH and MSI? Both anticipate morphological and syntactic errors as well as accurate realizations. For MSI, new parameter values are possible, but morphological mapping difficulties are to be expected. For RDH, learners beyond age nine are restricted to native parametric values, can only acquire misanalyzed L2 syntax (essentially learned as lexical items), and will show morphological errors as diagnostic of the syntactic deficit.

Chloe's production of nearly 500 verbs in the third interview is nearly perfect; she does not provide the morphological errors that would indicate a syntactic deficit. Furthermore, her accurate syntax (nominal clitics, adverb order) does not appear to indicate misanalysis. Rather, her target-like L2 morphological inflection and word order strongly indicate mastery of person / number / tense inflection and correct raising of thematic verbs and auxiliaries to check the tense and agreement features. The nearly 100% accuracy of the verbal aspects of her L2 grammar (contrasted, for example, with the lexical and gender agreement errors she makes) support the view that the functional features in French T and AgrS are correctly specified, supporting MSI over RDH. Her virtually error free production and nearly perfect GJs, give no indication of misanyalsis. More exactly, the results indicate she has gained the L2 split IP, (T and AgrS), to which she accurately raises all (correctly inflected) verbs. Further in support of MSI, her singular-plural and overgeneralization errors indicate mapping mistakes of performance, not permanently impaired morphosyntax. Her GJ errors corroborate Hawkins et al.'s (1993) observation that clustered properties of a parameter are not acquired simultaneously in L2A, and that acquisition of core negation precedes that of peripheral quantifiers (Herschensohn 2000).

6. Conclusion

This paper has compared two theoretical approaches to L2 uninterpretable functional features. RDH holds that a post-Critical Period inability to gain L2 functional feature values restricts parameter settings to the native ones, here no split IP, and causes surface L2 morphological errors. There is a direct link between specification of morphology and development of L2 syntax, with the functional feature deficit leading to underlying misanalyzed L2 syntax even if superficial syntax appears to be correct. MSI maintains that L2 parameter values may eventually be gained, and that inflectional errors are due not to syntactic deficits, but to difficulties in surface morphological realization, which may occur despite correctly specified L2 functional categories. In the current data, the highly accurate morphosyntax of anglophone L2 French learner Chloe indicates that she has gained the correct [+SIP] values of L2 Tense, supporting MSI's proposal of eventual L2 parameter resetting (Verb Raising) over RDH's restriction to L1 parameter values. Furthermore, her errors are performance based, not indicative of competence problems, another corroboration of MSI.

Notes

[1] Thráinsson gives compelling arguments against "feature strength" of uninterpretable features of T as the trigger for verb raising.

[2] The length of each interview increases during the nine month period, specifically, Sept 15, 1020; Dec 20, 1528; May 26, 2479 words.

References

Archibald, J., ed. (2000) *Second Language Acquisition and Linguistic Theory*. Oxford: Blackwell.

Chomsky, N. (2001) "Derivation by phase", in Kenstowicz, M. ed., 1-52.

——. (2002) *On Nature and Language*, Cambridge: Cambridge UP.

——. (2004) "Beyond explanatory adequacy", in Belletti, A. (ed), *Structures and Beyond*, Oxford: Oxford UP.

Emonds, J. (1978) "The verbal complex V'-V in French.", *Linguistic Inquiry* 9: 151-175.

Epstein, S. & N. Hornstein, eds. (1999) *Working Minimalism*, Cambridge, MA: MIT Press.

Franceschina, F (2001) "Morphological or syntactic deficits in near-native speakers? An assessment of some current proposals" *Second Language Research* 17: 213-247.

Hawkins, R. and C.Y-h. Chan. (1997) "The partial availability of Universal Grammar in second language acquisition: the failed features hypothesis" *Second Language Research* 13, 187-226.

——. and F. Franceschina. (2004) "Explaining the acquisition and non-acquisition of determiner-noun gender concord in French and Spanish", in Prévost and Paradis (eds.), 175-205.

——., R. Towell and N. Bazergui (1993) "UG and the acquisition of French verb movement by native speakers of English", *Second Language Research* 9, 189-233.

Haznedar, B. and B.D. Schwartz (1997) "Are there optional infinitives in child L2 acquisition?" in Hughes, E., Hughes, M. and Greenhill, A., eds, *Proceedings of the 21st Annual Boston University Conference on Language Development*. Somerville, MA: Cascadilla Press, 257–268.

Hendrick, R., ed. (2003) *Minimalist Syntax*, Malden, MA / Oxford: Blackwell.

Herschensohn, J. (2000) *The Second Time Around*, Amsterdam: J. Benjamins.

—. (2001) "Missing inflection in L2 French: Accidental infinitives and other verbal deficits", *Second Language Research* 17: 273–305.

Kenstowicz, M. ed. (2001) *Ken Hale: A life in language,* Cambridge, MA: MIT Press.

Koeneman, O. and A. Neeleman (2001) "Predication, verb movement, and the distribution of expletives", *Lingua* 111, 189-233.

Lardiere, D. (1998) "Case and tense in the fossilized steady state". *Second Language Research* 14, 1–26.

—. (2000) "Mapping features to forms in second language acquisition", in J. Archibald, ed., *Second Language Acquisition and Linguistic Theory,* 102-129.

Lasnik, H. (1999) *Minimalist Analysis*, Malden, MA / Oxford, Blackwell.

Ndayiragije, J. (1999) "Checking Economy", *Linguistic Inquiry* 30, 399-444.

Pesetsky, D. and E. Torrego (2001) "T-to-C Movement: Causes and consequences", in Kenstowicz, M., ed., 355-426.

Pollock, J-Y. (1989) "Verb movement, Universal Grammar and the structure of IP", *Linguistic Inquiry* 20, 365-424.

Prévost, P. and J. Paradis, eds., (2004) *The Acquisition of French in Different Contexts*, Amsterdam/Philadelphia: J. Benjamins.

—. and L. White (2000) "Truncation and missing inflection in second language acquisition" in Friedmann, M.A. and Rizzi, L., eds, *The Acquisition of Syntax*, London: Longman, 202–235.

Schwartz, B.D. and R. Sprouse (1996) "L2 cognitive states and the full transfer/full access model", *Second Language Research* 12, 40-72.

Smith, N. and I-M. Tsimpli (1995) *The Mind of a Savant: Language learning and modularity*, Oxford: Blackwell.

Thráinsson, H. (2003) "Syntactic variation, historical development, and minimalism", in Hendrick, 152-191.

Tsimpli, I–M. and A. Roussou (1991) "Parameter resetting in L2?", *University College London Working Papers in Linguistics* 3, 149–169.

SOME (*WH-*) QUESTIONS CONCERNING PASSIVE INTERACTIONS

CHRISTOPHER HIRSCH AND JEREMY HARTMAN

1. Introduction

English-speaking children are known to be delayed in their comprehension of passive sentences (Slobin, 1966; Turner & Rommetveit, 1967; Bever, 1970; Maratsos & Ambramovitch, 1975; Maratsos, Fox, Becker, & Chalkley, 1985; Gordon & Chafetz, 1990; Fox & Grodzinsky, 1998; Hirsch & Wexler, 2004a). Additionally, it has been noted that children's level of passive comprehension is in part determined by the type of verb used; children have significantly greater difficulty with passives involving "psychological" (subject-experiencer) verbs (1) than with passives of "actional" verbs (2), despite having no problems with either verb type in the active voice. This finding is confirmed in every study crossing voice and verb type (Maratsos, Kuczaj, Fox, & Chalkley, 1979; Maratsos, Fox, Becker, & Chalkley, 1985; Sudhalter and Braine, 1985; Gordon & Chafetz, 1990; Fox & Grodzinsky, 1998; Hirsch & Wexler, 2004a; Hirsch & Wexler, 2006).

(1) The boy was *loved / seen / remembered* by the girl.

(2) The boy was *kissed / kicked / held* by the girl.

It is this interaction of voice and verb type, which we refer to as the *Maratsos effect* after the seminal work by Michael Maratsos and colleagues, that primarily concerns us here. We examine three classes of theories offering potential explanations for this interaction. We concern ourselves with classes of theories, and not particular accounts, as we believe much can be gained from abstracting away from the details of specific theories, and focusing instead on various general approaches to the relevant phenomenon.

Three classes of theories are to be investigated: interaction/processing theories, frequency theories, and grammatical theories. The interaction/

processing theories state that both non-canonical word orders and psychological verbs incur processing costs greater than canonical word orders and actional verbs, but that alone neither causes noticeable comprehension difficulties for children, while both factors together impose a great processing burden. Frequency theories generally claim that children only comprehend structures to which they have been sufficiently exposed. Given evidence that children hear many more actional passives than psychological passives, children's comprehension asymmetry is taken to follow directly from the input asymmetry. Finally, grammatical theories claim that young children cannot comprehend certain grammatical structures because they cannot syntactically represent them. With respect to passives, such theories predict a general difficulty for all passives, irrespective of verb type, and as such, these theories tend to offer evidence that children are able to make use of a compensatory linguistic heuristic that provides a reasonable analysis for actional passives, but fails to do so for psychological passives. The predictions of each class of theories will be considered below, and subjected to experimental and conceptual review.

2. Interaction/Processing Theories Considered

Many theorists have argued that children have difficulty comprehending sentences with non-canonical word orders (for English, non-SVO word order). This might account for children's general difficulty with English passives (e.g., Bever, 1970; Sinclair & Bronckart, 1972)[1], but such a simple canonicity theory leaves the interaction between voice and verb type unexplained. If it could be demonstrated, however, that psychological verbs incur a greater processing cost than actional verbs, then an interaction/processing story could perhaps be maintained.[2] The hypothesis would be that while neither non-canonicity nor psychological verbs alone sufficiently tax children's processing resources, the combination of both proves too much for children, where it is further assumed that children have more limited processing resources than adults.

While we know of no particular theorists who have explicitly posited such an account in the published literature, it is by no means an obvious strawman theory. In fact, this sort of explanation is eminently plausible if the following are true: (1) non-canonical sentences and psychological verbs incur greater processing costs than their canonical and actional counterparts, (2) these costs draw upon the same pool of resources, and (3) children's pool of processing resources is great enough to handle either non-canonicity or psychological verbs, but not both simultaneously.

To examine whether such a class of theories can account for the Maratsos effect, we tested children's comprehension of a more common non-canonical construction: object-extracted *wh*-questions. If non-canonical word order alone is responsible for children's difficulties with passives, we should see a parallel deficit with object-extracted questions. Furthermore, if the Maratsos effect is due to a processing interaction of non-canonical word order and use of a psychological verb, then children should have significantly more difficulty with psychological object-extracted *wh*-questions compared to actional object-extracted *wh*-questions.

In order to test such predictions, we conducted a picture-question verbal-response task with four conditions, crossing question type (canonical subject-extracted vs. non-canonical object-extracted *who*-questions) and verb type (actional vs. psychological). For each experimental item, children were shown a set of three cards, depicting three characters interacting such that each character was both the agent/experiencer and patient/stimulus for a particular actional or psychological verb. For example, for the actional verb *wash*, the three pictures might consist of Piggy washing Bunny, Bunny washing Kitty, and Kitty washing Piggy (Figure 1). In an item testing the psychological verb *see*, the three pictures might depict scenes where Piggy sees Bunny, Bunny sees Kitty, and Kitty sees Piggy (Figure 2). After the three pictures were displayed, the child was then asked either a subject-extracted or object-extracted *who*-question about one interaction among the characters (e.g., *Who does Piggy wash?* or *Who sees Kitty?*). The experiment used two actional verbs (*push* and *wash*) and two psychological verbs (*see* and *hear*). To help minimize task demands, only three characters (*Piggy*, *Bunny*, and *Kitty*) were used throughout the experiment. Children were familiarized to these characters during the introduction to the experiment before any experimental items were presented. The entire experiment consisted of 24 total questions (six items per condition).

Figure 1

Figure 2

Each question was asked twice before children were allowed to respond, after which a pause was given for an answer. If no response was forthcoming, the question was repeated for the child indefinitely at 4- or 5-second intervals until an answer was received. Alternate names for the animals (e.g., *Rabbit* for *Bunny*, or *Cat* for *Kitty*) were accepted as correct answers. In the rare instance when a child responded that he was unsure, or took an unreasonable amount of time to provide an answer, he was asked whether he would like to come back to the item later; there was usually no problem the second time around. Rarely, a child would simply point to the correct character on the relevant card. In this case, the child was prompted to actually name the character, and the correct verbal response nearly always followed. Condition type was pseudo-randomized, with items of the same condition never appearing back to back.

42 children were tested, ranging in age from 3;1 to 5;8 (mean age of 4;6). Children were divided by age into two equal groups of 21 subjects each. The younger group ranged in age from 3;1 to 4;4, with a mean age of 3;10. The older group ranged from 4;6 to 5;8, with a mean age of 5;1. Subjects were recruited from daycares in the Boston area. All children were native English speakers and came from families of varying socioeconomic status.

The experimental results are summarized below in Table 1. Children performed extremely well on all four conditions. Across all subjects, all four conditions were answered at better than 92% accuracy. Importantly, there was no interaction of question type and verb type ($F(1,1004) = 0.082$, p = 0.775), nor even a main effect of structure ($F(1,1004) = 0$, p = 1).[3] When the children were split into the two equal groups by age, there was no hint of an interaction even in the younger (mean age 3;10) group ($F(1,500) = 0.514$, p = 0.474). In contrast to non-canonical psychological passives, children perform extremely well on non-canonical psychological object-extracted *who*-questions.

Table 1

Group	Question Type	Actional	Psychological
Younger Children	Subject	96.0%	87.3%
	Object	97.6%	92.1%
Older Children	Subject	98.4%	97.6%
	Object	96.0%	93.7%
Total	Subject	97.2%	92.5%
	Object	96.8%	92.9%

Children's excellent comprehension of object-extracted *who*-questions (both actional and psychological) demonstrates that non-canonicity itself is not responsible for poor performance. This finding fits neatly with previous corpus work demonstrating that children have no difficulty forming object-extracted questions, and that if anything, object-extracted questions appear slightly earlier in children's natural productions than subject-extracted questions (Stromswold, 1995). The total lack of an interaction between question type and verb type clearly speaks against any general interaction/processing explanation for the Maratsos effect.

Proponents of an interaction/processing theory, however, might object that we have not correctly defined "canonical" word order. While an object-extracted *wh*-question is certainly non-canonical compared to active transitive sentences, perhaps what matters for interaction theories is the type of non-canonical order involved. Passives, for example, have a non-canonical argument order of patient-verb-agent. Object-extracted *wh*-questions, on the other hand, have a non-canonical word order of patient-agent-verb. Since the Maratsos effect is noted in passives, but not in object-extracted *wh*-questions, one might try to "save" the interaction theory by refining it so that it says young children will only have problems with structures involving non-canonical word order of the passive type.

While this is certainly logically possible, the evidence available in the literature speaks strongly against such a hypothesis. The German word order for passives is patient-agent-verb, and it is known that children have trouble with passives in German (Grimm, Schöler, & Wintermantel, 1975; Bartke, 2004). Non-passive topicalized structures with the same word order, however, are known to be produced by very young German children (Poeppel & Wexler, 1993). Similarly for Japanese, passives are known to be delayed (Sugisaki, 1998; Sano, 2000), while sentences with the same surface word order derived by scrambling are comprehended without difficulty (Otsu, 1994). Thus, simple appeals to word order as accounts of children's difficulties with passives prove untenable.

3. Frequency Theories Considered

Some theorists have argued that syntactic structures are only acquired once enough examples have been heard in the input. Proponents of such frequency theories often tout "verb-by-verb" accounts of structure learning as part of the package (see Gordon & Chafetz, 1990; Tomasello, 1992, 2003). It is not hard to see why verb-by-verb acquisition is attractive to frequency theorists. If one assumes that children do not formulate general rules for structures, but rather verb-specific ones, it becomes easier to view frequency as the determining factor in children's comprehension. That is, if children represent rules on the level of the verb, it only makes sense that the verbs they hear should condition comprehension patterns.

As applied to passive acquisition, frequency theories claim that the passive will only be acquired once children hear enough token passive examples. The

Maratsos effect is to be accounted for by evidence that the passives children hear are overwhelmingly actional, as first reported by Gordon and Chafetz (1990). These authors use corpus searches to demonstrate that while passives are rare in the input to children, the vast majority of the passives children do hear (92%) are actional passives. The rarity of psychological passives in the input is thus taken as the explanation for children's problems comprehending them.

To examine whether a frequency-based theory could satisfactorily account for the Maratsos effect, we conducted a parallel corpus analysis to that of Gordon and Chafetz, searching the parental input for *wh*-questions. Just as Gordon and Chafetz compared the input frequencies of actional and psychological passives with children's comprehension of these same structures, we examined the degree to which the input of actional and psychological *wh*-questions predicts children's comprehension of such structures. If a frequency theory of any sort is to remain a tenable explanation for the Maratsos effect, it must account for any differences between the input-comprehension relationship in passives and the input-comprehension relationship in *wh*-questions.

We searched the parental input to Adam and Sarah (Brown, 1973), the same data used by Gordon and Chafetz, for *wh*-questions involving transitive verbs, classifying them by extraction position (subject vs. object) and verb type (actional vs. psychological).[4,5] Adam's data consisted of utterances he heard from 2;3 to 4;11 years-old, and comprised 26,178 total input utterances. Sarah's data consisted of utterances she heard from 2;3 to 5;1, and comprised 44,827 total input utterances. In both cases, the vast majority of the input was from the child's parents. So that our input counts would be most relevant to the hypotheses under consideration, and thus comparable to the comprehension data gathered in the *who*-question comprehension experiment, we adhered to a strict search procedure. Since the comprehension experiment only tested *wh*-questions with transitive verbs, we only counted object-extracted and subject-extracted *who* and *what* questions in the input containing transitive verbs. *What* when used like *which* (e.g., *What color did Bill see?*) was not counted. Likewise, NPs beginning with *whose* were not counted as legitimate instances of *who* (e.g., *Whose car did Mary take?*). Embedded questions were counted. Finally, immediate repetitions of utterances were not counted.

While subject-extracted and object-extracted questions with both *who* and *what* were analyzed, we were most interested in the input of actional and psychological object-extracted *who*-questions. This particular sentence type makes for a nice contrast with passives, as both are non-canonical structures involving displacement of the logical object of a transitive verb to sentence-initial position. Furthermore, *who*-questions are exactly the type of structure examined in our earlier comprehension experiment, and thus straightforward contrasts can be made between input frequency and comprehension levels. In order to make concrete numerical comparisons for passives, Gordon and Chafetz' passive input frequencies were compared to the passive comprehension accuracies in Hirsch & Wexler (2004a). These latter authors examined, among other things, comprehension of actional and psychological passives in 60 children aged 3 to 5, the same age range as the data for the Brown corpus input counts. The input frequencies for the *who*-questions were compared with the comprehension of these structures as determined by our *who*-question experiment. Again, the input searches for passives conducted by Gordon and Chafetz, and the input searches for *who*-object-extracted questions we carry out here are done for the very same children (Adam and Sarah from Brown, 1973). Furthermore, the comprehension data for passives taken from Hirsch & Wexler (2004a) and the comprehension data for *who*-questions all come from children of the same age range (3-5 years-old).

Before comparing the input frequencies of passives and *who*-questions with their respective comprehension levels, we must first settle on the relevant level of comparison. As noted earlier, Gordon and Chafetz find that 92% of the passives Adam and Sarah hear are actional passives. They take this asymmetry in the input to account for the noted asymmetry in passive comprehension (the Maratsos effect). Our experimental results for object-extracted *who*-questions demonstrate no significant comprehension asymmetry (96.8% actional vs. 92.9% psychological). Interestingly, there is no asymmetry in the input ratio of actional object-extracted *who*-questions and psychological object-extracted *who*-questions (59% actional vs. 41% psychological). At first glance, then, this would seem to constitute support for frequency theories: an asymmetry in input frequency leads to a comprehension asymmetry (passives), while a lack of asymmetry in input frequency leads to a lack of a comprehension asymmetry (object-extracted *who*-questions). This conclusion, however, is predicated upon the assumption that what determines the relevant comparison is the ratio of one type of structure to another, as opposed to simply the absolute frequency of a particular structure in the input.

Frequency theories, however, must work over absolute frequencies, and not mere ratios. This is obvious when one considers that, if what determined the Maratsos effect was simply that children hear more actional passives compared to psychological passives, one would expect children *never* to acquire psychological passives, since the ratio of the two passives remains the same into adulthood. Thus, the notion of frequency that must be used by such theories is that of absolute frequency, which Gordon and Chafetz readily accept. The relevant purpose of the data under consideration, then, is to determine the absolute frequency of actional object-extracted *who*-questions (16 examples in the corpus) and psychological object-extracted *who*-questions (11 examples).

The absolute frequencies of the *who*-questions share much more in common with the absolute frequency of psychological passives (7 examples in the corpus) than with actional passives (76 examples). Therefore, according to frequency theories, comprehension of both types of *who*-questions should pattern like psychological passives, which given the comprehension data, simply is not the case.

Once absolute frequencies are examined, it is clear that frequency accounts, at least as currently stipulated, cannot account for children's varying comprehension across different sentence structures. Comparing input and comprehension for *who*-questions with input and comprehension for passives reveals numerous instances where similar input frequencies simply do not produce anything resembling similar comprehension levels. By the age of 3;8, for instance, Adam and Sarah (henceforth A&S) have heard 11 psychological object-extracted *who*-questions in the corpus, and our data indicate that children at this age comprehend these questions perfectly (98% correct). At this same age (3;8), however, A&S have heard 7 non-actional passives in the corpus, yet children score very poorly on this sentence type (54% correct in Hirsch & Wexler, 2004a). To give another example: by age 5;1, A&S have heard 11 psychological object-extracted *who*-questions and 7 psychological passives (similar numbers), but while children score extremely well on psychological object-extracted *who*-questions at this age (94% for mean age of 5;1), they do very poorly on psychological passives (39% for a mean age of 5;3). Conversely, lower input frequencies can co-occur with higher comprehension levels: by age 5, A&S have heard 76 actional passives in the corpus, and children are 70% correct at comprehending these sentence types. By this age, A&S have heard many fewer actional object-extracted *who*-questions (only 30), but children are above 95% correct at comprehending these sentences. These data thus argue strongly against Gordon and Chafetz' claim that the Maratsos effect is a cumulative reflex of the types of passives children hear.

Perhaps we have been too conservative in counting only *who* questions (i.e., ignoring *what* questions). This is a real possibility, especially given that the input frequencies rise dramatically (by a factor of nearly 40) if the latter are included, and perhaps this increase is what accounts for the comprehension differences. But this raises a number of questions about the theoretical and psychological foundations of frequency theories, and points to the need for greater specificity in explicating just what allows language learners to generalize across structures.

The assumption here is that children acquiring a language can collapse *who* and *what* object-extracted questions for the purposes of formulating a general rule, but cannot collapse object-extracted *wh*-questions and passives. The first question for frequency theorists is, why draw the line here? After all, both object-extracted questions and passives involve movement of an object to sentence initial position. There is nothing inherent to frequency theories of rule-learning in the literature that posits a barrier to generalization here. Indeed, there is nothing inherent to frequency-based theories of rule-learning that posits particular barriers to generalization in specific places. (Of course, without *any* barriers to generalization, a frequency theory would not have much explanatory power at all, but that is a more fundamental concern.) Furthermore, if children can collapse *wh*-question types, what accounts for children's reluctance to collapse verbal and adjectival passives, which unlike *who* and *what* questions, are homophonous? As Gordon and Chafetz note, if adjectival passives are included in the input frequency counts, the strong actionality effect disappears. If nothing else, these issues highlight the need for frequency theorists to explain what counts as relevant input.

4. Grammatical Theories Considered

What are needed are theories able to distinguish the *syntactic types* of structures being tested. Once children are acknowledged to have deeper syntactic knowledge than is suggested by word order and frequency theories, motivated explanations arise for which structures children find (un)grammatical. Clearly passives and *wh*-questions are different syntactically, and the acquisition data strongly suggest that children are sensitive to these syntactic differences. A satisfactory account of the course of acquisition will thus by necessity involve explicit grammatical theories. Many grammatical theories have been posited over the years in an attempt to account for young children's general difficulty comprehending passive sentences: the A-Chain Deficit Hypothesis (Borer & Wexler, 1987), the External Argument Requirement Hypothesis (Babyonyshev, Ganger, Pesetsky, & Wexler, 2001), the Universal Phase Requirement (Wexler, 2004), and Smuggling (Hyams & Snyder, 2005). All of these particular grammatical theories are maturational theories, positing that children's early grammar lacks the syntactic means to represent passives due to biological immaturity. That is, while the syntactic mechanisms licensing passives in the adult grammar are assumed to be innately specified, it is hypothesized that these mechanisms are subject to biological development, appearing only in later childhood. Evidence that passives mature (as opposed to being "learned") comes from behavioral genetics (Ganger, Dunn, & Gordon, 2004), the apparent cross-linguistic universality of passive delay (see Crawford, 2005), and the particular detailed pattern on passive acquisition (Hirsch & Wexler, 2006).

If children's early grammar lacks the ability to represent/derive passives, then what accounts for the Maratsos effect, since the grammatical theories would appear to predict all passives to be uniformly delayed? The grammatical theories considered above all accept that English-speaking children make use of a strategy deriving a "passive-like" representation for actional passives, but not for psychological passives. The particular strategy involves children attempting to analyze verbal passives as adjectival passives. Since actional verbs, but not psychological verbs, form licit adjectival passives, children are able to arrive at a syntactic representation for actional passives, but not for psychological passives. There is much evidence that children's early (actional) passives are adjectival. Horgan (1978) provides evidence that children's early passives describe states, not events, as predicted on an adjectival analysis. Terzi & Wexler (2002) demonstrate that for a language in which the verbal passive and adjectival passive are not homophonous (Greek), the Maratsos effect does not obtain (Greek children perform very poorly on actional passives at ages where English-speaking children have nearly no problems). Finally, Hirsch & Hartman (2006) argue from experimental evidence that the class of passives acquired first is not that of paradigmatic actional verbs (e.g., *hit*), but that of object-experiencer verbs (e.g., *scare*). This is understandable in the context of an adjectival strategy, where object-experiencer verbs make even better adjectives than many actional verbs.

Further recommending (certain) grammatical theories is the fact that they straightforwardly account for (and predict) problems with other constructions involving similar syntactic dependencies, such as subject-to-subject raising (Froud, Wexler, & Tsakali, in preparation; Hirsch & Wexler, 2004b; Hirsch & Wexler, to appear) and unaccusatives (Babyonyshev, Ganger, Wexler, & Pesetsky, 2001; Lee & Wexler, 2001; Ito & Wexler, 2002; Hirsch & Hartman, 2006). Acquisition theories that lack linguistic sophistication fail to account for these correlations, while such correlations follow naturally from many grammatical theories.

5. Conclusions

Three classes of theories were considered in an attempt to explain why children find psychological passives more difficult to comprehend than actional passives. Interaction/processing explanations, it was shown, simply make the wrong predictions about comprehension of object-extracted *wh*-questions and thus offer little hope. Frequency theories, at least as currently construed in the literature, suffer from a number of conceptual difficulties and also make incorrect comprehension predictions based on the comparative frequencies of various constructions in the child's input. It is grammatical theories that best explain the available data and offer the most promising prospects of an empirically and conceptually satisfying account of the course of language acquisition.

Notes

*We gratefully acknowledge Ken Wexler for his detailed comments and discussion concerning this work. We would also like to thank Nadya Modyanova, Robyn Orfitelli, Alexandra Perovic, the entire Wexler ab/Normal Language Lab, the audiences at the Lisbon Workshop on Production versus Comprehension in the Acquisition of Syntax, and GALA 2005, as well as all the children who participated. The preparation of this article was supported in part by an NSF Graduate Fellowship awarded to the first author.

[1] We mean the base ordering of logical arguments. Another way of referring to such orderings is by thematic ordering, where canonical order for English is agent-verb-theme.

[2] While we know of no direct evidence that psychological verbs are harder (more costly) to process than actional verbs, this seems possible on the intuitively reasonable assumption that psychological verbs are less frequent than actional verbs, where token frequency relates to ease of retrieval (e.g., Howes & Soloman, 1951).

[3] A main effect of verb type was obtained ($F(1,1004) = 9.87$, p = 0.002). This appears to be driven by some children's isolated poor performance on questions involving the verb *hear*. Questions with the other verbs, including psychological *see* were all comprehended at above 95% correct, while accuracy for *hear* was at only 90.1%. This was likely due to some children having a difficult time interpreting the pictures associated with *hear*, which involved a relatively non-intuitive pictorial representation for hearing involving earmuffs.

[4] Sentences with non-actional, non-psychological verbs like *have* and *fit* were not counted.

[5] We omitted Eve, because her input data is only from 1;6 to 2;3. In comparing our numbers to those of Gordon and Chafetz, we have used only their combined Adam and Sarah totals.

References

Babyonyshev, M., J. Ganger, D. Pesetsky, and K. Wexler, (2001) "The Maturation of Grammatical Principles: Evidence from Russian Unaccusatives." *Linguistic Inquiry* 32, 1, 1-44.

Bartke, S. (2004) "Passives in German children with WS." in Bartke & Siegmuller, eds., *Williams syndrome across languages*. Amsterdam/Philadelphia.

Bever, T. (1970) "The cognitive basis for linguistic structures." in J.R. Hayes, ed., *Cognition and the Development of Language*. New York: Wiley, 279-362.

Borer, H., and K. Wexler, (1987) The maturation of syntax. in T. Roeper and E. Williams eds., *Parameter setting*. Dordrecht: Reidel.

Brown, R. (1973) *A first language: The early stages*. Cambridge: Harvard University Press.

Crawford, J. (2005) "The acquisition of the Sesotho passive: Reanalyzing a counterexample to Maturation." ms. BU

Fox, D., and Y. Grodzinsky, (1998) "Children's passive: A view from the by-phrase." *Linguistic Inquiry* 29, 311-332.

Froud, K., K. Wexler, and V. Tsakali, (in preparation) The Development of Raising.

Ganger, J., S. Dunn, and P. Gordon, (2004). "Genes take over when the input fails: A twin study of the passive." Poster presented at BUCLD 2004.

Gordon, P. and J. Chafetz. (1990) "Verb-based versus class-based accounts of actionality effects in children's comprehension of passives." *Cognition* 36, 227-254.

Grimm, H., H. Schöler, and M. Wintermantel, (1975) *Zur Entwicklung sprachlicher Strukturformen bei Kindern.* Weinheim: Beltz.

Hirsch, C., and K. Wexler. (2004a) "Children's passives and their resulting interpretation." Paper presented at GALANA 2004.

—., and K. Wexler. (2004b) "'Who' seems to rescue raising." Paper presented at GALANA 2004.

—., and J. Hartman. (2006) "Semantic Constraints on Passive Comprehension: Evidence for a Theory of Sequenced Acquisition." Paper presented at Latsis Colloquium. 2006.

—., and K. Wexler. (2006) "Acquiring Verbal Passives: Evidence for a Maturational Account." Paper presented at LSA 2006.

—., and K. Wexler. (to appear) "The late development of raising: What children seem to "think" about "seem"." Chapter from collection of papers from 2005 summer LSA workshop on raising and control.

Howes, D., and R. Soloman. (1951) "Visual duration threshold as a function f word probability." *Journal of Experimental Psychology* 41, 401-410.

Hyams, N., and W. Snyder. (2005) "Young children never smuggle: Reflexive clitics and the universal freezing hypothesis." Paper presented at BUCLD 2005.

Horgan, D. (1978) "The development of the full passive." *Journal of Child Language* 5, 65-80.

Ito, M., and K. Wexler. (2002) "The acquisition of Japanese unaccusatives." ms. MIT.

Lee, H., and K. Wexler (2001) "Nominative Case Omission and Unaccusatives in Korean Acquisition." in J. Ree, ed., *The Proceedings of the International Conference on Korean Linguistics.* Prague, 263-279.

Maratsos, M., and R. Abramovitch. (1975) "How many children understand full, truncated, and anomalous passives." *Journal of Verbal Learning and Verbal Behavior* 14, 145-157.

—., Fox, D., Becker, J., and M. Chalkley. (1985) "Semantic restrictions on children's passives." *Cognition* 19, 167-91.

—., S. Kuczaj, D. Fox, and M. Chalkley. (1979) "Some empirical studies in the acquisition of transformational relations: Passives, negatives and the past tense." in W.A. Collins, ed., *Children's Language and Communications.* Hillsdale, NJ: Lawrence Erlbaum Associates. 1-45.

Otsu, Y. (1994) "Early acquisition of scrambling in Japanese." in T. Hoekstra and B.D. Schwartz, eds., *Language Acquisition Studies in Generative Grammar.* John Benjamins. 253-264.

Poeppel, D., and K. Wexler. (1993) "The full competence hypothesis of clause structure in early German." Language 69, 1-33.

Sano, T. (2000) "Issues on unaccusatives and passives in the acquisition of Japanese." in *Proceedings of the Tokyo Conference on Psycholinguistics* 1, 1-21.

Sinclair, H., and J. Bronckart. (1972) "SVO—a linguistic universal." *Journal of Experimental Child Psychology* 14, 329-348.

Slobin, D. (1966) "Grammatical transformations and sentence comprehension in childhood and adulthood." *Journal of Verbal Learning and Verbal Behavior* 5, 219-227.

Stromswold, K. (1995) "The acquisition of subject and object wh-questions." *Language Acquisition* 4, 5-48.

Sudhalter, V., and M. Braine. (1985) "How Does Comprehension of Passive Develop? A comparison of actional and experiential verbs." *Journal of Child Language* 12, 455-470.

Sugisaki, K. (1998) "Japanese Passives in Acquisition." *University of Connecticut Working Papers in Linguistics* 10.

Terzi, A., and K. Wexler. (2002) "A-Chains and S-Homophones in Children's Grammar: Evidence from Greek Passives." Paper presented at NELS 32.

Tomasello, M. (1992) *First Verbs: A Case Study of Early Grammatical Development.* New York: Cambridge University Press.

—. (2003) Constructing a language: Harvard University Press, Cambridge.

Turner, E., and R. Rommetveit. (1967) "Experimental manipulation of the production of active and passive voice in children." *Language and Speech* 10, 169-180.

Wexler, K. (2004) "Theory of Phasal Development: Perfection in Child Grammar" *MIT Working Papers in Linguistics* 48, 159-209

EFFECTS OF L1 AND PROFICIENCY ON L2 PARSING

HOLGER HOPP

In the acquisition of second-language (L2) grammars, effects of the first language (L1) and proficiency level are well attested. This paper addresses the question whether L1 properties and proficiency also affect syntactic reanalysis in L2 on-line comprehension. 20 L1 English and 19 L1 Russian advanced to near-native speakers of German were tested on subject-object ambiguities in German. Section 1 outlines previous research on L1 and proficiency effects in L2 ambiguity resolution. Section 2 sketches the processing of subject-object ambiguities in German. Section 3 presents two experiments, and Section 4 discusses the findings.

1. L2 Syntactic Ambiguity Resolution: L1 and proficiency effects

Depending on parametrized syntactic processing principles, relative clauses like *He met the brother of the teacher who lived in Durham* preferentially attach to the second NP in English (i.e. low attachment), yet to the first NP in e.g. Greek, German, Spanish and French (i.e. high attachment). In eye-tracking studies, Frenck-Mestre (2002) finds that highly proficient English speakers have a native-like high attachment preference in L2 French, while a less proficient group of L1 English speakers shows a low attachment preference as in the L1. As for L1 effects, Felser et al. (2003) tested advanced Greek and German learners of English and report that the L1 groups did not differ in that (a) both showed the same preference for semantically biased sentences and (b) both did not show any preference in fully structurally ambiguous sentences. Papadopoulou and Clahsen (2003) obtain similar findings for advanced Spanish, German and Russian learners of Greek. In neither study did the L1s differ in attachment preferences, so that the studies do not directly speak to potential differential transfer of L1 properties in L2 parsing.

Reading-time studies on gap-filling effects in *wh*-movement by Williams et al. (2001) for advanced Chinese, German and Korean learners of English and Juffs (2005) for Chinese, Japanese and Spanish learners of English report that all L1 groups showed similar native-like gap-filling effects, irrespective of whether the L1 instantiates *wh*-movement. Yet, using cross-modal priming, Marinis et al. (2005) and Felser and Roberts (to appear) find no evidence of native-like reactivation of the filler at (intermediate) trace positions in L2 English long-distance *wh*-chains for any group of advanced Greek, German, Japanese and Chinese L2ers. Again, on-line performance of the L2ers in these studies did not differ according to whether the L1s employ overt *wh*-movement.

In sum, previous work on syntactic ambiguities has not attested L1 effects in L2 parsing for intermediate to advanced L2ers, while the study by Frenck-Mestre (2002) suggests that proficiency does affect L2 parsing strategies. This paper addresses these issues with respect to subject-object reordering in L2 German, comparing different L1 and proficiency groups.

2. Subject-Object Orders in German, Russian and English

In German and Russian, objects can optionally precede subjects, i.e. these languages have scrambling. The reordering of NPs in German (1b) and Russian (2b), indicated by the antecedent-trace relations, is overtly expressed by case marking on determiners (German) or nominal suffixes (Russian). English has neither case marking on full NPs nor scrambling.

(1) a. Maria glaubt, dass   der   Vater   den   Onkel schlägt.
       Maria thinks that   the-nom   father   the-acc uncle beats
       'Maria thinks that the father beats the uncle.'
    b. Maria glaubt, dass   [den   Onkel]$_1$ der   Vater t$_1$ schlägt.
(2) a. Utrom   dedushk-a   udaril   djadj-u
       In the morning   grandfather-nom   hit   uncle-acc
       'In the morning, the grandfather hit the uncle.'
    b. Utrom   [djadj-u]$_1$ udaril   dedushk-a t$_1$

Native speakers of German (e.g. Hemforth & Konieczny 2000) and Russian (e.g. Sekerina 2003) show a subject-first preference in reading clauses with multiple animate arguments. This preference is taken to reflect universal parsing principles (e.g. (3)).

(3) Minimal Chain Principle (de Vincenzi, 1991: 13).
    "Avoid postulating unnecessary chain members at S-structure, but do not delay required chain members."

In accordance with (3), the parser automatically constructs a subject-initial phrase structure upon encountering the first NP. Revision to an OS order is less economical, as the OS order contains more elaborate syntactic structure and movement chains than the SO default (cp. (1/2a) vs (1/2b)). The cost of reanalysis is measurable in garden-path effects, i.e. slowdowns and comprehension difficulties, for OS orders.

Due to syncretistic case morphology in German, the syntactic status of NPs can be locally ambiguous up to the agreement marking on the clause-final verb (4). In contrast to disambiguation to an OS order via case on NPs in (1b), which elicits fairly weak reanalysis effects, disambiguation only via verbal agreement in (4) gives rise to stronger garden-path effects (Meng & Bader 2000).

(4) ..., dass die Kellnerin$_{SG}$ die Kollegen$_{PL}$ gesehen haben$_{PL}$.
... that the-nom/acc waitress the-nom/acc colleagues seen have
'... that the colleagues saw the waitress.'

This difference between case and verbal agreement for disambiguation has been linked to their degree of informativity for reanalysis. According to the Diagnosis Model of reanalysis by Fodor & Inoue (1994, 2000), reanalysis is facilitated if the syntactic feature identifying a misparse redirects the parser to the original parsing error by grammatical relations and then leads to automatic repair of the parse.

To illustrate, accusative case marking on the first incoming NP in (1b) signals to the parser, first, that this NP is not the subject and, second, that the parser needs to create an additional slot for this NP to keep the subject position available for a following NP. Hence, a case cue signals a misparse (diagnosis) and automatically leads to the correct parse (repair). Now consider (4): Having filled the subject position with the singular NP *die Kellnerin* ('the waitress'), the parser encounters the plural verb *haben* ('have') and tries to coindex the two by way of an agreement relation. This leads to a number mismatch signaling an erroneous parse (diagnosis), yet it does not automatically imply the correct parse. In sum, verbal agreement is a negative symptom in that it diagnoses but does not repair a misparse, while case is a positive symptom that effects automatic repair (Fodor & Inoue 2000).

In ungrammatical sentences, case violations are harder to detect under time pressure than verbal agreement violations (Meng & Bader 2000). Judging a sentence to be ungrammatical means that no grammatical parse could have been constructed, i.e. that reanalysis has failed. Detecting a case mismatch in an ungrammatical sentence (e.g. nominative on more than one NP), however, appears to initiate an automatic attempt at repairing the mismatch by (erroneously) reanalyzing the parse towards an OS structure and – under time pressure – engenders false positive responses. By contrast, agreement mismatches (e.g. singular subject and plural verb) ensure more reliable ungrammaticality detection under time pressure since they do not initiate automatic repair processes in parsing.

Table 1. Interaction of syntactic feature of disambiguation and sentence type in parsing.

	Case	Verbal Agreement
	Accurate responses	
Grammatical OS sentences:	high	low
Ungrammatical sentences:	low	high

In sum, processing preferences and reanalysis effects in German native parsing are determined by the interaction of phrase-structural parsing principles and syntactic feature types (Table 1). Whether these varied effects also obtain in L2 German processing is investigated in two psycholinguistic experiments.

3. The experiments

Experiment 1 addresses the questions: (A) Do L2ers revise phrase structure incrementally according to syntactic features? (B) Do L2ers show a difference in reanalysis depending on type of syntactic disambiguation (case vs verbal agreement)? Experiment 2 asks: (C) Do L2ers show an interaction of syntactic feature type and accuracy in processing grammatical and ungrammatical sentences (Table 1)? Both experiments ask (D) whether reanalysis by syntactic features depends on the analogous L1 instantiation of features and/or on the level of L2 proficiency.

3.1. Subjects

Twenty L1 English and nineteen L1 Russian advanced to near-native speakers of German and 20 native German controls took part in the experiments. All L2 speakers of German had started learning German after age 11 and were residents in Germany. All L2ers completed a timed web-based C-test (Grotjahn 1996) to estimate their proficiency in German. Taking the median score in each L1 group as the cut-off point, the L2ers were divided into two proficiency groups, i.e. advanced (ADV; <67%) and near-native (N-N; ≥67%).

Table 2: Subject information by group (E = English, R = Russian).

		ADV E	N-N E	ADV R	N-N R	GER
N		**10**	**10**	**10**	**9**	**20**
C test	range	43-61%	67-81%	51-61%	66-81%	76-93%
(timed) (%)	aver.	**53%**	**71%**	**55%**	**73%**	**83%**
Years of exposure	aver.	24.2	22.2	14.9	13.0	
Years of residence	aver.	19.5	14.5	8.3	9.1	
Age	aver.	50.6	37.6	31.2	26.8	51.4

3.2. Experiment 1: Self-Paced Reading

For the self-paced reading task, 24 quadruplets of experimental sentences were constructed. Half of the quadruplets were disambiguated by case on determiners (e.g. (5)) and half by number agreement on the verb (e.g. (6)) (Factor *Ambiguity*). All sentences were initiated by a matrix clause. Embedded clauses were in SO or OS order (Factor *Order*); two additional versions within each quadruple set were constructed by reversing the position of the nouns (i.e. N1-N2 and N2-N1) to match potential effects of lexical semantics or pragmatics of the SO and OS manipulation. Further, all NP1-NP2 and NP2-NP1 combinations had been matched on plausibility, i.e. they had been judged to be semantically reversible in an off-line plausibility judgement pretest by a separate group of German natives.

(5) a. Er denkt, dass **der** Physiker am Freitag **den** Chemiker gegrüsst hat.
   He thinks that the-nom physicist on Friday the-acc chemist greeted has
   b. Er denkt, dass **den** Physiker am Freitag **der** Chemiker gegrüsst hat.

(6) a. Sie sagt, dass **die** Baronin am Freitag **die** Bankiers eingeladen **hat**.
   She says that the baroness-sg on Friday the bankers-pl invited has
   b. Sie sagt, dass **die** Baronin am Freitag **die** Bankiers eingeladen **haben**.
   She says that the baroness-sg on Friday the bankers-pl invited have

The quadruplets were matched in length of NPs and verbs (number of letters), gender, number, animacy, and in corpus frequency. In this way, the stimulus design ensured that case or number was the only cue for the syntactic function of the NPs. The quadruple sets were distributed across four lists with each list containing only one member of each set and an equal number of sentences in each condition. Each subject saw 24 items (plus 72 fillers), i.e. six per condition. A non-cumulative Moving Windows task (Just, Carpenter & Woolley 1982) was used. The rationale of the self-paced reading paradigm is that increased processing effort can be detected locally in higher reading times on a given segment compared to the same segment in a control condition. The experimental sentences were divided into seven segments (7). Subjects read each segment by pushing a button. As a segment appeared, the previous segment disappeared.

(7)   S1   S2   S3 (NP1)   S4 (adv.)   S5 (NP2)   S6   S7(V-fin)
      Er denkt | dass | der Physiker | am X | den Chemiker | gegrüsst | hat.

Each item was followed by a comprehension sentence to check for understanding. The subjects judged whether the comprehension sentence expressed the same meaning as the experimental item. For half of the experimental stimuli and the fillers, the comprehension sentence expressed the same meaning. Instructions and practice items preceded the task. Reading times were computed for all segments of all items, since at issue is how (non-native) subjects typically process sentences, rather than how they process the proportion of sentences they understand correctly.

Two mixed three-way Repeated Measures ANOVAs, both with **Order** and **Ambiguity** as within-subjects factors and with **Language** (German, English, Russian) and **Proficiency** (native, advanced L2 and near-native L2) as between-subjects factors, were performed on accuracy scores and on the reading times of all items by segment. The segments of interest were the regions of disambiguation, i.e. segments 3 (NP1) plus 4 (adverbial, to catch potential delayed effects), and segment 7 (finite verb). Comprehension judgements within 4000ms were recorded. Subjects' reading times of a segment above two standard deviations of the group mean were trimmed to the mean ±2sd. This affected less than 3% of the trials. Two subjects (one German, one near-native English) were excluded as their data sets were incomplete.

Table 3. Accuracy (A) & reading times (RT, segments): Experiment 1.

	SO (5a)		OS (5b)		SO (6a)		OS (6b)	
	A	RT S3&4	A	RT S3&4	A	RT S7	A	RT S7
GER	85%	1775ms	55%	1969ms	92%	976ms	29%	1573ms
ADV E	88%	2159ms	42%	2332ms	95%	1105ms	23%	1269ms
ADV R	85%	2288ms	42%	2345ms	92%	1033ms	23%	1223ms
N-N E	87%	1979ms	74%	2357ms	91%	1123ms	44%	1753ms
N-N R	91%	2053ms	61%	2344ms	96%	940ms	41%	1347ms

Table 3 gives the results (accuracy for sentences; reading times for relevant segments) of the self-paced reading task. As for comprehension accuracy, a between-subjects analysis of the accuracy scores on the comprehension questions yields a significant effect of Order ($F_1(1,52)$ 179.324, $p<0.001$;

$F_2(1,115)$ 342.953, p<0.001) and Ambiguity (F(1,52) 16.592, p<0.001), and an interaction of Order and Ambiguity (F(1,52) 65.193, p<0.001). There are no significant interactions with Language. The interaction between Order and Proficiency reaches significance ($F_1(2,52)$ 6.305, p=0.015; $F_2(2,115)$ 32.739, p<0.001), largely due to the better performance of the near-natives compared to the natives and to the advanced L2ers. In total, all groups prefer SO sentences over OS sentences, with the preference being considerably stronger when disambiguation is via verbal agreement. Pairwise comparisons show that the interaction between Order and Ambiguity is significant for each group.

As for reading times, the between-groups analysis shows a main effect of Order on segments 3&4 (NP1 + adverbial) ($F_1(1,52)$ 12.020, p=0.001; $F_2(1,115)$ 7.887, p=0.006), an interaction between Order and Ambiguity (F(1,52) 24.250, p<0.001) and, in the analyses by subject and marginally by item, between Order and Proficiency ($F_1(2,52)$ 4.866, p=0.032; $F_2(2,115)$ 3.420, p=0.067), yet, no interaction with the factor Language ($F_1(2,52)$ 0.061, p=0.807; $F_2(2,115)$ 0.182, p=0.677). On segment 7 (V-fin), there is a main effect of Order ($F_1(1,52)$ 26.211, p<0.001; $F_2(1,115)$ 27.926, p<0.001) and Ambiguity (F(1,52) 27.960, p<0.001) as well as an interaction between Order and Ambiguity (F(1,52) 10.729, p=0.002); there is no interaction between Order and Language ($F_1(2,52)$ 0.056, p=0.813; $F_2(2,115)$ 0.014, p=0.906), but the interaction between Order and Proficiency approaches significance in the analysis by item ($F_1(2,52)$ 2.446, p=0.124; $F_2(2,115)$ 3.827, p=0.053). Given the interactions with Proficiency, we analyze the data from each proficiency group separately.

Natives (GER) and near-natives (N-N) show a main effect of Order on segment 3&4 (GER: $F_1(1,18)$ 18.566, p<0.001; $F_2(1,23)$ 5.467, p=0.028; N-N: $F_1(1,17)$ 11.185, p=0.004; $F_2(1,23)$ 4.868, p=0.038); pairwise comparisons reveal a significant difference between (5a) and (5b) (GER: $F_1(1,18)$ -3.287, p=0.004; $F_2(1,11)$ -2.518, p=0.026; N-N: ($F_1(1,17)$ -5.345, p<0.001; $F_2(1,23)$ - 3.491, p=0.005). On segment 7, there are significant main effects of Order (GER: $F_1(1,18)$ 10.788, p=0.004; $F_2(1,23)$ 15.127, p=0.001; N-N: $F_1(1,17)$ 9.998, p=0.006; $F_2(1,23)$ 12.251, p=0.002) and Ambiguity (GER: F(1,18) 5.795, p=0.027; N-N: F(1,17) 11.575, p=0.003) as well as an interaction of Order and Ambiguity (GER: F(1,18) 4.642, p=0.045; N-N: F(1,17) 5.708, p=0.029); pairwise comparisons yield significant effects for sentence types (6a) and (6b) (GER: $F_1(1,18)$ -2.778, p=0.012; $F_2(1,11)$ -3.505, p=0.005; N-N: $F_1(1,17)$ - 2.939, p=0.009; $F_2(1,11)$ -4.093, p=0.002). By contrast, the advanced L2 group shows no main effects of Order on segment 3&4 ($F_1(1,19)$ 0, p=0.996; $F_2(1,23)$ 0.093, p=0.764) or Ambiguity (F(1,19) 0.1, p=0.755); pairwise comparisons between (5a) and (5b) unearth no significant differences ($F_1(1,19)$ -1.938, p=0.068; $F_2(1,11)$ -1.391, p=0.192). On segment 7, the advanced group approaches a main effect of Order in the analysis by subject ($F_1(1,19)$ 4.061, p=0.058; $F_2(1,23)$ 1.990, p=0.176) and shows a main effect of Ambiguity ($F(1,19)$ 10.249, p=0.005), yet no interaction between Order and Ambiguity ($F(1,19)$ 1.001, p=0.330); in pairwise comparisons, (6a) and (6b) are not significantly different ($F_1(1,19)$ -1.684, p=0.109; $F_2(1,11)$ -1.263, p=0.233). In sum, interactions of the factors Order and Ambiguity show that natives and near-natives evince locally specific slowdowns on segment 3&4 for OS orders disambiguated by case and on segment 7 for OS orders disambiguated by verbal agreement. Advanced speakers do not show either effect.

3.3. Experiment 2: Speeded Grammaticality Judgements

This task probed the processing of (un-)grammatical orders under time pressure to explore the status of case and verbal agreement violations in the detection of ungrammaticality. It included the following conditions: grammatical SO (8) and OS (9) orders disambiguated by case marking; case violations, i.e. sentences with double nominative (*der-der*) (10) and sentences with double accusative (*den-den*) (11); and violations of verbal agreement (number) in SO (12) and in OS (13) order.

(8)   Er glaubt, dass **der** Vater am Freitag **den** Onkel gegrüsst hat.
        He thinks that the-nom father on Friday the-acc uncle greeted has
(9)   Er glaubt, dass **den** Onkel am Freitag **der** Vater gegrüsst hat.
(10)   *Er glaubt, dass **der** Bäcker seit Jahren **der** Metzger beliefert hat.
        He believes that the-nom baker for years the-nom butcher supplied has
(11)   *Er glaubt, dass **den** Bäcker seit Jahren **den** Metzger beliefert hat.
(12)   *Er glaubt, dass **der** Bäcker seit Jahren **den** Metzger beliefert **haben**.
(13)   *Er glaubt, dass **den** Bäcker seit Jahren **der** Metzger beliefert **haben**.

The task comprised 36 experimental items, i.e. six per condition, and 66 fillers of various other types. In a partially factorial design, four lists were created: (8) and (9) according to the factor **Order** (SO and OS) and reversed noun position (i.e. N1-N2 and N2-N1); (10) to (13) according to the factor **Condition** (case violation, agreement violation) and reversed N position. All items were matched in and across conditions as in Experiment 1, so that case or number was the only cue for the syntactic function of NPs. In the task, the items were presented word-by-word for 250ms per word plus 17 ms per letter in the centre of a 15-inch TFT screen. After the final word of each sentence, the subjects made an immediate binary judgement. The rationale of the speeded judgement paradigm is that garden-path sentences elicit lower accuracy and higher response (judgement) times than comparable control sentences.

Three Repeated Measures ANOVAs with the factors **Order** (SO, OS) and **Condition** (grammatical, case violation, agreement violation) as within-subjects factors and **Language** (German, English, Russian) and **Proficiency** (native, advanced L2 and near-native L2) as between-subjects factors were performed on accuracy scores and on the reaction times. Data trimming was as in Experiment 1. Table 4 lists accuracy of responses and response times for (8) and (9). Other response times are not relevant for present purposes and will not be presented.

Table 4. Accuracy of responses and response times: Experiment 2.

	ADV E	ADV R	N-N E	N-N R	GER
(8) SOV	93% 1035ms	93% 940ms	92% 1008ms	94% 955ms	94% 770ms
(9) OSV	65% 1204ms	88% 1026 ms	83% 1194ms	87% 1087ms	75% 941ms
(10) *NOM-NOM	72%	75%	50%	22%	29%
(11) *ACC-ACC	65%	70%	52%	35%	38%
(12) *$S_{SG}O_{SG}V_{PL}$	28%	32%	28%	13%	12%
(13) *$O_{SG}S_{SG}V_{PL}$	25%	40%	22%	11%	8%

As for judgement accuracy, a between-groups comparison of the accuracy scores for sentences (8) and (9) shows a main effect of Order ($F_1(1,54)$ 19.419, $p<0.001$; $F_2(1,55)$ 14.466, $p<0.001$). There are no significant interactions with the factors Language or Proficiency, which shows that all groups demonstrate an SO preference compared to the OS order. In order to determine whether subjects make a difference between grammatical and ungrammatical case marking, comparisons of accurate judgements on (8) and (9) with the false positive judgements of (10) and (11) were run. These comparisons reveal a main effect of Condition ($F(1,54)$ 117.212, $p<0.001$) and significant interactions of Condition with the factors Language ($F(2,54)$ 4.596, $p=0.037$) and Proficiency ($F(2,54)$ 11.528, $p<0.001$). Subsequent analyses by proficiency group demonstrate that natives and near-natives reliably differentiate between grammatical OS orders and ungrammatical case marking ($p<0.001$), while the advanced group does not ($p\geq0.126$). These results show that the advanced group accepts case violations (10&11) as readily as grammatical case marking (8&9). Finally, the comparison of case (10&11) and number violations (12&13) yields a main effect of Condition ($F_1(1,54)$ 91.749, $p<0.001$; $F_2(1,115)$ 112.061, $p<0.001$), no interaction between Condition and Language, but an interaction between Condition and Proficiency ($F_1(2,54)$ 6.994, $p=0.011$; $F_2(2,115)$ 9.86, $p=0.002$). This interaction reflects the lower accuracy in detecting case violations by the advanced group. Analyses by proficiency group yield significant effects of Condition for each group (p≤0.004); i.e. each group achieves distinct accuracy on detecting case and verbal agreement violations. As for reaction times, a between-groups analysis of SO (8) and OS (9) orders yields an effect of Order ($F_1(1,54)$ 14.466, p<0.001; $F_2(1,55)$ 7.103, p=0.010), but no interactions with Language or Proficiency. Analyses by proficiency group show a main effect of Order for natives ($F_1(1,19)$ 8.777, p=0.008; $F_2(1,11)$ 6.966, p=0.023) and near-natives by subject ($F_1(1,18)$ 5.080, p=0.037; $F_2(1,11)$ 2.713, p=0.128). For the advanced group, there is no significant effect of Order ($F_1(1,19)$ 2.680, p=0.118; $F_2(1,11)$ 0.434, p=0.532).

4. Discussion

Two on-line experiments investigated syntactic reanalysis in the L2 processing of locally ambiguous OS clauses by English and Russian learners of German. Despite the fact that English and Russian differ in case marking and in word order optionality, the processing behaviour of English and Russian L2 German speakers turned out to differ less according to L1 than according to proficiency level. L1 effects only surfaced in the speeded processing of case by the near-natives (Exp. 2 (10&11)).

Irrespective of L1, the near-natives show an SO preference and incremental reanalysis effects in comprehension patterns and reading slowdowns (Exp. 1). The pattern of effects is modulated by the type of syntactic feature involved, which further interacts with the grammaticality of sentences, just as in native speakers (Exp. 2). Given that, in both experiments, all lexical, semantic, pragmatic and frequency-based cues to sentence interpretation were removed, the processing patterns observed for the near-natives strongly suggest that these L2ers, like natives, (a) employ a phrase-structural preference like the Minimal Chain Principle (5) (DeVincenzi, 1991), (b) establish syntactic agreement relations incrementally in parsing, and (c) attempt reanalysis by means of syntactic relations in parsing.

By contrast, the advanced L2ers, regardless of L1, demonstrate a general SO preference in judgement accuracies, yet no incremental reading delays (Exp. 1), response latencies or accuracies associated with native German reanalysis (Exp. 2). This suggests that native-like processing by syntactic features for subject-object ambiguities develops late, surfacing only at the highest proficiency levels, even for Russian speakers who have access to these features in their L1.

Nevertheless, even the advanced learners comprehend a significant proportion of OS orders accurately although disambiguation to the OS order is exclusively via syntactic features, and they demonstrate an interaction between sentence type and syntactic feature type (Table 1). This suggests they do use syntactic features differentially. Hence, the advanced L2ers appear to show a reduced sensitivity to syntactic features in parsing. The fact that the advanced groups diverge from the (near-)natives mostly in their failure to employ case information incrementally (Exp. 1) and under time-pressure (Exp. 2) suggests that their reduced sensitivity to syntactic features is due to the computational demands on real-time and speeded comprehension. Lardiere (2000) and White (2003) suggest in case studies on fossilized endstate learners that non-target-like suppliance of morphology in the L2 stems from increased computational demands in coordinating morphological forms and syntactic features. On the basis of ERP studies on phrase-structure violations, Hahne (2001) posits that the efficiency of integrating syntactic category information into phrase structure is reduced in L2 on-line comprehension. Using the same materials, Rossi et al. (to appear) find that highly proficient L2 Italian and L2 German learners of German and Italian, respectively, show native-like neurophysiological responses to phrase-structure violations, while less proficient groups showed a more divergent pattern. Similarly, the present results suggest that processing divergence by the advanced L2 group is due to lack of automaticity in coordinating different types of morphosyntactic information in the L2.

Computational problems in the present study were found to be relative to proficiency level and L1. At advanced proficiency levels, processing demands appear to curtail native-like use of syntactic features equally for both L1 groups (see Hopp, in prep., for results from L1 Dutch speakers of German). At the very high end of proficiency, the processing demands seem to have been mastered by all near-natives (Exp. 1). However, near-natives differ according to L1 in that solely the L1 Russian learners employ case information in a native-like way under speeded presentation ((10&11), Exp. 2). Under time-pressure, the Russian speakers appear to benefit from the L1 cue strength of case marking and/or the L1 automatized routines of mapping case features to syntactic function, while the L1 English near-natives experience difficulties.

The interaction between proficiency and L1 effects attested here echoes previous findings on L2 syntactic ambiguity resolution (Section 2), where advanced (but not near-native) speakers did not show different L2 processing behaviour across different L1s, while behaviour differed between proficiency groups (Frenck-Mestre 2002; Rossi et al. to appear).

Taken together, these findings suggest that L2 parsing is differentially modulated by proficiency and L1. Unlike the development of L2 grammar, where L1 effects are most visible at the initial stages, L2 parsing at lower proficiency levels seems to be relatively unaffected by L1 differences. In real-time comprehension of the target language (TL), learners face the task of coordinating multiple types of grammatical information incrementally to build a representation of the input. At first, the computational demands of this task might sometimes lead L2ers to resort to default processing strategies based on e.g. linear order or non-syntactic information, rather than to integrating different types of grammatical information incrementally in real-time processing. Assuming that computational demands on processing the TL tax L2 learners in general, one would expect to find L2ers regardless of L1s employing default processing strategies initially.

However, as proficiency increases and processing the TL becomes more automatized such that L2ers use syntactic features in on-line comprehension, L1 effects become visible. At this stage, the degree of automaticity in processing the TL will be affected by the properties of L1 processing: If the L1 makes use of the same features in parsing as the TL, L2 processing in this domain will benefit from the use of analogous processing routines in the L1. In the case of an L1-L2 mismatch, L2 learners will take longer to employ syntactic information in the L2 efficiently. Since the amount of exposure to the L1 and TL combined exceeds exposure to the TL, L2 learners who cannot make recourse to L1 processing routines on a given syntactic property might continue to show L1 effects well into very advanced stages of L2 acquisition (see also Sorace 2005). Indeed, protracted L1 effects at the procedural level might underlie persistent non-convergence on the TL. Further research will show if the sensitivity to other types of grammatical information in L2 processing varies by proficiency and L1 in the way attested in the present study.

References

De Vincenzi, M. (1991) *Syntactic Parsing Strategies in Italian.* Dordrecht: Kluwer.

Felser, C. and L. Roberts (to appear) "Processing Wh-Dependencies in a Second Language: a Cross-Modal Priming Study."

—., L. Roberts, T. Marinis and R. Gross (2003) "The Processing of Ambiguous Sentences by First and Second Language Learners of English," *Applied Psycholinguistics* 24, 453-489.

Fodor, J.D. and A. Inoue (1994) "The Diagnosis and Cure of Garden Paths," *Journal of Psycholinguistic Research* 24, 407-434.

—. and A. Inoue (2000) "Syntactic Features in Reanalysis: Positive and Negative Symptoms," *Journal of Psycholinguistic Research* 29, 25-36.

Frenck-Mestre, C. (2002) "An on-line Look at Sentence Processing in the Second Language," in R. Heredia and J. Altarriba, eds., *Bilingual Sentence Processing*, Elsevier, Amsterdam.

Grotjahn, R. (1996) *Der C-Test*, Brockmeyer, Bochum.

Hahne, A. (2001) "What's Different in Second-Language Processing? Evidence from event-related brain potentials," *Journal of Psycholinguistic Research* 30, 251–266.

Hemforth, B. and L. Konieczny (2000) *German Sentence Processing*, Kluwer, Dordrecht.

Hopp, H. (in prep.) *Grammatical Knowledge and Its Interfaces in Near-Native Interlanguage*, Doctoral dissertation, University of Groningen.

Juffs, A. (2005) "The Influence of First Language on the Processing of wh-Movement in English as a Second Language," *Second Language Research* 21, 121-151.

Just, M.A., P.A. Carpenter and J.D. Woolley (1982) "Paradigms and Processes in Reading Comprehension," *Journal of Experimental Psychology: General* 3, 228-238.

Lardiere, D. (2000) "Mapping Features to Form in Second Language Acquisition", in J. Archibald, ed., *Second Language Acquisition and Linguistic Theory*, Blackwell, Oxford.

Marinis, T., L. Roberts, C. Felser and H. Clahsen (2005) "Gaps in Second Language Sentence Processing," *Studies in Second Language Acquisition* 27, 53-78.

Meng, M. and M. Bader (2000) "Ungrammaticality Detection and Garden Path Strength: Evidence for Serial Parsing," *Language and Cognitive Processes* 15, 615-666.

Papadopoulou, D. & H. Clahsen (2003) "Parsing Strategies in L1 and L2 Sentence Processing: A Study of Relative Clause Attachment in Greek", *Studies in Second Language Acquisition* 24, 501-528.

Rossi, S., M.F. Gugler, A.D. Friederici and A. Hahne (to appear) "The Impact of Proficiency on Syntactic Second Language Processing of German and Italian: Evidence from ERPs," *Journal of Cognitive Neuroscience*.

Sekerina, I. (1997) *The Syntax and Processing of Split Scrambling Constructions in Russian*, Doctoral dissertation, CUNY.

Sorace, A. (2005) "Interfaces in Language Development," Talk at GALA, Siena, September 10.

Williams, J., P. Möbius and C. Kim (2001) "Native and Non-Native Processing of English Wh-Questions: Parsing Strategies and Plausibility Constraints," *Applied Psycholinguistics* 22, 509–540.

White, L. (2003) "Fossilization in Steady State L2 Grammars: Persistent Problems with Inflectional Morphology," *Bilingualism: Language and Cognition* 6, 129-141.

AN RI STAGE IN MALAGASY? IMPLICATIONS FOR THE ADULT GRAMMAR

NINA HYAMS

1. Introduction

Malagasy is an Austronesian language spoken on the island of Madagascar and is closely related to Philippine languages such as Tagalog. One of the most notable aspects of Malagasy grammar, which it shares with other Austronesian languages, is an elaborate voicing system. The voicing system has a distinctive morphology and it involves the promotion of an argument (*actor, theme, instrument*, etc.) to a referentially and syntactically prominent position, typically clause final position. Following Pearson (2001), and Schachter (1987)'s analysis of Tagalog, I refer to this prominent DP as the *trigger* and the promotion operation as *promotion to trigger* (PTT). The voice morphology on the verb identifies the grammatical function of the trigger, whether *actor, theme, instrument, location*, etc.

In this paper I discuss aspects of the acquisition of the Malagasy voicing system based on a longitudinal study of 3 children aged 19 to 32 months.[1] The question I address is whether there is evidence of a stage in Malagasy corresponding to the root infinitive (RI) stage found in many other child languages. Our findings have implications for acquisition theory: Are there universal stages in grammar development? And they also bear on an important debate in the Malagasy syntax literature: Is the trigger a subject (Guilfoyle, Hung & Travis 1992) or a clause-external topic (Pearson 2001, 2005) and the related question of whether PTT involves A-or A'-movement. To date, the latter issues have been looked at solely from the point of view of adult Malagasy. In this paper we examine them from a developmental perspective.

2. The Malagasy voicing system

The grammatical function of the trigger is encoded by voice morphology on the verb, as illustrated in (1) and (2) for the verb root *vidi* 'buy'. In (1) the verb is *mivídy*, the form that is used when the trigger is the actor (external argument). Following GHT and Pearson, we refer to this form as the AT (*actor-trigger*) form; (2) illustrates the TT (*theme-trigger*) form of the verb, *novidin*, i.e. the form that occurs when the trigger is the theme (internal argument).[2]

(1)   Mivídy   boky hoan'ny mpianatra *ny mpampianatra*.
       AT.Pfx.buy books for' Det   students Det teacher
       'The teacher bought books for the students.'

(2)   Novidin' ny mpampianatra hoan'ny mpianatra   *ny boky*.
       PST.buy.TT.LNK'Det teacher for' Det students Det books
       'The books, the teacher bought (them) for the students.'
or   'The books were bought by the teacher for the students.'

AT morphology involves the prefix *m-*, TT morphology the suffix *–in*. In addition to *m-*, the AT form contains another verbal prefix realized as *an-* or *i-*. In coding the acquisition data we treated this prefix as a voice morpheme. There are also some verbs that occur in a root form, that is to say, without voice or tense morphology, as in (3). These are mainly TT roots.

(3)   Haino-ko *izy*.
       listen-1SG.GEN 3SG.NOM
       'As for him, I listen(ed) to (him).'

In addition to voice morphology, the Malagasy verb is inflected for tense. All the tense morphemes are prefixes. Malagasy has 3 tenses: present, past, future. Present tense is unmarked. The past tense morpheme is *n-/no* and the future/irrealis marker is *h/ho-*. However, the future/irrealis morpheme is pronounced only in very careful speech.

2.1 Competing Analyses of the Malagasy Voice System

The traditional view of the PTT process is that it involves A-movement, either passivization (e.g. Keenan 1976), or raising to subject (GHT 1992). On this view, the trigger is a subject in Spec IP. A more recent proposal is that PTT involves topicalization or A'-movement (Pearson 2001, 2005, cf. also Richards 2000), in which the trigger is a right peripheral topic. These competing analyses are reflected in the two sets of translations for the sentences in (1) and (2).

GHT propose that in Malagasy both Spec VP and Spec IP are subject positions. The actor is generated in Spec VP and the theme internal to VP.

Either the actor or theme (or an oblique argument, cf. note 2) raises to Spec IP and maps onto the trigger function. As illustrated in the structure in (4), the verb adjoins to INFL, winding up at the left edge of the clause immediately preceding the actor. According to GHT, the voice affixes are case assigners that license all but one of the verb's dependents inside VP. The remaining argument raises to Spec IP to check nominative case.

(4)

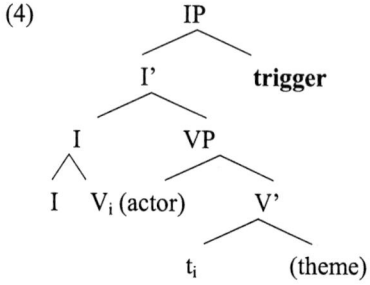

Pearson (2005) proposes instead that the trigger is a topic located in the C-domain. The trigger is base-generated in Spec TopP where it is licensed through coindexation with a null operator (*Op*) that raises to the specifier of WhP (also in the C domain) from an argument position inside VP, either actor, theme (or oblique.) position. Thus under Pearson's analysis, PTT involves A' movement. A simplified version of his structure is as in (5).

(5)

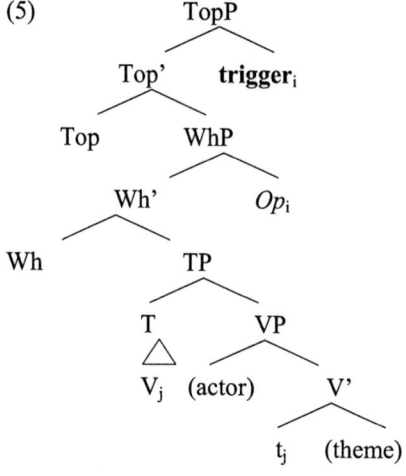

Like GHT, Pearson assumes that the base order is SVO, and he also takes voice morphology to be case related. He proposes that the voice morphemes spell out the case of the position from which the operator has moved: AT morphology is realized on the verb when the operator raises from the nominative case position to Spec WhP and TT morphology when it raises from the accusative case position.

Pearson proposes that Malagasy is a V2-like language in that (virtually) every clause contains a predicate external A'-position that must be filled. The trigger, like the Germanic topic, must be definite and is associated with 'aboutness'.[3]   An interesting property that Malagasy shares with the V2 languages is an optional rule of trigger drop, analogous to topic drop. In informal registers in the Germanic languages a discourse salient pronoun may be omitted when it occurs in topic position (and not otherwise), as illustrated in the German sentences in (6).

(6) a.   (Ich) hab' *(ihn) schon gesehen.   b.   (Ihn) hab' *(ich) schon gesehen.
         (I) have (him) already seen   (him) have I   already seen
         'I already saw him'   'Him, I already saw'

Pearson notes that a comparable pattern exists in Malagasy. In informal conversation a referential pronoun can be dropped, but only if it occurs in trigger position, as illustrated in (7).[4]

(7) a.   Mamangy an' i   Tenda   (*izy*)   c.   Vangian   i Naivo   (*izy*)
         AT.visit obj-Det Tenda   (3rd per.)   TT.visit Det Naivo (3rd per.)
         '(He) is visiting Tenda.'   (Him) Naivo is visiting.'
     b. Mamangy *(azy)   *i Naivo.*   d.   Vangian'- *(-ny)   *i Tenda.*
         AT.visit 3rd per.   Det Naivo   TT.visit   (3rd per.) Det Tenda
         'Naivo is visiting (him).'   'Tenda, (he) is visiting.'

GHT do not discuss trigger drop. However, because their analysis places the overt trigger in Spec IP (cf. 4), the omitted trigger would on their account presumably have to be analyzed as a null subject similar to the null subjects found in Romance and other pro drop languages.

The trigger drop phenomenon will be central to our analysis of the acquisition results presented in the following sections.

3. A Developmental Perspective

Various properties distinguish the acquisition of V2/topic drop languages from null subject languages. Perhaps the most significant difference in the developmental trajectory is that children acquiring V2/topic drop languages show a root infinitive (RI) stage, while children acquiring null subject languages do not (Sano and Hyams 1994; Rhee and Wexler 1995).[5] Some examples of RIs from the Germanic languages are provided in (8).

(8)

A		B	
a. Papa schoenen wassen.		d. Ook koek hebben.	(Dutch)
daddy shoes wash-INF		also biscuit have-INF	
b. Auf Teddy fenster gucken.		e. Wasser holen.	(German)
Teddy window look-INF		water get-INF	
c. Jag också hoppa där å där.		f. Bygge tåg.	(Swedish)
I also hop-INF there and there		build-INF train	

In languages such as Italian, Spanish, Catalan and Portuguese, we find few examples of the sort in (8) (Guasti 1993, 1994; Berger-Morales, Salustri and Gilkerson, 2005; Santos p.c.). The rate of RIs in these languages is typically under 10%, while in the V2 languages, RIs comprise between 40% and 50% of verbal utterances (Dutch: Wijnen 1997; Blom 2003; German: Poeppel & Wexler 1993; Becker and Hyams 2000; Swedish: Platzack 1995; Santelman 1995; Josefsson 2002; Norwegian: Plunkett & Strömqvist 1990). The generalization that null subject languages do not show an RI stage is not based solely on the Romance languages. Children acquiring null subject languages as typologically diverse as Hungarian and Slovenian also fail to show an RI stage. The percentage of RIs in these two languages is under 2% (Londe 2004; Rus and Chandra 2004).

The distribution of RIs differs from that of finite verbs in child language. Particularly relevant to the present discussion is the fact that RIs typically occur with null subjects. The RIs in (8A) contain overt subjects, but much more common are examples such as those in (8B). Table 1 reports the rate of subject omission in finite clauses vs. RIs in several of the V2 languages. Across children and languages, subject omission in finite clauses (i.e. null topics) averages around 23% while the average rate of subject omission in RIs is around 70%.[6]

Table 1: Percentage of subject omission with finite verbs and RIs

Language	Child	Finite verb	RI
Flemish (Krämer 1993)	Maarten	25% (23/92)	89% (89/100)
Dutch (Haegeman 1995	Hein	32% (1199/3768)	85% (615/721)
Danish (Hamann&Plunkett 1998)	Thomas	28% (165/596)	92% (246/267)
	Anne	11% (366/3379)	59% (394/667)
	Jens	23% (742/3173)	58% (539/937)
Total		23% (2495/11008)	70% (1883/2692)

3.1 Predictions for Malagasy

RIs are not specifically associated with V2/topic drop languages. They also occur in non-V2 languages such as English, French, and Russian. However, every V2/topic drop language studied thus far shows an RI stage. Conversely, there is no null subject language that shows an RI stage (cf. note 5). Given that Malagasy exhibits argument drop and cannot therefore be like English, French or Russian, there are two available options for the language. The first is that it is a null subject language, in which case we do not expect an RI stage and so we do not expect any relationship between trigger omission and verb finiteness. The second is that Malagasy is a V2-like language, in which case we expect it to show an RI stage, and the rate of null subjects in non-finite contexts should be significantly higher than in finite contexts, as is the case for other V2/topic drop languages. The developmental facts can therefore help to evaluate the competing analyses of adult Malagasy. Malagasy does not have an infinitival form but the omission of verbal inflection results in a bare verb (root) which is arguably an RI analogue.

Before turning to our results we provide some relevant information about our subjects and coding.

3.2. Subjects and coding conventions

The children in this study are from families that speak the Merina dialect spoken in and around the capital city, Antananarivo. Merina is also the basis for standard written Malagasy and has been the focus of much of the linguistic research on Malagasy. The tapes were coded and transcribed by Cecile Manorohanta, a native speaker of Malagasy, and independently reviewed by two non-native speakers of Malagasy. The 3 children are: Tsiorisoa 2;0–2;8 (MLU 1.68-4.5), Sonnia 1;6–2;2 (MLU 2.84-3.46) and Ninie 1;10-2;6 (MLU 3.09-4.09). The total number of coded utterances is 1618.

We coded for trigger (null or overt), voice and tense morphology, and case (on pronouns). Where an argument was null, we inferred identity from context, as is standard practice. When voice was not specified (a form we refer to as a 'bare verb') we used case marking, word order, context, and plausibility to determine type of voice. When tense morphology was specified we noted the tense. However, because present tense is not overtly marked[7] and the future morpheme is not pronounced in colloquial speech, past is the only tense that can be coded solely based on morphology in both AT and TT forms. However, children use past very infrequently (91 of 1444 verbs -- about 6%) and therefore systematic coding of tense was not possible.

4. An "RI stage" in Malagasy?

The children in our study used voice morphology productively (cf. Hyams et al. (2005)). In addition to verbs marked with voice morphology (both AT and TT),illustrated in (10),[8] the children also produced a high rate of bare verbs, exemplified in (11).

(10)   a.   M -i -ants Tsoso   Tsiorisoa, 2;3 (Adult: *m-i-anatra*,)
            AT -Pfx-study Tsiorisoa
            'Tsiorisoa studies/is studying.'

       b.   Ari-na   zondrina le manga (Tsorisoa 2;7) (Adult:*ari-an(a)*)

            throw away.TT dustbin Dem mango
            'As for this mango, (I) threw (it) in the dustbin.'

(11)   a.   Lomano   za   (Sonnia, 2;2) (Adult: *m-i-lomano*)
            swim   1sg. str.
            'As for me, I swim.'

       b.   Kapo mama   (Tsiorisoa, 2;7) (Adult: *kapoh-ana*)
            beat mommy
            'As for (me), mommy beat (me).

The rate of bare verbs used by the 3 children is given in Table 2. Imperatives are excluded from this analysis because the trigger (addressee) is unspecified in adult AT imperatives. Root verbs, that is, forms that are uninflected in the adult language (cf. 3), are also excluded.

Table 2. Percentage of bare verbs of all verbal utterances

Child	%
Tsiorisoa	38% (148/386)
Sonnia	41% (136/330)
Ninie	56% (147/285)
Total	43% (431/1001)

The 43% bare verb rate in our data falls within the range of RI rates found in the Germanic languages (between 40% and 50%), and is far higher than the <10% typically found in the null subject languages (cf. Hoekstra and Hyams (1998) for overview).

To confirm our hypothesis that the bare verb is an RI analogue we examined the relation between verb finiteness, viz. the specification of voice morphology, and two subject properties known to correlate with RIs in other child languages: null subjects (cf. Table 1) and strong subject pronouns. We first discuss strong subject pronouns.

Malagasy-speaking children use the strong form of the 1st person pronoun, *izaho*, as trigger (not possible in the adult grammar). Ntelitheos and Manorohanta (2005) observe that the strong pronoun occurs predominantly in bare verb contexts and the nominative form of the pronoun, *aho*, occurs predominately with finite verbs, as shown in Table 3.

Table 3. Distribution of *izaho* and *aho* with bare and finite verbs (from Ntelitheos and Manorohanta (2005))

	Finite	Bare
Aho	40 (**73%**)	15 (27%)
Izaho	5 (24%)	16 (**76%**)

This result is in line with those reported by Schütze (1997) for English and French speaking children, whose use of the default pronouns (*me, moi*) in subject position is largely restricted to non-finite contexts. Examples are given in (12). (In the Malagasy sentence in (12c/11a) *za* is a short form of *izaho*).

(12) a. Me got bean.
      b. Moi mettre ça comme Pol.
         me put that like Pol
         'I (want to) put it like Pol.'
      c. Lomano za (=izaho)   (Sonnia 26)
         swim 1SG.STR
         'I (want to) swim'

The high percentage of bare verbs in our data and the bare verb-strong pronoun contingency provide prima facie evidence of an RI stage in Malagasy, consistent with the V2/topic drop analysis of the language, but inconsistent with the hypothesis that Malagasy is a null subject language.

Our next prediction concerns the distribution of null triggers. If bare verbs are RI analogues then null triggers will substantially out number overt triggers. Table 4 shows that most triggers in bare verb sentences are null while in finite clauses most triggers are overt.

Table 4: Percentage of null triggers with finite and bare verbs

	Finite verbs	Bare verbs
Tsorisoa	40% (87/219)	52% (77/148)
Sonnia	50% (92/183)	69% (93/135)
Ninie	50% (100/202)	60% (81/134)
Total	46% (279/604)	60% (251/417)

The relationship between finiteness and trigger omission is marginally significant (p =.08 by a Friedman chi-square). The difference in percentage of null subjects in finite vs. non finite clauses is lower than in the languages in Table 1. In the next section we explore a possible explanation for the weaker effect found in Malagasy.

4.1 Metrical effects

We would like to propose that there are metrical effects of the sort proposed by Gerken (1994) and that this factor masks the null trigger-bare verb relation. Gerken has proposed that under production pressures, children may drop weak syllables (in iambic feet). Given the prosodic system of Malagasy we expect this kind of phonological reduction to affect prefixes but not suffixes. Suffixes form a tight unit with the verbal stem for purposes of stress assignment while prefixes form their own independent prosodic unit. Malagasy TT voice morphology is suffixal while AT voice morphology is prefixal. If prefixes are (also) being omitted for phonological reasons this would increase the number of bare AT forms relative to TT forms. Table 5 shows that this is indeed the case. There are proportionally many more bare AT verbs than bare TT verbs.

Table 5: Percentage omission of voice morphology in AT and TT clauses

	AT	TT
Tsorisoa	120/309 (39%)	28/77 (36%)
Sonnia	120/241 (50%)	16/89 (18%)
Ninie	107/262 (41%)	40/123 (33%)
Total	347/812 **(43%)**	84/289 **(29%)**

We thus propose that some percentage of bare AT verbs are actually finite with the voice morphology dropped in the phonology. This hypothesis leads to the prediction that the proportion of overt triggers will be higher in AT clauses (since some of these are hidden finites) than in TT clauses. This is shown to be confirmed in Table 6.

Table 6: Null/overt triggers in bare AT/TT clauses

	Null Trigger	Overt trigger
AT	190 (57%)	144 (43%)
TT	61 (73%)	22 (27%)

If we focus on the distribution of subjects of TT forms (controlling for the hidden finite factor), the null trigger rate is 73% and overt trigger rate 27%, very close to the (70/23%) difference found in the other RI languages (cf. Table 1).

We speculate that the 27% of bare TT verbs with overt triggers are cases in which PTT has not occurred. In other words, these are sentences in which the theme rests in situ in final position. The word order of the resulting surface string (VSO) is thus identical to one in which the theme moves to Topic position. If this hypothesis is confirmed (e.g. by spectrographic analysis showing an appropriate intonation break between the trigger and predicate), it would bring the Malagasy pattern further in line with the Germanic acquisition results, which show very few non-subject topics in RIs (which are thus overwhelmingly SOV) (cf. Poeppel & Wexler 1993; Haegeman 1995).

5. Crosslinguistic differences

One obvious difference between the Malagasy RIs and Germanic RIs is that the latter are verb final (SOV) while in Malagasy the bare verbs are clause initial (VSO). This means that in Malagasy there is V to T movement in non-finite clauses. How do we explain this difference between Malagasy and Germanic?

Recall that on Pearson's analysis voice morphology is a reflex of null operator movement to Spec WhP. The trigger, base generated in topic position, is licensed under coindexation with the null operator (cf. 5). We suggest that the absence of voice morphology in the children's bare verbs reflects *non-movement* of the operator. Without operator movement the (overt) trigger is not licensed. We thus derive the bare verb-null trigger relation. In Malagasy the locus of underspecification is voice. By our hypothesis, T is specified and thus V to T puts the verb at the left edge of the clause.[9] In Germanic RIs, in contrast, AGR/T is underspecified and hence the verb remains in situ. This difference in the domain of underspecification in Malagasy vs. Germanic RIs may be more apparent than real, however. In both instances it is the case-related categories that are underspecified.

6. Conclusions

The high rate of bare verbs in Malagasy is suggestive of an RI stage. The contingencies between bare verbs and (i) strong pronouns and (ii) null subjects further support this hypothesis. This is expected if Malagasy is a V2-like language. Our data also suggest that metrical effects are a contributing factor in the omission of AT prefixes in early Malagasy grammar and that some apparent bare verbs are hidden finite forms (similar proposals have been made for English (cf. Rizzi 2000; Blom 2003)). Our acquisition results may contribute to an understanding of the adult grammar in so far as we find that the data support a topic/A'-movement analysis of Malagasy voice system.

Notes

*For reasons of space many details and references are omitted. We apologize to the authors whose work we have not cited. For fuller discussions of the issues raised here see Hyams et al. (2005). Many thanks to Dimitris Ntelitheos and the GALA audience for their comments, and to Nathan Klinedinst for editorial and other assistance.
[1] This study was done in collaboration with Dimitris Ntelitheos (UCLA) and Cecile Manorohanta (Université Nord, Madagascar) and is part of a larger study of the acquisition of the voicing system of Malagasy (Hyams, Ntelitheos & Manorohanta, 2005).
[2] Malagasy also has a circumstantial voice, used when the trigger is an oblique nominal such as *instrument, location, manner*, etc. The children in our study produced almost no CT forms. See Hyams et al. for discussion of the acquisition of the different voice types.
[3] Pearson (2001) proposes that the trigger final order is derived through the fronting of TP to a left specifier position, a phrasal movement analogue to T to C in the V2 languages. Malagasy is thus a V2 language in this sense as well.
[4] Pronoun omission in (7d) is grammatical only under the interpretation that Tenda is being visited by some arbitrary person. The omitted pronoun does not have the definite reading associated with the null topic.

[5] Swahili, Greek and Kiché are apparent exceptions to the generalization that null subject languages do not show an RI stage. Pye (2001) claims that children acquiring Kiché exhibit an RI stage. In Kiché aspect and agreement morphology is prefixal and Pye notes that children typically produce only the last syllable of the verbal complex. This suggests an alternative explanation for the Kiché bare verbs as involving phonological reduction rather than underspecification of a verbal functional projection. Phonological omission is discussed in more detail in section 4.1.
Swahili is a null subject language and children do produce bare verbs, illustrated in (i), which Deen (2005) analyzes as RI analogues. Following Barrett-Keach (1986) and Buell (2005), we assume that Swahili subject agreement, object agreement, and tense markers comprise a separate Aux constituent, as in (ii), which children omit during the bare verb stage. The Swahili bare verb is thus analogous to the Italian bare participle, as in (iii), and not a non-finite main verb, as is found in the Germanic languages.

(i)   ∅- ∅-   ka   a   hapa   (child)
      a- na-   ka   a   hapa   (target)
      SA 3 PRS live IND here
(ii) [Aux a-na-] ka   a   hapa   (Barrett-Keach 1986; Buell 2005)
(iii) Disegno cascato
      picture fallen
      'The picture has fallen.'

A null aux analysis is also available for the 'bare subjunctive' form used by Greek children, e.g. Pío vavási 'Spiros reads' (cf. Varlokosta et al (1997), but cf. also Hyams (2002) for a different analysis).

[6] In these topic drop languages, subject omission in finite clauses refers to the dropping of a subject topic.

[7] Traditionally, m- has been analyzed as the present tense morpheme (Rajaona1972; Rajemisa-Raolison 1971). However, Pearson (2001, 2005) (cf. also Builles 1988; Travis 1994) argues persuasively that it is an AT voice marker and that present tense is unmarked in Malagasy. In our analysis we follow Pearson and take m- to be a voice marker.

[8] Malagasy-speaking children produce both AT and TT clauses just like children acquiring V2 languages produce both subject and object topics. The AT rate is higher than the TT rate for all children, also consistent with V2 languages in which subject topics are much more frequent than object topics in early language. (For discussion, see Hyams et al. (2005)).

[9] Though specified tense may be inaudible because, as noted earlier, present tense is not phonologically realized, future tense is audible only in careful speech, and there are very few past tense forms at this stage of development.

References

Barrett-Keach, C. (1986) "Word Internal Evidence from Swahili for AUX/INFL," *Linguistic Inquiry* 17(3), 559-564.

Becker, M. and N. Hyams, (2000) "Modal Reference in Children's Root Infinitives", *Proceedings of the Thirtieth Annual Child Language Research Forum*, 113-122.

Berger-Morales, J., M. Salustri and J. Gilkerson, (2005) "Root Infinitives in the Spontaneous Speech of Two Bilingual Children: Evidence for Separate Grammatical Systems," in J. Cohen, K. McAlister, K. Rolstad, and J. MacSwan, eds., *ISB4: Proceedings of the 4th International Symposium of Bilingualism*, Cascadilla Press, Somerville, MA.

Blom, E. (2003) *From Root Infinitive to Finite Sentence*, PhD Thesis, University of Amsterdam/LOT.

Buell, Leston (2002) "Swahili Amba-less Relatives Without Head Movement," In Torrence, Harald, ed., *UCLA Working Papers in Linguistics*, no. 8, 86-106.

Builles, J.-M. (1988) La Voix Agento-Stative en Malgache, in Etudes d'Ocean Indien, 9, Paris, INALCO.

Deen, K.U. (2005) *The Acquisition of Swahili*, J. Benjamins, Amsterdam.

Gerken, L.A. (1994) "A Metrical Template Account of Children's Weak Syllable Omissions from Multisyllabic Words", *Journal of Child Language* 21, 565-584.

Guasti, M. T. (1993/1994) "Verb Syntax in Italian Child Grammar: Finite and Non-finite Verbs", *Language   Acquisition* 3(1), 1-40.

Guilfoyle, E., H. Hung, and L. Travis (1992) "Spec of IP and Spec of VP: Two Subjects in Austronesian Languages", *Natural Language and Linguistic Theory* 10, 375-414.

Haegeman, L. (1995) "Root Infinitives, Tense, and Truncated Structures in Dutch", *Language Acquisition* 4(3), 205–255.

Hamann, C. and B. Plunkett, (1998) "Subjectless Sentences in Danish", *Cognition* 69, 35-72.

Hoekstra, T. and N. Hyams, (1998) "Aspects of Root Infinitives", *Lingua* 106, 81- 112.

Hyams, N. (2002) "Clausal Structure in Child Greek", *The Linguistic Review* 19, 225-269.

Hyams, N., D. Ntelitheos, and C. Manorohanta, (2005) "The Acquisition of the Malagasy Voicing System", to appear in *Natural Language and Linguistic Inquiry*.

Josefsson, G. (2002) "The Use and Function of Non-finite Root Clauses in Swedish Child Language", *Language Acquisition* 10(4), 273-320.

Keenan, E. L. (1976) "Remarkable Subjects in Malagasy", in C. Li, ed., *Subject and Topic*, Academic Press, New York, 249-301.

Krämer, I. (1993) "The Licensing of Subjects in Early Child Language", *MITWPL19*, 197-212.

Londe, Z. C. (2004) "The Hungarian Case of Root Infinitives: Too Many Cases No Place for Root Infinitives", ms., UCLA.

Ntelitheos, D. and C. Manorohanta, (2004) "Default Pronouns and Root Infinitives in Malagasy Acquisition," Proceedings of *GALANA 1*, 17-20/12/2004, Amin Center, University of Hawaii at Manoa.

Pearson, M. (2001) *The Clause Structure of Malagasy: A Mimimalist Approach*. UCLA Dissertations in Linguistics 21.

Pearson, M. (2005) "The Malagasy Subject/Topic as an A' –element," *Natural Language & Linguistic Theory* 23, 381–457.

Platzack, C. (1996) "The Initial Hypothesis of Syntax, A Minimalist Perspective on Language Acquisition", in H. Clahsen, ed., *Generative Perspectives on LanguageAcquisition*, John Benjamins, Amsterdam, 369-414.

Plunkett, K. and S. Strömqvist, (1990) "The Acquisition of Scandinavian Languages", in J. Allwood, ed., *Gothenburg Papers in Theoretical Linguistics*, Gothenburg, 59.

Poeppel, D. and K. Wexler, (1993) "The Full Competence Hypothesis of Clause Structure in Early German," *Language* 69, 1–33.

Pye, C. (2001) "The Acquisition of Finiteness in K'iche' Maya", *BUCLD 25 Proceedings of the 25th annual Boston University Conference on Language Development*, 645-656. Cascadilla Press, Somerville, MA.

Rajaona, S. (1972) Structure du Malgache. Etudes des Formes Prédicatives, Librairie Ambozontany, Fianarantsoa.

Rajemisa-Raolison, R. (1971) Grammaire Malgache (7ème Édition), Centre de Formation Pédagogique, Ambozontany, Fianarantsoa.

Rhee, J. and K. Wexler, (1995) "Optional Infinitives in Hebrew", *MIT Working Papers in Linguistics* 26, 383-402.

Richards, N. (2000) "Another Look at Tagalog Subjects," in I. Paul, V. Phillips and L, Travis, eds., *Formal Issues in Austronesian Linguistics*, Kluwer Academic Press, Dordrecht, the Netherlands, 105-116.

Rizzi, L. (2000) "Remarks on Early Null Subjects", in M.A. Friedemann and L. Rizzi, eds., *The Acquisition of Syntax: Studies in Comparative Developmental Linguistics*, Longman, Harlow, England, 269-292.

Rus, D. and P. Chandra, (2005) "Bare Participles are Not Root Infinitives: Evidence from Early Child Slovenian", *Proceedings of BUCLD 29*, Cascadilla Press, Sommerville, MA.

Sano, T. and N. Hyams, (1994) "Agreement, Finiteness, and The Development of Null Arguments", in M. Gonzàlez, ed., *NELS 24: Proceedings of the North East Linguistic Society* 2, 543-558.

Santelmann, L. (1995) *The Acquisition of Verb Second Grammar in Child Swedish*, unpublished PhD thesis, Cornell University.

Schachter, P. (1987) "Tagalog", in B. Comrie, ed., *The World's Major Languages*, Oxford University Press, Oxford.

Schütze, C. T. (1997) *INFL in Child and Adult Language: Agreement, Case, and Licensing*, PhD thesis, MIT.

Travis, Lisa. (1994.) "Event Phrase and a Theory of Functional Categories", in P. Koskinen, ed., Proceedings of the 1994 Annual Conference of the Canadian Linguistics Association, Toronto Working Papers in Linguistics, Toronto, pp. 559- 570.

Varlokosta, S., A. Vainikka and B. Rohrbacher, (1998) "Functional Projections, Markedness and 'Root Infinitives' in Early Child Greek", *The Linguistic Review* 15, 187-207.

Wijnen, F. (1997) "The Temporal Interpretation of Root Infinitivals: The Effect of Eventivity", in J. Schaeffer, ed., *Workshop on the Interpretation of Root Infinitives and Bare Nouns in Child Language*, MIT.

LEXICAL GROWTH AND GRAMMATICAL COMPETENCE: POTENTIAL RISKS FOR CHILDREN WITH A HEARING DEFICIENCY

JACQUELINE VAN KAMPEN

1. Normal language acquisition

Language acquisition is a step-wise process. Some features of the mother language are acquired earlier than others. The first utterances of the child consist of names and single words. In a next step, the child simplifies the input to (mainly) binary combinations of words with denotational content {e.g. *bear sweet*} and operator-like words with immediate situational deixis {e.g. *that bear*}. The combinatorial use of words enhances the opportunities to acquire new words. The number of words productively used within the binary constructions rises to something between 300 and 500 (*first lexical spurt*) (Bates, Dale and Thal 1995).

1.1. The acquisition of I-marking and D-marking in Dutch

Around the second birthday the binary utterances get systematically enriched by grammatical markings. The first set of markings are auxiliaries, modal verbs, copulas and finite verb endings. I will label them I(nfl)-marking. In the stage of binary constructions, Dutch children use at first modal verbs as a kind of pre-grammatical operator, see (1)a (Jordens 2002, Van Kampen 2005). These modal verbs have an affective and social value. They are speaker/hearer oriented in the situation at hand. It is only in the next stage that the use of modal verbs is extended as in (1)b. Moreover, I-marked predicates with finite lexical verbs now appear systematically.

(1) a. *wil* beer / *magwel* koekje eten   (wanna bear / (I) may cookie eat)
    b. beer {*is/wil/moet/gaat*} slapen   (bear is/want/must/goes sleep)
    c. beer slaap*t*   (bear sleeps)

The acquisition of I-marking can be captured in a longitudinal graph. The I°-graph in (2) marks Sarah's rising percentage of finite verbs towards the adult norm in some 20 weeks.

(2) Sarah (Van Kampen corpus)

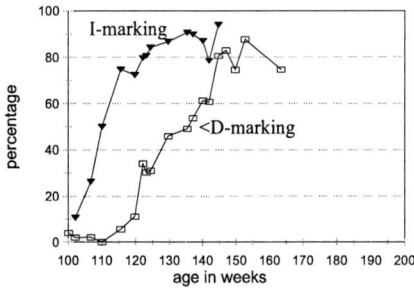

The rising percentage of I°-marking is partly based on auxiliary-type verbs (auxiliaries, modals and copulas), patterns (1)a and (1)b, and partly on the finite form of lexical content verbs, pattern (1)c. The columns S1, S2, S3 in (3) present the acquisition of I-marking by Sarah in the beginning, the middle and the end of the acquisition period. A trend-setting column M (mother), set on some 1000 consecutive I-marked predicates, has been added. The columns of Sarah show that the latter type (lexical V) is slower to take up its 28% share in the I-marking of the input (Evers and Van Kampen 2001).

(3) I-marking for Sarah (S) and her mother (M)

age in weeks	107-110 w. *S1*		115-122 w. *S2*		129-133 w. *S3*		*M*(other)	
auxiliary-types	86n	92%	140n	80%	297n	70%	731n	72%
lexical Vs	7n	8%	36n	20%	127n	30%	283n	28%

The rise of finite lexical verbs testifies a growing reliance on grammar. To make that step towards the grammaticalization of lexical verbs, the lexicon needs to have a certain extension (first lexical spurt), due to the pre-grammatical binary structures.

I-marking is followed by the acquisition of D(eterminer)-marking. The child starts to add articles to name-like parts of the utterances. The D°-graph in (2) marks Sarah's rising percentage of articles before nouns in (again) some 20 weeks. Like initial I-marking, initial D-marking is still situation-bound, as in (4)a. Dutch children refer to persons and things by means of demonstrative pronouns (*die/dat/dit/deze* "that/those/this/these") before they learn to apply articles and personal pronouns (Van Kampen 2004). Demonstratives have a clear deictic situation-bound value and are often gesture-sustained. It is only in the next stage that D-marking with articles and pronouns appears systematically in discourse-oriented grammar, as in (4)b.

(4) a. *die* (moet) slapen   (that (must) sleep)
    b. *de* beer/*hij* moet slapen (the bear must sleep)

Both I-marking and D-marking are indicative of the coherence of discourse. I-marking marks sentences as discourse units and D-marking indicates whether something has been mentioned before and is presupposed (*de/het* "the"). Due to these devices, language is no longer and necessarily *situation-bound*. It becomes *discourse-oriented*. This new orientation has in its turn a long-term effect on the further expansion of the lexicon.

The acquisition curve of articles, the D-graph in (2), coincides with the acquisition curve of personal pronouns (Van Kampen 2004). This simultaneity supports the view that both articles and pronouns are D-marking elements (Postal 1966). It also supports the view that D-marking is a matter of discourse reference tracking. It sets up a system of <± previously mentioned/±presupposed>, see (5).

(5) *De kleine beer* ging naar boven. **Daar** zag *hij het meisje. Die* lag in *zijn* bedje. *Ze* had *haar* ogen dicht. *Ze* bewoog niet. *Ze* sliep.

10 D-marked elements relate to each other across 6 I-marked units (sentences)
{ *het* meisje, *die, ze, haar, ze, ze*} { *de* beer, *hij, zijn* } { (boven), **daar** }
(*The little bear* went upstairs. **There**, *he* saw *the girl. That* (= she) was lying in *his* bed. *She* had *her* eyes closed. *She* didn't move. *She* was asleep.)

The acquisition of D-marking is a crucial step in human language acquisition. Discourse reference tracking is crucial for telling a story or maintaining a conversation. Moreover, the rising use of personal pronouns is the best indication that the speaker is oriented at earlier sentences and/or presupposition. A system equipped with D-marking allows attention to be directed at specific points. As such it delivers a powerful tool for the acquisition and maintenance of an extended lexicon.

2. Children with a hearing impairment

It stands to reason that hearing impairments in children will delay the identification and the acquisition of lexical items. Hearing impairments will in addition hamper the access to sentence structure and its discourse orientation. As a result, word finding is bound to remain slow and the use of language will continue to be an intellectual effort, rather than an intellectual short cut.

2.1. A neurolinguistic model of delayed language acquisition

Locke (1997) offers a neurolinguistic model for the switch towards grammar. His view is relevant for delays in acquisition. He holds the view that an early expansion of the lexicon (*first lexical spurt*) marks the shift towards a primary grammatical orientation. Grammatical frames offer a much better entrance to the lexicon, because they provide a more selective context. A slow extension of the lexicon, by contrast, will hamper a dominant grammatical orientation. The initial and crucial "rapid" extension of the lexicon may get stuck by a variety of factors (social, neural, perceptual), all leading to a more or less serious language specific impairment. Locke (1997) states this succinctly "A lexicon delayed is a grammar denied".

Grammatically marked language coincides with activities in the left brain hemisphere, as has been known from the earliest anatomical discoveries by Broca and Wernicke and has now been confirmed by electro-physiological techniques that localize neural activities in the brain. The child's early and grammatically still unmarked sentences (1st and 2nd stage), by contrast, correspond mainly with activity in the right brain hemisphere. This tallies well with the affective and social function of one- and two-word utterances. Affective and social values are better represented in the right hemisphere. This implies that the acquisition of formal grammar, the early grammaticalization between the 2nd and 3rd birthday, correlates with a shift in the major brain activity from the right to the left hemisphere. Locke (1997) explains this shift in the following way. Both brain sides process the incoming signals. The affective and social values of the signal provoke activity in the right hemisphere. An initial right-hemisphere dominance for such values is thereby enhanced. The grammatical markings for I^o and D^o (*is/de/het* etc.) are noticed only as mere phonological particularities, not reacted upon and left out. For that reason the grammatical markings are better noticed by the less involved left hemisphere.

The irrelevance of grammatical markings for affective and social values is counterbalanced by another type of prominence. Counts in child-directed speech (Van Kampen 2005) show how each of the grammatical markings has a frequency that is some 300 times higher than any arbitrary content word that is processed by the right hemisphere. The cognitive coherence between the meaningful content words {*beer/lief/weg/op/eten/slapen* "bear/sweet/away/ gone/eat/sleep"} begins with a limited number of stereotypes, as is stressed in Tomasello (2003), but when new content words stream in and the number of possible combinations increases accordingly, the holistic and cognitive understanding of the right hemisphere gets more difficult and slows down. As soon as the highly repetitive left-hemisphere phonological structures (order, stress, grammatical markings) begin to be recognized as schemes for coherence, there is a shift from right to left. The left-hemisphere phonetic image offers the abstract orientation for predication and argument structure. I-marking and D-marking offer a new entrance to the lexicon. This new entrance is far more effective. The grammatical orientation propels the child subsequently to a further and ultimately more than tenfold higher extension of her lexicon.

2.2. The acquisition of I-marking and D-marking: a Dutch child with otitis media

Perceptual factors that may lead to a delayed lexicon (and a grammar denied) are various hearing deficiencies before the 3rd birthday, such as persistent otitis media and a deficient function of the cochlea. These children are at risk to remain locked up in a limited frame of lexical orientation as they fail to develop a primary grammatical orientation based on merely phonetic clues in the sentence form. A case of that risk is recorded in the speech of a child L. that suffered from otitits media between 2 and 3½ years. Her acquisition graphs for I-marking and D-marking eventually reached normal levels, but with a shift in time due to a much slower rise. The stagnation period is (provisionally) marked with a straight line.

(6) Dutch child L. with otitis media

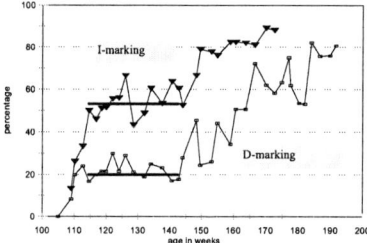

The columns in (7) represent L's acquisition of I-marking. The straight line through the graph for I-marking in (6) indicate a stagnation period. The columns

L2a and L2b reflect the I-marking at the beginning and the end of the stagnation period. The columns show that during the stagnation period there was no rise in the number of I-marked lexical verbs.

(7) I-marking (auxiliary-types + lexical V) for o.m. child (L) and mother (M)

age in weeks	110-115 *L1*	122-127 *L2a*	134-141 *L2b*	159-164 *L3*	*M*(other)
auxiliaries	72 n 94%	155 n 87%	156 n 88%	242 n 73%	690 n 69%
lexical Vs	5 n 6 %	18 n 13%	22 n 12%	88 n 27%	303 n 31%

Like the acquisition curve for articles (D-graph in (6)), the acquisition of personal pronouns shows a serious stagnation. L. "overuses" demonstratives for a much longer period than Dutch children with a normal language development.

Later on, this child with repeated otitis media, of normal intelligence and perfect hearing, turned out to have serious problems with reading, writing and word finding. She was diagnosed as dyslectic.

In sum, I- and D-marking establish the discourse network for lexical extension. Their rise follows from the pressure of new lexical items. Longitudinal graphs may support the thesis (Locke 1997) that "a lexicon delayed is a grammar denied". There is certain elasticity in the period that a grammar can be acquired, but this elasticity is limited. Children with a hearing deficiency before the age of three are at risk to run out of time. They may develop a serious language impairment. The child's lexical expansion will set in later and may be too slow to cause the shift towards a primary grammatical orientation. To check whether this is true, we need a detailed longitudinal picture of the actual progress of children with a hearing deficiency.

References

Bates, E., P. Dale and D. Thal (1995) "Individual differences and their implications for theories of language development," in P. Fletcher and B. MacWhinney, eds., *Handbook of Child Language*, 96-151, Blackwell, Oxford.

Evers, A. and J. van Kampen (2001) "E-language, I-language and the order of parameter setting," UiL OTS Working Papers 00105-SS, Utrecht University.

Jordens, P. (2002) "Finiteness in early child Dutch," *Linguistics* 40 (4), 687-765.

Kampen, J. van (2004) "Learnability order in the French pronominal system," in: R. Bok-Bennema et al., eds., *Selected Papers from Going Romance 2002*, 163-183, Benjamins, Amsterdam.

—. (2005) "Language-specific bootstraps for UG categories," *International Journal of Bilingualism* 9-2, 253-277.

Locke, J. L. (1997) "A theory of neurolinguistic development," *Brain and Language* 58-2, 265-326.

Postal, P. (1966) "On So-called Pronouns in English," in F. P. Dinneen, ed., *Monograph Series on Language and Linguistics* 19, 177-206, UP, Georgetown.

Tomasello, M. (2003) *Constructing a Language. A Usage-Based Theory of Language Acquisition*, Harvard University Press, Cambridge, MA.

SINGLE VALUE STEPS IN FIRST LANGUAGE ACQUISITION

JACQUELINE VAN KAMPEN AND ARNOLD EVERS

Abstract

Preferably, the properties of grammar can be derived from the following factors:
  (i)   The primary linguistic data as they are offered to the child.
  (ii)   A language acquisition procedure.
Hopefully, the language acquisition procedure is compatible with plausible assumptions about the neural abilities of human beings, but that is of no immediate concern here. The interaction of the primary data and the acquisition procedure can be studied by a closer look at the order of the child's acquisition steps. What does the child acquire first and why? What does she acquire later and why? This is empirically a promising and by no means trivial approach. At the same time, we will argue against an assumption that is quite common in computational studies and also in mere grammatical studies of child language. People from Gold (1967) to Yang (2002) assume that the acquisition procedure has simultaneous access to all data at once. Our point will rather be that the acquisition procedure implies a natural selection of data (not based on UG assumption). Child language can be reconstructed as the result of successive steps in input reduction. The result is a series of successive intermediate grammars. Each grammar causes a new data-selection from the same type of input. Data-selection turns the poverty of a diffuse input stimulus into a focused stimulus by highly selective intake. Eventually, it may be shown that generative grammar is learnable without the postulation of grammatical a priories.

1. Input reduction

Early child language is not only stereotype and repetitive, it is above all simplified. There is quantitative difference with the adult input. There are less lexical items, shorter sentences and less grammatical markings. More importantly, there is a qualitative difference as well. Certain grammatical properties are not present at all in early child language. They will not appear until other properties have been acquired first. This order in acquisition steps, first studied in Brown (1973), must be explained. Child language can be represented as a series of grammars G_i, each one one step more specified than its predecessor until the series ends with the target grammar G_n (Chomsky 1975: 119f).

(1) G_o ---- G_i $\Rightarrow$ G_{i+1} ---- G_n

Each step is an invention that makes sense due to the preceding grammar and due to a new selection of data from the input, see (2).

(2) $\left\{ \begin{array}{c} G_i \\ + D_{i+1} \end{array} \right\}$ $\Rightarrow$ G_{i+1}

The initial steps in the linear order offer the learner frames that determine the subsequent acquisition steps. The first steps are potentially relevant to all further steps and as such they are likely to have typological significance and to qualify as 'macro-parameters' (Baker 1996). For instance, the first evidence frames fit Greenberg's (1966) local frames for language typology: VSO (e.g. Celtic), SVO (e.g. French), SOV (e.g. Dutch). The later steps take place in a grammatical environment that is far more determined by previous acquisition steps. One may be more inclined to think about 'learning' in case of the latest steps than in case of the first steps. For example, when the verbal paradigm has been fully acquired, one may think about the irregular verbs as innocent substitutions that finally block the use of regular ones by sheer repetition. The regular verbal paradigm, also a fairly language-specific affair, looks more learnable if the category Verb, the auxiliary-verb restrictions and the φ-features on the subject are already acquired. In the same way, it can be argued that the language-specific markings for predicate-argument structure in the reduced data induce grammatical principles like EPP (subject obligation for inflection-marked predicates) and UTAH (standardized theta roles for fixed arguments), see Van Kampen (2006). Along this line, an innate UG need no longer be the source of parallels between grammars. The instructive force of input data is enhanced by the input reduction. Elementary distinctions are acquired by the force of an elementary reduced data set and child language itself testifies to the data reduction that is at issue. UG rather happens to be an outcome of an uninformed acquisition procedure.

    It is uncontroversial that the child begins its acquisition process with a radical reduction of the mother's (adult) input. The initial questions are formulated in (3).

(3) *Initial research questions*
  a. How does the child succeed to simplify the structures that she hears in a sensible way?
  b. Why are certain reductions repaired early and others later?

The first question (3)a can be answered by the provisionally simplified common sense principle in (4). We will give it a more subtle form in (8) below.

(4) *Principle for input reduction*
    Leave out what you cannot fit in.

The second question (3)b can be rephrased as in (5).

(5) How does a grammar G_i select the data D_{i+1} in order to reach the next and less reduced form G_{i+1}?

Note that the relevant data D_{i+1} are not covered by G_i itself. The data D_{i+1} are simply hidden in the mass of other unanalyzed input data. For that reason, we might say that the elements in D_{i+1} still are a poor and diffuse stimulus to reach G_{i+1}. How does the acquisition procedure get them out? Let us consider a simple case of reduction first.

Grammatical words or markings may be hundred or more times as frequent as any of the denotational (content) elements, yet they cannot be acquired without a grammatically interpreted context. This is because a grammatical element F_i indicates a grammatical relation between two phrases $[XP [F YP]_{FP}]$. It is a word that carries no meaning beyond the syntactic relation. The word *and* does not mean 'pair', the word *but* does not mean 'contrast', the word *is* does not mean 'property'. They express a certain relation between denotational terms X and Y.

When all grammatical elements are left out, pragmatic understanding of the utterances is the remaining option and binary constructions of denotational elements are best understood in a pragmatic situation-bound way. Early child language does indeed show something like that. The residue in child language is basically a set of binary constructions that lack grammatical elements. What remains is a set of denotational and name-like words like {*dance/daddy/shoe/milk/nice/warm/off/on/gone*} and a set of pragmatic operator-like words {*no/more/this/that/wanna*}. Denotational elements are acquired before grammatical elements, although each of the grammatical markings is several hundreds times more frequent. The acquisition order is imposed by the nature of the system the child is confronted with. Denotational words can be acquired without the support of a grammatical context.

(6)   *Typical reductions in early child language*

utterance

naming topic   comment

a.	(the)	bunny	(is)	dance(ing)
b.	(I keep the)	milk	(is)	warm
c.	(my)	shoe	(goes)	off
d.		daddy	(has)	gone

utterance

operator   comment

c.	(I)	wanna	play
d.	(you like)	more	milk
e.	(I put)	this	on
f.	(that is)	no(t)	nice

The initial denotational elements do not carry by themselves a referential or a predicative intention, nor are they marked by some I^o (inflection) for predication or some D^o (determiner) for reference. Such intentions are for the sympathetic listener to find out. This is the period that Lyons (1979) had in mind when he suggested that child language might have proto-predication as a forerunner of predication and also that child language might have proto-reference as a forerunner of reference. We propose the interpretation of Lyons (1979) in (7).

(7) a. proto-reference   ~ naming function
    b. proto-predication ~ comment/characterizing function
    c. proto-illocution ~ (pragmatic) operator function

The functions of naming and commenting are pragmatic and not yet grammatically marked. The same denotational meaning X can in principle be used for naming and for commenting alike, as one can see in the examples in (6)b,d. Because there is yet no grammatically marked relation, there need not be a distinction N/V either. One may assume that the child as well as any animal can make a distinction between things, events, properties, states and what not. It is hard to think of any consciousness at all when such distinctions are not available. The grammatical input reduction only means that such cognitive distinctions have not yet been related to fixed phonological forms. The point is that proto-grammar does not translate these cognitive qualities into grammatical forms, whereas the later grammars do. The proto-grammar seems a good candidate for G_0 in (1). It lacks any grammatically expressed relation between the denotational elements.

Since there is no grammar yet, the grammatical elements can be noticed as highly frequent, but they cannot yet be interpreted. Let such unknown, but highly frequent, elements be represented by <F?> (unidentified functional feature). It intends to cover any grammatical marking, whether by a separate grammatical word (*is*/*do*/*the*/*a*) or by a morphological affix (*-ing*/*-ed*/*-s*). The acquisition procedure may now start with the reduction operation in (8).

(8) *Reduction procedure*
 a. *reduction*: substitute <F?> for each grammatical marking still unknown
 b. *intake*: throw out all input sentences with more than one <F?>

A neuro-linguistic interpretation of the shift towards <F?> → <F_i> is present in Locke (1997 and references therein). Grammatically marked language coincides with activities in the left-brain hemisphere. The child's early and grammatically still unmarked sentences, by contrast, correspond mainly with activity in the right-brain hemisphere. This tallies well with the affective and social function of one- and two-word utterances. Affective and social values are better represented in the right hemisphere. It now happens that the acquisition of formal grammar, the early grammaticalization between the second and the third birthday, correlates with a shift in the major brain activity from the right to the left hemisphere. Locke (1997) explains this shift in the following way. Both brain sides process the incoming signals. The affective and social values of the signal provoke activity in the right hemisphere. Initial right hemisphere dominance for such values is thereby enhanced. The grammatical markings, e.g. for I^0 (finite verbs) and D^0 (articles), are noticed only as mere phonological particularities, not reacted upon and left out in the pragmatic exercise of the right hemisphere. For that reason, the grammatical markings (although uninterpreted) are better noticed by the less involved left hemisphere.

The cognitive coherence between the meaningful denotational words begins with a limited number of stereotypes (Tomasello 2003), but when new denotational words stream in and the number of possible combinations increases accordingly, the holistic and cognitive understanding of the right hemisphere gets more difficult and slows down. As soon as the highly repetitive left-hemisphere phonological structures (order, stress, grammatical markings) begin to be recognized as schemes for coherence, there is a shift from right to left. The left-hemisphere phonetic image offers the abstract grammatical orientation for predication and argument structure. The acquisition of I^0 and D^0 offers a new entrance to the lexicon. This new entrance is far more effective. The grammatical orientation propels the child subsequently to a further and ultimately more than tenfold higher extension of her lexicon. It is a shift from proto-grammar towards real grammar.

The topic-comment relation is underlined by a functional element. When the functional element is reinvented as marking the topic-comment function, one may say that the comment gets the (grammatical) predicate function and that it implies the subject/topic. What we have in mind is that all functional categories are acquired in that manner. They should all originate from a binary frame X and Y that is related by an initially not yet understood <F?>. Let us call such frames 'evidence frames'.

(9) *Evidence frame*
    a. pragmatically: an intuitively understood utterance
    b. syntactically: a binary phrase structure [XP [F? YP]$_{FP}$]$_{FP}$
    c. semantically: fully interpretable but for a single <F?>

The result of the input reduction will be that the intake to the acquisition procedure is a set of repetitive short sentences all containing a functional marking in the same position. The evidence frame may be represented as [XP <F?> YP], where XP and YP consist of fully recognizable items or phrases. When it is possible to figure out what the syntactic form and meaning of the evidence frame is, we have a minimal acquisition step. The category <F?> is learned. The question mark disappears and the result is an identified grammatical category <F$_i$>, as in (10)a, exemplified in (10)b.

(10) *Learning step*
    a. identify the pragmatically understood <F?> as <F$_i$> and attach <F$_i$> as a grammatical marker to the selectionally dominant element to left or right.

    b.
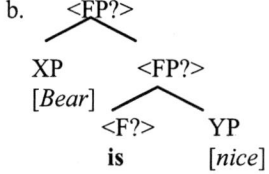

The present example [X [F$_i$ Y]$_{FP}$]$_{FP}$ needs additional motivation for why the functional category adjoins to Y rather than to X. One of the reasons is that [Fi Y]$_{FP}$ appears in the proto-grammar as a pragmatic operator + denotational word, see (6)e-f. Other arguments may follow from selection relations.

Besides the [specifier X–head F_i] relation, the acquisition procedure will need evidence frames for complements, attributes, movement and scope-bearing elements. Suppose now that such evidence frames can be found for the respective functional categories/features. Then we may arrive in the following world. The evidence frames select the relevant data from the input, and they focus the acquisition procedure on the grammatical category <F?>/F_i that relates to the binary evidence frame. The weak and diffuse stimulus that follows from the input sentences is now temporarily changed into a strong and exclusive stimulus that follows from the evidence frame.

The evidence frames are effective because they are minimal, but at the same time fully interpretable utterances. The relation between the parts XP and YP may have been recognized pragmatically as YP (*nice*) 'characterizes' XP (*Bear*). The label FP in (10)b implies that XP and YP are united by the relation <F?>. The binary structure, where <F?> combines to the right with [*nice*], is determined by the existence of the phrase type [*is nice*] in proto-grammar and because it is further related to stress and selection patterns (Van Kampen 2005). The more precise construction of viable evidence frames will be spelled out in the book. The central point is that the in-between grammars G_i in (1) have a data-selecting effect that supports the learnability of G_{i+1}. The basic claim that the intermediate (reduced) grammars select the data for the next acquisition step has been made before (Berwick and Weinberg's 'data-focus' 1984: 284). Here it is used as an argument against the poverty of the stimulus. The reduction turns a diffuse stimulus into an effective one.

As one may realize, the reduction procedure applies recursively. When <F?> has been identified as F_i, a new grammatical feature has been acquired. By consequence, the input reduction in (2) will now reapply to the same kind of input, but deliver a new kind of intake. F_i now passes the reduction filter. The next grammatical category F_{i+1} is singled out, etc. The successive input reductions that follow in this way should remind us of Clark's (1992: 90) 'Single Value Constraint' (cf. also Berwick 1985: 108). Notice though that the present acquisition procedure is not error-driven. It rather adds new specifications in a stepwise fashion. One may wonder why natural languages are so child-friendly to produce evidence frames that follow from systematic input reduction. A glib answer would be that grammatical systems of a less manageable type would fail to be learned and so fail to survive. A more constructive perspective is possible as well, and this is the perspective we ultimately want to explore. Let there be a type of formal systems that can be decoded by systematic input reduction. The decoding should ultimately arrive at a hierarchy of functional categories and their associated phrasal types. Is it possible that human core grammars are of that formal type? Main properties of human grammars, such as *locality* and *inclusiveness* as viewed in present day

Minimalism, are bound to be stable when they guarantee a natural learnablity of the system.

2. Order of acquisition steps

Language acquisition overcomes the radical underspecifications that result from the initial data reduction by adding grammatical features within a binary frame. The order of the successive acquisition steps can be shown by longitudinal graphs, as in (11).

(11)   Dutch Sarah: acquisition of I°-marking and D°-marking

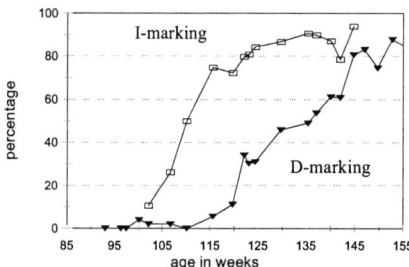

The graphs in (6) represent the acquisition of finite verbs (I°-marking) and determiners (D°-marking) by the Dutch child Sarah (Van Kampen 2004a). The graph for I°-marking shows the growing percentage of grammatical predicate marking {copula/auxiliary/modal/finite morphology}. The graph for D°-marking shows the growing percentage of argument marking {article/demonstrative/ possessor}.

Now the order of acquisition steps shows that Dutch Sarah applies systematic I°-marking almost half a year earlier than systematic D°-marking. The same order of appearance was found for English, French, and Rumanian. The amount of determiners outweighs the amount of finite verbs in the input data. Yet, children in various languages start to analyze predicate-argument structure by I°-marking. The less frequent I°-marking precedes the more frequent D°-marking in acquisition. The order I°→D° must be explained. Evers and Van Kampen (2006) show how the acquisition procedure follows the *Single Value Constraint* on evidence frames as proposed in (9), when initially sentences with both a D°-marked noun and an I°-marked verb are thrown out of the observation space. The feasibility of a mechanical reduction procedure was partly demonstrated by a computer simulation (Obdeijn 2004) that derived an order of intake frames in child language from a child-directed input.

The systematic I^o-marking and D^o-marking themselves give entrance to a whole series of further acquisition steps, beginning with a grammatical decision procedure on the category membership V versus N. This option, chosen in (Van Kampen 2005) for language acquisition, was implemented earlier in computational approaches to category assignment (Buszowski 1987). A general property of 'decoding' emerges as well. The successive evidence frames narrow down to a far more precise context and the speed of acquisition increases by an order of magnitude. The subject of the I^o-marked predicate (finite verb) initially lacks φ-features of person/number. In a subsequent step, the φ-feature content in D^o, {± person, ± number} on the subject, is figured out. However, the finite verb still doesn't show the correct agreement with the subject, see (12).

(12)   <u>de</u> clowntje<u>s</u><+plur> *heb*<+sing> oogjes   Sarah week 130
        (the clowns has eyes)

One step later, the initial I^o-marked predicate constitutes the local evidence frame for Agreement features, the copying of the φ-features on I^o. The finite verb now starts showing the correct agreement. Late acquisition of agreement has been reported for various languages, e.g. for Rumanian, Portuguese and Catalan.

The dense succession of the acquisition steps shows that the later steps are a matter of weeks whereas the earlier steps were a matter of months (Kampen 2006).

(13)   step I^o step D^o step $D^o(φ)$ step $I^o(φ)$
        20 wks   25 wks   5 wks (?)   5 wks

The more effective acquisition relates plausibly to the more precise frame that can be used to select the input. The selection of some binary combination of content signs is far more undetermined than the distributional relation between explicit grammatical markings such as φ-features and agreement. The later set of acquisitions is supported by a lexicon with categorial marking <+I> or <+D>. After step 1 and 2, the EPP (subject-<+fin>verb configuration) operates as an evidence frame.

3. A discovery procedure

Generative learnability theories in the 1980th were theoretical and somewhat defensive. They qualified the mathematical deduction in Gold (1967) that context-free rewriting grammars could not be identified or learned without negative data. As Wexler and Culicover (1980) argue, context free generative grammars and some transformational grammars are learnable from positive data as long as the relevant relations are sufficiently local. The main point was to argue learnability in principle for certain types of generative grammar. There was no reference to child language. The ongoing simplification of grammatical principles, pushed by Categorial Grammar, HPSG and the Minimalist Program, may re-inspire interest in their learnability. I mention four attempts into that direction. Fodor (1998), Yang (2002), Culicover and Nowak (2003) and our work (Evers and Van Kampen 2001).

Fodor (1998) and Yang (2002) assume that the child is confronted with the full variety of constructions in his language. The child meets this challenge with brilliant creativity. She comes up with all possible grammatical structures that the general theory of grammar would allow. The child's productivity in designing possible solutions is maybe comparable with his creativity in grasping visual or musical structures or maybe with the babbling phase that precedes the construction of phonological forms. Fodor as well as Yang's learner start with a variety of grammatical structures and work towards a minimal set of grammatical structures by comparing alternative solutions. Fodor's learner is sensitive to certain key-constructions (treelets) that betray the language type and Yang's learner is sensitive to rules that are too often involved in analyses that fail. The options that they compare are assumed to be a priori present from the human brain. Yang proposes an accounting system of 'penalties' for failing rules. Yang's bookkeeping of failures and Fodor's testing system could be characterized respectively as an effective *evaluation procedure* (Yang) and as an effective *decision procedure* (Fodor). Their learners start with all options offered by the theory. Both successfully simulate how the learner zeros in on the core grammar of the input language.

By contrast, we propose, like Culicover and Nowak (2003), that the young learner is unaware of any grammatical alternative that is available in the world outside. Our learning procedure could be characterized as a *discovery procedure*. Our young learner must reduce its initial attention to constructions assigned to pairs of adjacent content words and so he enters a maximally reduced observation space, as formulated in (8).

A learning procedure as in (10) that adds a grammatical feature to a category moves from a less restricted superset to a more restricted subset (Kiparsky 2002). The learning procedure starts with underspecifications, but the associative pressure of local contexts has a healing effect. The initial underspecifications are "blocked". Blocking effects are known from the very beginning of grammatical studies (Panini, Kiparsky 2005). This is a contentious issue in theories of language acquisition. Some try to reconstruct child language as subset language that is extended to the correct generalizations by positive data (conform the Subset Principle). Others believe that child language starts with overgeneralizations and narrows down by developing subcategories (Jakobson 1942; the present perspective: Van Kampen 1997, 2004b). Blocking in language acquisition can be traced by longitudinal graphs as we have seen. Blocking never works instantaneously. It takes some time and some quantification before the learner reacts. Blocking is more an effectiveness device. This reminds of Yang's (2002) penalty system, but Yang's system is more informed and intelligent. It chooses between innate alternative grammatical solutions. Our system is more stupid. It is pressured by input frequencies to add grammatical specifications to an underspecified frame.

4. The learnability of movement structures

The evidence frames are also effective for the learnability of scopal phenomena, like wh-marking and negation. When movement rules are seen as rules that reorder an underlying array of heads and phrases in order to arrive at the perceived surface structure, the learnability of movement rules offer at least the two problems in (14).

(14)   a.   *The gap* problem
           How can a phrase position be perceived as antecedent or gap?
      b.   *The distance problem*
           How are islands learned as phrases that do not allow a gap and an outside antecedent?

Both problems are more manageable in unification-based approaches that trade in the movement rule for a lexical feature matching between two sister-constituents Neeleman and Van de Koot (2002) derive such an approach from Minimality principles. The first sister is grammatically marked $<F_a, F_b>$, but beyond the usual licensing context. For example, wh-phrases in the Spec,C position are case-marked and preposition-marked as if they held an argument position. In the same line, the finite verb in the C^o position carries the tense/agr markings as if it were in the I^o position. The second sister of the construction should contain a grammatically definable gap $<+C\sim gap, F_a, F_b>$ that fails to carry the marking, $<F_a, F_b>$ see (15).

(15) $<+C>$ movement structure

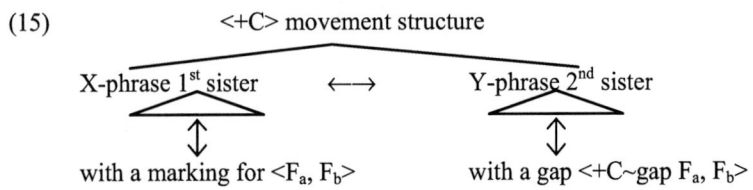

Obviously, the learnability of the antecedent ~ gap is on a promising track when the learner does already command a grammar that:

(16)   a.   spots the markings F_a, F_b orphaned in the first sister and spots
            their lack in the gap <+C~gap F_a, F_b> to the top label <+C>.
       b.   projects the markings <F_a, F_b> according to existing conventions.

Fortunately, the grammatical markings F_a, F_b, etc. that define the antecedent~gap relation have been acquired earlier in non-gapped structures. This is an empirical point and it fits (16)a. Does the grammar contain a procedure to project grammatical features? Sure, it was acquired when heads were subcategorized for grammatical properties of their complements. This fits point (16)b. The subcategorizing feature matching works for subcategorized complements, but not for subjects and adjuncts. The latter, subjects and adjuncts, happen to be islands, whereas the subcategorizing complements are in principle non-islands.

A grammatical complement property is reflected in a property of the head it is governed by, and [head complement] phrases that are complements themselves. This is equivalent with the more colorful description where a <+C/+wh>-marked constituent is first present in its argument position, moves up to the <+C> position, but requires a head~government path between <+C> and the gap as proposed in Kayne (1981). In both arrangements (Kayne 1981, Neeleman and Van de Koot 2002) the positions within a non-complement cannot be considered. This turns the notion island into a non-entity. It is not present in the grammar, hence it need not be learned.

The learnability of island constraints has been a topic of debate (Chomsky 1975, 1980: 319, Crain and Nakayama 1987, *Linguistic Review* 2002). In (17)a, the copula from the main clause is fronted. Copula movement out of a subject relative like (17)b is not possible (subject island).

(17)   a.   is$_i$ any ape that is brainy t_i talkative?
       b.   *is$_i$ any ape that t_i brainy is talkative?

It is a long debated issue how children learn that the movement is structure dependent, rather than linear dependent. Crain and Nakayama (1987), as well as Legate and Yang, Fodor and Crowther (2002) among others relate it to innate principles, whereas Pullum and Scholz (2002) prefer to see a hint in input percentages as sufficient. In the present view, it follows neither from innate principles, nor from input. It rather is a consequence from a feature projection system that has been acquired earlier (inclusiveness and sisterhood). The properties of the embedded copula will not reach the matrix projection line. *The ape* with subject status cannot do that. For that reason, preposing of the downstairs copula cannot be acquired. The grammar that has been acquired cannot figure that out, because there is no appropriate feature projection to lift the structure into comprehensibility. The discovery procedure proposed here must assume that the natural input allows a reduction to local frames and a terminal string that remains informative enough in spite of the reduction. Locality and local inclusiveness of grammatical information are present to guarantee a certain type of learnability, without grammatical a priories.

References

Baker, M.C. (1996) *The Polysynthesis Parameter*, Oxford University Press, Oxford.

Berwick, R. (1985) *The Acquisition of Syntactic Knowledge*, MIT Press, Cambridge.

—. and A. Weinberg (1984) *The Grammatical Basis of Linguistic Performance*, MIT Press, Cambridge MA.

Brown, R. (1973) *A First Language: the Early Stages*, Harvard University Press, Cambridge MA.

Buszkowski, W. (1987) "Discovery procedures for categorial grammars," in E. Klein and J. van Benthem, eds., *Categories, Polymorphism and Unification*, UvA.

Chomsky, N. (1975) *Reflections on Language*, Pantheon Books, New York.

Clark, R. (1992) "The selection of syntactic knowledge", *Language Acquisition* 2(2), 83-149.

Crain, S. and Nakayama, M. 1987. "Structure dependence in children's language", *Language* 62, 522-543.

Culicover, P. and A. Nowak (2003) *Dynamical Grammar: Minimalism, Acquisition and Change*, OUP, Oxford.

Evers, A. and J. van Kampen (2001) "E-language, I-language and the order of parameter setting," UiL OTS Working Papers 00105-SS, Utrecht University.

—. and J. van Kampen (2006) "Hierarchies of learning steps in first language acquisition," ms. UiL OTS Utrecht (monograph in preparation).

Fodor, J.D. (1998) "Unambiguous triggers," *Linguistic Inquiry* 29, 1-36.

—. and C. Crowther (2002) "Understanding stimulus poverty argument", *Linguistic Review 19* 1-2, 105-145.

Gold, E.M. (1967) "Language identification in the limit," *Information and Control* 10, 447-474.

Greenberg, J.H. (1966) "Some universals of grammar with particular reference to the order of meaningful elements," in J.H. Greenberg, ed., *Universals of Language*, MIT Press, Cambridge MA.

Jakobson, R. (1942) *Kindersprache, Aphasie und Allgemeine Lautgesetze*, Uppsula.

Kampen, J. van (1997) *First Steps in Wh-movement*, Eburon, Delft.

—. (2004a) "Learnability order in the French pronominal system," in R. Bok-Bennema et al., eds., *Selected Papers from Going Romance 2002*, 163-183, Benjamins, Amsterdam.

—. (2004b) 'An acquisitional view on optionality', *Lingua* 114, 1133-1146.

—. (2005) "Language-specific bootstraps for UG categories," *International Journal of Bilingualism* 9-2, 253-277.

—. (2006) "The acquisition of the standard EPP in Dutch and French," in J. Costa and M.C. Figueiredo Silva, eds., *Studies on Agreement*, 99-119. John Benjamins, Amsterdam.

Kayne, R. (1981) "ECP extensions", *Linguistic Inquiry* 12, 93-133.

Kiparsky, P. (2002) "On the architecture of Panini's grammar", Three lectures delivered at the Hyderabad *Conference on the Architecture of Grammar*.

—. (2005) "Blocking and periphrases in inflectional paradigms", in G.Booij and J. van Marle, eds., *Yearbook of Morphology* 2004, 113-135, Springer, Dordrecht.

Legate, J.A. and Ch.D. Yang 2002. "Emperical re-assessment of poverty arguments", *LinguisticReview 19* 1-2, 151-162.

Locke, J. L. (1997) "A theory of neurolinguistic development," *Brain and Language* 58-2, 265-326.

Lyons, J. (1979) "Deixis and anaphora," in T. Myers, ed., *The Development of Conversation and Discourse*, University Press, Edinburgh, 88-103.

Neeleman, A. and H. van de Koot (2002) "The configurational matrix," *Linguistic Inquiry* 33-4, pp. 529-574.

Obdeijn, A.: 2004, *Taalverwerving door Kinderen en Machines*, Master thesis University of Amsterdam, ILLC.

Pullum, G. and Scholz, B. (2002) "Empirical assessment of stimulus poverty arguments", *LinguisticReview 19* 1-2, 9-50.

Tomasello, M. (2003) *Constructing a Language. A Usage-Based Theory of Language Acquisition*, Harvard University Press, Cambridge MA.

Wexler, K. and P. Culicover (1980) *Formal Principles of Language Acquisition*, MIT Press, Cambridge MA.

Yang, C.D.(2002) *Knowledge and Learning in Natural Language*, O.U.P, Oxford.

VISIBLE VERSUS INVISIBLE EXTRACTION OR GAP INTERPRETATION?

LEONTINE KREMERS AND BART HOLLEBRANDSE[1]

Children obey relative clause barriers from an early age on for wh-movement but not for quantifier movement. Roeper and De Villiers (1993) explain this in terms of visibility of movement. The main goal of our experiment is to find out whether there is an alternative explanation for children's bad performance on quantifier movement. The alternative considered is a gap interpretation strategy, which predicts children to perform better on subject relatives than on object relatives, due to the relative position of the gap. The results of the experiment, however, show that children's performance cannot be related to gap interpretation nor to any type of movement strategy. The article concludes that the puzzle should be approached from a different angle, focusing more on the (qualitative) differences between distributivity and collectivity. An approach which is at present unfamiliar in both theoretical and acquisition research.

1. Introduction

There is a sharp distinction between sentences (1) and (2) below: (1) allows a so-called long-distance (LD) answer (*how did he go*), which is missing in the relative clause example in (2). Both allow short-distance (SD) answers (*how did he say/help*).

(1)   How did the Indian say that the man went to his wigwam?
(2)   How did the Indian help the man who went to his wigwam?

This observation is captured by Chomsky's Theory of Barriers, which states that "extraction" is blocked from relative clauses (2), but is allowed from complement clauses (1). Barriers also captures the observation that a quantifier inside a relative clause (3) lacks a wide-scope reading. For adults the quantified phrase "all cowboys" cannot have scope over the indefinite NP "a horse" and the distributive reading, where the cowboys are on different horses, is excluded.

The narrow-scope (collective) reading, where there is one particular horse that all the cowboys are sitting on, remains is the only available one.

(3)   There is a horse which all cowboys are sitting on."

Roeper and De Villiers (1993) show that children obey barriers for wh-movement (2), but possibly not for quantifier movement (3). A difference between (2) and (3) is that wh-movement is an operation in overt syntax and is therefore visible, whereas quantifier movement happens at Logical Form (LF), which is covert/invisible. The Barriers theory, not distinguishing between visible and invisible, predicts that children should handle (2) and (3) alike.

The object of the present study is to find out what causes children's bad performance on sentences like (3): does it really constitute a violation of relative clause barrierhood and therefore a problem with invisibility or can it be caused by something else? Before we present the results of an experiment designed to answer this question, we will provide you with some theoretical and acquisition background information (section 2 and 3 respectively). After that, we turn to our research question, experimental design and results (section 4), naturally finishing off with a discussion of the results and our conclusions (section 5 and 6).

2. Theoretical background

Chomsky's Barriers Theory (1986) states that NP's and CP's can be barriers for extraction, most commonly illustrated by the impossibility of long-distance wh-movement from relative clauses (see (2)), but also a possible explanation for the lack of a distributive reading in (3). The traditional explanation of how different interpretations of sentences containing quantifiers come about is Quantifier Raising (QR) (May, 1977). The sentence in (4) below has two possible interpretations.

(4)   All cowboys are riding on a horse.

To interpret this sentence QR has to take place at LF, which means that both the quantified phrase (*all cowboys*) and the indefinite noun phrase (*a horse*) have to be moved to the top node of the sentence (i.e. have to be adjoined to S). This can happen in either order: first quantified NP and then indefinite NP, which results in a collective reading (the indefinite NP having scope over the quantified NP), or the other way around which results in a distributive reading (quantified NP having scope over indefinite NP). May (1985) states that this invisible quantifier movement is constrained by the same constraints as overt movement, such as Subjacency. This way he explains the lack of a distributive interpretation in (3), repeated here in (5).

(5)   There is a horse that all cowboys are riding on.

It is not possible to move "all cowboys" cyclically to the top of the sentence without violating Subjacency. Therefore, "all cowboys" cannot get scope over "a horse" and the distributive reading is excluded.

In a recent version of QR Fox (2000) states that quantifier movement is constrained by economical motivations. He proposes two constraints (6) to account for the lack of a distributive interpretation for (5).

(6)   1. **Scope Economy**
        Scope-shifting operations cannot be semantically vacuous.
        2. **Shortest Move**
        QR must move a QP to the closest position in which it is interpretable.
        In other words, a QP must always move to the closest clause-denoting element that dominates it.

These constraints applied to (5) explain why "all cowboys" cannot escape its relative clause: Shortest Move tells you that "all cowboys" should be moved to the closest clause-denoting element that dominates it, which is right before the complementizer (*that*). However, at this point, there is no change in scope between "all cowboys" and "a horse", so Scope Economy forbids this movement operation to take place. Since Shortest Move forbids longer movement operations to take place "all cowboys" has no other option than to stay put and the only available interpretation is the collective interpretation.

Question is whether these theoretical accounts can explain children's difficulties with relative clause barrierhood when it comes to quantifier movement. Barriers Theory certainly cannot, as it treats visible and invisible movement alike. Quantifier Raising, in its traditional or modern form, can, but only by appealing to the difference between overt and covert movement. Moreover, as we will see in the next section, more elaborate acquisition data seem to indicate that it is more difficult than that.

3. Acquisition data

There has been a lot of research on children's acquisition of quantifiers, but not too much on children's acquisition of quantifier movement. Roeper and De Villiers (1993) concluded from results of several experiments testing bound-variable interpretations that constraints on quantifier movement are not in place until children are around 7 years old. Coles, De Villiers and Roeper (2004) tested a group of 21 African-American-English speaking children between 5;2 and 8;3 on their knowledge of relative clause barrierhood to both wh- and quantifier movement. They found that the relative clause as a barrier is respected for wh-movement but not for quantifier movement.[2]

This result is replicated for Dutch children by Hollebrandse and Kremers (2005). In an experiment that essentially followed the same rationale as Coles et al. (2004) twenty children between 4;6 and 6;2 (mean age 5;4) were tested. The experiment consisted of two parts: first, a question answering task for wh-movement, where a condition with complement clauses (7a) was contrasted with a condition with relative clauses (7b). For adults long-distance answers are possible for complement clauses but not for relative clauses. Second, a truth value judgment task for quantifier movement, where a condition with main clause sentences (8a) was contrasted with a condition with relative clauses (8b). Again for adults a distributive reading is available for main clauses, but not for relative clauses.

(7)   a. Hoe zei Kees dat de jongen gevallen was?
           "How did Kees say the boy fell?"
        b. Hoe hielp de sterke Indiaan de Indiaan die naar zijn wigwam ging?
           "How did the strong Indian help the Indian who went to his wigwam?"

(8)   a. Alle cowboys zitten op een paard.
           "All cowboys are sitting on a horse."
        b. Er is een paard waar alle cowboys op zitten.
           "There is a horse that all cowboys are sitting on."

The results of this experiment were striking: only 8% violations of the relative clause barrier with wh-movement (long-distance answers where not possible for adults) versus 28% violations of the relative clause barrier with quantifier movement. In these cases a distributive reading was accepted where it is not possible for adults.

One important difference between Coles et al. (2004) and Hollebrandse and Kremers (2005) is the type of relative clauses used. Coles et al. found significantly more violations of the relative clause barrier with object relatives than with subject relatives. Hollebrandse and Kremers (2005) used subject relatives in the wh-experiment and object relatives in the quantifier experiment, which might have influenced the data, especially since Coles et al. (2004) found this difference. The findings, however, did make us wonder why an object relative would lead to more violations than a subject relative. If it actually is something about object relatives that leads children to give a (for adults impossible) distributive interpretation to the sentence, then we would have an alternative explanation as to why children obey barriers for wh-movement and seem to disobey them for quantifier movement.

We believe such an alternative explanation to be available. Look at the sentences (9) and (10) below.

(9)   Er is een paard dat **e** alle cowboys draagt.
        "There is a horse that is carrying all cowboys."
(10)   Er is een paard waar alle cowboys **e** op zitten.
        "There is a horse that all cowboys are sitting on."

The difference between (9) and (10) is that (9) is a subject relative ("een paard" (*a horse*) is subject of the relative clause's predicate) whereas (10) is an object relative ("een paard" (*a horse*) is object of the relative clause's predicate). The most important difference between subject and object relatives is the position of the gap of the relative head in the relative clause. In (9) the gap is before "alle cowboys" (*all cowboys*), whereas in (10) the gap is after "alle cowboys". Suppose children interpret "een paard" (*a horse*) in its gap position rather than in its surface position; that would lead them to give a distributive interpretation to (10) but not to (9), so we would expect to find worse performance on object relatives than on subject relatives. The experiment reported on in this article is designed to distinguish which of the two explanations is correct, i.e. is it gap interpretation or movement?

4. Experimental design and results

4.1 Research question, experimental design and predictions

The question we try to answer in the present study is: "Is children's bad performance on relative clause barriers with quantifier movement caused by the 'invisibility' of quantifier movement or by a gap-interpretation strategy?" The movement hypothesis, in terms of the overt-covert distinction, can explain the difference between children's performance on relative clause barriers with wh-movement versus quantifier movement. The gap-interpretation hypothesis can also explain this difference: children employ a different strategy when interpreting sentences with quantifiers, so no correlation with their performance on wh-questions is expected. There are two indications for the existence of a gap-interpretation hypothesis: first, children seem to be aware of gaps and traces. And they want to fill them. A resumptive pronoun strategy is commonly found in child language (a.o. Perez-Leroux, 1993). Also for language that do not have a resumptive pronoun strategy for adults. This strategy clearly shows that children are aware of gaps, because they see the need to make them visible by filling them. Filled (intermediate) wh-traces are found by Thornton (1991) for English and Van Kampen (1997) for Dutch. Second, a gap-interpretation hypothesis would explain Coles et al. (2004)'s finding, which they left unaccounted for. A significant difference between subject and object relatives cannot be explained by a movement hypothesis, but can by a gap-interpretation hypothesis.

To find out which of the two hypotheses (if any) is the correct one, an experiment was designed consisting of a truth value judgment task with four conditions (a 2x2 design). The design is given in (11), the cells show the number of items in each condition.

(11)

Picture/type of relative	Subject relative	Object relative
Collective	3	3
Distributive	3	3

Different subject and object relatives were combined with either a collective or a distributive picture. To see which answer patterns both hypotheses predict, look again at the two types of relatives: the subject relative (12) and the object one (13).

(12)   Er is een paard dat **e** alle cowboys draagt.
        "There is a horse that is carrying all cowboys."
(13)   Er is een paard waar alle cowboys **e** op zitten.
        "There is a horse that all cowboys are sitting on."

Recall that for adults both sentences can only have a collective interpretation. For children, however, this might be different. The movement hypothesis predicts that, if children do not recognize the relative clause barrier due to the invisible nature of quantifier movement, children will accept both collective and distributive interpretations for both types of relatives. The gap-interpretation hypothesis predicts that, if children interpret the relative head in its gap position, children will accept only collective interpretations for subject relatives, since on that interpretation the indefinite NP ("een paard") has scope over the quantified NP ("alle cowboys"), whereas they will accept only distributive interpretations for object relatives, since interpretation in the gap position results in the quantified NP having scope over the indefinite NP. The predicted answers for each hypothesis and for each condition are given in the table in (14). The adult answer is given in the final column.

(14)

	Movement	Gap interpretation	Adult
Subj_col	Yes	Yes	Yes
Obj_col	Yes	No	Yes
Subj_distr	Yes	No	No
Obj_distr	Yes	Yes	No

The movement hypothesis predicts correct answers in both collective conditions and incorrect 'yes' answers in both distributive conditions. The gap interpretation hypothesis predicts correct answers in the subject_collective and subject_distributive condition, incorrect 'no' answers in the object_collective condition and incorrect 'yes' answers in the object_distributive condition.

4.2 Subjects and methods

Thirty-six Dutch children between age 5;8 and 6;11 (mean age 6;3) were tested, using a truth value judgment task (Crain and Thornton, 1998). The experiment used a handheld puppet called Timo who was said to come from the moon. Timo thought he already spoke Dutch very well, but sometimes he actually said very silly things. The children were asked to judge the puppet's utterances and correct him whenever he was wrong.

The children were told 15 stories (3 introductory stories and 3 per condition) accompanied by one introductory picture and one picture showing either a distributive or a collective interpretation of a quantified sentence. At the end of each story the puppet, played by another experimenter, gave a description of what he saw in the final picture using either an object or a subject relative. To illustrate this procedure further, an example is given in (15) below. The final pictures were combined with the test sentences in (12) and (13).

(15)

Experimenter:
Zie je deze cowboys? Ze willen gaan paardrijden.
"Do you see these cowboys? They want to go horse riding."

Experimenter:
Kijk, hier zijn ze klaar om te gaan paardrijden!
"Look here they are ready to go!"
Hand puppet:
Ja, ik zie het!
"O, I see!"

To control for ordering effects two different orders were used. Answers were scored by hand and if a child answered 'no' its response as to why was also noted to see whether the child said 'no' for the right, expected, reason. The experiment took about 10 minutes per child and the children were rewarded with a sticker.

4.3 Results

The experiment resulted in 12 answers per child (excluding the answers on the introductory stories) times 36 children is a total of 432 answers. After examination one child was left out because he answered two out of three introductory stories incorrectly. This resulted in a total amount of 420 answers (105 per condition). The results by condition are visually represented in the following graph.

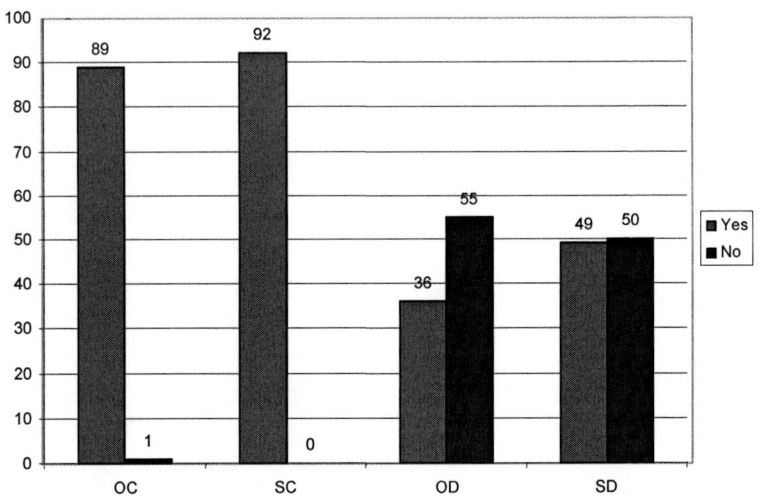

OC = object_collective   OD = object_distributive   Left bar = number of yes answers
SC = subject_collective   SD = subject_distributive Right bar = number of no answers

The first two conditions (OC and SC) are the ones where a subject or object relative was combined with a collective picture. The adult answer in these conditions is 'yes'. The children performed very well on these conditions: only one non-adult 'no' answer in the OC condition and no non-adult answers in the SC condition. The other two conditions (OD and SD), where a subject or object relative was combined with a distributive picture, do not show such good performance. The adult answer here is 'no' (the right bar). The children gave 55 and 50 adult 'no' answers and 36 and 49 non-adult 'yes' answers in OD and SD respectively. So the graph shows that children's performance on the collective conditions is much better than on the distributive conditions. The graph furthermore shows that it does not matter whether a distributive or collective picture is combined with a subject relative or an object relative. Performance on the two collective conditions seems to be equally well and performance on the two distributive conditions seems to be equally bad. These observations are confirmed by the results of a MANOVA – repeated measures: this gives a highly significant main effect of collective versus distributive picture

(F=38,148, p=0,00) but no effect for subject versus object relative and no interaction effect. There were no subject effects.

5. Discussion

Two conditions were considered: the gap interpretation hypothesis and the movement hypothesis. The gap interpretation hypothesis predicts correct answers when a subject relative is used and incorrect answers when an object relative is used. This is not the answer pattern we found (there is no effect of subject versus object relative), so how likely the gap interpretation hypothesis might be on the basis of the resumptive pronoun strategy, it has to be rejected. The movement hypothesis predicts correct answers in both collective conditions and incorrect answers in both distributive conditions. The answer pattern we found does approach this prediction, however, there is a problem. Although there are no incorrect answers in the collective conditions and much more incorrect answers in the distributive conditions, the pattern is not complete. It is not the case that children consistently answer correctly in the collective conditions and incorrectly in the distributive conditions, rather, they consistently answer correctly in the collective conditions and they answer inconsistently in the distributive conditions. In other words, the collective conditions show a clear pattern, but the distributive conditions show a very mixed pattern of answers; approximately half correct and half incorrect. This inconsistency is not due to subject effects and is not predicted by the movement hypothesis.

There are of course several ways to formulate the movement hypothesis and each formulation comes with its own predictions. In section 4 we used the movement hypothesis in such a way that it would result in an ambiguity for all test sentences for children; they do not recognize the relative clause barrier and therefore they can move the two quantified NP's in any order, resulting in the possibility of collective and distributive readings for both subject and object relatives. This ambiguity would lead them to give (adult) 'yes' answers when a relative was combined with a collective picture and (non-adult) 'yes' answers when combined with a distributive picture. This formulation of the movement hypothesis thus predicts consistent results, which we did not find in the distributive condition.

The second formulation of the movement hypothesis one can think of, is one where children only have one reading available. That is to say, they can only move in one particular way and therefore always end up with a collective reading or a distributive reading. If the only reading they can get is the collective reading, we expect correct answers in all conditions. If the only reading they can get is the distributive reading, we expect incorrect answers all conditions. Both options predict consistent answer patterns, which we did not find.

The final possible formulation of the movement hypothesis is one in which movement is optional for children: for every sentence it is the case that they can either move the quantified NP's in it or they can choose not to move them and interpret them in surface order. This would explain the inconsistent results we found in the distributive conditions, but it would predict the same inconsistency to show up in the collective conditions, where we did not find it. So neither of the formulations of the movement hypothesis predicts the answer pattern we found. The fact that we did not find any subject effects indicates that it can also not be the case that different children use movement in different ways.

6. Conclusion

In some way our study seems to make the puzzle more complicated: we still don't know why children obey the relative clause barrier in wh-movement but not in quantifier movement. We can conclude that it is not because they use a gap interpretation strategy in interpreting sentences with quantifiers. However, the results also show that it is not the case that they simply disobey the relative clause barrier all the time in quantifier raising. None of the three possible formulations of the movement hypothesis predicts the answer pattern found in this experiment. Nevertheless, we believe our results do not really complicate the puzzle further; rather, they indicate that the approach to the puzzle should be shifted. Recall the results, which show no problems or inconsistencies in the collective conditions. Problems show up in the distributive cases. There seems to be something characteristic of distributivity which makes it more difficult for children than collectivity. Quantifier Raising does not predict any qualitative difference between distributivity and collectivity to show up in child language. However, this data seems to support semantic analyses which take collectivity to be the more basic case. Distributivity is arranged by a (extra) distributivity operator (see o.a. Schwarzschild, 1996, Winter, 2000). Concluding we would argue that the differences and similarities between distributivity and collectivity need to be studied more thoroughly, both in theoretical and in acquisition research.

Notes

[1] We thank Jack Hoeksema, Holger Hopp, Angeliek van Hout for comments, as well as the audiences of the Language Acquisition Lab and the TaBudag in Groningen, the International Congress for the Study of Child Language in Berlin. All errors remain ours. We especially like to thank the children, parents and teachers of the Groninger Scholen

Vereniging for participating in the experiment. The work of Bart Hollebrandse was partly supported by a Alpha-stimulerings grant to the Faculty of Letters, Groningen. The work of Leontine Kremers by the Groninger Universiteitsfonds.
[1] In a recent BUCLD poster Syrett and Lidz (2005) show that children under completely different conditions QR out of tensed clauses.

References

Chomsky, N. (1986). *Barriers.* Cambridge: MIT Press.

Crain, S. and Thornton, R. (1998). *Investigations in universal grammar: a guide to experiments on the acquisition of syntax and semantics.* Cambridge: MIT Press.

Coles-White, D., T. Roeper and J. De Villiers (2004), "The emergence of barriers to Wh-movement, negative concord and quantification". In A. Burgos, L. Micciulla, and C.E. Smith, eds., *Proceedings of the 28th annual Boston University Conference on Language Development,* Cascadilla Press, Somerville, Massachusetts, 98-107.

Fox, D. (2000). *Economy and Semantic Interpretation.* Cambridge/London: MIT Press.

Hollebrandse, B. and J.L. Kremers, (2005). "Visible and invisible extraction." Paper at *Xth International Congress for the Study of Child Language (IASCL),* Berlin.

May, R.C. (1977). *The Grammar of Quantification.* Phd Thesis, MIT.

——. (1985). *Logical Form.* M.I.T. press, Cambridge, Massachusetts.

Perez-Leroux, A.T. (1993), *Empty Categories and the Acquisition of WH-movement,* G.L.S.A., Amherst, Massachusetts.

Roeper, T. and De Villiers, J. (1993). "The emergence of bound variable structures". in Reuland, E. and W. Abraham, eds., *Knowledge and Language,* Boston: Kluwer Academic Press, p.105-139.

Schwarzschild, R. (1996). *Pluralities.* Dordrecht: Kluwer Academic Publishers.

Syrett, K. and J. Lidz (2005), "Learning scope economy: why children will QR out of a tensed clause but adults won't." poster at BUCLD 30.

Thornton, R. (1991). *Adventures in Long Distance Moving: The Acquisition of Complex Wh-Questions.* Ph.D. dissertation, University of Connecticut.

Van Kampen, J. (1997). *First Steps in Wh-movement.* Ph.D. dissertation, Utrecht University.

Winter, Y. (2000). "Distributivity and dependency". Natural language semantics 8 (1), p.27-69.

CROSS-LINGUISTIC DIFFERENCES IN CHILD AND ADULT SPEECH OPTIONAL OMISSIONS: A COMPARISON OF DUTCH AND ITALIAN

JOKE DE LANGE, SERGEY AVRUTIN, AND MARIA TERESA GUASTI

1. Introduction

The goal of this study is to provide a unified explanation for the cross-linguistic (Dutch vs. Italian) differences observed in child speech and 'special registers' of unimpaired adult speech with respect to the optional omissions of determiners. The explanation is based on our analyses of the existing databases (CHILDES), on two databases of 1000 headlines each from Dutch and Italian newspapers and on experimental studies that we conducted with adult speakers. The paper starts with our findings on the investigation of the speech of 3 Italian and 3 Dutch children. Then it presents the investigation of the use of articles in Dutch and Italian newspaper headlines and the results of an experimental study in which Dutch and Italian speakers were asked to give relative acceptability judgments on actual and made-up headlines in which articles (definite and indefinite) were either used or omitted in different linguistic contexts. We will show that there are not only cross-linguistic differences in the patterns of optional omissions in Dutch and Italian child speech and headlines, but that there are also intriguing similarities if we look at the omission patterns in sentence initial and sentence internal position and the relation with the presence of a finite verb in the sentence.

In our conclusion we will come to a unified explanation for these cross-linguistic differences and between group similarities, based on an account that combines processing considerations and structural considerations.

2. Article omission in Dutch and Italian child language

A cross-linguistic study by Guasti, DeLange, Gavarro & Caprin (2004), using data from the Childes Database, for 3 Italian, 3 Catalan and 3 Dutch speaking children, based on 7 files for each child, showed that from stage 2 (the stage in which the child uses 101-200 different words) there is a difference in articles omitted in obligatory contexts: Dutch children omit articles in 54% of the obligatory contexts while Italian children omit articles in only 17% of the obligatory contexts (see Table 1).

	Stage 1 1-100 words		Stage 2 101-200 words		Stage 3 > 200 words	
	M	SD	M	SD	M	SD
Italian	.52	.24	.17	.19	.01	-
Dutch	.88	.16	.54	.14	.23	.12

Table 1: Omission in different periods of linguistic development

A comparison of the means showed that in stage 1 there was no difference amongst the languages, at stage 2 however Italian differed from Dutch (p=.05). Another important fact these figures show, besides the important cross-linguistic differences in omission is that omission of articles in child speech is optional, in Dutch as well as in Italian. From the earliest stages on, whenever an article is produced it is used correctly, it is always placed in the correct structural position in the presence of a nominal complement. This simple observation suggests that a child at this age does possess the relevant knowledge of the article system, however, there is some factor that prevents the child from always realizing it.

Taking as a point of departure this optionality in article omission we can make a further observation, related to the pattern of article omission. In Dutch child speech in sentence initial position 67 % of the obligatory articles were omitted while in sentence internal position 40% of the obligatory articles were omitted. In Italian child speech we find a similar pattern: in sentence initial position 36% of the obligatory articles were omitted while in sentence internal position 24% of the obligatory articles were omitted. So, both in Dutch and Italian child speech more articles are omitted in obligatory contexts in sentence initial position

3. Article omission in headlines

Not only children omit articles, sometimes adults omit articles too. They do so in the so-called 'special registers' like for example diary style (Haegeman 1990) and headlines (Avrutin 1999, Stowell 1999). Earlier generative linguistic studies on headlines concentrated on one language, mostly English. The present study discusses a completely new aspect of headlines as it gives insight into cross-linguistic differences in headlines. We selected 2000 headlines from 4 Dutch newspapers and 2 Italian newspapers. Table (2) shows the results:

Language	Articles Produced	Articles Produced + Standard Omissions	Nonstandard omission of articles
Dutch	7,9	12,9	87,1
Italian	58,3	72,1	27,9

Table 2: Percentages of article production and omission in the headlines examined (p < 0.0001)

On the one hand these data show that there is a striking difference between omissions of articles in Italian and Dutch. On the other hand they show that, in spite of the differences, article omission in headlines is a real existing phenomenon, in Dutch as well as Italian. And, again, like in child speech, we see that omissions are optional: sometimes articles are used, sometimes not.

The large difference between article omissions in Dutch and Italian headlines makes it clear that omission of articles in newspaper headlines is not ruled by functional motivations, like space restriction, alone, since space is restricted in Italian as well as in Dutch newspapers.

The observation that article omission in headlines is optional gives rise to further questions: Where and when are articles used? What is it that triggers the production of an article? To put it alternatively: Where and when are articles omitted? What is it that suppresses the production of an article? Let us first start with an analysis of the omission pattern of articles in headlines, and compare this with the pattern we found in child speech. The results of this analysis are shown in table (3):

	Dutch		Italian	
	Headlines	Child Speech	Headlines	Child Speech
Sentence initial	98	67	27	36
Sentence internal	85	40	18	24

Table 3: Percentages of article omission in obligatory contexts in sentence initial and sentence internal position.

As this table shows in both child speech and headlines, in Dutch as well as in Italian, we find a stronger tendency to omit articles from sentence initial position.

An experiment on headlines

We conducted an experimental study with adult Dutch and Italian speakers in which we asked participants to give relative acceptability judgments on actual and made-up headlines in which articles (definite and indefinite) were either used or omitted in different linguistic contexts (e.g. with/without finite verb, sentence initial/internal, Hanging Topic, Nouns in Isolation). The goal of our experiment was to see if people have intuitions about headlines.

Experimental design

Participants (50 native Dutch speakers, 35 native Italian speakers) were presented with a questionnaire. The test-sentences/headlines were based on actual headlines coming from our database. Participants were shown two versions of the same headline, and were asked to indicate their preference. If they had no preference for either of the two versions they could indicate this in a separate column. In order to find out whether the judgements of participants were influenced by the (linguistic) context in which the articles occurred we tested different conditions:

1. Headlines with finite verb and:
   -definite/indefinite article on subject, like in example (1):

   (1)   ITALIAN GOVERNMENT RISKS TO COLLAPSE
           THE ITALIAN GOVERNMENT RISKS TO COLLAPSE

   - definite/indefinite article on object, like in example (2):

   (2)   DICHIO UPSETS WELCOME COMMITTEE
           DICHIO UPSETS THE WELCOME COMMITTEE

2. Headlines with article on either the subject or the object, like in example (3)

   (3)   A GIANT WAVE KILLS FAMILY
           GIANT WAVE KILLS A FAMILY

3. Headlines with finite auxiliary/copular verb present or omitted, with/without article, like in example (4):

   (4a)   THE NEW TAX LAW IS ATTACKED BY BLUNKETT
           NEW TAX LAW IS ATTACKED BY BLUNKETT

(4b)   THE NEW TAX LAW ATTACKED BY BLUNKETT
NEW TAX LAW ATTACKED BY BLUNKETT

The results

1. Headlines with finite verbs and:
-definite article on subject (SD)- indefinite article on subject (SI)
-definite article on object (OD)- indefinite article on object (OI)

The results on this condition are presented in Table (4):

Condition	Dutch	Italian
SD	0.89	0.21
OD	0.80	0.19
SI	0.92	0.80
OI	0.84	0.46

Table 4: Results in the condition with finite verbs

On all conditions in this group we find a significant difference between Dutch and Italian (p<.05). The results show that for Dutch there is a strong preference for omission, both of definite and indefinite articles, and both for subject and object position. For Italian we observe a significant (p<.05) difference between the preferences in the conditions with the definite articles and the conditions with the indefinite articles: definite articles tend to be preferably present, while indefinite articles are preferably omitted, especially in the subject position.

2. Headlines with articles on either the subject or the object:
The results in this condition are presented in Table (5)

Condition	Preference for article used on:	Dutch	Italian
DEF	Subject	0.18	0.38
DEF	Object	0.72	0.42
IND	Subject	0.17	0.15
IND	Object	0.65	0.72

Table 5: Results in the condition with articles present on either the subject or the object position.

Dutch participants strongly preferred the version with the article present before the object and omitted before the subject (conform Stowell's (1999) findings for English headlines). The same pattern was found for Italian for the indefinite articles, however ,for the definite articles in Italian no strong preference for either two of the versions could be observed. In this group the difference between Dutch and Italian was significant in the conditions with the definite articles ($p<.05$), but not in the conditions with the indefinite articles.

3. Headlines with finite auxiliary/copular verb present or omitted, with/without article.

The results on this condition are presented in Table (6):

Condition	Dutch	Italian
No-AUX-Def	0.85	0.77
AUX-Def	0.63	0.13
No AUX-ind	0.90	0.44
AUX-Ind	0.62	0.13

Table 6: Results in the condition with auxiliaries or copula

As for the influence of the absence/presence of a finite auxiliary verb on the judgements: there was a significant effect in both languages: In Dutch as well as Italian there was a stronger preference for omission when the finite auxiliary verb was omitted ($p<.05$). However, this effect was stronger in Italian than in Dutch, especially in the case of the definite articles.

Let us summarize our results: Dutch participants showed a greater preference for article omissions in all contexts. By contrast, Italian subjects' preferences for article omissions depended on the linguistic context and on the type of article: in headlines without finite verbs omission is strongly preferred, in headlines including a finite verb:
- definite articles are strongly required both in subject as well as in object position
- indefinite articles are preferably omitted in subject position, while in object position we do not observe a preference for use or omission.
Moreover the experimental results confirmed the omission pattern found in Child Speech and in the Headline-database by showing that both Dutch and Italian speakers display a stronger preference for article omission before nouns in sentence initial position than before nouns in sentence internal position.

4. Child Language and Headlines compared

If we compare the data on child speech and headlines (database and experiment) we can come to the following generalizations:
(a) Overall we find more omissions in Dutch than in Italian, in both Child Speech and Headlines.
(b) We find more omissions in sentence initial than in sentence internal position.
(c) In the headlines database and experiment we find a finiteness effect, in the sense that preference for omission is higher in sentences in which the finite auxiliary or copular verb is omitted
(d) In the headlines experiment we observe a strong difference between the preferences for omissions of definite versus indefinite articles on subject position in Italian.
We will now discuss these findings more in detail:

(a.1): More omissions in Dutch than in Italian Child Speech:

We suggest that the differences we found in the overall pattern of omission in Child Speech are caused by the fact that there are differences in the processing resources required for the retrieval of an element from the article set in the lexicon. Retrieving an element from the Dutch article set is more difficult and requires more processing resources than retrieving an element from the Italian article set. In order to be retrieved from the lexicon, an element needs to be reliably distinguishable from its competitors. Following Kostic (2004) we suggest that distinguishability can be measured as Relative Entropy (Hr) of the system: the stronger the contrasts between the elements, the more conspicuous the elements are, the easier they can be distinguished and the lower Relative Entropy is. The calculation of Relative Entropy is based on the frequency distribution of articles found in corpora of spoken language. The calculation of Relative Entropy (Hr) of the Dutch and Italian article system, based on frequency data of articles in Corpus Gesproken Nederlands for Dutch and 'Corpus de Mauro' for Italian leads to the following results:

- Hr Italian: 0.71
- Hr Dutch: 0.94

This indicates that Italian articles are easier to distinguish from their competitors than the Dutch articles: in the Italian article set relative entropy is lower, as a consequence of this lower entropy value selection of an element costs less cognitive effort in Italian. By way of example of the computation the details of the calculation of Relative Entropy for the Dutch article system are included in Table (A) in the appendix in section 6 of this paper. What grows in children is the ability to cope with more and more uncertainty in the system. By uncertainty we mean the degree of distinguishability: how easy it is for an element to beat its competitors. Initially children can cope with the Italian (low) entropy, but not with the Dutch (high) entropy.

(a.2): More omissions in Dutch than in Italian Headlines:

Italian articles have a higher Informative Load (in a technical sense) than the Dutch articles. Informative load can be expressed as:

$$I_m = \left[-\log_2 \left(\sum_{j=1}^{k} \frac{\frac{F_m}{R_m}}{\frac{F_{m_j}}{R_{m_j}}} \right) \right]$$

In this equation I stands for the amount of information carried by a word form (m), F refers to frequency of a form expressed in terms of percentage, and R stands for the number of functions and meanings encompassed by a form. The resulting unit is the amount of information derived from the average frequency per function/meaning for a given word form. An example of the calculation of informative load of the Dutch articles is included in Table (B) in the appendix of this paper. For more details the reader is referred to studies of Kostic (2004) and Moscoso del Prado et al. (to appear) which have shown that the higher the informative load of what they call an 'ensemble', so a phrase, or a headline, the faster the processing speed per unit of information in that ensemble. Now what headline writers (unconsciously) are striving at is to accelerate the processing speed of a headline. To facilitate the processing it is necessary to increase the average amount of information per headline by omitting less informative elements. The lower informative load of Dutch articles means that omission of articles in Dutch will increase the average amount of information in a headline in a far stronger way than omission of articles in Italian, and that's why we find more omissions in Dutch headlines.

(b) The 'finiteness-effect': preference for omission is higher in headlines in which the finite auxiliary/copular verb was omitted.

Regarding finiteness, and more specific, tense in headlines an interesting observation can be made: a specific characteristic of tense in headlines is that present tense can be used to denote past events, see example (5)

(5) PITTBULL ATTACKS CHILD

Assume a system like the one proposed by Landau (2004) with a scale of finiteness based on the assignment of the features [T] and [Agr] to I^0. Suppose that in present clauses (of headlines) I^0 is assigned [–T, +Agr] when the interpretation of tense depends on the discourse context and that I^0 is assigned [+T, +Agr] in present clauses with independent interpretation, in past clauses and in copular sentences. According to Landau, dependent tense is selected by a matrix verb. This shows that in the language, present tense can be a dependent tense and headlines use this feature: in headlines, present tense can be selected and dependent on the discourse context. Past tense instead refers to past events and in copular sentences the copula is inserted to carry tense, referring to a state that is still occurring and that potentially can continue even in the future. For the interface between clause type feature and DP feature we also use Landau's ideas and say that whenever I^0 is specified for [+T, +Agr] it automatically comes to bear [+R], any other feature constitution of T and Agr will be associated with [-R]. When I^0 is assigned [+R] the clause requires a [+R] subject, a subject whose features are fully specified. A DP headed by an article is assigned the feature [+R]. Then, an I^0 with the feature [+R] requires a DP [+R] headed by an article to check its feature: this is what happens in headlines with past tense and in copular clauses. Therefore, in past tense and copular headlines, the subject must be a DP [+R]. In present tense headlines the subject can either be a DP fully specified or a DP with a null article.

The results for Dutch showed a strong preference for the headline without article also in the case of headlines specified for [+T,+Agr], so with a I^0 that is assigned a feature [+R] that has to be checked. We suggest that the mechanism by which the [+R] interpretation for bare plural and mass nouns in Dutch is derived is exploited in headlines for use with singular nouns. We suggest that the reason for this 'extrapolated' use in headlines of bare nouns in referential contexts lies in the low informative load of articles. As we already discussed in the previous section omission of elements with a low informative load speeds up the processing speed.

A fast processing speed is a requirement for reading of newspaper headlines (Van Dijk 1988) and it is this characteristic that makes the processing of newspaper headlines different from the processing of normal written (and spoken) language, and explains why it is not the case that Dutch speakers always omit articles.

Further it is important to note that only when the grammar allows for the option to give bare nouns a [+R] specification, this possibility will be exploited in special contexts for processing considerations.

(c) Difference sentence initial-internal:

Both in child speech and in headlines we found more omissions sentence initially, in the headlines experiment for Italian this could best be attested in the condition with the indefinite articles. This confronts us with two questions:
1. Why do we find a difference sentence initial – sentence internal?
2. Why do we find this difference in Italian headlines only for indefinite articles?

We will first discuss the second question: The results of the experiment showed that in Italian indefinite articles on subject position are preferably omitted, while definite articles on this same position are preferably used. Comparing judgements on: UN GIORNALISTA ATTACCA BIONDI ('a journalist attacks Biondi') versus GIORNALISTA ATTACCA BIONDI ('journalist attacks Biondi') we found a strong preference for the version of the headline in which the article was omitted. On the contrary, comparing judgements on: IL GOVERNO ATTACCA BIONDI ('the government attacks Biondi') versus GOVERNO ATTACCA BIONDI ('government attacks Biondi') we found a strong preference for the version of the headline with the article present. We propose an account for these findings based on Landau (2004). Suppose that present tense in headlines is dependent, again this hypothesis is very plausible, since it is very common in headlines to use present tense to refer to past events. This means that present tense in headlines is [–T], and this implies that the subject must be [–R]. Following Landau's argumentation that the criterion for [+T] is semantic (2004:839) we propose that presence of a semantic function is a criterion for [+R]. Since expletive meaning of the article implies the absence of a semantic function we argue that expletive meaning of articles means assignment of the feature [–R], just like the absence of a semantic function of dependent tense in clauses means that I^0 is assigned the feature [-T] (and hence will bear [-R]). Italian DEF articles can be used as expletives, so with a [–R] specification, for example when used before proper names (*Hai visto la Teresa?* 'Have you seen the Teresa?'). Italian INDEF articles cannot be used in an expletive, [–R] meaning. This means, that in [-T] headlines INDEF articles will preferably be omitted, since the [+R] specification of the DP is not compatible with the [-T] specification of I^0. DEF articles however can have a [-R] specification, so are allowed in the context of a [–T] headline.

Then we turn to the first part of the question: why do we find a difference between sentence initial versus sentence internal? One possibility to account for this difference is to recognize a special status to the first position of the clause in the same spirit that has been proposed by Rizzi (1997, 2004) for the Null-Root Subject Parameter. But, since we do find omissions not only from subject but also from object position, so omissions from object position are not impossible, but less frequent, we suggest that there may also be a processing account for these differences: Sentence initial position is the canonical topic position, here discourse information is encoded structurally: the information here is 'given, expected' information (Prince 1981). Since one of the functions of articles is the encoding of discourse information, it seems reasonable to argue that in situations of limited resources (like brain maturation) or in situations where a higher processing speed of information is required (like special registers) the same type of information will be encoded only once, not twice. So the discourse information will not be encoded in the article, this can either mean that the article will not be activated at all, or that it receives too little activation to be selected.

5. Conclusion

The overall differences in article omission in both child speech and headlines follow from the processing differences. These processing differences are related to differences in the article paradigm between Dutch and Italian, leading to differences in distinguishability of articles within the article sets, differences that can be expressed by Relative Entropy. The higher the Relative entropy, the higher the processing resources required to select an element out of the set. As for the differences in omission pattern depending on sentence type, position of the noun in the sentence and (for Italian) the type of article: For the finiteness effect we proposed an account based on the structural relation between the [R]-specification of the I^0 head and the DP. For the difference between omissions before nouns in sentence initial and sentence internal position we proposed an account based on structural and processing considerations.

6. Appendix

	freq.	p = rel freq		log p	p*log p
		RELATIVE ENTROPY DUTCH ARTICLES			
		(based on freq. 'Corpus Gesproken Nederlands)			
	freq.	**p = rel freq**		**log p**	**p*log p**
De	253210	0,478969311		-1,06199487	-0,508662953
Het	96327	0,182211116		-2,45631712	-0,447568284
Een	179119	0,338819573		-1,56141088	-0,529036566
	528656	1			-1,485267803
				H =	1,485267803
H MAX: if all articles have some probability:					
de		0,333333333		-1,5849625	-0,528320834
het		0,333333333		-1,5849625	-0,528320834
een		0,333333333		-1,5849625	-0,528320834
		1			-1,584962501
				H max =	1,584962501
		RELATIVE ENTROPY Dutch articles			
H r = H/Hmax	=	0,937099649			

Table A: Calculation Relative Entropy Dutch articles

			number of functions/ meanings	av.freq.per funct/m.= F/R	F/R det /sum F/R paradigm	$I = -\log_2$
		freq.				
De		253210	5	50642	0,3970964	1,3324389
Het		96327	3	32109	0,2517746	1,9897955
Een		179119	4	44780	0,351129	1,5099268
		528656		127531		

Table B: Calculation Informative Load Dutch artic

References

Avrutin, S. (1999) *Development of the Syntax-Discourse Interface,* Kluwer Academic Publishers, Dordrecht.

Guasti, M.T., J. de Lange, A. Gavarro and C. Caprin (2004) "Article Omission: across Child Language and across Special Registers," in J. van Kampen and S. Baauw, eds., *Proceedings of GALA 2003,* LOT, Utrecht, 199-210.

—., F. Foppolo, C. Luzzatti and C. Caprin (2004) "The priviledge of the first position in agrammatism, child language acquisition and headlinese," Poster presented at the Science of Aphasia, Potsdam.

Haegemann, L.(1990) "Non-overt subjects in diary contexts," in J. Mascaro and M. Nespor, eds., *Grammar in Progress,* Foris, Dordrecht, 167-174.

Kostiç, A. (2004) "The effects of the amount of information on processing of inflected morphology," ms., University of Belgrade.

Landau, I. (2004) "The Scale of Finiteness and the Calculus of Control," *Natural Language & Linguistic Theory* 22, 811-877.

Moscoso del Prado, M., A. Kostiç and H. Baayen (to appear) "Putting the bits together: An informational perspective on morphological processing," to appear in: *Cognition.*

Prince, E.F. (1981) "Towards a taxonomy of given-new information," in P.Cole, ed., *Radical Pragmatics,* Academic Press, New York, 223-256.

Rizzi, L. (2004) *The structure of CP and IP – The Cartography of Syntactic Structures,* Vol.2, Oxford University Press, New York.

—. (1997) "The Fine Structure of the Left Periphery," in L.Haegemann, ed., *Elements of Grammar,* Kluwer, Dordrecht.

Stowell, T. (1999) "Words lost and syntax found in Headlinese: The hidden structure of abbreviated English in headlines, instructions and diaries," paper presented at York University, Toronto.

Van Dijk, T. (1988) *News as Discourse,* Lawrence Erlbaum Associate Publishers, New Jersey.

OBJECT CLITICS AND DETERMINERS IN THE ACQUISITION OF ITALIAN AS L2 AND L1

CHIARA LEONINI

1. Introduction

In this paper we present a study in which we investigate the nature of the grammar developed by Italian learners in different acquisition contexts, namely L2 and L1, with respect to their mastering of functional categories. Specifically, we will be primarily concerned with the acquisition of object clitics and Def articles by adult L2rs of Italian with German as L1. Two different investigation methods will be used: 1) elicitation task procedure; 2) spontaneous production data.

Results will be then compared with original data from a monolingual Italian child (age 1,5; 3,0).

The main aim of the study is to demonstrate that the L2 learners under investigation here, show a different pattern of acquisition with regard to elements which share the same categorical status.

2. Theoretical background assumptions

We adopt Cardinaletti & Starke (1999)'s assumption of the existence of three classes of pronouns with different degrees of semantic, syntactic and morpho-phonological differences: strong, weak and clitic. The three forms are attested in Italian, while German has only strong and weak pronouns. We will thus investigate in an area where the two involved languages differ.

Following much recent research on Romance cliticization (Belletti, 1999 a.o.) we propose that 3rd person accusative Romance clitic belongs to the category D°, being the clitic a head of an impoverished DP structure containing only the clitic.

As a theoretical framework for the study of the development of the DP, we adopt the DP Hypothesis dated back to Abney (1987).

The relation between the acquisition of Italian object clitics and definite articles is thus made possible, as they both are D°. Furthermore, in Italian some forms of clitic pronouns have the same morphological form as determiners.

3. The study: participants and methods used

20 adult German-speaking learners of Italian participated in the elicitation task experiment. 15 of them have been identified as having intermediate (7) or advanced (8) level of proficiency, as determined by a standardized proficiency test. The remaining 5 were classified as near native speakers of Italian on the basis of length of residence and the amount of their use of Italian.

A control group of 10 native speakers of Italian were also tested.

As for the experimental design, we used the method already tested in Leonini and Belletti (2004).

The corpus for the analysis of spontaneous production data comes from 1 year-long recordings of the speech of a 23 y.o German girl. She had also participated in the previous experiment at the time of the first recording and was classified in the Intermediate group.

Data for L1 investigation comes from the spontaneous speech of 1 Italian-speaking child, followed from 1;5 to 3;0, who lived in the area of Siena.

4. Results on L2 elicited productions

4.1. Object clitics

General results on cliticization are given in (1) below:

(1)   Table 1. Comparison of clitic use in L2 subject and control group

Subjects	Clitic (+)	Clitic (-)	NPs	Str pron	Incompl
All Germans (Nr. 20)	28%	14%	52%	3%	3%
End State (Nr. 5)	61%	5%	32%	0	2%
Advanced (Nr. 8)	29%	16%	49%	2%	4%
Intermediate (Nr. 7)	2%	19%	69%	7%	3%
Control Subj (Nr. 10)	91%	0	8%	0	1%

Table 1 shows that clitics are often omitted; even more often the complement is realized as a full lexical NP; the use of a strong pronoun appears to be quite limited. Moreover, the learners adopt a generalised strategy that requires the use of full NPs instead of the clitic. Similar results have been reported by Leonini&Belletti (2004).

However, a developmental effect can be observed across the groups, as there is a clear difference between the native speakers and the lower group; the upper group seems to resemble the native speakers and differ from the lower group. This indicates that these L2rs are able to restructure their grammars, in contrast with those hypothesises, according to which interlanguage grammars suffer from some kind of permanent grammatical deficit (Beck 1998).

Furthermore, no misplacement errors of clitics in the provided answers have been attested; in contrast to some previous findings in L2 acquisition of object clitics in French. See a.o. Granfeldt & Schlyter (2004), Hamann & Belletti (2003).

4.2. Determiners

General results are shown in (2) below:

(2) Table 2: Definite articles in L2 groups: production vs omission

L2rs	Definite articles (+)		Definite articles (-)	
Near Natives	191/194	(98%)	3/194	(2%)
Advanced	253/262	(97%)	9/262	(3%)
Intermediate	183/187	(98%)	4/187	(2%)
Tot	627/643	(98%)	16/643	(2%)

Learners of all groups do not seem to have problems with Def articles. Our result thus confirm previous research on L2 showing that supplying article is not a major difficulty for L2rs, when the L1 has overt determiners (Granfeldt 2004).

5. Results on L2 spontaneous production data

5.1. Object clitics

General results, given in (3) below, shows that Heike has achieved a low degree of correctness in the mastering of cliticization:

(3)   Table 3: Use of object clitics in Heike

Stage	Cl (+)	Cl (-)	NPs	Strong P	Questo
1	4%	43%	30%	4%	17%
2	30%	40%	20%	10%	0
3	35%	39%	17%	4%	4%
4	42%	10%	5%	7%	5%
TOT	27%	36%	20%	8%	9%
Elicitation	9%	13%	69%	9%	0

Similarly to previous finding, clitics are not used frequently. However, when produced they are correctly positioned. A low use of strong pronouns is also attested.

Recall that Heike participated in the elicitation task experiment at the time of the first recording; therefore the comparison between results drawn from both experimental methods-specifically "Stage 1" and "Elicitation" in Table 3-is worth considering here. Such comparison shows that the mastering of cliticization is quite limited in both data, but that she seems to resort to different generalized strategies to avoid the use of object clitics in the two experiments. As a matter of fact, Heike prefers omissions in spontaneous production and DPs in elicited production.

5.2. Determiners

As visible in (4), Heike doesn't show a problematic performance in the use of Def articles here: a low rate of omission was found from the first stage (even though higher than in data from elicited production):

(4)   Table 4: Definite articles production vs. omission in Heike

File	Def Articles +		Def Articles -	
1	74/100	74%	26/100	26%
2	70/95	74%	25/95	26%
3	83/111	75%	27/111	25%
4	129/146	88%	17/146	12%
TOT	356/452	79%	95/452	21%
Elicitation	32/34	94%	2/34	6%

6. Object clitics and determiners in L1

The next step of the present study is an attempt to compare our L2 data with data from L1 acquisition of Italian. For this purpose, we investigated in the spontaneous production data of Denis (1;5, 3;0).

A preliminary analysis of the data reveals that determiners and object clitics show a parallel developmental path in Denis, as reported in (5) below:

(5): Table 5: Comparison % use of object clitics vs. determiners in Denis

Stage	Object clitic	Determiners
1;5-1;7	0	0
1;8-1;11	29%	28%
1;12-2;3	67%	57%
2;4-2;7	79%	95%
2;8-3;0	92%	97%

Our data are in partial contrast with previous findings on L1 acquisition of Italian and other languages, which do not provide evidence of a close parallel between the two phenomena (Bottari et al. 1993/94; Hamman 2003). Rather, they confirm those approaches which predict a direct comparison between the two developmental paths (Schaeffer 1997).

7. Conclusion

L2 data from both experimental methods provide evidence of a dissociation in the use of object clitics and def-articles in the L2rs tested here.

In adult L2 grammars under investigation here the process of cliticization is subject to development. This has been also reported in previous research (Granfeldt and Schlyter 2004, a.o.) and has been addressed as one of the aspects in which adult L2 acquisition differs from child L2 and L1 acquisition. On the contrary, definite articles seem to be acquired very rapidly and almost without errors.

Such dissociation is not attested in data from L1 reported here, where a close parallel in the acquisition of the two elements has been found.

A first comparison between data from Denis and those of L2 adult learners of Italian presented above shows that there are differences in the way cliticization is acquired in the two populations, thus confirming previous comparative works on cliticization and FCs in L1 and L2 acquisition (Prévost and White 2000).

References

Abney S. (1987) *The English Noun Phrase in Sentential Aspect*, MIT Dissertation.

Belletti A. (1999) "Italian/Romance clitics: Structure and derivation", in H. van Riemsdijk (ed) *Clitics in the Language of Europe*, Mounton de Gruyter.

—. and C. Hamman (2000) "Ça on fait pas! On the acquisition of French by two young children with different source languages", in *Proceedings of the 24th Annual Boston University Conference on Language Development*. Sommerville, MA: Cascadilla Press.

Bottari P. et al. (1998) "The Determiner System in a Group of Italian Children with SLI" *Language Acquisition 7*.

Cardinaletti A. and M. Starke (1999) "A typology of structural deficiency: A case study of three classes of pronouns, in H. van Riemsdijk (ed) *Clitics in the Language of Europe*, Mounton de Gruyter.

Granfeldt J. (2003) *L'acquisition des Catégories Fonctionelles. Etude comparative du Développement du DP Français chez des Enfants et des Apprendants Adultes,* PhD thesis, University of Lund.

Granfeldt J. and S. Schlyter (2004) "Cliticisation in the acquisition of French as L1 and L2" in Prévost P. and J. Paradis (eds), *The Acquisition of French in Different Contexts. Focus on functional categories*, Benjamins.

Guasti M.T. (1993/94) "Verb Syntax in Italian Child Grammar" *Language Acquisition 3*.

Leonini C. and A. Belletti (2004) "Adult L2 Acquisition of Italian Clitic Pronouns and 'Subject Inversion'/VS Structures", in *Proceedings of GALA 2003*, Utrecht University.

Prévost P. and L. White (2000) "Accounting for morphological variation in 2LA: Truncation or Missing Inflection?" in M-A. Friedemann and Rizzi (eds).

Schaeffer J. (1997) *Direct Object Scrambling in Dutch and Italian Child Language*, UCLA Dissertations in Linguistics. Nr. 17.

THE L-SYNTAX OF VERBS IN THE ACQUISITION OF L1 ITALIAN

PAOLO LORUSSO

1. Introduction

The general aim of this study is to investigate the syntactic features of verbs in acquisition. The analysis of overt subject distribution along verb classes in Italian spontaneous speech (Lorusso,Caprin &Guasti 2005) shows that overt subjects are distributed differently depending on the syntactic class of the verbs. Unaccusatives are produced preferentially with a post verbal overt subject, while unergatives and transitives with a null subject or a preverbal subject. This pattern of distribution strongly suggests that for informative or syntactic reasons children distinguish between verb classes. The VP projections in Italian also encode lexical aspectual information, such as telicity, depending on the presence of a quantified direct object (van Hout 1998). If children correctly attribute to the VPs an aspectual analysis they are supposed to have no problem to use aspectual marked morphology. In order to understand the characteristic of the l-syntax of verbs produced by children we performed two experiments about comprehension / production of verbs presenting perfective morphology. Children had to produce and comprehend perfective morphology applied to configurationally telic or atelic predicates (Lorusso 2005). The results show that children do not correctly analyse the perfective morphology with atelic predicates till a late stage, while they show no problems with telic predicates with an overt quantified object.

The general hypothesis we make is that children since earliest stages systematically use and acquire an adult-like l-syntax for different verb classes like the analysis of spontaneous speech confirms. Nevertheless, children do not use the aspectual perfective morphology in an adult like fashion along verb classes. This is linked to the fact that at syntax-semantics interface children are not able to use the structural information since earliest stages. We suggest that the acquisition of VP features responsible of the acquisition of such an interface relation proceeds in a step by step fashion.

2. Longitudinal Corpus: Overt Subject Distribution

The longitudinal corpus consisted of the productions of four Italian children aged between 18 and 36 months (Calambrone corpus, Diana Martina, Raffaello, Rosa CHILDES database MacWhinney & Snow 1985; Cipriani et al., 1989). The child corpora consisted in 17573 utterances of which 4733 include a verb; of these we examined only declarative sentences for a total of 2838 utterances. We also examined the speech of adults on a subset of the files that were used in the analysis of children speech. In this work, 2095 adult declarative sentences with verbal constructions were examined (Lorusso, 2003).

For each child we examined the use-omission of subject as a function of the syntactic frame of the verb: transitive, unaccusative and unergative verbs. When the subject was present, we examined whether it occurred in preverbal or postverbal position. We separately considered whether the verb was in a simple or compound tense and, in the last case, we kept trace of the auxiliary that was used. We distinguished among declarative, imperative and interrogative sentences, but in the analysis we retained only declarative sentences. The same analysis was performed on the speech of the caregivers during their interaction with children.

In table 1 we can examine the percentage of overt subjects as a function of the verb they occur with.

Tab.1 General Percentage of overt subjects distribution for every children and for adults depending on the class of the verb in the longitudinal corpus (Lorusso,Caprin & Guasti 2005)

Overt Subject Distribution along Verb Classes (Percentage)		
	Unaccusatives	Unergatives	Transitives
Diana	36%	22%	26%
Martina	41%	25%	32%
Raffaello	37%	23%	15%
Rosa	32%	30%	19%
Children	36%	25%	22%
Adults	41%	40%	20%

We can notice that all the children produce more overt subjects with unaccusatives than with other verb classes. Adults differ, in that they use overt subject more or less at the same rate with unergatives and unaccusatives. This different behaviour of subjects with unaccusative verbs with respect to the other two classes of verbs is also evident in the distribution of overt subjects in table 2.

Tab.2 Distribution of overt subjects with the three classes of verbs: unaccusatives, unergatives, transitives in the speech of children and adults in the longitudinal corpus (Lorusso,Caprin & Guasti 2005)

Overt Subject Position along Verb Classes (Percentage)

	Unaccusatives		Unergatives		Transitives	
	Preverbal Position	*Postverbal Position*	*Preverbal Position*	*Postverbal Position*	*Preverbal Position*	*Postverbal Position*
Diana	31%	69%	60%	40%	73%	27%
Martina	32%	68%	80%	20%	75%	25%
Raffaello	35%	65%	95%	5%	67%	33%
Rosa	37%	63%	73%	27%	74%	26%
Children	34%	66%	79%	21%	72%	28%
Adults	43%	57%	83%	17%	63%	37%

We observe a significant difference in the distribution of subjects as a function of the verb type in child speech (X2= 37.39 p<.005). With unaccusative verbs, subjects tend to occur in postverbal position, with transitive and unergative verbs they tend to be placed in preverbal position in both children and adult's speech. In summary, subjects are omitted less with unaccusative verbs than with the other two classes of verbs and overt subjects of unaccusative verbs occur more frequently in postverbal position. By these data we can conclude that children probably distinguish between verb classes and they project in different position the subject of unaccusatives and the subject or unergatives and transitives as the clausal realization show.

Another data Lorusso 2004 found in the corpus is linked to the presence of the perfective forms of passato prossimo with different verb classes. The *passato prossimo* in Italian is a past tense that adds to the predicates a perfective reading. It is derived in Italian as the *past perfect* in English: that is, the present form of the auxiliary 'avere' (to have) plus the past participle of the verbs. The age at which children first produce the forms of *passato prossimo* does not seem to be the same for all verb classes.

Tab.3 Age of first appearance of *passato prossimo* with different verb classes in the speech of children in the longitudinal corpus (Lorusso 2004)

	Age of first appearance of passato prossimo (yy,mm,dd)		
	First Compound Form with Unaccusatives	First Compound Form with Unergatives	First Compound Form with Transitives
Diana	01;08,05	02; 06	01; 10, 07
Martina	doesn't use auxiliary	02; 04,14	01; 07, 18
Raffaello	02; 03 14	02, 05, 13	01, 11
Rosa	02; 01, 14	03;00, 24	02; 05, 25

Children do not use in the early stages passato prossimo with unergatives. In our hypothesis it is linked with some l-syntactic characteristic that blocks the appearance of perfective morphology with atelic mono-argumental predicates. In order to understand the reason of such a delay we pass to describe the experiments about the production and comprehension of *passato prossimo* with (a)telic verbs.

3. Experiments on the "passato prossimo"

The experiments are organised in order to force the production/comprehension of the perfective marking of the *passato prossimo* in both the experimental activities. Both experiments were performed on ten native adult Italian speakers and fifty children participated in the study: ten 3 year-olds, ten 4 year-olds, ten 5 year-olds, ten 6 year-olds and ten 7 year-olds. The ten adults were tested at their homes in Conversano (Bari, Italy) and the children were tested at school 1° Circolo didattico "G. Falcone" also in Conversano (Bari, Italy).

3.1. Production task

This experiment is designed to recognize the pattern of expression of perfective/non perfective forms along ages and verb classes. The goal of the production task is to investigate when children start to produce passato prossimo with unergatives and transitives in a situation where children are forced to use this tense. Children in the early stage may not able to properly produce *passato prossimo* with unergatives, because they are not be able to identify the role linked to the presence/absence of a direct object in order to determine the compositional telicity as it happens for English and Dutch learners (van Hout 1998).The materials consisted of 8 silent digital videos in which a story was presented: the story involved four telic transitive verbs with an overt quantified object and five atelic unergatives without overt objects. Atelic events were represented with an endpoint in order to force a completed reading and, consequently, the use of *passato prossimo*. All events (telic and atelic) were presented in the same video in a random order. Then, children were asked to describe such actions in the past with the request: ''Describe what Marta did yesterday''. The result we present is the attribution of perfective/imperfective morphology to the general verb classes of telic Transitives (fig.1) on one hand and atelic Unergatives on the other (and fig.2).

Fig.1 Responses with Telic Transitives (percentage) in the production task (Lorusso 2005)

Fig.2 Responses with Atelic Unergatives (percentage) in the production task (Lorusso 2005)

Percentage of perfective forms with Telic Transitives

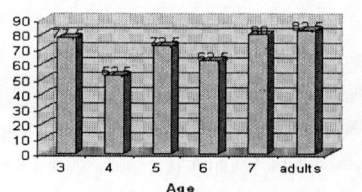

Percentage of Perfective Forms with Atelic Unergatives

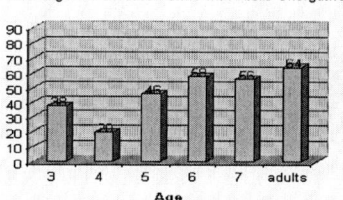

Adults seem to behave in the same way with both verb classes: they show the tendency in selecting the passato prossimo when the action depicted has an endpoint without any differences among the two verb classes. Children aged between 5 and 7 years also show the tendency to select passato prossimo for both verb classes. So, adults and children aged between 5 and 7 years respond as the experiment requires. 3/4-year olds show systematic difference in the responses for each verb class. Atelic unergatives are expressed with a preferential imperfective morphology, while telic transitives are expressed with a preferential passato prossimo. We propose that children, till the age of 5, fail in using perfective morphology with verbs that do not have an explicit direct object, since at 5 they start to analyze the presence/absence of object as a powerful aspectual markers.

4. Comprehension task

The comprehension experiment is a sentence picture-matching task. Eight digital video stories were presented to the subjects. Then a question in the passato prossimo was asked. The task was to identify the (completed) event. Subjects were shown the videos. Each of the videos presented the two characters performing the same action, one of the two girls completed the action (completed situation) while the other was still performing it (ongoing situation). At the end of the video subjects were shown a picture representing the ongoing situation and a picture presenting the completed situation. Then they were asked to choose the picture in order to answer the question "Who has verb-ed?" The completed situation was the correct answer in all cases. The results we present are relative to the completed interpretation assigned to the forms of *passato prossimo* with telic transitives (fig.3) and with atelic unergatives (fig.4).

Fig.3 Completed Readings with Telic Transitives (percentage) in the comprehension task (Lorusso 2005)

Fig.4 Completed Readings with Atelic Unergatives (percentage) in the comprehension task (Lorusso 2005)

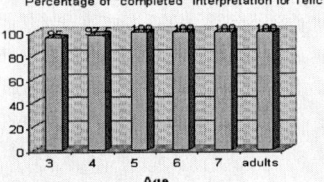

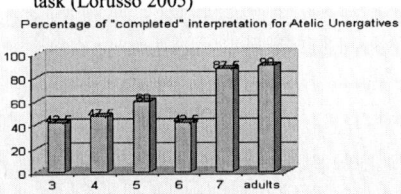

It seems clear by the results that children distinguish between the tensed forms of the two verb classes for the different readings they attribute to them systematically. So, between 5 and 7 years although children can produce perfective morphology they do not comprehend the aspectual meanings of the form of *passato prossimo* with atelic unergatives. This can be linked to the fact that they need to attribute a kind of semantic information to the structural positions of the VP and that they do not correctly derive aspect from structural relations.

5. Discussion

If we put together the results of both, the analysis of the longitudinal corpus of spontaneous speech and the production/comprehension experiments we can identify three different stages in the acquisition of verbs in Italian.

In the earliest stage, as we found in the analysis of the spontaneous speech, children show different modalities of expression of the subject depending on the verb classes (tab.1, tab.2) and this probably confirms that children differentiate between verb classes depending on the loci of generation of the subjects. They also do not systematically use the compounds perfective forms of 'passato prossimo' with unergatives till the age of 5, as it is confirmed by both the analysis of the spontaneous speech and the production task experiment. They do not assign aspectual value to verbs that do not present an overt object. They are not able to end up the derivation of passato prossimo since they link telic aspect to overt objects.

The second stage of acquisition of verbs in Italian is characterised by the fact that although children are able to derive perfective morphology for all verbs, they fail to comprehend the perfective morphology as it applies to atelic unergative predicates. Children are able to derive it morphologically for all verb classes, since it is a productive morphological mechanism, but they fail in attributing the completed reading to the forms of *passato prossimo* with atelic unergatives. They are not aware of the semantic features encoded in the structure of VP. When we talk about semantic features we refer for example to the flavours of VP (Folli, Harley 2002) or to the binary semantic non–configurational features of Mateu 2002 (central coincidence relation or terminal coincidence relation) that are assigned to structural elements of the VP and that determines telic or atelic reading infipendently from the presence of an overt object. This type of acquisition needs a mapping from semantic element to structural element in the VP.

Children get to the third stage (the adult like knowledge) at about 7 years with strong variation between individuals, as the results of the comprehension task show. When children are able to comprehend the perfective marking of the passato prossimo on atelic predicates, they do not have problems anymore in attributing the telic/atelic features as it is derived by the semantic features of the elements that enter into the VP. They start to analyse the lexical aspect not only compositionally. Contrary to the precedent stages which are syntactically driven, in the last one we have a semantic bootstrapping of lexical aspect, so that the interface relation between syntax and semantics are completely acquired.

6. Conclusion

We propose a three-stage model of acquisition of verb meaning, where we intend for verb meaning the mapping between structural syntactic positions and semantic features encoded in the VPs. Such a model is syntactically driven in two stages: the loci of generation of the subject and the characteristic of the direct object are the cues that help children in deriving verb meaning as an interface relation between l-syntax and semantics. The last stage is the only semantically driven one. Anyway, further studies are needed in order to isolate which are the semantic features responsible for the attribution of non compositional lexical aspect, and how they enter into the syntactic structures that children have already learnt in the previous stages. What we propose is just an attempt to understand the acquisition of verb meaning. Nevertheless, we can conclude that we are in front to a complex process of acquisition that involves different stages and that we have to hypothesize a mixed process of acquisition in which both semantics and syntax are implied at different stages and with different implications.

References

Folli, R. and H. Harley (2002) "Consuming results in Italian and English: flavors of v", to appear in P. Kempchinsky and R. Slabakova (eds.) *The Syntax, Semantics and Acquisition of Aspect*, Dordrecht, Kluwer.

van Hout, A. (1998). " On the role of direct objects and particles in learning telicity in Dutch and English", .in A Greenhills, (ed). *Proceedings of 22th BUCLD*, Sommerville, Cascadilla Press, 397-408

Lorusso, P. (2003) *L'Acquisizione dei verbi Inaccusativi: Studio sulla produzione spontanea dei parlanti.*, Tesi di laurea, Università degli studi di Siena.

—. (2004) *Caratteristiche dell'omissione del soggetto nell'Italiano Infantile:Evidenze da un'analisi longitudinale delle produzioni spontanee.* M.A. Dissertation, Università degli Studi di Siena

—. (2005) *The Development of VP Features. An analysis of the acquisition of Child Italian,* M.A. Dissertation, Universitat Autònoma de Barcelona

—., C. Caprin and M.T.Guasti (2005) "Overt Subject Distribution in early Italian Children" in BUCLD web proceedings

Mateu i Fontanals, J. (2002) *Argument Structure. Relational Construal at the Syntax-Semantics Interface*, PhD dissertation, Universitat Autónoma de Barcelona

DIRECT APPROACH TO INFERENCE IN CHILD LANGUAGE: A CASE STUDY OF *EVERY* [*]

UTAKO MINAI

1. Introduction

It has been widely known that the universal quantifier *every* yields an asymmetric entailment structure in its first and second arguments; the first argument of *every* (i.e., the NP) is a downward entailing (DE) environment, whereas its second argument (i.e., the VP) is a non-DE environment (e.g., Ladusaw 1979). As a consequence, *every* evokes asymmetric influences in each argument with respect to various aspects of a linguistic expression.

In particular, the asymmetric entailment structure that *every* creates in its arguments yields consequences that are represented at the level of individual sentence meanings. First, the DE environment in the first argument licenses an NPI such as *any*, whereas the non-DE environment in the second argument does not, as is shown in (1). Second, the DE environment in the first argument licenses a conjunctive interpretation of disjunction, whereas the non-DE environment in the second argument does not, as is shown in (2).

(1) Licensing of NPI: 1st argument (DE) does, while 2nd argument (non-DE) does not.
   a. Every boy who ate *any* vegetable may play outside.
   b. Every boy ate *any* vegetable.
(2) Licensing of conjunctive interpretation of disjunction: 1st argument (DE) does, while 2nd argument (non-DE) does not.
   a. Every boy who ate broccoli *or* (≈ and) a carrot may play outside.
   b. Every boy ate a broccoli *or* (*≈ and) a carrot.

The influence due to the entailment patterns is evident not only at the level of individual sentence meanings but also at the across-sentence level, i.e., it determines the relation of two truth conditional propositions. In particular, the DE environment in the first argument licenses an inference from a less restricted (set-denoting) expression to a more restricted (subset-denoting) expression, whereas the non-DE environment in the second argument licenses an inference from a more restricted (subset-denoting) expression to a less restricted (set-denoting) expression, as is shown in (3).

(3) Direction of inference licensed: 1st argument (DE) licenses an inference from set to subset, while 2nd argument (non-DE) licenses an inference from subset to set.
   a.   Every *boy* ate a carrot → Every *tall boy* ate a carrot
   a.' Every *tall boy* ate a carrot *→ Every *boy* ate a carrot
   b.   Every boy ate a *carrot* *→ Every boy ate a *small carrot*
   b.' Every boy ate a *small carrot* → Every boy ate a *carrot*

In the field of child language research, children's knowledge about *every* has been actively discussed these days. For example, a series of experimental studies (Meroni et al. 2000; Gualmini and Crain 2001; Crain et al. 2002; Gualmini 2005, among others) have proven that children could interpret sentences containing *every* with regard to licensing of the NPI *any* (as shown in (1)) and licensing of conjunctive interpretation of the disjunction operator *or* (as shown in (2)) under the DE environment in the first argument but not under the non-DE environment in the second argument. It thus suggests that children would possess the ability to compute the meaning of *every* with respect to the truth conditional semantics of individual sentences that contain it.

On the other hand, even if children understand individual sentences with *every* in an adult-like way, it is not obvious whether children are sensitive to the distinction between the valid and invalid inferences (cf., Philip and de Villiers 1992; de Villiers et al. 1998). Given that the previous studies described above have shown children's adult-like knowledge of various asymmetries between the arguments of *every*, it would be suggestive that children are aware of the entailment structure of *every*, and hence, that children should be able to tell which inferences involving *every* are valid. The present paper thus discusses children's awareness of the validity of inferences between minimal-paired sentences containing *every*, tested in three experiments.

2. Experiment I

We first ensure that children are able to interpret two premises containing *every* between which an inference is created. Therefore, the objective of this experiment is to investigate whether children have adult-like interpretations of sentences containing *every*.

In particular, we examined whether children can interpret the sentences containing *every* such as those in (4)-(5), which form a minimal pair with respect to the replacement of the set- / subset-denoting expressions in the first argument and the second argument of *every*, respectively.

(4) a.   Every *troll* ate a donut.
     b.   Every *yellow troll* ate a donut.
(5) a.   Every troll ate a *donut*.
     b.   Every troll ate a *chocolate donut*.

In designing the experiment, we focused on the fact that for the minimal-paired sentences such as these, there is a certain context that falsifies the entailing sentence, and that verifies the entailed one at the same time, due to the inclusion relations created regarding the set-denoting and subset-denoting expressions (Minai 2004; Minai and Crain to appear). In particular, for the minimal-paired sentences as in (4), the entailing sentence (4a) is false but the entailed sentence (4b) is true at the same time in the same context as schematized in (6); for the minimal-paired sentences as in (5), the entailed sentence (5a) is true but the entailing sentence (5b) is false at the same time in the same context as schematized in (7).

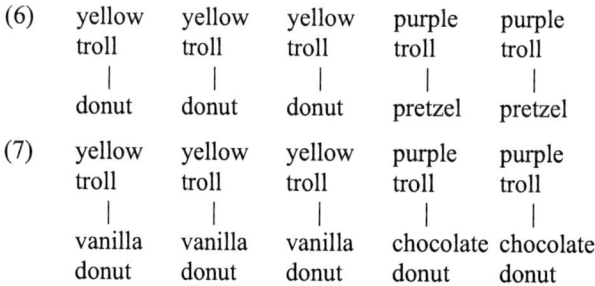

(6)   yellow   yellow   yellow   purple   purple
      troll   troll   troll   troll   troll
       | | | | |
      donut   donut   donut   pretzel   pretzel

(7)   yellow   yellow   yellow   purple   purple
      troll   troll   troll   troll   troll
       | | | | |
      vanilla   vanilla   vanilla   chocolate   chocolate
      donut   donut   donut   donut   donut

In taking advantage of this fact, we used the Truth Value Judgment task (Crain and Thornton 1998) in this experiment. There were two experimenters: one was the storyteller who acted out stories using the toy characters and props; the other manipulated the puppet, such as Kermit the Frog, which watched stories along with the child. In the end of each story, the puppet was supposed to describe what he thought happened in the story, and the child was asked to evaluate whether the puppet's description was right or wrong. Each target sentence in the minimal pair like (4) and (5) was presented as the puppet's description in the end of the story, whose ending was the context like (6) and (7), respectively.

Twenty English-speaking children whose mean age was 4;10 participated in this experiment, who showed adult-like performance. The following table shows the results.

Table 1: The Percentages of Children's Acceptance			
"True" Sentences		"False" Sentences	
(4b)	100% (20/20)	(4a)	10% (2/20)
(5a)	95% (19/20)	(5b)	0% (0/20)

Thus, Experiment I demonstrated children's adult-like truth value judgments of the sentences containing *every*, influenced by the inference/entailment patterns evoked by it.

Note that at this point it is not yet obvious whether they can compute the inference between two premises. Given the positive results found in Experiment I, however, we can now step further ahead toward the logical aspects of children's knowledge about entailments involving *every*. In particular, we would like to test whether children are aware of the inference between premise and consequence presented at once, as well as the truth values of the independently presented sentences.

3. Experiment II

Given the results in Experiment I, Experiment II directly examines children's inferences evoked by *every*, examining whether children are sensitive to the valid and invalid inferences arising from the premises containing *every*. In this experiment, we test environments in which one *every*-sentence was presented as a premise, which would either license or not license a subsequent outcome in the trial, depending on children's assumptions about the entailments licensed in each argument of *every*.

We utilized a newly developed experimental task, in which the premise was orally presented and the consequence was subsequently presented in the act-out, in order to examine children's ability to follow the logical reasoning, rather than their ability to evaluate the truth conditional matching between the context and the stimulus sentences.

The detailed design of this task is as follows. Among the two experimenters, one was the storyteller, and the other operated the puppet that was said to be practicing storytelling. The storyteller first leads-in each story, introducing the characters that are involved. He/she then gives an instruction to the puppet, letting him act out the final outcome of the story by moving the toys. The premise was narrated by the storyteller in the instruction to the puppet, and the consequence was portrayed in the puppet's act-out. The child's task was to check the puppet's act-out step by step, and to make a correction if the puppet acts out invalidly based on the premise.

The two experimental conditions were set out by different combinatorial patterns of premises and consequences: the "Valid" Condition in which the premise and the consequence follow a valid inference; the "Invalid" Condition in which the premise and the consequence follow an invalid inference. The following tables show the paradigm.

Table 2: "Valid" Condition	
Premise (to be orally presented)	Consequence (to be acted out)
Every *troll* eats a donut (≈(4a))	Every *yellow troll* ate a donut (=(4b))
Every troll eats a *chocolate donut* (≈(5b))	Every troll ate a *donut* (=(5a))

Table 3: "Invalid" Condition	
Premise (to be orally presented)	Consequence (to be acted out)
Every *yellow troll* eats a donut (≈(4b))	Every *troll* ate a donut (=(4a))
Every troll eats a *donut* (≈(5a))	Every troll ate a *chocolate donut* (=(5b))

The detailed process of the entire trial in the "Valid" Condition is outlined as follows.

Storyteller: This is a story about hungry yellow and purple trolls, who came to the grocery store. (Showing the toys of trolls in the workspace.) In the end, the following thing will happen. Move the toys and show it to us. "Every *troll* eats a donut."

Puppet's act-out: (Giving a donut to the trolls in the following order:)
yellow → yellow → *yellow* → purple → purple

Note that at the point which the third yellow troll got a donut (boldfaced above), the outcome "every yellow troll eats a cookie" was acted out. The child was expected to let the puppet finish the act-out until the end (the purple trolls' receiving a cookie).

The following is the outline of a sample trial in the "Invalid" Condition.

Storyteller: This is a story about hungry yellow and purple trolls, who came to the grocery store. (Showing the toys of trolls in the workspace.) In the end, the following thing will happen. Move the toys and show it to us. "Every *yellow troll* eats a donut."

Puppet's act-out: (Giving a donut to the trolls in the following order:)
yellow → **purple** → yellow → purple → yellow

Note that at the point which the purple troll received a cookie (boldfaced above), the consequence in which "Every troll ate a cookie" has started to be acted out, which is invalid based on the premise that is given. The child was expected to correct the puppets' act-out at this point, or point it out after completing all the act-out. Crucially, it would be predicted that children should not correct the puppet at this point, if they did not know *every*'s first argument is DE, as it could be consistent with non-DE entailment, i.e., subset to superset relation.

Twenty English-speaking children whose mean age was 5;1 participated in this experiment. The results are shown in the following table.

| Table 4: The Percentages of Children's Correction ||
"Valid" Condition	"Invalid" Condition
0% (0/40)	95% (38/40)

As the table shows, children never corrected the consequences acted out validly on the basis of the premise, and corrected the invalid consequences, which would suggest their awareness of the validity of inferences.

However, a couple of points should be made. Our interpretation was that children ruled out the act-out based on their own assumption about the entailments. From another perspective, however, an alternate interpretation of children's correction in the "Invalid" Condition would be plausible, which is that children ruled out the act-out based on the mismatch between the storyteller's "command" and the puppet's "fulfillment of the command". In particular, children might have corrected the puppet's giving a donut to the purple troll because the purple troll was not referred to in the storyteller's command (i.e., the premise), which was "Make it happen that every yellow troll eats a donut". In order to tease apart these two alternate interpretations, another methodology would be needed, in which (i) the premise and the consequence both should be presented in the sentences, not in the act-out, and (ii) the consequence should be felicitously presented as a rephrase of the premise, in order to be logically evaluated.

4. Experiment III

In response to the points that arose above, Experiment III was conducted, in which the minimal-paired sentences are presented sequentially in the conversation of two puppets, Merlin the Magician and Kermit the Frog. The improved task is illustrated as follows. Kermit was a frog who wants to be a magician, and Merlin the Magician showed some magic tricks to the child and Kermit. Before performing each magic trick, Merlin introduced the characters (e.g., yellow trolls and purple trolls), and described what would happen to them, which presented the premise. Then, as part of his practice to be a magician, Kermit considered what else he could say about what will happen without being wrong, which presented the consequence. The child's task was to determine whether what Kermit said sounds good or it sounds odd.

The experimental conditions were set out by different combinatorial patterns of premises and consequences, as in Experiment II. The paradigms are repeated in the following tables.

Table 5: "Valid" Condition	
Premise (by Merlin)	Consequence (by Kermit)
Every *troll* will eat a donut (≈(4a))	Every *yellow troll* will eat a donut (≈(4b))
Every troll will eat a *chocolate donut* (≈(5b))	Every troll will eat a *donut* (≈(5a))

Table 6: "Invalid" Condition	
Premise (by Merlin)	Consequence (by Kermit)
Every *yellow troll* will eat a donut (≈(4b))	Every *troll* will eat a donut (≈(4a))
Every troll will eat a *donut* (≈(5a))	Every troll will eat a *chocolate donut* (≈(5b))

The sample trial in the "Valid" Condition is outlined as follows.

Merlin: We have yellow trolls and purple trolls here (showing the toys in the workspace). I promise you to make the following happen: *every troll will eat a donut.*

Kermit: Merlin said that every troll would eat a donut. So that must mean that I can also say **that *every yellow troll will eat a donut.***

Note that the premise and the consequence (boldfaced above) constitute a valid inference with regard to the first argument of *every*. The child was expected to accept Kermit's rephrase, by saying "you can say it, Kermit".
The following is the outline of a sample trial in the "Invalid" Condition.

Merlin: We have yellow trolls and purple trolls here (showing the toys in the workspace). I promise you to make the following happen: *every yellow troll will eat a donut.*

Kermit: Merlin said that every troll would eat a donut. So that must mean that I can also say that *every troll will eat a donut.*

Note that the premise and the consequence (boldfaced above) constitute an invalid inference regarding the first argument of *every*. The child was expected to reject Kermit's rephrase, by saying "you cannot say it" or "you said something weird".

Seven English-speaking children whose mean age was 5;9 participated in this experiment. The results are shown in the following table.

Table 7: The Percentages of Children's Acceptance	
"Valid" Condition	"Invalid" Condition
86% (5/7)	14% (2/7)

As the table shows, the ratio of children's adult-like responses was above chance, which would suggest children's adult-like ability to distinguish the valid and invalid inferences concerning *every*.

In response to the methodological problems pointed out in Experiment II, the task in Experiment III was designed conservatively to let the child evaluate a consequence on the basis of a premise that preceded it. One drawback was that the task was too hard for the younger children to complete. In particular, the following two points should be made, regarding why this might be. First, towards children, Kermit's task in the game was to make a prediction based on what Merlin said. However, what Kermit did was simply rephrase what Merlin said, which would not sound like making a prediction for children. It might have blurred what the child was expected to do in the end of the task, and they, for this reason, might have been confused. Second, Kermit's response was led by the following phrase: "It must mean that I can also say …". At the performance level, such a phrase might have been too complicated for children.

To address these concerns, another new task has been developed to allow us to involve younger children, which is already in progress in a follow up study.

5. Conclusion

In the present paper, we reported three experiments to examine children's ability to compute logical inferences between sentences, with respect to the universal quantifier *every* which asymmetrically influences them towards the opposite direction. Experiment I demonstrated children's adult-like judgments of the truth values of the antecedent and consequence of potential entailments, i.e., reflect of the inference/entailment patterns associated with *every*. Building upon the results from Experiment I, Experiments II and III suggested that children are able to distinguish the valid and the invalid inferences created between the sentences containing *every*. Thus, the findings in the three experiments would suggest the conclusion that children are sensitive to the valid and invalid inferences between sentences, as well that they are aware of the entailment structure that the universal quantifier *every* evokes. As has been pointed out above, however, some methodological elaboration is required to provide stronger empirical evidence for children's sophisticated knowledge about logical inferences related to the universal quantifier, and to further illustrate their adult-like knowledge of the semantics of *every* from a logical point of view.

Notes

[*] I would like to thank Paul Pietroski, Ivano Caponigro, Jeff Lidz, Stephen Crain, Jill de Villiers, Robert Fiorentino, Anastasia Conroy, the audience of GALA 2005, and the children, staff and parents at the Center for Young Children at UMCP. Needless to say, all errors are mine.

References

Crain, S., A. Gardner, A. Gualmini and B. Rabbin (2002) "Children's Command of Negation", *Proceedings of the Third Tokyo Conference on Psycholinguistics*, Tokyo, Hituzi Publishing Company.
—. and R. Thornton (1998) *Investigations in Universal Grammar: A Guide to Experiments on the Acquisition of Syntax and Semantics*, Cambridge, Massachusetts, The MIT Press.
de Villiers, J., L. Curran, H. DeMunn and W. Philip (1998) "Acquisition of the Quantificational Properties of Mental Predicates", *Proceedings of Twenty-second Boston University Conference on Language Development*, Boston University, Boston.
Gualmini, A. (2005), *The Ups and Downs in Child Language*, New York, NY, Routledge.

—. and S. Crain (2001) "Downward Entailment in Child Language", *University of Maryland Working Papers in Linguistics* 11, 112-133.

Ladusaw, W. A. (1979) *Polarity Sensitivity as Inherent Scope Relations*, Doctoral Dissertation, University of Texas at Austin

Meroni, L., A. Gualmini and S. Crain (2000) "A Conservative Approach to Quantification in Child Language", *University of Pennsylvania Working Papers in Linguistics* 7(1), 171-182.

Minai, U. (2004) "Semantic Interaction in Child Language: Quantifiers, Entailment and Truth", LING895 Doctoral research paper, Submitted to University of Maryland, College Park.

—. and S. Crain (to appear) "Semantic Interaction between Quantificational Expressions in Child Language", *Proceedings of the First Generative Approaches to Language Acquisition North America*, University of Hawai'i at Manoa.

Philip, W. and J. de Villiers (1992) "Monotonicity and the Acquisition of Weak Wh-Island", *Twenty-fourth Stanford Child Language Conference*, Stanford University, CSLI.

PARAMETERIZING NEGATION: INTERACTIONS WITH COPULAR CONSTRUCTIONS IN ITALIAN AND ENGLISH CHILDREN

VINCENZO MOSCATI

1. Introduction

The main goal of this study is to provide a more precise picture of the pattern of copular omission attested in Italian and English child grammar through a closer investigation of negative contexts. If copular omissions could be considered as a reflex of a "defective" inflectional system, in the sense that certain functional projections could be left underspecified in the first stages of linguistic development, then looking at them in negative utterances will give us other material helpful to understand the shape of the early IP system and of the principles governing it.

In the next section the results of two recent studies will be presented, in order to illustrate the phenomenon of copular omissions in Italian and English and to give a general idea of its consistency. The picture which emerges is of a fundamental symmetry between the two languages in declarative contexts. In the following section a new count will be made, in order to assess if the same behaviour could be found also in negative utterances. Quite surprisingly, the omission rate varies considerably between the two languages, and an interesting alchemy arises between those principles responsible for omissions in declarative contexts and the additional projection NegP, considered as one of the *loci* of parametrical variations. A good account for the difference found in Italian and English negative utterances must then consider both the common principle responsible for omissions in declarative utterances and the variations in the syntax of negation. This result can be achieved adopting a developmental theory along the lines proposed in Rizzi (1994) combined with a well documented cross-linguistic difference in the structural realization of NegP.

2. Copular omissions in declarative sentences

Between the second and the third year, early grammar allows specific constructions that are absent in the target language, the specific grammar to be learned. One good example is constituted by the sentences reported below, taken from three children whose corpora are available through CHILDES:

(1)   a. He on a horse. (Nina 2;1.22)
       c. there my cow. (Eve 2;2)
       d. it a lady (Eve 1;11)

Those sentences are not well formed in adult English, where a finite form of the verb *be* must be obligatorily present, even if the option to leave the copular verb unexpressed is attested in several other languages, such as Russian, Hebrew and also African American English. The possibility to have a null copula in other adult grammars might suggest that sentences as in (1) can be accounted for an instance of parametrical mis-setting, but this option, which may look attractive, has its limits. A first, conceptual one, is that such an explanation would be extremely construction-specific, unable to integrate this kind of omissions into a model of the early Inflectional System. Moreover this hypothesis is directly disconfirmed by the empirical data. In fact the parametrical mis-setting hypothesis predicts that the rate of null copulas should be constant across declarative and negative sentences as well as wh-questions. This is not the case, as it will be shown in this the paper.

Another possibility is to explain the presence of null copulas through more general properties of child grammar. Let's assume, together with many authors (Moro 1988, Becker 2004), that copular verbs are not lexical verbs, since they don't assign any θ-role but are best considered as the spell-out of Tense features. In this case it could be possible to relate copular omissions (i.e. Tense omissions) with other phenomena observable in early grammar, usually explained in terms of Tense underspecification, as Root Infinitives. This seems a viable hypothesis, supported by the fact that null copulas disappear at around the same age as Root Infinitives.

In order to illustrate the phenomenon of copular omission in English, we report in Table 1 some of the results of Becker 2000.

Tab.1. Omission rate in relation to predicates in the High Omission Period				
	age	nominals	locatives	adjectives	average
Nina	2;0-2;6	26%	86%	47%	53%
Peter	2;0-2;3	19%	73%	58%	50%
Naomi	2;0-2;7	10%	62%	40%	37%
Adam	2;7-3;4	46%	95%	58%	66%
Eve	2;1-2;3	60%	45%	80%	62%
Tot.		**36%**	**72%**	**56%**	**53%**

Those results refer to selected files from the reported speech of five American English children and show the phenomenon at its peak[1]. I will refer to this period as the High Omission Period (HOP). One effect found by Becker and reported in table 1 is that the omission rate varies in function of the predicate class, differentiating between stage/individual level predicates. I won't talk at length about this aspect, since this distinction is not relevant for our purposes and no similar effect can be found in Italian. What is important is the magnitude of the phenomenon: if we average the omission rate across the predicate classes, we see that it ranges between the 37% in Naomi's and the 66% in Adam's production.

Those findings are in part replicated for Italian children in a recent study by Elisa Franchi (2004), who found a similar omission rate in the speech of three two-years old children, Martina, Raffaello and Rosa (CHILDES). She individuated 692 copular contexts, 235 of them without an overt copula. Those results are summarized in table 2.

Tab 2. Omissions in the production of 3 Italian children			
	omission rate (n. on total)		temporal development
Martina	35%	(69/197)	1;7- 1;11 **49%**
			2;1- 2;7 17%
Raffaello	27%	(30/113)	1;7- 2;4 **65%**
			2;5- 2;11 17%
Rosa	36%	(136/382)	1;7- 2;5 **81%**
			2;6- 3;3 26%
Tot	**34%**	**(235/692)**	

Table 2 gives an indication of the temporal course of the phenomenon[2], distinguishing between an early stage, that we may think as corresponding to the High Omission Period of Table 1, where omission ranges between 49% and 81%, and a later stage where omissions tend to disappear. It is worth noticing that the in the case of Raffaello and Martina, the last transcription ends before the third year of life, when omissions have not completely disappeared.

Those results take into consideration only sentences with an overt subject, leading to an underestimation of the occurrences of null copulas. This point will be made clear by considering some examples. Take the following sentences, extracted from the child corpora:

(2) a. quetto Ø Giovanni (Martina 2;7.15)
        this   Giovanni

    b. questo Ø bianco (Raffaello 2;04.29)
       this   white

Those sentences require an inflected form of the verb *essere* 'to be' in order to be grammatical:

2a': questo è Giovanni
     this be-3pres/s G.

2b'. questo è bianco
     this be-3pres/s white

Since they are not well-formed in adult Italian, there is less doubt that they are best analyzed as genuine instances of omission. But there is also another possibility, related to the *pro*-drop nature of Italian. This language allows the subject to be left unexpressed, a fact that slightly complicates the task of individuating null copulas, since in an early grammar where both the options of having a null subject and a null copula are given, one word sentences like (3) could also be considered as omissions:

(3) *pro* Ø bianco

Since utterances such as (3) can be interpreted either as elliptical sentences or copular sentences with a *pro* subject, they have been left out from the count of copular omissions.

A last set of data, worth mentioning, is concerned with the lack of omissions in wh-utterances. In this syntactic contexts as shown in table 3, the percentage of null copulas is negligible, with only two cases out of more than 400 utterances.

Tab. 3. Omission in Wh-sentences			
	age	n/totali	rate
Martina	1;7-2;7	1/51	2%
Raffaello	1;7-2;11	0/78	0%
Rosa	1;7-3;3	1/290	0.3%
Tot		2/419	0.48%

This fact suggests that the clause type, in this case declarative vs. interrogative, may affect the distribution of overt copulas and we may suspect that also other clausal types could have the same effect. In order to refine the omission pattern, we conducted a new analysis looking at negative contexts.

3. Asymmetry in negative sentences

Negative sentences differ from declaratives in that they need to project an extra functional head, the one which host the sentential negative marker. This trivial consideration leads us to ask if this extra projection present in the IP system may have consequences on the omission pattern.

To provide an answer to this question, the same corpora chosen by Becker and Franchi were analyzed, selecting the negative utterances characterized by the presence of the sentential negative marker *not*/*non*[3]. Between them, only the ones unambiguously identifiable as copular from the context of occurrence where taken into consideration and in the case of English an additional requirement was added: only sentences with an overt subject where included.

With those criteria, 98 negative copular sentences were found in the High Omission Period, and between them, 67 present a null copula. In (4) some example are reported:

(4) a. this not Jesus (Adam 10)
    b. the dolls not in your briefcase (Eve 11)
    c. this not yours (Naomi 60)

The results relative to all the five children examined are reported in table 5.

Tab. 5. Omissions in negative sentences – HOP			
	nominals	**locatives**	**adjectives**	**total**
Nina	-	-	1/1	1/1
Peter	1/1	-	0/3	1/4
Naomi	-	-	2/12	2/12
Adam	23/32	1/1	16/24	40/57
Eve	15/16	1/1	7/7	23/24
Tot	39/49	2/2	26/47	**67/98**
%	80%	100%	55%	**68%**

Comparing negative with positive utterances, presented respectively in tables 5 and 1, it is clear that negation doesn't limit the distribution of null copulas in English. However, in the period under examination, only 98 negative utterances where found. In order to enlarge the database, all the files available from the corpora of the 5 children were included into the count, until the last one (if available) where omission is attested. In this case it is possible to find 393 negative copular sentences, 84 of them with a silent copula. Table 6 summarizes those findings. It is interesting to notice that no difference related to the predicate class can be found.

Tab. 6. Omissions in negative sentences - all files			
	nominals	**locatives**	**adjectives**	**total**
Nina	3/79	1/10	3/37	7/126
Peter	3/86	0/12	2/51	5/138
Naomi	1/9	0/1	2/21	1/31
Adam	22/33	1/1	16/22	39/56
Eve	16/17	4/4	10/10	30/31
Tot	45/224	6/28	33/141	**84/393**
	20%	21%	23%	**21.4%**

Those results clearly indicate that also in negative contexts copular omissions are consistently attested in English.

Now we turn to Italian. Remember that by virtue of its *pro*-drop nature, choosing only sentences with an overt subject, we are excluding potential omissions, underestimating their occurrence. The same situation holds in the case of negative utterances. Consider the following examples:

(6) a. Gianni non ø verde
      John   not   green

b. non verde
   not   green

Sentence (6a) is ungrammatical in adult Italian and can be unambiguously considered as a genuine instance of omission. In the case of (6b), instead, where the subject is left unexpressed, another option exists. In fact, (6b) is perfectly natural if considered as a normal elliptical sentence where only the negative constituent is overt. It can be felicitously uttered in response to a question, for instance. Consider the exchange in (7):

(7) A: Di che colore comprerai il cappotto?
     'Of which colour will you buy the trench coat ?'

    B: Non verde ~~comprerò il cappotto~~
       Not green I'll buy the trench coat

It is clear that 7B is a different possible analysis for (6b). In those cases it is very hard to choose between the ellipsis interpretation and the null copula one, where 6b receives instead the following representation:

(8) *pro* non Ø verde

Including also ambiguous sentences of the kind in (6b) into the count, we may overestimate the omission rate, given that also elliptical sentences can be ascribed within the set of omissions. Nevertheless, they will be included for two reasons. The first reason is that in this way we can obviate the paucity of negative copular constructions in the corpora examined, not being forced to exclude sentences with a null subject. The second is that in this way we will maximize the omission rate in Italian, adopting the most permissive counting procedure. Remember that in English, instead, we have excluded sentences without an overt subject. In this way we can obtain the highest omission rate possible for Italian and the lowest for English[4].

The transcriptions from Martina, Raffaello and Rosa where checked for negative utterances, and then controlled in order to isolate copular ones.

Tab.7 Omissions in negative contexts. Martino, Raffaello and Rosa			
	age	overt	covert
Martina	1,7 - 2,7	3	0
Raffaello	1,7- 2,11	2	0
Rosa	1,7 - 3,3	6	0
Tot		**11**	**0**

Only 11 where found, and in none of them a null copula appears. The problem is that the total number of the negative copular utterances is not enough to give us more than an indication. To enlarge the database, the transcriptions of all the other Italian children available through CHILDES where examined, plus the corpus of Lisa, provided by Flavia Adani. In this way as many as 63 negative copular contexts were attested, and none of them contained any copular omission, either of the form (6a) or (6b). Table 8 provide the results for Italian.

Tab.8 Omissions in negative contexts. 11 Italian children.			
	age	overt	covert
Martina	1,7 - 2,7	3	0
Raffaello	1,7 - 2,11	2	0
Rosa	1,7 - 3,3	6	0
Guglielmo	2;2 - 2;11	6	0
Diana	1;8 - 2;6	7	0
Viola	1;11 - 2;10	1	0
Lisa	1;5 - 2;7	4	0
Camilla	2;2 - 3;4	16	0
Gregorio	1;7 - 2;1	2	0
Marco	1;5 - 2;1	0	0
Elisa	1;10 - 2;3	16	0
Tot.		**63**	**0**

If we compare those results with the English data presented in tab. 6, a sharp asymmetry is evident: omissions are absent in Italian negative copular constructions, while they are attested in the same English constructions. Table 9 summarizes the relevant contrast.

Tab. 9. Omission in negative contexts: Italian and English		
	%	n. on total
Italian	0%	(0/63)
English	21%	(84/393)

A complex picture than emerges, which leaves us with an interesting puzzle to explain. If omission of the copula is a genuine option for early grammar, as seems to be confirmed by cross-linguistic analysis of declarative sentences, why is it the case that Italian negative sentences block this option? In the next section we will sketch a proposal that tries to unify the lack of omissions in both questions and negative utterances under the same general principle.

4. An explanation: the C-selection Parameter

It is possible that copular omission is not an isolated phenomenon in early grammar but that it follows from other general principles. In particular, since copular verbs may be considered to be the bare expression of a Tense (and Agreement) due to their inability to assign θ-roles, they could be omitted for whatever reason leads the children to underspecify the Tense projection (Rizzi 1994, Wexler 1998). This will explain the distribution of null copulas in both Italian and English declarative sentences. What still needs to be explained is the asymmetry found in negative contexts. The difference in the omission rate reported in tab.9 suggests that negative sentences don't constitute exactly the same syntactic context in the two languages and a different parametrical choice is already made at the age when children were investigated. Selecting the right parameter is not an easy task, but a good candidate can be the relative position of the Negative Phrase with respect to other functional projections[5]. Many authors (Laka 1990, Ouhalla 1990, Zanuttini 1997) have suggested that NegP could be realized in certain languages below the Tense projection, while in others it occupies an higher position. To illustrate this possibility, I report the following pair taken from Ouhalla 1990:

(11) a. Jan elmarlar-i ser-**me**-di-0   *TUR*
      John apples-ACC like-Neg-Past-Agr

    b. **Ur**-ad-y-xdel Mohand dudsha   *BER*
      Neg-Fut-Agr-arrive M.   tomorrov

In the Turkish example in (11a) the negative marker *–me* appears closer to the verbal stem than the morpheme expressing tense *–di*. Assuming Baker's Mirror Principle (Baker, 1985), the linear order of morphemes suggests that the position where *–me* is generated lower than the Tense projection. In the case of Berber in 11b, instead, the temporal morpheme *–ad* appears closer to the verbal stem than the negative morpheme *–ur*, reversing the order of the functional projections. Ouhalla takes this fact as an indication that the relative order of TP and NegP is a dimension of parametrical variation:

(12) C-Selection Parameter.
    A: NegP > TP
    B: TP > NegP

We have thus individuated one possible factor that could be useful to explain the observed contrast in negative sentences between Italian and English children. Following Chomsky (1995) and Laka (1990), we can assume that English has the parameter set on value B, while Italian, following Belletti (1990) seems to have the same parameter set on value A. The order of the two projection results opposite, a fact that, combined with a theory of acquisition along the lines of Rizzi 1994, may provide us an explanation for the omission pattern observed in negative contexts.

Rizzi proposed that children have the option not to project the whole functional structure up to CP, but to choose an arbitrary projection XP as the highest one. One important restriction is that every functional projection below XP must be present and its requirements must be satisfied. Given variation in the ordering of projections, this means that when Italian children produce negative copular sentences, they can truncate the structure right above NegP (14), but they still have TP, whose features require checking by an overt copula. On the other side, due to a different functional order, English children can truncate the structure above NegP (13), leaving aside all the other higher functional projections, including TP. In this case, no feature on TP exists and no overt copula is required.

(13) Eng

(14) Ita

This account also has the advantage that it explains the lack of null copulas in wh-sentences. In fact they behave as the Italian negative ones, forcing the Tense projection to be present in the syntactic representation. This explanation will be further supported if also in English wh-sentences a low rate of omission were found, but this must be left to further research.

5. Conclusions

In the previous sections some new data concerning the phenomenon of null copula relative to negative contexts were presented, and it was shown that a difference between Italian and English emerges. In order to explain this difference, I assumed that a C-selectional parameter, the one regulating the structural position of NegP, presents a different setting in the two languages. This fact, combined with Rizzi's proposal that children may optionally truncate the structure lower than the CP, allows us to explain the complex omission pattern of null copulas. In particular, under this account, the optionaliy of copular omissions in declarative sentences, their ban from wh-sentences and the observed asymmetry between Italian and English   negative sentences can receive a straightforward explanation.

Notes

1. The time period under exam (HOP) is delimited between the first file where copular sentences appear and the last file where the omission rate in locative constructions is attested above 50%.
2. The distinction between the two periods is made by individuating the first file where a monotonic decrease of the omission rate starts.
3. One might expect that another strategy is available to English children, namely the use of the clitic negative form "*n't*". With the exception of Eve, none of the children uses it in the relevant period, as illustrated in the following table.

Use of is/are/was/were + n't		
Nina	7-13	0
Peter	6-11	0
Naomi	35-68	0
Adam	10-28	0
Eve	15-20	9
Tot		**9**

4. This procedure, could be adopted also for declarative sentences. In this case the omission rate is slightly higher than the one presented in Table 2 (see Franchi 2004). A fact that is not crucial for the present discussion.
5. This last claim militates against the view that a universal hierarchical organization of functional heads exist. The relative position of NegP doesn't seem to be unique and also Cinque (1999) is forced to treat this projection as a special case.

References

Belletti, A. (1990) *Generalized Verb Movement: Aspects of Verb Syntax*, Rosenberg e Sellier, Torino.
Baker, M. (1985) "The Mirror Principle and morphosyntactic explanation" *Linguistic Inquiry* 16: 373-415.

Becker, M. (2000). *The development of the copula in child English: The lightness of be*. Doctoral dissertation, UCLA.

——. (2004) "Is isn't be". *Lingua 114*, 399–418

Chomsky, N. (1995) *The minimalistic program*, Cambridge, MA, MIT Press.

Cinque, G. (1999) *Adverbs and Functional Heads*, New York, Oxford University Press.

Franchi, E. (2004). *Piena competenza e assenza di competenza linguistica:una distinzione messa in evdenza dalla logogenia. Essere copula e ausiliare in italiano infantile e in un sordo profondo prelinguale non segnante.* Doctoral dissertation, Università di Firenze.

Guasti, T. (1993/94) "Verb Syntax in Italian Grammar: Finite and Non-finite Verbs", *Language Acquisition*, 3: 1-40.

Haegeman, L., and R. Zanuttini (1991). Negative heads and the neg criterion. *The Linguistic Review 8*:233-251

Laka, M. I. (1990). *Negation in syntax: On the nature of functional categories and projections*. Ph.D. dissertation, MIT.

MacWhinney, B.and C. Snow (1985) "The child language data exchange system", *Journal of Child Language 12*, 271-296.

Moro, A. (1988). "Per una teoria unificata delle frasi copulari", *Rivista di Grammatica Generativa*, vol.13, 81-110

Ouhalla, J. (1991). *Functional categories and parametric variation*. Routledge.

Rizzi, L. (1994). "Some notes on linguistic theory and language development: The case of root infinitives". *Language Acquisition 3*, 371–393.

Schütze, C. T. (2004). "Why nonfinite *be* is not omitted while finite *be* is" in *Proceedings of the 28th BUCLD*, 506-521.

Wexler, K. (1994) "Optional Infinitives, Head Movement and the Economy of Derivations in Child Grammar", in Lightfoot and Horstein, eds., *Verb Movement*, Cambridge University Press.

——. (1998) "Very early parameter setting and the Unique Checking Constraint: A new explanation of the Optional Infinitive stage". *Lingua* 106:23-79.

Zanuttini, R.(1997). *Negation and clausal structure*. Oxford, Oxford University Press.

FOCUS-TO-STRESS ALIGNMENT IN 4 TO 5-YEAR-OLD GERMAN-LEARNING CHILDREN

ANJA MÜLLER, BARBARA HÖHLE, MICHAELA SCHMITZ, AND JÜRGEN WEISSENBORN

1. Introduction

Children do not only have to learn how to express and to interpret the propositional content of a sentence, but also what is supposed to be common knowledge for the interlocutors and what is new information. Previous research has shown that from the beginning of multi-word utterances children seem to adequately use the prosodic, lexical and syntactic means of the target language to mark information structure, like for example focus stress, focus particles, and word order to indicate the focused element (e.g. Jannedy, 1997; Penner, Tracy & Weissenborn, 2000; Nederstigt, 2001). On the other hand, studies looking at comprehension performance suggest that children have difficulties, possibly beyond preschool age, interpreting a sentence containing focus particles like *only,* or with the interpretation of stress as a focus marker (e.g. Drozd, 2005; Drozd & van Loosbroek, 1998; Bergsma, 2002; Gualmini, Maciukaite & Crain, 2003; Paterson, Liversedge, Rowland & Filik, 2003; Hüttner, Drenhaus, van de Vijver & Weissenborn, 2003).

Why do 4-5 year and older children still have problems interpreting a given sentence in context correctly? One of the reasons for this may be that they have difficulties determining what is given and what is new, i.e. focused information with respect to the preceding linguistic context[1]. In order to investigate this hypothesis, we started from two widely accepted assumptions. First, that the focus of a particular sentence, as a rule, can be determined on the basis of the preceding context, and second, that there is a systematic relation between the informational focus of the sentence and its intonation, in the sense that the prominent accent (nuclear accent) has to be assigned to the rightmost element of the focused constituent, a principle called Focus-to-Stress-Alignment (FSA) by Nespor and Guasti (2002) following Jackendoff (1972). That contextual information and prosodic information, i.e. nuclear sentence accent are essentially overlapping, as observed among others by Büring (to appear), is shown by the fact that when reading aloud a text, we automatically and rather consistently assign the appropriate focus intonation to it.

Thus, exploiting this redundancy, one way to find out whether a child is able to correctly determine the information structure of a given sentence in context, more specifically whether she is able to identify the new, i.e. the focused information, is to investigate whether she is able to realize the corresponding Focus-to-Stress Alignment.

A linguistic context with respect to which the semantic focus of the following sentence can be unambiguously determined is constituted by the question in a wh-question-answer pair[2]. That is, the focused constituent of the answer corresponds to the constituent in the scope of the wh-phrase in the question and thus has to be assigned the nuclear accent. This is illustrated by the following examples:

(1)   a. What happened? *John bought a CAR.*
        b. What did John do? John *bought a CAR.*
        c. What did John buy? John bought *a CAR.*
        d. Who bought a car? *JOHN bought a car.*

The constituent underlined is focused, the large capitals mark the constituent carrying the nuclear accent. Thus in (1a) the focus consists of the answer as a whole, the so-called "broad focus", in (1b) of the VP, and in (1c) and (1d), of the object and the subject respectively, the so-called "narrow focus".

In a sentence with broad focus like (1a) which could also be uttered out of any context, the nuclear accent universally seems to fall on the rightmost element of the prosodic structure, whereas the syntactic constituent structure realizes the unmarked, canonical order, corresponding for example to SVO in languages like English, German, and Italian. We may consider the way focus-to-stress alignment (FSA) is realized in (1a) as the default, or unmarked case.

But languages vary in how they realize FSA in case of narrow subject focus. They may basically be differentiated with respect to whether they tend to maintain either the unmarked, canonical prosodic structure by choosing a word order that places the focused element at its right edge where nuclear accent is assigned according to the regular stress rule, as for example in Italian, or, alternatively, whether they assign the nuclear accent to the focused element in its syntactic position, thus abandoning the unmarked, canonical prosodic structure, as for example in English (e.g. Nespor & Guasti, 2002; Samek-Lodovici, 2005; Valldují, 1993). This division basically corresponds to the traditional distinction between flexible/free and rigid/fixed word-order languages. Languages like German in which both word order and the position of nuclear accent are relatively flexible, occupy an intermediate position. These different strategies are illustrated by the following examples from English, Italian, and German:

(2)   a. Who bought a car? *JOHN* bought a car. vs. * bought a car *JOHN.*
      b. Chi comprò una machina? (Una machina,) la comprò *GIOVANNI.*
      c. Wer kaufte ein Auto? *PETER* kaufte ein Auto. *or* Ein Auto kaufte *PETER.*

Thus in English, the FSA is satisfied by stress movement, in Italian by movement of the subject from the canonical to the post-verbal, final position where nuclear accent is assigned according to the regular stress rule, whereas German has both options.

But on the other hand, German has less flexible word order in intransitive sentences than Italian as shown in (3) (e.g. Nespor & Guasti, 2002):

(3)   a. Chi è morto?   È morto CALVINO
      b. Wer ist gestorben *ist gestorben HANS
      (Who has died?   has died Hans)

Summarizing so far we can say that the language-specific FSA pattern that we observe in the answers to narrow focus subject wh-questions make apparent which are the principles of FSA underlying these pattern, i.e. nuclear stress movement or focus movement. This also means that investigating the intonation pattern that German-learning children of age 4-5 assign to prosodically neuter test-sentences, displaying the different legitimate word-order pattern which are licensed by the preceding narrow focus subject and object wh-questions, should allow us to tell not only whether the children have correctly identified the focus of these sentences, i.e. what constitutes new information with respect to the preceding context, but also, whether they have acquired the principles determining FSA in German.

If they have, they should assign nuclear accent, i.e. the most prominent pitch accent to the focused constituent, and they should do so independently of whether the focused constituent occupies the sentence final position, where nuclear accent is canonically assigned by the regular stress rule, or whether it occupies a non-final sentence position, where nuclear accent can only be assigned through movement of the main prominence.

What would we predict if the children were not able to determine the focus structure of the answer-sentences? One possibility could be that they then analyze the sentence as unrelated to the preceding context, as an "out of the blue" utterance, or like a sentence with broad focus answering the question "What happened?". We have seen that these focus-neuter sentences universally realize main prominence on the rightmost constituent. This should then also be the predominant intonation pattern realized by the children. We would also predict that in this case, given that focus-neuter sentences, as a default, realize the canonical word order pattern of the given language, children should then possibly reorder non-canonical orders such that they conform to the canonical word order of German, i.e. SVO, when repeating the test sentence independently of whether the reordered element in the given context should be focused or not.

2. Method

2.1 Participants

Fifteen monolingual German children with a mean age of 4;09 years were tested (range: 4;01 years to 5;10 years).

The 7 girls and 8 boys attended different kindergartens in Potsdam. According to a questionnaire filled out by the parents none of the children had ever shown any indications of an impairment or delay in language acquisition.

Furthermore, a control group consisting of 14 female adult speakers was tested.

2.2 Design and Material

All in all there were 32 simple target sentences, which were presented orally and which were to be repeated by the participants. All sentences consisted of a subject, a direct object and a verb. The sentences differed with respect to their constituent order and with respect to the focused constituent. Half of the sentences were syntactically canonical (subject-verb-object) and the other half was syntactically non-canonical (object-verb-subject). The subject was the focused constituent in half of the sentences while it was the object in the other half. Both factors (focus / word order) were completely crossed leading to the four experimental conditions shown in Table 1. 8 test sentences were constructed for each condition.

	Syntactically canonical	Syntactically non-canonical
Subject focus	8 items (FS)O *Eva* kauft die Gurke. *Eva* buys the cucumber. subject object	8 items O(FS) Den Opa begrüßt *Peter.* The grandfather greets *Peter.* object subject
Object focus	8 items S(FO) Eva putzt *die Fenster.* Eva cleans *the windows* subject object	8 items (FO)S *Die Treppe* fegt Peter. *The staircase* sweeps Peter object subject

Table 1: Experimental conditions
S=subject, O=object. F= focus
(FS)= subject should be focus marked
(FO)= object should be focus marked

For each of the 32 target sentences a short comic strip consisting of three pictures each was drawn. In addition, a short three-sentence story related to the pictures was created that provided the relevant contextual information. The story was followed by a question related to the last picture of the sequence. This question was followed by the answer to exactly this question (see Figure 1). This answer served as the target sentence for the imitation task.

All verbal material for the experiments – except the target sentence – was recorded by a female native speaker of German. She was instructed to produce the sentences in a lively, child directed manner. To avoid any focus related prosodic information in the target sentences, these were spliced together from words recorded in isolation. For these means, the same female speaker that recorded the contexts and questions recorded all words necessary for the target sentences from a list in which these words had been ordered randomly. After recording, the single words were spliced out and put in the order of the target sentences. These sentences were again manipulated using a PRAAT script, so that the F0-value for each word of the sentence was set to 150 Hz.

All visual and acoustic material necessary for the experiment was transferred to a notebook that displayed the comic strips as well as the corresponding verbal stimuli.

Morgen hat die Mama von Peter und Eva Geburtstag. Beide wollen deshalb für die Mama eine Überraschung vorbereiten.

Tomorrow is Peter's and Eva's mother's birthday. Therefore they want to surprise their mother.

Eva möchte Plätzchen backen.

Eva wants to bake cookies.

Was backt Peter?
Peter backt Kuchen.

What does Peter bake?
Peter bakes a cake.

Figure 1: Example for the material

The study was designed as an elicited imitation task. This kind of procedure seemed especially useful for our study out of the following reasons. First, elicited imitation does not reflect a parrot-like passive reproduction of the stimulus but clearly reflects the linguistic competence of the child by systematic changes between the stimulus and the child's output (Höhle et al, 2001; Lust, Flynn & Foley, 1996). This might be especially true when – as it is the case in our study – the stimulus sentence lacks any sentence intonation. Since it would be quite unnatural to produce a sentence without intonation the spontaneous addition of prosodic information can be expected.

The experiment took place in a separate room of the children's kindergarten. Each child was tested two times. The first time the child got to know the experimenter. Also during this first session two pre-tests were conducted to check whether the child understood wh-questions and whether the child was able to produce sentences with non-canonical word order. All children tested were able to perform both tasks. At the end of this first session a hand-puppet, a rabbit, was introduced to the child. The rabbit talked to the child and said that next week he would bring a wonderful comic strip with him into the kindergarten for the child to see.

One week later the experimenter came a second time to the kindergarten. But this time the rabbit had a bandage on his head and of course the children asked what had happened. And then the rabbit told them that he was a bit ill at the moment, but that he nevertheless wanted to have a look at the comic strip together with the child. But because of the bandage the rabbit had some problems in understanding and therefore he asked the child to help him and repeat some things, because he might not understand every detail in the comic strip and in the story. If the child gave her consent, the rabbit and the child looked together at the comic strip, but after presenting the question and the target sentence the rabbit touched the child and said: "Oh, I didn't understand that," prompting the child to repeat the target sentence for the rabbit, using the prosody she thought to be appropriate.

For the adult control group there was only one test session because there were no pre-tests. In the test session we used exactly the same procedure for the control group as for the children. That means that the adults were also asked to help the rabbit and so they had to speak with him. All participants were tested individually and each test session lasted approximately 20-25 minutes. The verbal responses to the sentence to be imitated were recorded.

2.4 Data analysis and results

For the analysis all responses of the subjects were digitized for a further prosodic analysis using PRAAT as well as orthographically transcribed for an analysis of word order.

Both groups of subjects produced a high number of complete and literal repetitions of the target sentences (see Figures 2 and 3). The number of literal repetitions was statistically analyzed by a 2x2 factorial ANOVA (canonicity x subject/object focus) for the two groups of participants separately. The analysis of the children's data showed a significant main effect for the factor canonicity ($F_{(1,14)}$ = 11.18; $p < 0.05$). No other effects reached significance. The same pattern emerged for the adults with the only significant effect for canonicity ($F_{(1,13)}$ = 8.12; $p < 0.05$).

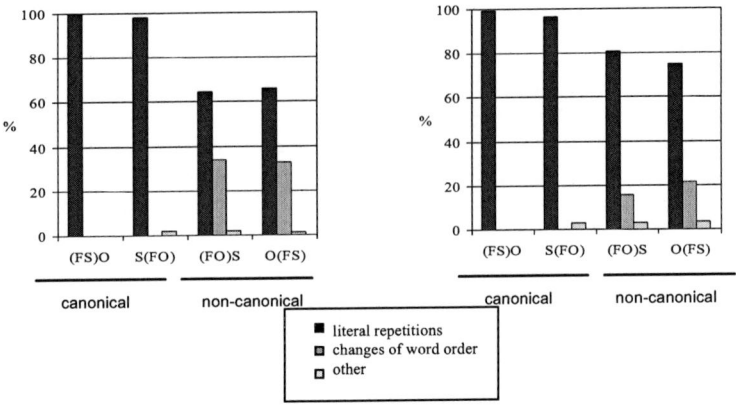

Figure 2: Adults - Types of responses

Figure 3: Children - Types of responses

Only the complete and literally imitated sentences were included in the prosodic analysis. We were able to conduct the prosodic analysis for all children but only for 10 of the adult controls. The other four adult participants systematically changed the word order in one of the non-canonical sentence conditions to a canonical word order so that for one sentence condition there is no analyzable material. We decided therefore to exclude these participants from the prosodic analysis.

Using PRAAT the pitch contour over the subjects and the objects of the imitations produced by the children and by the adults was determined. These pitch values were than averaged over the subjects and objects for the sentences belonging to the same experimental condition (see Figures 4 and 5).

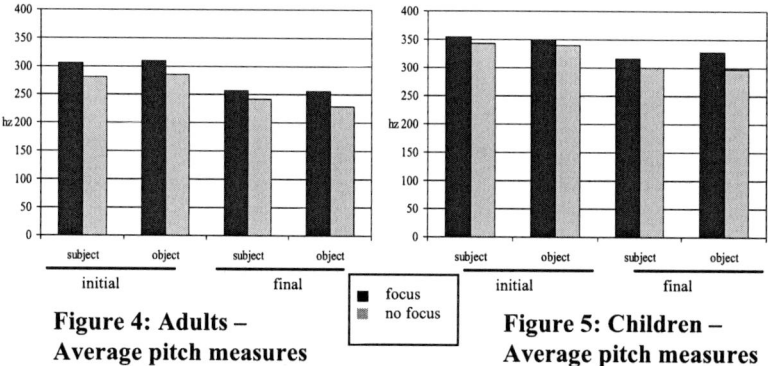

**Figure 4: Adults –
Average pitch measures**

**Figure 5: Children –
Average pitch measures**

The statistical analysis of the data was conducted by a 2x2x2 (position x subject/object x focus) factorial ANOVA separately for the two groups of participants. The analysis for the children's data showed significant main effects for the factors position ($F_{(1,14)}$ = 70.16; $p < 0.001$) and focus ($F_{(1,14)}$ = 18.42; $p < 0.001$). All other effects or interactions failed to reach significance. The results of the adults' data revealed the same picture with significant main effects for position ($F_{(1,9)}$ = 35.08; $p < 0.001$) and focus $F_{(1,9)}$ = 9.33; $p < 0.05$) and no further significant results.

Furthermore, we analyzed the number of changes of constituent order in our experimental conditions. Only responses that reversed the constituent order by keeping the subject/object functions of the arguments were considered in this analysis. As can be seen in Figures 2 and 3 neither the children nor the adults produced any changes of the constituent order in the conditions in which a canonical sentence had to be imitated. All changes of constituent order were observed in the non-canonical conditions changing a non-canonical target sentence to a canonical output. The number of these changes was numerically higher for the adults than for the children but there was no significant difference between the groups ($t_{(df=27)}$ = 1.12; $p = 0.27$). The tendency for the children to produce more changes in constituent order in the subject focus condition than in the object focus condition also failed to reach significance ($t_{(df=14)}$ = 1.13; $p = 0.27$).

3. Discussion

Summarizing our results we found that in the utterances of German 4-year-olds as well as German adults a focused element carries a higher pitch than an unfocused element with the same syntactic function and the same position within an utterance. In addition we found a strong effect of position with respect to pitch: in both groups the initial constituent of the utterances always carries a higher pitch than the final one, irrespective of being focused or not. A second main finding of our study is the strong tendency for the production of sentences with canonical word order: the children as well as the adults show a tendency to produce canonical word order (SVO) irrespective of whether the subject or the object is being focused.

First of all, our results indicate that previous findings according to which English-learning children's productive behavior reflects an early mastery of the prosodic devices of focus marking (MacWhinney & Bates, 1978; Hornby & Hass, 1970; Jannedy, 1997) can be extended to children learning German. This suggests that the fact of the higher flexibility that German allows with respect to changes of word order or nuclear stress position does not necessarily make the task of acquiring the FSA rules harder. In addition, our experimental data suggest that children of the age we tested have no problems in using contextual information – at least in restricted contexts like question-answer pairs – for the identification of the focus of an utterance. This suggests that the problems children of the same age still show with the interpretation of sentences containing focus particles reported in the introduction (Gualmini et al., 2003) are not due to a general inability to infer information structure from given contexts.

In addition, our results suggest that children use linguistic means to express information structure – at least in the area under investigation, namely focus stress – adequately. This is worth noting since – as our pitch analysis also reveals – the focused constituent in a sentence must not carry the highest average pitch in the sentence. As our data have shown, the sentence initial constituent is systematically higher pitched than a final constituent. This fact is probably due to declination, i.e. the typical continuous decrease of the F0-contour within an intonational phrase due to physiological facts (e.g. Cohen & t'Hart, 1967). This means that the listener cannot simply rely on pitch peaks to identify the prosodic focus in a sentence but she must take declination into account to compute the most salient constituent in a sentence. Adult listeners seem to compensate for this declination easily: in a flat intonational contour a later appearing element is rated as being more stressed than an earlier one (Liberman & Pierrehumbert, 1984). The child must have these compensatory processes available by a very early age otherwise it would be hard to figure out that focused elements in a sentence are prosodically highlighted. The fact that the children show the same effect for position and focus as the adults suggests that they have mastered the interplay of declination and focus stress in the planning and the motoric execution of the intonational pattern of a sentence.

This early mastery of prosodic means of focus marking might be supported by specific features of infant-directed speech. Fernald and Mazzie (1991) as well as Fischer and Tokura (1995) found a much more consistent placement of focused words on pitch peaks of the utterance in infant-directed speech as compared to adult-directed speech. In addition, in adult-directed speech prosodic prominence was conveyed by a variable composite of acoustic features, including pitch, duration and amplitude while pitch was the most prominent feature for focus marking in their infant-directed speech samples. This could suggest that infant-directed speech is characterized by features that make the signal more transparent with respect to form-function relations, which helps the infants to track the relevance of a single cue for specific functions.

For the moment, we only looked at pitch as one of the prosodic correlates that mark stress, because according to Pierrehumbert & Hirschberg (1990) the pitch accent marks the most prominent, i.e. in our case the focused lexical item. But further analysis should be extended to other cues that have been discussed as being relevant as acoustic correlates of prosodic prominence such as for example durational cues and intensity.

The second main result from our study concerns the strong tendency to produce canonical sentence structures that is obviously not influenced by the sentence's information structure. This result is remarkable since the children as well as the adults deviated in their reactions from the target sentence even though this was a clear violation of the directions given. The strong preference for the canonical word order is not only evidenced by the changes of the constituent order if the target sentences had a non-canonical structure but also by the fact that changes of constituent order did not in a single case occur when a canonical sentence was the target sentence.

This finding is remarkable given the fact that German – as described in the introduction – is a language in which both the constituent order as well as the placement of the nuclear stress are relatively flexible. Nevertheless, the results of our task suggest that both options are not equally acceptable or equally likely to be produced at least in the kind of experiment and for the type of sentences used. A follow-up experiment we did with 18 adult speakers suggests that it is not simply the task of reproducing the sentences or the experimental situation involving the "hearing impaired" rabbit that invoked the preference for canonical structures. In this follow-up, the experiment was run in the same fashion except that the subjects had to answer the question spontaneously and not to repeat the answer to the questions. In this task there were only three cases out of 576 answers that had a non-canonical word order. Overall, this suggests that, in the types of sentences we used, a more rigid word order seems to win over a rigid placement of the nuclear stress, putting German closer to languages like English than to languages like Italian. Further research should be extended to other structures in German, especially on the ordering of dative and accusative objects within the middle field where a higher variability of word order might be expected. In addition, factors like animacy and definiteness are highly relevant for constituent ordering in German. These factors also might have contributed to the strong tendency for canonical sentences observed in our data.

Notes

[1] For an operational definition of „given" see Schwarzschild (1999).

[2] It is not excluded that a sentence in a given context may have more than one potential semantic focus as noticed by Bolinger (1972) cited in Büring (to appear).

Acknowledgements

This study was supported by the German Research Foundation (DFG) as part of the SFB 632 "Information structure: the linguistic means for structuring utterances, sentences and texts" with a grant to Barbara Höhle and Jürgen Weissenborn. We thank our student assistants for their help in collecting and analyzing the data and Elizabeth Medvedovsky for assistance with the English text.

References

Bergsma, W. (2002) "Children's interpretations of Dutch sentences with the focus particle alleen ('only')," in I. Lasser, ed., *The Process of Language Acquisition. Proceedings of the GALA '99 Conference*, Peter Lang, Frankfurt (Main).

Bolinger, D. (1972) "Accent is predictable if you're a mind reader," *Language* 48, 633-644.

Büring, D. (to appear) "Intonation und Informationsstruktur," *Akten der IDS Jahrestagung 2005*, Mannheim.

Cohen, A. and J. 't Hart. (1967) "On the anatomy of intonation," *Lingua* 19, 177-192.

Drozd, K. F. (to appear) "Children's Interpretation of Quantification," Special Issue of *Language Acquisition* 13 (3-4).

—. and E. van Loosbroek (1998) "Dutch Children's Interpretation of Focus Particle Constructions," *Poster presented at the 23rd annual Boston University Conference on Language Development*, Boston, MA.

Fernald, A. and C. Mazzie (1991) "Prosody and focus in speech to infants and adults," *Developmental Psychology* 27(2), 209-221.

Fisher, C. and H. Tokura (1995) "The Given-New Contract in Speech to Infants," *Journal of Memory and Language* 34(3), 287-310.

Gualmini, A., S. Maciukaite, and S. Crain (2003) "Children's Insensitivity to Contrastive Stress in Sentences with *ONLY*," in S. Arunachalan, E. Kaiser, and A. Williams, eds., *Proceedings of PLC 25* (Vol. PWPL 8.1).

Höhle, B., J. Weissenborn, M. Schmitz, and A. Ischebeck (2001) "Discovering Word-Order Regularities: The Role of Prosodic Information for Early Parameter Setting," in J. Weissenborn and B. Höhle ,eds., *Approaches to Bootstrapping: Phonological, Lexical, Syntactic and Neurophysiological Aspects of Early Language Acquisition* (Vol. 1), John Benjamins Publishing Company, Amsterdam.

Hüttner, T., H. Drenhaus, R. van de Vijver, and J. Weissenborn (2003) "The acquisition of the German Focus Particle *auch* 'too': Comprehension does not always precede production", in A. Brugos, L. Micciulla, and C. E. Smith, eds., BUCLD 28 Proceedings Supplement, Boston, MA.

Hornby, P. A. and W. A. Hass (1970) "Use of contrastive stress by preschool children," *Journal of Speech and Hearing Reserach* 13, 395-399.

Jackendoff, R. (1972) *Semantic interpretation in generative grammar*, MIT Press, Cambridge, MA.

Jannedy, S. (1997) "Acquisition of Narrow Focus Prosody," in *Language Acquisition, Knowledge Representation and Processing. Proceedings of the GALA '97 Conference*. Edinburgh, Edinburgh University Press.

Liberman, M. and J. Pierrehumbert (1984) "Intonational invariance under changes in pitch range and length," in M. Aronoff and.R. Oehrle, eds., *Language and Sound Structure* MIT Press, Cambridge, MA.

Lust, B., S. Flynn, and C. Foley (1996) "What Children Know about What They Say: Elicited Imitation as a Research Method for Assessing Children's Syntax," in D. McDaniel, C. McKee, and H. Smith Cairns, eds., *Methods for Assessing Children's Syntax*, MIT Press, Cambridge, MA.

MacWhinney, B. and E. Bates (1978) "Sentential devices for conveying giveness and newness: A cross-cultural developmental study," *Journal of Verbal Learning and Verbal Behavior* 17, 539-558.

Nederstigt, U. (2001) "The Acquisition of Additive "Focus Particles" in German," in A. H.-J. Do, L. Domínguez, and A. Johansen, eds., *Proceedings of the 25th annual Boston University Conference on Language Development, Cascadilla Press,* Somerville, MA.

Nespor, M. and M. T. Guasti (2002) "Focus-stress alignment and its consequences for acquisition," *Lingue e Linguaggio* 1, 79-106.

Paterson, K. B., S. P. Liversedge, C. Rowland, and R. Filik (2003) "Children's comprehension of sentences with focus particles," *Cognition* 89, 263-294.

Penner, Z., R. Tracy, and J. Weissenborn (2000) "Where scrambling begins: Triggering object scrambling at the early stage in German and Bernese Swiss German," in C. Hamann and S. Powers ,eds., *The Acquisition of Scrambling and Cliticization*, Kluwer, Dordrecht.

Pierrehumbert, J. and J. Hirshberg (1990) "The Meaning of Intonation in the Interpretation of Discourse," in P. Cohen, J. Morgan, and M. Pollack, eds., *Intentions in Communication*, MIT Press, Cambridge, MA.

Samek-Lodovici, V. (2005) "Prosody-syntax interaction in the expression of focus," *Natural Language & Linguistic Theory* 23, 687-755.

Schwarzschild, R. (1999) "GIVENness, AvoidF and other Constraints on the Placement of Accent," *Natural Language Semantics* 7, 144-177.

Vallduví, E. (1993) *The informational component*, Garland, New York

On the Null Subject Stage in Non-Null Subject L1 Acquisition

Katérina Palasis-Jourdan and Michèle Oliviéri

Children acquiring a non-null subject language (French, English, etc.) systematically produce subjectless sentences, until the approximate age of 3;0. This paradoxical phenomenon is well-known as the "null subject stage" (e.g. Hyams (1986) and Rizzi (1998), among many others).

(1) Examples of children's null subjects[1] and their adult equivalents:

_ veux les roues.	(Mat, 3;0)	"<u>je</u> veux les roues/<u>I</u> want the wheels"
_ viens à côté de toi.	(Raph, 2;7)	"<u>je</u> viens à côté de toi/<u>I</u> come next to you"
_ est là.	(Ali, 2;8)	"<u>il</u> est là/<u>he</u> is there"
_ sais pas.	(Tho, 2;4)	"<u>je</u> (ne) sais pas/<u>I</u> don't know"
_ a lion.	(Thi, 2;9)	"<u>il</u> y a un lion/<u>there</u> is a lion"

The bounds between grammaticality and ungrammaticality (noted * in the above examples) are defined by the application of the Null Subject Parameter which classifies French, English, etc. as non-null subject languages. Our research therefore presents two steps in order to account for the child null subject stage in non-null subject languages. First of all, we re-examine the Null Subject Parameter criteria as defined by Rizzi (1997), collating them with French oral data. This step allows us to put forward some of the actual characteristics of the oral data young children hear daily (= input to acquisition) and show that the dichotomy between null subject languages and non-null subject languages is not clear-cut. Secondly, we study the language young children produce (= output), regarding this language as a proper linguistic system, working as a dialectologist discovering a new dialect[2] and hence considering the null subject stage as logical within this system.

1. Input

Hereafter we review two of the four Null Subject Parameter criteria formalized by Rizzi (1997), i.e. licensing of null pronominals and identification of null pronominals[3]. As shown in table (2) hereunder with Italian, French and English examples, these two criteria traditionally allow to part languages in two groups, i.e. null subject vs. non-null subject languages. However, it is observable that counterexamples to this classification exist on both sides. French for instance also allows grammatical null subject sentences, especially with the imperative paradigms and some defective verbs, as in (3).

(2) Licensing and identification of null pronominals:

Languages	Criteria		Language type
	pro licensing (no pronominal subject)	*pro* identification (rich verbal agreement)	
Italian	Yes	Yes	Null subject
	_ *parla* _ *piove*	6 different verbal forms: *parl-o, parl-i, parl-a, parl-iamo, parl-ate, parl-ano*	
French/ English	No	No	Non-null subject
	* _ *parle* * _ *speaks* * _ *pleut* * _ *rains*	Only 3 forms: Only 2: *parl-,* *speak-,* *parl-ons,* *speak-s* *parl-ez*	

(3) French counterexamples:
All imperatives: _ *fais attention* "_ be careful".
Some defective verbs, e.g. *falloir* "have to": _ *faut faire ça* _ "have to do that".

The above sentences show that French displays *pro* licensing —like Italian does— under certain conditions. On the other hand, null subject languages like Italian also display counterexamples to the classification illustrated in table (2). Adams (1987) for instance has noted that certain subjunctive forms in standard Italian require the presence of a pronoun, e.g. _ *parta* "(that) I/he/she leave/s" vs. *tu parta* "(that) you leave". In addition to this fact, it has also been noticed[4] that Northern Italy dialects present an intermediary situation. For example, all the pronouns, except 1sg, are obligatory in Fiorentino, and Trentino displays 5 obligatory forms. As a first conclusion, we hence note that the dichotomy with regard to *pro* licensing is not clear-cut and we propose to qualify this criterion, suggesting an intra-linguistic variation rather than an inter-linguistic one[5].

As far as *pro* identification is concerned, the situation is similar as counterexamples to the classification also exist. For instance, all French imperatives display rich verbal agreement. Indeed, imperatives always present 3 different forms out of 3, e.g. *fais* "do 2sg", *faisons* "let's do", *faites* "do 2pl" (*faire* "do/make"). French present paradigms can also show rich verbal agreement. The verbs "to be" in French and Italian for instance display the same number of different forms (5 out of 6), i.e. *suis, es [e], est [e], sommes, êtes, sont* vs. *sono, sei, è, siamo, siete, sono.* We conclude that the dichotomy with regard to *pro* identification can also be qualified. Consequently, we claim that the input data French children hear daily are therefore misleading with regard to the putative dichotomy established by the Null Subject Parameter. This could then represent one of the reasons why young children produce about 25 % of null-subject sentences.

2. Output

Our data point up that young children do not use many different verbs. Indeed their recurrent verbs amount to twelve in the present corpus[6], as detailed in (4).

(4) **The main verbs in our corpus:**

Verbs	Glosses	%	Conjugation types	%
être	"be"	48.7		
vouloir	"want"	17.2		
faire	"make/do"	16.2	3rd and *être/avoir*	94.9
avoir	"have"	7.0		
savoir	"know"	3.6		
voir	"see"	2.2		
e.g. *manger*[7]	"eat"	1.5	1st	5.1

Next we considered thirteen possible subject referents, corresponding to the different French pronouns, as detailed in (5). We noted the realized pronouns as well as the omitted ones in our corpus. As far as the singular pronouns are concerned (98.8 % of the sentences), our data show that the children's system mainly consists of the first person (35 %) and the third person (60.9 %). If we cross this information with the data about the verbs present in the children's lexicon, we obtain table (6) of actually occurring verbal forms.

(5) **Pronoun occurrences in our corpus:**

Pronouns		Glosses	% of the sentences		% present	% absent
1sg	*je*	"I"	35		52.8	47.2
2sg	*tu*	"you"	2.9		81.8	18.2
	il	"he"	23.4		86.7	13.3
	il expl	"it/there"	2.2	98.8	11.8	88.2
	elle	"she"	4.3		66.7	33.3
3sg	*c'*	"it"	23.4		78.3	21.7
	ça	"this/that"	2.5		100	0
	on	"one/we"	5.1		100	0
1pl	*nous*	"we"	0		0	0
2pl	*vous*	"you"[8]	0	1.2	0	0
	ils	"they ms"	0.7		100	0
3pl	*elles*	"they fm"	0.5		100	0

(6) **Actual verbal forms in the children's system:**

	être	*vouloir*	*faire*	*avoir*	*savoir*	*voir*	*1st conj*
1sg	sɥi	vø	fe	e	se	vwa	mᾶʒ
3sg	e	vø	fe	a	se	vwa	mᾶʒ
%	**48.7**	17.2	16.2	**7.0**	3.6	2.2	5.1

We notice that in more than half of the sentences (55.7 %, with *être* and *avoir*, plus the sentences with defective verbs), the children are using a system comparable to a null subject language system with regard to the rich agreement criterion, in the sense that the expected impoverished agreement of French does not apply to the majority of their sentences. Indeed, within their system, *est là* "is there" (Alizée, 2;8) for instance can only be 3sg in a system where the other possible form is *suis là* "am there" (1sg). Output is therefore also misleading with regard to the Null Subject Parameter classification.

3. Conclusion

We explain the children's null subjects in a non-null subject language like French[9] thanks to two factors : misleading input as well as misleading output with regard to the Null Subject Parameter classification. Firstly, non-null subject languages do not only provide non-null subject sentences (e.g. imperatives). Secondly, the French system of children under 3;0 presents characteristics similar to a null subject system like Italian. Therefore, null subjects are grammatical in the children's system as long as this system is reduced in terms of persons (1sg and 3sg) and verbs (mainly irregular). The French children fix the value of the Null Subject Parameter correctly (most of their sentences are correct). However, the input as well as the output data being contradictory, the children need additional linguistic experience to analyse precisely where the null subjects are grammatical in the adult system in order to consequently reduce the proportion of null subjects in their production. This usually happens when the children are approximately 3;0.

Notes

[1] From our corpus. For further details, cf Palasis-Jourdan (2005).

[2] Cf Dalbera (2002).

[3] The two other criteria, i.e. free subject inversion and long subject extraction, are considered in Palasis-Jourdan (2005) and a simplification of the Parameter is proposed.

[4] Cf Brandi & Cordin (1989) and Manzini & Savoia (2002).

[5] Cf for example Kayne (1996) and Oliviéri (2004) on micro-variation.

[6] The data are filtered. Of course, the occurrence of certain verbs depends on the context and on the children so other studies are foreseen.

[7] The other verbs are *rouler* "roll", *jouer* "play", *tomber* "fall", *cacher* "hide" and *marcher* "walk/work".

[8] *vous* has two possible referents: "you plural" and "you polite".

[9] We propose that these arguments might be transposable to other languages.

References

Adams, M. (1987), "From Old French to the Theory of Pro-Drop", *Natural Language & Linguistic Theory*, Vol. 5, n° 1, p. 1-32.

Brandi, L. & P. Cordin, 1989, "Two Italian Dialects and the Null Subject Parameter", in *The Null Subject Parameter*, in O Jaeggli,. & K. Safir, eds., Dordrecht: Kluwer Academic Publishers, p. 111-142.

Dalbera, J. P. (2002), "Le corpus entre données, analyse et théorie", *Corpus*, Vol. 1.

Hyams, N. M., (1986), *Language Acquisition and the Theory of Parameters*, Dordrecht: D. Reidel Publishing Company.

Kayne, R. S., (1996), "Microparametric Syntax. Some Introductory Remarks", in *Parameters and Universals*, in R. S. Kayne, ed., Oxford: Oxford University Press, 2000, p. 3-9.

Manzini, M. R. and L. M. Savoia (2002), "Parameters of Subject Inflection in Italian Dialects", in P. Svenonius ed., *Subjects, Expletives and the EPP*, Oxford: Oxford University Press.

Oliviéri, M. 2004, "Y a-t-il des frontières dialectales en syntaxe ?", *Etudes corses*, Vol. 59, p. 77-94.

Palasis-Jourdan, K. (2005), *Problèmes d'acquisition et le Paramètre du Sujet Nul*, Mémoire de Master, Université de Nice-Sophia Antipolis.

Rizzi, L. (1997), "A Parametric Approach to Comparative Syntax: Properties of the Pronominal System", in Haegeman, L. ed., *The New Comparative Syntax*, Harlow: Addison Wesley Longman, p. 268-285.

Rizzi, L. (1998), "Remarks on Early Null Subjects", in Friedemann, Marc-Ariel and L. Rizzi, eds., *The Acquisition of Syntax. Studies in Comparative Developmental Linguistics*, London: Longman, 2000, p. 269-292.

DP ACQUISITION AS STRUCTURE UNRAVELING

MAREN PANNEMANN AND FRED WEERMAN[1]

1. Introduction

This paper focuses on the development and extension of the Determiner Phrase (DP) in first language (L1) acquisition. Cross-linguistically, it has been observed that in the one-word-stage, bare nouns are the first DP elements to emerge. In a subsequent stage, nouns start to combine with other DP elements such as determiners and adjectives. Previous studies have accounted for this observation by assuming that in an initial stage, functional categories are absent and only the lexical category N is projected (Radford 1990). Subsequently, the DP structure expands bottom-up in a strictly stepwise fashion (Clahsen et al. 1994, Müller 1994, Hulk 2004). The stages of DP extension in this structure-building hypothesis are summarized in (1).

(1)

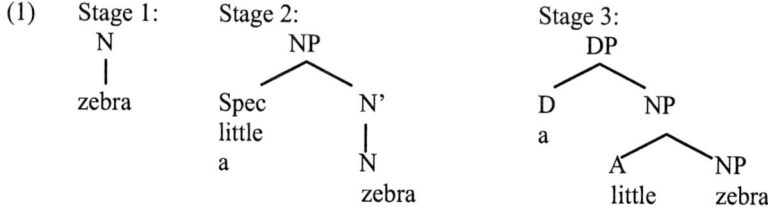

Although this approach captures the emergence of complex nominals in child language, it presupposes structures in child grammar that are in conflict with principles in adult grammar. We propose an alternative model based on Jackendoff's tripartite parallel architecture (Jackendoff 1997) that can account for the observed emergence of the DP while maintaining conformity with principles that hold for adult grammar.

2. Challenges to a model of DP acquisition

The structure-building hypothesis is challenged both by empirical observations and theoretical objections. First, the structure-building approach suggests that DP acquisition is a process of rule-based learning. It has been argued that S-shaped developmental curves—thus curves that display a rather abrupt increase of the overt production of a particular grammatical element—are evidence of the acquisition of rules (cf., e.g., Van Kampen 1997). However, it has been observed in a number of cross-linguistic studies that the production of overt determiners increases gradually and does not show the pattern of an S-curve (Van den Berg 2001, Granfeldt 2000 and others). This suggests that the acquisition of the determiner is a lexical learning process rather than rule acquisition.

Second, the structure-building model as summarized in (2) presupposes the existence of grammatical structures in child language that violate principles in adult grammar. In stage 1, bare nouns are represented as projections of N. Such a structure would lead to a violation of semantic principles. For instance, Vergnaud and Zubizaretta (1992) have argued that only the D-layer can establish reference to particular items whereas the N-layer denotes reference to kinds. This would imply that bare nouns in children's speech could only refer to kinds, which is very unlikely. Furthermore, in stage 2, determiners and adjectives are hosted in the same position. However, such a node, generalizing over determiners and adjectives, is non adult-like and forces an extension of the theory of possible categories if continuity between child and adult grammar is to be upheld.

To conclude, a theory of DP acquisition should be in line with the observation that the overt production of determiners increases gradually while at the same time adhering to principles that hold for adult grammar. In the next sections, we will propose an alternative account of DP acquisition that can deal with these requirements.

3. Mismatches between syntax and phonology in adult language

Jackendoff (1997) proposes a tripartite architecture of grammar, consisting of a phonological, a syntactic and a conceptual component. These independent modules are connected by correspondence rules. The representation of the word *zebra* is, for instance, as in (2), where a correspondence rule connects the phonological information, the syntactic representation and the conceptual interpretation of the lexical entry. (The subscript *w* refers to the phonological unit *word*.)

(2)   /ziːbr@/_w ←→ N ←→ "horse-like mammal with stripes etc."

The tripartite system offers a new perspective to account for phenomena in adult and child language since there is not always a 1:1 relation between phonological words and syntactic categories. In other words, mismatches are possible. As Jackendoff argues, phonological units do not necessarily have to correspond to terminal nodes at the syntactic level but can also correspond to units smaller or larger than heads. Instances where lexical entries are smaller than heads are for example productive derivational or inflectional morphemes. Conversely, phonological units can also be larger than terminal nodes. This means that words at the phonological level can correspond to phrases at the syntactic level. Jackendoff argues for this type of mismatch based on evidence from idiomatic expressions (1997: 158). Weerman and Evers-Vermeul (2002) argue that pronouns also correspond to maximal projections. For instance, the Dutch pronoun *mijnes* "mine" cannot be combined with other DP internal material (cf. 3 vs. 4). The same holds for its English equivalent.

(3)   a. Mijnes   is niet   zo goed   Dutch
       b. Mine   is not   so good   English

(4)   a. *mijnes   (twee) (mooie) boeken   Dutch
       b. *mine   (two) (nice)   books   English

Weerman and Evers-Vermeul take this as evidence that *mijnes* corresponds to a DP at the syntactic component. Notice that there is an important contrast with theories based on lexical insertion: *mijnes* is not a D or an N, leaving the rest of the structure empty. The phonological unit /mɛInəs/_w *corresponds* to the maximal projection DP; it is not inserted in that position (cf. 5) (we disregard the semantic information of this pronoun (cf. 2) as it is not relevant for the argumentation). In syntax, the whole DP structure is available.

(5)   /mɛInəs/ _w ←→

4. Mismatches between syntax and phonology in child language

If we take a look at determiner omissions in first language acquisition, we find that the state of affairs is highly similar to the situation in (4): children pass through a stage where they produce nouns without any other DP internal material (here illustrated with data from French L1 acquisition, cf. 6).

(6)   mettre tracteur su - cuillère sur tracteur   French, Daniel (1;10.14)
        put   tractor on - spoon on tractor

Above we have argued that words at the phonological level can correspond to phrases at the syntactic level in adult language (cf. 5). Given that this is possible in adult grammar, it makes sense that child grammar also allows for mismatches between phonology and syntax. If we assume for child language that a bare noun like *tracteur* in (6) is mapped onto a DP at the syntactic component (cf. 7), the absence of other DP material can be explained. Notice that this assumption is perfectly in line with the claim that only DPs can function as arguments (Szabolcsi 1987, Longobardi 1994). Furthermore, this explains why a bare noun in child language can denote a particular instance in the sense of Vergnaud and Zubizaretta (1992) because even though there is no determiner, the D-layer is active.

(7)   /tRaktœR /$_w$ ←→ DP

The initial setting of the correspondence rule for the lexical item *tracteur* differs from the target setting, where the phonological unit /tRaktœR/$_w$ is associated with a noun (N) in syntax. This accounts for the observation that the children's output deviates from adult language. The question then arises as to how the child departs from this initial hypothesis. In the course of development, the child acquires the phonological and semantic properties of a lexical item and becomes more sensitive to its occurrences in the input. Since the determiner is nearly obligatory in French, entities like /tRaktœR/$_w$ are consistently preceded by a determiner in adult language. The initial setting of the correspondence rule in (7) cannot accommodate this input property. Consequently, the correspondence rule must be reset such that /tracteur/ corresponds to a projection lower than DP, e.g. NP, in order to have enough structural space to host the determiner. Hence, /tRaktœR/ $_w$ will be associated with an NP. If the child again encounters DP internal material that cannot be accommodated within the current setting of the correspondence rule, such as adjectives, he will again retune the correspondence rule. In this way, the child unravels the DP structure top down, layer by layer (cf. 8). Given that lexical items can correspond to non-terminal nodes at the syntactic level in adult language, the subset principle actually dictates a top-down acquisition of syntactic structure.

(8)   /tRaktœR/ $_w$ ←→ DP
       /tRaktœR/ $_w$ ←→ ...
       /tRaktœR/ $_w$ ←→ N

We argue that the whole DP structure is available in syntax and that the child will unravel lower layers of the DP only if there is relevant evidence in the input. The retuning of the correspondence rules takes place per individual item. In other words, it is a process of lexical learning. This explains why the development of overt determiners is rather gradual and does not display the pattern of S-curves.

5. Conclusion

The assumption that there is not always a 1:1 relation between phonological items and syntactic categories does not only account for phenomena in adult language, as previous studies have shown. These mismatches between phonology and syntax offer a new perspective on omissions in L1 acquisition. The advantage of this approach is that we can account for non adult-like omissions without being forced to postulate non adult-like structures. The DP structure is present from the onset of L1 acquisition. At the same time, this model accounts for the fact that children start to use DP elements gradually. In our model, the gradual extension of the DP does not reflect a bottom-up process of structure building. Instead, it expresses how the child gains stepwise access to lower syntactic layers of the DP, a process of structure unraveling.

Notes

[1] We thank Elisabeth van der Linden and Holger Hopp as well as the audience at the GALA 2005 conference for helpful comments and discussion and Robert Cloutier for correcting our non-native English. All remaining errors are ours.

References

Berg, M. Van den (2001) *L'Acquisition de l'Article par des Enfants Francophones, Néerlandophones et Bilingues*, Master thesis, University of Amsterdam.

Clahsen, H., S. Eisenbeiß, & A. Vainikka (1994) "The Seeds of Structure: A Syntactic Analysis of the Acquisition of Case Marking," in T. Hoekstra and B. D. Schwartz, eds., *Language Acquisition Studies in Generative Grammar*, John Benjamins, Amsterdam.

Granfeldt, J. (2000) *Le Développement Morphosyntaxique du Syntagme Nominal chez des Enfants et des Adultes - Approche Générativis*, PERLES 9, Lund University.

Hulk, A. (2004) "The Acquisition of the French DP in a Bilingual Context," in J. Paradis and P. Prévost, eds., *The Acquisition of French in Different Contexts. Focus on Functional Categories*, John Benjamins, Amsterdam, Philadelphia.

Jackendoff, R. (1997), *The Architecture of the Human Language Faculty*, MIT Press, Cambridge, MA, London.

Kampen, J. Van (1997) *First Steps in WH-Movement*, Doctoral dissertation, Utrecht University.

Longobardi, G. (1994) "Reference and Proper Names: A Theory of N-Movement in Syntax and Logical Form," *Linguistic Inquiry*, 25, 609-665.

Müller, N. (1994) "Gender and Number Agreement within D," in J. M. Meisel, ed., *Bilingual FirstLanguage Acquisition. French and German Grammatical Development*, John Benjamins, Amsterdam, Philadelphia.

Radford, A. (1990) *Syntactic Theory and the Acquisition of English Syntax: the Nature of Early Child Grammar of English*, Blackwell, Oxford.

Szabolcsi, A. (1987) "Functional Categories in the Noun Phrase," in I. Kenesei, ed., *Approaches to Hungarian* 2, Szeged: JATE, 160-190.

Vergnaud, J.R., Zubizaretta, M. L. (1992) "The Definite Determiner in French and in English,"*Linguistic Inquiry* 23, 595-652.

Weerman, F. and J. Evers-Vermeul (2002) "Pronouns and Case,"*Lingua* 112, 301-338.

MORPHOLOGICAL CUES IN L2 SENTENCE PROCESSING: EVIDENCE FROM SUBJECT/OBJECT AMBIGUITIES IN GREEK AS L2

DESPINA PAPADOPOULOU AND IANTHI MARIA TSIMPLI

1. Introduction

In this paper, we examine the role of two morphological cues, S-V agreement and Case on DPs, in L2 sentence processing by using on-line data collected from native speakers (NS) as well as L2 learners of Greek. Recently, there is a growing interest in L2 parsing in order to investigate any differences between native and non-native sentence processing strategies (Felser et al., 2003; Papadopoulou & Clahsen, 2003 among others). The aim of this study is to further explore L2 parsing by testing how surface morphological cues are employed (a) to detect (un)grammaticality on-line and (b) to process the L2 input. The phenomenon used involves a temporal ambiguity, which arises when the verb of a pre-posed adverbial clause is optionally transitive and, therefore, the NP that follows could be either the object of the subordinate verb or the subject of the main verb:

(1a)   While she was eating the biscuits she fell on the floor.
(1b)   While she was eating the biscuits fell on the floor.

All parsing theories (cf. Frazier, 1987; Pritchett, 1992) predict that (1b) causes a garden-path effect and conscious reanalysis, due to either Late Closure or θ-constraints. This prediction has been supported in English as L1 (cf. Mitchell, 1987; Pickering & Traxler, 2003 among others) and L2 (Juffs, 1998) and in French as L2 (Frenck-Mestre, 2002).

2. The present study

The data we report come from two self-paced reading experiments conducted with 80 NS (50 women and 30 men; age range: 20-40 years) and 20 L2 learners (14 women and 6 men; age range: 18-55 years) of Greek. The proficiency level of the L2 learners has been tested in a cloze-test, which involved a text taken from a Greek newspaper with 50 gaps that should be completed with functional free morphemes. All the L2 learners participating in this study scored only within 10% below the NSs' score in the same cloze-test. In addition, their mean time of residence in Greece is 18,76 years (age range: 2-28 years; SD: 7,26). Based on the scores from the cloze-test and the time of residence in the country, we can conclude that the L2 learners tested are very advanced speakers of Greek. The L2 learners of this study have various L1s (English (8), French (2), Swedish (2), German (3), Spanish (2), Serbian, Arabic, Italian). In addition, four subjects have grown up as bilinguals, 3 English/Greek and 1 German/Greek, in that they were raised in a foreign country by Greek parents. The rest of the subjects started learning Greek as adults.

The method used in both experiments is the self-paced reading paradigm, in which the sentences were presented in a word-by-word fashion on a computer screen. The subjects controlled the appearance of each word by pushing a specified button on the keyboard and when they did so the previous word disappeared from the screen. At the end of each sentence the subjects had to perform a grammaticality judgment task. The dependent variables were (a) the reading times (RT) for each word, (b) the response times and (c) the accuracy scores for the grammaticality judgment task.

In each experiment there were 96 trials, 24 of which involved critical items and 72 fillers. The critical items were divided into four conditions (6 items per condition), two investigating on-line (un)grammaticalities and two parsing strategies. (Un)grammaticalities have been tested with intransitive subordinate verbs (cf. (2a&b) and (4a&b), whereas optionally transitive verbs have been used to investigate parsing strategies (cf. (3a&b) and (5a&b)). The two experiments differed in the morphological cue involved: in the first task, the subjects had to use S-V agreement morphology to decide on the (un)grammaticality of the critical sentences and/or to disambiguate them, whereas in the second task, they had to rely on the morphological case on DPs.

From the data to be reported below, we have excluded all erroneous responses and all RTs that were above 2000ms and 1,5SD above the overall mean per condition. Moreover, none of the subjects included in the study was accurate less than 60%. In what follows we will present the data from each experiment. In this paper, we only present the RTs on the critical segments for both experiments.

3. The Agreement experiment

The critical sentences of this task involved a pre-posed adverbial clause with either an intransitive (cf. 2a&b) or an optionally transitive (cf. 3a&b) verb followed by a DP, which was unmarked for gender, *ta makaronja*. The main verb was marked either for 3rd person singular (cf. 2b&3b) or 3rd person plural (cf. 2a&3a):

(2a) Kathos etrehe   ta   makaronja kaik**an**   stin katsarola.   (IS)
     while   ran-IMP the spaghetti-PL burnt-3PL in the pot
(2b) *Kathos etrehe   ta   makaronja kaik**e**   stin katsarola.   (IO)
     while   ran-IMP the spaghetti-PL burnt-herself-3SG in the pot

(3a) Kathos majireve   ta   makaronja   kaik**an**   stin katsarola. (TS)
     while   cooked- IMP the spaghetti- PL burnt-3PL in the pot
(3b) Kathos majireve   ta   makaronja   kaik**e**   stin katsarola. (TO)
     while   cooked- IMP the spaghetti- PL burnt-herself-3 SG on the pot

(2b) is ungrammatical, because the number feature of the main verb forces an object analysis for the DP, *ta makaronja*, which is not possible due to the intransitivity of the subordinate verb. The number feature of the subordinate verb in (3a) forces a subject analysis of the DP *ta makaronja*, whereas in (3b) the same DP should be analysed as the object of the subordinate clause. The critical segment in this experiment was the main verb, any ungrammaticality and ambiguity resolution arises there. The RTs for the main verb per condition are presented in Table 1:

Table 1. Agreement Experiment: Mean RTs on the main verb per condition for each group.

Group	IS	IO	TS	TO
NS	547,65	619,20	574,69	590,64
L2 learners	847,42	900,20	903,11	834,96

For both groups the ungrammatical condition (IO) was significantly longer than the grammatical one (IS) (NS: t(38)= 3,896; p<0,001; L2 learners: t(19)=2,409; p<0,03), which indicates that the NS as well the L2 learners successfully used S-V agreement and argument structure to detect ungrammaticalities on-line. On the other hand, there was no significant difference between the TS and the TO condition in the NS data, whereas the L2 learners showed a garden path-effect in that the TO condition was read significantly faster than the TS condition (t(19)=2,454; p<0,03).

The results from the main verb indicate that the NS do not experience a garden-path when processing sentences like (3a), which contrasts with the findings from NS of English. These cross-linguistic differences might be due to the fact that in Greek morphology plays a crucial role in parsing and may override processing strategies such as Late Closure (cf. Papadopoulou & Tsimpli, 2005). On the other hand, the L2 learners were able to use morphological features to detect (un)grammaticalities on-line, but they seem to resort on more general parsing routines, like Late Closure, when ambiguity arises.

4. The Case experiment

In this experiment, the critical sentences also involved a pre-posed adverbial clause with an intransitive (4a&b) or an optionally transitive (5a&b) verb, but the DP that followed the subordinate verb was marked for either nominative or accusative case:

(4a)   Kathos etrehe i   astaki   kaikan   stin katsarola.   (IS)
       while   ran-IMP the lobsters-NOM burnt-3PL in the pot

(4b)   *Kathos etrehe tus astakus   kaike   stin katsarola.   (IO)
       while   ran-IMP the lobsters-ACC burnt-herself-3SG in the pot

(5a)   Kathos majireve   i   astaki   kaikan   stin katsarola. (TS)
       while   cooked- IMP the lobsters- NOM burnt-3PL in the pot

(5b)   Kathos majireve   tus astakus   kaike   stin katsarola. (TO)
       while   cooked- IMP the lobsters-ACC burnt-herself-3 SG on the pot

In this task, the critical segments are the determiner and the noun, *i/tus astaki/astakus*, because the morphological case features of the DP result in ungrammaticality in (4b) and resolve the ambiguity towards the subject reading in (5a) and towards the object reading in (5b). The data on the determiner are presented below:

Table 2. Case Experiment: Mean RTs on the determiner per condition for each group.

Group	IS	IO	TS	TO
NS	450,22	461,66	467,45	438,30
L2 learners	578,95	627,05	583,62	623,99

In the L2 learners data, the determiners marked for nominative case were read faster than the ones marked for accusative case (F $(1,14)=5,948$; $p<0,03$). This might be due to the salience of the nominative case. In contrast, the NS exhibited a garden-path effect, in that the TO condition was significantly shorter than the TS condition ($t(39)=4,111$; $p<0,001$), while the L2 learners showed a garden-path effect in the opposite direction, which provides additional evidence for the salience of the nominative case.

In Table 3 we present the data from the noun:

Table 3. Case Experiment: Mean RTs on the noun per condition for each group.

Group	IS	IO	TS	TO
NS	481,39	545,11	526,53	503,58
L2 learners	747,73	881,29	796,33	761,58

Both groups showed evidence that they detected the ungrammaticality on the noun, since the IO condition was significantly longer than the IS condition (NS: $t(39)=4,109$; $p<0,01$; L2 learners: $t(19)=2,156$; $p<0,05$). Moreover, the L2 learners data indicated a preference to expect a direct object after encountering the subordinate verb, which did not reach significance ($t(19)=1,783$; $p=0,096$). Such an effect was not found in the NS data, probably due to the fact that the direct object expectation has arisen earlier, on the determiner, and therefore, has already decayed on the noun.

Overall, the results from the determiner and the noun provide evidence that two stages are involved in the processing of such constructions. During the first stage, which is evident on the determiner, the NS show an expectation for a direct object, in accordance with Late Closure, and no thematic effects, whereas the only effect shown with the L2 learners is the salience of the nominative case. During the second stage, evident on the noun, the thematic information from the verb is made available for both groups resulting in the grammaticality effect.

5. Conclusion

The present findings are interesting, because they indicate that morphological cues can override general parsing routines in L1 sentence processing, whereas this was not found in the L2 data. On one hand, there seem to be cross-linguistic differences in sentence processing and on the other, L2 sentence processing differs from L1 in that morphological features cannot be used on-line to trigger parsing preferences.

References

Felser, C., L. Roberts, R. Gross and T. Marinis (2003) "The processing of ambiguous sentences by first and second language learners of English," *Applied Psycholinguistics* 24, 453-489.

Frazier, L. (1987) "Theories of sentence processing," in J. Garfield, ed., *Modularity in Knowledge Representation and Natural Language Understanding*, MIT Press, Cambridge, MA. (pp. 291-307)

Frenck-Mestre, C. (2002) "An on-line lok at sentence processing in the second language," in R.R. Heredia and J. Altarroba, eds., *Bilingual sentence processing*, Elsevier, Amsterdam. (pp. 218-236).

Juffs, A. (1998) "Some effects of first language argument structure and morphosyntax on second language processing," *Second Language Research* 14, 406-424.

Mitchell, D.C. (1987) "Lexical guidance in human parsing: Locus and processing characteristics," in M. Coltheart, ed., *Attention and Performance XII: The Psychology of Reading*, Erlbaum, Hillsdale, NJ. (pp. 601-618)

Papadopoulou, D. and H. Clahsen (2003) "Parsing Strategies in L1 and L2 Sentence Processing: A Study of Relative Clause Attachment in Greek," *Studies in Second Language Acquisition* 25, 501-528.

Papadopoulou, D. and I. Tsimpli (2005) "Morphological cues in children's processing of ambiguous sentences: a study of subject / object ambiguities in Greek," in A. Brugos, M.R. Clark-Cetton and S. Ha, eds., *BUCLD 29: Proceedings of the 25th annual Boston University Conference on Language Development*, Cascadilla Press, Somerville, MA. (pp. 471-481)

Pickering, M.J. and M.J. Traxler (2003) "Plausibility and recovery from garden-paths: An eye-tracking study," *Journal of Experimental Psychology: Learning, Memory and Cognition* 24, 940-961.

Pritchett, B.L. (1992) "Parsing with grammar: Islands, heads, and garden paths,".in H. Goodluck and M. Rochemont, eds., *Island Constraints: Theory, Acquisition, and Processing*, Kluwer, Dordrecht. (pp. 321-349)

PROCESSING OF MORPHOLOGICAL MARKERS AS A CUE TO SYNTACTIC PHRASES BY 10-MONTH-OLD GERMAN-LEARNING INFANTS

LYDIA PELZER AND BARBARA HÖHLE

1. Introduction

In order to learn the syntactic regularities of a language, the learner has to find out about the boundaries of linguistically relevant units like clauses, phrases and words in this language. There is much evidence that first language learners as well as adult second language learners make use of prosodic patterns to detect the boundaries of units larger than a word in their speech input (e.g. Morgan et al. 1987; Jusczyk et al. 1992; Mandel et al. 1994; Soderstrom et al. 2003; Nazzi et al. 2000).

However, since prosodic phrasing is strongly influenced by non-syntactic factors like, for example, the length of an utterance, speech tempo and pragmatic information (e.g. Grosjean, Grosjean & Lane, 1979; Nespor & Guasti, 2002) prosody is not always a reliable source of information for finding syntactic boundaries. Therefore learners must also rely on other means such as distributional regularities to gain knowledge about the locus of phrase and clause boundaries. One source of information that has been suggested is the distribution of functional elements within the child's input (e.g. Christophe et al., 1997; Gerken 1996; Valian & Levitt 1996). Across languages, function words typically appear at the edges of syntactic phrases (e.g. English: *The* little girl *has* eaten *the* red apple; French: *la* jeune fille *a* mangé *la* pomme rouge). This suggests that they could serve as a further cue that signals the syntactic boundaries in the input. But given the late appearance of functional elements in children's production there have been doubts that young infants are able to perceive and process these elements (e.g. Gleitman & Wanner, 1982). Meanwhile, there is converging evidence that infants are able to process function words long before they produce them. By 7.5 months of age, for example, German infants are able to recognize free functional morphemes like articles and prepositions in continuous speech (Höhle & Weissenborn, 2003). By 11 months of age English-learning infants are even able to discriminate between two versions of a continuous text containing either real English function words or nonsense syllables instead of function words (Shafer et al., 1998). About a year later they also seem to use free functional morphemes for sentence interpretation (Gerken & McIntosh, 1993). Consequently, the fact that function morphemes are mostly short and unstressed does not per se constitute a disadvantage for infants to perceive these elements since the recognition of these elements is possible at the same age as the recognition of monosyllabic content words (e.g. Jusczyk & Aslin, 1995). Furthermore, from 14 months of age on infants are able to use determiners for categorization of new words that appear together with these elements (Höhle et al., 2004).

A further cue for syntactic phrasing might be provided by bound grammatical morphemes. A number of languages have morphologically concordant phrases, i.e. syntactic phrases in which all elements are marked by the same affix (e.g. Spanish: *los gatos negros [the black cat]*, Italian: *una cioccolata calda [one hot chocolate]*, German: *diesen reichen Mädchen [those rich girls]*). For adults' distributional analysis the relevance of this cue has been investigated in studies of artificial grammar learning (Morgan et al., 1987; Meier & Bower, 1986). These studies show that adults are better at learning structural regularities of strings in which syntactic phrases are marked by concordant markings. As bound grammatical morphemes also appear quite late in children's productions we have to ask again whether children have the prerequisites to process these cues. Even though the processing of bound grammatical morphemes is not as well studied as the processing of freestanding morphemes, there is evidence that infants also have the ability to perceive these elements earlier than they produce them. Studies by Soderstrom et al. (2001), for example, show that by 19 months English infants are sensitive to the 3rd person singular marking in English which is realized by the bound morpheme – *s*. Furthermore, Santelmann & Jusczyk (1998) demonstrated that English learning 18–month-olds are already sensitive to the morphosyntactic dependencies between the freestanding auxiliary *is* and the bound morpheme – *ing*.

One of the first studies to investigate the role that concordant morphology plays in infants' first language acquisition was conducted by Blenn et al. (2003). In a cross-linguistic experiment with German and English-learning infants, they found that German-learning 10-month-olds already seem to be sensitive to concordant markings that are realized as suffixes. In an experiment with the Headturn Preference paradigm (Juszyk and Aslin, 1995) the infants were familiarized with two isolated German grammatical noun phrases, one concordant and one non-concordant (e.g. *seinen grossen Katzen [his big cats]*, *dieser faulen Henne [this lazy hen]*). During the test, four different short texts were presented, one containing the familiar concordant phrase, one containing the familiar non-concordant phrase, the other two containing either an unfamiliar concordant or an unfamiliar non-concordant phrase. The infants significantly preferred listening to the texts containing a concordant phrase over those containing a non-concordant phrase in the unfamiliar condition. This finding was interpreted as evidence that even infants this young seem to be sensitive to concordant morphology. In a follow-up study Pelzer & Höhle (2006) showed that English-learning infants whose target language does not make use of concordant markings seem to be sensitive to this feature when it appears at the beginning of words like it is the case in Swahili (e.g. *ki-le ki-su ki-pya [each new knife]*). These data suggest that infants seem to be sensitive to recurring bound functional elements regardless of whether their target language uses concordant markings or not.

In our study reported here we want to explore the role concordant morphology plays in infants' speech processing by asking whether infants at the age of 10 months are not only sensitive to concordant markings but also show evidence of actually using this sensitivity for phrase segmentation. Only if this is the case it is possible that infants might profit from concordant markings when trying to derive the grammatical regularities of their target language.

2. Experiment 1

2.1 Methods

2.1.1 Participants

Thirty-seven infants from monolingual German speaking households were tested. The infants (19 girls and 18 boys) had a mean age of 10 months and 15 days (age range: 0;10.03 – 0;11.00) and no known hearing deficits. In addition 5 more infants were tested but were excluded from the final analysis because of mean listening times shorter than three seconds.

2.1.2 Materials

Four pairs of German noun phrases consisting of a determiner, an adjective and a noun were constructed. The members of one pair of phrases only differed with respect to the morphological markers within the phrase. Half of the phrases were concordant, ending in the German suffix [-en] (e.g. *seinen grossen Katzen [her big cats], solchen dünnen Suppen [those watery soups]; diesen faulen Hennen [these lazy hens]; ihren jungen Meisen [her young titmice]*) whereas the other half of the phrases were non-concordant, having varying suffixes (e.g. *seiner grossen Katze [his big cat], solcher dünnen Suppe [this watery soup], dieser faulen Henne [this lazy hen], ihrer jungen Meise [her young titmouse]*). Both the concordant and the non-concordant phrases are grammatical in German with perfectly congruent morpho-syntactic markers. Both types of phrases are identical with respect to case (dative) but they differ systematically in number, the concordant phrases being marked as plural and the non-concordant phrases as singular.

For two of the pairs of phrases a five-sentence text passage was constructed. Each sentence provided a grammatical context for each phrase of a pair so that the passages containing the concordant phrases were identical to those containing the non-concordant phrases. Thus, the only difference between the concordant and non-concordant passages was the morphological marker on the critical phrases.

Example of a text passage containing a concordant phrase:
Der Bauer erwartet von diesen faulen Hennen mehr Leistung. Er gibt deshalb diesen faulen Hennen viel Bewegung auf dem Hof und am Waldrand. Dummerweise jagt diesen faulen Hennen am Abend ein Iltis hinterher. Dabei wird diesen faulen Hennen Angst und Bange. Bis auf ein paar ausgerissene Federn ist diesen faulen Hennen aber wirklich nichts passiert.

Equivalent text passage containing a non-concordant phrase:
Der Bauer erwartet von dieser faulen Henne mehr Leistung. Er gibt deshalb dieser faulen Henne viel Bewegung auf dem Hof und am Waldrand. Dummerweise jagt dieser faulen Henne am Abend ein Iltis hinterher. Dabei wird dieser faulen Henne Angst und Bange. Bis auf ein paar ausgerissene Federn ist dieser faulen Henne aber wirklich nichts passiert.

A female native speaker of German recorded the four text passages as well as the eight isolated phrases. She was encouraged to read the texts in an infant-directed manner with a lively voice. These recordings were digitized for presentation during the experiment. The mean length of the passages was 23.4 seconds. Each sound file for the passages contained three different instances of the text and a silent pause of one second was inserted between these instances.

The eight sound files containing the isolated phrases had a mean length of 30.6 seconds. Each file contained twelve different tokens of the same phrase. Between the single instances of the phrase a silent pause of 500 msec was inserted. Additionally, there were 50 msec of silence at the beginning as well as at the end of each sound file.

2.1.3 Design and Procedure

A variation of the Headturn Preference paradigm developed by Jusczyk and Aslin (1995) was used. In this method, an initial familiarization phase is directly followed by a test phase. During the experiment the infant is seated on the lap of a caregiver sitting on a chair in the center of a test booth. The caregiver listens to masking music over enclosed headphones in order to prevent any bias. Inside the booth three lights are attached approximately at the infant's eye level: a green light on the center panel and two red lights on each of the side panels. Directly above the green light on the center panel is a hole for a video camera to record the experiment. A loudspeaker is mounted behind each side panel at the same height as the red lights.

Each experimental trial began with the flashing of the green light in the center of the booth. When an infant orientated towards the green light it extinguished and one of the red lights on the side panel began to flash. When the infant turned her head towards the flashing red light, the speech stimuli began to play. The speech stimuli were presented only from one of the two loudspeakers, namely from the side where the red light was flashing. The presentation of the speech stimulus was stopped when an infant turned her head away from the light for more than two consecutive seconds or when the speech file ended. If an infant turned away for less than two seconds, the presentation of the speech file continued, but the time spent looking away was subtracted from her listening time.

The passages were used during the familiarization. The infants were familiarized with one passage containing a concordant phrase in each sentence and one passage containing a non-concordant phrase in each sentence. The two passages used for familiarization stemmed from different pairs (e.g. concordant: *diesen faulen Hennen*; non-concordant: *seiner grossen Katze*) so that there was no overlap in the lexical elements of the phrases. The participants varied with regard which pair of phrases were embedded in the passages they heard Thus, half of the infants listened to the passages containing the phrases *diesen faulen Hennen* and *seiner grossen Katze* and the other half of the infants listened to the passages containing the phrases *seinen grossen Katzen* and *dieser faulen Henne* during familiarization.

During the test phase, the four isolated phrases were presented to the infants in four trials each. This resulted in a total of sixteen test trials. Two of these phrases, one concordant and one non-concordant, had already appeared in the passages presented during the familiarization. The other two phrases had not appeared in a passage beforehand. Again, one of the two unfamiliar phrases was concordant whereas the other was non-concordant. Depending on the version of the experiment an infant in the test phase either listened to the isolated phrases *seinen grossen Katzen, dieser faulen Henne, solchen dünnen Suppen* and *ihrer jungen Meise* or to the corresponding (non)-concordant counterpart for each phrase. In addition, the order as well as the side of presentation of the different phrases were varied between subjects.

2.1.4 Hypotheses

If infants at the age of 10 months make use of concordant markings for segmenting the phrases out of the passages, we expect better recognition of the familiar concordant phrases than the familiar non-concordant phrases. This should be evidenced by longer listening times for the familiar concordant phrase than for the familiar non-concordant phrase. Furthermore, if a preference for the familiar concordant phrase is really the product of the recognition of the phrases from the familiarization phrase and not a simple preference for concordant over non-concordant phrases, longer listening times for the familiar concordant than for the unfamiliar concordant phrases are expected.

2.2 Results

For each infant, mean listening times were calculated for each type of phrase over the four trials in which it appeared. The infants listened to the familiar concordant phrase for 10864 msec (SD = 7929 msec) and to the familiar non-concordant phrase for 8051 msec (SD = 3466 msec). In the unfamiliar conditon they listened to the concordant phrase for 7770 msec (SD = 2981 msec) and to the non-concordant phrase for 9798 msec (SD = 4528 msec). A two-by-two factorial ANOVA with the factors familiarity and concordance was conducted. This resulted in a significant interaction of the two factors familiarity and concordant morphology ($F_{(1;36)}$ = 11.94 p < 0.01). No main effects were observed, neither for concordant morphology ($F_{(1;36)}$ = 0.26 p = 0.62), nor for the factor familiarity ($F_{(1;36)}$= 0.77 p = 0.39). Pairwise comparisons showed that infants listened significantly longer to the familiar concordant phrases than to the familiar non-concordant phrases ($t_{(df=36)}$ = 2.14, p < 0.05). Furthermore, the listening times for the familiar concordant phrases were significantly longer than for the unfamiliar concordant phrases ($t_{(df=36)}$ = 2.45, p < 0.05). In addition, the preference for the unfamiliar non-concordant phrases over the unfamiliar concordant ones also proved to be significant ($t_{(df=36)}$ = 3.02, p < 0.01).

Figure 1: Mean looking times for the phrases in the test phase

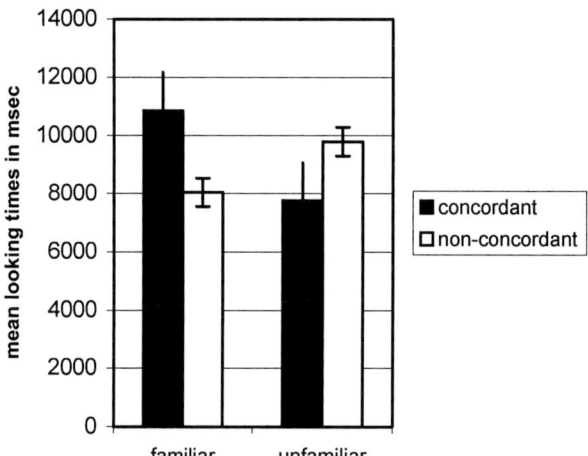

3. Discussion

Summarizing our results, we found that German-learning infants at the age of 10 months prefer to listen to noun phrases in which all elements carry the same affix over noun phrases with different endings that had been presented before in the continuous speech of passages. In addition, they show longer listening times to those concordant phrases they had been familiarized with within the passages than to new unfamiliar concordant phrases.

First of all, these results are in line with our previous findings (Blenn et al. 2003) according to which German infants as young as 10 months do process grammatical morphemes. Even though these elements appeared as unstressed endings and only involve the reduced shwa-vowel infants detect and attend to these elements in continuous speech. This is parallel to results concerning freestanding grammatical morphemes and shows again that infants perceive and process grammatical morphemes – freestanding as well as bound ones – long before they produce them. Our results provide further evidence for the assumption that the structural information carried by functional elements might already play a crucial role in early language processing and early language acquisition, as has been proposed by a number of researchers (e.g. Golinkoff et al., 2001, Valian & Coulson, 1988; Gerken, 1996).

The main aim of our study was not only to show that infants are sensitive to suffixes but also that concordant markings of syntactic phrases may help the infant to segment these units out of running speech. Our findings provide the first pieces of evidence for this assumption: infants only show longer listening times for familiar phrases over unfamiliar phrases when these are marked concordantly but not when the concordance marker is missing. This suggests that the children did recognize the phrases from their previous presentation within the passages and thereby that they did segment the phrases from the passages. The interpretation of the preference as reflecting the recognition of the phrases is in line with studies looking at the role of prosodic information for phrasal or clausal segmentation. In these studies, infants once again preferred to listen to word sequences that had been presented as prosodic units in a familiarization phase as compared to word sequences that contained a prosodic boundary (Nazzi et al., 2000; Soderstrom et al., 2003).

It is likely that infants' reaction to the concordant markings results from statistical learning mechanisms that identify recurrent patterns in speech and track the co-occurrences of elements (Bonatti et al., 2005; Newport & Aslin, 2004, Saffran, 2001; Saffran et al., 1996). The appearance of identical segments within a relatively small domain seems to be a salient feature for infants, which might make this domain stick out of the surrounding context and thereby might help to extract the corresponding phrase from the input. Another possibility is that the recurring parts of the string support the memorization and consequently the recognition of the phrases. The determination of the exact source of this supportive effect has to be a matter for further research. Parallel to our findings for infants, we found a similar supporting effect of concordant markers in adults' processing of a foreign language (Pelzer & Höhle, 2006). Together with the findings on the effect of concordant markers in adults' artificial grammar learning (Meier & Bower, 1986; Morgan et al., 1987), this suggests a high degree of continuity in the processing skills of infants and adults.

However, the pattern of results that appeared for the unfamiliar phrases is somewhat unexpected. The infants showed longer listening times to the non-concordant unfamiliar over the concordant unfamiliar phrases. First of all, the observed interaction between familiarity and concordance supports our interpretation that infants' preference of the familiar concordant over the familiar non-concordant phrases has to do with the previous presentation of the phrases within the passages and reflects the recognition of at least the concordant phrase from the familiarization phase. The pattern of results for the unfamiliar phrases shows that the effect we found for the familiar phrases does not simply reflect a general preference for phrases with recurring endings over phrases without these recurring parts.

But it is hard to explain why the infants listened longer to the unfamiliar non-concordant than to the concordant phrases. This pattern seems to reflect a novelty effect in which the longer attention for the non-concordant phrases might be caused by the higher degree of acoustic variability within the non-concordant phrases than within the concordant phrases which shared crucial parts of their acoustic material. We know from other studies that familiarity as well as novelty effects can show up in experiments using habituation or familiarization paradigms depending on factors like the age of the children tested, the number of familiarization trials and the complexity of the material used in the experiment (e.g. Hunter & Ames, 1988, Roder et al., 2000; Schilling, 2000). The exact nature of the factors leading to the one or the other direction of infants' preferences is still unclear and an important aspect of further research. Our results show that preferences in both directions can even appear within the same experiment. This could suggest that the processing of the unfamiliar and the familiar phrases tapped different levels of cognitive or perceptual skills (c.f. Roder et al., 2000).

Notice that the feature concordant morphology as we have described it crosslinguistically has only been observed within noun phrases. Therefore another area than segmentation where concordant markings might be useful is categorization. Once a child realizes that all phrases that are marked by concordant affixes belong to the same syntactic category, namely noun phrases, she could then use this knowledge for further detailed analysis of these phrases with regard to their distribution in sentences.

Whether this is really something that can already be performed by infants and also whether concordant morphology actually facilitates infants' learning of grammatical regularities of the target language has to be a matter of further research. Possibly the way in which a language realizes concordant affixes also plays an important role. In German the relevant affixes for concordant markings always contain the weak vowel [ə] whereas in other languages like for example Spanish and Italian the relevant markers contain full vowels which might be much easier to perceive for infants. Consequently it is possible that the impact concordant markings have on infants' speech processing might be greater in languages like Italian and Spanish than in languages like German.

Despite these still open questions, the data from our experiment suggest that infants are able to perceive bound functional elements from early on and that recurring speech segments can be used for phrase segmentation from a continuous speech stream. Nevertheless, we do not want to suggest on the basis of our data that infants at the age of 10 months already have a representation of the morphosyntactic features of these functional elements; rather, they seem to pay attention to these repeatedly occurring elements and use them to break up the speech stream into smaller units which in turn might support grammatical learning.

Notes

This research was supported by a grant to Lydia Pelzer by the graduate school 275: "Economy and complexity in language" by the German Science Foundation (DFG) and by a grant to Barbara Höhle by the German Science Foundation (DFG, HO 1960/6-1). We thank Michaela Schmitz, Sonja Bartels and Anne Rosenthal for their help in preparing and running the experiments and Jürgen Weissenborn for his scientific support.

References

Blenn, L., A Seidl,.and B. Höhle (2003) "Recognition of phrases in early language acquisition: The role of morphological markers. In Beachley", in B., A. Brown and F. Conlin, eds., *Proceedings of the 27th Annual Boston University Conference on Language Development*, Somerville: Cascadilla Press, 138-149.

Bonatti, L. L., M Peña,., M.Nespor,and J.Mehler (2005) "Linguistic Constraints on Statistical Computations: The Role of Consonants and Vowels in Continuous Speech Processing", *Psychological Science* 16, 451 - 459.

Christophe, A., R.Guasti,, M. Nespor, E.Dupoux, and B.Van Oyen (1997) "Reflections on phonological bootstrapping: Its role for lexical and syntactic acquisition", *Language and Cognitive Processes* 12, 585-612.

Gerken, L. (1996) "Phonological and distributional information in syntax acquisition", in J. L. Morgan and K. Demuth, eds., *Signal to Syntax: Bootstrapping from Speech to Grammar in Early Acquisition*. Mahwah: Erlbaum.

Grosjean, F., L. Grosjean, and H. Lane, (1979) "The patterns of silence: Performance structures in sentence production", *Cognitive Psychology* 11, 58-81.

Jusczyk, P. W., K.Hirsh-Pasek, , D. G Kemler Nelson,. L.Kennedy, A Woodward,. and J.Piwoz, (1992) "Perception of acoustic correlates of phrasal units by young infants", *Cognitive Psychology* 24, 252-293.

—., and R. N. Aslin, (1995) "Infants' detection of the sound patterns of words in fluent speech", *Cognitive Psychology* 29, 1-23.

Höhle, B. and J. Weissenborn, (2003) "German-learning infants' ability to detect unstressed closed-class elements in continuous speech", *Developmental Science* 6, 122-127.

—., J.Weissenborn, D. Kiefer, . A.Schulz and M Schmitz, (2004) "Functional elements in Infants' Speech Processing: The Role of Determiners in the Syntactic Categorization of Lexical Elements", *Infancy* 5, 341-353.

Hunter, M. A., and   E. W Ames. (1988) „A multifactor model of infant preferences for novel and familiar stimuli", in L. P. Lipsitt & C. Rovee-Collier eds., *Advances in Infancy Research, Vol. 5*. Stanford: Alex Publishing Corporation.

Mandel, D. R., P. W Jusczyk, and   D. G. Kemler Nelson (1994) "Does sentential prosody help infants organize and remember speech information?", *Cognition* 53, 155-180.

Meier, R. P., and G. H Bower, (1986)" Semantic Reference and Phrasal Grouping in the Acquisition of a Miniature Phrase Structure Language", *Journal of Memory and Language* 25, 492-505.

Morgan, J. L., R. P Meier,. and E. L. Newport (1987) "Structural Packaging in the Input to Language Learning: Contributions of Prosodic and Morphological Marking of Phrases to the Acquisition of Language", *Cognitive Psychology* 19, 498-550.

Nazzi, T., D. G Kemler Nelson,. P. W Jusczyk,, and A. M Jusczyk. (2000) „Six-month-olds' Detection of Clauses Embedded in Continuous Speech: Effects of Prosodic Well-Formedness", *Infancy* 1, 123-147.

Nespor, M. and M. T Guasti. (2002) "Focus-stress alignment and its consequences for acquisition", *Lingue e Linguaggio* 1, 80-106.

Newport, E. L. and R. N Aslin, (2004) "Learning at a distance I. Statistical learning of non-adjacent dependencies", *Cognitive Psychology* 48, 127-162.

Pelzer, L. and B: Höhle   (2006) "The Impact of Morphological Markers on Infants' and Adults' Speech Processing", in B. Beachley, A. Brown and F. Collin, eds., *Proceedings of the 30ᵗʰ Annual Boston University Conference on Language Development*. Somerville: Cascadilla Press.

Roder, B. J., E. W Bushnell,. and A. M Sasseville. (2000) "Infants' preferences for familiarity and novelty during the course of visual processing", *Infancy* 1, 491-507.

Saffran, J. R. (2001) "The Use of Predictive Dependencies in Language Learning", *Journal of Memory and Language* 44, 493-515.

—., R. N.Aslin , and E.Newport, (1996) "Statistical learning by 8-month-old infants", *Science,* 274, 1926-1928.

Santelmann, L. and P. W Jusczyk. (1998) "Sensitivity to Discontinuous Dependencies in Language Learners: Evidence for Processing Limitations", *Cognition* 69, 105-134.

Schilling, T. H. (2000) "Infants' looking at possible and impossible screen rotations: The role of familiarization", *Infancy* 1, 389-402.

Shafer, V. L., D. W Shucard., J. L.Shucard and L. Gerken (1998) "An Electrophysiological Study of Infants' Sensitivity to the Sound Patterns of English", *Journal of Speech, Language and Hearing Research* 41, 874-886.

Processing of Morphological Markers as a Cue to Syntactic Phrases
                by 10-month-old German-Learning Infants

Soderstrom, M., K.Wexler and P. W. Jusczyk,(2001) „English-Learning Toddlers' Sensitivity to Agreement Morphology in Receptive Grammar", in B. Skarabela & S. Fish eds., *Proceedings of the 26th Annual Boston Conference in Language Development*. Somerville: Cascadilla Press.

—., A.Seidl, D. G.Kemler Nelson, and P. W. Jusczyk (2003) "The prosodic bootstrapping of phrases: Evidence from prelinguistic infants", *Journal of Memory and Language* 49, 249-267.

Valian, V. and S. Coulson (1998) "Anchor Points in Language Learning: The Role of Marker Frequency", *Journal of Memory and Language* 27, 71-86.

—. and A. Levitt (1996) "Prosody and Adults' Learning of Syntactic Structure", *Journal of Memory and Language* 35, 497-516.

KNOWLEDGE OF BINDING IN SERBO-CROATIAN SPEAKERS WITH DOWN SYNDROME

ALEXANDRA PEROVIC

1. Introduction

Down syndrome (DS) is a neurodevelopmental disorder caused by an abnormality of chromosome 21. It occurs in 1 in 700-900 live births, which makes it one of the most common impairments in the population with intellectual disabilities. Language development in DS has been traditionally viewed as an instance of a common delay, such that whatever problems with language that are observed, have been taken as being caused by general delays in cognitive development. This view has, unfortunately, contributed to generating little interest in DS in the linguistic literature. Contrary to the traditional view, however, studies have revealed an incredibly limited grammatical development in DS, more limited than what might be expected if it resulted from the general cognitive impairments in this population (Fowler, 1990). Severe deficits in morphosyntax, as well as lack of complex syntactic structures in spontaneous speech of children with DS led Fowler (1990) to conclude that the ultimate linguistic achievement in individuals with DS rarely surpasses that of a typically developing (TD) two-and–a-half- or three-year-old. Rondal and Lambert (1985) report that only 50% of all utterances by the adolescents and adults with DS in their sample were grammatical. In this way, DS can be viewed as another example of a dissociation between language and cognition, with language lagging behind general cognitive development – the opposite to what is reported for Williams syndrome.

In view of the fascinating facts surrounding the development and the end linguistic knowledge in DS, it is surprising that DS has hardly received any attention in the generativist framework. Linguistically motivated accounts of other linguistic impairments, developmental (e.g. Specific Language Development), or acquired (e.g. aphasia), have proved vital in furthering our knowledge of both the language disorders and the study of linguistic theory. If linguistic theories are neurologically plausible, the testing of principled theoretical accounts by applying them to language impairments is crucial. In the hope of shedding more light on the issue of how a deficit in atypical language such as that of DS surfaces crosslinguistically, the goal of this study is to assess the knowledge of binding in individuals with DS who are speakers of a language rarely investigated in the literature on atypical language. Binding is a module of grammar known to pose difficulties at later stages of acquisition in TD children, so it seems fit to be studied in DS, in view of the controversies surrounding the issue of 'delayed' language in this population. For the same reason, this investigation focuses on adult speakers with DS, whose linguistic development is deemed complete.

2. Binding in DS: Results from English and Predictions for Serbo-Croatian

Binding Principles (Chomsky, 1981; 1986) are responsible for the distribution and interpretation of nominal expressions, and as such constitute a major component of adult syntactic knowledge. Principle A of standard Binding Theory governs the distribution and interpretation of reflexive pronouns, whereas Principle B is concerned with personal pronouns. Studies have shown that TD children acquire Principle A much earlier than Principle B. English speaking children are reported to allow illicit coreference in (1) around 50% of the time, even at the age of 6 (Jakubowicz, 1984; Chien & Wexler, 1990), however they have no difficulty ruling out (2):

(1) * Mary$_i$ is washing her$_i$.

(2) * Mary$_i$ is washing herself$_{*j}$.

Different accounts have been offered, but the agreed interpretation of the data seem to be that children do know syntactic binding, regulated by syntactic constraints, but may have trouble with coreference, which is regulated by pragmatic or processing constraints (Chien & Wexler, 1990; Grodzinsky and Reinhart, 1993). The abundance of studies crosslinguistically and the interesting results that show asynchronies even in typical development of pronominal reference make the acquisition of this module of grammar particularly interesting to study in atypical language, and, especially in DS, in view of the traditional 'slow but normal' characterization of language development in this disorder. If it is the case that language is merely delayed in DS, then patterns in the acquisition of binding in this population should be parallel to those in typical development: Principle A should pose few problems, but Principle B should yield interpretive difficulties until later stages of development. This prediction is proven incorrect in Perovic (2001) who investigated the knowledge of binding in four adult English speakers with DS. These individuals showed a perfect performance on sentences involving personal pronouns, but had inordinate difficulties interpreting anaphors. In a truth-value judgement task, they correctly rejected illicit coreference in examples such as (3) 80-100% percent of the time. However, they correctly interpreted the anaphor in (4) only 25 to 55% of the time. Note that the poor performance on the test conditions involving anaphors was seen in both 'yes' and 'no' answers (match and mismatch conditions), thus no positive or negative bias was evidenced.

(3) Is Mickey Mouse$_i$ washing him $_{*i/j}$?

(4) Is Mickey Mouse$_i$ washing himself $_{i/*j}$.?

This performance is in striking contrast to the results in typical development, discussed earlier. Even in the rare studies that show some difficulties with the interpretation of anaphors in very young children (Franks and Connell, 1996), the pattern where children should know the coreference but not syntactic binding, is not attested. The pattern in DS reported by Perovic, and later replicated in younger English-speaking individuals with DS by Ring & Clahsen (2003), clearly indicates that grammar in DS is not (just) delayed, but also deficient. Using the theoretical framework of Reflexivity of Reinhart and Reuland (1993), Perovic (2001) interpreted the revealed pattern in DS as revealing a deficit in forming the syntactic dependency between the anaphor and its antecedent, with the conditions on binding, as defined in this framework, intact. What follows is a grossly simplified introduction to the framework of Reflexivity of Reinhart and Reuland (1993) (thereon, R&R), needed to account for the data both in English and Serbo-Croatian; the reader is referred to the original paper for a detailed account. In this framework, binding conditions are not concerned with governing the syntactic relation of binding, but the structural position of pronouns and reflexives fall out of conditions on reflexivity of predicates. According to R&R, the conditions on binding are defined as (5) and (6).

(5) **Condition A:** 'A reflexive-marked predicate must be reflexive.'

(6) **Condition B:** 'A reflexive predicate must be reflexive-marked.'
        (where the predicate is reflexive if its arguments are co-indexed)

Anaphors and pronouns are classified according to two characteristics, referential independence, and ability to reflexive-mark a predicate. These properties decide which pronominal elements can appear as coarguments of predicates. Whether an element is fully specified for referential features (i.e. grammatical features such as gender, number, person and structural Case) determines if it can enter the chain formation (this property is not crucial for our analysis so it will not receive much further attention). Elements that have the function of reflexive-marking are able to reflexivize transitive predicates – e.g. anaphors *himself/herself* in English. Elements that are not reflexive-markers cannot appear as arguments of transitive predicates – e.g. English pronouns *him/her*.[1] In (7), the predicate is reflexive: the anaphor functions as a reflexive-marker, satisfying Condition A given in (5) above whilst the pronoun is ruled out by Condition B in (6).[2]

(7) John$_i$ loves himself$_i$/*him$_i$.

The other type of predicates, inherently reflexive predicates, are marked so in the lexicon. In English, these predicates are intransitive,[3] while in Romance inherent reflexivity is marked through inflection system, where the reflexive clitic is a sign that the predicate has undergone a valency reduction (Reinhart, 1996).[4]

(8) John behaves.

(9) Gianni si lava.
    Gianni *si* washes
    Gianni washes himself.

Since the predicates in (8) and (9) are inherently reflexive, there is no need for them to be reflexive-marked in syntax by the (complex) anaphor; the conditions on reflexivity are satisfied. The important consequence of Binding Conditions is that they account for the distribution of anaphors and (together with the revised chain theory) pronouns, without stating any restrictions on their structural domains.

Turning back to the performance reported in the adult English speakers with DS earlier, their good performance on sentences such as (3) shows that they obey Condition B, as defined in (6): they correctly reject a reflexive predicate that is not reflexive-marked: (3) contains no anaphor that will reflexivize the transitive predicate 'wash'. In contrast, their poor performance on sentences containing anaphors sheds no light on whether the participants obey Condition A, i.e. whether the reflexive-marked predicate must be interpreted as reflexive, but it certainly indicates an extremely serious problem in interpreting anaphors. The anaphor still needs to be interpreted as being in a syntactic relation with its antecedent however.

To investigate whether the participants know Condition A, their knowledge of inherently reflexive predicates needs to be tested, e.g. examples such as (8) above. The number of these predicates in English is quite limited so a safer bet would be to investigate a language that has a more transparent way of marking inherent reflexivity, such as Serbo-Croatian. Serbo-Croatian (SC) has both full and clitic forms of personal pronouns and the reflexive pronoun. In the R&R terms, pronouns and pronominal clitics do not have a reflexive-marking function, and so cannot appear as arguments of reflexive predicates:[5]

(10)   *Marija$_i$ nju$_i$/je$_i$ voli.
       Marija her/her-clitic loves
       'Marija$_i$ loves her$_i$.'

I consider the anaphor 'sebe' to be a complex anaphor: it lacks most referential features, not being marked for number, person or gender[6] and is therefore able to occupy the foot of the chain (in R&R terms), while its reflexive-marking function means that it can appear as a coargument of a transitive reflexive predicate. Both are illustrated in (11).

(11)   Marko$_i$ sebe$_i$ voli.
       Marko self loves
       'Marko$_i$ loves himself$_i$.'

As argued for Romance (Kayne, 1975), the reflexive clitic *se* in SC is not an object clitic. It does not enter anaphoric relations: it is not an argument, but a morphological marker of an arity operation that reduces the internal theta role of the verb, making the verb inherently reflexive, in the sense of Reinhart (1996) and earlier approaches discussed there.[7] Thus it is unable to reflexive-mark a transitive predicate in syntax the way the complex anaphor 'sebe' can:

(12)   Marko$_i$ *se$_i$/sebe$_i$ voli.
       Marko se loves
       'Marko$_i$ loves himself$_i$.'

There are two types of predictions to be made for the SC speakers with DS. More generally, if it is the case that grammar in DS is only delayed, but no real deficiencies are found, we should expect no difference in the performance of adult individuals with DS and TD controls. However, if the grammar in this disorder is deficient, the patterns in DS may be very different to those seen in TD. On the basis of what is seen in English individuals with DS, where Perovic (2001) claimed that conditions on binding, as defined in R&R, are available in DS, but a deficit may concern the forming of the syntactic relation between the anaphor and its antecedent, interesting predictions may be made: participants may show difficulties interpreting the reflexive pronoun, but not personal pronouns or pronominal clitics. Furthermore, it can be hypothesized that the participants will only find the full anaphor difficult to interpret, but *not* the reflexive clitic. The following section will establish whether these predictions are borne out.

3. Experiment

Six SC speaking adults with DS, aged 19-29 (mean 23.3), took part in the study. Their average non-verbal IQ was 63.5, and verbal IQ 58, as measured by Yugoslav standardization of Wechsler Adult Intelligence Scales. Their mean MLU in words was 4.8 (7 words in an average SC-speaking adult). The participants were individually matched on non-verbal MA to TD controls aged 5 and 6;11. A truth-value judgment task, used in Perovic (2001) with English speakers with DS, itself an adaptation from Chien and Wexler (1990), was translated into SC. This design has been used extensively in studies on the acquisition of pronominal reference crosslinguistically, both with TD children and those with developmental disorders. Participants are first presented with a picture of two cartoon characters involved in some action, and after introducing the characters, a yes-no question is presented: '*This is Cinderella. This is Snow White. Is Cinderella washing her?*' The SC version contained additional test conditions so that both full and clitic forms of pronouns and reflexives could be tested. The same verbs used in Perovic (2001) were used: 'dirati' (touch), 'prati' (wash) and 'brisati' (dry). As can be seen from the examples below, experimental questions reflected the umarked word order in SC: full pronouns and full reflexives were placed in the unmarked preverbal position whilst clitic forms occupied the obligatory second position. In addition to experimental questions that contained full or clitic form of a pronoun or reflexive, control conditions involving only proper names were used. To control for a positive (or negative) bias, for each test condition, there were eight questions that matched the picture and eight questions that did not match the picture. The total of 172 test questions was presented in the course of two or three experimental sessions.

Full pronoun/reflexive – referential antecedent:

(13)Da li Snežana nju/sebe pere?
comp prt Snow White *her/self* washing
'Is Snow White washing her/herself?'

Pronominal/reflexive clitic - referential antecedent:
(14)Da li je/se Snežana pere?
comp prt *her-cl/se-cl* Snow White washing
'Is Snow White washing her/herself?'

Full pronoun/reflexive – quantified antecedent:
(15)Da li svaka veštica nju/sebe pere?
comp prt every witch *her/self* washing
'Is every witch washing her/herself?'

Pronominal/reflexive clitic – quantified antecedent
(16)Da li je/se svaka veštica pere?
comp prt *her-cl/se-cl* every witch washing
'Is every witch washing her/herself?'

Control conditions involved both questions assessing participants' attention, e.g. 'Is Father Christmas sleeping?' where he is standing next to a bed, and questions that contained only proper names, in referential or quantified contexts: 'Is Snow White/every witch washing Cinderella?'

4. Results

The results are given in Tables 1-5. A mixed repeated measures ANOVA revealed significant effects for both the group (F $(1,10)$=13.99, p=0.004) and sentence type (F $(20,200)$=12.89, p<0.001), as well as a significant interaction (F $(20,200)$=2.27), p=0.002 between the two.

Table 1: Percentage correct on control conditions, match and mismatch

Group	name match	quant match	name mismatch	quant mismatch	attention mismatch
DS	95.9	91.6	100	83.4	91.6
TD	100	97.9	100	91.6	97.3

Table 2. Percentage correct on *match* conditions, full forms

Group	name pron	name reflex	quant pron	quant reflex
DS	89.6	89.6	91.6	91.6
TD	97.9	100	100	95.9

Table 3. Percentage correct on *match* conditions, clitic forms[8]

Group	name prn-cl	name refl-cl	quant prn-cl	qnt refl-cl
DS	87.5	97.9	89.6	89.6
TD	89.6	100	100	93.8

Control participants performed at ceiling on all conditions. Participants with DS also performed well on a number of test conditions. Their good performance on control conditions, which did not involve any pronouns or reflexives (Table 1), indicates that they understood the task and were able to answer both yes (match) and no (mismatch) questions appropriately. They also scored high on experimental match conditions with full forms of the pronouns and the reflexive (Table 2) and match conditions with clitic forms (Table 3). Independent samples t-test revealed no statistically significant differences between the two groups on these conditions.

The crucial results are in Table 4: while control children still performed at ceiling, participants with DS performed only slightly above chance on the mismatch conditions (requiring a negative answer) that involved the full form of the anaphor 'sebe': when the anaphor was bound by a referential antecedent (*name reflexive*), they reached 60% correct, and in contexts with quantified antecedents (*quantifier reflexive*), 66.6% correct. This is in stark contrast to their performance on the sentences involving personal pronouns, *name pronoun* and *quantifier pronoun* conditions, where they reached at least 90% correct. The independent samples t-tests confirmed that the scores of participants with DS differed significantly to those of the TD controls: $t(5)= -3.8$, $p=0.01$ for name-reflexive, and $t(5)= -3.63$, $p=0.01$ for quantifier-reflexive, both mismatch conditions. The difference between the group with DS and the matched controls on name-pronoun mismatch condition was also significant ($t(5)= -3.16$, $p=0.025$), even though the group with DS reached 91.6% correct on this condition.

Table 4. Percentage correct on mismatch conditions, full forms

Group	name pron	name reflex	quant pron	quant reflex
DS	91.6	60.4	89.6	66.6
TD	100	100	97.9	97.9

Table 5 shows that, in contrast to their poor performance on the full reflexive 'sebe' seen earlier, the group with DS showed good scores on the mismatch conditions that involve the reflexive clitic 'se': between 80 and 95% correct. They showed a generally good performance on pronominal clitic conditions, but their performance was lower on *quantifier pronominal clitic* condition ('quant prn-cl'): only 70.9% correct. On closer examination of individual scores it was revealed that this was due to one participant who got only 1 out of 8 correct on this condition (the standard deviation for this condition was 3.01).

Table 5. Percentage correct on mismatch conditions, clitic forms

Group	name prn-cl	name refl-cl	quant prn-cl	qnt refl-cl
DS	83.4	94.9	70.9	80
TD	97.9	93.6	97.9	93.6

To summarize, the participants with DS showed no particular difficulties with any of the test conditions except for those involving the anaphor 'sebe'. The control group performed at ceiling on all conditions.

5. Discussion

The findings of our study confirm the predictions made in section 2. We predicted that the SC-speaking participants with DS would show a performance parallel to that of the English-speaking individuals studied in Perovic (2001). They would obey conditions on reflexivity of predicates, as given in the framework of R & R, but show difficulties establishing the syntactic relation between the anaphor and its antecedent. These predictions are borne out. The participants correctly rejected a reflexive predicate that is not reflexive-marked, ruling out full pronouns and pronominal clitics when coarguments of reflexive predicates. This is in accordance with Condition B. Their knowledge of Condition A, that a reflexive-marked predicate must be reflexive, is seen in their correct interpretation of predicates involving the reflexive clitic. These are inherently reflexive predicates, already marked so in the lexicon. However, their performance on mismatch conditions involving the anaphor 'sebe' revealed a considerable difficulty with the interpretation of this element, which can only be interpreted as a deficit in establishing the syntactic relation between the anaphor and its antecedent. Future investigations, in English and crosslinguistically, are needed to shed more light on the nature of the deficiency in the grammar of DS and how these can be related to the deficiencies observed in the domain of syntactic binding.

A more general prediction stated earlier concerns the nature of language development in the population with DS. If the traditional characterisation of grammar in DS is correct, namely that language in DS is merely delayed, or at least, at the level of children matched on non-verbal MA, we should see no difference between the TD controls and our six adult participants with DS. Our data patently support the opposite view: the performance pattern seen in DS is *not* observed in TD controls who excelled in all test conditions. This makes the 'slow but normal' view of grammatical development in DS untenable.[9]

One issue worth of our attention is the difference in the performance pattern of English as opposed to SC-speaking individuals with DS. Notice that the parallel between the SC speakers' pattern here and that of English speakers in Perovic (2001) is observable in the mismatch *name reflexive* conditions only. English speakers with DS showed a poor performance in both the match and mismatch contexts – even when they were asked to provide a seemingly easier 'yes' response. One may suggest that SC-speaking participants were showing a stronger positive bias. If this were the case, their performance in mismatch conditions should be poorer than what was observed. It is more likely that these differences are due to different language-particular strategies the speakers of English and SC are using to interpret the anaphor. Let us assume that English-speaking participants treated the anaphor as a pronoun. As well as incorrectly accepting the non-local interpretation for the anaphor on mismatch conditions, they also incorrectly rejected the local interpretation of the anaphor on match conditions. This second pattern in fact reveals English participants' knowledge of Condition B: assuming that they treat the anaphor as a pronoun, this pattern shows that the participants know that a) pronouns are not reflexive-markers; and that b) coindexation of a pronoun and a referential antecedent must be ruled out.

The SC-speaking participants with DS did not seem to employ this strategy, if they did, they would have shown a high percentage of negative answers to the match reflexive conditions, as these questions would have been interpreted as violations of both Condition B, the knowledge of which they have. The difference in the performance patterns can be attributed to the different grammatical properties of anaphoric elements in English and SC. English anaphors are complex anaphors, consisting of both the 'self' element and the pronoun marked for all phi features. Thus it is possible that the English participants ignored the 'self' element, paying attention to the pronoun part and in effect ruling it out in accordance with the Condition B. The SC anaphor 'sebe' is morphologically simpler and does not contain a pronoun. Although marked for case, it is not marked for number, person or gender. These properties of 'sebe' make it impossible for the SC-speaking participants with DS to treat it as a pronoun and match it to any particular antecedent based on phi features agreement between the anaphor and its antecedent.[10] To determine the reference of the anaphor, they could choose its antecedent on the basis of its accessibility in the discourse (in terms of hierarchy of the discourse prominence of the antecedent of Ariel, 1990). The most accessible antecedent is the one provided in the experimental question: 'Is Snow White *sebe* washing?' In the mismatch contexts, where the Snow White is being washed by someone else, the participants would give an incorrect 'yes' answer. In the match contexts, where Snow White is indeed involved in the action of washing herself, this is a correct answer. The choice of the 'correct' local antecedent need not reveal the knowledge of anaphoric binding but the same strategy of choosing the most accessible/discourse prominent antecedent. The SC-speaking participants therefore reveal the same deficit in anaphoric binding as their English counterparts, but distinct grammatical properties of anaphors in SC and English force them to adopt different strategies in attempting to interpret the anaphoric element, resulting in slightly different performance patterns on our experimental task.

6. Conclusions

This paper provides further evidence for a syntactic deficit in DS, in speakers of SC, supporting and extending the findings of Perovic (2001) and Ring & Clahsen (2003) in English DS. It was shown that adult speakers of SC with DS obey the conditions on reflexivity as given in the framework of R&R, but have difficulties forming the syntactic dependency of anaphoric binding. These findings have important implications for the theory of binding. They support the proposed fractionation of binding into syntactic and extra-syntactic components, as proposed in R&R (1993), Grodzinsky and Reinhart (1993). Here the interpretation of anaphoric elements is limited to syntax proper, whereas the coreferential interpretation of pronouns is governed by extra-grammatical constraints. While the literature on the acquisition of binding in TD supports this fractionation in one direction, by documenting that TD children have difficulties in applying the extra-grammatical constraint, the data presented here run in the opposite direction: our participants with DS revealed an inability to interpret anaphoric elements, a task in the realm of syntax proper.

Notes

*I would like to thank all the participants and staff at 'Milan Petrovic' secondary school, 'Radosno Detinjstvo' kindergarten in Novi Sad, Serbia, and the art workshop 'Pohvala Ruci' in Belgrade, Serbia. This work is based on my PhD thesis completed at University College London in 2004. I am grateful to GALA 2005 audience for helpful comments.

[1] Note that for the full classification of pronominal elements in world's languages both properties must be taken into account. See R&R for details of how the interplay of these properties can explain the tripartite distinction of pronominal system in Dutch. Dutch has two anaphoric elements: 'zichzelf' and 'zich', but only 'zichzelf' is a reflexive marker.

[2] The pronoun is also excluded by the revised Chain Condition, see R&R.

[3] Everart (1986) argues that some English verbs are ambiguous between being inherently reflexive and purely transitive predicates (e.g. *shave*, *wash*), with each of these occurrences listed separately in the lexicon.

[4] See Reinhart & Siloni (2005) for an updated view of how reflexive predicates are generated in Romance.

[5] They are also excluded from this position by the Chain Condition.

[6] The anaphor is not fully specified for structural case: like all anaphors, it lacks Nominative.

[7] According to Reinhart & Siloni (2005), SC belongs to the group of languages where arity operations affecting the syntactic valency of the predicate, including reflexivization, apply in syntax, and not in the lexicon. This implies that reflexivization is a productive process, where the reflexive clitic *se* is able to appear with any transitive predicate. The productivity of this operation in SC is questionable, however. The SC data discussed in Reinhart & Siloni that shows the availability of the clitic with ordinary transitive predicates is not readily accepted by all native speakers of SC. The example 12 shows the ungrammaticality of the reflexive clitic with an experiencer verb 'love', but this is not limited to experiencer verbs only – the clitic is unacceptable, if not completely ungrammatical, with any verb that is not inherently reflexive:
(i) 'Jovan ???se/sebe crta.'
   Jovan se/self draws
   Jovan draws himself.
The same holds of the ECM contexts, another diagnostics of Reinhart and Siloni where the reflexive clitic signals that reflexivization in a language takes place in syntax:
(ii) 'Jovan *se/sebe smatra pametnim
   Jovan se considers clever
   Jovan considers himself clever.

[8] Only the data on the conditions involving the verbs 'dry' and 'wash' are given for the conditions involving the reflexive clitic, due to a possible confounding reading that allows both reflexive and non-reflexive reading with the verb 'touch' (see Perovic 2004a for this effect in young TD children and the explanation based on Rivero, 1999; Stojanovic, 2002).

[9] One could argue that comparing the results of participants with DS to controls whose ceiling performance suggests binding is fully acquired (regardless of the matching done

on non-verbal MA) is not informative. Perhaps the grammatical development in the individuals with DS is somehow 'arrested' so parallels can be found with earlier stages of typical development, in very young children acquiring SC. This in fact is not the case: Perovic (2004b) reported data from an identical experiment with four groups of TD children acquiring SC, the youngest being 3;6, and the oldest 7. Difficulties with anaphors but not with other pronominal elements, seen in DS, were not detected in any of the TD groups.

[10] See Perovic (2004a) for a discussion on whether the SC anaphor could be treated in the fashion of the Japanese logophoric element 'zibun'.

References

Ariel, M. (1990) *Accessing Noun-phrase Antecedents*. Routledge, London.

Chien Y-C. and K. Wexler, (1990) "Children's knowledge of locality conditions in binding as evidence for the modularity of syntax and pragmatics." *Language Acquisition* 1: 225-295.

Chomsky, N. (1981) *Lectures on Government and Binding*. Dordrecht: Foris.

—. (1986) *Knowledge of Language: Its Nature, Origin and Use*. New York: Praeger.

Everaert, M. (1986) *The Syntax of Reflexivization*. Dordrecht: Foris.

Fowler, A. (1990) "Language abilities in children with Down syndrome: evidence for a specific delay." In D. Cicchetti and M. Beeghley, eds., *Children with Down syndrome: A Developmental Perspective*. Cambridge: Cambridge University Press.

Franks, S. and P. Connell, (1996) Knowledge of binding in normal and SLI children. *Journal of Child Language, 23.2,* 431-464.

Grodzinsky, Y. and T. Reinhart, (1993) "The innateness of binding and coreference." *Linguistic Inquiry* 24: 69-101.

Jakubowicz, C. (1984) "On markedness and binding principles." In C. Jones and P. Sells, eds., *NELS 14*. Amherst: University of Massachusetts.

Kayne, R. (1975) *French Syntax. The Transformational Cycle*. Cambridge Mass: MIT Press.

Perovic, A. (2001) Binding Principles in Down Syndrome. *UCL Working Papers in Linguistics 13*.

—. (2004a) *Knowledge of Binding in Down Syndrome: Evidence from English and Serbo-Croatian*. PhD Thesis, University College London.

—. (2004b) *Acquisition of Binding in Serbian: More on the (lack of) Delay of Principle B Effect*. Presented at Formal Approaches to Slavic Linguistics 13.

Reinhart, T. (1996) Syntactic Effects of Lexical Operations: Reflexives and Unaccusatives. *OTS Working Papers in Linguistics. University of Utrecht.*

—. and T. Siloni, (2005) The Lexicon-Syntax Parameter: reflexivization and other arity operations. *Linguistic Inquiry* 36.3.

—. and E. Reuland, (1993) "Reflexivity." *Linguistic Inquiry* 24: 657-720.

Ring, M. and H. Clahsen (2003) *Syntactic Dependencies in Down's Syndrome (and Williams Syndrome): New Results from Passives and Binding.* Paper presented at Generative Approaches to Language Acquisition. UiL OTS/Utrecht University.

Rivero, M. (1999) On impersonal *się* in Polish: A simplex expression anaphor. *Journal of Slavic Linguistics* 8.1.

Rondal J. and J. Lambert, (1985) The speech of mentally retarded adults in a dyadic communication situation: Some formal and informative aspects. *Psychologica Belgica* 23:49-56.

Stojanović, D. (2002) *The Acquisition of Pronominal Categories.* Ms. University of Ottawa.

THE PUZZLE OF MIXED AGREEMENT IN EARLY CODE MIXING[*]

CRISTINA PIERANTOZZI, CATERINA DONATI, LAURA BONTEMPI, AND LETIZIA GASPERONI

1. Introduction

The Minimalist Program had a very profound impact on our understanding of many linguistic phenomena, and language mixing is no exception. Its essential methodological lesson, basically that of scientific parsimony, was particularly important in a field where empirical facts were traditionally accounted for by simple stipulations of ad hoc constraints and 'principles' (see McSwan 2001 for a critical review). On a more conceptual ground, the reduction of grammar to a computational procedure operating on a lexicon, led MacSwan (2001; 2005) to a model of the bilingual competence in which code mixing is the result of selecting and computing lexical items belonging to two different lexicons (i.e. two languages). As a consequence, "nothing constrains code switching apart from the requirements of the mixed grammars" (MacSwan 2001, 43).

This paper discusses how such an elegant and simple framework might account for some puzzling asymmetries observable in mixed DPs. It reports the first results of a vast project aiming at comparing the code-mixing productions of early bilinguals in languages crucially differing in the features they realize.

Starting from the generalization proposed by Spradlin et al. (2003) that in mixed DPs bilinguals prefer the D endowed with more uninterpretable F's (section 1), section 2 verifies its crosslinguistic validity on a set of bilingual children (two French/English, one Dutch/English, one Italian/Spanish): after excluding external factors such as language dominance, the results are discussed, which point to a weaker version of the initial claim. Section 3 focuses on the curious phenomenon of mixed agreement, where a determiner in language A agrees with the covert equivalent in the same language of the noun actually selected in language B. Section 4 discusses these facts as an argument against lexicalism and draws some conclusions.

2. Preferences in mixed DPs

The point of departure is an interesting observation reported in Spradlin et al. (2003) with respect to 4 Spanish/English bilingual children, who all display a strong preference (close to 100%) for the Spanish D + English N pattern (1a) over the opposite (1b).

(1)   a. esta bike (Simon 2;6.)
        b. this niña (Manuela 1;11.)

Analogous preferences rates are reported in adult Spanish/English bilinguals (Myers-Scotton (2002), Moro (2001)). Spradlin et al. (2003) propose the following generalization to account for this asymmetry.

(2)   GENERALIZATION: In mixed DPs children prefer the D endowed with more uninterpretable F's.

3. Verifying the generalization

In order to check the crosslinguistic validity of the generalization in (2), we studied the natural production of a number of children, basically belonging to two groupings: the 'English grouping', made of two French English boys (Gene 1;10.26 - 3;7.17 and Olivier 1;10.5 - 3;06.14: Genesee and Paradis (1995)), and one Dutch English girl (Kate 2;7.12- 3;3.16: De Houwer (1990)), all CHILDES files; the 'Italian grouping', consisting of two German Italian children (Leucò from 2;0 and Rebecca from 2;1), and one Italian Spanish girl (Lucia from 1;6.25: Bontempi (2006)), whose data are still being collected. For the second group we shall present here only the data concerning Lucia.

The idea under such data collection is that of comparing the mixing patterns in the DP domain in two main groups of bilinguals: one acquiring languages realizing an equal number of phi-features in the nominal domain (Italian/Spanish) and the other one acquiring languages realizing a different number of phi-features (English/French, English/Dutch, Italian/German).

In order to be sure that our conclusions have some general validity, we need first to exclude that any asymmetry we might observe is due to some external factor, such as language dominance. In other words, if a subject X shows a preference for determiners in language A in mixed DPs, we need to be sure that this is not due to X being dominant in A

In order to do so, we adopted two strategies. First, we relied on external factors, selecting children raised in a One Parent One Language (OPOL) environment, the most likely to yield balanced simultaneous bilingualism;

second, we measured their relative competence in the two languages with a battery of standard criteria (adapted from Genesee and Paradis (1995))[1]. The data concerning all the subjects are comparable in that they are all are essentially balanced. More precisely, Gene is perfectly so; Olivier is slightly French dominant; Kate is slightly English dominant; Lucia is slightly Italian dominant. We can therefore exclude that any generalization we might draw from the data is due to an external factor such as dominance.

We then need to be sure that our subjects are indeed producing a relevant number of mixed DPs, i.e. that the phenomenon is really productive. Our data display a robust mixing in the DP domain, as shown in the table (3).

(3)   (4)

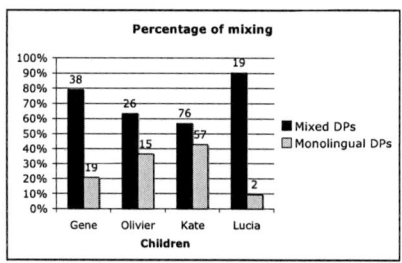
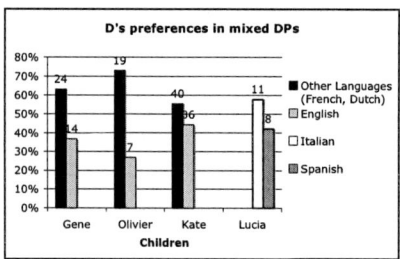

Given that all four children do massively mix the DPs they produce[2], we can proceed to verify the validity of the generalization (2) we started from. Consider table (4) reporting the relevant data both in absolute numbers and in percentages[3].

Some examples are given in (5) for Kate, Gene, Olivier, and Lucia, respectively.

(5)   a.   in de kitchen (k09 3;0.06)
           in the kitchen
      b.   une ball (gen23b07f 2;06.29)
           a   ball
      c.   in la house (oli23b06m 2;06.03)
           in the house
      d.   l'avión (Lu20 2;00.19)
           the airplane

All four children display some asymmetry in their mixed DPs. In particular the French/English children present a preference that seems to confirm the generalization in (2): they appear to prefer the determiner endowed with more uninterpretable features (i.e. French) over the English one. Lucia, on the other hand, acquiring two languages with a very similar determiner system, does not show any significant preference, as predicted.

The results concerning Dutch are however problematic: while Dutch determiners are indeed endowed with more uninterpretable features (displaying the gender vs. non gender distinction) they are not significantly preferred by Kate. This might be due to an extra factor conditioning mixing directionality, namely frequency in the input. While French (and Spanish) determiners are much more frequent than the English ones because they cannot be virtually omitted, this asymmetry does not hold for Dutch determiners, which exhibit more ore less the same omission possibilities as the English counterparts. If this factor is really what is responsible for the flatness of the Dutch data, then the explicative power of (2) might turn out to be much weaker. As for the difference between the two French/English children, the more dramatic preference displayed by Olivier might be a byproduct of his slight French dominance.

As a conclusion of this quick crosslinguistic testing, the generalization proposed by Spradlin et al. (2003) does not seem to hold very strongly. In Spanish/English and French/English children, where the predicted asymmetry is indeed observed, it might be due to some acquisitional factor: either the frequency in the input, as suggested by the Dutch data, or those other factors which make acquiring determiners in French and Spanish easier for monolinguals as well (Kupisch (2003);(2006); Chierchia et al (1999, 2001)).

4. Understanding mixed agreement

Rather than pursuing asymmetries that do not seem to hold very robustly, it is worth looking at what appears to be a systematic and rather peculiar phenomenon of mixing in the DP domain: what we might call mixed agreement.

Recall first of all that frequently (if not dominantly) mixed DPs combine a determiner displaying an uninterpretable feature with a noun lacking such a feature. An interesting question is how feature checking might go in this frequent situation, and how come such a 'mismatch' is tolerated by grammar.[4] Besides this theoretical issue, there is also an empirical question that arises in relation to agreement in mixed DPs: specifically, when a child uses a determiner displaying gender features together with a genderless noun, what gender does the determiner realize?

Before looking at the agreement patterns in mixed DPs and answer these questions, we need to check whether the children under investigation are indeed competent in realizing agreement in monolingual DPs. Tables (6) through (9) illustrate such competence respectively in Kate, Gene, Olivier, Lucia[5].

(6) Kate

Age	Dutch DP		English DP	
	agree	mismatches	agree	Mismatches
2;7.12 - 2;9	82 (91%)	8 (9%)	6 (75%)	2 (25%)
2;10.05 - 3;0.17	102 (84%)	19 (16%)	9 (100%)	0 (0%)
3;01.06 - 3;03.16	86 (83%)	18 (17%)	17 (100%)	0 (0%)
Tot.	270 (86%)	44 (14%)	32 (94%)	2 (6%)

(7) Gene

Age	French DP		English DP	
	agree	mismatches	agree	mismatches
1;10.28 - 1;10.26	8 (89%)	1 (11%)	0 (0%)	0 (0%)
2;6.29 - 2;7.05	24 (100%)	0 (0%)	1 (100%)	0 (0%)
3;0.14 - 3;0.20	9 (100%)	0 (0%)	3 (100%)	0 (0%)
3;7.17 - 3;7.09	14 (93%)	1 (7%)	3 (100%)	0 (0%)
Tot.	55 (96%)	2 (4%)	7 (100%)	0 (0%)

(8) Olivier

Age	French DP		English DP	
	agree	mismatches	agree	mismatches
1;10.05 - 1;11.15	57 (92%)	5 (8%)	1 (100%)	0 (0%)
2;03.20 - 2;6.03	140 (89%)	17 (11%)	0 (0%)	0 (0%)
2;09.03 - 2;11.15	90 (94%)	6 (6%)	7 (70%)	3 (30%)
3;06.09 - 3;06.14	51 (96%)	2 (4%)	1 (50%)	1 (50%)
Tot.	338 (92%)	30 (8%)	9 (69%)	4 (31%)

(9) Lucia

Age	Italian DP		Spanish DP	
	agree	mismatches	agree	mismatches
1:6.25 - 1;7.28	2 (67%)	1 (33%)	6 (100%)	0 (0%)
1:8.04 - 1;9.14	10 (100%)	0 (0%)	4 (100%)	0 (0%)
1:10.00 - 1;11.23	25 (93%)	2 (7%)	27 (93%)	2 (7%)
2:00.01 - 2;02.02	71 (100%)	0 (0%)	27 (96%)	1 (4%)
Tot.	108 (97%)	3 (3%)	64 (96%)	3 (4%)

As the tables show, all four children display a very low percentage of errors, with the relative exception of Kate, who produce respectively a 17% error rate in Dutch in her third stage (see De Houwer (1990) for details)[6]. We can conclude from this survey that all four children have a good agreement competence in the DP domain.

We can now face the empirical question raised above: how does agreement manifest in mixed DPs when the determiner displays gender features and the noun does not? Let us keep aside the Spanish/Italian case for a moment, where such a problem does not hold.

A first possibility that comes to mind is that children might exploit a default strategy, therefore realizing the determiner in a default gender: masculine in French, gender in Dutch. This does not seem to be the case, however: although the default gender is more frequent in children production, the non default one is also attested. Therefore, the issue of what the source of gender agreement is turns out to be a real one.

A second possibility is that the bilingual child gets the gender of the determiner from the gender of the covert equivalent of the noun selected in the mixed DP. By covert equivalent, we mean the noun of the non selected language which is semantically closer to the noun actually uttered in the selected language. To clarify, in the example in (5.c) the gender displayed by the French determiner (feminine, hence not default) matches the gender of *maison*, the covert equivalent of the selected English *house*.

We checked this hypothesis, verifying how frequently the gender lexicalized on the determiner agrees with the (covert) equivalent. In the following tables we reported the agreement patterns in mixed DPs for the three English grouping children, respectively: we counted in how many cases the gender selected on the determiner matches the covert equivalent of the selected English noun.

(10) Kate

Age	D (Dutch) + N (English)	
	agree	mismatches
2;7.12 - 2;9	17 (89%)	2 (11%)
2;10.05 - 3;0.17	9 (75%)	3 (25%)
3;01.06 - 3;03.16	11 (79%)	3 (21%)
Tot.	37 (79%)	8 (21%)

(11) Gene

Age	D (French) + N (English)	
	Agree	mismatches
1;10.28 - 1;10.26	7 (100%)	0 (0%)
2;6.29 - 2;7.05	6 (100%)	0 (0%)
3;0.14 - 3;0.20	3 (75%)	1 (25%)
3;7.17 - 3;7.09	5 (71%)	2 (29%)
Tot.	21 (88%)	3 (12%)

(12) Olivier

Age	D (French) + N (English)	
	agree	mismatches
1;10.05 - 1;11.15	0 (0%)	0 (0%)
2;01.29 - 2;06.03	14 (82%)	3 (18%)
2;09.03 - 2;10.29	1 (100%)	0 (0%)
3;06.09 - 3;06.14	1 (100%)	0 (0%)
Tot.	16 (84%)	3 (16%)

As the tables show, the mixed DPs display what we might call mixed agreement: the determiner matches its gender feature with the covert equivalent of the selected noun. Notice also that the error rate reported in the tables includes number mismatches, as well as gender mismatches. This means that mixed gender agreement might be even more systematic.

What these data show is that bilingual children are capable of deducing a feature needed for computation, i.e. gender, from a lexical item superficially not selected in the computation itself. This possibility, which appears to be rather systematic, sheds a surprising light on the mechanisms involved in mixing and in computation in general.

Before getting to the discussion of what theoretical consequences we might draw from this, let us see what happens when the two languages involved share all the relevant features in the DP domain: Italian and Spanish are a good illustration. If that of accessing the silent lexicon were a kind of an emergency strategy for computing weird DPs and get a missing feature, we would expect this never to happen when there is no feature mismatch in mixed DPs, as is the case with Spanish and Italian, where both the determiner and the noun agree for gender and number.

Notice that not all Italian nouns and all Spanish nouns overlap in their gender: although rare, there are cases of gender non-correspondence between the noun selected in the mixed DP and the covert equivalent. What will be the gender the determiner agrees with in these cases? That of the actually selected noun or that of the covert equivalent? We counted all the (few) cases of mixed

DPs involving nouns belonging to gender mismatching pairs. There are only three relevant cases in Lucia's corpus, all produced in the last two stages and belonging to the Italian D+Spanish NP pattern.

(13) a.   Il flor (Lu20 2;00.19) (la flor/il fiore)
          the flower
     b.   Le zapatos (Lu17 2;00.01) (los zapatos/le scarpe)
          the shoes
     c.   Il plátano (Lu18 2;00.01 twice) (el plátano/la banana)
          the banana

Although there are so few relevant cases, they are enough to show that the mixed agreement pattern is indeed available to the bilingual child even when it is not needed as a repair strategy: in (13), Lucia chooses to match the selected determiner with the covert equivalent in (a) and (b), in what seems to be a free choice with respect to the alternative (c).

5. Theoretical considerations and conclusions

The agreement patterns displayed in mixed DPs show that the derivation of a DP can access grammatical information from two lexical items available to the bilingual child: the two corresponding nouns in the two languages associated with the determiner. More precisely, in order to derive a DP like (13a) *il flor*, Lucia must compute at the same time the morpho-phonological features associated with the Spanish lexical entry (*flor*) and the gender feature associated with the Italian lexical entry (*fiore*). This seems to be a clear and systematic component of the bilingual competence, as shown by the mixed agreement pattern displayed by all the children we have investigated.

This kind of data might provide an argument against a lexicalist approach to computation, where syntax is driven and governed by the necessity of checking the features of fully inflected lexical items (Chomsky (1995)). Cases like (13a) presuppose a dissociation between the *form* of the word selected and its *grammatical feature* (e.g. gender), which seems to support on the contrary a "late insertion" model *à la* Distributed Morphology, where the lexicalization is dissociated from the features computed in the derivation (Marantz (1997)).[7]

To clarify this point, let us compare two possible implementations of the two approaches with respect to the bilingual competence. (14) is a tentative modification of Harley and Noyer (1999), which is to be compared to the classical bilexicon model proposed in MacSwan (2001).

(14)

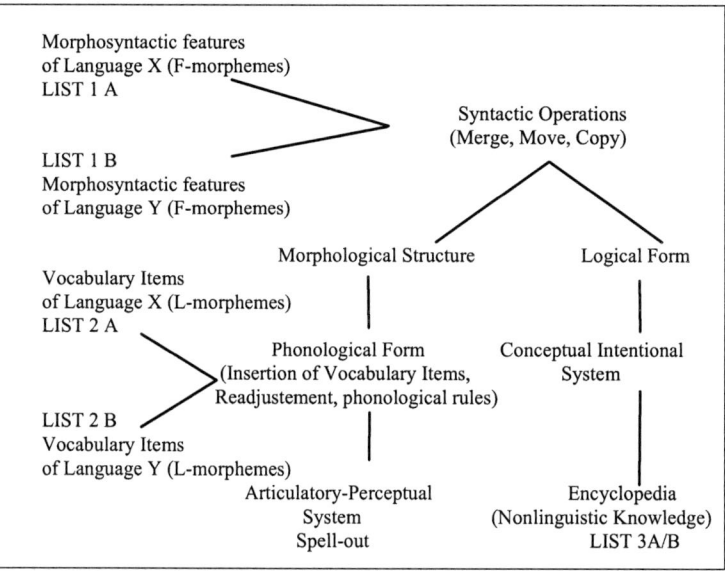

As for McSwan's model, which is lexicalist in spirit, there is no way for the child to dissociate the features available to computation: they all come in bundles (i.e. lexical items) from either lexicon A or lexicon B. The patterns of mixed agreement described in last section are thus underivable from the architecture of grammar unless we posit special mixing rules departing from the minimalist program.

As for the model in (14), it can easily derive the relevant pattern if the child can select an array of F-morphemes from list 1 in language A, and lexicalize them selecting the corresponding L-morphemes from list 2 in language B. This model, positing a double list for each level of insertion, may run the opposite risk of being too powerful and overgenerate. In what follows let us try to list the possible combinations given such a model and to figure out what are their actual realizations, if any.

The first possible combination, (15), where all the features at both levels are taken from one language list, clearly triggers monolingual DPs.

(15) Morphosyntactic Level: List 1A
      Vocabulary Item: List 2A

All the remaining combinations trigger some kind of mixing at different levels. As for the combination in (16), where the uniform selection of formal features from one and only language list corresponds to a mixed lexicalization, it triggers what we have called mixed agreement patterns, such as, say, *la house*, *il flor* or *le zapatos*.

(16) Morphosyntactic Level: List 1A
      Vocabulary Item: List 2A + List 2B

(17) sketches another possible combination: the selection of F-morphemes from language A is entirely lexicalized with L-morphemes in language B.

(17) Morphosyntactic Level: List 1A
      Vocabulary Item: List 2B

This combination might correctly characterize a frequent phenomenon in bilinguals, namely syntactic calque, as illustrated by strings such as *the house green* uttered by a French/English bilingual.

Another possible combination, listed in (18), might trigger a case such as *el flor*, which is superficially monolingual, but shows a mixed agreement pattern (recall that *flor* is feminine while *fiore* is masculine). This kind of pseudo-monolingual production is indeed attested in our corpus (Lucia 20 2;00.19).[8]

(18) Morphosyntactic Level: List 1A + List 1B
      Vocabulary Item: List 2A

As for the last a priori possible combination (19), it can be interpreted as the pattern underlying such productions as *il plátano*, where a mixed lexicalization corresponds to a mixed grammatical agreement (recall that *plátano* is masculine while *banana* is feminine).

(19) Morphosyntactic Level: List 1A + List 1B
      Vocabulary Item: List 2A + List 2B

From this overly quick review of the predictions of the late insertion model proposed, we can simply say very tentatively that it appears to be able to generate the patterns of mixing that are attested. What the model cannot predict, on the other hand, is a hierarchy of the different types of mixing. More precisely, the model does not predict the kind of asymmetry we started the paper from, namely the preference for the determiner endowed with more formal features, very robustly attested in some language pairings (e.g. Spanish/English,

French/English) and less so in others (e.g. Dutch/English, Italian/Spanish). If we suppose however that being able to use lists belonging to different languages is a salient characteristic of a bilingual I-language (cf. the Bilingual Mode: Grosjean (2001)), then we might interpret this preference as a preference for the only way to realize those mixed agreement patterns which are as the core manifestation of this specific competence.

Notes

* We need to thank the audience of the GALA conference for precious comments and suggestions, together with the students of the Seminar of linguistics of Urbino, where an earlier version of the talk was presented. Thanks are also due to Jürgen Meisel, Regina Köppe, Maria Goldbach and Tanja Kupisch for their comments and critiques. Finally, the paper benefited from some observations by the editors of the volume, whom we thank.
[1] For Gene and Olivier, similar measurements have been realized by Genesee and Paradis (1995); for Kate see De Houwer (1990). For sake of uniformity, we nevertheless calculated again the performance of all subjects, which we cannot report here for obvious reasons of space. All the details about the actual criteria and all the graphs reporting the relevant measurements for all subjects are however available for consultation at www.uniurb.it/docenti/donati/pubblicazioni.
[2] Notice that Kate produces less mixed DPs than the other children (table (7)). This might be simply due to the fact that her recordings start later (age 2;7 vs. Gene 1;10, Olivier 1;11.10, Lucia 1;6). See Meisel (1994) and Köppe and Meisel (1995) showing that mixings are especially productive in the very first stages of acquisition.
[3] Since our study was only focused on DPs internal structure, we extracted the DPs from their context without paying any attention to such factors as the syntactic position, the completeness of the utterance etc. For the graphs (3) and (4) we counted as determiners: definite and indefinite articles and protoarticles, quantifiers, demonstratives and possessives. For reasons made clear in note 5, we adopted slightly different criteria in relation to tables (6) through (9), evaluating the agreement competence in monolingual DPs for the various children: see note 5. In all cases, we excluded all the DPs which were compatible with an analysis in both languages, namely the ones containing words belonging to both lexicons, e.g. *water* for English/Dutch; *toast* for English/French, and the many words shared by Italian and Spanish; *mano, casa, piscina* etc.
[4] MacSwan faces this potential problem for his bi-lexicon approach in MacSwan (2005, 18), proposing a technical solution which does not go very far. See also Radford et al. (to appear).
[5] In order to dress the tables in (6) through (9) we included in the counting only the determiners displaying overt agreement given the agreement rules of the various languages. This means that for French, Italian and Spanish we included: definite and indefinite articles, demonstratives and possessives; for English only demonstratives; for Dutch definite and indefinite articles (the latter only in combination with an adjective) and demonstratives.
[6] Olivier displays a 50% error rate in his third stage, but this does not seem to be very significant given that it is calculated on the basis of only two DPs.

[7] See Liceras et al. (2005) for a recent revision of the generalization in (2) in the DM framework.

[8] This kind of (apparently) monolingual DPs have been counted in the tables above among the "mismatching monolingual DPs".

References

Bontempi, L. (2006) *Lucia, una bambina bilingue*, MA Thesis, University of Urbino.

Chomsky, N. (1995) *The minimalist program*, Cambridge, Mass, MIT Press.

Chierchia, G., M. T. Guasti and A. Gualmini (1999) "Early omission of articles and the syntax/semantics map", paper presented at Gala, Potsdam.

—., M. T. Guasti and A. Gualmini (2001) "Nouns and articles in child grammar and the syntax/semantics map", Manuscript, University of Milan/University of Siena/University of Maryland, College Park.

De Houwer, A. (1990) *The acquisition of two languages from birth, a case study* Cambridge, Cambridge University Press.

Gasperoni, L. (2005) *I veux conter mon story*, MA Thesis, University of Urbino.

Grosjean, F. (2001) "The bilingual's language modes", in J. L. Nicol (eds.) *One mind, two Languages: bilingual language processing*, Oxford, Blackwell, 1-22

Harley, H. and R. Noyer, (1999) "Distributed morphology", *GLOT International* 4.

Liceras, J.M, K.T. Spradlin and R. Fernández (2005) "Bilingual early functional-lexical mixing and the activation of formal features". *International Journal of Bilingualism*, 9, 227-253.

Köppe, R. and J. Meisel, (1995) "Code-swiching in bilingual first language acquisition", in L. Milroy & Muysken, eds, *One speaker, two languages*, Cambridge, Cambridge University Press, 276-301.

Kupisch, T. (2003) "The DP. A vulnerable domain?", in N. Müller (ed.), *(In)vulnerable domains in multilingualism*, Amsterdam, Benjamins, 1-39.

—. (2006) "The emergence of article forms and functions in the language acquisition of a German-Italian bilingual child", in Lleò, C., ed., *Interfaces in multilingualism*, Amsterdam, Benjamins, 139-177.

MacSwan, J. (2001) "The architecture of the bilingual language faculty, evidence from intrasentential code-switching", *Bilingualism, Language and Cognition* 8, 1-22.

—. (2005) "Codeswitching and generative grammar, A critique of the MLF model and some remarks on 'modified minimalism", *Bilingualism, Language and Cognition* 3, 37-54.

MacWhinney, B. (2000) *The CHILDES project, tools for analyzing talk*, Hillsdale, NJ, Erlbaum.

Marantz, A. (1997) "No escape from syntax. Don't try morphological analysis in the privacy of your own lexicon", in A. Dimitriadis, L. Siegel et al. (eds.) *Proceedings of the 21 Annual Penn Linguistics Colloquium*, University of Pennsylvania Working Papers in Linguistics 24, 201-225.

Meisel, J. (1994) "Code-Switching in young bilingual children, the acquisition of grammatical constraints", *Studies in second Language Acquisition*16, 413-441.

Moro, M. (2001) "The semantic interpretation and syntactic distribution of determiner phrases in Spanish/English code switching", paper presented at the 3rd International Symposium on Bilingualism (ISB3), Bristol UK.

Paradis, J. and F. Genesee (1995) "Language differentiation in early bilingual development", *Journal of Child Language* 22, 611-631.

Radford, A., Kupisch, T., Köppe, R. and Azzaro, G. (to appear) "Concord, Convergence and Accomodation in Bilingual Children", *Bilingualism, Language and Cognition*.

Spradlin, K. T., J. Liceras and R. Fernandéz, (2003) "Functional-Lexicon Code-Mixing patterns as evidence for language dominance in young bilingual children, a Minimalist approach", in J. M. Liceras et al., eds., *Proceedings of 6th Generative Approach to Second Language Acquisition Conference (GASLA 2002)*, Somerville, MA, Cascadilla Proceeding Project, 298-307.

THE ACQUISITION OF OBJECT CLITICS IN FRENCH L1: SPONTANEOUS VS. ELICITED PRODUCTION

MIHAELA PIRVULESCU

1. Introduction

Results from research on spontaneous speech found that there is an important delay in the acquisition of object clitics when compared to other clitic elements such as pronominal subject clitics, reflexives and determiners (Hamann et al. 1996, Müller et al. 1996, Jakubowicz et al. 1996, Jakubowicz et Rigaut 1997, Van der Velde et al. 2002, Friedemann 1992, Hamann 2003, Mueller 2004). What are the children using while object clitics are not yet fully acquired? Previous research suggests contradictory answers according to whether one looks at spontaneous versus elicited production data; more specifically, it seems that in spontaneous production children prefer DPs (Jakubowicz et al. 1996, 1997 ; van der Velde et al. 2002) while in elicited production they prefer omissions (Pérez-Leroux et al. 2005, Schmitz et al. 2004; Jakubowicz et al. 1996). The divergent results bear on the status of null objects in child grammar while clitics are not yet fully acquired. The debate is whether the child grammar allows free object deletion without clitic recoverability, as opposed to adult grammar.

In this paper I will take a closer look at the rates of omission in two new spontaneous corpora and compare them with previous results from spontaneous and elicited production. I will show that the difference between the rates of omission in spontaneous versus elicited production is the result of the decision on what counts as the context for the production of clitics in spontaneous production. When a common methodology is used, there is no contradiction in the data: omission across modality is a robust phenomenon in early French.

2. The object clitic construction

Constructions requiring/permitting object pronominalization in French express this object as a pronominal clitic surfacing at the left of the finite verb of the clause as in (1):

(1) A: Tu veux ce livre ?   "You want this book?"
     B: Oh ! Mais je l'ai déjà lu.   "But I already read it."

Extensive research on the early acquisition of French reveals that pronominal clitics in object position are acquired later than other clitics (such as subject pronouns, reflexives and determiners). While the object clitics are not fully acquired, one can find in child production omissions where a pronominal clitic would be expected according to adult performance as in the following example from Müller et al. 1996 (the underlined gaps are placed where pronominals would be expected on the surface):

(2) Adult: On peut le manger, l'oeuf?   "Can we eat it, the egg?"
     Child: Tu peux _ manger, oui.   "You can eat _, yes."

What is the status of these constructions? In order to properly explore this question, a look at adult possibilities is required. Studies of spoken French show that similar constructions exist in adult French. Such constructions are identified as "latent objects" (Larjavaara 2000), "definite null complements" (Lambrecht and Lemoine 2004) or "clitic-drop constructions" (Cummins and Roberge 2005). Examples are provided in (3) below (from Larjavaara 2000):

(3) a. On lui tendit une main. Pas besoin d'aide. Vexé, il _ négligea et se releva...
        "A hand was extended to him. Don't need help. Annoyed, he ignored _ and got up..."
     b. A: Maîtrisez-vous vos interviews? C'est capital, les interviews.
        B: Je _ maîtrise.
        "Do you master your interviews? Interviews are very important."
        "I master _."

Constructions such as (3) seem to be freely available to adults, as the constraints on their use seem to be mainly stylistic or pragmatic. The adult use of this type of construction "results from a choice on the part of the speaker, the null pronoun alternating with an overt lexical or pronominal expression." (Lambrecht and Lemoine 2004:21). Current literature on the issue stresses two important facts: first, that this construction is equivalent to one in which a clitic would normally be used; and second, that the non-realized object in (3) has syntactic reality, i.e. there is a null-instantiated complement in argument position (Lambrecht and Lemoine 2004, Cummins and Roberge 2005).

From the perspective of language acquisition the constructions in (2) and (3) raise several questions. First, from the empirical point of view: what is the importance of constructions such as (2) in child production, and with respect to adult ones? Are these constructions abundant or are they insignificant? Is there a trade-off between omissions and clitics or between DPs and clitics? Second, from the theoretical point of view: what is the proper syntactic analysis of the construction in (2)? What is the relation between a child construction as in (2) and an adult construction such as (3)? Is (2) the result of a grammatical option that is used by the child in an adult-like manner?

Before tackling the theoretical question, there is still need, as I will show in the next section, to clarify what the answer is for the first question: what is the importance of omission constructions in child language and what is the child using while he has not yet mastered the pronominal clitic?

3. Previous studies

3.1. Comparing results from spontaneous vs. elicited production

In this section I will review the results coming from both spontaneous and elicited production. The picture that emerges is a contradictory one: while the low rate of clitic production is associated with a high rate of DP use in spontaneous production, in elicited production it is associated with a high rate of omissions.

3.1.1. Spontaneous production

Data coming from spontaneous production show that during the period when clitics are scarce, children favour DPs: "instead of accusative clitics, the three children produce lexical DPs [...]" (Van der Velde et al. 2002: 122; also Jakubowicz et al. 1996, 1997). An example is given below:

(4)   Adult: tu l'aimes cette chanson? "Do you like this song?"
      Child: j'aime Aladdin.
               "I like Aladdin." (Victor, 2;5.29;
                                Van der Velde et al. 2002: 122)

This spontaneous production data comes from the interaction of three children. These children were recorded in monthly 45 minutes sessions. The age for the children ranged between 1;8 and 2;5. The omissions are scarce, between 10-15% while the use of DPs rises as high as 70%. These results support an analysis where the clitics appear later because of their structural deficiency (van der Velde et al. 2002 ; Jakubowicz et al. 1998, Jakubowicz and Nash 2001, Jakubowicz and Nash to appear). Accusative clitics are DP arguments without a root layer (an NP) due to the lack of the feature [animacy]. Children have difficulties merging as arguments non-canonical or categorical deficient elements such as clitics. Instead of clitics, the children prefer lexical DPs, which conform to the canonical argument type.

3.1.2. Elicited production

Elicited production data contain a high rate of omissions. These studies use an elicited production paradigm (Schaeffer 2000) where the experimenter asks a question to a puppet introduced as unreliable, and the child is asked to help in correcting the puppet's factual mistakes. The goal is to establish the introduced object as the definite topic of the discussion, which is a context where a clitic should be used if one wants to refer again to this object. Constructions with null arguments without identification by clitics are frequent; instead of clitics, the children favour null objects (Perez-Leroux et al. 2005, Schmitz et al. 2004; Jakubowicz et al. 1996). An example is provided below:

(5) Context: the story included an explicit mention of the direct object, to introduce it as a possible discourse antecedent.
Question: Qu'est ce que le père fait avec la balle ?
"What is the father doing with the ball?"
Expected answer: Il la frappe. "He hits it."
Child's answer : frappe. "Hits."(Nathaniel, 2;8; Perez-Leroux et al. 2005)

The rate of omissions goes as high as 60%, while the production of DPs is about 30% (comparable to the adult responses in an elicitation setting). The proposed analyses for these results adopt a (parametric) discontinuity view (Müller et al. 1996, Müller 2004, Schmitz et al. 2004, Pérez-Leroux et al. 2005). Essentially, these analyses propose that the child starts with an unmarked option, either from the different values of a null object parameter or from the null elements available in the target grammar. They are thus proposals about the status of null objects in early grammar, and therefore are in sharp contrast with the type of analysis offered for the data coming from spontaneous speech production.

To recapitulate, there are two sets of data used in evaluating children's acquisition of object clitics: from the spontaneous production data it seems that the delay in the apparition of object clitics was compensated by a massive use of DPs; a low percentage of omissions was found[1]. In the elicited production data, in the absence of object clitics the children favoured omissions; a high percentage of omissions was found. Thus, the picture that emerges is an asymmetry in the use of object omission in spontaneous versus elicited production.

Why do we find such a difference between children's behaviour in spontaneous versus elicited production? One possibility, as mentioned by Jakubowicz et al. (1996: 384) is that elicited production might have a negative effect on the children, such that they tend to omit more objects when compared to spontaneous interaction: "We believe that the high percentage of object omissions [...] is a by-product of the task itself. If these children assumed that French allowed object deletion, they would have omitted objects also in spontaneous interaction data. As shown [...] this did not happen." There is however, another possibility: the low rate of omissions in spontaneous discourse might be a consequence of the methodology used to count these omissions. Therefore, before firmly concluding that the elicitation task is favouring object omission (which if true, is an interesting matter to further investigate), we need to look more clearly at the methodology used to calculate object omissions in spontaneous production.

3.2 Methodology

Let's examine closely the denominator used in calculating object omission vs. object realization across the two modalities, spontaneous versus elicited production. In spontaneous production, the base for calculating object omissions/realizations is the verb's lexical transitivity: obligatory/optional transitives (Müller et al. 1996, Müller & Hulk 2001), the complement context (Hamann 2002) or the objects of transitive verbs (van der Velde et al. 2002, Jakubowicz et al 1996, 1997). To cite one of these works: « The percentage for accusative and reflexive clitics was calculated dividing the actually produced cases by the number of transitive and pronominal verbs, respectively. » (Van der Velde 2002 : 118). In elicited production, on the other hand, the base for identifying object omissions/realizations is the context that requires clitic use according to adult behaviour (Pérez-Leroux et al. 2005, Schmitz et al. 2004; Jakubowicz et al. 1996); see example (5). Therefore, it seems plausible that the difference between the rate of omissions in spontaneous vs. elicited production is due to what was counted as necessary context for the appearance of clitics.

4. New study

4.1. The clitic context

It is well known that clitics are not required by verbal transitivity alone, but by a certain discourse situation. The pronominal clitic must be specific, i.e. it must have an antecedent in the preceding discourse (according to the interpretation of the term "specific" provided by Cardinaletti and Starke (1999) and references therein) and, while it can have a token-reading or a type-reading, it must be an entity that can be presupposed (Lopez 2003). Previous studies on spontaneous production seem to have included contexts where clitics are not required as in (6) below (from Van der Velde et al. 1999: 122):

(6)   a. situation: Hugo's mother is preparing the animals to construct a
                      farm.
      Child :   je fais une ferme. "I'm making a farm" Hugo, 2;5.5
      b. Adult :   tu l'aimes cette chanson? "Do you like this song?"
      Child: j'aime Aladdin. "I like Aladdin."   Victor, 2;5.29
      c. Adult: qu'est-ce que tu veux faire?
                      "What do you want to do?"
      Child: je vais pêcher les poissons. "I am going to catch the
                      fish"   Chloé, 2;4.1

The observation that I would like to make is the following: in order to verify that early grammar permits "object deletion" (Jakubowicz 1996) we need to look only at contexts where a clitic is permissible/necessary: these are the contexts in which we can talk about object deletion and which were used in elicited production. From the examples in (6), at least (6a) and (6c) do not seem to be contexts where a clitic is possible in adult language.

I would like to propose the notion of "clitic-context", based on the different types of recoverability proposed by Cummins and Roberge (2005); in French, this is a context where a clitic appears in order to identify the features (person, number, gender) of the null element *pro* in argument position (in line with a *pro* analysis of clitic constructions, cf. Sportiche 1998); this null element refers to a definite and specific antecedent which is the topic of the discourse (presupposed):

(7)   A: Tu veux ce livre ?   "You want this book?"
      B: Oh ! Mais je l_i'ai déjà lu $\varnothing_i$.   "But I already read it."
                                         (Cummins and Roberge, 2005)

In the clitic context, the null element might not be identified by the clitic ("clitic-drop construction") as in (3a,b).

The clitic context can be applied in children's spontaneous production: "the referent is the topic of the discussion; it is contained in the question/assertion in the immediately preceding discourse."[2] (Pirvulescu and Roberge 2005, pp.10). There are three types of elements which may appear in the clitic context in children's spontaneous production: clitics, omissions and DPs. An example of each is provided in (8a-c) (from York corpus, Mona and Para files, CHILDES database):

(8) a.   Adult: elle n'est pas sèche [la pâte à modeler] "it is not dry."
         Child: moi va l'couper. "Me cut it."   Max, 2;2.22
    b.   Adult: tu ne veux pas le mettre dans l'eau [le canard]?
                  "You don't want to put it in the water?"
         Child: _ mettre ici. "put here"   Max, 2;0.14
    c.   Adult: c'est le couteau qui est tombé?
                  "Is it the knife that fell?"
         Child: attends! Toi cherche couteau?
                  "Wait! You look for knife?"   Anne,   2;2.20

The context used in previous experimental work is the clitic context; see example (5). Therefore, what is needed is an analysis of the spontaneous production using the notion of "clitic-context". In section 4.2 I present the new data from spontaneous production coded and analyzed for the clitic-contexts and the percentage of omissions vs. pronominal clitics. In section 4.3 the results from the children will be compared with the results from adult spontaneous child-directed speech.

4.2. Child Data

The child data come from the York database (CHILDES). Two corpora were analyzed: the corpus PARA (Paris, France) and the corpus MONA (Montréal, Canada). These are the only two corpora available on the CHILDES database in which recordings start early enough and were made regularly, every two weeks for 30 minutes at a time. The children were Anne (PARA files); and Max (MONA files). The percentages of omissions and pronominal clitics for each child are reported in Table 1 and Table 2 respectively (only the recordings with more than 2 clitic-context occurrences are shown).

Table 1: Null objects and clitics in clitic-context; Anne (Paris; PARA files)

MLU	AGE	NUL	CL	Cl contexts (tokens)
2.58	2;2.30	62.50%	25.00%	8
2.83	2;4.2	50.00%	16.66%	6
3.01	2;4.20	33.33%	0.00%	3
2.61	2;5.4	25.00%	0.00%	4
3.25	2;5.18	25.00%	37.50%	8
3.38	2;6.2	28.00%	57.14%	7
3.21	2;6.18	70.58%	11.76%	17
2.87	2;7.1	20.00%	60.00%	5
2.85	2;8.3	42.85%	42.85%	7
3.66	2;8.20	40.00%	50.00%	10
3.56	2;9.15	16.00%	83.00%	12
3.59	2;10.18	8.00%	92.00%	25

For Anne, Table 1 shows a rate of omissions as high as 62.5%[3]. The drop in the rate of omission seems to coincide with the increased frequency of accusative clitics.

Table 2 Null objects and clitics in clitic-context; Max (Montréal, MONA files)

MLU	AGE	NULL	CL	Cl contexts (tokens)
1.78	2;0.14	50.00%	25.00%	8
1.83	2;0.28	40.00%	40.00%	5
2.11	2;1.16	40.00%	0.00%	5
2.73	2;2.9	27.27%	36.36%	11
2.47	2;2.22	40.00%	40.00%	5
2.51	2;3.20	57.14%	42.85%	7
2.98	2;4.4	20.00%	80.00%	5
3.21	2;4.18	16.66%	66.66%	6
3.73	2;5.1	27.27%	54.54%	10
3.29	2;5.15	20.00%	80.00%	10
3.46	2;5.29	0.00%	100.00%	4
3.68	2;6.12	33.33%	61.11%	18

For Max, Table 2 shows that clitics appear early; however, the rate of omissions is as high as 50%. The drop in the rate of omission seems to coincide with the increased frequency of accusative clitics.

What these figures show is that object omission in clitic context is an important phenomenon in early child language and that the rate of omissions is much higher than previously thought. There seems to be a trade-off between the increasing use of clitics and the drop in the rate of omissions. Another important new finding is that we know these omissions are in a well-identified context, the clitic-context. In other words, we have eliminated omissions that are presumably of a different type. These omissions are the ones in deictic contexts ("the null object refers to an entity that is salient in the extralinguistic context but not necessarily present in the discourse" Cummins and Roberge 2005:22), and omissions in the case of "absolute" use ("generic" or "indefinite null objects"). Examples for the two types of omissions are in (9a,b) respectively (from Lambrecht and Lemoine 2004):

(9) a.   Upon hearing the doorbell: Va ouvrir! "Go open up."
     b.   Maman est occupée; elle coud. "Mom is busy; she is sewing."

It is important to isolate the context types where a clitic will not be normally used. The analyses of adult omissions in (9a,b) are presumably different from the one in which clitics are required (see Cummins and Roberge 2005 among others). Therefore, if the target grammar is to be taken into consideration, we need to separate those contexts.

As seen in examples (3a,b) in section 2, a clitic-context in adult production might appear without a clitic. While qualitative research on the constructions shows the extent and the limits of the usage, to the best of my knowledge there is no quantitative study across adult populations. A quantitative comparison between children and adults is important in deciding whether child omissions in this context are deviant from adult ones. Therefore, I conducted an analysis of adult child-directed speech data following the same methodology used for the child data.

4.3. Children vs. adults

In this section I compare children's omissions with those of adults in comparable clitic-contexts. While constructions where the null argument is not recovered by the clitic are attested in adult French (cf. examples 3a and b) we don't yet know how frequent these constructions are. In this paper I report a preliminary result of the analysis of child-directed adult spontaneous production. These results will be compared to the ones from the two children in order to fully answer the first question as presented in section 2: what is the importance of constructions such as (2) in child production? We saw that the percentage of omissions is very high; however we still need to know what adults do in comparable contexts. The data comes from child-directed speech from the mothers in the two analyzed CHILDES files. There were 8 recordings and 109 clitic-contexts[4]. The results are shown in Figure 1.

Figure 1. Null objects, clitics and NPs in clitic-context: adult child-directed speech

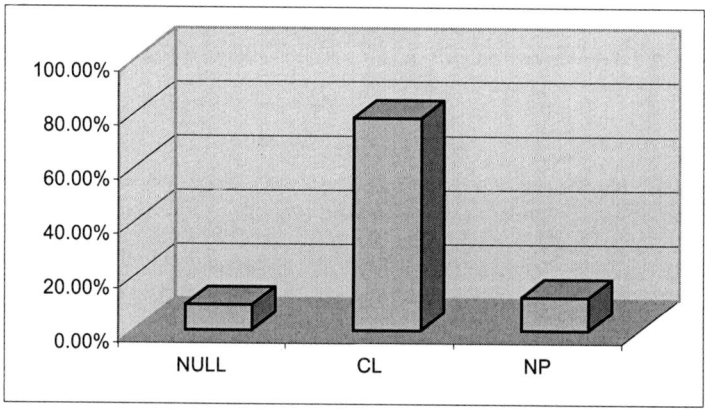

Figure 1 shows around 10% omissions for adults, compared to 62.5% and 50% for children. There is therefore a substantial quantitative difference between adults and children.

5. Discussion

The study of spontaneous production in a specific context, the clitic-context, confirms what was found in elicited production: there is an important rate of omissions in a context that requires the use of a clitic (Table 1 and 2). Moreover, the rate of omissions is much higher in children than in adults (Table 1 and 2 and Figure 1). For children, the drop in the rate of omissions seems to coincide with the increased frequency of accusative clitics. These observations seem to warrant the following statement: in clitic-contexts, early grammar does allow null objects not identified by clitics. The data from spontaneous and elicited production converge[5]. The possibilities for analyzing these results are to be found among those proposed to explain high rates of omission. The omission of the clitic in child speech have received different types of explanations. First, according to a parametric discontinuity view, children's grammar allows at the beginning null objects not identified by clitics: "free object omission" of the type found in a topic-drop language such as Chinese (Müller et al. 1996, Müller

2004, Schmitz et al. 2004). Second, taking into consideration the availability of the construction in adult grammar, Pérez-Leroux et al. 2005 propose that the early grammar starts with a VP which contains a null N, which is the minimal type of null object; this N is recovered through pragmatically inferred reference. The child does not yet identify the context that requires the clitic (Pérez-Leroux et al. 2005). And third, under a continuity the child grammar is analogous to the adult grammar; however the morphophonological paradigm is not yet acquired (Fujino and Sano 2002, Borer and Rohrbacher 2002).

6. Conclusion

In this paper I wanted to stress the following methodological point: the study of the acquisition of object clitics must take into consideration the contexts that require object clitics in both spontaneous and elicited production: children's omissions vary according to the semantics. This is an extremely important point, considering the fact that empirical studies until now have yielded contradictory results. The study of spontaneous production has limitations due to the availability of the construction: it is not easy to come about clitic-contexts in the speech of young children, and too few recordings of French-speaking children are available. More data is indeed needed.

Acknowledgement

I would like to thank Cécile De Cat, Ana Pérez-Leroux and Yves Roberge for their comments and suggestions. This research is funded in part by a SSHRC grant (410-05-0239).

Notes

[1] A higer rate of omission is reported in Hamann (2002, 2003) who discusses data from one child, Augustin. The age period studied is from 2;0.2 to 2;9.30. The omissions in range from 40% to 14.4% in the 10 samples examined. Although the incidence of null objects tends to decline with age, it is still around 20% in three of the last four samples (between 2;4.22 and 2;9.30). Therefore, there seem to be different rates of omission even in data coming from spontaneous production alone.

[2] A similar notion is used in Paradis (to appear) : a permissible context for direct object pronominalization is one where the referent for the direct object was mentioned within the previous 10 lines in the transcript.

[3] At the age of 2;6.18, Anne use a lot of constructions with sentential topics: the majority of omissions are in this construction and this accounts for the 70% omissions.

[4] An individual analysis was performed first for each corpus, and the results were very similar. Therefore, the results for the two corpora have beed collapsed.

[5] The difference between spontaneous vs. elicited production seems to be manifested as a delay in the use of clitics in elicited production.

References

Borer, H. and B. Rohrbacher, (2002) "Minding the absent: Arguments for the Full Competence Hypothesis". *Language Acquisition 10(2)*: 123–175.

Cummins, S. and Y. Roberge, (2005) "A Modular Account of Null Objects in French". *Syntax* 8: 44-64.

Hamann, C., Rizzi, L. and U. Frauenfelder, (1996) "On the acquisition of subject and object clitics in French". In *Generative Perspectives on Language Acquisition*, ed. Harald Clahsen, 309-334. Amsterdam/Philadelphia: Benjamins.

—. (2002) *From syntax to discourse, Pronominal clitics, null subjects and infinitives in child language*, Kluwer: Dordrecht.

—. (2003) Phenomena in French normal and impaired language acquisition and their implications for hypotheses on language development, Probus 15, 91-122.

Jakubowicz C., N. Müller, O. Kang, B. Riemer and C. Rigaut, (1996) "On the acquisition of the pronominal system in French and German". *Proceedings of the 20th BUCLD* ,ed., by Andy Springfellow, Dalia Cahana-Amitay, Elizabeth Hughes & Andrea Zukowski, 374-385. Somerville, Mass.: Cascadilla Press.

—., N. Müller, B. Riemer and C. Rigaut, (1997) The case of subject and object omissions in French and German, *Proceedings of the 21st BUCLD*, ed., by Elizabeth Hughes, Mary Hughes & Annabel Greenhill, 331-342. Somerville, Mass.: Cascadilla Press.

—., L. Nash, C. Rigaut et G. Christophe-Loic, (1998) Determiners and clitic pronouns in French-speaking children with SLI, Language acquisition 7 :113-160.

—., and L. Nash, (2001) Functional categories and syntactic operations in (ab)normal language acquisition, Brain and Language 77, 321-339.

Lambrecht, K. and K. Lemoine, (1996) "Vers une grammaire des compléments zéro en français parlé". *Absence de marques et représentation de l'absence*, ed.,by Jean Chuquet & Marc Frid, 279-309. Rennes: Presses universitaires de Rennes.

Larjavaara, M (2000) Présence ou absence de l'objet. Limites du possible en français contemporain. Helsinki: Academia Scientiarum Fennica.

López, L. (2003) Steps for a well-adjusted dislocation. *Studia Linguistica* 57 (3): 193-231.

MacWhinney, B. (2000) The CHILDES Project: tools for analysing talk. Mahwah: Lawrence Erlbaum.

Müller, N., B. Crysmann and G. A. Kaiser, (1996) Interactions between the acquisition of French object drop and the development of the C-system, *Language Acquisition* 5(1), 35-63.

—. and A. Hulk, (2001) "Crosslinguistic influence in bilingual language acquisition: Italian and French as recipient languages", *Bilingualism: Language and cognition* 4: 1-21.

—. (2004) Null-arguments in bilingual children, in Paradis, J. and Ph. Prévost, eds., *The acquisition of French in different contexts*, John Benjamis: Amsterdam.

Perez-Leroux, A., Pirvulescu M. and Y. Roberge, (2005) Early object omission in child French and English, submitted to Proceedings of LSRL 35.

Pirvulescu, M. and Y. Roberge, (2005) "Licit and Illicit Null Objects in L1 French". Volume of selected papers from LSRL 34, ed., by in Ed Rubin & Randall Gess. Amsterdam: John Benjamins.

Schmitz, K., K. Cantone, N. Mueller and T. Kupisch, (2004) "Clitic realizations and omissions in early child grammar : a comparison of Italian and French", paper delivered at the workshop *The Romance Turn, Workshop on the Acquisition of Romance Languages*. Madrid, Spain.

Sportiche, D (1998) *Partitions and atoms of clause structure*, London: Routledge.

Van der Velde, M., C. Jakubowicz, and C. Rigaut, (2002) The acquisition of determiners and pronominal clitics by three French-speaking children. In *The Process of Language Acquisition*, ed., Ingeborg Lasser, 115-132. Frankfurt/ Berlin: Peter Lang Verlag.

CHILD SLOVENIAN IMPERATIVES: ROOT INFINITIVE ANALOGUES?

DOMINIK RUS AND PRITHA CHANDRA

1. Introduction

Early Root Nonfinites (ERNs) have received a great deal of attention in the child morphosyntactic acquisition literature in the last decade or so. It has been noted that besides producing correctly-inflected finite V(erb)s in root contexts, where a finite form denoting T(ense) and/or Agr(eement) is required in adult systems, children also produce various ERNs, specifically: (a) English, Swahili and Inuktitut-speaking children produce a high number of Bare Verb stems (BVs) (see Deen 2002 for reviews on English and Swahili; Swift 2004 for Inuktitut); (b) children speaking other non-null subject Germanic languages (Dutch, German, and Swedish), French, and Russian produce a high number of Vs with infinitival morphology, i.e., R(oot) I(nfinitive)s (see Guasti 2002 for reviews); (c) children speaking null subject Romance (Catalan, Italian, and Spanish) and Slovenian produce a high number of B(are) P(articiple)s, i.e., active past participles not supported with auxiliaries (see Montrul 2004 for a review on Catalan and Spanish; Guasti 2002 for Italian; Rus & Chandra 2005 for Slovenian); (d) Greek-speaking children produce a high number of nonfinite participle-like Vs with perfective morphology and meaning (see Varlokosta et al. 1998)—forms which Hyams (2002, 2003) refers to as B(are) Perf(ective)s.

We have learned a great deal about early morphosyntactic systems since the conception of the "RI program". First, it has been noted that early grammars exhibit a wide *variety* of ERNs and that *not all* children go through an RI stage, though it is still not well understood whether there is an "RI-like" (i.e., RI-analogue) stage cross-linguistically. Specifically, it is not clear why there seems to be a clear cut between RI and non-RI languages and what developmental (linguistic) mechanism(s) is/are responsible for that, if any, and if null subjecthood and the richness of verbal morphology play a role in this cut (Hyams 2003). Second, it has become clear that the rate of ERNs *varies considerably* not only across (similar) languages (from 3% to as much as 90%

of all early Vs), but also *within* a language (see Guasti 2002 for a review). Third, it seems that the properties generally associated with RIs are the following (after Hyams 2003): (a) the presence of nonfinite morphology (infinitive, bare V stem, or participle/perfective); (b) the lack of occurrence with T/Agr-related elements (e.g., subject clitics, reflexive clitics, and modals), as well as C-related elements (*wh*, focus/topic subject, and object DPs); (c) eventivity constraint (i.e., expressing events rather than states); (d) irrealis semantic meaning (i.e., expressing volition and intention).

Some of the most influential studies on ERNs have attempted to *unify* early grammatical systems by proposing a more or less specific *structural deficit* (e.g., Rizzi 1993/4; Wexler 1994, 1998), sometimes resorting to the syntax/semantics interplay (e.g., Hyams 2003). Various "unification accounts" have appeared in the acquisition literature in the recent years, based on various early languages, most notably: (a) BVs as RIs (Wexler 1994, on the basis of English); (b) BPs as RIs (Varlokosta et al. 1998, on the basis of Greek); (c) BPerfs as RIs (Hyams 2003, on the basis of Greek); and (d) Imperatives (IMPs) as RIs (Salustri & Hyams 2003, on the basis of Italian).

We believe that the "BVs as RI-analogues" and "BPs as RI-analogues" hypothesis have both been refuted successfully (see Hoekstra & Hyams 1998 for the former and Hyams 2002, 2003 and Rus & Chandra 2005 for the latter). This paper evaluates the last position (i.e., the "IMPs as RI-analogues" hypothesis), concluding that it *cannot* hold cross-linguistically for null subject languages with rich verbal morphology, contra Salustri & Hyams (2003). Bringing forth empirical facts from child Slovenian (SLO hereafter), this paper argues that SLO children's IMPs do *not* lack the TP/AgrP projection(s) because they show perfect [Person] and [Number] Agr. Independently, in the syntactic accounts of adult Slovenian, IMPs have never been treated as tenseless structures, but full CPs with a fully-blown (i.e., nondefective) CP-AgrP/TP-VP structure. Furthermore, our data on child IMPs show that early IMPs also appear in constructions with object scrambling and clauses with post-IMP clitics, which in the present minimalist paradigm require a full clausal structure, contra Salustri & Hyams' (2003) "missing/eliminated functional heads" account.

2. The "Imperative as an RI-Analogue" Hypothesis (IRIAH)

The analysis presented by Salustri & Hyams (S&H hereafter) commences with the *prima facie* "RI-like" characteristics of child Italian IMPs, namely they are tenseless structures; they express irrealis semantic interpretation; and they occur mainly with eventive predicates. S&H make the following two predictions for the IRIAH: (a) in null subject languages with rich morphology, IMPs will occur significantly more often in the child language than in the corresponding adult language; and (b) IMPs will occur significantly more often in null subject child languages than in the RI languages.

Let us unpack some of the details of the S&H' analysis. First, as observed correctly by S&H, IMPs seem to be among the first and most frequently used V forms in child Italian; compare the frequency rates in child speech with those of the adult target language in the two tables below:

Frequency Rates of IMPs and RIs in Early Italian (from S&H)				
Child	Age	%RI (mean)	% IMP (mean)	Total Verbs
Denis	2;0-2;7	2.8	31;1	318
Martina	2;1-2;7	0	17.5	513
Diana	2;0-2;7	0	16.4	863
Viola	2;1-2;7	0.2	30	198

Frequency Rates of IMPs in Adult Italian (all forms) (from S&H)			
Discourse context	IMP Tokens	IMP%	Total Verbs
Adult-directed	36	5.6	950
Child-directed	82	14.9	550

Child IMPs peak at approximately 40%, in direct contrast with 15% in adult grammar, thus validating the first prediction. Second, the frequency of IMPs in child German remains constant at around 10% (between the ages of 1;6 and 2;7) even though child-directed German contains around 36% of IMPs.

S&H's next objective is to provide a "uniform" structural description for IMPs and RIs, only "apparently different" forms. A defining character of IMPs is V-raising to C, illustrated below in (1). Compare an IMP in (1a) with an indicative (IND) in (1b):

(1) a. Prendi-la.   b. La prendi.
        take-it-cl.   it-cl.-take
        'Take it!'   'You take it.'

Adopting Han's (2001) analysis of IMPs, S&H suggest (2) as the underlying representation for IMPs:

(2)

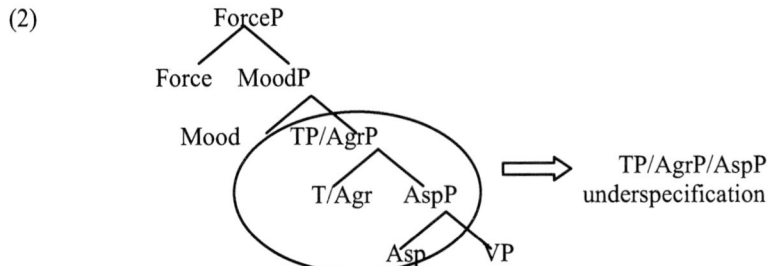

IMP Vs have an irrealis feature that must be checked against MoodP in a local configuration (i.e., head-head, spec-head, or head-complement). To satisfy locality, there must be no intervening heads/projections between MoodP and the IMP V. IMPs are unmarked for T and arguably unspecified for Agr as well, suggesting that the intermediate projections are *eliminated* in the structure like the one in (2) above. The irrealis feature on the V is thus checked locally against MoodP and subsequent movement of the V to Mood allows the "directive" feature to be in a local checking relation with Force.

V-raising in IMPs is hence obligatory for feature checking and is achieved via underspecification. On the other hand, IND Vs bear T/Agr morphology, hence eliminating TP/AgrP/AspP is not a possibility. Crucially, the technology adopted for IMPs is the same as for RIs. Infinitivals have an irrealis feature that is checked against MoodP and a local checking relation is rendered possible only by the underspecification. IMPs and RIs are thus outcomes of the same underlying structures and subsequently share temporal, modal, as well as aspectual interpretations.

Finally, RIs and IMPs (though with a very low frequency) can *co-exist* within a single language. To explain the preference for RIs over IMPs—as evident in child German, for example—S&H appeal to *economy* considerations and assume movement to be a last resort operation. Since feature checking on the infinitival V can be done at a distance without actually moving the V into the domain of MoodP (by merely underspecifying the intermediate projections), RIs stand out as *more economical* derivations over IMPs, which require the V's movement to the checker's domain.

However, as we will see below, S&H's claim about IMPs being RI-analogues *cannot* be extended to all non-RI/null subject languages. Child SLO IMPs show perfect [Person] and [Number] Agr, allow focalized and topicalized subject and object DPs in pre-IMP positions, and appear in structures with post-

IMP clitics, with the clitic climbing onto the IMP V. These facts, which we present in details below, all argue against S&H's "missing/eliminated functional heads" account for child IMPs in null subject languages.

3. The Study

The present study investigates IMPs in very early child SLO (age 1;3–2;0; mean age: 1;7; MLU 1;4–2;31; mean MLU: 1.94), trying to shed light on the IRIAH. The data for the study are taken from Rus & Chandra (2005), which is part of a larger corpus of child SLO, originally reported in Kranjc (1999). Before turning to child SLO IMPs, let us review some of the crucial morphosyntactic properties of adult SLO IMPs, commonly assumed in the syntactic literature. We review the IMP morphology, subject use, as well as the clitic placement in SLO IMPs, showing that IMPs are full CP-TP-VP clauses with no defective Infl-related projection or defective Infl-related features. This review will serve as the basis for our argument against the IRIAH. In the subsequent section we then explore these properties in the child system.

4. Adult Slovenian Imperatives

According to traditional descriptive grammar, SLO distinguishes among three moods, namely IND, IMP, and exclamative (Toporišič 2000). The IND and the IMP have *distinct* V morphology. The table below shows the IMP conjugation paradigm, contrasted with the present IND one, which has 9 cells. The IMP has a restriction in allowing only for 2SG, 1DU/PL, and 2DU/PL forms:

Slovenian Imperative Paradigm				
	2SG	1DU	2DU	1PL	2PL
Present Indicative	delaš you-work	delava we two-work	delata you two-work	delamo we work	delate you work
Imperative	delaj you-work!	delajva let us two-work!	delajta you two-work!	delajmo let us three-or more work!	delajte you three-or more work!

On the basis of SLO, Milojević Sheppard & Golden [S&G hereafter] (2002) argue against Platzack & Rosengren's [P&R hereafter] (1997) hypothesis about IMP clauses being tenseless, where the term tenseless is not to be understood merely as non-finite (in which case T would carry a feature [–finite]), but rather as a clause completely lacking the TP projection.[1] What S&G have in mind when arguing against the lack of T in IMPs is that the presence of an overt C (SLO *da*) indicates that there must be a complement clause to the head C, namely a TP. Furthermore, they show that in SLO, the complementizer *da* (just like *that* in English) never c-selects a [–finite] clause, as seen below in (3):

(3)   a.   Ukazal mi je, (da) naj delam.
           ordered me is (that) *naj* work-1SG PRES IND
           'He ordered me to work/He told me that I must work.'
      b.   Ukazal mi je delati.
           ordered me is work-INF
           'He ordered me to work.'
      c.   *Ukazal mi je, *da* delati.
           ordered me is that work-INF
           'He ordered me to work.'

From the examples above, we see that the *da* c-selects either a [+finite] T (3a) or a [–finite] T (3b). However, it cannot be complemented by an infinitival clause with the presence of the overt *da* (3c).[2]

Let us now turn to the subject use. In SLO, the syntactic subject in matrix IMPs need not be expressed, just like in English. Syntactically, it is restricted to 2SG, 1DU/PLs, and 2DU/PL, as noted above. Semantically, the subject is either the same as the addressee or quantifies over the addressee, again just like in English (Han 2001). Hence, either the hearer addressed by the speaker must be present or one or more persons the action is directed to must be present when the utterance containing an IMP V is uttered. The subjects of SLO IMPs seem to exhibit *the same* syntactic characteristics as the subjects of *finite clauses*: they can bind an anaphor in VP (4a), control the *pro* subject of non-finite complements (4b), and agree with predicatively used adjectives and past participles (4c) in both matrix as well as embedded contexts (cf. S&G 2002):

(4)   a.   Kupi   si   kolo.
           buy-2SGIMP *pro* yourself bicycle
           'Buy yourself a bicycle!'
      b.   Navadita   se   pospraviti svojo sobo.
           get used-2DUIMP *pro* refl *PRO* to clean up your   room
           '(You-two) get used to clean up your room!'
      c.   Bodite   previdni   v gozdu!
           be-2PLIMP *pro* careful-PLMASC in wood
           '(You three-or more) be careful in the woods!'

Overt subjects are, of course, possible (either full NPs or pronouns), generally denoting contrast or emphasis:

(5) Ti   si   kupi   kolo,   ne Marija.
     you yourself *pro* buy-2SGIMP bicycle not Mary
     'You (must) buy yourself a bicycle, not Mary!'[3]

If we assume that subject Agr features are shared by *pro*—a standard assumption in the literature—then *pro* must be *referential*. This seems to rule out P&R's proposal on the absence of Agr or finiteness in IMP clauses.[4] From these facts, we conclude that IMPs *cannot* be tenseless clauses and we take them as *tensed forms*, having *the same* structure as *finite clauses* (CP-TP-VP).

SLO is a null subject second position (2P) (Wackernagel) clitic (CL) language with raised IMP Vs preceding the CLs. Though SLO is a language with 2P clitics (6a), pronominal CLs can sometimes be sentence-initial. However, clitics *cannot* precede the IMP V (**CL+V-IMP*) in matrix clauses, where the only possible word order is *V-IMP+CL*:

(6) a.   *Ga   poslušaj,   če hočeš.
          him-CL-DAT   listen-2SGIMP   if want-2SGPRESIND
          'Listen to him if you want!'
     b.   Poslušaj   ga,   če hočeš.
          listen-2SGIMP him-CL-DAT if want-2SGPRESIND
          'Listen to him if you want!'

In interaction with negation, structures with CLs yield the *Neg+V-FIN+CL* word order. In matrix IMPs, the word order is exactly the same. Hence, as regard to clitic placement, SLO matrix IMPs show *the same* word order as CL placement in IND clauses. The following is the proposed phrase structure for SLO IMPs from Rus (2005)[5]:

(7) a.   [CP [MP V-IMP [TP CL^0]   /matrix clauses/
     b.   [CP V-IMP CL [MP ... [TP ...]   /matrix clauses w/ V raising/
     c.   ... [CP C [MP CL V-IMP [TP ...] /embedded clauses/

Let us now proceed to child Slovenian IMPs in some detail.

5. Imperatives in Child Slovenian

Very early child SLO shows an extremely high number of IMPs (56% of all V forms) and BPs (16.3 % of all V forms), with practically no RIs (<1%), as the table below shows (from Rus & Chandra 2005):

Child Slovenian Verbal Forms				
Sentence Type	IMPs	Past Participles	Finite Vs	Other
Total #	679	197	187	142
%	56.4	16.3	15.5	11.8

Hence, frequency-wise, we confirm S&H's claims about the frequency of IMPs in null subject languages with rich morphology. However, our data also show perfect [Person] and [Number] Agr, as shown in the following table:

Agreement Correct on Imperative Verbs in Child Slovenian	
Total # IMPs	679
Agr correct	673/679 (99.1%)

We see that there are only six Agr errors in early IMPs in our data. There are three different errors (with different Vs), all of which are phonological reductions of the IMP forms (i.e., generally, base stems without affixes). Compare the children's errors in with the correct adult-like forms on the right in (8) below:

(8) a. *Pu. (Pusti!)   (Katja, 1;11)   cf.   Pust(i)!⁶
       leave-IMP2SG
       'Leave this/it/me!'

    b. *Maga, ohh! (Pomagaj!) (Lenart, 1;9)   cf.
       Pomagaj!/Pomagi!
       help-IMP2SG
       'Help (me).'

    c. *Dej ne.(Dej, nehaj!)   (Kaja, 1;11)   cf.   Dej, nehaj/nehi!
       give-IMP2SG stop-IMP2SG
       'Come on, stop it.'

Constructions with IMP Vs appear with a number of Vs, both transitive as well as intransitive in various constructions, as seen below:

(9)   a.   Glej   jih!   (Lenart,   1;11)
            look-IMP2SG   them.ACC

'Look at them!'

b. Čaki!   (Vesna, 1;7)
    wait-IMP2SG
    'Wait!'

d. Noter   dej   to.   (Lenart,   1;11)
    inside   put-IMP2SG   this
    'Put this inside!'

e. Tuki   makni   tole.   (Kaja, 1;11)
    here   move-IMP2SG this
    'Move this in here!'

We see that IMP constructions appear even in very elaborated structures with Foc and Top DPs and APs (for the issue on "productivity" in terms of IMP morphology, see Rus & Chandra in press).

Overt sentential subjects in IMPs are extremely rare, showing correct target null subject setting. Just like in adult SLO, subjects in child SLO appear when the speaker wants to add emphasis or contrast (cf. (5) above for adult SLO):

(10) a. Goga,   pejt!⁷   (Vesna, 1;7)
         Goga.NOM   go-IMP2SG
         'Go, Goga!'
     b. Vesna   (d)ej   men.   (Doroteja, 1;11)
         Vesna.NOM   give-IMP2SG me.DAT
         'Vesna, give it to me!'

Some constructions show object scrambling, i.e., constructions where the object DP appears in pre-IMP position.⁸ If the IMP raises to C via (M and) T, as assumed in the syntactic literature, then these constructions provide a good piece of evidence that the phrase structure in early IMPs does *not* lack Infl-related projections, and broadly, that the phrase structure contains a complete set of functional projections above VP. In (11) below, we show a couple of examples of object scrambling that appear in our data:

(11) a. Tole   pokaž.   (Katja, 1;11)
         this.ACC   show-IMP2SG
         'Show me this!'
     b. Bončka jej.   (Tomaž, 1;11)
         candy.ACC   eat-IMP2SG
         'Eat the candy!'

There are a couple of cases with reflexive CLs, such as the following:

(12) Se   obuj   teta.   (Vesna, 1;7)
      refl   put on shoes-IMP2SG   auntie.NOM
      'Put on your shoes, auntie/woman!'

Morphologically, the CLs in IMPs are correctly-inflected for case and correctly-placed in post-IMP position (for more examples, see Rus & Chandra in press):

(13) Biba, biba,   lej   jo.   (Katja, 1;10)
      creepy–crawley.NOM look-IMP2SG it.ACCFEMSG
      'Creepy–crawley, look at it!'

6. Child Slovenian Imperatives: A Reanalysis

The data presented in the previous section unveil the overgeneralization eminent in the IRIAH. *Not all* null subject languages with rich morphology will exhibit IMPs as RI-analogues (if this is the right analogy after all!), child SLO being a prime example in this regard, where IMPs abound, but appear with rich and correct morphological marking. We take this as strong evidence against the IRIAH and propose (14) as the structural representation for Child SLO IMPs:

(14)

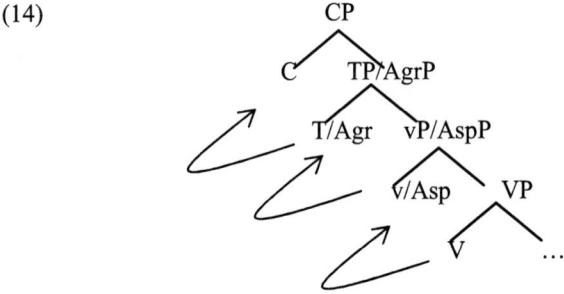

We assume that CP has an irrealis/mood feature that must be checked obligatorily by V-raising. This is accomplished by successive-cyclic movement of the V via v/Asp and T/Agr heads, which also explains correct Agr facts. Note that our analysis also assumes a locality constraint on feature checking—there must be no intervening heads between C and the V. The IMP V's movement to T/Agr to check the phi-features on the latter places it in a local relation to C, whereby it undergoes further movement into it, checking and deleting the target's uninterpretable feature in the process.[9] Our analysis has two immediate advantages. First, it adequately captures the Agr facts in child SLO, and second, it is explanatorily more desirable, as it undermines superfluous operations like TP/AgrP/AspP underspecification in child grammars.

6. Conclusion

The presence of T/Agr suffixes, the use of pronominal and reflexive clitics, topicalized/focalized DPs, post-verbal object clitics, and scrambled object DPs in pre-verbal positions in constructions with finite Vs have all been taken in the field to be evidence for a complete set of functional projections in both adult and child grammatical systems. SLO IMPs show all these properties. Independently, it has also been argued in the syntactic literature that on the basis of word order facts with clitics, Agr morphology, as well as subjects, SLO IMPs are fully-fledged clauses rather than structures with defective T/Agr. Hence, we cannot but conclude that Slovenian children IMPs are perfect analogues of their adult counterparts. These facts argue against Salustri & Hyams' (2003) hypothesis that IMPs are nonfinite structures, analogous to RIs.

Notes

[1] P&R state: "*Imperatives do not seem to be related to time (…), so we assume that there is no tense-feature in their lexical entry and hence no TP*" (italics ours).

[2] IMPs as full CP-TP clauses also occur in embedded contexts in SLO (cf. Rus 2005). These are not crucial for the present study as our data contain no embedded examples.

[3] The same restrictions apply in embedded IMPs, where there are no speaker-hearer restrictions like in matrix clauses, but the IMP subjects still show the same restrictions as those in matrix IMPs, i.e., they must be 2SG, 1DU/PL, or 2DU/PL (cf. Rus 2005).

[4] P&R explicitly claim that subject Agr (and Asp) features are *unrelated to finiteness* and that would mean that in the system we are proposing, the subject Agr features have *no* referential role. This seems to be counterintuitive to standard assumptions of reference between subject Agr features and *pro*, though we leave this issue aside here (cf. also S&G).

[5] This approach assumes that all IMPs check IMP morphology via V-to-M movement in both matrix and subordinate clauses. In matrix clauses only, the movement can be longer, with the V moving all the way to C°. This operation may arise for independent reasons, e.g., when a CL is in P1 position in [Spec, CP] with the IMP V in C^0, or when there is a phrase in P1 providing a host for a clitic in P2 as a consequence of the Wackernagel effect. The CL in both cases climbs together with the V and adjoins to C.

[6] The forms in brackets are the ones that the investigator recorded in the original transcription, indicating that the context required the IMP form. The V *pustiti* (leave, stop) has *pusti* as the perfective form and *puščaj* as the imperfective one. Some SLO Vs have two distinct IMP forms, one ending in *-i* and one in *-aj/-ej* for 2SG, though most Vs only have the *-aj/ej* form. Moreover, in colloquial SLO the *-i* in *pusti (consonant cluster + -i)* is not pronounced in some dialects.

[7] *pejt* is a colloquial/dialectal form of *pojdi*, the IMP form of *iti*, 'to go'. Some Vs have irregular IMP morphology.

[8] Interestingly, the same (non-adult) word order is attested in constructions with finite Vs and bare past participles (Rus in print; Rus & Chandra 2005), indicating the presence of a complete set of functional heads above the VP (i.e., CP-TP/AgrP).

[9] This analysis is also consistent with the phrase structure and technology proposed in Rus (2005) for adult SLO IMPs, though Rus assumes that IMP Vs need not move all the way to C, but must move at least to MoodP to check off/license morphological mood, where MoodP immediately dominates TP. Hence, the technology adopted there is the same (i.e., resting on successive cyclic movement).

References

Deen, K. (2002) *The Acquisition of Nairobi Swahili: the Morphosyntax of Inflectional Prefixes and Subjects*. Ph.D. Dissertation. UCLA.

Guasti, M.T. (2002) *Language Acquisition: The Growth of Grammar*. Cambridge, MA: MIT Press.

Han, C.H. (2001) "Force, negation and imperatives," *The Linguistic Review* 18: 289-325.

Hoekstra, T. & N. Hyams (1998) "Aspects of root infinitives," *Lingua* 106: 81-112.

Hyams, N. (2002) "Clausal structure in child Greek," *The Linguistic Review* 19: 225-269.

—. (2003) "Child non-finite clauses and the mood-aspect connection: Evidence from child Greek," to appear in *Aspectual Inquiries*, eds., R. Slabakova & P. Kampechinsky. New York: Springer.

Kranjc, S. (1999) *Razvoj Govora Predsolskih Otrok* [*Language Development of Pre-School Children*] Ljubljana: Znanstveni Institut Filozofske Fakultete Ljubljana.

Montrul, S. (2004) *The acquisition of Spanish. Morphosyntactic Development in Monolingual and Bilingual L1 Acquisition and Adult L2 Acquisition*. Amsterdam: John Benjamins.

Platzack, C. & I. Rosengren (1997) "On the subject of imperatives: A minimalist account of the imperative clause," *The Journal of Comparative Germanic Linguistics* 1: 177-224.

Rizzi, L. (1993/1994) "Some notes on linguistic theory and language development: The case of root infinitives," *Language Acquisition* 3: 371-393.

Rus, D. (In press) "Early root nonfinites and the acquisition of finiteness in child grammar: Evidence from early child Slovenian," to appear in *Proceedings of*

Formal Approaches to Slavic Linguistics (FASL) XIV: the Princeton Meeting.

—. (2005) "Embedded imperatives in Slovenian," in *Georgetown Working Papers in Theoretical Linguistics IV*, eds., C. Brandstetter & D. Rus, 153-183. Georgetown University Department of Linguistics. Washington DC.

—. & P. Chandra. (In press) "Child language imperatives: Questioning the 'imperative as root infinitive analogue' hypothesis," to appear in *Proceedings of the 30th annual Boston University Conference on Language Development*. Somerville, MA: Cascadilla Press.

—. & P. Chandra (2005) "Bare participles are *not* root infinitives: Evidence from early child Slovenian," in *Proceedings of the 29th annual Boston University Conference on Language Development*, eds., A. Brugos, M. Clark-Cotton & S. Ha, 493-503. Somerville, MA: Cascadilla Press.

Salustri M. & N. Hyams (2003) "Is there an analogue to the RI stage in the null subject languages?," in *Proceedings of the 27th annual Boston University Conference on Language Development*, eds., B. Beachley, A. Brown & F. Conlin, 692-703.Somerville, MA: Cascadilla Press.

Sheppard M. & M. Golden (2002) "(Negative) imperatives in Slovene," in *Modality and its Interaction with the Verbal System*, eds. S. Barbiers, F. Beukema & W. Wurff, 245-259. Amsterdam/Philadelphia: John Benjamins.

Swift, M.D. (2004) *Time in Child Inuktitut: A Developmental Study of an Eskimo-Aleut Language*. Mouton de Gruyter.

Toporišič, J. (2000) *Slovenska Slovnica*. Maribor: Založba Obzorja.

Varlokosta, S., B. Rohrbacher & A. Vainikka (1998) "Functional projections, markedness, and 'root infinitives' in early child Greek," *Linguistic Review* 15: 187-207.

Wexler, K. (1994) "Optional infinitives, head movement and economy of derivation," in *Verb movement*, eds., N. Hornstein & D. Lightfoot, 301-350. Cambridge: CUP.

—. (1998) "Very early parameter setting and the unique checking constraint: A new explanation of the optional infinitive stage," *Lingua* 106: 23-79.

Disjoint Reference of Pronominal Binding in Adult L2 English by Japanese Learners

Tetsuya Sano and Maki Yamane

This study investigates how disjoint reference of pronominal binding is exhibited in adult L1-Japanese/L2-English interlanguage grammar. By comparing simple clauses and ECM constructions, we exclude a possibility of L1 transfer and demonstrate that the adult L2 learners obey Binding Principle B although its effect is not evident in L1 Japanese. We also argue that, in our study, pronouns in the adult interlanguage have the property of SE anaphors. Since SE anaphor is found in natural languages such as Dutch, this suggests that even adult interlanguages are UG-constrained (duPlessis, Solin, Travis and White 1987; Schwartz and Sprouse 1994, among others) regarding pronominal binding.

1. Disjoint reference of pronominal binding in child L1

In this study, we will discuss disjoint reference of pronominal binding and we will show that L2 English by Japanese learners exhibits the same pattern as L1 child English. In order to move forward to this goal, first of all, let us review findings in child L1 studies.

1.1 Otsu (1981)

In the past literature of generative acquisition, Otsu (1981) is the first study which investigated whether children obey Binding Principles. In his experiment, Otsu asked English-speaking children to act-out sentences with pronouns and anaphors. As a result, children mostly obeyed Binding Principle A and C, but there were some mistakes regarding disjoint reference of a pronoun. Specifically, some children assigned reflexive interpretation to stimulus sentences such as (1).

(1) The rabbit patted him.

This could suggest that children do not obey Binding Principle B in L1 acquisition of English, but Otsu did not provide any analysis and the phenomenon was left open for further investigation.

1.2 Chien and Wexler (1990)

Chien and Wexler (1990) later demonstrated that children mostly succeed in rejecting a reflexive interpretation for a stimulus sentence such as (2).

(2) Every bear is touching her.
(3) Mama Bear is touching her.

In their experiment of yes/no question task with pictures, children showed good understanding of a quantifying expression *every* at the age of 5, and at that age, children's rejection rate of the reflexive reading is as high as around 85% for a sentence such as (2), while it is around 50% for a sentence such as (3).

The difference between (2) and (3) is the subject NP: in (2), the subject is a quantifying NP *every bear* and in (3), it is a referential NP *Mama Bear*. Reinhart (1983) points out that anaphora between a referential antecedent and a pronoun is ambiguous between variable binding and pragmatic coreference, as exemplified in (4).

(4) Mama bear likes her dog and Goldilocks does, too

When the pronoun *her* takes *Mama Bear* as its antecedent in (4), (4) is ambiguous between the so-called bound variable reading and pragmatic coreference reading. When what Goldilocks likes is Goldilocks' dog, it is called bound variable reading, and when what Goldilocks likes is Mama Bear's dog, it is called pragmatic coreference reading. Reinhart (1983) also points out that, in pronominal anaphora with a quantifying antecedent, there is a bound variable reading only. Consider (5) for example.

(5) Every bear likes her dog and Goldilocks does, too

In (5), what Goldilocks likes is Goldilocks' dog only and it can't be any other dog. Thus, in (5), there is bound variable reading only when the pronoun *her* takes *every bear* as its antecedent.

Reinhart (1983) argues that Binding Principle B, stated in (6), applies to bound variable anaphora only (i.e., not to pragmatic coreference). Based on this, Chien and Wexler (1990) claim that children obey Binding Principle B because they are good at rejecting the reflexive interpretation for (2).

(6) Binding Principle B: a pronominal must be free in its Governing Category.

As for the errors with examples such as (3), Chien and Wexler (1990) suggest that they should be attributed to children's difficulty with a pragmatic principle which excludes coreference (i.e., not variable binding) in instances such as (3). Thus, according to Chien and Wexler (1990), if we want to investigate whether Binding Principle B is respected or not, we should examine variable binding only. That is, we should examine the interpretation of a pronoun with a quantifying antecedent, such as (2), rather than the interpretation of a pronoun with a referential antecedent, such as (3). We will follow this guideline in our experiment for L2 acquisition.

1.3 Baauw and Cuetos (2003)

Baauw and Cuetos (2003) found an exception to Chien and Wexler's generalization that children are good at respecting binding constraints with variable binding. With the truth-value judgment task, they examined Spanish kids' behavior of disjoint reference with clitic pronouns. The examined kids were good at rejecting the reflexive interpretation for simple clauses such as (7) (see Mckee 1992 for a similar result in child Italian).

(7) *La niña$_i$ la$_i$ señala. (Good performance)
    the girl her points-at
    (The girl is pointing at her.) rejected 90%

This is in conformity with Chien and Wexler's finding, because clitic pronouns exhibit variable binding only and the reflexive interpretation for (7) is excluded by Binding Principle B. In addition to this, Baauw and Cuetos examined the ECM construction such as (8).

(8) *La niña$_i$ la$_i$ ve bailar. (Poor performance)
    the girl her sees dance
    (The girl sees her dancing) rejected only 60%

The same kids' rejection rate for (8) was only around 60%, which is significantly lower than the 90% for (7). Thus, Baauw and Cuetos (2003) discovered that children are poor at exhibiting the disjoint reference in variable binding between the matrix subject and the embedded subject in the ECM construction.

1.4. Sano and Crain (2004)

Sano and Crain (2004) examined if Baauw and Cuetos (2003)'s finding would be replicated in English variable binding with a quantifying antecedent. With a truth-value judgment task, they tested children's interpretations of simple clauses such as (9) and ECM constructions such as (10).

(9) *Every rabbit$_i$ brushed him$_i$. (Good performance, 95% rejection)
(10) *Every troll$_i$ believes him$_i$ to be a good jumper. (Poor, 45% rejection)

As a result, it was found that kids (aged 4-6) were poor at rejecting the local binding in the ECM construction (10), while the same kids were good at rejecting the local binding in the simple clause (9). Thus, here again, children are poor at exhibiting the disjoint reference in variable binding between the matrix subject and the embedded subject in the ECM construction. The source of this error will be discussed later in section 6.

To sum up section 1, we have seen that children obey Binding Principle B in variable binding in the simple clause but they are poor at exhibiting the disjoint reference in variable binding between the matrix subject and the embedded pronominal subject in the ECM construction.

2 Previous studies (adult L2)

To our knowledge, there have been no studies that directly test Binding Principle B in adult L2 English by Japanese learners. (Some relevant studies are: Finer and Broselow (1986), Kanno (1997), Perez-Léroux and Glass (1999), but they do not directly test Binding Principle B.) Since there are no previous studies, we attempt to conduct a preliminary study that investigates Binding Principle B in adult L2 English by Japanese learners. To be specific, we will investigate if adult L2 English patterns the same as child L1 English regarding disjoint reference in pronominal binding.

3. Excluding a possibility of L1 transfer

When we examine whether Binding Principle B is respected in adult L2 English by Japanese learners, we must take care of a difference of pronominals between English and Japanese. In English, a third-person pronoun can be a bound variable. That is, a third-person pronoun can be bound by a quantifier when Binding Principle B is irrelevant, as in (11).

(11) Every rabbit thinks he is smart.

Thus, we can posit a feature [+ bound variable] for English third-person pronouns. In contrast, a Japanese overt third-person pronoun, *kare*, can never be a bound variable (Saito and Hoji 1983). Even when Binding Principle B is irrelevant, as in (12), *kare* cannot be bound by a quantifier *dono usagi mo* 'every rabbit'.

(12) dono usagi$_i$-mo kare$_{*i/j}$-ga kashikoi to omotte-iru.
      every rabbit   he-NOM smart COMP think
      (Every rabbit thinks he is smart)

Thus, we can posit a feature [- bound variable] for Japanese *kare*. Because *kare* has the feature [- bound variable], the effect of Binding Principle B is opaque in Japanese. Although *kare* cannot be bound by its local antecedent in the simple clause (13), it does not necessarily demonstrate the effect of Binding Principle B in Japanese, because *kare* cannot be bound by a quantifier even when Binding Principle B is irrelevant, as in (12).

(13) dono usagi$_i$-mo kare$_{*i/j}$-o tataita.
      every rabbit   he-ACC pat-PAST
      (Every rabbit patted him)

Given this, even when a Japanese adult rejects the reflexive interpretation for (14), we are not sure if Binding Principle B is respected in L2 English.

(14) Every rabbit$_i$ patted him$_{*i/j}$.

The rejection of (14) could be because of transfer from L1 Japanese. If a Japanese adult transfers the [- bound variable] feature from Japanese *kare* to English *him/he*, (14) can be rejected on the basis of the [- bound variable] feature on *him*, without any reference to Binding Principle B.

Here, recall that L1 English-speaking children are poor at rejecting pronominal binding in the ECM construction such as (15).

(15) *Every troll$_i$ believes him$_i$ to be a good jumper. (Poor, 45% rejection)

Although in adult English the embedded clause subject *him* cannot be bound by the matrix subject *every troll* in the ECM construction (15), Sano and Crain (2004) report that English-speaking children, aged 4-6, cannot reliably reject the bound interpretation for (15).

Now, suppose that the pattern of L1 English is replicated in L2 English by Japanese learners. Then, the bound reading is allowed in (15). This means that the third-person pronoun, such as *him*, has the [+ bound variable] feature in L2 English, and the [- bound variable] feature of *kare* is not transferred from L1 Japanese to L2 English. Thus, if the bound reading is allowed in (15) in L2 English, just as in L1 child English, it is demonstrated that there is no transfer of [- bound variable] feature from L1 Japanese. Also, if the pattern of L1 English is replicated in L2 English by Japanese learners, the reflexive reading will be rejected for the simple clause such as (14), where *him* is bound by a quantifier antecedent in its Governing Category. Since the possibility of transfer of [- bound variable] feature on *him* has been excluded by the acceptance of the bound reading in (15), the rejection of the reflexive reading in (14) should now clearly indicate that Binding Principle B is respected in L2 English.

In this way, by replicating the finding in child L1 English, we can examine the effect of Binding Principle B in L2 English by Japanese learners. Specifically, our argument can be summarized as in (16).

(16) If it is shown that the bound reading is allowed in (15) but not in (14), we can claim that Binding Principle B is respected in L2 English by Japanese learners.

Below, we will report our experiment which lends support to this claim.

4. Experiment

We administered a grammaticality judgment task to 22 native Japanese adults (age; 21-22) who were learning English as a second language. There were four targets as shown in (17):

(17) a. *Every rabbit$_i$ brushed him$_i$. (Simple clause with bound reading)
    b. Every rabbit$_i$ brushed him$_j$. (Simple clause with disjoint reading)
    c. *Every troll$_i$ believes him$_i$ to be a good jumper.
       (ECM construction with bound reading)
    d. Donald believes Lisa to be a good cook.
       (ECM construction with real names)

We tested the subjects' knowledge of the Binding Principle B in (17)-a and (17)-b. But their performance in (17)-a and (17)-b does not necessarily reflect their knowledge of the principle, because they can successfully deal with them through positive L1 transfer as discussed above. Target (17)-c is relevant to see whether the L1 transfer actually exists there. If the subjects correctly rule out the bound reading in (17)-c, it is due to either their pure knowledge of binding or due to L1 transfer. However, recall that (17)-c is the structure where L1-English children allow bound reading. If the adult L2 learners of this study replicate the child-L1 pattern, *him* in (17)-c is [+ bound variable] in their grammars, while Japanese equivalent *kare* is [- bound variable]. If this is the case, the possibility of L1 transfer is excluded. Target (17)-d is to see whether the subject could handle the ECM construction itself.

There were two sentences for each target in the experiment. The task was given in written form. The subjects were asked to read stories in Japanese and judge whether the English sentence following the story correctly reflects it. An example is shown in (18):

(18) Story (originally written in Japanese):
Grover and three trolls are playing. A troll says, "Let's have a jumping contest. Here we have five medals. A good jumper can get medals."
First, Grover goes. "Look, I can do somersault! Uh-oh, I stumbled. I give up."
Second, the blue troll goes. "I'm very fast!" But he knocks over the fence.
Next, the green troll goes. "I'm careful. I don't knock over anything. Now I'm done."
Last, the yellow troll goes. "Look, I can spin around! I made it!"
They start talking: "Now, let's decide who gets medals. Give a medal to the jumper who you believe is good."
Grover says, "I don't know what to do. Do I get a medal?"
The blue troll says, "I believe I am a good jumper since I was very quick. So I give myself a medal. And I also believe Grover is quite good. So I give him a medal, too."
The green troll says, "I believe I am a good jumper since I finished without bumping anything. So I give myself a medal. And, I am also impressed by Grover. So I give him a medal, too."
The yellow troll says, "Well, there is only one medal left. What shall I do? Grover was good, but he didn't finish. If you don't finish, you are not a good jumper. I believe I am a good jumper since successfully finished. I give myself a medal."
Target (written in English): Every troll believes him to be a good jumper.
(False)

5. Result and discussion

The results of the experiment are shown in Graph 1.

Graph 1: Results of grammaticality judgment task

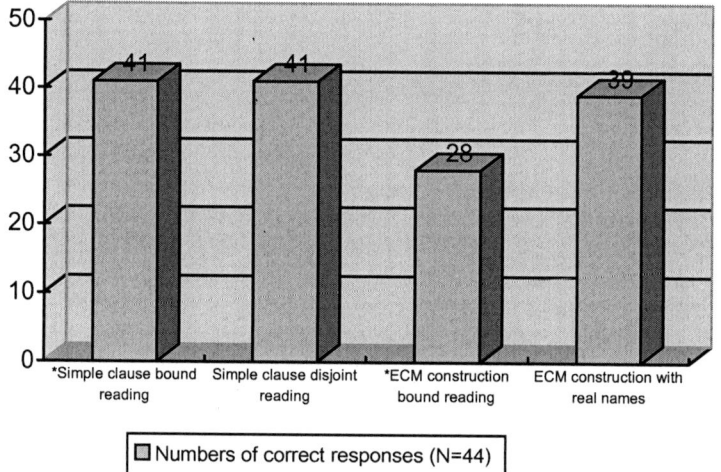

As for "simple clause with bound reading" ((17)-a) and "simple clause with disjoint reading" ((17)-b), the correct response rates were over 93%. That is, the majority of subjects correctly ruled out the bound reading and ruled in the disjoint reading in simple clauses. On the other hand, the number of correct responses in "ECM construction with bound reading" (17-(c)) was significantly smaller than that in "simple clause with bound reading" (17-(a)) ($\alpha<0.001$, one-way ANOVA within subjects). This indicates that quite a few number of subjects treated the pronominal as a bound variable in ECM constructions. It is not because they were confused in dealing with the ECM construction itself, since the correct response rate in "ECM construction with real names" (17-(d)) was over 88%, which is again significantly larger than that of "ECM construction with bound reading" ($\alpha<0.001$).

6. Discussion and Conclusion

The data support our hypothesis (16). The results of the experiment show that the bound reading is allowed in ECM constructions. This demonstrates that the adult L2 learners treated a pronominal as [+ bound variable], where they would have treated it as [- bound variable] if they had been under the influence of L1 Japanese. Hence, the possibility of L1 transfer is excluded, and their rejection of reflexive reading in simple clauses can be interpreted as pure knowledge of syntactic binding.

Then, what accounts for their ambiguous interpretation between the bound reading and the disjoint reading in ECM constructions? Here, we apply the same analysis as Baauw and Cuetos (2003) and Sano and Crain (2004) that the learners treat a pronominal in the ECM construction as a SE anaphor. SE anaphor (e.g., *zich* in Dutch) does not allow pronominal binding in simple clauses as exemplified in (19), but it allows pronominal binding in ECM constructions as in (20):

(19) *Peter$_i$ wees naar zich$_i$.
Peter pointed at   SE
(Peter pointed at SE)
(20) Het jongetje$_i$ zag zich$_i$ dansen.
the boy   saw   SE   dance
(The boy saw him(self) dancing)

Sano and Crain (2004) refer to the framework of Reinhart and Reuland (1993) as in (21), and argue that L1-English children are not able to specify the case/number feature for the pronominal element. That is, they have yet to acquire [+ Referentiality] of the pronominal. Hence, the pronominal element behaves like SE-anaphor in environments like ECM constructions.

(21) Reinhart and Reuland (1993)
    a. Co-indexing in anaphora creates an A-chain.
    b. The tail of an A-chain must be [- Referential].
    c. Principle B: semantically reflexive predicate must be reflexive
marked.
    (ECM predicate is NOT a semantically reflexive predicate.)

	Referentiality	Reflexive marked
SELF anaphor	-	+
SE anaphor	-	-
Pronoun	+	-

Like L1 children of Sano and Crain (2004), adult L2 learners may not be able to specify the Φ-feature of pronouns at an early stage of acquisition.

Then, what is relevant here is a morphological issue, but not a syntactic issue: the adult L2 learners do have knowledge of binding, and what they have yet to learn is a morphological feature of the L2 pronominal elements.

And this study also supports the broadly accepted claim that even adult interlanguages are UG-constrained: they employ grammatical options that are found neither in L1 nor L2, but that are found in other natural languages (duPlessis, Solin, Travis and White 1987; Schwartz and Sprouse 1994).

Notes

We would like to thank Yoko Ikeda and Miwako Momiyama for conducting the experiment. We would also like to thank members of TPL for comments and discussions. All the remaining errors are our own.

References

Baauw, S. and F. Cuetos, (2003) "The interpretation of pronouns in Spanish Language acquisition and breakdown: evidence for the 'Principle B Delay' as a non-unitary phenomenon," *Language Acquisition 11*, 219-275.

Chien, Y. and K. Wexler, (1990) "Children's knowledge of locality conditions in binding as evidence for the modularity of syntax and pragmatics," *Language Acquisition 1*, 225-295.

duPlessis, J., Solin, D., Travis, L. and L. White, (1987) "UG or not UG, that is the question: a reply to Clahsen and Muysken," *Second Language Research 3*, 56-75.

Finer, D. and E. Broselow, (1986) "Second language acquisition of reflexive-binding," in *Proceedings of the North Western Linguistic Society 16*.

Kanno, K. (1997) "The acquisition of null and overt pronominals in Japanese by English speakers," *Second Language Research 13*, 265-287.

Perez-Léroux, A. and W. Glass, (1999) "Null anaphora in Spanish second language acquisition: probabilistic versus generative approaches," in E. Klein and G. Martohardjono, eds., *The development of second language grammars: a generative approach*, John Benjamins, Amsterdam.

Otsu, Y. (1981) "Universal Grammar and syntactic development in children: toward a theory of syntactic development," doctoral dissertation, MIT, Massachusetts.

Reinhart, T. (1983) *Anaphora and Semantic Interpretation*, Croon Helm, London.

—. and E. Reuland, (1993) "Reflexivity," *Linguistic Inquiry 24*, 657-720.

Saito, M. and H. Hoji, (1983) "Weak crossover and move-alpha in Japanese," *Natural Language and Linguistic Theory 1*, 245-259.

Sano, T. and S. Crain, (2004) "A developmental delay of 'Principle B' in variable binding: the case of English ECM constructions," poster presented at Generative Approach to Language Acquisition North America 2004.

Schwartz, B. and R. Sprouse, (1994) "Word order and nominative case in nonnative language acquisition: a longitudinal study of (L1 Turkish) German interlanguage," in T. Hoekstra and B. Schwartz, eds., *Language Acquisition Studies in Generative Grammar*, John Benjamins, Amsterdam.

GETTING IN FOCUS: THE ROLE OF THE NSR IN CHILDREN'S INTERPRETATION OF SENTENCES WITH FOCUSED PREVERBAL MATERIAL

ANA LÚCIA SANTOS

1. Introduction

This paper discusses the comprehension of sentences with the focus operator *só* "only" by European Portuguese (EP) children between 2;9 and 4;11. Two main facts about *só* will be crucial for the discussion in this paper: the fact that *só* associates with focus and the fact that it introduces a presupposition.

Só associates with focus to the extent that the scope of *só* and the focus of a sentence generally coincide. On the other hand, since Horn (1969) it is assumed that *only / só* introduces a presupposition. In this paper, I suggest that the interpretation of *só* presents two independent problems for children: one problem is the definition of the scope of *só*; the other problem is the recognition of the presupposition.

2. Focus, acquisition and the Nuclear Stress Rule

In this section, I present Cinque's (1993) formulation of the Nuclear Stress Rule (NSR) and I make explicit its predictions for acquisition. I review the main findings concerning children's sensitivity to focus and show that the majority of these findings are in agreement with the predictions of Cinque's NSR.

2.1. Focus and Cinque's Nuclear Stress Rule

Cinque (1993) develops a theory of phrase and sentence stress assignment according to which there is no language specific NSR. Cinque claims that nuclear stress is assigned in all languages to the most embedded constituent, the relevant notion of embedding being determined by the direction of recursion. I.e. the constituent bearing the most prominent stress in a sentence is the most embedded one on the recursive side of a tree. This means that, when there are sister nodes, the most embedded one is the one that is selected by the other. Cinque's achievement is the fact that, according to this definition of the Nuclear Stress Rule (NSR), nuclear stress is always assigned to the embedded object in VO as well as in OV languages, and hence there is no need for a language-specific NSR. Reinhart (1995), and also Neeleman and Reinhart (1998), propose that each sentence is associated with a set of possible focus readings, as in (1). When, by the application of the NSR, stress falls on the object, the focus set is defined as in (1'b). The discourse context will determine which member of the focus set is appropriate.

(1) The focus set of IP consists of the constituents containing the main stress of IP.

(1') a. $[_{IP}$ Subject $[_{VP}$ V *Object*$]]$
    a'. $[_{IP}$ Subject $[_{VP}$ *Object* V$]]$
    b. *focus set*: {IP, VP, Object}

The way Cinque (1993) defines the NSR makes it possible to claim that the NSR is innate (cf. Reinhart, *to appear*). If the NSR is not language specific, it is *a priori* plausible that is not learned. Maturational factors aside, this leads to the prediction that children should manifest this knowledge from a very early stage.

In addition to the NSR, which assigns neutral stress and which is the default strategy of stress and focus assignment, languages use different strategies to depart from the NSR and to assign a focus interpretation to other constituents. The stress shift strategy is one of these strategies. When a constituent is focused that does not belong to the focus set derived by the NSR, there is a "stress shifting" strategy which may apply and give rise to a different focus reading. This is the case in (2), where the subject is focused. This focus reading is obtained through marked stress and, in this case, only the subject focus reading is possible (cf. Neeleman and Reinhart, 1998).

(2) Q: Who went to the US yesterday?
    A: PETER went to the US yesterday.

Languages have also syntactic strategies of focus shifting. For instance, in (3) the subject, which does not necessarily receive contrastive stress, is interpreted as focused because it is associated with the focus adverb *only / só*.

(3) Só   o   Pedro foi   ontem para   os EUA.
    only the   Pedro went yesterday to   the USA
    'Only Pedro went to the US yesterday.'

In (4), the subject is interpreted as focused because it is clefted.

(4) Foi   o Pedro que viajou   ontem   para   os EUA.
     was   the Pedro that traveled yesterday   to   the USA
     'It was Peter who traveled to the US yesterday.'

It is plausible that, although the NSR is not learned, the specific strategies that allow to establish readings not determined by the NSR are acquired on a case by case basis through the observation of the input. It is also possible that strategies of "focus shift" are computationally more complex than the NSR: Reinhart (*to appear* a, b) claims that stress shift (one strategy of focus shift) is computationally complex, whereas the NSR is computationally simple. We will return to this later in this paper.

2.2. Previous results concerning children's sensitiveness to focus

Children's recognition of focus positions in their language has indeed been at the center of current debate. Much of this debate concerns children's interpretation of sentences containing the focalization adverb / quantifier *only*. Using different types of tasks, various researchers have tried to evaluate children's knowledge of the scopal properties of *only*. The predominant result in these studies is compatible with the claim that children are sensitive to the NSR from the earliest stages of language acquisition.

Gualmini, Maciukaite and Crain (1992) show that English speaking children do not have an adult interpretation of sentences with *only* and stress shift within the VP: differently from adults, children seem to ignore the effects of stress shift and associate *only* to the most embedded constituent in the VP. Szendrői (2003) shows similar facts. She shows that 9 out of 23 Dutch speaking children (4;1-6;10) fail to interpret sentences with stress-shift within the VP: instead of interpreting *alleen* "only" as associating with the constituent with the main stress, they interpret *alleen* as associated with the VP. Costa and Szendrői (2004) replicate the same finding with EP children (3;11-5;9). The important fact is that the VP focus reading in Szendrői's and in Costa and Szendrői's studies can be obtained without stress-shift. According to Neeleman and Reinhart's definition of the focus set (cf. 1), VP focus is one of the possible readings if stress is on the most embedded XP, i.e. the position determined by the NSR. So it may be that in these cases as well children are merely interpreting sentences according to the NSR. Philip (1999) presents compatible evidence. He shows that Norwegian children (4;5 to 6;9, mean age 6;0) apply an object focus reading to VSO sentences in which the subject is under the scope of *bare*, but they do not do the inverse.

Other studies tested children's ability to interpret sentences in which *only* associates with a preverbal subject. Crain et al. (1992) tested 3 to 6-year-old children (mean age: 4;9) on their comprehension of sentences in which *only* associates with a preverbal subject and sentences in which *only* is in preverbal position and associates with the postverbal object. They notice that some children overuse a focus subject reading and others overuse an object focus reading.

Paterson et al. (2003) carried out a large scale study on English-speaking children's and adults' comprehension of sentences with *only* in a picture-choice task. They compared the performance of 4- to 12-year-olds and adults on sentences with *only* preceding a preverbal subject and sentences with *only* preceding a VP – cf. (5a, b). Their results indicated that the majority of errors corresponded to cases in which the children interpreted sentences with *only* as if *only* were not present in the structure. For example, they interpret (5a) or (5b) as (6). There was also a group of responses indicating that children misanalyze the scope of *only*: in these cases, children interpret (5a) as (5b) or the opposite (as in Crain et al.'s 1992 results).

(5) a. The fireman is only holding a hose.
    b. Only the fireman is holding a hose.

(6) The fireman is holding a hose.

More recently, Endo (2004) presents results on children's interpretation of the focus particles *dake* 'only' and *sika-nai* 'nobody except / nothing but' in SOV sentences in Japanese. Endo shows that, although the majority of children have an adult interpretation of the sentences in which the focus particles are attached to the object, they do not have an adult interpretation of the sentences in which the focus particles are attached to the subject. The typical non-adult reading of a sentence in which the focus particle was attached to the subject was a reading in which the children interpreted the focus particle as if it was attached to the object.

Although the results across these different studies are not identical and although they have received different interpretations, the predominant response is the one indicating that children interpret *only* as associated with the unmarked position of stress, i.e. the most embedded position. In this paper I develop the hypothesis that this predominant response reflects the fact that children initially interpret focus according to the NSR. They then later acquire language specific strategies of focus shift. The hypothesis developed here is stated in (7):

(7) Default Focus Hypothesis (DFH)
Children start with a default focus assignment strategy, which corresponds to the application of a universal NSR.

3. The experimental setting

We tested a group of 20 monolingual EP speakers aged 2;9 up to 4;11 (mean age 3;8) and a group of 16 adult controls with no background in linguistics on their interpretation of sentences with *só*. The experimental subjects were presented with simple situations acted out with props in which experimenters offered different types of food to two animals and the animals accepted or refused it. The test was a Truth Value Judgment Task (Crain and Thornton, 1998), in which children were presented with yes-no questions. The following three types of structures were tested: *só* in pre-VP position, *só* associated with a preverbal subject, and *só* associated with a preverbal subject that was focused by an inverted *é que* pseudo-cleft – Condition 1, Condition 2 and Condition 3, respectively. In each condition, children were presented two test questions (along with filler questions); one of the test questions expected an affirmative answer and the other expected a negative answer. The situation and the test questions in Condition 1 is presented in (8).

(8) Condition 1:
The pig is eating a cookie and a banana; the cow is eating a cookie and has refused the banana.
a. First question
Lead-in: O   porco   só   quer   a banana?
            the   pig   only   wants   the banana
            'Does the pig only want the banana?'
Target answer: NO
b. Second question
Lead-in: A   vaca   só   quer   a   bolacha?
            the   cow   only   wants   the   cookie
            'Does the cow only want the cookie?'
Target answer: YES

By comparing the answers in the two test questions, we arrive at more secure conclusions about the readings that children attribute to the different questions. We identify four different readings: not only object focus and subject focus, but also sentence focus and a reading in which *só* "only" is ignored. Namely, if the child answers "no" to both questions, the child may be allowing *só* to associate with the whole sentence, a case of "sentence focus reading". A sentence focus

reading in Condition 1corresponds to the reading: "the only thing that happens /
happened is / was that the pig wants the banana". Finally, an affirmative answer
to both questions would indicate an interpretation in which *só* is ignored (*yes*
bias excluded on the basis of filler and warming-up questions). In this case, the
first question in Condition 1 would be interpreted as "Does the pig want the
banana?".

Table 1 synthesizes the four possible answer patterns in Condition 1.

Table 1 - Answers to questions in Condition 1 and their interpretation

Question 1	Question 2	Reading
Negative	Affirmative	→Object focus reading
Affirmative	Negative	Subject focus reading
Negative	Negative	Sentence focus reading
Affirmative	Affirmative	*Só* is ignored

In (9) and (10), I present the settings and the questions in conditions 2 and 3.

(9) Condition 2

*The pig is eating an apple and has refused the orange; the cow is eating an
apple and an orange.*

    a. First question

Lead-in:	Só	o	porco	quer	a	maçã?
	Only	the	pig	wants	the	apple

               'Does only the pig want the apple?'

Target answer: NO

    b. Second question

Lead-in:	Só	a	vaca	quer	a	laranja?
	Only	the	cow	wants	the	orange

               'Does only the cow want the orange?'

Target answer: YES

Table 2 - Answers to questions in Condition 2 and their interpretation

Question 1	Question 2	Reading
Affirmative	Negative	Object focus reading
Negative	Affirmative	→Subject focus reading
Negative	Negative	Sentence focus reading
Affirmative	Affirmative	*Só* is ignored

(10) Condition 3

*The pig is eating lettuce and a carrot; the cow is eating lettuce and has
refused the carrot.*

    a. First question

Lead-in: Só   o   porco é que quer   a   cenoura?

Only   the   pig   is that wants the   carrot

'Is it only the pig that wants the carrot?'

Target answer: YES

b. Second question

Lead-in: Só   a   vaca   é que quer   a   alface?

only   the   cow   is that wants the   lettuce

'Is it only the cow who wants the lettuce?'

Target answer: NO

Table 3 - Answers to questions in Condition 3 and their interpretation

Question 1	Question 2	Reading
Negative	Affirmative	Object focus reading
Affirmative	Negative	→Subject focus reading
Negative	Negative	Sentence focus reading
Affirmative	Affirmative	*Só* is ignored

In order to avoid possible effects of order of presentation, the children were presented with the 3 conditions in different orders. For 9 children the order of presentation was Conditions 1, 2, 3; for 11 children the order was Conditions 2, 1, 3. No effects of order of presentation were found.

4. Results: two major response patterns

In this section, I present the results, starting with the adult controls. Figure 1 presents the results of the adult controls.

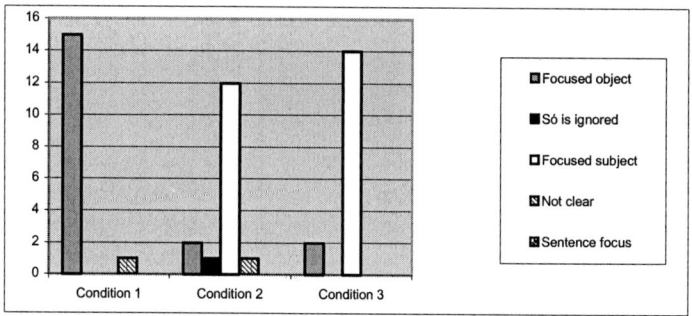

Fig. 1 – Results of EP adult controls interpretation of focus

Most adult controls (12 out of 16) performed as expected. When adults did not perform as expected, they tended to interpret the test questions in Condition 2 and 3 (the subject focus conditions) according to an object focus reading. Although only 3 adults consistently gave this reading (two of them only in one of the subject focus conditions), 3 other adults first interpreted sentences in Condition 2 according to an object focus reading and then reformulated their interpretation according to the adult subject focus interpretation. We will come back to these adult errors in section 5.

In Figure 2, I present children's results.

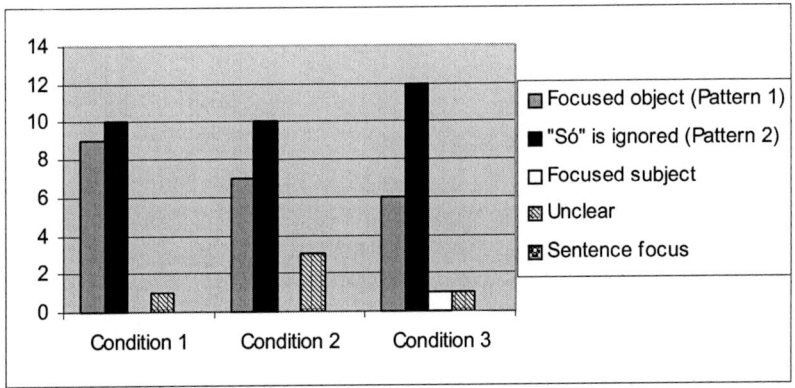

Fig. 2 – Results of EP children's interpretation of focus (age 2;9-4;11)

The child results can be summarized as follows:

(i) Children do not assign a subject focus reading either in cases in which this is the target reading (Conditions 2 and 3) or in cases in which this reading is not expected (Condition 1). The only exception is one child (one of the oldest) who performed adult-like in interpreting *só* as focusing the subject in Condition 3.

(ii) Independent of the exact structure that was tested, children's answers fell into one of two patterns: either they interpret *só* in all sentences as associating with the post-verbal object DP (we refer to this as *Pattern 1*) or they answered 'yes' to all test questions, although they answer 'no' when relevant in filler trials (we refer to this as *Pattern 2*).

Most children were fairly consistent in their responses, conforming to either the object focus reading (Pattern 1) or Pattern 2 across test conditions. The distribution of children across response types is given in Figure 3.

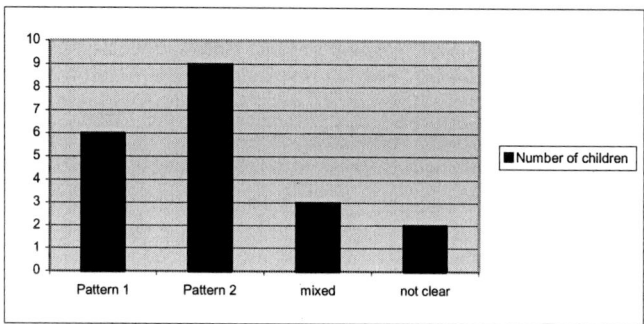

Fig. 3 – Distribution of children across response types

5. Discussion

5.1. The default focus reading (Pattern 1)

Pattern 1 corresponds to a reading in which *só* associates with the post-verbal object DP. Six children use this pattern across the different conditions, i.e. also in Conditions 2 and 3, in which this is not an expected reading. The following is a typical justification associated with this type of reading:

(11) Condition 3
Lead-in: Só   o   porco   é que   quer   a   cenoura?
        only   the   pig   is that wants   the   carrot
        'Is it only the pig that wants the carrot?'
        (Target answer: yes)

Child: Não.   Quer # folha de alface   e   cenoura.
        no   wants   lettuce   and   carrot
        'No, he wants lettuce and carrot.'

The responses of Pattern 1 children are in agreement with the DFH (cf. 7). Children interpret *só* as associated with the embedded object even in cases in which *só* associates with the subject in the target grammar (cf. Condition 2 and 3). The results are consistent with the claim that children start with the NSR as a default strategy of focus interpretation.

Reinhart (*to appear* a, b) proposes a parsing explanation for children's difficulty with focus in stress shift contexts. However, the particular results we are discussing here cannot be accounted for by a processing explanation. A strict processing account of the results obtained is possible if we show that children have the relevant competence; the results obtained in this experiment suggest that children do not have the knowledge necessary to interpret preverbal material as focused, but rather interpret focus strictly according to the DFH. However, it is possible that, after having acquired strategies of shifting focus from its default position, children show processing difficulties of the type suggested by Reinhart. It is possible that this bigger processing load associated with non-default focus readings explains the few errors in the adult control group, which also reveal a preference for the object focus reading.

Finally, let us return briefly to the fact that Crain et al. (1992) and Patterson et al. (2003) obtained subject focus readings in object focus contexts. This could be a problem for the DFH that we propose in this paper. However, the children in Crain et al.'s and Patterson et al.'s studies are older than in the experiment reported in this paper (mean age in Crain et al.'s study is 4;8 and 5;0; the youngest children in Patterson et al.'s study are 4- to 5-year-old children). So it is possible that some of the children in these studies had already acquired the non-default focus positions and, at some point, overuse a subject focus reading.

5.2. Pattern 2

Pattern 2 corresponds to cases in which children answered affirmatively to all test questions, although they answered *no* appropriately in filler questions. Therefore, I maintain that these are not cases of a "yes" bias. Instead, I argue that in these cases children interpret sentences as the corresponding sentence without *só*. Patterson et al. (2003) first noticed this type of answer and claim that this is a strategy English-speaking children use to interpret sentences with *only*. The hypothesis that Pattern 2 children interpret sentences as the corresponding sentence without *só* is supported by some of the justifications provided by children:

In answer to the first test question in Condition 2:
(12) Lead-in: Só   o   porco   quer   a   maçã?
                 only   the   pig   wants the   apple
                 'Does only the pig want the apple?'
                 (Adult answer: Não.)
     Child: Sim.   Quer uma   maçã.
              Yes   wants a   apple
              'Yes. He wants an apple.'

As an explanation for Pattern 2, we hypothesize that children (at least up to 4;11, according to our data) may have a problem dealing with *só* that is independent from the identification of focus: children do not understand that a sentence with *só* introduces a presupposition. We call this the Presupposition Difficulty Hypothesis (PDH). Sentences with *only* introduce presuppositions. For instance, the sentence in (12) introduces the presupposition "the pig wants the apple", i.e. (12) can only be uttered in a context in which it is assumed to be true that the pig wants the apple. So what is under discussion in (12) is whether no other animal but the pig want the apple, not whether the pig wants the apple. If children do not recognize the presupposition, in the sense that they take the presupposition as an assertion, they will interpret the question in (12) as asking also the sub-question "does the pig want the apple?". This sub-question is always compatible with a "yes" answer because the situations in which a question such as (12) can be felicitously asked are situations in which it is true that the pig wants the apple. Thus, when children systematically answer affirmatively to the test questions in our experiment, our hypothesis is that they are taking the presupposition as an assertion.

5.3. The co-existence of "default focus" and "presupposition difficulty"

In the previous section, I argued that children in the age range of the subjects in our experiment have a problem identifying as such the presupposition introduced by *só*. On the other hand, I also argued that children in the same age range have difficulty accessing focus interpretations that are not derived by the NSR. Therefore, these children cannot interpret as focused a preverbal subject.

Note now that the fact that the presupposition problem and the default focus problem are independent interpretation problems makes it possible that the two problems co-exist in the same child. In fact, Pattern 1 and Pattern 2 groups are not related to different age groups and therefore it is implausible that Pattern 1 and Pattern 2 correspond to different developmental stages. I would like to suggest that all the children in this study may have both interpretation problems, irrespective of whether they perform according to Pattern 1 or to Pattern 2. To clarify the hypothesis, I outline children's interpretation of one of the test questions. My hypothesis is that all the children in our study take as an assertion the presupposition introduced by *só*, and hence interpret (13) as asking the two sub-questions in (13a and b).

(13) Só   o   porco   quer   a   maçã?
     Only   the   pig   wants   the   apple
     'Does only the pig want the apple?'
     a.   Does the pig want the apple?
     b.   Does the pig only want the apple?

In addition, the children are unable to interpret the preverbal subject as focused, and hence may formulate the sub-question in (13b) as a question in which *só* associates with the VP or the embedded object. Thus, if children choose to answer (13a) they manifest the presupposition difficulty, if they choose to answer (13b) they manifest the default focus strategy. The fact that there exists a group of three mixed children (cf. Fig. 3), i.e. children that interpret some questions according to the default focus strategy and some others according to the Pattern 2 strategy is in agreement with the idea that the two problems may co-exist in the same child.

6. Conclusion

In this paper, I argue that children do not have adult knowledge of the interpretation of *só* "only". First, they start with a more limited set of possibilities as far as the definition of the scope of *só* is concerned: children start by restricting the scope of *só* to the constituents that are identified as focus according to the NSR. Second, I argue that children do not know that *só* introduces a presupposition (in the sense of Horn, 1969) and they can take as an assertion the presupposition introduced by *só*.

Acknowledgment

This work would not have been done without systematic discussion with Nina Hyams and Inês Duarte. I am also grateful to the audience of the "Psychobabble Meeting" at UCLA, where I presented an earlier version of this paper. Of course, all errors are mine. Thanks also to Nélia Alexandre and Susana Correia, who helped with data collection and to the teachers and children at CEPI 5 de Outubro. This work was supported by Fundação para a Ciência e Tecnologia (research grant SFRH / BD / 19829 / 2004).

References

Cinque, G. (1993) "A Null Theory of Phrase and Compound Stress", *Linguistic Inquiry.* 24.2: 239-297.

Costa, J. and K. Szendrői (2004) "Acquisition of focus marking in European Portuguese: evidence for a unified approach to focus", paper presented at the 2nd Lisbon Meeting on Language Acquisition. Universidade de Lisboa.

Crain, S., W. Philip, K. F. Drozd, T. Roeper and K. Matsuoka (1992). "Only in Child Language", ms., University of Connecticut, Storrs, CT.

—. and R. Thornton (1998) *Investigations in Universal Grammar. A Guide to Experiments on the Acquisition of Syntax and Semantics*, The MIT Press, Cambridge, Mass.

Endo, M. (2004) "Developmental issues on the interpretation of focus particles by Japanese children." In A. Brugos, L. Micciulla & C. E. Smith (eds.) *Proceedings of the 28th Annual Boston University Conference on Language Development.* Vol. 1. Somerville, Mass.: Cascadilla Press.

Gualmini, A., S. Maciukaite and S. Crain (2002) "Children's insensitivity to contrastive stress in sentences with ONLY", in *PWPL* 9.1: Proceedings of the 26th Annual PLC. University of Pennsylvania.

Horn, L. R. (1969) "A Presuppositional Analysis of *only* and *even*", in R. I. Binnick et al., eds., *Papers from the Fifth Regional Meeting of the Chicago Linguistic Society.* University of Chicago.

Neeleman, A. and T. Reinhart (1998) "Scrambling and the PF interface", in M. Butt and W. Geuder, eds., *The Projection of Arguments. Lexical and Compositional Factors*, CSLI Publications, Stanford.

Paterson et al. (2003) "Children's comprehension of sentences with focus particles", *Cognition*, 89.3, 263-294.

Philip, W. (1999) "Children want Only a right-conservative determiner", *University of Massachusetts Occasional Papers in Linguistics 24*, University of Massachusetts, Amherst.

Reinhart, T. (*to appear* a) "The Processing Cost of Reference-set Computation: Acquisition of Stress Shift and Focus", *Language Acquisition.*

—. (*to appear* b) *Interface Strategies – Reference Set Computation*, The MIT Press

Szendrői, K. (2003) "Acquisition evidence for an interface theory of Focus", in J. Van Kampen and S. Baauw, eds., *Proceedings of GALA 2003*, LOT, Utrecht.

L2 ACQUISITION OF DEFINITENESS AND SPECIFICITY IN ENGLISH BY ADVANCED JAPANESE AND SPANISH LEARNERS

NEAL SNAPE[*]

Abstract

Ionin (2003) has claimed that languages with a two-article system (like English *the/a*) either use articles to mark definiteness (English) or to mark specificity (Samoan), and that this is a function of a UG-determined 'article choice parameter'. The present study addresses the proposal of an article choice parameter by comparing learners of English whose L1 is Japanese (article-less) and Spanish (which has definiteness-marking articles). Additionally, it examines article choice in two different nominal contexts: with count singular and plural NPs. Fluctuation in the choice of *the/a* by the Japanese speakers is expected in indefinite specific count NP contexts (singular and plural) and in the case of the Spanish speakers, fluctuation between *the/a* is not expected due to L1 transfer effects.

1. Introduction

A recent approach to article classification has been offered by Ionin & Wexler (2003) using the definiteness and specificity distinction. They suggest that there is an article choice parameter determining the distribution of articles and claim that L2 learners from articleless languages fluctuate between definiteness and specificity when they are learning an L2 that has the features [+definite] and [+specific]. My study investigates the use of articles in count singular and plural contexts by advanced Japanese and Spanish L2 learners of English.

2. The Article Choice Parameter (ACP)

Ionin (2003) claims that there are two settings of ACP where a language, which has two articles, will have one value or the other:

(1)   Setting I. Articles are distinguished on the basis of specificity
         Setting II. Articles are distinguished on the basis of definiteness

(taken from Ionin 2003, p.85)

Ionin's informal definition of definiteness and specificity is in (2):

(2)   Definiteness and Specificity
         If a Determiner Phrase (DP) of the form [D NP] is...
         (a) [+definite], then the speaker and hearer presuppose the existence of a unique individual in the set denoted by the NP
         (b) [+specific], then the speaker intends to refer to a unique individual in the set denoted by the NP, and considers this individual to possess some noteworthy property

According to Ionin the features [+definite] and [+specific] are discourse-related. The crucial difference between the two features is that [+definite] is a shared state of knowledge between speaker and hearer and [+specific] is knowledge only held by the speaker. Their proposal of specificity in (1b) is based Fodor and Sag (1982), who claim that relative clause (RC)-modification biases an indefinite in favour of the specific reading:

(3)   A: Kylie went to Tim's party
         B: Did she have fun?
         A: She met *a man who I know at school.*

Ionin & Wexler tested subjects from languages without articles – 30 L1 Russian speakers and 40 L1 Korean speakers who are all intermediate and advanced L2 learners of English. It is predicted that L2 learners of English without articles in their L1's will fluctuate between the two settings under the ACP in the absence of L1 transfer effects. Ionin suggests that L2 learners may adopt neither the L1 nor the L2 parameter settings, but a possible setting from some third language i.e. Samoan.

The Fluctuation Hypothesis is formulated by Ionin (2003) in (4):

(4)   The Fluctuation Hypothesis (FH) for L2-English article choice:
  (1) L2 learners have full UG access to the two settings of the Article
  Choice Parameter
  (2) L2 learners fluctuate between the two settings of the Article
  Choice Parameter until the input leads them to set this parameter to
  the appropriate value

(taken from Ionin 2003, p.86)

My study differs to Ionin & Wexler (2003) because one group is Japanese (a language without an article system) and the other group is Spanish (a language with an article system). I assume that the Japanese L2 learners, like Ionin's Russian and Korean L2 learners, may adopt a setting from a third language owing to the absence of L1 transfer effects. I predict that the Spanish L2 learners will behave differently to the Japanese because of L1 transfer effects in that the Spanish will not fluctuate between the features [+definite] and [+specific] because Spanish, like English, has articles for marking [±definite]. The Japanese L2 learners may still fluctuate in indefinite specific contexts because they associate *the* as a [+specific] marker.

3. Empirical Study: Forced-choice elicitation task

The test consisted of 92 short dialogues in total. The participants were asked to read the short dialogues where there are four possible items that could fill a gap. They were asked to choose the item that they felt was most appropriate to fill the gap and put a circle around it. RC-modification was used to force an indefinite specific reading for singular and plural contexts, as in Ionin & Wexler (2003). There were four short dialogues for each context and the contexts were randomised.

3.1 Research Hypothesis

H[1]   Japanese L2 learners tend to overuse *the* in indefinite specific
singular and plural contexts as they fail to set the Article
Choice Parameter and associate *the* with specificity.

3.2 The participants

The participants in our study were 13 advanced Japanese L2 learners of English, 13 advanced Spanish L2 learners of English and 13 native control speakers. Even though all the participants have taken TOEFL and have scores equivalent of 575 or above, they were asked to take the Oxford Quick Placement Test in order to obtain their current proficiency level.

3.3 Results

The native control speakers (NS) performed as expected in each context with 90% or above accuracy rates. Table 1 shows the results of one-way ANOVAs with post-hoc Tukey HSD tests.

Table 1. Use of articles by Japanese and Spanish advanced groups

	use of *the*	use of *a*	use of *Ø*
definite specific singular	F = 2.591	F = 2.483	1.000
indefinite specific singular	F = 8.237**	F = 8.955**	F = 1.000
indefinite specific plural	F = 10.377***	F = 0.00	F = 10.377***

*p <.05. **p <.01. ***p <.001.

The shaded areas in table 1 show that the advanced Japanese L2 learners are overusing *the* in indefinite specific singular and plural contexts significantly more than the advanced Spanish L2 learners and native controls. The results fully support Hypothesis (1) as the Japanese L2 learners overused *the* in indefinite specific singular and plural contexts.

4. Conclusion

Ionin claims that L2 learners have full access to UG's semantic features definiteness and specificity and they fluctuate between the two parameter settings of the ACP. I found that there is likely to be L1 transfer from Spanish to English because Spanish is a language that has morphemes for encoding definiteness, whereas Japanese is not. The advanced Japanese L2 learners continued to fluctuate even though they had years of exposure to English. One question that arises from my results and Ionin & Wexler's (2003) results is how much input is needed to set the ACP? If L2 learners have full access to UG, restructuring of their interlanguage grammars continue until the Primary Linguistic Data leads them to set the ACP to [+definite], which is the correct setting for English. However, they may not fully converge on the target language grammar because as Ionin (2003) states, the triggers from input are particularly subtle[1]

Notes

* This research is being funded by the ESRC, award no PTA-030-2003-01043. A version of the present study was presented at the Japan Second Language Association (J-SLA) conference, 2005. I would like to thank Roger Hawkins, Yan-kit Ingrid Leung, Bonnie Schwartz, Rex Sprouse and Tania Ionin for helpful comments and advice. Any shortcomings are mine alone.

[1] I thank Bonnie Schwartz and Rex Sprouse (*p.c*) for making the point that my results are consistent with the Full Transfer/ Full Access model (Schwartz and Sprouse 1996) in that L2 learners do not have to fully converge on the target grammar even at advanced stages of acquisition.

References

Fodor, J and I. Sag. (1982) "Referential and quantificational indefinites", *Linguistics and Philosophy* 5, 355–398.

Ionin, T. (2003) *Article semantics in second language acquisition*, Doctoral dissertation, MIT. Distributed by *MIT Working Papers in Linguistics*.

—. and K. Wexler (2003) "The Certain Uses of *the* in L2-English", paper presented at the 6th Generative Approaches to Second Language Acquisition Conference, University of Ottawa.

Schwartz, B. and R. A. Sprouse (1996) "L2 cognitive states and the Full Transfer/Full Access model", *Second Language Research* 12, 40–72.

INTERFACES IN L2 DEVELOPMENT

ANTONELLA SORACE

1. Introduction

One of the most significant shifts in recent theoretical and experimental research on adult second language (L2) acquisition is that it has become part of the wider effort to understand human cognition. Within this broader picture, data from L2 acquisition can be compared with data from other domains of language development as different manifestations of the language faculty and of its modes of interactions with other cognitive systems. It has emerged that there are striking parallels - in terms of developmental stages, effects of one language system on the other, and determinacy of outcomes - between L2 acquisition and other developmental domains such as first language (L1) attrition and bilingual L1 acquisition: one can observe similar patterns of optionality and indeterminacy that are apparently restricted to the interface(s) between syntax in a 'narrow' sense and other cognitive systems. The investigation of these phenomena therefore requires an understanding of the interplay of grammatical and extragrammatical factors and, in particular, a closer focus on the interaction among formal constraints on grammatical representations, discourse constraints on the contextual interpretation of language, and processing constraints on real-time language comprehension and production. In this respect, recent L2 research on the most advanced ('near-native') endstate of L2 acquisition marks a radical departure from previous L2 acquisition studies, which were almost exclusively concerned with the nature of L2 grammatical representations. Linguistic theory still provides a fundamental contribution: it directly addresses the question of interfaces between language and language-external systems (Chomsky 1995; Rizzi 2004); it accounts for variation in terms of features and lexical choices (Adger and Smith 2005); it formalizes discourse conditions on syntactic realization (Belletti 2004a, 2005a); and it allows a formal differentiation among different interfaces (Tsimpli and Sorace 2006). However, a theory of language processing is also needed to explain L2 development: the range of options available to the L2 speaker is grammatically based, but their actual selection in particular contexts is affected by processing principles. This paper focuses primarily on the development of the syntax-discourse interface in null subject languages, with a special emphasis on the interpretation and production of subjects.[1] The structure of the paper is as follows. First, some recent findings are summarized from L2 acquisition and L1 attrition research, showing that the syntax-discourse interface exhibits optionality in both developmental domains. A potential explanation is then presented in terms of feature undespecification and crosslinguistic influence at the level of the representations in the bilingual speaker's grammar. The last part of the paper concentrates on a different type of account that identifies sub-optimal processing, rather than underspecified representations, as a source of interface optionality.

2. The syntax-discourse interface

As is well known, Italian and English differ with respect to the range of pronominal subjects available: Italian allows null subjects whereas English does not.[2] In standard generative grammar theory, such differences are due to parametric variation between the two languages in terms of the value instantiated for the Null Subject Parameter (Rizzi 1982, 1986). Furthermore, the selection of a null or overt subject in Italian is sensitive to discourse conditions. Null subject pronouns are typically used when a condition of co-referentiality with the current topic holds, whereas overt subject pronouns are used to indicate a shift in reference to a non-topical antecedent (Grimshaw and Samek Lodovici 1998). As shown in (1), the preferred antecedent for the null pronoun is the matrix subject 'Gianni', which is the most prominent topic (although the object 'Pietro' is also possible, but dispreferred, in this context), whereas the overt pronoun is normally interpreted as referring either to the object, or to an extralinguistic antecedent, both of which are lower on the topicality scale (Ariel 1994).

(1) Gianni$_i$ ha salutato Pietro$_k$ quando *pro$_i$* / lui$_{?i/k/j}$ è arrivato.
    Gianni has greeted Pietro when   pro / he   is arrived

In null subject languages, postverbal subjects are traditionally regarded as possible as an implication of the [+null subject] value of the parameter.[3] The placement of the subject with respect to the verb, however, is regulated by a number of semantic conditions. For example, postverbal subjects in Italian are typically motivated by the need to mark focus, as shown in (2) where 'il presidente' is the focus of the new information that is conveyed by the sentence. The choice of postverbal over preverbal subjects is also modulated by other semantic factors, such as the definiteness of subject (cf. Belletti 1988) and the thematic properties of the verb (Pinto, 1997).

(2) Chi ha parlato?   Ha parlato   il presidente.
    who has spoken?   Has spoken the president

A further property related to the respective position of subject and verb is the partitive interpretation of indefinite preverbal subjects (Pinto 1997). Preverbal indefinite subjects tend to be interpreted as 'old' information (topic) whereas postverbal subjects are ambiguous between the focus and the topic readings, as shown in (3).

(3) La Marina americana ha stazionato due navi nel   Golfo.
    the navy American   has placed   two ships in the Gulf
    a. La notte scorsa una nave è affondata.
       the night last   a   ship   is sunk   (= one of the ships)
    b. La notte scorsa è affondata una nave.
       the night last   is sunk   a ship   (= one of the ships OR
                                                        some other ship)

3. Pronominal subjects in near-native Italian

Native and non-native speakers of Italian diverge in their production and comprehension of pronominal subjects: this divergence is manifested in the greater optionality shown by non-native speakers (Belletti, Bennati and Sorace 2005; Filiaci 2003; Sorace 2003, 2005a,b; Sorace and Filiaci 2006a; see also Tsimpli and Sorace 2006 for data on L2 Greek).[4] In production, near-native L2 Italian speakers optionally utter sentences such as (4b), with a 'redundant' overt pronoun, whereas a monolingual Italian speaker would produce (4c) with a null pronoun.

(4) a. Perchè Giorgio si è licenziato?   "Why did Giorgio resign?"
    b. Perchè lui non sopportava più il direttore.
    c. Perchè ø non sopportava più il direttore.
       because ø/he not stand-3s anymore the boss
       "Because he couldn't stand his boss anymore"

In contrast, errors involving the production of null pronouns in inappropriate contexts are unattested; for example, when a new referent is introduced (as in (5), or when the sentence is explicitly contrastive (as in (6).

(5) a. Perchè Giorgio si è licenziato? "Why did Giorgio resign? "
    b. *Perchè Ø non lo   aveva promosso   (Ø = "il direttore)
       because Ø not him-CL had promoted

(6) a. Maria ha detto che passava a prendere Paolo?
     Maria has said that she was going to pick up Paolo?
    b. *No, Ø ha detto che   passava a prendere lei   (Ø = Paolo)
      No, Ø said that he was going to pick her up.

It is important to note that the greater optionality in near-native grammar affects not only L2 speakers' production, but also their interpretation of pronominal subjects. Their divergent interpretations are particularly clear with respect to intersentential anaphora involving a main clause that includes equally plausible antecedents and a subordinate clause containing an overt pronoun. In forward anaphora (where the main clause precedes the subordinate clause, as in (7)) Italian near-native speakers often interpret the overt pronominal subject of the embedded clause as coreferential with the lexical subject of the main clause (7a). In contrast, native speakers interpret the overt pronoun in this context as referring to the complement (7b).

(7) a. Paola$_i$ andrà a trovare Marta$_k$ quando lei$_i$ avrà tempo.
    b. Paola$_i$ andrà a trovare Marta$_k$ quando lei$_k$ avrà tempo.
     Paola will go to visit Marta when she will have time

In backward anaphora (i.e. with the subordinate-main clause order, as in (8)), native speakers typically interpret the overt subject as referring to an extralinguistic antecedent (8b); near-natives, on the other hand, have a strong preference for establishing a dependency between the overt pronoun and the matrix subject (8a).

(8) a. Quando lei$_i$ era in vacanza, Paola$_i$ è andata a trovare Maria$_k$.
    b. Quando lei$_j$ era in vacanza, Paola$_i$ è andata a trovare Maria$_k$.
     When she was on holiday, Paola went to visit Maria

Subject placement in near-native Italian also presents more optionality compared to native Italian. In all-focus sentences, Italian near-native speakers optionally produce (9b), where a monolingual Italian speaker would normally produce (9c):[5]

(9) a. Che cosa è successo? 'What happened?'
    b. Il criceto   è   scappato.
     the hamster is-3s run away
    c. E'   scappato il criceto
     is-3s run away the hamster

The same speakers may also overuse preverbal subjects (often stressed) in contexts in which it would be more natural to use a postverbal subject because the DP is in narrow focus:

(10) a. Chi è scappato? "Who has run away?"
     b. Il criceto   è   scappato.
      the hamster is-3s run away

Near-native speakers may also interpret the preverbal subject in (11b) as conveying new information instead of the native preference for a partitive reading.

(11) a. La Marina Americana ha stazionato tre navi nel Golfo.
     the American Navy placed three ships in the Gulf
    b. La notte scorsa una nave è affondata.
     Last night a ship sank

4. An asymmetric overgeneralization

Descriptively, the patterns found in the performance of near-native speakers of Italian can be summarized as follows:
• Overt subject pronouns/preverbal subjects may optionally replace null subjects/postverbal subjects in both production and interpretation, but not vice versa.
• Near-native Italian speakers have fully acquired a null-subject grammar: they can – and often do - use null subjects and postverbal subjects correctly.
Thus, the problem is not related to the L2 speakers not having acquired a null subject grammar. Their indeterminacy appears to be at the level of the discourse conditions on the distribution of pronominals and on the placement of subjects. Let us first examine the implications of this assumption for the representation of pronominal subjects in the near-native grammar.
As seen earlier, null subject pronouns in null-subject languages are syntactically licensed but their distribution is governed by discourse-pragmatic factors. The identification of pronouns is therefore dependent on the on-line computation of these factors in processing, as argued in recent syntactic theory (see e.g.

Holmberg 2005; more on processing below). A number of developmental studies have drawn a similar, but more general distinction between syntax in a narrow sense and interfaces between syntax and other (semantic, discourse, lexical) cognitive systems (Avrutin 1999, 2004; Tsimpli, Sorace, Heycock and Filiaci; 2004; Tsimpli and Sorace 2006). According to this view, uninterpretable features in 'narrow syntax' drive syntactic derivations (and may be parameterized); interpretable features at interfaces (such as [Topic Shift] and [Focus]) 'exploit' parametric options and have interpretive effects, as they can be 'read' by the conceptual/intentional systems of cognition. These two types of features appear to be dissociated in near-native L2 grammars: uninterpretable features are acquirable, but interpretable features are not.[6] One possible reason is that these features remain underspecified in the non-native grammar, and this underspecification generates optionality. Using an extension of Cardinaletti and Starke's (2001) typology that includes interpretable features, the L2 Italian grammar can be represented as having a tripartite distinction where the monolingual Italian grammar has a binary one ((consistent with recent formal accounts of variation, e.g. Adger and Smith 2005; see also Cardinaletti 2005). The non-native grammar has more choices available than the native grammar, as seen in Table 1.

Native grammar	Near-native grammar
OVERT = STRONG = [+TS]	OVERT = STRONG = [+TS]
NULL = WEAK = [-TS]	OVERT = WEAK = [-TS]
	NULL = WEAK = [-TS]

Table 1: Range of subject pronouns in native and non-native Italian

According to this view, the residual optionality in near-native L2 grammars therefore involves interpretable features linked to a parametric choice that differs between the L1 and the L2. An interpretable feature that is specified in L2 in a particular syntactic structure remains unspecified due to the absence of a similar interpretable feature in L1 in the same syntactic context. This underspecification gives rise to ambiguity and optionality. L2 grammars are then expected to show more "ambiguity" since conflicting options associated with L1 and L2 will be accessible at the interface. In contrast, uninterpretable feature values that distinguish between the parametric choices of L1 and L2 do not show residual optionality. No optional "syntax" is therefore expected to be found.

A similar dissociation between formal licensing conditions and discourse conditions has been reported in recent studies on near-native speakers of Italian ((Belletti and Leonini 2004; Belletti, Bennati and Sorace, 2005) that show a discrepancy between the general availability of null subject pronouns in these speakers' performance and the reduced availability of postverbal subjects. Postverbal subjects are in fact produced significantly less frequently than null subjects. The explanation offered is that the availability of null-subject *pro* is a necessary, but not a sufficient condition to license postverbal subjects. An interpretation within the 'cartographic' framework (Belletti 2004a; Rizzi 2004) assumes that the postverbal subject, which is the focus of new information, fills a dedicated position in the VP periphery of the clause. In these structures, the (relevant) preverbal subject position is filled by pro. This is shown in (13), corresponding to (12b); see Belletti 2004a, 2005a, 2005b for details of this analysis.

(12) a. Chi ha telefonato?
        who has telephoned
    b. Ha telefonato Gianni
        has telephoned Gianni

(13) [CP ...[TP pro ...ha telefonato ... [TopP [FocP Gianni [TopP [VP ...]]]]]

Thus, the formal conditions licensing pro are a prerequisite for the VS order; but the postverbal subject crucially requires the activation of the VP periphery in specific discourse conditions. This analysis, besides allowing an interpretation of the near-native data, also provides a key to revisiting some asymmetries between null and postverbal subjects that have been found in previous L2 studies: for example, L1 English learners of L2 null subject languages show developmental delays in accepting/producing postverbal subjects (Liceras and Diaz 1998); L1 Spanish/Italian/Greek learners of L2 English do not transfer VS (Tsimpli and Roussou 1991).

It should be stressed that these interface phenomena do not involve strong ungrammaticality and categorical choices, but rather contextual inappropriateness and preferences. Although native and non-native speakers behave significantly differently from each other, these differences are best defined in terms of strength of preferences than presence vs. absence of a given behaviour.

5. Convergences: L1 attrition

The same overgeneralization of overt pronouns and postverbal subjects is exhibited by native Italian speakers after prolonged exposure to English: this is the developmental domain known as 'L1 attrition' (Tsimpli et al. 2004). However, a comparison of Italian near-natives, native Italian speakers under attrition, and monolingual Italian controls (Sorace and Filiaci 2006b) indicates that the magnitude of the overgeneralizations is different in the three groups: the production rates and preferences for redundant overt subject pronouns and for preverbal subjects of the speakers under attrition are consistently intermediate between those of monolinguals (which are the lowest) and those of near-native speakers (which are the highest).

The convergence between attrition and acquisition prompts a number of considerations. First, it indicates that the syntax-discourse interface is developmentally unstable: it may not be acquired completely in a second language and it is prone to change in a native language due to attrition from another language. Second, the directionality of crosslinguistic effects in bilingual speakers does not appear to be always from the L1 to the L2; rather, the language that instantiates the least restrictive option affects the other, but not vice versa. Therefore, L2 acquisition involves neutralization of target L2 distinctions towards the less restrictive L1 option, whereas L1 attrition involves neutralization of native distinctions towards the less restrictive L2 option. As a result, both Italian near-native speakers and Italian speakers under attrition have a wider range of options available to them than monolingual speakers typically have. Crucially, however, there is no formal incompatibility between these options and the parametric settings of Italian syntax. One could in fact predict that in the symmetrically opposite developmental situations of native Italian near-native speakers of L2 English and native English speakers under attrition from L2 Italian, the extension of the null subject option to English should be impossible, since it would be incompatible with the negative value of the null subject parameter (see Belletti, Bennati and Sorace 2005 for further discussion). Such an extension is indeed unattested.

To sum up so far, data from two developmental domains suggest that there is a split between narrow syntax and interface properties in terms of completeness of acquisition and vulnerability to change: in short, interface properties are more unstable than narrow syntactic properties. A possible account for these data was presented based on differences between native and non-native grammar representations with respect to the specification of interpretable interface features; it was suggested that optionality is due to the coexistence in the bilingual speaker of two grammars that differ in their inventory of interpretable features. However, crosslinguistic influence may not be the only cause of optionality.

6. Processing interface structures

Let us focus in particular on pronominal subjects and let us suppose that optionality is related not (only) to the underspecification of the interface features regulating the mapping between levels of representation, but rather to the integration of information from different domains, which must take place in real time whenever a subject is produced or encountered in a particular context in languages like Italian. The efficiency of integration may remain, at least occasionally, problematic for adult bilingual speakers. In this perspective, structures that require not only knowledge of different types of information but also the ability to coordinate them in real time are more 'complex', or more costly in processing terms, than structures that require only one type of information. It follows that processing interface structures should in general be more costly than processing narrow syntax structures. Referential subject pronouns in Italian, in fact, qualify as 'complex', since they demand mastery of both morphosyntactic properties and discourse conditions. In contrast, referential subject pronouns in English are less complex because they do not involve a selection among different forms depending on discourse conditions. Moreover, differences in processing complexity between languages should be reflected in the directionality of influence (from less complex to more complex) of one language on the other in bilingual speakers. Furthermore, even monolingual speakers, or bilingual speakers of languages that do not differ in terms of syntax-discourse interface mappings, should occasionally experience integration problems.

Why do near-native L2 speakers have residual difficulty with the integration of different types of information? One possibility is the fact that syntactic information - even if has been acquired -- is not processed in the same way by non-native speakers as by native monolinguals. Much recent research on L2 processing provides evidence in favour of this argument. Data from on-line psycholinguistic (Felser et al. 2003; Kilborn 1992) and neuroscience experiments (particularly ERPs - see Hahne and Friederici 2001; Sabourin 2003) indicates that syntactic processing continues to be less efficient than for native speakers even at advanced levels. A more refined recent hypothesis is that that syntactic processing in (advanced) L2 speakers may be 'shallower' than for native speakers (Clahsen and Felser 2006 and comments therein). Shallow processing dispenses with syntactic parsing, over-relying on semantic and pragmatic information instead. Importantly, shallow processing is an option available to the human processor and it is used sparingly even by adult monolinguals; thus, it is possible that the difference between native and non-native speakers may be a matter of degrees of optionality. L2 speakers of Italian whose L1 is English may (optionally) fail to activate the VP-internal focus position required by focalization in Italian, even though this is part of their grammar. The result is the use of focus in-situ: an L1-based strategy that is more economical because it involves an "activated" DP-internal focus position (see Belletti 2005b; Belletti, Bennati and Sorace 2005; Sorace 2006a for details). The over-production and misinterpretation of overt subject pronouns may be compounded by shallow processing of the interface features governing the use of overt subjects (e.g. the obligatory mapping of the feature 'topic shift'; see Tsimpli et al. 2004). The result is the use of 'redundant' overt subject pronouns and, since is the only possibility available in the speakers' L1, there is a 'conspiracy of factors' favouring this option.

We have seen, however, that the same productions or misinterpretations are, on occasion, found in native speakers of Italian. Let us further explore this similarity between native and non-native speakers and entertain another possible, and more general, reason behind optionality at interfaces. In particular, let us assume that native speakers may also occasionally deviate from target production/comprehension because of communicative demands that momentarily exceed their processing capacity. Indeed, recent psycholinguistic research on anaphora resolution in native speakers lends support to this argument. Carminati (2002, 2005) provides experimental evidence that null and overt pronouns in Italian have distinct and complementary functions, manifested in their distinct biases for antecedents in different syntactic positions. Null pronouns have a strong bias towards an antecedent in Spec IP (normally – but not exclusively – the subject), whereas overt pronouns prefer an antecedent in positions lower in the phrase structure (normally – but not exclusively – a complement): this is referred to as the 'Position of Antecedent Strategy' (henceforth PAS). Thus, the initial antecedent assignment in anaphora resolution is structurally based, but if the predicate is pragmatically biased to contradict the PAS, reanalysis is necessary but incurs a measurable processing cost. For example, the sentence in (14b) elicits longer reading times than the sentence in (14a). Similarly, phi-features (gender, person and number) may be consistent or inconsistent with the initial parse based on the PAS: incongruences between the PAS and these features (as in (15a) with an overt pronoun and (15b) with a null pronoun) are costly in processing terms (examples 14-16 are adapted from Carminati 2000).

(14) a. Quando Paola$_i$ ha telefonato a Luisa, ø$_i$ le ha dato la buona notizia.
         when Paola$_i$ has telephoned Luisa, ø$_i$ to her has given the good news.
         'When Paola$_i$ telephoned Luisa, she$_i$ gave her the good news.'
      b. ?Quando Paola ha soccorso Luisa$_k$, ø$_k$ era svenuta.
         When Paola aided Luisa$_k$, she$_k$ was unconscious.

(15) a. Quando Luigi$_i$ parla con Teresa$_k$, ø$_i$ / ?lui$_i$ è contento.
         When   Luigi$_i$ speaks with Teresa$_k$, ø$_i$ / ?he$_i$ is happy-M
      b. Quando Luigi$_i$ parla con Teresa$_k$, ?ø$_k$ / lei$_k$ è contenta.

When   Luigi$_i$ speaks with Teresa$_k$, ?$\emptyset_k$ / she$_k$ is happy-F

The PAS is a highly efficient processing principle that belongs to the interface between syntax and discourse. As Carminati herself suggests, not only is there a reliable correspondence between the structural position Spec IP and the notion of topic, but also pragmatic principles are the core of antecedent preferences. So, for example, using an overt pronoun to refer to a topic antecedent would represent a violation of Grice's maxim of quantity, because since another form – the null pronoun - is available for the same purpose, the comprehender assumes that it should have been used instead.

Crucially, however, there is a difference between null and overt pronouns with respect to the strength of the PAS. Carminati's experimental data indicate that while the preference of the null pronoun for subject antecedents is very robust, the overt pronoun shows more flexibility in its antecedent preferences: a weaker processing cost may be incurred if an overt pronoun takes a subject antecedent than if a null pronoun takes a non-subject antecedent. The antecedent preferences of overt pronouns appear to be sensitive to contextual factors: the native grammar is more tolerant of PAS violations in unambiguous sentences, in which the potential for miscommunication is low. It appears, therefore, that native speakers may be occasionally unable or unwilling to engage in full processing when they know that the context is sufficiently unambiguous, as in (16b), in which there is only one referent, or (16c), in which the pronoun agrees in number with only one of the two antecedents; in these cases they may produce a sentence with an unnecessary, or redundant overt pronoun which does not impair antecedent assignment in comprehension.[7] An overt pronoun would be much less likely to be produced in the ambiguous context of (16a).

(16) a.   Paola$_i$ passava molto tempo con Luisa$_k$ quando lei$_{??i/k}$ era in vacanza.
         'Paola$_i$ used to spend a lot of time with Luisa$_k$ when she$_{??i/k}$ was on holiday.
     b.   Giorgio$_i$ ha detto che lui$_i$ non voterà alle prossime elezioni.
         'Giorgio$_i$ has said that he$_i$ will not vote at the next election'.
     c.   Quando Carlo$_i$ ha visto i suoi amici, lui$_i$ era molto contento.
         'When Carlo$_i$ saw his friends he$_i$ was very happy'

Thus, overt pronouns may be used inappropriately when the speaker does not pay enough attention to making the utterance ideal from the comprehender's perspective, or is otherwise unable to do so when, for example, the processor is overloaded: in this case, the PAS is relaxed, although comprehensibility is not compromised. It is plausible to think (although on-line experiments are needed to test this hypothesis) that non-native speakers, whose processing resources are more restricted, may resort to relaxing the PAS in a wider range of contexts and with less consideration for overall potential ambiguity. The overt pronoun may therefore be a kind of default form used to relieve processing demands when these become temporarily unmanageable. If these assumptions are correct, one would expect that these patterns of overgeneralization in Italian should be produced not only by non-native speakers whose L1 is English, but also by non-native speakers from different language background, including languages that have a similar pronominal system to that of Italian Supporting evidence comes from studies of low and intermediate proficiency Spanish learners of Italian (Bini 1993) whose overproduction of overt subject pronouns (as in examples 17 and 18, taken from Bini) is not related in any obvious way to to L1 transfer.[8]

(17) a. Quanti anni ha Pedro?
     How old is Pedro?
     b. Lui ha ventitre.
     He is twenty-three

(18)   Mia sorella e mio cognato escono per il lavoro e loro lavorano a Paseo de la Castellana.
       My sister and my brother-in-law go out to work and they work at Paseo de la Castellana

   To sum up, the evidence from processing research suggests, at least as a working hypothesis, that the optionality manifested in the L2 speakers' overuse of overt pronouns magnifies the flexibility of interface principles that already exists in native Italian: the residual optionality found in the pronominal subjects of L1 English near-native speakers of L2 Italian may be the result of less-than-optimal interface processing strategies to link pronouns to their antecedents. These processing deficiencies, however, appear not to be exclusive to non-native speakers of Italian from a non-null subject language, such as English; more research is needed to establish whether they are found more generally in bilingual speakers, regardless of their particular combination of languages. Processing strategies may be the most vulnerable aspect of the pronominal system of Italian speakers in the initial stages of individual attrition due to long-term contact with a second language. Finally, the processing account is not incompatible with the representational account based on feature underspecification that was outlined in Section 4: on the contrary, processing principles determine which, among the options that are grammatically legitimate in non-native grammars, are favoured in performance. The combined effect of such underspecification and inadequate processing abilities may contribute to a greater magnitude of overgeneralization effects in L1 English near-native speakers of Italian than in non-native Italian speakers from null-subject language backgrounds.

7. Conclusions

Near-native speakers of Italian exhibit residual optionality in structures that involve the interfacing of syntax and other cognitive domains. Their residual difficulties at interfaces may result from both representational factors in their grammar and insufficient grammatical processing resources. Processing and structural factors interact: processing factors may strengthen particular options among those that are syntactically legitimate in the L2 grammar. The multiple convergences between L2 acquisition and other domains of language development confirm that L2 acquisition has a place in the wider context of research on language and cognition.

Notes

[1] For an extension of the arguments developed in this paper to the syntax-lexicon interface underlying split intransitivity, and specifically on the choice of perfective auxiliaries in native and non-native Italian, see Sorace 2006b.

[2] The fact that null subjects may be possible, albeit with a much more restricted distribution, in certain registers and varieties of English (as well as in child English) will not be considered within the scope of this paper (see Haegeman 2001). Furthermore, there has been a significant debate in the generative literature on a formal redefinition of the null subject parameter, the complexity of which cannot be given full justice in this paper (see e.g. Holmberg 2005).

[3] As pointed out by Roberts and Holmberg (2002), however, the lack of a perfect correlation between null subjects and postverbal subjects across languages indicates that there is a more indirect link, rather than a hierarchical relationship, between the two properties; they refer to this a 'independent parameter interaction'.

[4] As this section and the remainder of the paper are intended to provide a summary outline of the findings emerging from recent studies, the actual data and statistical significance analyses are not reported. The reader is referred to the original studies for full details of these.

[5] The data in Belletti et al, however, indicate that preverbal subjects are significantly less frequent with unaccusative verbs; this suggests that there may be a difference between a discourse-related mechanism for 'inversion', which is problematic in the near-native grammar, and a lexical mechanism, which is responsible for VS with unaccusatives and is less problematic. See the original paper for full discussion.

[6] Some theories of L2 acquisition (e.g. Hawkins and Chan 1997) assume a 'representational deficit' that prevents L2 learners from acquiring functional features not instantiated in the L1. A different version of this position (Tsimpli 2003) holds that only uninterpretable features are unacquirable in L2. However, neither of these positions has

been tested on near-native speakers; while such features may present developmental delays, there is therefore no evidence that they cannot be acquired.

[7] Engelhardt, Bailey and Ferreira (in press) report experimental evidence that speakers often produce 'overdescriptions', that is, they provide more information that is necessary to the correct identification of referents, but they seldom produce 'undedescriptions' which lack sufficient information. Overdescriptions (like redundant overt subject pronouns in unambiguous contexts) have a much less dramatic impairing effect on comprehenders than underdescriptions.

[8] I am leaving aside without further discussion the possibility of that Italian and Spanish might be different types of null subject languages, as has been indicated in the literature (e.g. Ordóñez and Treviño 1999), and that L1 transfer from Spanish to Italian may therefore occur. Carminati (2002) also hints to potential microvariation among null subject languages in the antecedent assignment possibilities for overt subjects.

References

Adger, D. and J. Smith, (2005) Variation and the minimalist program. In L. Cornips and K. Corrigan, eds., *Syntax and Variation. Reconciling the Biological and the Social*. Amsterdam: John Benjmins.

Ariel, M. (1994) Interpreting anaphoric expressions: a cognitive versus a pragmatic approach. *Journal of Linguistics* 30, 3-42.

Avrutin, S. (1999) *Acquisition of the Syntax-Discourse Interface*. Dordrecht: Kluwer.

—. (2004) Beyond narrow syntax. In L. Jenkins, ed., *Variation and Universals in Biolinguistics*. Amsterdam: Elsevier.

Belletti, A. (1988) The case of unaccusatives. *Linguistic Inquiry* 19.1-34.

—. (2004a) Aspects of the low IP area. In L. Rizzi, ed., *The structure of CP and IP. The cartography of syntactic structures, Volume 2,* 16-51. New York: Oxford University Press.

—., ed, (2004b) *Structures and beyond. The cartography of syntactic structures, Volume 3.* New York: Oxford University Press.

—. (2005a) Extended doubling and the VP periphery. *Probus* 17: 1-35.

—. (2005b) Answering with a cleft: the role of the null subject parameter and the VP periphery. In   L.Brugè, G.Giusti, N.Munaro, W.Schweikert, G.Turano, eds, *Proceedings of the Thirtieth "Incontro di Grammatica Generativa*, 63-82, Venezia: Cafoscarina.

—. and C. Leonini, (2004) Subject inversion in L2 Italian. In S. Foster-Cohen, M.Sharwood Smith, A.Sorace, M.Ota, eds., *Eurosla Yearbook*, 95-118. Amsterdam: John Benjamins.

—., Bennati, E. and A. Sorace, (2005) Theoretical and developmental issues in the syntax of subjects: evidence from near-native Italian. Ms, University of

Siena and University of Edinburgh (submitted).

Bini, M. (1993) La adquisicíon del italiano: mas allá de las propiedades sintácticas del parámetro pro-drop. In J. Liceras, ed., *La linguistica y el analisis de los sistemas no nativos*, 126-139. Ottawa: Doverhouse.

Cardinaletti, A. (2005) La traduzione: un caso di attrito linguistico. In A. Cardinaletti and G. Garzone, eds., *L'italiano delle traduzioni*, 59-84. Milano: Franco Angeli.

—., and M. Starke, (1999) The typology of structural deficiency. A case study of the three classes of pronouns. In H. van Riemsdijk, ed., *Clitics in the languages of Europe*, 145-233. Berlin: Mouton de Gruyter.

Carminati, M. N. (2002) The Processing of Italian Subject Pronouns, PhD Thesis, University of Massachusetts Amherst.

—. (2005) Processing reflexes of the Feature Hierarchy (Person > Number > Gender) and implications for linguistic theory. *Lingua* 115, 259-285.

Clahsen, H. and C. Felser, (2006) Grammatical processing in first and second language learners. *Applied Psycholinguistics* 27: 3-42.

Chomsky, N. (1995) *The Minimalist Program*. Cambridge, MA: MIT Press.

Engelhardt, P.E., Bailey, K. and F. Ferreira, in press. Do speakers and listeners observe the Gricean Maxim of Quantity? To appear in *Journal of Memory and Language*.

Felser, C., Roberts, L., Marinis, T. and R. Gross, (2003) The processing of ambiguous sentences by first and second language learners of English. *Applied Psycholinguistics* 24: 453-489.

Filiaci, F. (2003) The acquisition of the properties of Italian null and overt subjects by English native speakers. MSc. Dissertation, University of Edinburgh.

Grimshaw, J. and V. Samek-Lodovici, (1998) Optimal subjects and subject universals. In Barbosa, P., Fox, D., Hangstrom, P., McGinnis, M. and Pesetsky,D., eds., *Is the best good enough? Optimality and competition in syntax*, 193-219. Cambridge, Mass.: MIT Press.

Haegeman, L. (2001) Adult null subjects in the non-pro-drop languages: two diary dialects. *Language Acquisition* 9: 329-346.

Hahne, A. and Friederici, A. 2001. Processing a second language: late learners' comprehension mechanisms as revealed by event-related brain potentials. *Bilingualism: Language and Cognition* 4: 123-141.

Hawkins, R. and C.Y.Chan. (1997) The partial availability of Universal Grammar in second language acquisition: The 'failed functional features hypothesis'. *Second Language Research* 13/3: 187-226.

Holmberg, A. (2005) Is there a little pro? Evidence from Finnish. *Linguistic Inquiry* 33: 533-564.

Kilborn, K. (1992) On-line integration of grammatical information in a second language. In R.J. Harris ,ed., *Cognitive Processing in Bilinguals*. Amsterdam: Elsevier Science.

Liceras, J. and L. Díaz, (1998) On the nature of the relationship between morphology and syntax: inflectional typology, *f*-features and null/overt pronouns in Spanish interlanguage. In M. Beck (ed.) *Morphology and its Interfaces in Second Language Knowledge*. Amsterdam: J. Benjamins.

Montrul, S. (2004) Second language acquisition and first language loss in adult early bilinguals: exploring some differences and similarities. *Second Language Research* 20.

Ordoñez, F. and E. Treviño, (1999) Left dislocated subjects and the pro-drop parameter: a case study of Spanish. *Lingua* 107: 39-68.

Pinto, M. 1997. Licensing and interpretation of inverted subjects in Italian. Ph.D. dissertation, University of Utrecht.

Rizzi, L. 1982. *Issues in Italian Syntax*. Dordrecht: Foris.

—. 1986. Null objects in Italian and the theory of *pro*. *Linguistic Inquiry* 17:501-557.

—., ed., (2004) *The Structure of CP and IP. The cartography of syntactic structures, Volume 2*. New York: Oxford University Press.

Roberts, I. and A. Holmberg, (2002) Null subjects and the structure of parametric theory. Ms., University of Cambridge.

Sabourin, L. (2003) Grammatical gender and second language processing. Ph.D. dissertation, University of Groningen.

Sorace, A. (2003) Near-nativeness. In M. Long and C. Doughty, eds., *Handbook of Second Language Acquisition*, 130-152. Oxford: Blackwell.

—. (2005) Selective optionality in language development. In L. Cornips and K.P. Corrigan, eds., *Syntax and Variation. Reconciling the Biological and the Social*, 55-80. Amsterdam, John Benjamins.

—. (2006a) Possible manifestations of shallow processing in advanced second language speakers. *Applied Psycholinguistics* 27: 88-91.

—. (2006b) Gradience and optionality in mature and developing grammars. In G. Fanselow, C. Fery, M. Schlesewsky and R. Vogel, eds., *Gradience in Grammars: Generative Perspectives*. Oxford: Oxford University Press.

—. and F. Filiaci, (2006a) Anaphora resolution in near-native speakers of Italian. To appear in *Second Language Research*.

—. and F. Filiaci, (2006b) On the convergence between L2 acquisition and L1 attrition. Ms., University of Edinburgh.

Tsimpli, I.M. (2003) Clitics and Determiners in L2 Greek. *Proceedings of Generative Approaches to Second Language Acquisition*. Cascadilla Press.

—. and A. Roussou, (1991) Parameter resetting in L2? *University College*

London Working Papers in Linguistics 3: 149-169.
—. and A. Sorace, (2006) Differentiating interfaces: L2 performance in syntax-semantics and syntax-discourse phenomena. *Proceedings of BUCLD 30.*
Tsimpli, T. Sorace, A., Heycock, C. and F. Filiaci, (2004) First language attrition and syntactic subjects: a study of Greek and Italian near-native speakers of English. *International Journal of Bilingualism* 8: 257-277.

COMPUTATIONAL COMPLEXITY AND THE PRODUCTION OF LONG DISTANCE WH-QUESTIONS IN CHILD FRENCH[*]

NELLEKE STRIK

1. Introduction

The purpose of this paper is to provide evidence for the idea that the development of Long Distance (henceforth LD) wh-questions in French is constrained by the Computational Complexity Hypothesis (Jakubowicz 2003, Jakubowicz 2004, Jakubowicz 2005). Computational Complexity is determined by the nature and the number of syntactic operations involved in the derivation.

To this effect, we report the results of an elicited production task of LD wh-questions with 3, 4 and 6 year-old children and adults. These results show that 1) children produce few LD questions, in comparison to adults; 2) children on the age of 3 are able to produce target-like wh fronted LD questions, but 3) however, particularly the younger children produce "exceptional" Partial Movement wh-questions. We will give a detailed description of these Partial Movement questions and compare them to similar questions in other languages.

This paper is organized as follows: first, we give a typology of LD wh-questions in French. We then turn to the Computational Complexity Hypothesis and the predictions for the acquisition of LD wh-questions in French. After a description of the methodology, we discuss the findings of our elicited production task and we end with a short conclusion.

2. LD questions in French and the Computational Complexity Hypothesis

2.1. Typology of LD wh-questions in French

It is currently admitted that there exist several different strategies to make a LD wh question in French. In the most "standard" or normative one the wh word is fronted and there is subject-verb inversion (see (1)).

(1) a. **Où$_i$ Q$_{uf}$** crois$_j$-tu (crois$_j$) (où$_{if-i}$) que Marie va (où$_{if-i}$) ?[1]
where believe you   that Marie goes
"Where do you believe that Marie goes?"

   b. **Qui$_i$ Q$_{uf}$** penses$_j$-tu (penses$_j$) (qui$_{if-i}$) qui (qui$_{if-i}$) lit des histoires ?
who   think you   that reads histories
"Who do you think reads histories?"

   c. **Que$_i$ Q$_{uf}$** penses$_j$-tu (penses$_j$) (que$_{if-i}$) que je mange (que$_{if-i}$) ?
what   think you   that I eat
"What do you think that I eat ?"

Adopting the Minimalist Program (e.g. Chomsky 1999), we assume that each interrogative sentence is marked by an uninterpretable Q(uestion)-feature in its left periphery and that the wh-word moves to the left periphery to check this feature.

It is also possible that the wh-word is fronted without having subject-verb inversion. In (2a-b) there is a simple wh-word and in (2c) the wh-word *que* is followed by the expression *est-ce que*, to form the complex wh-constituent *qu'est-ce que* (see for instance Munaro & Pollock (2001) for a possible, non-cleft, analyses of *qu'est-ce que*).

(2) a. **Où$_i$ Q$_{uf}$** tu crois (où$_{if-i}$) que Marie va (où$_{if-i}$) ?
where you believe   that Marie goes
"Where do you believe that Marie goes ?"

   b. **Qui$_i$ Q$_{uf}$** tu penses (qui$_{if-i}$) qui (qui$_{if-i}$) lit des histoires ?
who think you   that reads histories
"Who do you think reads histories ?"

   c. **Qu'est-ce que$_i$ Q$_{uf}$** tu penses (*qu'est-ce que$_{if-i}$*) que je mange (*que$_{if-i}$*) ?
what *is it that* you think   that I eat
"What do you think that I eat ?"

A third possibility is to leave the wh-word in-situ (see (3)), although one has to note that the status of these questions is unclear. According to some authors (Cheng & Rooryck 2000) they are not grammatically correct, according to others they are (Obenauer 1994, Blanche-Benveniste pc). In any case, they are attested in our adult-data (those presented here and previous data (Strik 2002)).

(3) a. Q_{uf} Tu crois que Marie va où$_{if}$?
you believe that Marie goes where ?
"Where do you believe that Marie goes ?"
b. Q_{uf} Tu penses que **qui**$_{if}$ lit des histoires ?
you think that who reads histories
"Who do you think reads histories ?"
c. Q_{uf} Tu penses que je mange **quoi**$_{if}$?
you think that I mange what
"What do you think (that) I eat ?"

In the wh in-situ questions, the uninterpretable Q-feature is checked by the Agree relationship between the feature and the unmoved wh-word.

2.2. The acquisition of LD wh-questions in French

Very few research has been done about the acquisition of LD wh-questions in French. Besides the comprehension study of Weissenborn, De Villiers & Roeper (1991) – in which it's shown that 3 year-old children are able to interpret LD wh-movement – we can mention Oiry (2002), Strik (2002) and Strik (2003). Strik (2003) reports data that result from the same experimental task as the one presented in this paper. The results of Strik (2002) (which can be considered as a pilot study of the work presented here) and Oiry (2002)[2] show that 3, 4 and 5 year-old French-speaking children produce much more wh fronted than wh in-situ LD questions, wh in-situ questions being rather rare. In addition to wh fronted and wh in-situ questions, children produce a certain number of LD questions in which the wh-word occupies an intermediate position, in the left periphery of the embedded sentence (see (4)).

(4) Tommy, tu penses **quoi** que Lala préfère ?   (Arno 4;11.18)
Tommy, you think what that Lala prefers
"Tommy, what do you think that Lala prefers ?"

Interestingly, similar phenomena have been observed in other child languages, like in English. The results of an elicited production task of LD wh-questions with English-speaking children (Thornton 1990, Crain & Thornton

1998) show that some of them produce Partial Movement (henceforth PM) questions, with the wh-word in the left periphery of the embedded sentence and also an overt wh scope-marker *what* in the left periphery of the matrix sentence (see (5)).

(5) *What* do you think **which animal** says "woof woof"?   (Tiffany, 4;9)

2.3. The Computational Complexity Hypothesis and Predictions

Given the different LD strategies in French, we ask the following questions: which strategy do children acquiring French prefer? Is there an acquisition order and if yes, how could we explain this order? We assume that there is an order and make the hypothesis that this order is constrained by the Computational Complexity of the derivation. In Jakubowicz (2004) the Computational Complexity Hypothesis (henceforth CCH) is formulated as follows:

(6)**CCH:**
   ("<" indicates "less complex than")
   A. Merge < Move.
   B. Moving a constituent α n times < Moving α n+1 times.
   C. Moving n constituents < Moving n+1 constituents.

We are now able to make a hierarchy of LD strategies, based on the Computational Complexity of each construction. For instance, a wh in-situ question (merger of the Q-feature and the wh-word and agreement between these two) is syntactically less complex than a wh fronted question (merger of the Q-feature and the wh-word and movement of the wh-word to the left periphery). Second, a wh fronted root question (movement of the wh word by one cycle) is syntactically less complex than a wh fronted LD question (movement of the wh-word by two cycles). Third, a wh fronted question without subject-verb inversion (only movement of the wh-word) is syntactically less complex than a wh fronted question with inversion (movement of both the wh-word and the verb). The CCH gives rise to the following predictions:

(7) **Predictions:**
   1. Wh in-situ questions will emerge before wh fronted questions.
   2. Root and "exceptional" Partial Movement questions - in the spirit of Crain & Thornton (1998) - will emerge before (adult-like) LD questions.
   3. Questions without subject- verb inversion will emerge before questions with inversion.

3. Methodology

To test our predictions an elicited production task of root and LD questions, inspired by the work of Crain & Thornton (1998), has been used[3]. The task includes four LD conditions, namely object, subject, adjunct (with the locative wh word *où-where*) and derived subject LD wh-questions. The matrix verb in all items is *penser* (*to think*) or *croire* (*to believe*). There are four test items per condition. The task consists in asking questions to a robot, about life on the robot's planet, about what the robot thinks about life on earth and about a guessing game that is part of the experiment. There are two investigators: one who talks and plays with the child and introduces the questions and one who plays the role of the robot. An example of an object LD questions is given in (8) and an example of a subject LD question in (9).

(8) *Investigator :*
    Voyons ce que Tommy croit que tu bois. Demande lui.
    "Let's see what Tommy believes what you drink. Ask him."
    Possible (expected) responses :
    a. Qu'est-ce que tu crois que je bois ?
    b. Que crois-tu que je bois ?
    c. Tu crois que je bois quoi ?
    "What do you believe I drink ?"

(9) *Investigator :*
    Voyons qui Tommy pense qui mange des os.
    "Let's see who Tommy thinks eats bones. Ask him."
    Possible (expected) responses :
    a. Qui tu penses qui mange des os ?
    b. Qui penses-tu qui mange des os ?
    c. Qui est-ce que tu penses qui mange des os ?
    d. Tu penses que qui mange des os ?
    "Who do you think eats bones ?"

Three groups of twelve children each and one adult control group participated in the task. The subjects are all monolingual French native speakers. The age range, mean age and Standard Deviation (SD) of each group are reported in Table I.

Table I

Group	N	Age range	Mean Age	S.D.
3 years	12	3;2 - 3;8	3;5	1,7
4 years	12	4;0 - 4;6	4;2	1,8
6 years	12	6;4 - 6;8	6;6	1,3
Adults	24	19 - 28	23	2,8

4. Results and discussion

4.1. General Overview

First, Figure 1 shows that LD wh-questions are not frequent in all the child groups. Children produce much more root than LD questions. Although the frequency of LD questions increases with age, the difference between children and adults remains important, even for the 6 year-olds.

Figure 1

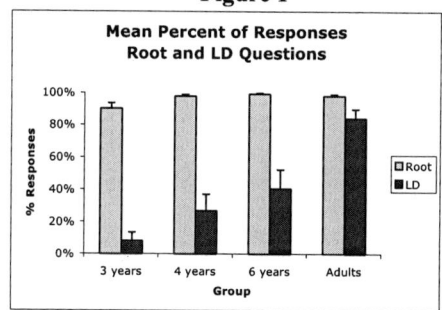

Figure 2 shows the distribution of the different types of LD strategies in all the categories of LD questions mixed up together[4]. In all age groups wh in-situ LD questions are rare. The 4 and 6 year-old children and the adults clearly prefer the wh fronted construction. In addition to these two constructions, subjects of all age groups produce PM questions.

Figure 2

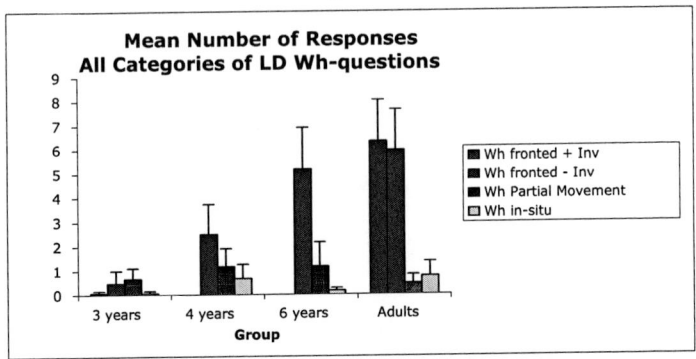

The PM questions can be divided in two types. On the one hand 3 and 4 year-old children produce PM questions of the type cited in (4) above, with or without the complementizer *que* (see (10)). In one case, an overt copy of the wh-word has been left in-situ (see (11)).

(10)   *Tu penses **quoi** (que) je mange ?
       you think what (that) I eat ?
       "What do you think I eat ?"

(11)   *Tu crois **quoi** que je bois **quoi** ?
       you believe what that I drink what
       "What do you believe I drink ?"

On the other hand, 6 year-old children and adults produce grammatically correct PM questions with a cleft wh word in the intermediate position:

(12)   Tu penses que **c'est quoi** qui est caché dans la boîte ?
       you believe that it is what that is hidden in the box ?
       "What do you believe is hidden in the box ?"

The total number of LD questions and the total number of PM questions produced in each age group are reported in Table II:

Table II

	Total number of LD wh-questions	PM	PM Cleft
3 years (n=12)	16	7 (44%)	-
4 years (n=12)	52	13 (25%)	-
6 years (n=12)	78	2 (2%)	12 (15%)
Adults (n=24)	323	-	11 (3%)

With respect to subject-verb inversion, Figure 2 shows that children don't produce questions with inversion (except from two cases), while adults do produce them in about half of the wh fronted questions.

4.2 Partial Movement questions

The PM questions reflect the successive steps of LD wh-movement. That is that the wh-word moves only one time, to the left periphery of the embedded sentence (see (10) repeated in (13)). Contrary to what happens in wh-fronted LD questions, the wh-word doesn't move a second time, to the left periphery of the matrix sentence.

(13) $[_{CP} Q_{uf} [_{IP}$ tu penses $[_{CP}$ **quoi$_i$** $[_{C°}$ que $[_{IP}$ je mange (quoi$_i$)]]]]]
             you think   what   that   I eat what

The French PM questions differ from the English ones (see (5) repeated in (14)) in the sense that the former lack an overt scope marker in the left periphery of the matrix sentence.

(14) $[_{CP}$ **what** Q_{uf} $[_{C°}$do $[_{IP}$ you think $[_{CP}$ **which animal$_i$** $[_{C°}$ $[_{IP}$ (which animal$_i$) says "woof woof"]]]]]]^5

PM questions like (13) are not legitimate in adult French, nor are PM questions like (14) in adult English, but they are legitimate in other adult languages. Fanselow (to appear) gives an exhaustive typology of PM constructions attested in different languages and discusses the analyses that have been proposed for these constructions. He distinguishes PM movement without a scope-marking element – which he calls Simple Partial Movement – from PM movement with a scope-marking element. Simple PM is attested in for instance Bahasa Indonesia (Saddy, 1991) or Slave (e.g. Basilico 1998) (see (15)). The French PM questions are of the Simple PM type.

(15)   Raymond [**judeni** Ri Jane yili] kodhishi ?
        Raymond   where FOC Jane is   knows
        "**Where** does Raymond know that Jane is?"

German is a well-known example of a language with PM movement with a
scope-marking element (e.g. McDaniel, 1989), but Fanselow also cites several other
languages, like Frisian (Hiemstra 1986), Hindi (e.g. Mahajan 1990) and Hungarian
(e.g. Horvath 1997). In German the scope-marking element is the most unmarked
wh-word: *was* (*what*) (see (16))[6]. The English PM questions correspond to this type
of PM.

(16)   **Was** glaubt Hans **mit wem** Jakob jetzt spricht?
        what believes Hans with who Jakob now speaks
        "**What** does Hans believe with **who** Jakob speaks now? "

McDaniel (1989) proposes a Direct Dependency analyses to account for the
German facts. This means that there exists a direct dependency relationship between
the partially moved "real" wh-constituent *mit wem* and the neutral wh-word *what*.
The wh scope-marker is an expletive element that fills up the left periphery position
of the matrix sentence and serves to assign matrix scope to *mit wem*. The two wh-
words are linked to the same wh-chain and thus have the same LF representation as
complete LD wh-movement[7].
   Fanselow (to appear) mentions a relationship between Simple PM questions
and wh in-situ questions. On the basis of Simple PM constructions in the
different languages he observed, he established the following generalizations: 1)
If a language tolerates Simple PM, it also tolerates wh-elements in-situ and
allows full movement. 2) If a construction is grammatical with Simple PM, it
can also be constructed with a wh-word in-situ. The French PM questions
perfectly fit in with these generalizations. It is well known that in French the
wh-word can be either in-situ or fronted, at least in root questions (see (17)).
Recall that the status of wh in-situ LD questions remains unclear (see section
2.1).

(17)   a. Tu vas **où** ?
           you go where
        b. **Où** tu vas ?
           where you go
           "Where do you go ?"

Furthermore French allows full LD movement (which is the most frequent LD
strategy) and the Simple PM construction in (13) can also be constructed with the wh-

word in-situ (see (18)). This type of construction is attested in our data, although it is not so frequent.

(18)   Tu penses que je mange **quoi** ?
        you think that I eat what
        "What do you think that I eat?"

The fact that the wh-word can stay in-situ in French means that the left periphery of a (root or LD) wh-question can be empty, in overt syntax, and that the Q-feature in the left periphery can be checked by an agree relationship (see section 2.1). This is also what we get in Simple PM questions and in the cleft PM questions. In these questions, the left periphery of the matrix clause is not filled by an overt wh-element neither. The Q-feature in the left periphery of the matrix sentence is checked by an agree relationship between this feature and the partially moved wh-word in the left periphery of the embedded sentence:

(19)   [$_{CP}$ Q$_{uf}$ [$_{IP}$ tu penses [$_{CP}$ **quoi**$_i$ [$_{C°}$ que [$_{IP}$ je mange (quoi$_{if-i}$)]]]]]

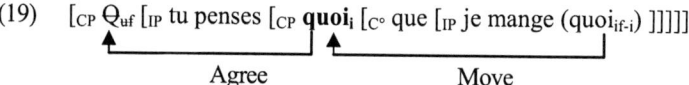

                Agree   Move

Given that in English the wh-word cannot remain in-situ, it is not surprising that the English children tested by Thornton (1990) and Crain & Thornton (1998) don't produce Simple PM questions, but that they produce PM questions with an overt scope marker[8].

Thornton (1990) and Crain & Thornton (1998) adopt McDaniel's (1989) analyses to account for the PM questions in English and they analyze the matrix wh-word *what* as an wh expletive that assigns matrix scope to the partially moved wh-word in the embedded sentence. They note that the non-adult LD questions in English are consistent with the principles of the Universal Grammar. Although not grammatically correct in the target language English, they are in other languages and thus reflect parameter settings of other languages. We assume that the same holds for French. The non-adult PM questions in French comply with UG options available in other languages, like Bahasa Indonesia and Slave.

4.3 Unexpected responses

The number of LD wh-questions being low, the question arises what kind of responses subjects produce instead of LD questions. In all age groups, subjects produce the root question corresponding to the LD question they are supposed to ask (see (20)). This is the most frequent unexpected response type in all (the) children groups.

(20)   Qu'est-ce que je bois ?
       "What do I drink ?"

The most frequent unexpected response type for adults are root questions preceded (or followed) by the expressions *à ton avis* or *d'après/selon toi* (*according to you*), which are semantically similar to LD questions with the matrix verb *think* or *believe* (see (21)). Children don't produce this response type at all.

(21)   A ton avis Tommy, qu'est-ce que je bois ?
       "According to you Tommy, what do I drink ?"

A third type of unexpected responses are indirect wh questions (see (22)). This response type is especially frequent in the 6 year-old's group.

(22)   Tu sais **ce que** je bois ?
       "Do you know what I drink ?"

Finally, especially 3 year-old but also 4 year-old children sometimes give the answer to the question, instead of asking it (see (23)). In Dos Anjos (2004) it is shown that children producing this kind of response have not yet acquired the Theory of Mind.

(23)   Je lis Peter Pan.
       "I read Peter Pan."

In addition to these four unexpected response types, children – especially the youngest ones – produce a certain number of irrelevant responses, among others yes/no questions. The unexpected responses show a hierarchy in the sense that the younger children produce the less appropriate responses and that the number of more appropriate responses increases with age. For more details about the nature and the exact frequency of the unexpected responses, the reader is referred to Strik (2003).

5. Conclusion

In the preceding section we have seen that the children who participated in our experiment produce more root questions than LD questions (cf. Figure 1). In the majority of the LD questions produced by the 4 and 6 year-old children the wh-word is fronted (cf. Figure 2). The 4 and also the 3 year-old children also produce a relatively big number of PM questions and a certain number of wh in-situ questions. The relative number of PM questions decreases with age. Furthermore, children produce root questions (among others) instead of LD questions. These facts were predicted by the CCH. Indeed, it turns out to be less complex to move the wh-word one time, as is the case in root and PM questions, than two times, as is the case in wh fronted LD questions.

One point that might be surprising is the fact that the French children produce only a few number of wh in-situ LD questions, although this strategy is the less complex option. Wh in-situ LD questions – no movement of the wh-word at all – are syntactically still less complex than PM questions and therefore children should prefer them to PM questions. Possibly the low number of wh in-situ LD questions is due to the unclear status of these questions in French (see section 2.1) and French children avoid to use this strategy.

On behalf of subject-verb inversion we can be short. Children virtually don't produce questions with inversion (while adults do) and it is clear that they prefer questions without inversion, involving less syntactical operations. The prediction that questions without inversion will emerge before questions with inversion is borne out.

To summarize, our data show an evolution, in the sense that children start with constructions implying less computational complexity (PM questions and to a lesser extent wh in-situ LD questions) and that they use more and more constructions implying a higher computational complexity (wh fronted LD questions) when they get older. We therefore conclude that the development of LD questions in French is constrained by the CCH.

Notes

* I am very grateful to Celia Jakubowicz, for her help and comments concerning all aspects of the research presented in this paper. Furthermore, I thank Marlies van der Velde for useful comments, Catherine Rigaut for assistance with statistical analyses and the "Catharine van Tussenbroek Fonds" and the "Prins Bernhard Cultuurfonds" for financial support in 2004 and 2005.
[1] Uf: uninterpretable feature; if: interpretable feature. The words between brackets are unpronounced copies.
[2] Oiry (2002) uses the same but slightly modified experimental protocol as Strik (2002).
[3] The research protocol has been developed in the team directed by Celia Jakubowicz at the LPE, CNRS-FRE 2929, Université Paris 5.
[4] Recall that the experimental task contains four LD conditions (object, subject, derived subject and adjunct wh-questions) and that there are four items per condition. This makes that the total number of LD questions that a subject can produce is 16.
[5] Unfortunately, the examples cited by Thornton (1990) are subject LD questions and the movement of the wh-word is not clearly visible. The wh-word could also be in-situ.

[6] In other languages, the scope-marking element can be another wh-word than *what* or a question particle.
[7] On the other hand, we can cite the Indirect Dependency analyses. A well-known version of it is the analyses proposed by Dayal (2000) for Hindi. Under this analyses, the German sentence in (16) should contain two independent root questions, that are linked by an indirect dependency relationship, namely co-indexation between the matrix wh-word *was* and the CP of the embedded sentence. The wh-word *was* is not an expletive but rather an argumental wh-word, that can assign scope to complete clauses (here the embedded sentence) and not to individuals.
[8] In the French data reported here, no PM questions with an overt scope-marking element have been found. However, this type of PM does exist in French too. It is attested in the data of a more recent study of LD questions we conducted with French children (see Strik 2006).

References

Basilico, D. (1998) "Wh-movement in Iraqui Arabic and Slave". *The Linguistic Review* 15, pp. 303-339.

Cheng L., J. Rooryck, (2000) "Licensing *Wh*-In-Situ", *Syntax* 3:1, pp. 1-19.

Chomsky, N. (1999) *Derivation by Phase*. MIT Occasional Papers in Linguistics, Cambridge (Mass.).

Crain, S. & R. Thornton, (1998) *Investigations in Universal Grammar, A Guide to Experiments on the Acquisition of Syntax and Semantics*. Cambridge, Mass.: MIT Press.

Dayal, V. (2000) "Scope Marking: Cross-linguistic Variation in IndirectDependency". In U. Lutz, G. Mueller and A. von Stechow, eds., *Wh-Scope Marking*, J. Benjamins.

Dos Anjos, C., (2004) *L'acquisition des questions à longue distance chez des enfants normaux et chez des enfants atteints de Dysphasie de Développement. Quel rôle la théorie de l'esprit joue-t-elle ?*. Mémoire de maîtrise, Université Paris 5, Boulogne-Billancourt.

Fanselow, G. (to appear). "Partial Movement". In Everaert, M. & H. van Riemsdijk (in prep). SYNCOM (The Syntax Companion): An electronic encyclopaedia of syntactic case studies. The LingComp Foundation.

Hiemstra, I. (1986) "Some aspects of wh-questions in Frisian". *NOWELE* 8, pp. 97-110.

Horvath, J. (1997) "The status of 'Wh-Expletives' and the Partial Movement Construction of Hungarian". *NLLT* 15, pp. 509-572.

Jakubowicz, C. (2003) "Hypothèses psycholinguistiques sur la nature du déficit dysphasique". Y. Brun & Ch.L. Gérard (eds.), *Les Dysphasies*. Paris: Masson.

—. (2004) "Is Movement Costly? The Grammar and the Processor in Language

Acquisition". Presentation, JEL, Journée d'Etudes Linguistiques, Nantes.

—. & C. Rigaut, (2005) Formulation and interpretation of Wh-questions by typically developing French-speaking children and children with SLI: Derivational complexity and "spell out". Presentation 9th EUCLDIS' Conference, Royaumont.

Mahajan, A. (1990) *The A/A-bar distinction and movement theory*. Doctoral dissertation, MIT, Cambridge, Mass.

McDaniel, D. (1989) "Partial and multiple wh-movement". *Natural Language and Linguistic Theory* 7, pp. 565-604.

Munaro, N. & J.-Y. Pollock (2001) *Qu'est-ce que* (qu)-est ce que? *A Case Study in Comparitive Romance Interrogative Syntax*. Unpublished manuscript.

Obenauer H.-G. (1994) *Aspects de la Syntaxe A-Barre, Effets d'Intervention et Mouvements des Quantifieurs*. Thèse d'Etat, Université Paris 8.

Saddy, D. (1991) "Wh-Scope Mechanisms in Bahasa Indonesia". *MIT Working Papers in Linguistics* 15, pp. 182-218.

Strik N. (2002) *L'Acquisition de Questions Wh Objet et Sujet chez les Enfants Francophones Agés de 4 et de 5 ans*, Mémoire de Maîtrise, Universiteit van Amsterdam & LPE, Université Paris 5.

—. (2003) *Où tu as caché ton sac? Qu'est-ce que tu penses que je lis? Acquisition des Questions Wh chez les Enfants Francophones de 3 à 6 Ans*, Mémoire de DEA, Université Paris 8 & LPE, Université Paris 5.

—. (2006) *Scope-marking strategies in the acquisition of LD Wh-questions in French and Dutch*. Presentation, Latsis Colloquium, Genève.

Thornton, R. (1990) *Adventures in long distance moving: The acquisition of complex wh-questions*. PhD, University of Connecticut.

Weissenborn, J., De Villiers J. & T. Roeper, (1991) "The Acquisition of Wh-Movement in German and French". *Papers in the Acquisition of Wh-questions, Proceedings of the Umass roundtable*, May 1990, Amherst, eds., T.L. Maxfield & B. Plunkett, p. 43-78. Amherst, Mass.: GLSA Publications.

DEVELOPMENTAL PATHS IN L1 AND L2 PHONOLOGICAL ACQUISITION: CONSONANT CLUSTERS IN THE SPEECH OF NATIVE SPEAKERS AND TURKISH AND DUTCH LEARNERS OF GREEK[1]

MARINA TZAKOSTA

1. Introduction

Cluster simplification, fusion and epenthesis tend to be the major strategies employed during the process of syllable acquisition cross-linguistically (cf. Broselow et al. 1998, Broselow & Xu 2004, Barlow 1997, Fikkert 1994, Gnanadesikan 2004, Pater & Barlow 2002, Steele 2002). Markedness (examples (1a), (1b)), positional faithfulness (examples (1e), (1f)) and contiguity (examples (1c), (1d)) seem to be the phonological principles satisfied in these repair processes.

(1) a. drum → [dʌm] 'drum' (1;8.24)
   b. sky → [kaɪ] 'sky' (1;9.17)   (Pater & Barlow 2003)
   c. blokken → ['lɔ.kə] 'bricks' (1;10.24)
   d. slak → [lɑk] 'leaf' (1;10.24)   (Van der Pas 2004)
   e. friɣa'nula → ['fu.la] 'cracker-dim' (D: 2;03.07)
   f. ɣli.'ko → [ɣo] 'sweet' (D: 2;01.09)   (Revithiadou & Tzakosta 2004)

In this paper, the focus is on two-member /obstruent + liquid/, /obstruent + obstruent/, /s/ + obstruent, obstruent +/s/[2] clusters in all word positions, stressed and unstressed syllables, in order to examine their shape in child production. The innovation of the present study is that it investigates and theoretically evaluates the realization of syllabic structure in L1 and L2 simultaneously. The research questions consist in, first, observing how consonant clusters are realized in Greek L1 and L2 and what the repair strategies followed by language acquirers and language learners are, second, in examining whether a consonant cluster exhibits equivalent patterns in all word positions in L1 and L2 and, third, in questioning to what extent L1 acquisition influences L2 learning. A goal related to the third question is to demonstrate that L1 and L2 can be modeled within the same theoretical framework. My proposal is that the model of *Multiple Parallel Grammars* (hereafter MPGM, Tzakosta 2004) offers a unified account of L1 and L2.

According to the MPGM, a model initially proposed for the acquisition of stress in Greek L1, multiple grammars, which shape language learning, are activated during the same developmental phase. Learning is completed in three major phases. In the initial phase, M constraints outrank F constraints[3] resulting in the prevalence of unmarked forms in L1 and L2. In the intermediate phase, multiple grammars, which are the product of constraint permutation, are adopted in parallel by learners and acquirers. In the final phase, F constraints outrank M constraints and faithful forms start being produced more frequently. Employing multiple grammars means that children make use of various learning mechanisms, which lead to multiple output forms. The statistical prevalence of certain grammars is due to universal principles in combination with input frequency. 'Core grammars' are theoretically and statistically more prominent and obey principles satisfied cross-linguistically. 'Peripheral grammars' are subsets of the core grammars and satisfy language-specific principles. Activation of parallel grammars gives an explanation regarding why variation is systematic in Greek child speech. The MPGM allows faithful productions to emerge together with the simplified forms, given that the grammar of the final state is also available to the learner in the intermediate phase.

Two assumptions are made regarding L2 learning. According to the first one, L2 learners of Greek employ the same intermediate grammars that native speakers employ. These grammars constitute the second language learners' interlanguage. Given the second assumption, L2 learners use a subset of the grammars adopted by L1 acquirers. L2 learners employ a smaller or bigger set of developmental grammars compared to native speakers, depending on the complexity of the system of their L1. In the present study, the data show that the less complex the phonological system of L1 is, the fewer the activated grammars in L2 are.

2. Research methodology

The study draws on data from three corpora. Corpus 1 consists of longitudinal L1 data from four children, two boys (B.T., D.) and two girls (Me., B.M.) raised in monolingual Greek environments whose age range is 1;07-3;05 years. Data were collected through a technique of picture naming during free interaction of the experimenter with the child. Corpus 2 consists of production

data from 13 Turkish pupils of elementary education who live in the Western
part of Thrace, Greece, and whose age ranges between ten and twelve years.
Data were collected through spontaneous interviews taken in class settings.[4]
Finally, corpus 3 consists of natural data, from ten Dutch monolingual adults,
who range in age between 25 and 60 years and are in intermediate proficiency
level. Data were collected by means of structured questionnaires, which the
subject were asked to read.

3. L1 Data

Before we move to the presentation of the data, it is essential to provide
some basic information regarding the cluster phonotactics of the languages
under discussion, beginning with Greek. Greek allows (CCC)V(C) syllables, it
permits onsetless and/ or codaless syllables, as well as complex onsets. The
latter may consist of maximally triconsonantal clusters. Two-member clusters
consist of [obstruent + liquid], [obstruent + obstruent], [s + obstruent],
[obstruent + s], [nasal + nasal], [obstruent + nasal], [obstruent + glide] (cf.
Malikouti-Drachman 1984). Three-member clusters allow /s/ + [obstruent +
liquid], [obstruent] + [obstruent + liquid] combinations. Codas can maximally
consist of one segment word medially (/n,r,l/) or word finally (/s/).

The first set of Greek developmental data given in (2) and (3) demonstrate
that CL and CC clusters are simplified irrespective of whether they are in initial
(2a), ((2c-e), (3a-c), (3f)), or medial position ((2b), (3d-e)), whether they belong
to stressed (2b-c), (2e), (3a), (3d), (3f) or unstressed syllables ((2a), (2d), (3b-c),
(3e)). Cluster simplification is accomplished by means of vowel insertion ((2a),
(3c, e)), cluster reduction ((2b-d), (3a-f)), fusion (2e), and contiguity (3f).
Cluster reduction may be driven by positional faithfulness (3b, e, f) and/ or
markedness ((3a), (3d)). Multiple outputs may correspond to one target form
((3e)-(f)).

(2) a. /ˈkli.ˈðja/ → [kə.li.ˈðja]   'keys'   (Me: 2;03.14)
    b. /o.ˈbre.la/→ [o.ˈbe.la]   'umbrella'   (D: 2;03.21)
    c. /ˈfru.ta/ → [ˈfu.ta]   'fruits'   (BT:1;10)
    d. /ˈfri.ɣa.ˈŋa/ → [fi.ɣa.ˈŋa]   'biscotte'   (D: 2;06.29)
    e. /ˈkle.i/ → [ˈte.i]   'cry-3SG.PRES.'   (B.M.: 1;09.22)

(3) a. /ˈxte.na/→ [ˈte.na]   'brush'   (B.T.: 1;11.10)
    b. /fte.ˈra/→[fe.ˈla]   'wings'   (D:2;02.24)
    c. /xti.ˈpa.i/→ [ɣə.ti.ˈba.i]   'hurt-3SG.PRES.'   (Me: 2;00.26)
    d. /o.ˈxto/→ [o.ˈto]   'eight'   (B.M.: 2;06.19)

e. /'pe.fti/→ ['be.fi], ['pe.fə.ti]   'fall-3SG.PRES.'   (B.M.: 2;07.09)
f. /'vɣa.lo/→ ['ɣa.lo], ['va.lo]   'take out-1SUBJ.'   (B.M.: 2;03.19)

The picture is the same, regarding SC clusters, as shown in (4). Again, the main strategy used is *cluster reduction* ((4a-4c)), and *cluster reduction* combined with *stopping* (4d). All cluster types are susceptible to the same repair processes.[5]

(4) a. /'spi.ti/→['pi.ti], ['bi.ti]   'house'   (BT:1;10)
   b. /ste.fa.'na.ci/→ [te.ta.'na.ci]   'crown-DIM.'   (Me: 1;08.31)
   c. /pi.'sto.li/→ [te.'to.li], [be.'to.li]   'gun'   (D: 2;01)
   d. /pa.sxa.'li.tses/→ [paka'li.teθ]   'ladybugs'   (Me: 1;11.13)

The data in (5) show that faithful forms (32.2%) may emerge together with the simplified forms (67.8%). Cluster simplification takes place in all word positions, stressed and unstressed syllables. M constraints exercise some influence during advanced stages of language development, as exemplified in ((5a-5d)), since M constraints govern hybrid grammars that link primitive and advanced phases of language learning (Revithiadou & Tzakosta 2004). I consider the clusters in (5) to be faithfully produced regarding the number of the realized consonants, however markedness drives faithful cluster realization.

(5) a. /a.'fto/→[a.'pto],[a.'fto]   'this-DEM.PR.'   (B: 1;11.27)
   b. /sxo.'li.o/→ [θxo.'li.o]   'school'   (D: 2;07.06)
   c. /o.'bre.la/→ [ku.'ble.la]   'umbrella'   (Me: 1;11.22)
   d. /'pa.sxa/→ ['pa.θka]   'Easter'   (B.M.: 2;09.25)

In terms of OT, the facts described above need to be explained by a specific set of constraints. These constraints are drawn out of the categories of M constraints, as well as F constraints of the IDENT type and are presented in (6) below. Apart from the more general M and F constraints, I have made use of more specific positional M and positional F constraints, to refer to certain positions in the word.

(6) Constraints (adjusted)
- ***COMPLEX**: CV syllables
- **M**: Avoid sonorous/marked segments in onset position
- **DEP**: No insertion
- **IDENT**: Be faithful to the featural composition of the target segment
- **#C/.C**: Retain the initial segment of a word/ syllable

- **CONTIGUITY**: Retain the adjacent to the nucleus cluster member
- **IDENT (MAN₁&PL₂)/(MAN₂&PL₁)**: Retain either manner or place of articulation of each member of the cluster (fusion)
- **AGREE-MAN/PL**: agree in manner and/or place of articulation

Within the MPGM, constraint permutation generates a huge number of grammars (39.916.800 grammars (!)), which are the potential developmental paths children can follow during their phonological acquisition. However, only the rankings in (7) make up the real set of grammars adopted by Greek children. This fact raises the question what are the factors that determine which grammars are activated and which are not. The answer lies in a combination of factors. Even though UG provides a huge number of developmental paths, the set of activated grammars is restricted by the statistical and theoretical/ typological predominance of certain grammars. Consequently, the final small set of grammars will successfully lead learners to the faithful realization of the target clusters.

(7) Involved rankings:
    a.   *COMPLEX >> M, #C >> ... >> F (deletion/M/PF)
    b.   *COMPLEX >> F(IDENT), DEP, M >> ... F (insertion/M)
    c.   *COMPLEX >> CONTIGUITY >> ... >> F (contiguity)
    d.   *COMPLEX>>IDENT(MAN₁&PL₂)>>M>>...>>F (fusion)
    e.   AGREE-MAN,AGREE-PL>>F>>*COMPLEX (harm./assim.)
    f.   M, F >> *COMPLEX (partial M/partial F/anaptyxis)
    g.   F₁ >> M, *COMPLEX (L1 grammar)

4. L2 Data

4.1. Turkish

Turkish phonotactics are simpler compared to those of Greek. Complex syllables are disallowed in Turkish. Turkish syllables take a (C)V(C) shape. Word-medial consonantal sequences are syllabified in different syllables. VC syllables are more frequent word-initially. The examples in (8) and (9) demonstrate that Turkish learners of Greek exhibit equivalent patterns to those of native speakers. Target clusters of all major categories are simplified due to either deletion of one member of the cluster (8), or vowel epenthesis (9). Fusion, however, is absent. Cluster reduction is, in all cases in (8), driven by markedness considerations.

(8) a. /ma.**kri**.'a/→[ma.**ci**.'a]   "far-ADV."   (Esra, 5th grade)
   b. /e.ti.'ma.**sti**.ce/→[ti.'ma.ti.ce]   "get ready-3PAST.SG" (Ksamdi, 2nd gr.)
   c. /'**spi**.tja/→ ['**pi**.ti.a]   "house-PL."   (Hatis, 6th gr.)

(9) a. /'ma.**vra**/ → ['ma.**və.ra**]   "black-ADJ.NOM.PL."   (Esra, 5th gr.)
   b. /xo.'**dri**/→ [xo.**də.ri**]   "fat-ADJ.NOM.SG."   (Esra, 5th gr.)
   c. /'ðen.**dra**/→ ['de.**də.ra**]   "tress"   (Hatis, 6th gr.)

In general, target forms are simplified by analogy to the phonological system of Turkish. (10) provides examples on faithful production of target clusters.

(10)   a. /'**tro**.o/→ ['**tro**.o]   "eat-1PR.SG."   (Okan, 4th gr.)
   b. /**tra**.'γu.dja/ → [**tra**.'γu.di.a]"song-ACC.PL."   (Anife, 6th gr.)
   c. /'**pra**.si.na/→ ['**pra**.si.na]   "green-NOM.ADJ.PL."   (Emir, Xanthi)
   d. /'**kse**.ro/→ ['**kse**.o]   "know-1PR.SG."   (Hatis, 6th gr.)
   e. /**ksi**.'pni.si/ →[**ksi**'pni.si]   "wake up-3SG.SUBJ."   (Emir, Xanthi)
   f. /'**spi**.ti/→ ['**spi**.ti]   "house-NOM.SG."   (Hatidz, 6th gr.)
   g. /za.'li.**sti**.ce/→ [za.'li.**sti**.ce] "get dizzy-3PAST.SG."(Emir, Xanthi)
   h. /'**vle**.po/→ ['**vle**.po]   "see-1PR.SG."   (Emir 4th gr.)
   i. /'**γri**.γo.ra/→ ['**γri**.γo.ra]   "fast-ADV."   (Okan, 4th gr.)
   j. /o.'**xto**/ → [o.'**xto**]   "eight"   (Safetim,2nd gr.)

The overall picture is that together with the simplified forms (16%), target clusters are faithfully produced (84%). The high rate of faithful productions is attributed to the advanced proficiency level of Turkish learners. The children who participated in our survey are raised in Greece and are in the final grades of the Greek-Turkish primary school. The data exhibit equivalent rates of faithful word initial (52%) and word medial clusters (48%). CL, CC, SC and CS combinations constitute the majority of attempted forms (72%), compared to Gj clusters (22%) and affricates (6%). Clusters in stressed syllables exhibit a higher degree of faithfulness (96%) compared to clusters in unstressed syllables. However, faithful production of unstressed syllables clusters is very high (83%). Clusters in word medial position exhibit higher reduction rates (42%) compared to word-initial position (6%). The picture is obscure between different cluster types, though; the more 'popular' CL clusters have a rate of 45% faithful productions in word-initial position and 58% in word-medial position. At the same time, CL clusters exhibit the highest rate of reduced forms (86%). Consequently, markedness together with input frequency determines the rates of faithful and/ or reduced realizations.

Regarding the grammars involved in the learning process, we notice that
only a subset used by L1 acquirers, provided in (11a), (11b), (11d), are
employed by L2 Turkish learners. The speech of Turkish learners is also ruled
by the grammar of their mother language given in (11c). F_1 corresponds to the
constraints that rule the grammar of Turkish L1, whereas F_2 reflects on the F
constraints of the ambient language. The existence of (11c) indicates the
influence of L1 in L2 learning.

(11)   Involved rankings:
      a.   *COMPLEX >> M, #C >> ... >> F (deletion/M/PF)
      b.   *COMPLEX >> F(IDENT), DEP, M >> ... F (insertion/M)
      c. F_1 >> M, *COMPLEX (L1 grammar)
      d. F_2 >> M, *COMPLEX (L2 target grammar)

4.2. Dutch

Dutch is the most complex language at the level of syllabic phonotactics.
Word-initial and -medial syllables may consist of up to five segments,
appendices included. Word-final syllables may consist of up to nine segments.
Ill-formed clusters may consist of sequences that violate the Sonority Scale or
sequences of adjacent segments on the SS, and sequences of identical segments.
/s/ is allowed in the combinations /sp/, /st/, /ps/, /ts/. In three-member clusters,
/s/ is always involved. The possible combinations are /spl/, /spr/, /str/. Finally,
ill-formed sequences are allowed only in word-final position (cf. van der Hulst
1984).
Turning to the L2 data, we observe that only a few errors occur. However,
both vowel insertion (12a) and cluster reduction (12b) are reported for all cases
of cluster simplification (examples in (12), (13)), as was also illustrated for
Greek L1 data of native speakers and L2 data of Turkish learners. Moreover,
there are cases of clusters emerging in unexpected positions, as shown in (14).
This is a form of *cluster anaptyxis* reported only on the Dutch corpus; I call the
resulting clusters *non-existing*, because they are not part of the input/ target
form. Nevertheless, such clusters are grammatical in either the native or the
second language or both. Since Dutch is more complex compared to Greek at
the syllabic level, Dutch learners produce Greek forms by analogy to the
phonology of Dutch. As a result, CV target syllables (examples in (14)) are
realized as more complex (C)CCV. Finally, clusters may also be faithfully
produced together with the simplified clusters. Interestingly, in the latter case
faithful clusters are 'Dutch-like', because they have undergone devoicing (15a,
b, d,) or stopping (15c).

(12) a. /θo.ri.'kto/→ [fo.ri.ti.'ko]   "tanker"   (Ju)
     b. /e.vðo.'ma.ða/ → [e.to.'maː.ða]   "week"   (Ol)

(13) a. /'a.ni.ksi/ → ['a.ni.si] (Jo, Els), ['a.ni.zi]   "spring"   (Marg)

(14) a. /θo.ri.'kto/→ [fri.'kto]   "tanker"   (Ju)
     c. /u.ra.'nos/ → [i.ɣra.'nos]   "sky"   (Els)
     d. /e.po.'ci/ → [e.'po.ksi]   "season"   (Jo)
     e. /'ci.ni.si/ → ['kli.si]   "circulation"   (Ma)

(15) a. /fo.to.ɣra.'fi.a/→ [fo.to.xra.'fi.a] "photo"   (Ol)
     b. /gri.'ŋa.ris/→ [kri.ni.'a.ris]   "nasty-ADJ.MASC.SG" (Ju)
     c. /e.vðo.'ma.ða/ → [e.vdo.'ma.da]   "week"   (Ol)
     d. /'tza.mi/ → /'tsa.mi/   "glass"   (Ju)

Put in a nutshell, CL, CC, SC and CS clusters constitute the majority of faithfully produced clusters (91%), with affricates (6%) and Cj (3%) clusters following them. Only 6% of the attempted forms are reduced. They are never simplified in initial position and they exhibit a low reduction rate in medial position (4%). Clusters are reduced in unstressed (87%) rather than stressed syllables (13%). CL and SC clusters are never reduced, probably due to the fact that they are frequent both in Greek and Dutch. 3% of the produced combinations consist of non-existing clusters primarily found in medial positions (62%) and unstressed syllables (62%). Such clusters seem to reinforce the production of 'weak' constituents. The majority of non-existing clusters consist of CL clusters (62%), a fact which underlines their unmarked character.

The grammars involved in L2 learning are provided in (16). Compared to the grammars adopted by Greek native speakers and Turkish learners given in (7) and (11), respectively, Dutch learners adopt a subset of grammars of the former, but a superset of the latter. Dutch learners employ the grammar in (16d), not used by Turkish learners, which is responsible for the realization of non-existing clusters.

(16) Involved rankings:
   a. *COMPLEX >> M, #C >> ... >> F (deletion/M/PF)
   b. *COMPLEX >> F(IDENT), DEP, M >> ... F (insertion/M)
   c. F_1 >> M, *COMPLEX (L1 grammar)
   d. F_2 >> F_1 >> M, *COMPLEX (non-existing clusters)
   e. F_2 >> M, *COMPLEX (L2 target grammar)

5. L1 and L2 Data in light of the MPGM

If the initial phase in L1 acquisition is one where M >> F, the question is whether the nature of the initial state is the same in L1 and L2. Two hypotheses hold regarding the L2 initial state. One is that it resembles the final state of the learners' L1 (cf. Grijzenhout 2000), i.e. the learners' starting point in L2 is the end-state of L1. According to the hypothesis proposed here, L2 learning is characterized by the intermediate and final states only; the initial M >> F state is only characteristic of L1. It cannot be active in L2 because L1 highly affects L2. If the former assumption were the correct one, we would not expect developmental paths shared by L1 and L2. However, it is proved that the grammars effective in L1 are also active in L2 and their impact, which is evident throughout the learning process, depends on the influence of the learners' native language.   Moreover, if we accept that the same constraints hold cross-linguistically, then, native speakers and learners of Greek adopt developmental grammars out of the same pool of grammars. Consequently, L1 acquirers and L2 learners exhibit equivalent production patterns.

My claim here is that L2 learners adopt a subset of the grammars employed by L1 learners. The limited amount of grammars in L2 intermediate phase is due to the fact that L2 learning is restricted by the phonological system of L1 (see figure 1, section 6). The data provide intuitions regarding the quality of grammars activated in distinct 'interlanguages'. Speakers of languages with simpler syllabic structure than the ambient language, like Turkish, adopt fewer grammars than speakers of languages with more complex syllabic structure compared to Greek, like Dutch. This becomes obvious if we compare the sets of grammars adopted by native speakers, Turkish and Dutch learners provided in (7), (11), and (16), respectively. We would expect that, if the phonological system of the learners' L1 is more complex than that of the ambient language, learners would employ fewer grammars compared to other learners whose L1 is simpler than the ambient language. Nevertheless, Dutch learners employ a superset of grammars compared to Turkish learners; this happens because, here, we deal with more general M and F constraints, and, as a result, with more general grammars. The case may be different if we need to bring more refined grammars into play. This is an issue amenable to future discussion.

6. Conclusions

In this paper I investigated the realization of two-member consonant clusters in Greek L1 acquisition and L2 learning. The L1 and L2 data reveal that native speakers and learners of Greek simplify target clusters, by means of, first, reduction to the least sonorous/ unmarked segment due to dominant well-formedness constraints or to the initial segment due to positional faithfulness effects and, second, vowel insertion. In other words, Greek acquirers and learners adopt similar repair strategies. These processes are reported for all clusters, irrespective of their segmental composition. They are also reported to occur in clusters in all word-positions, initially, medially or finally, as well as stressed and unstressed syllables. However, simplification strategies are more dominant in weak positions, i.e. medial and unstressed syllables.

The data reveal that multiple surface forms may occur for one and the same target form. Variation in L1 and L2 is determined by cross-linguistic phonological principles, as well as input frequency. Variation is attributed to the parallel activation of multiple grammars during the acquisition process. Such grammars conform to various states of the adult grammar, as well grammars mirroring real languages of the world. Depending on whether phonological principles or input frequency rule output forms, the predominance of specific grammars is ascertained.

The discussion has further highlighted that, within the MPGM, L2 learners adopt a subset of the grammars adopted by L1 learners; this happens because the phonological system of L1, UG principles and input frequency in L1 and L2 restricts the set of possible grammars. The number of activated grammars further depends on the acquisition/learning phase and the level of proficiency in the second language.

Figure 1

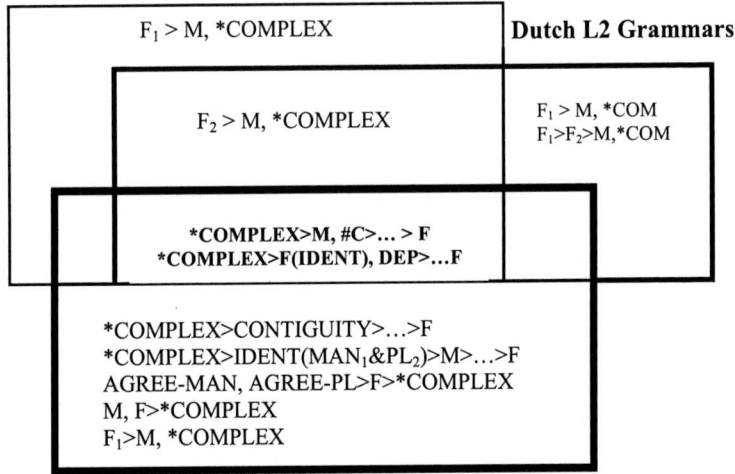

Turkish L2 Grammars

F_1 > M, *COMPLEX

Dutch L2 Grammars

F_2 > M, *COMPLEX

F_1 > M, *COM
F_1>F_2>M,*COM

*COMPLEX>M, #C>... > F
*COMPLEX>F(IDENT), DEP>...F

*COMPLEX>CONTIGUITY>...>F
*COMPLEX>IDENT(MAN$_1$&PL$_2$)>M>...>F
AGREE-MAN, AGREE-PL>F>*COMPLEX
M, F>*COMPLEX
F_1>M, *COMPLEX

Greek L1 Grammars

Notes

1. I wish to thank the audience of GALA 2005, as well as the participants of the 1st Workshop on Greek Phonology for useful discussion and feedback. All errors remain mine.

2. My aim is not to exhaustively compare the internal structure of different consonant clusters categories, but to examine the repair processes these clusters undergo in the process of language acquisition.

3. M stands for Markedness/ Well-formedness constraints, while F stands for Faithfulness constraints, as these are defined within Optimality Theory.

4. I thank dr. A. Fragoudaki and dr. S. Moschona who kindly allowed my access to the data of the project "Education of Muslim Pupils of Western Thrace, 2002-2004", conducted under the auspices of the EE and the Greek State.

5. There are no instances of CS clusters in the L1 corpus of data.

References

Avivit, B. D. (2001) *Language Acquisition and Phonological Theory: Universal and Variable Processes Across Children and Across Languages*. Ms. Tel-Aviv University.

Barlow, J.A. (1997) *A Constraint-based Account of Syllable Onsets: Evidence from Developing Systems*. Ph.D. Dissertation. Indiana University.

Broselow, E. Su-I Chen, and C. Wang (1998) "The Emergence of the Unmarked in Second Language Phonology", *SSLA 20*, 261-280.

Broselow, E. and Z. Xu (2004) "Differential Difficulty in the Acquisition of Second Language Phonology", *International Journal of English Studies* 4(2), 135-163.

Kirk, C. and K. Demuth (2003) "Onset/Coda Asymmetries in the Acquisition of Clusters", in B., Beachley, A. Brown and F. Conlin, eds., *Proceedings of the 27th Annual Boston University Conference on Language Development*, Somerville, Cascadilla Press, 437-448.

Fikkert, P. (1994) *On the acquisition of Prosodic Structure*. Doctoral Dissertation, HIL/Leiden University. The Hague: Holland Academic Graphics.

Gnanadesikan, A. (2004) "Markedness and Faithfulness Constraints in Child Phonology", in R. Kager, J. Pater, and W. Zonneveld, eds., *Constraints in Phonological Acquisition*. Cambridge: C.U.P. 73-108.

Goad, H. and Y. Rose (2004) "Input Elaboration, Head Faithfulness and Evidence for Representation in the Acquisition of Left-edge Clusters in West Germanic". in R. Kager, J. Pater and W. Zonneveld, eds., *Constraints in Phonological Acquisition*. Cambridge: C.U.P, 109-157.

Grijzenhout, J. (2000) *Constraint Demotion and Constraint Transfer in Language Acquisition*. Paper read at the 4th Utrecht Biannual Phonology workshop.

Hulst van der, H. (1984) *Syllable Structure and Stress in Dutch*. Ph.D. Dissertation. Leiden University.

Kornfilt, J. (1997) *Turkish*. London: Routledge.

Malikouti-Drachman, A. (1984) "Syllables in Modern Greek", in W.U. Dressler et al., eds., *Phonologica 1984. Proceedings of the 4th International Phonology Meeting*. C.U.P.

Pas van der, B. (2004) "Contiguity in Phonological Acquisition", in S. Baauw and J. van Kampen, eds., *Proceedings of GALA 2003. Generative Approaches to Language Acquisition,* Vol. 2, LOT Occasional Series 3, 353-364.

Pater, J. and J. Barlow (2003) "Constraint Conflict in Cluster Reduction", *Journal of Child Language* 30, 487-526.

Revithiadou, A. and M. Tzakosta (2004) "Markedness Hierarchies vs. Positional Faithfulness and the Role of Multiple Grammars in the Acquisition of Greek", In S. Baauw and J. van Kampen, eds., *Proceedings of GALA 2003. Generative Approaches to Language Acquisition,* Vol. 2, LOT Occasional Series 3 377-388.

Steele, J. (2002) *Representation and Phonological Licensing in the L2 Acquisition of Prosodic Structure.* Ph.D. Dissertation. McGill University.

Tzakosta, M. (2004) *Multiple Parallel Grammars in the Acquisition of Stress in Greek L1.* Ph.D. Dissertation. ULCL/HIL. LOT Dissertation Series 93.

Tzakosta, M. (2005) "Positional and Qualitative Asymmetries of Consonant Clusters in Greek L1". Handout of a talk delivered at the 17th International Conference of Theoretical and Applied Linguistics, Thessaloniki, School of English, Aristotle University of Thessaloniki.

Tzakosta, M. (in prep.). "Phonological errors in the speech of Dutch learners of Greek". Ms. University of Patras & University of the Aegean.

SETTING THE WH-MOVEMENT PARAMETER[*]

AKIRA WATANABE

The goal of this paper is to point to a specific parametric combination that cannot be handled by error-driven parameter setting models. The Cue-Based Learner of Dresher (1999), on the other hand, is shown to face no problem in acquiring the parametric pattern in question.

1. Models for Parameter Setting

Various models of parameter setting can be classified in terms of whether they are error-driven or not. Let us review some major models proposed in the literature.

The important characteristics of the Cue-Based Learner (Dresher and Kaye 1990 and Dresher 1999) crucial for our discussion are summarized in (1).

(1) Cue-Based Learner (Dresher 1999, pp. 28-29)
  A. UG associates every parameter with a cue.
  B. A cue is not an input sentence or form but is something that can be derived from input.
  C. Cues must be appropriate to their parameters in the sense that the cue must
     reflect a fundamental property of the parameter, rather than being fortuitously related to it.
  D. A parameter value that has a default state remains in it until the learner detects its cue, which acts as the trigger to move to the marked setting.
  E. Cues are local in the sense that each decision depends on finding a specific
     configuration in the input, which the learner acts on without regard to the final result. Hence, *learners are not trying to match the input*.

As italicization highlights, this model is not error-driven. The learner does not care about whether the input can receive a full structural analysis or not. In this model, each parameter acts as an agent which seeks to be valued.

Fodor's (1998, 2001) Structural Triggers Learner is very close to the Cue-Based Learner in its emphasis on the UG-specified relation between the parameter setting and its trigger. See the quotation in (2) below. The Structural Triggers Learner, however, is error-driven, since it incorporates the clause in (2c).

(2) Structural Triggers Learner (Fodor 1998, p. 19)
   Triggers, then, are small structural templates that are innate, are stored by the language faculty, and constitute the parametric options offered by UG for languages to make use of if they choose to... The learner's task is
   (a) to find these bits of structure in the sentences of the input;
   (b) to adopt a trigger structure into the current grammar if it is indubitably present in an input sentence; but
   (c) *not to adopt a trigger structure if the input sentence has any analysis, on any grammar not yet decisively ruled out, that does not include it.*

Gibson and Wexler's (1994) Triggering Learning Algorithm also belongs to the error-driven class, as italicization in (3) indicates.

(3) Triggering Learning Algorithm (Gibson and Wexler 1994, pp. 409-410)
   Given an initial set of values for n binary-valued parameters, the learner attempts to syntactically analyze an incoming sentence S. *If S can be successfully analyzed, then the learner's hypothesis regarding the target grammar is left unchanged. If, however, the learner cannot analyze S, then the learner uniformly selects a parameter P (with the probability 1/n for each parameter), changes the value associated with P, and tries to reprocess S using the new parameter value.* If the analysis is now possible, then the parameter value change is adopted. Otherwise, the original parameter value is retained.

The same is true with Clark and Roberts' (1993) Genetic Algorithm Learner, summarized in (4).

(4) Genetic Algorithm Learner (Clark and Roberts 1993)
   A. a representation of hypotheses in terms of strings
   B. a set of reproduction operators, namely, crossover and mutation, that combine or alter existing "parent" hypotheses in order to produce new "offspring" hypotheses.
   C. a measure of fitness of hypotheses in terms of their performance in an environment with respect to *violations*, superset penalty, and elegance

"Hypotheses" in (4) mean particular combinations of parametric values. The fitness metric measures success in parsing the input with respect to whether UG principles are violated among others, so this model again is error-driven.

One may say that the error-driven models look at the learning task from the perspective of the input data. The Cue-Based Learner, on the other hand, emphasizes the tight relation between the theory of UG and the learning algorithm, as Dresher (1999, p. 64) observes. The Structural Triggers Learner tries to cover the middle ground by taking both into account. The two perspectives each have their own intuitive appeal. But there is a particular parametric option which turns out to be deadly to any error-driven models.

2. Data Patterns that Falsify Error-Driven Parameter Setting

The problem arises in acquisition of the plain wh-movement when the target grammar allows scrambling. Consider the configuration in (5).

(5) Potential structural analyses of a preposed wh-phrase
     wh_i subject t_i V

There are two ways of analyzing it. One is to say that preposing of the wh-phrase over the subject is due to scrambling, concluding incorrectly that the strategy for wh-questions in the target grammar is wh-in-situ. The other, correct alternative is to say that overt wh-movement takes place in (5). For a language with scrambling and wh-movement, the first option must be ruled out in parameter setting.

Let me lay out the background assumptions that play important roles in our discussion. First, wh-in-situ is taken to be the default value. In the absence of input data, children start with the non-movement setting. (See Harada (1999) for discussion in relation to Modern Japanese.) Second, I assume that UG allows at least some kind of scrambling to raise a wh-phrase. Third, scrambling is acquired quite early, as shown in Murasugi and Kawamura 2004, and Sano 2005. Murasugi and Kawamura report that even two-year-old children learning Modern Japanese can handle scrambling pretty successfully. Since children of this age learning English start to produce correct wh-questions without failure of movement (Guasti 2002), the ambiguity of analysis is real for (5).

I will discuss the first two assumptions in more detail in the next section. Let us now examine how the three error-driven models reviewed in section 1 fare in the face of the challenge posed by a language with overt wh-movement and scrambling.

The Structural Triggers Learner will never adopt the wh-movement value, regardless of whether the scrambling parameter is already set correctly. This is because there is no way of ruling out the scrambling analysis of (5) decisively prior to setting the wh-movement parameter, as long as the target grammar has scrambling. In other words, the input of the form in (5) remains ambiguous till the wh-movement parameter is set. But since setting the wh-movement parameter is the very task that faces children, the default wh-in-situ option will be retained forever.

The situation is slightly different in the case of the Triggering Learning Algorithm. If the scrambling option is adopted prior to the encounter with (5), the default wh-in-situ value will be kept, since (5) can be analyzed as an instance of scrambling. If, on the other hand, children are not yet aware that the target grammar has scrambling, children have a chance of arriving at the target grammar, depending on how the dice is thrown. So the problem for the Triggering Learning Algorithm is that there is no guarantee that children will acquire the target grammar correctly.

Finally, for the Genetic Algorithm Learner, the problem is essentially the same as in the case of the Triggering Learning Algorithm. The [+scrambling, – wh-movement] setting and the [+scrambling, +wh-movement] are rated as on a par by the fitness metric, as far as the number of the violations of the UG principles is concerned, since both settings can parse the input of the form in (5) successfully. Thus, there is no guarantee that children will reach the target grammar.

One might invoke the Subset Principle of Berwick (1985), built into the Genetic Algorithm Learner, to avoid the problem. The [+scrambling, –wh-movement] setting generates the language that is a superset of the one generated by the [+scrambling, +wh-movement]. This is because the position of the wh-phrase is fixed in the [+scrambling, +wh-movement] language whereas it is not in the [+scrambling, –wh-movement] language, on the assumption that the scrambling option in question can apply to the wh-in-situ. The [+scrambling, – wh-movement] setting incurs a superset penalty and therefore is disfavored.

The Subset Principle, however, has been found to be incompatible with incremental learning (Fodor and Sakas 2005). More significantly, though, the Subset Principle favors the [+scrambling, +wh-movement] setting over the [+scrambling, –wh-movement] setting prior to looking at actual wh-question sentences. It follows that children start with the [+wh-movement] value once they realize that the target grammar has scrambling. This consequence is directly in conflict with the idea that wh-in-situ is the default value. As will be shown in sections 3.1 and 4, [–wh-movement] as the default is crucial in accounting for the loss of wh-movement in Old Japanese. For these reasons, invoking the Subset Principle is not a viable solution to the problem posed for error-driven learning.

To summarize, the heart of the problem for error-driven parameter setting is that a parametric choice with an appropriate type of scrambling can analyze a preposed wh-phrase as due to scrambling without requiring wh-movement. The possibility of this alternative analysis prevents the learner from adopting the wh-movement analysis without fail.

3. Justification of the Background Assumptions

To show that the problem for error-driven parameter setting is not hypothetical but real, let us take up the background assumptions and consider their empirical justifications in detail.

3.1. Loss of wh-movement in Old Japanese

The assumption that wh-in-situ is the default is motivated by the loss of wh-movement in Old Japanese, as discussed in Watanabe (2002). The wh-question and the yes-no question in the seventh and eighth centuries obeyed the word order restriction shown in (6a), where the focused expression marked by the particle *ka* is found between the *ha*-marked topic and the nominative subject. This word order restriction is illustrated by (6b, c), where the focused phrase is put in italics. In (6b), the focus is a wh-phrase. (6c) is a yes-no question. See the Appendix for the statistical data that substantiate the restriction in question.

(6) a. Topic (...) Wh-/Non-wh-focus (...) Subj$_{Nom}$... V

b. ... *izuku-yu-ka*   imo-**ga**   iriki-te   yime-ni   mie-tsuru?
where-through-KA wife-nom enter-conj   dream-loc   appear-perf
"From where did my wife come and appear in my dream?"
(Man'youshuu #3117)

c. ... Hatsuse-no kawa-**ha**   *ura*   *na-mi-ka*   fune-**no**
Hatsuse-gen river-top shore absent-ness-KA boat-nom yori-ko-nu?...
approach-come-neg
"Is it because Hatsuse River has no shore that no boat comes near?"
(Man'youshuu #3225)

Watanabe (2002) analyzes this phenomenon in terms of the structure in (7), a modification of Rizzi's (1997) proposal, claiming that the wh-phrase (as well as the non-wh focus) was raised to Spec of FocP during the relevant period.

(7)   [$_{TopP}$ Spec [$_{FocP}$ Spec [$_{FinP}$ [$_{TP}$ Subj VP T°] Fin°] Foc°] Top°]

Old Japanese was a wh-movement language.

Wh-movement had been lost by the end of the tenth century, though the exact dating of the loss is impossible due to the lack of sufficient documentation during the ninth century. Examples like (8) are found in the *Tales of Genji*, attributed to the beginning of the eleventh century.

(8)   Ito   ayashiki mi-kokoro-**no**,   geni,   *ikade*
       very curious   hon-character-nom indeed how
       naraha-se-tamahi-kemu?
       develop-hon-hon-would.have
       "How has his curious character developed indeed?"

(Tales of Genji, Ukifune)

Note that the wh-phrase follows the nominative subject in (8). Thus, as far as the wh-movement parameter is concerned, the grammatical system of this period is the same as that of Modern Japanese.

This change was not accompanied by any radical social upheaval. The major cause of the loss of wh-movement, therefore, must come from the mechanism of parameter setting. In other words, there must be a preference for wh-in-situ imposed by UG and the associated language acquisition device. A reasonable hypothesis is that the default status of wh-in-situ is exactly what is needed here.

A complete account of the loss of wh-movement is provided in section 4. For now, let us note that it is this preference for wh-in-situ over wh-movement that creates the problem for error-driven parameter setting discussed in the previous section. Acquisition of wh-movement is made all the more difficult if wh-in-situ is preferred.

3.2. Scrambling

Another important assumption is that UG allows a particular kind of scrambling to apply to wh-in-situ. This type of scrambling is instantiated by Modern Japanese, as illustrated in (9), where the wh-phrase is raised to various positions.

(9)   a. John-wa   *dare-ni*   sono   hon-o   ageta no?
           John-top   who-dat   that   book-acc gave Q
           "Who did John give the book to?"
       b. John-wa   sono hon-o   *dare-ni*   ageta no?
       c. *Dare-ni*   John-wa   sono hon-o   ageta no?

Scrambling was also found in the seventh and eighth centuries. This movement operation results in adjunction to various positions. The examples in (10) show that the scrambled phrase, indicated by italics, can appear between the wh-phrase and the nominative subject.

(10)   a.   Ikani-ara-mu   hi-no-toki-ni-**ka**-mo   *kowe shira-mu   hito-no*
            how-be-will   day-gen-time-loc-KA-MO   sound know-will person-gen
            hiza-no-he   wa-**ga**   makuraka-mu
            knee-gen-top   I-nom   sleep-will?
            "When will I sleep on the knee of someone who recognizes my
            sound?"   (*Man'youshuu* #810)
       b.   ... nani-su-to-**ka** ...   *okutsuki-ni* imo-**ga**   koya-se-ru?
            what-do-quot-KA   tomb-loc   woman-nom lie-hon-perf
            "How on earth has the woman come to lie in the tomb?"
                                                              (*Man'youshuu* #1807)

The landing site can be higher than the wh-phrase, as in (11).

(11)   a.   ... hototogisu *Kenashi-no   Woka-ni*   itsu-**ka**   ki-naka-mu?
            cuckoo   Kenashi-gen hill-loc   when-KA come-sing-will
            "When will a cuckoo come and sing at Kenashi Hill?"
                                                              (*Man'youshuu* #1466)
       b.   *Kasugano-no   fuji-ha   chiri-ni-te*   nani-wo-**ka**-mo
            Kasugano-gen wisteria-top fall-perf-conj what-acc-KA-MO
            mikari-no   hito-no   wori-te   kazasa-mu?
            hike-gen   person-nom pick-conj wear-on-the-hair-will
            "Since the wisteria flowers at Kasugano are gone, what should hikers
            pick and wear on the hair?"   (*Man'youshuu* #1974)

It can be even higher than the topic, as in (12).

(12)   a.   ... *samuki yo-ni*   wa-ga senokimi-**ha**   hitori-ka   nura-mu?
            cold   night-loc I-gen   husband-top   alone-KA sleep-will
            "Is my husband sleeping alone on the cold night?"(*Man'youshuu*
#59)
       b.   *Miyabiwo-ni*   ware-**ha** ari-keri.
            graceful.man-pred I-top be-past
            "I was a graceful man."   (*Man'youshuu* #127)

   One cannot tell whether the type of scrambling found during this period is
applicable to wh-in-situ, because the wh-phrase was obligatorily raised to Spec
of FocP, and also because there are not a sufficient number of multiple wh-
questions attested which may provide examples of wh-in-situ. It should also be
noted that scrambling must be prevented from applying to the wh-phrase
already raised to Spec of FocP, since it would produce the ungrammatical wh
topic order.   Nevertheless, given that Old Japanese and Modern Japanese differ
only minimally in the setting of the wh-movement parameter, it is reasonable to

suppose that the type of scrambling found in Old Japanese is the same as the one in Modern Japanese. At least, children have a good chance of hypothesizing that the target grammar allows scrambling to apply to wh-in-situ before realizing that it has wh-movement. The analytical ambiguity in the configuration in (5), repeated below, is thus real.

(5) Potential structural analyses of a preposed wh-phrase
    wh_i subject t_i V

4. How is Wh-Movement Acquired?

The discussion so far has concentrated on showing that error-driven parameter setting cannot deal with the grammar with scrambling and overt wh-movement. We now need to ask whether there is a valid alternative.

4.1. How was wh-movement lost?

To consider how children set the wh-movement parameter, it is instructive to examine how they fail to acquire wh-movement, namely, the loss of wh-movement. Recall first of all that the absence of overt wh-movement is the default value. The loss of wh-movement, then, implies that the trigger for the [+wh-movement] value becomes unavailable. In my earlier (2002) work, I suggested that this is exactly what happened in the history of Japanese. The fact that the wh-phrase is consistently found in the configuration in (5) leads linguists to posit wh-movement. Suppose that the situation is essentially the same for children, except that they do not make use of negative evidence. In the grammatical system of Old Japanese, there are two ways in which the configuration in (5) becomes unavailable. First, topicalization of the subject would place it above the wh-phrase as in (13), since the position of the topic is higher than the focus.

(13)   *subj-top   wh t_{subj} t V

Second, the use of a null subject makes it impossible to detect (5). Watanabe (2002) pointed to the increase in subject topicalization as the major factor. In addition to the observation discussed there, one may note that the ratio of non-topicalized subjects was exceedingly high when Old Japanese used to have overt wh-movement. In *Man'youshuu*, a collection of verse texts where wh-movement is attested, there are about ninety examples in which the *ka*-marked focused expression including both wh- and non-wh-cases precedes an overt nominative subject (see the Appendix). At least about one third of these ninety cases should instead have a topicalized subject in the Modern Japanese rendition. At some point in the history, the ratio of subject topicalization must have risen up. I conjectured that this increase is a precondition for the loss of wh-movement. This conjecture is backed up by Aoki's (1954) data concerning one form of the nominative case marker. She counted the number of the examples in which the subject is topicalized and also of the cases where the subject is marked with one of the nominative case particles, namely, *ga*. Unfortunately, she did not take up the other nominative case particle *no*. The picture is, therefore, partial. But her data is dramatic enough to warrant my conjecture. I reproduce the relevant figures in (14), which gives the raw number of examples.

(14)   Subject marking in root clauses with the unambiguously adnominal ending

nominative marker (*ga*) / topic marker (*ha*)

Man'youshuu (7-8 c.)	52	47
Genji (c. 1000)	2	161

Since wh-movement requires the adnominal form of the predicate as the clause ending, only those root clauses with the unambiguously adnominal ending are included. The difference in subject marking is remarkable. The nominative case marker *ga* had almost disappeared from root clauses in the *Tales of Genji*, where wh-movement no longer takes place.

My own counting of wh-questions in the first four volumes of *Genji* leads to the same conclusion. I looked at all the wh-questions, regardless of whether the clause ending is unambiguously adnominal or not. I also included both *ga* and *no* as the nominative subject marking. The result is given in (15).

(15)   Subject marking in wh-questions in the first 4 volumes of *Genji*
        topicalized subjects: 15 examples
        nominative subjects: 0 examples
        bare subjects: 6 examples

The overt nominative subject is quite rare in wh-questions in *Genji*.

Deprived of the opportunity to encounter the configuration in (5), children stick to the default value of the wh-movement parameter, namely, wh-in-situ. Note also that the Subset Principle, which favors [+scrambling, +wh-movement] over [+scrambling, –wh-movement], should not play a role here.

4.2. The Cue-Based Leaner

If the encounter with input sentences of the form in (5) triggers the [+wh-movement] value, it follows that the parameter setting mechanism simply ignores the fact that the scrambling analysis of (5) is possible in principle. This is exactly the crucial characteristic of the Cue-Based Learner. Recall also that positing the default value is a possibility allowed under this model (1D).

The configuration of the form in (5) is the only cue for SOV languages, but not for SVO languages. Otherwise, null subject languages like Italian are incorrectly predicted to be unable to have overt wh-movement. For SVO languages, the presence of an overt subject is not that important. Objects and other complements are placed postverbally in SVO languages. Preposing of these postverbal elements necessarily crosses the main predicate, which should be sufficient for setting the [+wh-movement] value. Thus, we can say that the wh-movement parameter is sensitive to word order cues, putting aside complications that other word order types may create. (16) is the schematic summary.

(16)   Word order cues for setting [+ wh-movement]

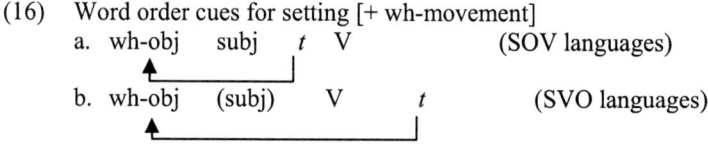

      a. wh-obj   subj   *t* V   (SOV languages)

      b. wh-obj (subj)   V   *t*   (SVO languages)

5. Conclusion

To wrap up the discussion, I have demonstrated that error-driven learning cannot handle grammars with overt wh-movement and scrambling. One weakness of this demonstration is that the example of such languages taken up here is Old Japanese, of which there is no native speaker alive. Languages with overt wh-movement and scrambling, however, do not seem to be so unusual, judging from Dryer's (1991) sampling data concerning the relation between word order typology and wh-movement, given in (17).

(17)   Word order typology and wh-movement (Dryer 1991)

	wh-in-situ	initial-wh	total
V-final	56 (68%)	26 (32%)	82
SVO	31 (60%)	21 (40%)	52
V-initial	6 (21%)	23 (79%)	29

Overt wh-movement is not rare, though not predominant, among verb-final languages (32%). And there is no reason to expect that all of these languages lack scrambling. Thus, the problem for error-driven learning is real. The Cue-Based Learner, which is not error-driven, seems to be the way to go.

At the same time, it is too naïve to think that a single learning model suffices for all the cases of parameter setting. There may be a domain where error-driven learning takes place. It is an interesting empirical question for future research to sort out what kind of parameter setting model is indeed used for which domain.

It has also turned out that the Subset Principle is problematic in accounting for the loss of wh-movement in the history of Japanese. It is necessary to reexamine the empirical content of the Subset Principle.

Appendix: Wh-Movement and Scrambling in Old Japanese

Here, I present the crucial statistic data on wh-movement and scrambling in Old Japanese.

The word order restriction during the seventh and eighth centuries can be seen in Nomura's (1993) data on the position of the *ka*-marked focus in interrogative sentences in *Man'youshuu*, given in (A1), which shows that the focused expression, whether wh or not, is located between the position occupied by the topicalized subject and that occupied by the nominative subject.

(A1)   Ordering of the subject and the *ka*-marked phrase in *Man'youshuu*
 I.   Nominative subject
      XP-ka ... Subj-no/ga ... V(adnominal form):   approximately 90
      Subj-no/ga ... XP-ka ... V(adnominal form):   5

II. Topicalized subject
    XP-ka ... Subj-ha ... V(adnominal form):   3
    Subj-ha ... XP-ka ... V(adnominal form):   approximately 50

What is important about *Man'youshuu* is that it is a collection of contributions by various authors. Thus, the data indicates that speakers uniformly had a grammar with overt wh-movement at that time. Out of the eight exceptions, three are by an author who is conjectured to be an immigrant from the Korean Peninsula on other grounds, reinforcing the idea that the word order restriction reflects the grammatical knowledge of native speakers of Old Japanese. The appropriate parameter setting model must guarantee the uniform behavior on the part of the speech community.

My own data on scrambling in *Man'youshuu* is based on the text edited by Satake et al. (1998), together with the concordance by Koten Saku'in Kankou-kai (2003). I assume that scrambling takes the form of adjunction to a maximal projection. For some additional discussion of scrambling in Old Japanese, see Watanabe (2005). Out of about the ninety cases of (A1I), where the focus precedes a nominative subject, something intervenes between the subject and the focus in 12 examples. Of the same ninety cases, some scrambled phrase appears higher than the focus in 16 examples. Out of the about fifty cases of (A1II), six have some phrase intervening between the topicalized subject and the following focus. For adjunction to TopP, I only counted the first half of *Man'youshuu*, which turned up 88 such cases, excluding cases where an adjunct clause or a phrase marked by the discourse particle *mo* appears in front of the topic. (A2) gives the summary.

(A2)   Scrambling in *Man'youshuu*
        I.   adjunction to FinP/TP   12 (out of 90)
        II. adjunction to FocP
             a. YP   XP-ka ... Subj-no/ga ... V   16 (out of 90)
             b. Subj-topic   YP ... XP-ka ... V   6 (out of 50)
        III. adjunction to TopP   88 in the first half

Notes

I would like to thank the audiences at Osaka University (2004) and GALA2005, including Masao Ochi, Luigi Rizzi, and Ken Wexler, for useful comments.

References

Aoki, R. (1954) "Shugo shousetsu-no *ha* joshi nitsuite", *Kokugo to Kokubungaku* 31(3), 41-54.

Berwick, R. C. (1985) *Acquisition of Syntactic Knowledge*, Cambridge, Mass., MIT Press.

Clark, R. and I. Roberts (1993) "A computational model of language learnability and language change", *Linguistic Inquiry* 24, 299-345.

Dresher, B. E. (1999) "Charting the learning path: Cues to parameter setting", *Linguistic Inquiry* 30, 27-67.

——. & J. D. Kaye. (1990) "A computational learning model for metrical phonology", *Cognition* 34, 137-195.

Dryer, M. S. (1991) "SVO languages and the OV:VO typology", *Journal of Linguistics* 27, 443-482.

Fodor, J. D. (1998) "Unambiguous triggers", *Linguistic Inquiry* 29, 1-36.

——. (2001), "Setting syntactic parameters", in M. Baltin and C. Collins, eds., *The Handbook of Contemporary Syntactic Theory*, 203-225. Oxford, Blackwell.

——. and W. G. Sakas (2005) "The Subset Principle in syntax: costs of compliance", *Journal of Linguistics* 41, 513-569.

Gibson, E. and K. Wexler (1994) "Triggers", *Linguistic Inquiry* 25, 407-454.

Guasti, M. T. (2002) *Language Acquisition*, Cambridge, Mass., MIT Press.

Harada, K. I. (1999) "On the acquisition of covert and overt wh-movement", in M. Muraki and E. Iwamoto, eds., *Linguistics: In Search of the Human Mind*, Tokyo, Kaitaku-sha, 708-736.

Koten Saku'in Kankou-kai (ed.) (2003) *Man'youshuu Saku'in* (Man'youshuu Concordance), Tokyo, Hanawa Shobou

Murasugi, K. and T. Kawamura (2004) "On the acquisition of scrambling in Japanese", *Language and Linguistics* 5, 131-151.

Nomura, T.(1993) "Joudaigo no *no* to *ga* nitsuite", *Kokugo-Kokubun* 62(2),1-17, 62(3), 30-49.

Rizzi, L. (1997) "The fine structure of the left periphery", in L. Haegeman, ed., *Elements of Grammar*, Dordrecht, Kluwer, 281-337.

Sano, T. (2005) "The acquisition of Japanese topicalization and the role of discourse context", in *BUCLD 29 On-line Proceedings*. Boston University.

Satake, A., M. Kinoshita, and N. Ogawa (1998) *Man'youshuu Honbun-hen*, Emended edition, Tokyo, Hanawa Shobou.

Watanabe, A. (2002) "Loss of overt wh-movement in Old Japanese", in D. W. Lightfoot, ed., *Syntactic Effects of Morphological Change*, Oxford, Oxford University Press, 179-195.

—. (2005) "*So/Zo* in Old Japanese", in *The World of Linguistic Research: A Festschrift for Kinsuke Hasegawa on the Occasion of his Seventieth Birthday*, Tokyo, Kaitaku-sha, 3-13.

Triggering V2: The Amount of Input Needed for Parameter Setting in a Split-CP Model of Clause Structure

Marit R. Westergaard

1. Introduction

In this paper I argue that children generally need relatively little input evidence to set word order parameters. Within a type of Split-CP model of clause structure, where different clause types are assumed to have different heads in the CP domain, I suggest that children make no global search of the primary linguistic data, but scan the input for designated word order cues, focusing exclusively on the relevant clause type. I investigate child and adult data from a dialect of Norwegian (Tromsø), where there is verb movement and verb second (V2) word order in some clause types, but not in others. The findings show that target-consistent word order is attested early in the different clause types, regardless of input frequencies, and that there is no overgeneralization of word order from one construction to another. This is argued to be due to the heads in the CP domain providing separate input cues for word order in the different clause types.

2. The Word Order of Norwegian

Norwegian is a V2 language with the finite verb generally appearing in second position in main clauses. This is standardly assumed to be the result of verb movement to the C position of the clause (see e.g. Vikner 1995). Since Norwegian is an SVO language, the V2 requirement in subject-initial declaratives is only visible if there is a sentence adverb or negation present. This is illustrated in (1), where the finite verb is assumed to have moved across negation. In non-subject-initial declaratives we see verb movement across the subject, as in example (2). Verb movement is also required in *yes/no*-questions, as shown in (3).

(1) Vi **drikker ikke** fransk vin/*vi ikke drikker fransk vin.
     we drink   not French wine
     'We don't drink French wine.'
(2) Italiensk vin **drikker vi** ofte/*italiensk vin vi ofte drikker.
     Italian   wine drink · we often
     'Italian wine we often drink.'
(3) **Drikker han** mye vin?
     drinks   he   much wine
     'Does he drink much wine?'

But non-V2 word order is found in certain clause types in the language, both
in standard Norwegian and in the Tromsø dialect, which is the variety of the
language spoken by the children and adults in this study. Sentence (4) shows
that there is generally no verb movement across an adverb or negation in
embedded clauses,[1] and example (5) illustrates that there is no verb movement
across the subject in embedded questions. Also exclamatives require non-V2, as
illustrated by the example in (6).

(4) Det finnes noen studenter [som **aldri drikker** vin
                                             /*som drikker aldri vin].
     there exist some students   who never drink   wine
     'There are some students who never drink wine.'
(5) Jeg lurer på [hva **han drikker**]/[*hva drikker han].
     I wonder on what he   drinks
     'I wonder what he drinks.'
(6) Kor stor **du er** blitt!/*Kor stor er du blitt!
     how big you are become
     'How big you have become!'

Furthermore, many dialects of Norwegian do not have a strict V2
requirement in *wh*-questions, and Vangsnes (2004) argues that the dialect
variation is based on several microparameters. In the Tromsø dialect, the word
order distinction is dependent on the length of the *wh*-constituent. While
questions introduced by disyllabic *wh*-words or full *wh*-phrases always appear
with the verb in second position, non-V2 word order is possible (alongside V2)
after the monosyllabic *wh*-words *ka, kem* and *kor* ('what', 'who' and 'where').
In Westergaard (2003), I investigated a sample of spontaneous adult speech and
argued that the choice of V2 vs. non-V2 in these questions is dependent on the
information structure of the sentence, more specifically on whether the subject
conveys given or new information. This is reflected in certain (statistically
significant) patterns for subject and verb types in the two constructions, V2

being preferred with full DP subjects and the verb *være* 'be', while non-V2 is typically chosen with pronominal subjects and all other verbs. Some examples from the adult speech sample are provided in (7) and (8).[2]

(7)   kor   **er mitt fly**? (INV, file Ole.17)
      where is my   plane
      'Where is my plane?'
(8)   kor   **vi lande** henne? (INV, file Ole.17)
      where we land   LOC
      'Where do we land?'

Summarizing, in the Tromsø dialect, there are some clause types that require V2 and some that require or allow non-V2, as illustrated in Table 1.

Table 1: Overview of clause types with V2 and non-V2 in Norwegian (Tromsø).

V2	Non-V2
Subject-initial declaratives with Neg/Adv	Embedded clauses with Neg/Adv
Non-subject-initial declaratives	Embedded questions
Yes/no-questions	Exclamatives
Certain matrix *wh*-questions	Certain matrix *wh*-questions

In a cue-based approach to acquisition and change, such as Lightfoot (1999, 2006), the evidence for verb movement in V2 languages will be expressed by the presence of a particular syntactic structure in the input. In a syntactic model with an unsplit CP, Lightfoot (2006, p. 86) formulates the cue for V2 syntax as in (9), which is a piece of structure "where a phrasal category occurs in the Specifier of a CP whose head is occupied by a verb."

(9) $_{CP}$[XP $_C$V...]

Lightfoot's cue-based approach to acquisition and change seems to be founded on very sound principles and historical data. However, I think that the cue as it is formulated in (12) is somewhat too simple and would cause confusion for a child learning the Tromsø dialect of Norwegian (and any mixed V2 grammar), where the evidence for verb movement is expressed in the input in some clause types and not in others. That is, the children are exposed to a C position that is only sometimes filled by a verb. In a grammar with an unsplit CP, one would expect that mixed input such as the target structures in the Tromsø dialect could cause overgeneralization from one clause type to another, depending on the frequency of the cue in the primary linguistic data the child is exposed to. The next section will therefore look at the frequency of the various clause types in some typical child-directed speech.

3. Input Frequencies

In order to get an indication of what child-directed speech may consist of in terms of frequency of syntactic constructions, a sample of the adult material from the child language corpus (see section 4 below) was investigated in detail. This is the production of the investigator in a one-hour recording of spontaneous conversation with a child around the age of two and a half. In this file, the investigator produced a total of 793 utterances, out of which there were 668 complete (matrix and embedded) clauses. The different clause types and corresponding frequencies are provided in Table 2.

Table 2: Clause types with V2 and non-V2 in a sample of child-directed speech, the investigator in the file Ole.14 (age of child 2;6.21), with percentages calculated relative to the total number of complete (matrix and embedded) clauses (N=668).[3]

V2		Non-V2	
Subject-initial declaratives with Neg/Adv	6.4% (43)	Embedded clauses with Neg/Adv	0.9% (6)
Non-subject-initial declaratives	19.6% (131)	Embedded questions	1.6% (11)
Yes/no-questions	28.4% (190)	Exclamatives	1.0% (7)
Certain *wh*-questions	2.4% (16)	Certain *wh*-questions	4.2% (28)
Total evidence for V2	**56.8% (380)**	**Total evidence for non-V2**	**7.7% (52)**

As we see from Table 2, the most frequent sentence types are *yes/no*-questions and non-subject-initial declarative main clauses, which make up as much as 28.4% and 19.6% of all complete clauses in the file respectively. In addition, there is 6.4% evidence for verb movement in subject-initial declaratives containing negation or an adverb, as well as a number of *wh*-questions with V2, making the total evidence for V2 word order in the input sample reach a percentage of 56.8%.

The evidence for non-V2 in the constructions that require this word order is much more sparse. Embedded *wh*-questions are very infrequent, attested only 1.6% in the adult data. Exclamatives are even less frequent, occurring 1.0% in the sample, while *wh*-questions with non-V2 make up 4.2% of the total number of complete sentences. Embedded declaratives with negation or an adverb are the least frequent of all non-V2 constructions, occurring in only 0.9% of the sample. This means that altogether the evidence for non-V2 word order is attested in 7.7% of the input data, considerably lower than the evidence for V2. However, there is also one example of a negated non-V2 main *wh*-question in the file, increasing the evidence for the lack of verb movement across negation or adverbs in Norwegian, but only by 0.1% (and is thus not included in Table 2). This example is provided in (10). [4]

    (10) kem som **ikkje får** kjøre? (INV, file Ole.14)
           who that not   gets drive
           'Who doesn't get to drive?'

The sample of adult data reported here is of course very small, and furthermore, only produced by one person. However, similar findings have been attested for V2 constructions in much larger samples of Swedish input data in Josefsson (2004). A larger sample of the Norwegian input data on the non-V2 constructions was investigated in Westergaard&Bentzen (2005), and the frequencies were found to be parallel to the findings in the small sample investigated here.

Given these frequencies in the input sample, it seems safe to conclude that there is ample evidence for V2 in the input to North Norwegian children, while the evidence for the non-V2 constructions is relatively sparse. Based on frequency, it could therefore be expected, in a model with an unsplit-CP, that there might be some overgeneralization of V2 in early child language. In the next section, we will therefore turn to the production of the Norwegian children.

4. The Child Data

The corpus used for this study was collected in Tromsø in 1997/98 and consists of altogether 70 recorded sessions of three children, most of them lasting about an hour. Table 3 gives an overview of the corpus, specifying the age of the children and the total number of files and child utterances.

Table 3: Overview of the Norwegian child language corpus, Tromsø dialect.[5]

Name of Child	Age	Files	Child Utterances
Ina	1;8.20-3;3.18	Ina.01-27	20,071
Ann	1;8.20-3;0.1	Ann.01-21	13,129
Ole	1;9.10-2;11.23	Ole.01-22	13,485
Total			46,685

As expected from the input frequencies, V2 word order is attested from the earliest occurrences of multi-word utterances (see also Westergaard 2005a). This is illustrated by the subject-initial declarative with negation in (11), the non-subject-initial declarative in (12), and the *yes/no*-question in (13).

(11) ho mamma **er** **ikke** på jobb. (Ole, age 1;10.0)
DET mom be.PRES not at work
'Mom is not at work.'

(12) så **tegne** æ mamma. (Ina, age 1;10.4)
then draw.INF/PRES I mommie
'Then I draw mommie.'

(13) **ser** **du** nokka? (Ann, age 2;1.7)
see.PRES you something
'Do you see anything?'

Furthermore, the children were found to produce *wh*-questions with both V2 and non-V2 from a relatively early age, with the same patterns for subject and verb types as in the adult grammar, as illustrated in (14) and (15), cp. examples (7) and (8) from the adult data. Given the inconsistent and relatively sparse input evidence for the word order in *wh*-questions, this suggests that children are sensitive to patterns of information structure from early on (see Westergaard 2003, 2005a).

(14) kor **e** **babyen**? (Ina, age 2;1.0)
where be.PRES baby.DEF
'Where is the baby?'

(15) ka **du skal** finne? (Ina, age 2:0.5)
what you shall find
'What do you want to find?'

But what about the other non-V2 constructions that are attested even less frequently than the *wh*-questions in the input? Embedded questions, which were found in 1.6% of the input sample, appear in the child corpus with target-consistent non-V2, as illustrated in (16), cp. example (5) from the adult data. That is, there is no evidence of overgeneralization from main clause questions. Exclamatives, which are even less frequent in the input data, are also infrequent and appear relatively late in the child data. Nevertheless, exclamatives occur with non-V2 as soon as they appear in the children's own production, as shown in (17), cp. example (6) above.

(16) se   her   ka   **Ina gjør.** (Ina.04, age 1;11.22)
look here what Ina does
'Look here what Ina is doing.'
(17) kor   store mage   **han har.** (Ina.27, age 3;3.18)
where/how big   stomach he   have.PRES
'What a big stomach he has!'

Finally, we will consider embedded clauses containing negation or an adverb, where the target language requires non-V2. Although there are relatively few embedded clauses in the child corpus, due to the young age of the children, a number of cases of overgeneralization of V2 word order are attested, as illustrated in (18), cp. example (4) above (see also Westergaard 2005a). Another construction where the target language does not have verb movement across negation or an adverb is the non-V2 main clause *wh*-questions, as was shown in (10) above. In the child corpus there is only one such question containing negation, and in this example the verb has indeed moved across negation. Thus, the word order of (18) and (19) indicates that there *is* overgeneralization of verb movement in these cases. Similar examples are attested in the production of somewhat older children acquiring the Tromsø dialect in Bentzen (2003) and Westergaard&Bentzen (2005), where it is shown that these children move the verb past negation in several embedded non-V2 contexts, *that*-clauses, relative clauses, and adverbial clauses, as well as the non-V2 main clause *wh*-questions. A small experiment reported on in Westergaard&Bentzen (2005) suggests that children do not consistently produce the target non-V2 word order in these constructions until after the age of six.

(18) det er   ho mamma som **har**   **også** tegna. (Ina, age 3;2.05)
it be.PRES DET mommie who have.PRES also draw.PART
'It is mommie who has also drawn.'
Target form: Det er ho mamma som også har tegna.'
(19) kem som **vil ikkje** være ilag   med han? (Ina, age 3;1.8)
who that will not   be   together with him
'Who doesn't want to be with him?'
Target form: Kem som ikkje vil være i lag med han?

To summarize this section, all the clause types listed in Table 1 appear in the child data with target-consistent word order, the ones in the left-hand column with V2, the ones in the right-hand column with non-V2. Thus, regardless of the very different input frequencies, there seems to be no overgeneralization from one clause type to another. The only exception to this is the appearance of verbs in front of negation or adverbs in non-V2 contexts such as embedded clauses and main clause non-V2 *wh*-questions. In the next section, I account for the child data within a Split-CP approach to clause structure, where different clause types have different heads in the CP domain, and consequently different cues for verb movement.

5. Syntactic Analysis

The syntactic framework adopted in this paper is a Split-CP model of clause structure, originally developed in Westergaard&Vangsnes (2005) and somewhat revised in Westergaard (2005a). The model is inspired by Rizzi (1997, 2001) and other work on Italian syntax (e.g. Poletto 2000 and Benincà&Poletto 2004), but is in many ways different from these models. For example, the ForceP of Rizzi's model is replaced by different heads for different clause types. Some of the relevant heads present in the CP domain of the clause are given in (20):

(20) $_{CP}$[(Int° Pol° Top°...) ... [(Wh°) Fin° $_{IP}$[...

Not all functional heads are present in all clauses, and clause typing is dependent on the topmost head in the structure - e.g. if the head Int° is present, the sentence is a *wh*-question, whereas if the head Top° is present, the sentence is a declarative, either a subject-initial or a non-subject-initial clause, see Table 4. As embedded clauses do not have the same illocutionary force as main clauses, declaratives are assumed to be bare FinPs and embedded questions bare WhPs.

Table 4: Examples of syntactic heads and corresponding clause types.

Syntactic Head	Clause Type
Int°	*Wh*-questions
Pol°	*Yes/no*-questions
Top°	Declaratives
Fin°	Embedded declaratives
Wh°	Embedded questions
etc.	

V2 word order in this model is the result of an EPP *head* feature ($[X°_{EPP}]$) on syntactic heads in the CP domain, which attracts the verb. This means that there may be several sources for V2 word order, and this accounts for different V2 grammars. For example, English must have a requirement for a filled Int° head, but no such requirement for a filled Top°, and this accounts for subject-auxiliary inversion in questions and the lack of it in declaratives. Certain dialects of Norwegian, e.g. Nordmøre (see e.g. Westergaard&Vangsnes 2005), exhibit V2 in all types of declaratives but not in any kinds of *wh*-questions. These dialects are therefore assumed to have the EPP head feature on Top° but not on Int°, exactly the opposite requirements of English. The head involved in exclamatives must lack the EPP feature in Norwegian, while e.g. Danish presumably has it, since this language displays verb movement in exclamatives. Finally, the lack of the EPP feature on the Fin° and Wh° heads in Norwegian accounts for the non-V2 word order in embedded contexts. By comparison, Belfast English displays V2 in embedded questions (see Henry 1995), and must therefore have the EPP feature on the Wh° head.

The word order of the Tromsø dialect, illustrated in section 2, can thus be accounted for by the presence or absence of the feature $[X°_{EPP}]$ on different heads in the CP domain: Those clause types which display V2 are endowed with this feature, while those clause types which do not, lack it. The two different word orders possible in *wh*-questions with monosyllabic question words must then be due to the requirements of a lower CP head, which attracts elements with low information value (pronominal subjects or *be*), see Westergard (2005a). This could e.g. be the lower Top° head of Rizzi (1997, 2001).[6] The reason why children acquire this so quickly, as was illustrated by examples (14) and (15) in section 4, is argued to be an early sensitivity to information structure (see Westergaard 2003, 2004, 2005a).

The functional architecture outlined in Table 4 is assumed to be provided by UG, while children obviously have to learn from the input which CP heads have the $[X°_{EPP}]$ feature. In this process, they rely on certain cues in the input, in the sense of Lightfoot (1999, 2006).[7] Recall that he formulated the cue as in (9), repeated here:

(9') $_{CP}[XP\ _CV...]$ (from Lightfoot, 2006, p. 86)

Within the present split-CP model, there must be several cues expressing V2 word order, depending on clause type. For example, the cue for V2 in *wh*-questions must be a structure with a *wh*-element followed by a verb filling the head position in the IntP, while the cue for V2 in declaratives must be an XP followed by a verb in the TopP. English-speaking children will encounter the former in the primary linguistic data that they are exposed to, but not the latter, while children growing up in Nordmøre will have evidence for the latter, but not the former. Both English and Norwegian-speaking children will be exposed to the cue for verb movement in *yes/no*-questions, while this will not be the case in e.g. standard Italian, where the word order of *yes/no*-questions is identical to that of declaratives. The cues for verb movement to the FinP and WhP will not be manifested in the input to Norwegian children, while the latter should be present in the input to children acquiring Belfast English. Table 5 gives a first approximation of some of the cues for V2 syntax.

Table 5: Examples of cues for V2 in a split-CP model.

Cue	Presence in the Input
$_{IntP}[wh\ _{Int°}V...]$	+ (English, Standard Norwegian) - (Nordmøre dialect)
$_{TopP}[XP\ _{Top°}V...]$	+ (Norwegian, German etc.) - (English, Italian etc.)
$_{PolP}[\ _{Pol°}V...]$	+ (Norwegian, German, English etc.) - (Italian)
$_{WhP}[(wh)\ _{Wh°}V...]$	+ (Belfast English) - (Norwegian, English)
etc.	

According to this model, then, there is no global cue for V2 syntax, but separate cues for each clause type. When children scan the primary linguistic data for word order cues, this is presumably a selective process where only a particular clause type is relevant. When searching the linguistic input for possible cues for verb movement to Int°, for example, children will only consider *wh*-questions and ignore other clause types such as declaratives or imperatives. Likewise, only *yes/no*-questions would be focused on for a possible cue for the Pol° head. This means that no transfer of feature values is predicted from one clause type to another. That is to say, realizing that there is a $[X°_{EPP}]$ head feature on e.g. Pol° does not make the child grammar automatically assume that the feature specification is the same on other heads in the CP domain.[8]

But how do we then account for the relatively persistent overgeneralization of verb movement across negation or adverbs attested in embedded contexts and non-V2 *wh*-questions, illustrated in (18) and (19) in section 4? In Westergaard (2005a) and Westergaard&Bentzen (2005) this is argued to be due to an economy principle in language acquisition, which causes the child grammar to move elements only as high up in the structure as there is evidence for in the input. In the sample of child-directed speech (see Table 2), there is ample evidence of verb movement across negation or adverbs in subject-initial declarative main clauses, and given the tendency for economy, the child grammar will only move the verb to the lowest position which ensures that it appears in front of these elements, which is a head in the IP domain. This means that the child grammar misinterprets the word order in subject-initial declaratives in Norwegian to be the cue for V-to-I movement. Missetting this parameter to the wrong value will cause a word order where the verb precedes negation or adverbs also in non-V2 contexts, i.e. all embedded clauses and main clause non-V2 *wh*-questions. In all other constructions, the verb will move to a C-head, and this will make verb movement to the IP domain invisible. In Westergaard&Bentzen (2005), it is argued that the children will only reset this parameter after they have been exposed to a large number of embedded contexts where the verb follows negation or adverbs, and given that these constructions are extremely infrequent in the input (cf. Table 2), this is a process that may take some time.

For the purpose of the present paper, what is crucial about this word order overgeneralization is that it occurs in the IP domain, where all clause types are assumed to have identical projections. Thus, transferring a feature value from one clause type to another, in this case from subject-initial declarative main clauses to non-V2 *wh*-questions and all embedded contexts, would in fact be expected. This is in contrast to the CP domain, where all clause types are assumed to have different heads. Consequently, the lack of word order overgeneralization in this domain is expected.

Finally, if this idea of a selective cue-searching process is on the right track, then that would also mean that the cues for word order are much more robustly expressed in the various constructions than the percentages in Table 2 suggest. In fact, for most of the functional heads, e.g. *yes/no*-questions or exclamatives, the cue would be expressed in 100% of the relevant utterances in Norwegian. This idea of a selective search may thus also explain why word order tends to be acquired so early and why there in general does not seem to be any overgeneralization of feature values from one construction type to another.

6. Conclusion

So how much triggering experience is needed to set word order parameters? The answer to that question is presumably "very little", as even clause types that are extremely infrequent in typical child-directed speech are acquired with target-consistent word order from early on. The Split-CP model that has been presented in this paper accounts for the early acquisition of word order in languages where different clause types have different word orders, such as the Tromsø dialect of Norwegian. If children are assumed to focus exclusively on the relevant clause type when searching the primary linguistic data for syntactic cues, then this also explains why there is no word order overgeneralization from one clause type to another.

Notes

[1] V2 word order is possible, but not preferred, in certain embedded clauses in Norwegian, mainly in complements to so-called bridge verbs (see Vikner 1995 and Bentzen 2003).

[2] The adult speech sample has been taken from one of the investigators in the acquisition corpus (see sections 3 and 4).

[3] The figures in Table 2 do not add up to 100%, as constructions that do not provide evidence for either word order have been disregarded here, e.g. imperatives or subject-initial declaratives without Neg/Adv.

[4] This is an example of a subject question, which in the Tromsø dialect requires the insertion of the relative complementizer *som* in second position. Subject questions thus always occur with non-V2 word order. The element *som* is also obligatory in embedded subject questions, in the dialect as well as in standard Norwegian.

[5] Apart from 10 files that have been collected and transcribed by the author, the corpus has been collected by Merete Anderssen.

[6] In Westergaard&Vangsnes (2005) and Westergaard (2005a) the optional word order of *wh*-questions in Norwegian dialects was argued to be due to the Foc° head.

[7] This is in contrast with what is argued in some recent work, e.g. the variational model of grammar competition in Yang (2002), where children are assumed to pay attention to statistical frequencies in the input and keep several grammar types in the hypothesis space for an extended period of time. According to his model, V2 falls into place relatively late, around age 3;0-3;3.

[8] In Westergaard (2005b) I discuss the loss of V2 in declaratives in Old and Middle English, and in Westergaard (2005c) the optional word order in *wh*-questions in two present-day Norwegian dialects is given an analysis in terms of a diachronic change in progress towards loss of V2. In both situations, only one of the CP heads is affected by the change (Top° in English, Int° in Norwegian), providing some further support for this type of Split-CP approach.

References

Benincà, P. and C. Poletto (2004) "Topic, Focus and V2: Defining the CP Sublayers," in L. Rizzi, ed., *The Structure of CP and IP: The Cartography of Syntactic Structures* 2, Oxford University Press, Oxford and New York, 52-75.

Bentzen, K. (2003) "V-to-I Movement in the Absence of Morphological Cues: Evidence from Northern Norwegian," *Nordlyd: Proceedings from the 19th Scandinavian Conference of Linguistics* 31.3, University of Tromsø, 573-588.

Henry, A. (1995) *Belfast English and Standard English: Dialect Variation and Parameter Setting*, Oxford University Press, New York.

Josefsson, G. (2004) "Input and Output: Sentence Patterns in Child and Adult Swedish," in G. Josefsson, C. Platzack and G. Håkansson, eds., *The Acquisition of Swedish Grammar* [Language Acquisition and Language Disorders 33], John Benjamins, Amsterdam, 95-133.

Lightfoot, D. (1999) *The Development of Language: Acquisition, Change and Evolution,* Blackwell, Malden, MA and Oxford.

—. (2006) *How New Languages Emerge,* Cambridge University Press, Cambridge.

Poletto, C. (2000) *The Higher Functional Field: Evidence from Northern Italian Dialects.* Oxford University Press, New York and Oxford.

Rizzi, L. (1997) "The Fine Structure of the Left Periphery," in L. Haegeman, ed., *Elements of Grammar: Handbook of Generative Syntax,* Kluwer, Dordrecht, 281-337.

—. (2001) "On the Position 'Int(errogative)' in the Left Periphery of the Clause," in G. Cinque and G. Salvi, eds., *Current Studies in Italian Syntax,* Elsevier, Amsterdam, 287-296.

Vangsnes, Ø. A. (2004) "On *Wh*-questions and V2 across Norwegian Dialects: A Survey and Some Speculations," *Working Papers in Scandinavian Syntax* 73, 1-59.

Vikner, S. (1995) *Verb Movement and Expletive Subjects in the Germanic Languages,* Oxford University Press, Oxford and New York.

Westergaard, M. R. (2003) "Word Order in *Wh*-questions in a North Norwegian Dialect: Some Evidence from an Acquisition Study," *Nordic Journal of Linguistics* 26.1, 81-109.

—. (2004) "The Interaction of Input and UG in the Acquisition of Verb Movement in a Dialect of Norwegian," *Nordlyd: Tromsøl Working Papers in Language Acquisition* 32.1, 110-134.

—. (2005a) *The Development of Word Order in Norwegian Child Language: The Interaction of Input and Economy Principles in the Acquisition of V2.* Dr. philos. dissertation, University of Tromsø.

—. (2005b) "Norwegian Child Language and the History of English: The Interaction of Syntax and Information Structure in the Development of Word Order," in K. McCafferty, T. Bull, and K. Killie, eds., *Contexts - Historical, Social, Linguistic. Studies in Celebration of Toril Swan,* Peter Lang, Bern, 293-410.

—. (2005c) "Optional Word Order in *Wh*-questions in Two Norwegian Dialects: A Diachronic Analysis of Synchronic Variation," *Nordic Journal of Linguistics* 28.2, 269-296.

—. and K. Bentzen (2005) "The (Non-) Effect of Input Frequency on the Acquisition of Word Order in Norwegian Embedded Clauses," paper presented at DGfS, Köln, February 23-25, submitted to the SOLA series, Mouton de Gruyter.

—. and Ø. A. Vangsnes (2005) "*Wh*-questions, V2, and the Left Periphery of Three Norwegian Dialects," *Journal of Comparative Germanic Linguistics* 8, 117-158.

Yang, C. (2002) *Knowledge and Learning in Natural Language,* Oxford University Press, Oxford and New York.

SCRAMBLING AND CHILDREN'S INTERPRETATIONS

OF SCOPE INTERACTIONS[*]

KYOKO YAMAKOSHI

1. Introduction

It has been pointed out by Musolino (1998) that children interpret sentences involving quantifiers differently from adults. In a sentence such as "Every horse didn't jump over the fence," adults accept both the surface (every>not) and the inverse scope readings (not>every), but children accepted only the surface scope reading (Isomorphism effect.) This paper reports an opposite case, in which children do not prefer a surface scope reading in a certain case of the interaction between *WH* and *every* (henceforth *WH/every* interaction) in Japanese. Two types of *WH/every* interaction are given in (1) and (2):

(1) Type I: Dare-ga   dono-hito-mo /dare-mo-o   aisiteimasu ka?
         who-nom every-person/everyone-acc love   Q
         "Who loves everyone?" (Subject *WH* and object *every*)

     a. Mary-ga   dono-hito-mo/dare-mo-o   aisiteimasu.
        Mary-nom   every-person/everyone-acc   love
        "Mary loves everyone."   (individual answer) (^{ok}WH > every)

     b. * Mary-ga   Ichiro-o, Kate-ga   Matsui-o,   Sarah-ga
        Mary-nom Ichiro-acc Kate-nom   Matsui-acc Sarah-nom
        Nomo-o   aisiteimasu. (pair-list answer)   (*every > WH)
        Nomo-acc love
        "Mary loves Ichiro, Kate loves Matsui and Sarah loves Nomo."

(2) Type II: Dare-o$_i$ dono-hito-mo / dare-mo-ga t_i aisiteimasu ka?[1]

who-acc   every-person/everyone-nom   love   Q
"Who does everyone love?" (Object *WH* and subject *every*)

a.   Ichiro-o$_i$ dono-hito-mo/dare-mo-ga t_i aisiteimasu.
     Ichiro-acc   every-person/everyone-nom   love
     "Everyone loves Ichiro." (individual answer) (^{ok}WH > every)

b. * Mary-ga   Ichiro-o,   Kate-ga   Matsui-o,   Sarah-ga
     Mary-nom   Ichiro-acc   Kate-nom   Matsui-acc Sarah-nom
     Nomo-o   aisiteimasu.   (pair-list answer)   (*every > WH)
     Nomo-acc love
     "Mary loves Ichiro, Kate loves Matsui, and Sarah loves
     Nomo."

For the Type I question (1), only an individual answer (1a) (WH>every) is
possible and a pair-list answer (1b) (every>WH) is not allowed as it is in
English. For the Type II question (2), only an individual answer (2a)
(WH>every) is possible. A pair-list answer (2b) (every>WH) is not normally
allowed in Japanese (Hoji 1985), unlike English.[2] Our experiment examined
whether children acquiring Japanese could give the same interpretations as
adults for *WH/every* interaction.

2. Experiment

The subjects were 10 children acquiring Japanese (4;4–6;9) and 10 adults.
Two children (5;2 and 5;4) were excluded because they could not the
experiment. The numbers of the subjects in each age group were as follows: 2
four-year-olds (4;4, 4;6), 3 five-year-olds (5;2, 5;3, 5;10) and 3 six-year-olds
(6;7, 6;3, 6;9).

The method was the question-answering task. The experimenter acted out a
short story such as (3) in Japanese using stuffed animals and materials such as
flowers, sweets and vegetables drawn on small pieces of paper. At the end of the
story, the experimenter asked either a Type I question or a Type II question to a
child, and the child was expected to give an answer. We used stories in which
either the individual or the pair-list answer was possible.

(3) Experimenter: A mouse, a pig and a panda came to the garden. There were (three) sunflowers, (two) tulips and (a) rose. The mouse said, "Beautiful flowers! I want (some)," and he took a sunflower. The panda took a sunflower, a tulip and a rose. The pig took a sunflower and a tulip. Ok, I want to ask (child's name),

a.Experimenter: Dare-ga   dono-hana-mo   totta   kana? (Type I question)
                who-nom   every-flower   took   Q
                "Who took every flower?"

    Child (Expected answer): Panda-san.   (individual answer)
                     Panda

b. Experimenter:
   Nani-o$_i$ dono-doubutu-mo t_i totta   kana?   (Type II question)
   what-acc   every-animal   took   Q
   "What did every animal take?"
   Child (Expected answer): Himawari. (individual answer)
                       Sunflower

Children could see every animal and the things they took at the end of the story. 3 Type I questions and 3 Type II questions were asked. We also included 2 WH-questions which did not involve quantifiers as fillers.

The results of the experiment are shown in Table 1:

Table 1: Percentages of the correct individual answers

	Children	Adults
Type I: WH(subj) – every (obj)	87.5% (21/24)	92.6% (25/27)
Type II: WH(obj) – Every (subj)	0.0% (0/24)	100% (27/27)

The children produced correct individual answers for Type I questions 87.5% of the time, whereas they could not produce correct individual answers for Type II questions at all. The children's wrong answers for Type II questions were mainly categorized into the following three types:

(4)   a. Pair-list answers
      Usagi-wa   ringo-to   banana,kuma-wa ringo-to   mikan,
      Rabbit-top apple-and banana,bear-top apple-and   orange,
      zou-wa   ringo-to   banana. (TN 6;9)
      elepant-top apple-and banana.
      "The rabbit (took) an apple and a banana, the bear (took) an apple and an orange, and the elephant took an apple and a banana."
   b. Listing the objects (perhaps a portion of a pair-list answer)

Ringo-to banana,ringo-to   mikan-to,   ringo-to   banana.
apple-and banana,apple-and orange-and, apple-and banana.
(DY 4;4)
"Apple and banana, apple and orange, and apple and banana."
  c. Answering for "who", similar to an answer for the Type I question,
     not for "what."
     Kuma-san. (Bear) (MN 6;8)

3. Discussion: Scrambling and Rigidity

Our results have shown that the children were good at Type I questions but
not Type II questions. In Type II questions, it appears crucial that *nani-o*
("what-acc") is scrambled and moved to the sentence-initial position as shown
in (3b).

Hayashibe (1975) and others have pointed out that it is not easy for children
to interpret sentences involving scrambling correctly (cf. Otsu 1994). [3] If
children have problems with scrambled sentences, the children may also have
problems with Type II questions involving scrambling.

Sano (2004) has conducted an experiment regarding children's
interpretations with two quantifiers (*some* and *every*) and scrambling as in (5):

(5) a. Dareka-ga   dono-neko-mo tukamaeta.
       someone-nom   every-cat   caught
       "Someone caught every cat."

                                   (^{ok}some>every, *every>some)
    b. Dono-neko-mo dareka-ga   tukamaeta.
       every-cat   someone-nom caught
       "Every cat, someone caught."

                                   (^{ok}some>every, ^{ok}every>some)

When the word order is canonical as in (5a), only the surface scope reading
(some>every) is possible. In contrast, when the object *dono-neko-mo* is
scrambled as in (5b), not only the surface but also the inverse scope reading
(every>some) become possible. Sano (2004) tested 20 children (4;1-6;5) using
the truth value judgment task and showed that most of the children did not
change the interpretations between (5a) and (5b). [4]

Sano argues that children may treat the scrambling in (5b) as A'-movement.
In Japanese, short scrambling changes the scope relation as in (5b), but long
scrambling as in (6b) does not change the scope relation (Tada 1993):

(6) a. Dareka-ga [John-ga   daremo-o   aisiteiru-to]   omotteiru.
      who-nom   John-nom   everyone-acc love-comp   think
      "Someone thinks that John loves everyone."
                                      (^{ok}some>every, *every>some)
    b. Daremo$_i$-o   dareka-ga   [John-ga t_i aisiteiru-to] omotteiru.
      everyone-acc someone-nom John-nom   love-comp   think
      "Everyone, someone thinks that John loves."
                                        (^{ok}some>every, *every>some)

In (6b), *daremo-o* ("everyone-acc") moves out of the embedded clause and *daremo* ("everyone") is higher than *dareka* ("someone"), but *daremo* cannot take wide scope over *dareka*. Only *dareka* ("someone") takes wide scope over *daremo* ("everyone"). Long scrambling as in (6b) has been considered as A'-movement (Saito 1992), so the scope change does not occur in A'-movement. It is said that short scrambling as in (5b) can be A-movement, so the scope change occurs in the case of A-movement in adult grammar. Sano (2004) argues that children acquiring Japanese may treat short scrambling in (5b) as A'-movement, not A-movement, and thus the children did not change the scope relation in (5b).

Sano's (2004) analysis can be applied to the type II question of *WH/every* interaction in (7), in which the object *nani-o* ("what-acc") is scrambled. If children treat this scrambling as A'-movement unlike adults, children's wrong responses for Type II questions are explained by the Rigidity Condition (8).

(7) Type II: Nani-o$_i$ dono-doubutu-mo t_i totta kana?   (= (3b))
           what-acc every-animal   took Q
           "What did every animal take?"
(8) Rigidity Condition (Lasnik and Saito 1992):
      Suppose that Q_1 and Q_2 are operators (quantified NP or *WH*.)
      Then Q_1 cannot take wide scope over Q_2 if t_2 c-commands t_1.
(9)   a. Adult: [$_{CP}$ nani$_1$-o [$_{TP}$ dono-doubutu-mo$_2$ [$_{TP}$ t'_1 [$_{TP}$ t_2 t_1 totta]]]
           kana?]
      b. Child: [$_{CP}$ nani$_1$-o [$_{TP}$ dono-doubutu-mo$_2$ [$_{TP}$ t_2 t_1 totta]] kana?]

(9a) is the LF structure of (7) for adults. First, *nani-o* is scrambled and moved to the position of t'_1. Next, *dono-doubutu-mo* is adjoined to TP because of Quantifier Raising. Then *nani-o* moves to the specifier of CP due to LF wh-movement. According to Murasugi and Saito (1992), only variables are relevant to the Rigidity Condition. t_1 is not subject to the Rigidity Condition in adult grammar since it is a trace of short scrambling (i.e. A-movement) and an

NP-trace. t'_1 c-commands t_2 and thus *nani-o* (Q_1) can take wide scope over *dono-doubutu-mo* (Q_2) (i.e. the surface scope reading / individual answer).

In contrast, if the scrambling of *nani-o* in child grammar is A'-movement, not A-movement, the LF structure of (7) for children is like (9b). *Nani-o* is moved from the position of t_1 to the specifier of CP directly by A'-scrambling. In this case t_1 is subject to the Rigidity Condition since it is a trace of A'-movement. Because t_2 c-commands t_1, *nani-o* (Q_1) cannot take wide scope over *dono-doubutu-mo* (Q_2) due to the Rigidity Condition. Moreover, *nani-o* (Q_1) is higher than *dono-doubutu-mo* (Q_2), thus *dono-doubutu-mo* (Q_2) cannot take wide scope over *nani-o* (Q_1) either. In summary, if children treat the scrambling of *nani-o* as A'-movement and if they are sensitive to the Rigidity Condition, they cannot interpret (7): neither the individual reading (WH>every) nor the pair-list reading (every>WH) is possible. Due to this problem, it is possible that children could not interpret the Type II questions as various wrong answers were given.

If our perspective is on the right track, why do children treat the scrambling of WH in Type II questions as A'-movement, not A-movement? It is well known that children have difficulties in constructions involving A-movement such as passives. Borer and Wexler (1987), Babyonyshev et al (2001) among others propose that the delay of passives is due to the maturation of A-chain (A-chain Deficit Hypothesis: ACDH). In contrast, Sano, Endo and Yamakoshi (2001) have argued against ACDH. They have shown that unaccusatives in Japanese involving A-chain are acquired early by conducting an experiment. Sano (2004) suggests that children's A-chain maturation could be observed in constructions which show both A and A'-properties such as short scrambling. To find what kind of A-chains are difficult for children and why are important issues for further research.

Notes

* I thank Noriko Imanishi, Barbara Lust, Tetsuya Sano, Yasuhiro Shirai, John Whitman for their valuable comments. I am grateful to the children and the staff of the Mihara Kindergarten. This study is supported by the grant in 2004 towards "The study of the scope interaction of WH and quantifiers" from Senshu University. All errors are my own.
[1] Hoji (1985) has pointed out that the non-scrambled order of (2) is awkward.
[2] A functional answer such as "Everyone loves his mother" is also possible in Japanese and English, but we do not deal with it here.
[3] Otsu (1994) has shown that children could interpret scrambled sentences correctly (89.6%) when an another sentence was added prior to the scrambled one to show that the scrambled phrase was the topic. However, when the additional sentence was not given, the scrambled sentences were difficult for children (45.8%). Such contexts are not

needed for adults, hence there is a difference between children and adults.
[4] The number of the children who correctly rejected the inverse scope reading (ISR) (every>some) of (5a) was 6, and of those, 5 incorrectly rejected the ISR of (5b). The number of the children who incorrectly accepted the ISR of (5a) was 14, and among these, 13 accepted the ISR of (5b).

References

Borer, H. and K. Wexler (1987) "The Maturation of Syntax," in T. Roeper and E.Williams, eds., *Parameter Setting*, Dordrecht, Reidel.
Babyonyshev, M., R. Fein, J. Ganger, D. Pesetsky and K. Wexler (2001) "The Maturation of Grammatical Principles: Evidence from Russian Unaccusatives," *Linguistic Inquiry* 32, 1-44.
Hayashibe, H. (1975) "Word Order and Particles: A Developmental Study in Japanese," *Descriptive and Applied Linguistics* 8, 1-18.
Hoji, H. (1985) *Logical Form Constraints and Configurational Structures in Japanese*, Doctoral Dissertation, University of Washington.
Lasnik, H. and M. Saito (1992) *Move α*, MIT Press, Cambridge, Massachusetts.
Murasugi, K. and M. Saito (1992) "Quasi-adjuncts as Sentential Arguments," *The Proceedings of Western Conference on Linguistics* 22, 251-264.
Musolino, J. (1998) *Universal Grammar and the Acquisition of Semantic Knowledge: An Experimental Investigation of Quantifier-Negation Interactions in English*, Doctoral Dissertation, University of Maryland at College Park.
Otsu, Y. (1994) "Early Acquisition of Scrambling in Japanese," in T. Hoekstra and B. Schwartz, eds., *Language Acquisition Studies in Generative Grammar*, John Benjamins, Amsterdam.
Saito, M. (1992) "Long distance scrambling in Japanese," *Journal of East Asian Linguistics* 1, 69-118.
Sano, T. (2004) "Scope Relations of QP's and Scrambling in the Acquisition of Japanese," in van Kampen, J. and S. Baauw, eds., *The Proceedings of GALA2003 (Generative Approaches to Language Acquisition)*, University of Utrecht.
—., M. Endo and K. Yamakoshi (2001) "Developmental Issues in the Acquisition of Japanese Unaccusatives and Passives," in A. Do, L. Domínguez, and A. Johansen Somerville, eds., *The Proceedings of the 25th Boston University Conference on Language Development*, 668-683, Cascadilla Press, Massachusetts.
Tada, H. (1993) *A/A-bar Partition in Derivation*, Doctoral Dissertation, MIT.

NON-UNIFORM DEVELOPMENT OF WH-WORDS IN ENGLISH SPEAKERS' L2 ACQUISITION OF CHINESE WH-QUESTIONS[*]

BOPING YUAN

1. Wh-questions in Chinese and English

This paper reports on an empirical study examining behaviours of different wh-words in English speakers' L2 acquisition of Chinese wh-questions. Unlike English wh-questions, in which the wh-word has to move to the sentence initial position, the Chinese wh-word remains *in situ*, as *shenme* in (1). Chinese uses a particle *ne* as a wh-question particle but it is phonetically optional. Another characteristic of Chinese wh-questions is that the wh-word can be located inside islands, such as a complex NP (CNP), as in (2), and a sentential subject, as in (3). Obviously, wh-words cannot be extracted from these islands in English.

(1) Ni xiang chi shenme (ne)?
    you want eat what   Q
    "What would you like to eat?"
(2) Ta xihuan [shei xie de] shu (ne)?
    he like   who write DE book Q
    "*Who$_i$ do you like the book [that t_i wrote]?"
(3) [Shei qu Beijing] bijiao   heshi (ne)?
    who go Beijing relatively   suitable Q
    "*Who$_i$ is [t_i to go/goes to Beijing] more appropriate?"

However, when a Chinese wh-word in the island is a wh-adverb rather than a wh-argument, the sentence becomes ungrammatical, as shown in (5), which is in contrast with (2) and (4), where the wh-words in the island are wh-arguments.

(4) Ni xihuan [xie shenme shu de] ren   (ne)?
    you like   write what book DE person Q
    "*What book$_i$ do you like the person [who wrote t_i]?"

(5) *Ni xihuan [ta weishenme xie   de] shu (ne)?
    you like   he why   write DE book Q
    "*Why$_i$ do you like the book [that he wrote t_i]?"

Chinese wh-words corresponding to "when" and "where", which are
generally regarded as adjuncts, can also appear in islands and do not cause
ungrammaticality to the sentences, as shown in (6) and (7).

(6) Ni xihuan [ta (zai) shenmeshihou xie   de] shu (ne)?
    you like   he (at) when   write DE book Q
    "*When$_i$ do you like the book [that he wrote t_i]?"
(7) Ni xihuan [ta zai nar   xie   de] shu (ne)?
    you like   he at where write DE book Q
    "*Where$_i$ do you like the book [that he wrote t_i]?"

Huang (1982) suggests that wh-words "when" and "where" are NPs in
Chinese as they can be preceded by a preposition *zai* "at", as in (6) and (7). In
this sense, "when" and "where" in Chinese can be distinguished from "why" by
the distinction between nominals and adverbs. The Chinese wh-word "how"
patterns with nominals in Chinese as well. As we can see in (8), it can be
located inside a CNP.

(8) Ni xihuan [ta zenmeyang   zuo   de] dangao (ne)?
    you like   he how   make DE cake   Q
    "*How$_i$ do you like the cake [that she makes t_i]?"

In his split-CP proposal, Rizzi (1997) argues that CP should be split up into
separate structural layers, one of which is a Force Projection. According to
Rizzi, *force* encodes clause-type information and is responsible for
distinguishing various clause types such as declarative, interrogative, etc. In
this paper, I follow Cheng and Rooryck (2000, 2002), Simpson (2000) and
Rizzi (1997) in assuming that C^0 in wh-questions is essentially unvalued with
respect to specification of *force*, and that unvalued C^0 must be valued. In
Chinese wh-questions, the valuation of *force* is carried out by the Chinese wh-
particle *ne*, which is merged into the head of CP. The wh-particle *ne* in C^0 has a
dual function: it disambiguates the *force* of the sentence and at the same time it
also licenses the wh-word *in situ*. I also follow Tsai (1994a,b, 1999) and Cheng
and Rooryck (2002) in assuming that the wh-adverb *weishenme* "why" in
Chinese has an operator but wh-nominals don't. The operator of the wh-adverb
has to raise to CP for feature checking. In English, C^0 of wh-questions is valued
by the wh-word which is moved from its base-generated position to Spec CP.

Will English speakers' L2 Chinese grammars use the Chinese wh-particle *ne*, rather than wh-movement, to value the *force* of Chinese wh-questions? If they do, will the merging of *ne* into C^0 make wh-movement unnecessary in their L2 Chinese wh-questions? Another question we ask is whether English speakers' L2 Chinese grammars can make a distinction between wh-nominals and wh-adverbs so that wh-nominals can stay *in situ* inside islands such as CNPs or sentential subjects while wh-adverbs cannot. If the distinction can be made, we can assume that the wh-nominal and the wh-adverb have different sets of morphological features attached to them in learners' L2 Chinese grammars, with the set of the latter having an operator, which is absent in the former. The operator of the wh-adverb has to undergo movement and the movement is subject to Subjacency.

2. Empirical Study

The empirical study involves 107 English speakers as subjects. It also includes 20 native speakers of Chinese as controls. On the basis of their performance in a Chinese cloze test, the English speakers were divided into five Chinese proficiency groups. Information about each of the 6 groups is given in Table 1. An ANOVA result shows that there is a significant difference between all groups in their performance in the cloze test, (F=855.619, p<0.001) and the following-up scheffé tests indicate that except for the advanced group, each learner group is significantly different from the native Chinese group and that all the learner groups are significantly different from each other.

Table 1: Information about each group

Groups	No. of subjects	Average Age	Average months of studying Chinese	Average months in China	Mean scores in the cloze test (total=40) (ranges in brackets)
Beginners	20	22	4	1	4 (1-6)
Post-beginners	20	23	10	3	11 (7-15)
Intermediate	28	22	29	6	22 (16-25)
Post-intermediate	25	27	83	18	30 (26-34)
Advanced	14	36	207	44	36 (35-39)
Native Chinese	20	28	N/A	N/A	39 (38-40)

Each subject has to do an acceptability judgment test, which includes control sentences and corresponding experimental sentences. Subjects are asked to judge the acceptability of each sentence by circling a number on a scale as given in (9).

(9)

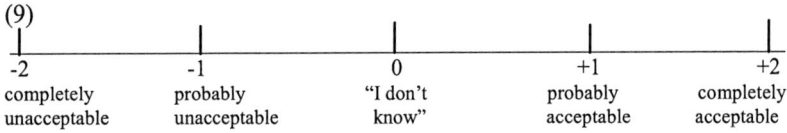

-2	-1	0	+1	+2
completely unacceptable	probably unacceptable	"I don't know"	probably acceptable	completely acceptable

3. Results

As shown in Table 2, except for the Beginner Group, all learner groups, like the native Chinese Group, accept Chinese wh-questions with the wh-particle *ne*. Moreover, as the data in Tables 2 and 3 show, those groups who accept Chinese wh-questions with *ne* reject ungrammatical wh-questions with the wh-word moved from its base-generated position to the sentence initial position.

Table 2 also shows that all learner groups including the beginner group, like the Native Chinese Group, accept Chinese wh-questions without phonetically realised *ne*. It seems that valuation of C^0 of Chinese wh-questions by phonetically unrealised *ne* is preferred by L2 Chinese grammars at least at beginner levels.

Table 2: Mean scores in the judgment of Chinese wh-questions with/without *ne* and with wh-argument moved

	Beginner	Post-beginner	Intermediate	Post-intermediate	Advanced	Chinese
With *ne*	0.7	1.13	1.46	1.53	1.89	1.89
*Wh-movement	-1.15	-1.25	-1.48	-1.72	-1.8	-1.49
Without *ne*	1.69	1.88	1.86	1.84	1.98	1.96

Table 3: Mean scores in the judgment of simple Chinese wh-questions with "when/where/how/why" *in situ* or moved

	Beginners	Post-beginners	Intermediate	Post-intermediate	Advanced	Chinese
In situ	1.1	1.76	1.88	1.82	1.71	1.9
*Moved	-0.24	-0.89	-1.02	-1.59	-1.64	-1.69

Similar results are obtained in the groups' judgments of simple Chinese wh-questions with *shenmeshihou* "when", *nar* "where", *zenmeyang* "how" and *weishenme* "why". All learner groups accept these wh-words *in situ* in Chinese wh-questions, as shown in the second row in Table 3, and they, except for the

Beginner Group, reject or tend to reject wh-questions with this type of wh-words moved to the sentence initial position, as shown in the third row in Table 3.

Now let's look at the judgment data of wh-words embedded in islands to see whether there is any evidence showing operator raising in English speakers' L2 Chinese wh-questions. The data in the second row of Table 4 are from subjects' judgment of sentences with a CNP but without any wh-word. This type of sentence is used as a control to distinguish subjects who have mastered the basic structure of the sentence with an embedded CNP from those who have not. As we can see, all groups, except for the Beginner Group, have mastered the basic sentence structure with an embedded CNP in Chinese. So we have to ignore the Beginner Group's judgment and concentrate on the other groups' judgment of wh-questions which correspond to the control sentences.

Table 4: Mean scores in the judgment of Chinese wh-questions with a wh-word inside CNP

	Beginner	Post-beginner	Intermediate	Post-intermediate	Advanced	Chinese
Control	0.68	1.43	1.94	1.87	1.89	1.93
Wh-argument	0.55	1.43	1.46	1.58	1.56	1.71
"When/where"	-0.31	0.15	0.55	1.06	1.13	1.16

From the third row in Table 4, we can see that all learner groups, except for the Beginner Group, accept Chinese wh-questions with a wh-argument embedded inside a CNP. It seems that so long as L2 Chinese grammars can handle the basic sentence structure, there is no problem for wh-arguments to stay inside a CNP in L2 Chinese wh-questions. This suggests that Subjacency is irrelevant here as no movement is involved in this type of wh-questions in L2 Chinese.

However, the wh-words *shenmeshihou* "when" and *nar* "where" inside a CNP do not seem to be so acceptable to L2 Chinese grammars at post-beginner and intermediate levels. As we can see from the fourth row in Table 4, the Post-beginner and Intermediate Groups, who are shown to have mastered the basic sentence structure and who accept wh-arguments inside a CNP, do not accept Chinese wh-questions with *shenmeshihou* "when" and *nar* "where" embedded in a CNP. We can take this as evidence that wh-arguments and the wh-words such as *shenmeshihou* "when" and *nar* "where" do not develop in a uniform fashion in L2 Chinese grammars. It seems that only at post-intermediate and advanced levels does it become acceptable in L2 Chinese grammars to allow *shenmeshihou* "when" and *nar* "where" to stay *in situ* inside a CNP. L2 grammars at beginner, post-beginner and intermediate levels seem to be unsure of the status of *shenmeshihou* "when" and *nar* "where" and they seem to be uncertain whether these wh-words should share the same behaviour as wh-arguments in Chinese wh-questions.

How do wh-words *zenmeyang* "how" and *weishenme* "why" behave in L2 Chinese wh-questions? The data in Table 5 suggest that all groups, except for the Beginner Group, can handle the basic sentence structure for testing wh-questions with *zenmeyang* "how" and *weishenme* "why", as these groups accept the control sentences with a CNP, as shown in the second row in Table 5.

However, as shown in the third row in Table 5, none of the learner groups, including the advanced group, accepts Chinese wh-questions with *zenmeyang* "how" embedded inside a CNP, which forms a striking contrast with the judgment of the native Chinese group. A careful examination of the data reveals that with regard to wh-questions, the status of *zenmeyang* "how" in L2 Chinese grammars remains variable throughout the acquisition process as the subjects in all groups optionally accept and reject wh-questions with *zenmeyang* "how" embedded inside a CNP. This variable status seems to be permanent in English speakers' L2 Chinese grammars as the variability continues even at a very advanced level.

Table 5: Mean scores in the judgment of Chinese wh-questions with *zenmeyang* "how" or *weishenme* "why" inside a CNP

	Beginners	Post-beginners	Intermediate	Post-intermediate	Advanced	Chinese
Control	0.73	1.71	1.89	1.97	1.82	1.93
"How"	-0.15	-0.09	0.06	0.22	0.27	1.19
*"Why"	-0.41	-1.16	-1.47	-1.49	-1.59	-1.65

In contrast to the variable behaviours of *zenmeyang* "how", the behaviour of *weishenme* "why" in English speakers' L2 Chinese wh-questions seems to be rather consistent. As we can see from the fourth row in Table 5, all groups, except for the Beginner Group, reject Chinese wh-questions with *weishenme* "why" embedded inside a CNP. This could be due to the fact that as the case in the native Chinese grammar, *weishenme* "why" in L2 Chinese grammars has an operator which has to move to Spec CP in wh-questions. Since *weishenme* "why" in the test sentences is embedded in a CNP and since the movement of the operator of *weishenme* "why" out of a CNP would violate Subjacency, L2 Chinese grammars reject wh-questions with *weishenme* "why" embedded in a CNP.

Can we get similar results from wh-questions with a wh-word embedded in a sentential subject? This type of sentence is also useful for testing possible wh-movement in L2 grammars as any movement out of the sentential subject would violate Subjacency. The data in the second row in Table 6 are mean scores of the groups' judgment of control sentences, i.e. sentences with a sentential subject but without a wh-word. These data suggest that sentences with a sentential subject are acquired very late and that only those subjects at post-intermediate and advanced levels can handle this type of sentences. This forces us to concentrate only on these two groups' judgment of wh-questions with a wh-word embedded in a sentential subject.

As we can see from the third row in Table 6, the Advanced Group accept Chinese wh-questions with a wh-argument embedded in a sentential subject. A similar result can also be seen in the fourth row in Table 6, which indicates that the Advanced Group accept Chinese wh-questions with *shenmeshihou* "when" or *nar* "where" embedded in a sentential subject. The post-intermediate group also accept this type of sentences although not as strongly as the Advanced Group.

Table 6: Mean scores in the judgment of Chinese wh-questions with a wh-word inside a sentential subject

	Beginners	Post-beginners	Intermediate	Post-intermediate	Advanced	Chinese
Control	0.43	0.26	0.33	1.11	1.48	1.84
Wh-argument	0.24	-0.35	-0.45	0.38	1.11	1.73
"When/where"	0.06	-0.15	0.22	1	1.54	1.81
"How"	-0.25	-0.06	-0.02	0.52	0.36	1.4
*"Why"	-0.09	-0.11	-0.46	-0.94	-1.04	-1.34

However, when the wh-word *zenmeyang* "how" is embedded in a sentential subject of a wh-question, the judgment of the sentences by the learner groups becomes variable, as shown on the fifth row in Table 6. A careful examination of the data reveals high degrees of variability in the judgment of this type of sentences by the subjects as the subjects in these groups optionally accept and reject this type of sentences. The results suggest that the wh-word *zenmeyang* "how" in English speakers' L2 Chinese grammars is far from being native-like even at very advanced levels and that it can serve as an example of fossilization in English speakers' L2 Chinese grammars.

The wh-word *weishenme* "why" seems to behave differently from the other wh-words in English speakers' L2 Chinese grammars. As we can see from the sixth row in Table 6, the Advanced Group and Post-intermediate Group reject or tend to reject wh-questions with *weishenme* "why" embedded in a sentential subject. The native Chinese group also reject this type of sentences.

Table 7 provides a summary of all the groups judgment.[1] The second row of Table 7 shows that the Beginners have not mastered the basic sentence structures with an embedded CNP or with a sentential subject in Chinese. The second column and the last column of Table 7 suggest that, except for beginners, English learners generally allow wh-arguments to stay inside islands and that they reject ungrammatical Chinese wh-questions with the wh-adverb "why" embedded inside an island.

However, as we can see from the third column in Table 7, the Post-beginner and Intermediate Groups, who have mastered the basic sentence structures and who accept wh-arguments in islands, do not accept Chinese wh-questions with "when" and "where" embedded in islands. We can take this as evidence that wh-arguments and the wh-words such as "when" and "where" do not develop in a uniform fashion in L2 Chinese grammars. A closer examination of the data indicate that post-beginner and intermediate learners variably accept and reject Chinese wh-questions with "when" or "where" embedded inside islands.

Table 7: Summary of English speakers' judgment of different Chinese wh-words inside CNPs and inside sentential subjects

	shei "who", shenme "what"	shenmeshihou "when", nar "where"	Zenme(yang) "how"	*weishenme "why"
Beginners	N/A	N/A	N/A	N/A
Post-beginners	√	?	?	X
Intermediate	√	?	?	X
Post-intermediate	√	√	?	X
Advanced	√	√	?	X
Native Chinese	√	√	√	X

Note: *N/A=learners have not mastered the basic sentence structure; "√" = accept; "X"=reject; "?"= variable.*

How about the behaviour of *zenme(yang)* "how" in L2 Chinese? As shown in the fourth column in Table 7, none of the learner groups, including the advanced group, accepts Chinese wh-questions with *zenme(yang)* "how" embedded inside islands. A careful examination of the data reveals that subjects in all learner groups variably accept and reject wh-questions with *zenme(yang)* "how" embedded inside islands.

4. Discussion

Our results indicate that C^0 of wh-questions in English speakers' L2 Chinese grammars is valued by the merging of the Chinese wh-particle *ne* into C^0. There is no L1 transfer in this aspect of L2 grammars as no wh-movement is found in English speakers' L2 Chinese although it is generally required in their L1. This finding does not support the transfer part of the Full Transfer and Full Access model proposed by Schwarts and Sprouse (1994, 1996). The findings here confirm our hypothesis that once C^0 of Chinese wh-questions is valued by the wh-particle *ne*, the C^0 thus specified and valued will become a wh-licenser for the wh-word *in situ* and the principle of economy in L2 Chinese grammars will make any wh-movement unnecessary and impossible in L2 Chinese.

However, wh-words do not develop in a uniform fashion in L2 Chinese. Why do Chinese wh-words behave differently at different Chinese proficiency levels? And what are the underlying mental representations of the wh-words in English speakers' L2 Chinese grammars? To facilitate our analyses, let us first make distinctions between three types of wh-words in the native Chinese grammar in (10).

(10) Type A: Wh-words with [+argument] and [+nominal] features
                (e.g. *shei* "who" and *shenme* "what");

Type B: Wh-words with [-argument] but [+nominal] features
                (e.g. *shenmeshihou* "when", *nar* "where" and *zenmeyang* "how");

Type C: Wh-words with [-argument] and [-nominal] features, i.e. wh-adverbs (e.g. *weishenme* "why").

It is likely that at beginner and intermediate levels, English speakers' L2 Chinese grammars are indeterminate as to whether the operator should be attached to wh-words with the [-argument] feature or to wh-words with the [-nominal] feature (although they seem to know it has to be attached to something minus). This indeterminacy leads to optional attachment of the operator to wh-words such as "when" and "where" as they have the [-argument] but [+nominal] features. When wh-words with the [-argument] feature are attached with the operator, wh-words "when" and "where" are not allowed to stay inside islands because the operator attached to them requires raising to Spec CP but the Subjacency constraint makes that impossible. However, when the operator is attached to wh-words with the [-nominal] feature, "when" and "where" are allowed to stay inside islands in L2 Chinese grammars as both the learners' L1 English and the L2 Chinese input can tell their L2 Chinese lexicons that these wh-words can serve as object of a preposition (e.g. "from where" and "since when"). Therefore, they should have the [+nominal] feature and thus have no operator. In other words, the wavering between the [-argument] feature and the [-nominal] feature for the operator attachment in L2 Chinese grammars is believed to be the source of the variability at the surface level in the Post-beginner and Intermediate groups' L2 Chinese wh-questions.

The wh-word "why" has both the [-nominal] feature and the [-argument] feature in learners' L1 English and their L2 Chinese input can also show that it is the case in the target language. As a result, Chinese wh-questions with *weishenme* "why" embedded inside islands is rejected by L2 Chinese grammars whether the operator is attached to wh-words with the [-nominal] feature or to wh-words with the [-argument] feature because the wh-adverb "why" has both of these two features.

The wavering between these two features for the operator attachment will not lead to variable behaviours of *shei* "who" and *shenme* "what" at the surface level either. This is because the two wh-words have both the [+argument] and [+nominal] features. Consequently, learners at these early stages accept wh-questions with *shei* "who" or "what" *shenme* embedded inside islands. This amounts to saying that the stable behaviours of the Chinese wh-words "who", "what" and "why" in these groups' judgment are only superficial because the underlying mechanism concerning the behaviours of these wh-words is still indeterminate in these English speakers' L2 Chinese grammars.

The English wh-word "how" has both the [-argument] and [-nominal] features. If English beginner and intermediate learners of Chinese take the wh-word *zenmeyang* "how" as the Chinese counterpart of the English wh-word "how", we would expect this Chinese counterpart to have both the [-argument] and [-nominal] features in the learners' L2 Chinese lexicons. This would allow the Chinese wh-word *zenmeyang* "how" to behave in the same way as the wh-word *weishenme* "why" at these early stages. However, learners are exposed to positive evidence in their L2 Chinese input that the Chinese wh-word *zenmeyang* "how" can be embedded inside islands. The two sources of information, i.e. the positive evidence in the Chinese input and the L1 transfer, are likely to make the operator optionally attached to *zenmeyang* "how" in these learners' L2 Chinese grammars, which can account for their wavering between accepting and rejecting Chinese wh-questions with *zenmeyang* "how" embedded inside islands.

If we look at the third column in Table 7, we can see that the variability in the Post-beginner and Intermediate Groups' judgment concerning Chinese wh-words "when" and "where" disappears in the Post-intermediate and Advanced Groups. This suggests that from the post-intermediate level onward, feature attachment to L2 Chinese wh-words has been reassembled and that the Chinese wh-words "when" and "where", which have the [-argument] and [+nominal] features, no longer have an operator. This implicates that in these learners' L2 Chinese grammars, the [+/-argument] feature has lost the function of distinguishing wh-words with an operator from those without, and that the only feature that the L2 Chinese grammars use for making such a distinction is the [+/-nominal] feature. This reassembly of features in Chinese wh-words can be triggered by learners' observation that all wh-words that appear in islands in Chinese have one thing in common, that is, they all have the [+nominal] feature.

This type of positive evidence can force L2 Chinese lexicons to reassemble the features attached to Chinese wh-words and to remove the operator from wh-words with the [-argument] feature and only attach the operator to wh-words with the [-nominal] feature. Then why does the reassembly not take place earlier? This is probably because, due to the complexity of the sentence in the input involving islands, earlier L2 Chinese grammars are unable to perceive the generalization of the [+nominal] feature to all Chinese wh-words inside islands, and as a result, this piece of positive evidence cannot be taken in by L2 Chinese grammars until a later stage.

Then why is the behaviour of *zenmeyang* "how" persistently variable, even in advanced learners' L2 Chinese wh-questions? In the English lexicon, the wh-word "how" has the [-nominal] feature. However, the wh-word *zenmeyang* "how" in the native Chinese lexicon has the [+nominal] feature. There seem to be reasons to assume that the wh-word *zenmeyang* "how" may have two different representations co-existing in English speakers' L2 Chinese lexicons; one is a Chinese counterpart of the English wh-word "*how*" with the [-nominal] feature and the other is the proper Chinese wh-word *zenmeyang* "how" which has the [+nominal] feature. The acquisition of the latter is made possible by the positive evidence that the Chinese wh-word *zenmeyang* "how" can stay *in situ* inside islands. As there is no positive evidence in the input data which can help remove the Chinese counterpart of the English wh-word "how" from English speakers' L2 Chinese lexicons, the two representations of *zenmeyang* "how" permanently co-exist in English speakers' L2 Chinese lexicons, leading to persistent variability in their L2 syntax.

5. Conclusion

In this paper, I have analysed my data on the basis of a lexical morphology account. If we adopt the view of the Minimalist Program that the computational system takes words from the lexicon along with their morphological information and forms LF and PF representations via a derivational procedure, we can assume that a wh-word selected from L2 Chinese lexicons with a deficient morphological feature can have syntactic implications. In my study, this deficit is manifested in beginner and intermediate learners' optional attachment of the operator to wh-words with the [-argument] feature and wh-words with the [-nominal] feature, which lead to variable syntactic behaviours of wh-words such as *shenmeshihou* "when" and *nar* "where" in their L2 Chinese wh-questions. At post-intermediate and advanced levels, the deficit can be seen in the co-existence of two representations of *zenmeyang* "how" in English speakers' L2 Chinese lexicons; one is a Chinese counterpart of the English wh-word "how" with the [-nominal] feature and the other the Chinese wh-word *zenmeyang* "how" with the appropriate [+nominal] feature, the result of which, again, is variable syntactic behaviours of *zenmeyang* "how" in post-intermediate and advanced learners' L2 Chinese wh-questions. All this has demonstrated that the lexical morphology-syntax interface is a possible locus of variability in L2 acquisition. A considerable research has been reported in the L2 research literature regarding the relationship between the acquisition of overt morphological inflection and the acquisition of underlying properties, such as functional categories and their features. This is an important issue in L2 research. However, it is equally important to examine the relationship between lexical morphological features and syntax in L2 acquisition. We cannot take it for granted that features of lexical items can be acquired by L2 learners.

Notes

* The research reported in this paper is part of a project funded by the Economic and Social Research Council in England (Grant reference number: RES-000-22-0180). I gratefully acknowledge the financial support for the project from the ESRC.
[1] To a large extent, the data in Table 7 are based on the groups' judgment of Chinese sentences with wh-words embedded inside a CNP. This is because English speakers seem to be able to handle Chinese sentences with a CNP earlier than sentences with a sentential subject.

References

Cheng, L. L.-S. and J. Rooryck, (2000) "Licensing wh-in-situ," *Syntax* 3, 1-19.
—. and J. Rooryck, (2002) "Types of Wh-in-situ", ms., Leiden University.
Huang, C.-T. J. (1982) *Logical Relations in Chinese and the Theory of Grammar*, doctoral dissertation, MIT, Cambridge, Massachusetts.
Rizzi, L. (1997) "The fine structure of the left periphery," in L. Haegeman, ed., *Elements of Grammar: Handbook of Generative Syntax*, 281-337. Kluwer Academic Publishers, The Netherlands.
Schwartz, B. and R. Sprouse, (1994) "Word order and nominative case in non-native language acquisition: a longitudinal study of (L1 Turkish) German Interlanguage," in T. Hoekstra and B. Schwartz, eds., *Language acquisition studies in generative grammar: papers in honour of Kenneth Wexler from the 1991 GLOW workshop*, 317-368. John Benjamins, Amsterdam.
—. and R. Sprouse, (1996) "L2 cognitive states and the full transfer/full access model," *Second Language Research* 12, 40-72.
Simpson, A. (2000) *Wh-movement and the Theory of Feature-checking*. John Benjamins, Amsterdam.

Tsai, W.-T. D. (1994a) "On nominal islands and LF extractions in Chinese," *Natural Language and Linguistic Theory* 12, 121-175.

—. (1994b) *On Economizing the Theory of A-bar Dependencies*, doctoral dissertation, MIT, Cambridge, Masachusetts.

—. (1999) "On lexical courtesy," *Journal of East Asian Linguistics* 8, 39-73.